CKPezzarossi

Comprehensive Textbook of Psychotherapy

Oxford Textbooks in Clinical Psychology

Comprehensive Textbook of Psychotherapy

Theory and Practice

Edited by

BRUCE BONGAR

*Stanford University School of Medicine
and the Pacific Graduate School of Psychology*

LARRY E. BEUTLER

University of California, Santa Barbara

New York   Oxford
OXFORD UNIVERSITY PRESS
1995

Oxford University Press

Oxford   New York   Toronto
Delhi   Bombay   Calcutta   Madras   Karachi
Kuala Lumpur   Singapore   Hong Kong   Tokyo
Nairobi   Dar es Salaam   Cape Town
Melbourne   Auckland   Madrid

and associated companies in
Berlin   Ibadan

Library of Congress Cataloging-in-Publication Data
Comprehensive Textbook of Psychotherapy:
theory and practice /
edited by Bruce Bongar, Larry E. Beutler.
p.   cm.— (Oxford textbooks in clinical psychology ; v. 1)
Includes bibliographical reference and index.
ISBN 0-19-508215-X
1. Psychotherapy.
I. Bongar, Bruce Michael.
II. Beutler, Larry E.
III. Series.
[DNLM: 1. Psychotherapy.   Wm 420 f771 1994]
RC480.F67   1994   616.89′14   dc20
DNLM/DLC   for Library of Congress   94-12593

9 8 7 6 5

Printed in the United States of America
on acid-free paper

To my son,
Brandon Fortune Bongar.
Dum Vivimos, Vivamos!—B.B.
With thanks
and appreciation
to Margaret—L.E.B.

Preface

Over one hundred years have passed since Freud's talking cure dramatically changed the shape of our world. The past century has witnessed the development of numerous modifications of Freud's psychoanalysis, along with hundreds of new theories and clinical models—and at least as many books that describe these theories and models. These diversities have often been profound and have produced a field that is filled with vitality as well as controversy. Unfortunately, it has become the bane of psychotherapy that the richness of theoretical diversity has never been matched at the level of practice. While theoretical constructs are varied and elaborate, leading one to believe that the adoption of a particular theoretical framework will lead to a discriminating method of practice, the usual observation has been that therapists from different schools do similar things with similar results.

At present, the variability of our clinical practice appears to be more dependent on each therapist's level of experience and on the setting in which the interventions are applied than on any particular theoretical model that is assumably guiding the process. In a time of consumer advocate groups, managed health care, and the

specter of national health care, this has led to a popular assumption that psychotherapy is psychotherapy is psychotherapy—that theoretical models, practitioners, and the population on which each model is applied are all interchangeable.

As if to perpetuate such a belief, textbooks on psychotherapeutic theories have traditionally devoted only small sections of each chapter to reviewing research findings and practical applications. Thus, practical guidelines are neither easily nor directly derived from theoretical treatises. If the richness of theoretical developments are to have an impact on the lives of our patients and to advance the mission of health care, these matters must be translatable to practical applications that are distinctive and focused. The value of training practitioners in various theories must be proven by evidence of distinctive levels of benefit or differential outcomes when applied to different populations and problems. This fact has been recognized in the recent development of manuals or guidebooks, developments that have arisen directly from the evolution of psychotherapy research.

Furthermore, when compared to psychotherapy practice, psychotherapy research is a relatively recent derivation. Applications of scientific methods to validating the efficacy and to understanding the processes of psychotherapy are now in only their fifth decade. For most of this time, this research has had the important but relatively unstimulating task of testing the belief that psychotherapy is an effective way to alter emotional distress and disorders. However, in the past two decades increasing research attention has been paid to translating theoretical differences into distinctive psychotherapy practices. The result has been the development of psychotherapy manuals, along with measures by which to assess a given therapist's compliance and skill in applying a chosen theory. These manuals provide guidelines for practice and direct the therapist in the selection of theory-consistent procedures that are designed to effect improvement in the patient's life. While the stated goals of these manuals are to facilitate research that tests the relative efficacy of different theories and extends our knowledge of which patients can be most effectively treated by each model, manuals also have revitalized psychotherapy training. These manuals have accomplished this task by providing clear goals, methods of application, and standards by which one can determine and compare therapists' levels of proficiency and skill. With the pending development of national health care and the challenges posed by consumer advocate groups, there has never been a greater necessity of integrating the theory, practice, and science of psychotherapy than there is at present.

This book is not just a book of theories. It is a book of theories and psychotherapy manuals. It is designed to serve the needs of a broad audience—from undergraduate students who are taking their first course in psychotherapy to graduate students and practitioners who are trying to apply these principles in practice. The first chapter by Orlinsky and Howard sets the stage for the scope of chapters presented by placing psychotherapy, psychotherapy research, and psychotherapy practice within a historical context. The chapters in Part I represent major theoretical approaches in which standard manuals have either been developed or are in the process of development. Psychodynamic Psychotherapy, Behavior Therapy, Experiential and Existential Therapies, Cognitive Therapy, Group Therapy, Systems Therapy, and Integrative-Eclectic Therapy were chosen to represent the major themes and models in the field. Each of these theoretical approaches are represented in this book by two chapters. The first chapter on each theory presents the historical developments, variations of the model, and major theoretical concepts of the theory. This historical chapter also provides an overview and selective review of the research that is available on the efficacy of the therapeutic model. These historical and theoretical chapters will be of greatest interest to beginning students or practitioners who wish to refresh their memory about an alternative viewpoint to their own.

The second chapter on each theory serves as a mini-manual for applying one of the general theoretical models to practice. This latter chapter defines the assumptions that are extracted from the broad theoretical framework, and outlines distinguishing characteristics of the format, length, and therapeutic procedures utilized. This chapter also defines for whom the approach is considered to be most usefully applied, the limitations of the approach, and requirements of the model for training and research. This set of chapters will be of most interest to graduate students and practitioners who are seeking to apply theories, learn new skills, and achieve advanced proficiency.

The authors of the chapters in Part I are distinguished contributors to theory and research, and each was selected because of his or her contributions to knowledge in a specific theoretical area or therapeutic philosophy.

Part II of this book is comprised of a series of chapters on psychotherapeutic applications to special populations and circumstances. We have included chapters on the treatment of women, members of ethnic and minority groups, children and adolescents, older adults, and people who are in crises. These approaches are not accompanied by separate treatment manuals because of the broad focus of the topics. The concepts presented are designed to cut across theoretical approaches. The authors of these chapters were selected because of their breadth of experience and knowledge, and because each has made significant contributions to research and practice within the area of their presentation.

Part III is designed to provide an extension and integration of the material presented in the earlier chapters. The authors who contributed to this part were selected because of the breadth of their perspectives and their wisdom in the broad domain of science and practice. While research implications, training methods and considerations, and professional issues are addressed in each part as applied to each specific theory or topic, the contributions in this section focus on cross-theoretical issues. In this spirit, the final chapter provides an overview of the field with a view toward the future. This chapter aptly caps the presentation and brings the historical reviews and the contemporary practices into focus.

We wish to thank the authors of the chapters in this volume. We have enjoyed working with them and appreciate their willingness to comply with deadlines, tolerate our pressure, and let us critique their ideas. They were congenial, forgiving, and prompt, making our jobs much easier than expected and by far easier than has been our experience with any other edited volume. We also thank Ms. Lynn Peterson, Drs. Ray William London and Julia Shiang, Captain Robert Bigler, and Ms. Peggy Goodale for their persistence, assistance, and support. Most of all, we have enjoyed coming to know one another through this process. We enjoyed ourselves.

August 1994
Marina Del Rey, California   B. B.
Santa Barbara, California   L. E. B.

Contents

Part II. Psychotherapy for Special Populations and Circumstances

Part III. Research Methods, Professional Issues, and New Directions

Contributors

BARBARA BALLINGER
Department of Psychiatry and Behavioral Sciences
Stanford University School of Medicine
Stanford, California

LARRY E. BEUTLER
Program in Counseling/Clinical/School Psychology
Graduate School of Education
University of California, Santa Barbara
Santa Barbara, California

JEFFREY L. BINDER
Georgia School of Professional Psychology
Atlanta, Georgia

BRUCE BONGAR
Pacific Graduate School of Psychology
Palo Alto, California
Department of Psychiatry and Behavioral Sciences
Stanford University School of Medicine
Stanford, California

ANNETTE M. BRODSKY
Department of Psychiatry
Harbor UCLA Medical Center
Torrance, California

JAMES F. T. BUGENTAL
Emeritus Clinical Faculty
Stanford University School of Medicine
Stanford, California

DANIEL CARPENTER
Department of Psychology in Psychiatry
Cornell University Medical College
Ithaca, New York

J. MANUEL CASAS
Program in Counseling/Clinical/School Psychology
Graduate School of Education
University of California, Santa Barbara
Santa Barbara, California

JOHN F. CLARKIN
Department of Psychology in Psychiatry
Cornell University Medical College
Ithaca, New York

ANDRÉS J. CONSOLI
Program in Counseling/Clinical/School Psychology
Graduate School of Education
University of California, Santa Barbara
Santa Barbara, California

LINDA WILCOXON CRAIGHEAD
Department of Psychology
University of North Carolina at Chapel Hill
Chapel Hill, North Carolina

W. EDWARD CRAIGHEAD
Departments of Psychiatry and Psychology
Duke University Medical Center and Duke
    University
Durham, North Carolina

KEITH S. DOBSON
Department of Psychology
University of Calgary
Calgary, Alberta, Canada

ROBERT ELLIOTT
Department of Psychology
University of Toledo
Toledo, Ohio

DOLORES GALLAGHER-THOMPSON
Department of Psychiatry and Behavioral Sciences
Veterans Affairs Medical Center
Palo Alto, California
Department of Psychiatry and Behavioral Sciences
Stanford University School of Medicine
Stanford, California

MARVIN R. GOLDFRIED
Department of Psychology
State University of New York at Stony Brook
Stony Brook, New York

LESLIE S. GREENBERG
Department of Psychology
York University
North York, Ontario, Canada

RICHARD P. HALGIN
Department of Psychology
University of Massachusetts at Amherst
Amherst, Massachusetts

WILLIAM P. HENRY
Department of Psychology
University of Utah
Salt Lake City, Utah

KENNETH I. HOWARD
Department of Psychology
Northwestern University
Evanston, Illinois

STEPHEN S. ILARDI
Department of Psychology
Duke University
Durham, North Carolina

BERTRAM P. KARON
Department of Psychology
Michigan State University
East Lansing, Michigan

ALAN E. KAZDIN
Department of Psychology
Yale University
New Haven, Connecticut

PHILIP C. KENDALL
Department of Psychology
Temple University
Philadelphia, Pennsylvania

GERALD P. KOOCHER
Department of Psychiatry
Children's Hospital and Harvard Medical School
Boston, Massachusetts

ROBERT P. LIBERMAN
Department of Psychiatry
University of California, Los Angeles
Los Angeles, California

MICHAEL J. MAHONEY
Department of Psychology
University of North Texas
Denton, Texas

BRUCE MCBEATH
St. Mary's Graduate School
Novato, California

DONALD H. MEICHENBAUM
Department of Psychology
University of Waterloo
Waterloo, Ontario, Canada

KIM T. MUESER
Department of Psychiatry
Dartmouth Medical School
Hanover, New Hampshire

ROBERT A. MURPHY
Department of Psychology
University of Massachusetts at Amherst
Amherst, Massachusetts

JOHN C. NORCROSS
Department of Psychology
University of Scranton
Scranton, Pennsylvania

DAVID E. ORLINSKY
Committee on Human Development
University of Chicago
Chicago, Illinois

SUSAN M. PANICHELLI
Department of Psychology
Temple University
Philadelphia, Pennsylvania

KATHLEEN M. PATTERSON
Program in Counseling/Clinical/School Psychology
Graduate School of Education
University of California, Santa Barbara
Santa Barbara, California

MICHAEL ROHRBAUGH
Department of Psychology
University of Arizona
Tucson, Arizona

MAX ROSENBAUM
Nova Southeast University
Palm Beach, Florida

BRIAN F. SHAW
Department of Psychiatry
The Toronto Hospital and University of Toronto
Toronto, Ontario, Canada

JULIA SHIANG
Pacific Graduate School of Psychology
Palo Alto, California
Department of Psychiatry and Behavioral Sciences
Stanford University School of Medicine
Stanford, California

VARDA SHOHAM
Department of Psychology
University of Arizona
Tucson, Arizona

CAROL SPUNGEN
Couples Alcoholism Treatment Project
Graduate School of Education
University of California, Santa Barbara
Santa Barbara, California

SUSAN L. STEINBERG
Veterans Administration Outpatient Clinic
Los Angeles, California

PETER STEINGLASS
Ackerman Institute for Family Therapy
New York, New York

HANS H. STRUPP
Department of Psychology
Vanderbilt University
Nashville, Tennessee

LARRY W. THOMPSON
Department of Psychiatry and Behavioral Sciences
Veterans Affairs Medical Center
Palo Alto, California
Department of Psychiatry and Behavioral Sciences
Stanford University School of Medicine
Stanford, California

ANMARIE J. WIDENER
Department of Psychology
Michigan State University
East Lansing, Michigan

REBECCA E. WILLIAMS
Program in Counseling/Clinical/School Psychology
Graduate School of Education
University of California, Santa Barbara
Santa Barbara, California

IRVIN YALOM
Department of Psychiatry and Behavioral Sciences
Stanford University School of Medicine
Stanford, California

I
THEORIES AND PRACTICES OF PSYCHOTHERAPY

1

Unity and Diversity Among Psychotherapies: A Comparative Perspective

David E. Orlinsky
Kenneth I. Howard

Until recently, it was customary to find psychotherapies discussed as competing claimants to fundamental truths about human nature, and as rival systems for healing the ills and solving the personal problems of modern individuals. Each therapeutic ideology depended on the allegiance of believers who assumed that, if their system was right, the others must be wrong. Disagreement on point of view and with respect to procedure soon led to schism and the multiplication of separate "schools." As with the religious sects of former times, adherents of the various therapeutic schools turned inward to their own communities for mutual support and ranged in their attitudes toward other systems from studied indifference to intemperate criticism.

Fortunately for those who prefer debate to radiate light rather than heat, several factors have led to a significant change in this situation. One is the growing number of variants on the major psychotherapeutic systems, which seem to divide and subdivide and combine endlessly into a plethora of particular treatment approaches. The sheer multiplicity of psychotherapies has effectively undermined the credibility of absolute claims that any one of them might assert.

A second factor inducing change in the psychotherapeutic scene is the growing number of psychotherapists. Many of these fourth-, fifth-, or sixth-generation practitioners, feel less need to seek professional security within closed communities, and are inclined to find useful ideas and procedures in more than one of the psychotherapies. Relatively few seem to have either the personal need or the ideological disposition to be "true believers" in a single system. They are more committed to helping their patients than to doctrinal purity, with the possible exception of some extreme groups such as the Lacanians in France (e.g., Turkle, 1978). Large numbers of psychotherapists follow a pragmatic policy of using what seems to be helpful to their clients and describe themselves as "eclectic" or "integrative" in their practice (Beutler, 1983; Garfield, 1980; Norcross, 1986; Norcross & Goldfried, 1992).

A third factor leading to a new perspective on the psychotherapies is the significant growth of empirical research on psychotherapy, which has accelerated strikingly in the past decade (e.g., Orlinsky, Grawe, & Parks, 1994). In the beginning, this research was undertaken by clinicians to defend psychotherapy against the attack of critics like Eysenck (1952) or to prove the efficacy or superiority of a particular therapeutic system. By the mid-1980s, a growing body of evidence seemed to have demonstrated the first of these points but to have failed consistently to support the second. Psychotherapies in general were shown in a large number of controlled studies to have a significant positive effect on most patients in comparison to untreated persons (e.g., Lambert & Bergin, 1994; McNeilly & Howard, 1991; Shapiro & Shapiro, 1982; Smith, Glass, & Miller, 1980). However, none of the therapeutic systems studied showed consistent superiority over the others, and such differences as were found could usually be explained more plausibly in terms of circumstances having to do with research methodology.

All these factors have brought about a state of ferment and uncertainty in contemporary psychotherapy. Old dogmatisms now seem more bark than bite, and self-sufficient catechisms have been declawed. Research has led many clinicians to adopt an attitude that is more confident and modestly open-minded, yet the same research so far has not provided effective guidance for clinical practice. Accordingly, therapists have continued to experiment personally in order to find what works best for them and for their patients.

Under these circumstances, how can students of the psychotherapies gain a comprehensive overview of the field and an understanding of its essential features? What do the various psychotherapies have in common? Why are there so many psychotherapies? What basic features link them and yet differentiate them as a group from other forms of caregiving and professional practice? How can they be systematically compared to one another?

Help in answering these questions may be found in another recent development that has not been adequately appreciated by clinical researchers,[1] that is, the growth of a comparative ethnographic and historical literature on equivalents to modern psychotherapies in other cultures and other times. This has led to a new perspective that highlights the essential coexistence of culture and psychotherapy, illuminating the psychotherapeutic element in culture, as well as the cultural element in psychotherapy, and the responsiveness of therapeutic systems to historical changes that have taken place in contemporary societies.

The remainder of this chapter is divided into four sections. The first provides a quick sketch of the factors that make psychotherapy, in one form or another, a universal function found in all human cultures. The next section focuses on the distinctive features of modern (and modernizing) societies and examines the cultural form of psychotherapy that has evolved to meet the needs of people who live within them. The third section focuses on the specific forms of psychotherapy in modern societies, and considers the factors and forces that have led to their differentiation. Finally, the last section offers an integrative framework for the comparative study of therapeutic processes found in modern psychotherapies. We hope that taking an overall view of the field will help students of the psychotherapies gain a deeper insight into their foundations.

PSYCHOTHERAPY AS A UNIVERSAL FUNCTION OF CULTURES

Psychotherapeutic activities, or their equivalents, no doubt have been carried on since time immemorial. Examples of these are plentiful. Preliterate shamans journeyed into the spirit world in order to combat the supernatural beings that possessed their fellow tribesmen (Eliade, 1964; Levi-Strauss, 1967a). David eased the melancholic fits of King Saul with music, and in later times biblical scribes in Judea advised troubled congregants on how to conduct their lives in accordance with God's law (Weber, 1921/1952). Sophist philosophers in classical Athens used their rhetorical skills for a fee, presenting rational arguments to persuade depressed citizens out of melancholic moods (Lain Entralgo, 1970). Throughout the ancient Mediterranean world, mystagogues led their devotees through esoteric rituals designed to loosen their souls from astrological bondage to the fate-determining stars (Dodds, 1965). During the Middle Ages, priestly confessors heard sinners' admissions of their transgressions and prescribed penances to cleanse their souls (Clebsch & Jaekle, 1967; McNeill, 1951). Individual mystics everywhere engaged in ascetic practices to achieve release from the desires and suffering evoked by the material world (Weber, 1922/1963), and the communal symbolism of tragic drama or sacred mass or revivalistic prayer meetings has provided emotional catharsis throughout the ages for their participants by purging them vicariously of anxiety and guilt (Aristotle, 1954; LaBarre, 1969; Warner, 1961). Healing rituals and traditional medical and religious practices with significant psychotherapeutic effects are found in tribal, traditional, and modern societies around the world (e.g., Burridge, 1969; Fabrega & Silver, 1973; Kakar, 1983; Kiev, 1964; Kleinman 1980, 1988; Lévi-Strauss, 1967a, 1967b; Lewis, 1971; McGuire, 1988; Métraux, 1972; Obeyesekere, 1981; Turner, 1969; Wallace, 1956).

Every culture has devised activities of some sort to provide guidance, relief, or consolation to vulnerable individuals in ordinary times, and to ordinary individuals in times of extraordinary stress (Berger, 1967; Geertz, 1973; Rieff, 1968). The examples cited above can be seen as true antecedents and functional equivalents of modern psychotherapy. Alternatively, and more precisely, the modern scientific psychotherapies can be seen as modes of healing that have been reinvented to suit the secular, rational, and technological culture that predominates among the middle and elite strata of urban industrial society.

Magical, religious, or secular practices that have a psychotherapeutic function can be found in every culture. The reason for this is that every culture posits an ideal type of personality, or a set of related ideal types, which Rieff (1968) referred to as its "character ideal." Every culture also posits an ideal life cycle, or a set of related life cycle patterns, usually differentiated according to gender and social class or caste.

Individuals are valued and, more important

for their mental health, experience themselves as worthy of appreciation to the extent that they embody appropriate character ideals. Similarly, the lives that individuals lead are viewed by others and are experienced by themselves as meaningful to the extent that they approximate personally significant life cycle ideals.[2]

Yet every culture also confronts a range of individual differences in its members based on variability in their biological inheritance and constitution, their different socialization experiences, their occupation of diverse roles in the adult division of labor, and (always and everywhere) the random play of accident or fortune (e.g., Dunn & Plomin, 1990; Runyan, 1984). These differences mean that almost all individuals will deviate to some extent from the cultural ideals of character and life cycle development (whatever their content) and that a few individuals will deviate greatly from those ideals.

Minor deviations from cultural ideals are so common that they are taken for granted as normal and are dealt with, for the most part, in commonsense[3] ways. Major deviations are rarer by definition, but constitute socially problematic forms of deviance that usually require the elaboration of specialized cultural procedures.

The sociologist Talcott Parsons (1964) described the conditions under which societies interpret behavioral deviance as illness calling for therapeutic measures (rather than as crime, disloyalty, or sin). He noted that "the primary criteria for mental illness must be defined with reference to the social role-performance of the individual"; that "it is as an *incapacity* to meet the expectations of social roles that mental illness becomes a problem in social relationships . . . for both the sick person and others with whom he associates" (p. 258; emphasis added).

This criterion has a double aspect. The individual's capacity for participation involves self-management skills as well as interpersonal skills, as the sociologist Erving Goffman (1967) pointed out. For example, self-understanding and self-control are just as essential for social participation as are the capacities for affiliation, assertiveness, and accommodation.

Wherever it lies, the incapacity in question must be viewed by all concerned as essentially involuntary:

> One of the principal criteria of illness [is] that the sick person "couldn't help it." Even though he may have become ill or disabled through some sort of carelessness or negligence, he cannot legitimately be expected to get well simply by deciding to be well, or by "pulling himself together." Some kind of underlying reorganizing process has to take place, biological or "mental," which can be guided or controlled in various ways, but [the incapacity] cannot simply be eliminated by an "act of will." On the other hand, both obedience to norms and fulfillment of obligations . . . are ordinarily treated as involving "voluntary" decisions; the normal individual can legitimately be "held responsible." (Parsons, 1964, p. 271)

Using Parsons' general formula, we can define intentional psychotherapeutic activities, no matter what their form, as efforts that are made to guide and control the "underlying reorganizing process[es]" necessary to restore (and refine) the individual's *capacity* to participate in normal social relationships. Since that capacity has both *intra*personal and *inter*personal aspects, therapeutic measures might focus primarily on problems in one or the other or both of those areas.

It is, of course, essential to note that what is regarded as normal depends on the *expectations* that individuals have for their participation in significant relationships. This, in turn, depends in part on the expectations that others have of them. Thus, what seems to be a tolerable level of deviance in some social settings and for some persons may be experienced in other settings or by other persons as sufficiently distressing to require some form of special therapeutic intervention. It is quite possible, and in fact not uncommon, that individuals who are not grossly abnormal or deviant may seek psychotherapy. For example, persons in situations that demand extraordinary interpersonal sensitivity and skill are likely to find that the development

of their capacities to a merely ordinary extent fails to meet the need.

If psychotherapies exist in some form in every culture, so too must individuals who can be described as professional therapists. Following the general sociological formula proposed above, professional psychotherapists can be defined as persons who become *expert* at guiding and controlling "underlying reorganizing process[es]" and who practice that expertise as part of their *vocation*. They may appear as shamans, healers, priests, doctors, or counselors, depending on the cultural pattern that predominates in their society. Typically, they belong to some sort of professional community (e.g., a healing society, a church, or an occupational association) that regulates their activities and provides a healing ideology to legitimate (i.e., explain and justify) those activities.

In modern societies, of course, the dominant psychotherapeutic systems are legitimated by invoking the unqestioned cultural authority of science. Every modern psychotherapy represents itself as having some sort of scientific warrant and grounds itself symbolically (through its terminology and manner of practice) either in an already established discipline or in a new science that it claims to have discovered. Accordingly, the archetypal psychotherapist is a doctor of medical or psychological science or some other sort of university-trained professional (e.g., counselor or social worker) with an advanced postgraduate degree.

From a global perspective, psychotherapy in this modern sense has become a familiar and widespread phenomenon in a relatively small group of countries concentrated mainly in Europe and North America. Of course, modern psychotherapists practice in other countries too; in fact, they are found wherever Western culture predominates (e.g., Argentina, Australia, Israel, South Africa) or wherever a substantial segment of a traditional non-European population has been educated in Western cultural ways (e.g., India, Japan, Korea, Taiwan). However, there are also many countries without psychotherapists or psychotherapy in the modern sense, and it is important to remember that there are significant populations within even the most modern countries for whom traditional religious and folk healing practices still constitute viable forms of psychotherapeutic intervention (e.g., McGuire, 1988).

PSYCHOTHERAPIES IN URBAN TECHNOLOGICAL SOCIETIES

The similarities among those nations in which modern psychotherapies have gained general acceptance rest on the fact that they are urban technological societies. Urban technological societies are distinguished by several related characteristics (Berger, Berger, & Kellner, 1974; Parsons, 1969; Weber, 1958; Wirth, 1938). Large concentrations of population live and work in cities or their suburbs. Economic production and distribution, management, transportation, and communications media all depend on advanced mechanical and electronic technologies. Private enterprise, government, and social administration generally are organized rationally or bureaucratically, basing their authority on explicitly formulated goals and rules of procedure rather than on time-honored tradition or the charisma of inspired leaders. Social strata are differentiated in terms of lifestyles centering on the consumption of material and symbolic goods and services. Collective activities and civic identity are construed primarily in terms of secular values and ideologies.

The characteristics of urban technological societies mentioned above refer mainly to the public sphere—social, economic, and political institutions. However, the common feature of these societies that is most significant for understanding the modern psychotherapies is the polarization of life into public and private spheres. As noted by the French historian Philippe Ariès (1989):

> The problem of private life in the modern era must be approached from two directions. One approach should focus on the opposition between the public servant and the private individual and the relations between the state and what would ultimately become the domestic preserve. The other should focus on the transition from an anonymous form of sociability, in which notions of public and private were confounded, to a more fragmented sociability that combines remnants of the old anonymous form with relations based on professional affinities and with the equally private relations born of domestic life. (p. 11)

The public sphere of life is vast in scale and confronts individual members of society as massive and complex beyond comprehension. Individuals are linked to these public institutions in their everyday lives mainly through their occupational roles and through exposure to mass media, and more occasionally (though equally vitally) through the impact of their rights and duties as citizens.

In contrast, private life is typically composed of a small number of close personal relationships, mainly with immediate family members plus a few intimate friends or companions. For most people, private life centers on domestic relations, bodily activities and experiences, and leisure-time pursuits. The hallmark of this private sphere is that it is experienced as *personal* This is the sphere where individual personality and intimate relationships are cultivated and expressed, in counterpoint to the public sphere, where a norm of impersonality predominates (although the boundary is sometimes blurred at crucial points of interface between the private and public spheres, as shown by the tendency of many professional workers to invest their sense of identity and personal self-esteem in their occupational roles).

In urban technological societies, the sphere of private life is where the individual is supposed to develop and maintain a valued sense of personal identity, achieve a positive balance of emotional satisfaction and frustration, and carry on a spiritually meaningful existence. Frustrations and failures in these matters are viewed as problems of private life,[4] and those problems have been viewed as signs or symptoms of "illness" (as defined by Parsons) to the extent that they seem to result from *involuntary* difficulties in the individual's *capacities* "to meet the expectations of social roles" in the private sphere.

An intensely personal and relatively segregated private life of this sort is so common, and so much the center of everyday life, that it is hard to realize that it is a historically conditioned rather than a universal feature of human existence. Yet ethnographic and historical research has abundantly demonstrated that private life as we know it is largely the creation of urban technological society; that it is broadly associated with the cultural emergence of a heightened individuality and consciousness of self in personality; and that it is essentially a new sphere of existence with distinctive developmental challenges, satisfactions, and stresses.

Creation of an intensely differentiated sphere of private life occurred through the convergence of several factors. To understand these, it is necessary to remember that urban technological societies emerged historically from preexisting traditional societies in which the majority of the population was engaged in agriculture, lived on farms or in rural villages, and understood the world primarily in religiously defined terms. This transformation was relatively gradual in some countries and precipitous in others, but everywhere it occurred, it wrought massive changes in the scope, scale, and quality of social life and radically altered the conditions under which individual members of society conceive, construct, and seek to control their personal lives.

A critical change was the physical and institutional separation between workplace and household brought about by the factory system. A related change was the emergence of the small nuclear family (Parsons 1954; Shorter 1975; Zaretsky 1973). Still another was the creation of anonymous population masses in urban centers (Simmel 1950a; Wirth 1938). These trends had their source in the concentration of industry in areas having ready access to sources of energy and transportation and the demand of the occupational system for a mobile work force. Other changes also had convergent effects. For most people, work has been rationalized and depersonalized to the point where it provides little sense of personal meaning, especially for those who have "jobs" rather than "careers" (Bell, 1960; Marx 1844/1978). On a cultural level, the "disenchantment" of nature

through expansion of a secular scientific world view has made the cosmos seem a place devoid of life and inhospitable to human feeling (Berger et al., 1974; Weber, 1904/1958), whereas once, through religion, the cosmos provided an imperative and transcendent sense of familial connection (Freud, 1930/1961; Warner, 1961).

In the long run, these changes had the effect of concentrating the individual's emotional energies and needs for meaningful attachment and identity into a highly concentrated sphere consisting of a small number of close but individually negotiated (and therefore always somewhat fragile) personal relationships (e.g., Mauss, 1985; Simmel, 1950b). Family ties still provide a more or less stable network of social relations for many people, if only because blood relatives are inherited rather than acquired, but this factor is mitigated by the voluntary and vulnerable nature of the marital bond. Traditional religion also still provides a symbolic safety net for many, but with denominational pluralism and separation between church and state, religious congregations have become voluntary organizations that people may join or not, based on individual preference, rather than being compelling and inclusive sources of meaningful orientation (Luckmann, 1967). This further magnifies the importance for most people of a few fragile, intimate relationships as areas of private life within which most individuals hope to find a sense of personal identity, emotional fulfillment, and meaningful community. These few attachments, mainly focused within the nuclear family, assume great importance as the sources of support and control in the individual's life. Yet, because they are so few and because each is so important, they are often difficult to manage and leave the individual peculiarly vulnerable to experiences of conflict and loss.

People growing up and leading their adult lives in urban technological societies are subjected to chronic or recurrent stresses generated by the urban technological pattern of life. Among the conditions that generate stress are geographic and social mobility, anonymity, rapid intergenerational change, and powerlessness associated with a social life led among masses of unknown people rather than among familiar individuals. These same conditions also erode the institutional supports of traditional community life in ways that create widespread problems in living for individuals, couples, and family groups and engender addictive, psychosomatic, or emotional illnesses in individuals with specific vulnerabilities. The inherent difficulty of marital, parental, filial, and sibling attachments, and the constant erosion of friendship attachments in a highly mobile society, leave many individuals in need of help.

In such circumstances, individuals are likely to have to cope with demoralization and disorientation, frustration and violence, psychological regression, and painful states of self-alienation. Certainly the conditions of life in traditional and tribal societies generate problems too, often much worse than ours, but people in those societies have other types of problems and other cultural forms to help cope with them. They have shamans and priests, folk healers and mystagogues. Local versions of those types of helpers remain active to some degree in urban technological societies among the least urbanized and, in cities, least educated, least affluent, and technologically least sophisticated segments of the population. But what of the more educated, urbanized, technologically sophisticated, relatively affluent segments of the population—who are too sophisticated to be "holy rollers" and too secular,[5] to hope for divine intervention? Where do they turn for help?

The answer is that they turn to modern scientific psychotherapies, which are offered as expert services by professionals trained in disciplines that provide a relevant knowledge base for therapeutic intervention. These therapies have evolved as ways to cope with the causes of, and problems engendered by, those stresses, frustrations, and failures of private life that exceed the ameliorative and corrective resources of common sense and ordinary social support. The modern psychotherapies address themselves to problems and disorders that are manifested as symptoms, inhibitions, and anxieties—directly in the sphere of private life (e.g., intimate relationships or psychosomatic disor-

ders), and in other areas of personal functioning insofar as they influence or are influenced by the sense of self that is sustained in the sphere of private life (e.g., educational or work performance). These therapies represent various approaches to understanding and treating these disorders, each focusing on one or more type of personal dysfunction, offering a specialized viewpoint on its causes, and proposing a set of techniques for its remedy (Beutler & Clarkin, 1990).

Thus, the modern psychotherapies may be described generically as involving a *professional service* that provides *personal help* in the sphere of *private life* under the symbolic authority and guidance of *scientific knowledge*. As a professional service, psychotherapy is a contractual business relationship engaged in by recognized experts, for a fee or as an entitlement, with clients who wish to avail themselves of that expertise. It is an occupation and form of employment for the therapist and an economic transaction for the client.

By contrast, in providing personal help, the modern psychotherapies derive ultimately from the culture's ideal model of caring parental love[6] (e.g., Halmos, 1970). They concentrate on the personal dysfunctions, problematic feelings, and developmental needs of the patient (selflessly "putting baby first") and require—as an ethical principle—that therapists limit the expression of *their* personal needs to their *own* private lives while consistently monitoring their personal involvement in treatment in order to avoid conflicts of interest.[7]

This combination of professional service with personal attachment as contrasting and even contrary social structural elements[8] into a single relationship is a distinctive feature of the modern forms of psychotherapy. The professional service relationship (rooted in economic exchange) imposes a formal contractual framework on psychotherapy and requires that therapists have an explicit apparatus of technical expertise. The helping personal attachment (rooted in a sense of community) makes psychotherapy an engagement between human beings and emphasizes the nature of the bond that forms between them. This contrast between the business and personal aspects of the modern therapies[9] is further reflected in a striking asymmetry in relationship. Patients bare the intimate details of their private lives for therapeutic examination and intervention, whereas the private lives of therapists remain largely cloaked in professional anonymity.

Another distinctive feature of modern psychotherapies is their attunement to the secular-scientific sphere of culture, as distinct from its traditional institutionalization in the ministry and its persistent presence in ethnic folk-healing practices. In terms made familiar by the sociologist Max Weber (1978), the modern therapies operate under the aegis of the rational authority of science, rather than traditional authority (e.g., the ordination of priests by bishops) or charismatic authority (e.g., a special spiritual gift of healing powers).[10] The modern psychotherapies strive to be *scientific* in two distinct senses of the term.

They are scientific, first, in the sense that the theories they propound about psychological illnesses and therapeutic interventions must be strictly *naturalistic*. Only conditions, forces, and agents recognized as present in nature or society may be invoked. Thus, although there is considerable disagreement as to whether personal problems are due to genetic defects, traumatic experiences, conflicts between internal drives and defenses, faulty cognitive habits, inadequate interpersonal skills, existential dilemmas, or various combinations of these factors, there is complete agreement that such explanations may *not* invoke benign or malevolent divinities, ancestral spirits, or other supernatural agencies.

The second sense in which the modern psychotherapies are constrained to be scientific is the use of *empirical research* to provide the knowledge base for their operations and to demonstrate their clinical effectiveness. This aspect of scientific culture has only recently begun to be felt by practitioners,[11] and even now not by all. Nor is there yet agreement, even among researchers, as to which sciences—cognitive, behavioral, biological, social, linguistic, and so on—provide the most relevant bases for therapeutic practice. The current psychotherapeutic scene accordingly supports a wide range of treatment models, each of which claims to be scientific in some respect.

THE VARIETY OF PSYCHOTHERAPIES AND PSYCHOTHERAPISTS

Professional psychotherapies are typically distinguished in terms of their theoretical orientations or therapeutic ideologies. A very rough delineation of modern therapeutic orientations finds four broad categories or streams, each with significant variations and internally conflicting currents. These are the analytic or psychodynamic therapies, the behavioral or cognitive-behavioral therapies, the experiential or humanistic therapies, and the systemic or structural-strategic therapies.[12]

The *analytic-dynamic* psychotherapies include classical psychoanalysis and its early variants (Adler, 1956; Freud, 1963; Fromm-Reichmann, 1950; Jung, 1966; Luborsky, 1984; Thomä & Kächele, 1985, 1988) as well as various analytically oriented therapies (Eagle, 1984) that have developed under the influence of existential philosophy (Laing, 1965), interpersonal theory (Sullivan, 1953), linguistics (Lacan, 1978), object-relations theory (Greenberg & Mitchell, 1983), ego psychology (Hartmann, 1964), and self-psychology (Kohut, 1984). What they have in common is an emphasis on the salience of motivational forces (hence the term *psychodynamic*), particularly motivations of which patients are unaware, and situations of conflict between motives. They typically aim to provide patients with insight into their unconscious motivations as a means toward resolving conflicts and redirecting energies toward current adaptational tasks.

The *cognitive-behavioral* therapies include two broad streams: those based primarily on classical conditioning, operant conditioning, or social learning theory (e.g., Bandura, 1969; Goldfried & Davison, 1976; Kanfer & Phillips, 1970; Wolpe, 1958) and those based on combinations of cognitive and behavioral principles, such as Kelly's (1955) personal construct theory, Beck's (1976) cognitive therapy, and Ellis'

(1962) rational-emotive therapy. What these have in common is a shared emphasis on maladaptive habits caused by faulty learning and also, in the cognitive therapies, by faulty reasoning. These treatments typically aim to correct maladaptive patterns of behavior and thought by weakening or suppressing old habits (e.g., through extinction, logical demonstration, or counterconditioning) and reeducating or retraining patients with more effective cognitive and interpersonal skills (e.g., assertiveness training).

The *experiential-expressive* therapies include client-centered psychotherapy (Rogers, 1951, 1961), gestalt therapy (Perls, 1976), focusing (Gendlin, 1981), Zen therapies (Watts, 1961), the symbolic-experiential therapy of Whitaker and others of the Atlanta school (Whitaker & Malone, 1953), imagery therapies such as guided affective imagery and eidetic therapy (Singer & Pope, 1978), logotherapy (Frankl, 1967), dialogical or conversational therapy (Hobson, 1985), and bioenergetic or other neo-Reichian body therapies (Lowen, 1975). What these have in common is an emphasis on concrete, nonrational or prerational, symbolic aspects of experience—emotion, bodily sensation and feeling, imagery, and imaginative fantasy—and the failure to give these adequate expression in consciousness and behavior. Such therapies aim to restore or attain psychological well-being through creative self-expression, the reattunement or recentering of consciousness in the flow of immediate sensory and affective experience, and the rebalancing or harmonizing of personal energies.

The *strategic-systemic* therapies originated mainly among analysts of communications and social transactions, practitioners of marital and family therapy, and hypnotherapists (e.g., Berne, 1961; Bowen, 1978; Haley, 1963, 1973; Minuchin, 1974; Ruesch & Bateson, 1951; Satir, 1964; Watzlawick, Beavin, & Jackson, 1967; Watzlawick, Weakland, & Fisch, 1974). One finds a common emphasis among them on the exchange and processing of information, conflict in the flow of influence among intimates, and an active but indirect approach to resolving problems.

To complicate the picture further, contemporary therapies are also differentiated in terms of their format and in terms of the special problem populations they serve. Thus, there are individual, couple, family, group, and milieu therapies. There are specialized forms of child psychotherapy (e.g., play therapy), geriatric therapy (e.g., life reminiscence), feminist therapy, training groups, encounter groups, self-help groups, associational and residential treatment communities for alcohol abuse and drug addiction, and so forth.

Still more variation is added by the fact that, although there are many professional psychotherapists, there is as yet no coherent and unified profession of psychotherapy (Henry, Sims, & Spray, 1971). Members of a number of different professions claim the right to practice psychotherapy as subspecialty fields within their basic professions. In the contemporary United States, for example,[13] one finds psychotherapy offered both in institutions and in private practice by *some* (but by no means all) psychiatrists, clinical psychologists, clinical social workers, and psychiatric nurses. As specialists in psychotherapy, they represent the most visible but not the only mental health service delivery system (e.g., Taube, Mechanic, & Hohmann, 1989). There is an educational system in which counseling psychologists and school social workers are primary providers. Primary care physicians in the general medical service delivery system provide a substantial amount of pharmacological and nonspecialized psychosocial mental health services to less psychologically sophisticated patients. In addition, one finds trained professional marital counselors connected to the courts or other institutional systems. Even less visible to secular psychotherapists and researchers is an important pastoral care system sponsored by religious denominations in which ministers and ordained pastoral therapists are primary providers (e.g., Abbott, 1988; Holifield, 1983). Finally, there is an extensive network of specialized self-help groups (e.g., Hurvitz, 1974) in which professional therapists are sometimes used as consultants.

A certain proportion of subjectively distressed, functionally impaired, and/or socially deviant persons take varied pathways into these mental health service delivery systems (e.g., Kadushin, 1969; Phillips, 1985; Ryan, 1969; Saunders & Resnick, 1992). The individual's gender, age, level of education, occupational status, religion and degree of religiosity, ethnic background, area of residence, and psychological sophistication are all factors in this process. A national survey of the utilization of outpatient mental health services in 1980 found that in the United States:

> white people have almost double the probability of a mental health visit than people of other races; females have a 40 percent higher probability than males have; proportions with visits are highest among adults 25–64 years of age. . . . Adults (over 17 years of age) with 13 or more years of education have a 54 percent higher probability of an ambulatory mental health visit than those with less education have . . . [and] had an average of 58 percent more visits than those with less education. (Taube et al., 1984, p. 3)

Among those who reach the mental health service system, educational and socioeconomic status also are influential factors in determining continuance in treatment (Garfield, 1986). Most of those who enter therapy have a brief experience, averaging approximately five or six sessions. A relatively small subgroup of patients becomes committed to longer treatment and utilizes a disproportionate number of sessions (e.g., Howard, Davidson, O'Mahoney, Orlinsky, & Brown, 1989). Yet, in the words of a popular journalist (Hunt, 1987), it appears, despite all these selective factors, that "Psychotherapy . . . is no longer the avant-garde fad of an elite. It has become instead an essential component of our service economy, a commodity that a large segment of the population needs in order to deal with problems of contemporary living."

But why are there so many and such diverse forms of psychotherapy in modern societies? A plausible explanation for this state of affairs can be found in the fact that urban technological societies are highly differentiated social and cultural systems. Advanced division of labor in economic affairs results in a great degree of occupational specialization. Large populations in urban areas are typically ethnically diverse and culturally pluralistic, with consequent diversification of beliefs and values. The prevailing pattern of individualized, voluntary mate selection and the ubiquitous presence of mass communications tend to ensure a thorough mixing of parental backgrounds and cultural models. With regard to personality, these factors foster a broad range of inherited temperaments, favor wide differences in childhood socialization, and promote individuation in styles of adult identity.

This situation may be clarified by comparing the specific types of psychotherapy to a group of biological *species* that belong to the same *genera* (i.e., are generically the same) but have evolved differentially in adapting to diverse niches or microenvironments in a complex social-cultural system. The different species of psychotherapy have adapted, first of all, to variations in the type of problem or disorder from which patients suffer. Psychoanalysis originally evolved as a treatment model for hysterias and obsessive-compulsive neuroses. Interpersonal therapy, as developed by Sullivan, Fromm-Reichmann, and Searles, evolved as a treatment model for schizophrenias. Behavior therapy evolved as a treatment model for phobias. Cognitive therapy evolved as a treatment model for depression. And so forth.

A second source of variation to which specific psychotherapies have adapted are the different social circumstances, subcultures, personality types, and life conditions of patients. Thus, Freud's patients tended to be relatively young, upper-middle-class adults. Jung did much work with middle-aged patients, who also differed in cultural background from Freud's clients. Adler was committed to treating working-class patients. Melanie Klein worked with very young children. By contrast, Rogers worked in university settings, typically (and most successfully) with highly educated, introspective, self-directed clients. As a further contrast, Goldstein developed a structured behavioral model in working with relatively uneducated, nonintrospective clients (Goldstein & Stein, 1976), and Ayllon and Azrin (1968) evolved a behavioral token-economy model in working with institutionalized persons.

A third source of the differences among species of psychotherapy can be traced to variations in belief and value commitments, and in personality types, among psychotherapists. Some therapists are more contemplative, while others are more action-oriented; some are more rational and organized, others more intuitive; some are more extroverted, others more private; and so forth.

Thus the individuation and variability of human character, life conditions, and sociocultural environments that are so typical of the contemporary United States, but are also found in other countries, create a diversity of legitimate psychotherapeutic challenges. The spirit of experimentation, innovation, and progress that imbues modern culture[14] ensures that a variety of psychotherapeutic systems will to continue to evolve in response to these challenges. Since, under these conditions, there is not likely ever to be a single specific psychotherapy serviceable for all disorders, all patients, and all therapists, what is needed is a comparative framework that encourages the comparative study of psychotherapies in terms of their generic features.

A COMPARATIVE FRAMEWORK FOR THE STUDY OF PSYCHOTHERAPIES

Over the past two decades, a conceptual framework has gradually evolved in response to opportunities we have had to review and synthesize a rapidly expanding body of research evidence relating psychotherapeutic process to outcome (Howard & Orlinsky, 1972; Orlinsky, Grawe, & Parks, 1994; Orlinsky & Howard, 1978, 1986). This research-based view of psychotherapy has been successful in integrating more than 2,300 empirical findings into a coherent view of therapeutic process. We called it the *generic model* of psychotherapy because it focuses on the essential characteristics shared by the various specific psychotherapies (Orlinsky, 1989, 1992, 1994; Orlinsky & Howard, 1987a, 1987b). Understanding how the generic model may be used as a systematic framework for comparing the specific therapies requires clarification of the difference between *research therories* of psychotherapy and *clinical or treatment theories* of psychotherapy.

The primary purpose of any clinical theory is to guide therapists in conducting treatment with their patients. Every clinical theory provides a set of concepts that enables the therapist to interpret the subjective complaints and behavior of patients in terms of certain underlying problems. Every clinical theory also provides a repertory of specialized techniques, and rules for their use, to help the therapist intervene beneficially in the patient's situation.

Of course, different clinical theories construe patients' problems in different terms and suggest different modes of intervention. Yet, to be a psychotherapist, one must have practical mastery of *some* clinical theory. Mastery of a clinical theory provides the specialized language and expert knowledge that separate the professional therapist from the ordinary layperson who tries to be helpful. It also helps the therapist earn membership in a recognized community of professional psychotherapists. Having a professional community is essential for a psychotherapist, both as a source of referrals for potential patients and as a source of emotional support to counteract the stresses of therapeutic work.

A research theory of psychotherapy has very different functions. The primary purpose of a research theory is to guide investigators in conducting controlled studies of a phenomenon. Research theories provide a conceptual scheme of variables and rules for their detection that will enable the investigator to simplify complex phenomena and make systematic observations of their basic features. Another vital function of research theories is to suggest questions and hypotheses about the relationships among basic variables that can guide the design of specific studies. Finally, research theories help investigators explain the results of their observations and understand these results in relation to what has been established by earlier studies.

Thus, while there may be contrasts and conflicts between various clinical theories of psychotherapy, there is no inherent conflict between research theory and clinical theories. In linguistic terms, research and clinical theories are simply different modes of discourse. Research and clinical theories are tools of thought designed to accomplish different goals. However, research and clinical theories of psychotherapy are not unrelated. Insofar as clinical theories influence the interpretations and actions of therapists vis-à-vis their patients, the therapist's treatment model (i.e., clinical theory) may be viewed as one of the variables to be considered by a research theory of psychotherapy.[15]

Research theory thus, in principle, encompasses the whole variety of clinical theories, viewing them from a higher level of abstraction as alternative states of a specific variable. This research variable can be called the *therapist's treatment model*. Research theory enables investigators to ask how, how much, and under what conditions, the therapist's treatment model contributes to shaping the process and outcome of psychotherapy. By the same token, research theory provides a conceptual standpoint from which it is possible to have a systematic overview of clinical treatment models.

The generic model of psychotherapy is an example of a research theory. It was conceived for a different purpose, and at a different level of abstraction, than specific treatment theories. It can be used as framework for making systematic comparisons among the various specific approaches to therapy. Research to date has led us to distinguish six aspects or facets of the therapeutic process, each of which represents a broad category of variables but all of which operate concurrently and jointly define the parameters of any treatment.

First, the formal aspect of the process is usually called the *therapeutic contract*. This defines the respective goals and roles of the patient and therapist and specifies formal characteristics of the treatment, such as the fre-

quency and duration of sessions, the length of the treatment, whether it will be conducted as individual or group therapy, and so forth. The *therapist's treatment model* is a key element in the therapeutic contract, especially as it shapes the form and content of the therapist and patient roles. This treatment model consists of the following elements: a *philosophical anthropology*, presenting a more or less explicit conception of human nature and optimal human functioning; a *psychodiagnostic scheme* that enables therapists to make expert evaluations of the information and problems presented to them by their patients; a *repertory of intervention methods* that can be used to ameliorate or resolve patients' problems; and a *case management style* or recommended manner vis-à-vis patients as a guide to forming a safe and helpful mode of involvement.

Second, the instrumental or technical aspect of the process consists of *therapeutic operations* that are performed by the patient and therapist. This involves the *patient's presentation* of information to the therapist, both verbally and nonverbally, and the therapist's *expert evaluation* of that information in terms of the diagnostic and explanatory constructs provided by the therapist's treatment model. Based on this assessment of the patient's underlying problem, the treatment model indicates which *technical intervention* should be most helpful. Finally, to be successful, any type of therapeutic intervention requires a complementary mode of *cooperation* from the patient. Thus, if the problem the patient presents is judged to be caused by dynamically unconscious conflicts of motivation, then interpretation of the latent content of the patient's preconscious associations is a relevant technique for "making the unconscious conscious," and spontaneous free association is the optimal way for the patient to cooperate with this procedure.

Third, the interpersonal aspect of the process is called the *therapeutic bond*, since it focuses on the person-to-person relationship between patient and therapist. In group therapy, where the bond is multilateral rather than bilateral, this is described in terms of cohesiveness and group atmosphere. The quality of the bond is manifested in two ways. One is through the caliber of *therapeutic teamwork*—the participants' personal investment and ability to coordinate action in their respective roles. Another is the quality of their *personal rapport*—the resonance of their communication and the feelings they elicit in each other.

The fourth aspect of the therapeutic process is intrapersonal rather than interpersonal and reflects immediate states of personality functioning. Participants' *self-relatedness* refers to the way persons respond to themselves in the course of responding to the people, things, and forces around them. It includes the way persons experience their internal activation; formulate their self-awareness; control and direct their ideas, feelings, and urges; and evaluate themselves. In therapy, this is often referred to globally as *openness vs. defensiveness*. Individuals in an open state can absorb what is offered or available to them in their surroundings, adapting to take advantage of what is useful. Individuals in a defensive state need to screen and filter their responses more stringently—in order to maintain their self-control, self-esteem, or inner sense of safety—and they are able to avail themselves only of what matches the limitations they impose on themselves.

The fifth aspect of the therapeutic process that researchers have focused on concerns the immediate clinical productivity of therapeutic work, that is, *in-session impacts* such as insight, emotional relief, and remoralization. These *therapeutic realizations* of the patient's presumably have an intimate connection with the treatment outcome, yet they cannot be counted as outcome until they are effectively applied by the patient in problematic life situations outside of therapy. In-session impacts also include the personal rewards and frustrations that accrue to therapists as a result of their efforts to help their patients.

The sixth and final aspect of the therapeutic process is temporal in nature, and may be thought of in terms of strands of process that unfold as *sequential events* during sessions and that combine over blocks of sessions to define the distinctive *phases of treatment*. These sequential strands of process represent successive intersections of the other aspects of process, a series of momentary configurations of the contract, operations, bond, self-relatedness, and in-session impacts that cumulatively determine the overall course of treatment. The salience of this temporal aspect is demonstrated, for example, through interaction effects indicating that the character of events is partly determined by whether they occur early, middle or late within a session—or early, middle, or late in the course of treatment.

Figure 1.1 presents a conception of how the first five (nontemporal) aspects of the therapeutic process function as a system. These are represented in the middle, or *process*, level of the diagram. The top, or *input*, level indicates the preliminary requirements for therapy: a patient, a therapist, and a treatment setting that is part of a mental health service delivery system. These are necessary but not sufficient conditions for therapy to occur. They must be brought together and set in motion by a *therapeutic contract* between the parties by means of which the patient (or someone acting on behalf of the patient) engages the therapist for the specific purpose of treating the patient. Thus, the therapeutic process starts with the contract, but, of course, the contract must also remain in effect for the process to continue. Negotiation of the contract includes explicit agreement on such practical matters as when, where, and how often therapy sessions will take place; who will take part in those sessions; how much those sessions will cost; and who will pay. The concrete goals and methods of treatment, as well as how long the treatment will last, may or may not be discussed explicitly (depending on the sophistication of the patient and the treatment model and customary practice of the therapist). Once the patient freely enters into the contract, it is part of the therapist's job to protect its integrity so that treatment can be brought to a successful conclusion or, at any rate, be terminated only for legitimate reasons.

Two other aspects of the therapeutic process are initiated as direct consequences of the therapeutic contract. Formal *therapeutic operations* are begun in accordance with the therapist's

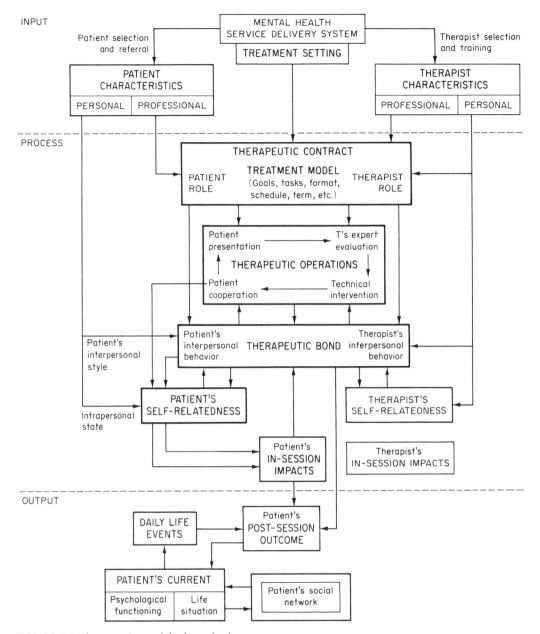

FIGURE 1.1 The generic model of psychotherapy.

treatment model. The patient is encouraged to present relevant information about his or her condition and experiences for the therapist's expert evaluation, on the basis of which the therapist initiates some type of intervention. The patient's cooperative participation (or lack of it) elicits further information for the therapist to evaluate and may also stimulate further elements of therapeutic processes. At any rate, the overt technical work of treatment follows this cyclical pattern.

Another aspect of the process that follows

directly from the therapeutic contract is the start of a person-to-person relationship between the patient and therapist. This *therapeutic bond* may be kept in the background and given only limited recognition or it may become an important focus on treatment, depending mainly on the therapist's treatment model and the patient's personal input. However, whether the bond is overtly emphasized or not, research has shown that it is centrally related to the therapeutic outcome (e.g., Horvath & Symonds, 1991; Orlinsky et al., 1994). Good outcomes seem to result when the therapeutic bond is characterized by mutual affirmation, empathy, and personal investment; poor outcomes when mistrust, misunderstanding, and superficiality prevail. The human qualities of the bond are determined largely through the interaction of the patient's and therapist's *inter*personal behaviors (Benjamin, 1974; Carson, 1969; Kiesler, 1982), but what the patient and therapist consider proper behavior in their roles with one another also influences the way that the bond develops.

In contrast to therapeutic operations and the therapeutic bond, the process element of *self-relatedness* does not depend directly on the therapeutic contract. Patient and therapist self-relatedness depend instead on the *intra*personal states of the participants during sessions. However, patient and therapist self-relatedness are not uninfluenced by what goes on during sessions. Experience of a safe and stimulating therapeutic bond enhances the participants' openness; by contrast, a bond that evokes anxiety or boredom results in constricted or unfocused states of self-relatedness.

The quality of self-relatedness is particularly important in regard to the most derivative and variable aspect of therapeutic process, which is *in-session impact*. Figure 1.1 shows this by representing patient self-relatedness as a filter[16] through which the effects of therapeutic operations and the therapeutic bond must pass. For example, a therapist's interpretation that could yield a helpful insight as an in-session impact might be misconstrued or quickly forgotten due to the patient's defensiveness. Given the same

quality of therapy, open patients are more likely than defensive ones to experience positive in-session impacts, since they are better able to take in and digest the therapist's interventions and the supportive atmosphere of the therapeutic bond.

The bottom, or *output*, level of Figure 1-1 suggests the factors that affect the influence of in-session therapeutic processes on the patient. During the period immediately following each therapy session the *postsession outcome* reflects what the patient retains of in-session session impacts. A good therapeutic bond also affects the postsession outcome by boosting the patient's morale. The length of time involved may vary from a few moments to several hours or days. This is determined largely by the nature of daily life events. While it lasts, however, the postsession outcome has an impact on the patient's current life situation and psychological functioning, and these, in turn, also influence the nature of daily life events. By this means, continuing positive output from therapy sessions can have a cumulative impact on the patient's life situation and psychological functioning. But, of course, other factors such as positive or negative changes in the patient's social network (family, friends, work situation, neighborhood) also have an impact on the patient's life situation and psychological functioning. Being involved in psychotherapy is just one part of the patient's life, but when it is effective, therapy can help the patient make the best of the opportunities and challenges that those other parts of life continually bring.

With the generic model as a comparative framework, students of the modern psychotherapies can raise a number of basic questions about each of the specific clinical approaches and about the empirical research that is relevant to each. The following are examples of some of these questions.

How does each approach formulate its *therapeutic contract*? What is its basic clinical theory or treatment model (philosophical anthropology, psychodiagnostic scheme, repertory of intervention methods or techniques, recommended style of case management)? How explicitly does it deal with issues of the therapeutic contract during therapy sessions? What special measures (if any) does it take to protect the psychological and ethical integrity of the contract?

How are actual *therapeutic operations* initiated and carried on? What type of information from patients is viewed as relevant to treatment, and how are patients helped to present that information? How do therapists formulate and utilize their expert evaluations? Are these communicated to the patient or just used as the basis for making interventions? Does the therapist formulate an explicit treatment plan or intervention strategy? Is there a typical sequence of interventions? To what extent, and in what terms, are treatment processes explained to patients? What steps (if any) are taken to promote the patient's cooperative participation?

How much recognition is given to the *therapeutic bond?* Are any specific methods available to enhance the quality of the bond? What explicit use (if any) is made of the bond during therapy sessions? How formal or informal are therapists in their manner of participating in the bond?

How much emphasis does each approach place on the patient's *self-relatedness?* On the therapist's self-relatedness? Are any special methods used to foster openness or counteract defensiveness in patients? In therapists?

What positive *in-session impacts* does each approach seek to achieve for patients? What negative in-session impacts does it recognize (if any)? To what are these attributed? How are they dealt with? What methods (if any) are used to help patients maintain positive in-session impacts after they leave the therapy session?

How are *sequential events* in therapy organized by each approach? How long is a typical treatment session? How frequently are sessions scheduled? How long is a typical course of treatment? Is the duration of treatment specified in advance? What stages or phases of therapy are recognized? How is the termination of treatment handled?

Finally, how does each approach *integrate* the various aspects of the therapeutic process?

What is the relative emphasis given to each? How are they organized or combined to achieve optimum effectiveness with respect to the goals that are sought?

Acknowledgment

Work on this chapter was partially supported by Research Grant R 01 MH42901 from the National Institute of Mental Health.

NOTES

1. With the notable exception of Jerome Frank (1961/1973; Frank & Frank, 1991).

2. By the same token, individuals tend to experience themselves as worthless (and to be rejected by others) insofar as they deviate from an accepted character ideal, and tend to experience their lives as stressful or meaningless insofar as they fail to follow a recognized life cycle ideal.

3. The idea of common sense as a cultural domain has been interestingly explored by Geertz (1983).

4. Except during times of widespread personal distress, when it may be interpreted as symptomatic of disorder in the cultural community at large, that is, as a problem in the public sphere primarily rather than in the private sphere alone.

5. This group includes the majority of liberal adherents of mainstream denominations in all religious communities, as well as humanists, agnostics, and atheists. It does not include fundamentalist groups within each religious community who reject modern culture and adhere fervently to a more traditional, supernaturalistic world view.

6. Similar if not identical to the *agape* of Christian theology (e.g., D'Arcy, 1956; De Rougemont, 1940; Tillich, 1960; Warner, 1961; Williams, 1938).

7. A major challenge of performing the therapist role is finding an effective balance between personal care and professional detachment. The optimal balance will vary somewhat with each patient–therapist pair, and even for each patient–therapist pair it will vary somewhat over the course of treatment. However, loss of vital balance in the therapeutic relationship in either direction (excess intimacy or excess impersonality) will likely result in therapeutic failure.

8. Implied here is Tönnies' (1887/1957) distinction between personal community *(gemeinschaft)* and economic society *(gesellschaft)*, which parallels

the fundamental categories of other writers who have been concerned with the contrast between traditional and modern societies, such as Durkheim's (1893/1964) distinction between *mechanical* and *organic* modes of social solidarity, and Maine's (1861/1960) concepts of *status* and *contract*.

9. In this regard, an instructive if irreverent parallel has been remarked by some observers (sotto voce) between professional psychotherapy and professional prostitution.

10. Nevertheless, tradition and charisma are significant informal phenomena in psychotherapeutic communities, as when psychoanalysts trace their lineages through training analysts back to their founding fathers (Freud's original disciples or Freud himself) or when new sects and schisms form around extraordinary personalities with influential "prophetic" visions (e.g., Kohut, Lacan, Laing).

11. While the origin of scientific psychotherapies in the first sense may be dated to the publication of Breuer and Freud's *Studies on Hysteria* in 1895, it was more than a half century before sustained empirical research on psychotherapeutic processes and outcomes was undertaken.

12. Even within a single orientation, historical circumstances have created significant differences across national boundaries (e.g., Kurzweil, 1989).

13. Striking differences in the historical development and interrelations of psychotherapeutic professions, and in mental health service delivery systems, exist even within culturally closely related countries, such as the United States and Great Britain. In some countries, particular professions are associated with specific therapeutic orientations, such as clinical psychologists with cognitive and behavioral therapies but not with psychoanalysis. In other countries, the professional specialities have evolved differently—for example, in Germany, where a medical specialty of psychosomatics and psychotherapy is represented in medical schools alongside more traditional departments of psychiatry (since the latter did not promote psychotherapeutic practice). Moreover, at the time this is being written, a major overhaul of the entire health care system is being planned in the United States, which is certain to have a significant impact of the delivery of mental health services, including psychotherapy.

14. To these may be added a spirit of commercial competitiveness which emphasizes marginal differentiation and purely symbolic distinctiveness among basically similar products and services in order to gain market share.

15. Reciprocally, research-based theories also

may provide therapists with knowledge that is useful in treating patients.

16. Therapist self-relatedness functions in a similar way.

REFERENCES

Abbott, A. (1988). *The system of professions: An essay on the division of expert labor.* Chicago: University of Chicago Press.

Adler, A. (1956). *The individual psychology of Alfred Adler* (H. & R. Ansbacher, Eds.). New York: Basic Books.

Ariès, P. (1989). Introduction. In R. Chartier (Ed.), *A history of private life: Vol. III. Passions of the Renaissance.* Cambridge, MA: Harvard University Press.

Aristotle (1954). *Poetics.* New York: Modern Library.

Ayllon, T., & Azrin, N. H. (1968). *The token economy: A motivational system for therapy and rehabilitation.* New York: Appleton-Century-Crofts.

Bandura, A. (1969). *Principles of behavior modification.* New York: Holt, Rinehart, & Winston.

Beck, A. T. (1976). *Cognitive therapy and the emotional disorders.* New York: New American Library.

Bell, D. (1960). Work and its discontents. In D. Bell, *The end of ideology* (pp. 227–272). Glencoe, IL: Free Press.

Benjamin, L. S. (1974). Structural analysis of social behavior. *Psychological Review, 81,* 392–425.

Berger, P. (1967) *The sacred canopy.* Garden City, NY: Doubleday Books.

Berger, P., Berger B., & Kellner, H. (1974). *The homeless mind: Modernization and consciousness.* New York: Vintage Books.

Berne, E. (1961). *Transactional analysis in psychotherapy.* New York: Grove Press.

Beutler, L. E. (1983). *Eclectic psychotherapy: A systematic approach.* Elmsford, NY: Pergamon Press.

Beutler, L. E., & Clarkin, J. F. (1990). *Systematic treatment selection: Toward targeted therapeutic interventions.* New York: Brunner/Mazel.

Bowen, M. (1978). *Family therapy in clinical practice.* New York: Jason Aronson.

Breuer, J., & Freud, S. (1959). *Studies on hysteria.* In J. Strachey (Ed.), *The standard edition of the complete psychological works of Sigmund Freud* (Vol. 2). London: Hogarth Press. (Original work published 1895)

Burridge, K. (1969). *New heaven, new earth.* New York: Schocken Books.

Carson, R. C. (1969). *Interaction concepts of personality.* Chicago: Aldine.

Clebsch, W. A., & Jaekle, C. R. (1967). *Pastoral care in historical perspective.* New York: Harper & Row.

D'Arcy, M. C. (1956). *The mind and heart of love.* New York: Meridian Books.

De Rougemont, D. (1940). *Love in the Western world.* New York: Pantheon Books.

Dodds, E. R. (1965). *Pagan and Christian in an age of anxiety.* New York: Norton.

Dunn, J., & Plomin, R. (1990). *Separate lives: Why siblings are so different.* New York: Basic Books.

Durkheim, E. (1964). *The division of labor in society.* New York: Free Press. (Original work published 1893)

Eagle, M. N. (1984). *Recent developments in psychoanalysis: A critical evaluation.* Cambridge, MA: Harvard University Press.

Eliade, M. (1964). *Shamanism: Archaic techniques of ecstasy.* Princeton, NJ: Princeton University Press.

Ellis, A. (1962). *Reason and emotion in psychotherapy.* New York: Lyle Stuart.

Eysenck, H. J. (1952). The effects of psychotherapy: An evaluation. *Journal of Consulting Psychology, 16,* 319–324.

Fabrega, H., & Silver, D. (1973). *Illness and shamanistic curing in Zinacantan.* Stanford, CA: Stanford University Press.

Frank. J. D. (1973). *Persuasion and healing: A comparative study of psychotherapy.* New York: Schocken Books. (Original work published 1961)

Frank. J. D., & Frank J. B. (1991). *Persuasion and healing: A comparative study of psychotherapy* (3rd ed.). Baltimore: Johns Hopkins University Press.

Frankl, V. E. (1967). *The doctor and the soul: From psychotherapy to logotherapy.* New York: Bantam Books.

Freud, S. (1961). The future of an illusion. In J. Strachey (Ed.), *The standard edition of the complete psychological works of Sigmund Freud,* Vol. 20. London: Hogarth Press. (Original work published 1930)

Freud, S. (1963). *Therapy and technique* (P. Rieff, Ed.). New York: Collier Books.

Fromm-Reichmann, F. (1950). *Principles of intensive psychotherapy.* Chicago: University of Chicago Press.

Garfield, S. L. (1980). *Psychotherapy: An eclectic approach.* New York: Wiley.

Garfield, S. L. (1986). Research on client variables in psychotherapy;. In S. L. Garfield & A. E. Bergin (Eds.), *Handbook of psychotherapy and behavior change* (3rd ed., (pp. 213–256). New York: Wiley.

Geertz, C. (1973). Religion as a symbolic system. In C. Geertz, *The interpretation of culture* (pp. 87–125). New York: Basic Books.

Geertz, C. (1983). Common sense as a symbolic system. In C. Geertz, *Local knowledge: Further essays in interpretive anthropology* (pp. 73–93). New York: Basic Books.

Gendlin, E. T. (1981). *Focusing.* Toronto and New York: Bantam Books.

Goffman, E. (1967). The nature of deference and demeanor. In E. Goffman, *Interaction ritual: Essays on face-to-face behavior* (pp. 47–95). Garden City, NY: Anchor Books.

Goldfried, M. R. & Davison, G. C. (1976). *Clinical behavior therapy.* New York: Holt, Rinehart, & Winston.

Goldstein, A. P., & Stein, N. (1976). *Prescriptive psychotherapies.* Elmsford, NY: Pergamon Press.

Greenberg, J. R., & Mitchell, S. A. (1983). *Object relations in psychoanalytic theory.* Cambridge, MA: Harvard University Press.

Haley, J. (1963). *Strategies of psychotherapy.* New York: Grune & Stratton.

Haley, J. (1973). *Uncommon therapy: The psychiatric techniques of Milton H. Erickson.* New York: Norton.

Halmos, P. (1970). *The faith of the counsellors: A study in the theory and practice of social case work and psychotherapy.* New York: Schocken Books.

Hartmann, H. (1964). *Essays on ego psychology: Selected problems in psychoanalytic theory.* New York: International Universities Press.

Henry, W., Sims, J., & Spray, L. (1971). *The fifth profession.* San Francisco: Jossey-Bass.

Hobson, R. F. (1985). *Forms of feeling: The heart of psychotherapy.* London and New York: Tavistock.

Holifield, E. B. (1983). *A history of pastoral care in America: From salvation to self-realization.* Nashville, TN: Abingdon Press.

Horvath, A. O., & Symonds, B. D. (1991). Relation between working alliance and outcome in psychotherapy: A meta-analysis. *Journal of Counseling Psychology, 38,* 139–149.

Howard, K. I., Davidson, C. V., O'Mahoney, M. T., Orlinsky, D. E., & Brown, K. P. (1989). Patterns of psychotherapy utilization. *American Journal of Psychiatry, 146,* 775–778.

Howard, K. I. & Orlinsky, D. E. (1972). Psychotherapeutic processes. *Annual review of psychology*, Vol. 23. Palo Alto, CA: Annual Reviews.

Hunt, M. (1987, August 30). Navigating the therapy maze: A consumer's guide to mental health treatment. *The New York Times Magazine*.

Hurvitz, (1974). Peer self-help psychotherapy groups: Psychotherapy without psychotherapists. In P. M. Roman & H. M. Trice (Eds.), *The sociology of psychotherapy* (pp. 84–138). New York: Jason Aronson.

Jung, C. G. (1966). *The practice of psychotherapy*. New York: Pantheon Press.

Kadushin, C. (1969). *Why people go to psychiatrists*. New York: Atherton.

Kakar, S. (1982). *Shamans, mystics and healers: A psychological inquiry into India and its healing traditions*. Boston: Beacon Press.

Kanfer, F. H., & Phillips, J. S. (1970). *Learning foundations of behavior therapy*. New York: Wiley.

Kelly, G. A. (1955). *The psychology of personal constructs*. New York: Norton.

Kiesler, D. J. (1982). Confronting the client–therapist relationship in psychotherapy. In J. C. Anchin & D. J. Kiesler (Eds.), *Handbook of interpersonal psychotherapy*. New York: Pergamon Press.

Kiev, A. (Ed.). (1964). *Magic, faith, and healing: Studies in primitive psychiatry today*. New York: Free Press.

Kleinman, A. (1980). *Patients and healers in the context of culture: An exploration of the borderland between anthropology, medicine, and psychiatry*. Berkeley: University of California Press.

Kleinman, A. (1988). *Rethinking psychiatry: From cultural category to personal experience*. New York: Free Press.

Kohut, H. (1984). *How does analysis cure?* (A. Goldberg & P. Stepansky, Eds.). Chicago: University of Chicago Press.

Kurzweil, E. (1989). *The Freudians: A comparative perspective*. New Haven, CT: Yale University Press.

LaBarre, W. (1969). *They shall take up serpents*. New York: Schocken Books.

Lacan, J. (1978). *The four fundamental concepts of psycho-analysis*. New York: Norton.

Lain Entralgo, P. (1970). *The therapy of the word in classical antiquity*. New Haven, CT: Yale University Press.

Laing, R. D. (1965). *The divided self: An existential study in sanity and madness*. Baltimore: Pelican.

Lambert, M. J., & Bergin, A. E. (1994). The effectiveness of psychotherapy. In A. E. Bergin & S. L. Garfield (Eds.), *Handbook of psychotherapy and behavior change* (4th ed.) (pp. 143–189). New York: Wiley.

Levi-Strauss, C. (1967a). The effectiveness of symbols. In C. Levi-Strauss, *Structural anthropology* (pp. 181–201). New York: Basic Books.

Levi-Strauss, C. (1967b). The sorcerer and his magic. In C. Levi-Strauss, *Structural anthropology* (pp. 161–180). New York: Basic Books.

Lewis, I. M. (1971). *Ecstatic religion: An anthropological study of spirit possession and shamanism*. Harmondsworth, England: Penguin Books.

Lowen, A. (1975). *Bioenergetics*. Harmondsworth, England: Penguin Books.

Luborsky, L. (1984). *Principles of psychoanalytic psychotherapy: A manual for supportive-expressive treatment*. New York: Basic Books.

Luckmann, T. (1967). *The invisible religion: The problem of religion in modern society*. New York: Macmillan.

Maine, H. S. (1960). *Ancient law: Its connection with the early history of society, and its relation to modern ideas*. New York: Dutton. (Original work published 1861)

Marx, K. (1978). Economic and philosophical manuscripts of 1844: Estranged labour. In R. C. Tucker (Ed.), *The Marx–Engels reader* (pp. 66–125). New York: Norton. (Original work published 1844)

Mauss, M. (1985). A category of the human mind: The notion of person; the notion of self. In M. Carrithers, S. Collins, & S. Lukes (Eds.), *The category of the personal: Anthropology, philosophy, history* (pp. 1–25). Cambridge: Cambridge University Press.

McGuire, M. B. (1988). *Ritual healing in suburban America*. New Brunswick, NJ: Rutgers University Press.

McNeill, J. T. (1951). *A history of the cure of souls*. New York: Harper & Bros.

McNeilly, C. L., & Howard, K. I. (1991). The effects of psychotherapy: A reevaluation based on dosage. *Psychotherapy Research*, 1, 62–73.

Métraux, A. (1972). *Voodoo in Haiti*. New York: Schocken Books.

Minuchin, S. (1974). *Families and family therapy*. Cambridge, MA: Harvard University Press.

Norcross, J. C. (Ed.). (1986). *Handbook of eclectic psychotherapy*. New York: Brunner/Mazel.

Norcross, J. C. & Goldfried, M. R. (Eds.). (1992). *Handbook of psychotherapy integration* (p. 15). New York: Basic Books.

Obeyesekere, G. (1981). *Medusa's hair: An essay on personal symbols and religious experience*. Chicago: University of Chicago Press.

Orlinsky, D. E. (1989). Researchers' images of psychotherapy: Their origins and influence on research. *Clinical Psychology Review, 9,* 413–441.

Orlinsky, D. E. (1992). La recherche quantitative en psychothérapie: État acutel et perspectives. *Nervure: Journal de Psychiatrie, 5,* 29–33.

Orlinsky, D. E. (1994). Learning from many masters: Toward a research-based integration of psychotherapy treatment models. *Der Psychotherapeut, 1,* 2–9.

Orlinsky, D. E., Grawe, K., & Parks, B. K. (1994). Process and outcome in psychotherapy—noch einmal. In A. E. Bergin & S. L. Garfield (Eds.), *Handbook of psychotherapy and behavior change* (4th ed.) (pp. 270–376). New York: Wiley.

Orlinsky, D. E., & Howard, K. I. (1978). The relation of process to outcome in psychotherapy. In A. E. Bergin & S. L. Garfield (Eds.), *Handbook of psychotherapy and behavior change* (2nd ed.) (pp. 283–329). New York: Wiley.

Orlinsky, D. E., & Howard, K. I. (1986). Process and outcome in psychotherapy. In A. E. Bergin & S. L. Garfield (Eds.), *Handbook of psychotherapy and behavior change* (3rd ed.) (pp. 311–381). New York: Wiley.

Orlinsky, D. E., & Howard, K. I. (1987a). A generic model of psychotherapy. *Journal of Integrative and Eclectic Psychotherapy, 6,* 6–27.

Orlinsky, D. E., & Howard, K. I. (1987b). A generic model of process in psychotherapy. In W. Huber (Ed.), *Progress in psychotherapy research: Selected papers from the 2nd European conference on psychotherapy research* (pp. 445–458). Louvain-la-Neuve: Presses Universitaires de Louvain.

Parsons, T. (1954). The kinship system of the contemporary United States. In T. Parsons, *Essays in sociological theory* (pp. 177–196). Glencoe, IL: Free Press.

Parsons, T. (1964). Mental illness and "spiritual malaise": The role of the psychiatrist and of the minister of religion. In T. Parsons, *Social structure and personality* (pp. 292–324). New York: Free Press.

Parsons, T. (1969). *The system of modern societies.* Englewood Cliffs, NJ: Prentice-Hall.

Perls, F. S. (1976). *The Gestalt approach and eyewitness to therapy.* New York: Bantam Books.

Phillips, E. L. (1985). *Psychotherapy revised: New frontiers in research and practice.* Hillsdale, NJ: Erlbaum.

Rieff, P. (1968). *The triumph of the therapeutic.* New York: Harper & Row.

Rogers, C. R. (1951). *Client-centered therapy: Its current practice, implications, and theory.* Boston: Houghton Mifflin.

Rogers, C. R. (1961). *On becoming a person: A therapist's view of psychotherapy.* Boston: Houghton Mifflin.

Ruesch, J., & Bateson, G. (1951). *Communication: The social matrix of psychiatry.* New York: Norton.

Runyan, W. M. (1984). *Life histories and psychobiography: Explorations in theory and method.* New York: Oxford University Press.

Ryan, W. (Ed.). (1969). *Distress in the city.* Cleveland: Case Western Reserve University Press.

Satir, V. (1964). *Conjoint family therapy.* Palo Alto, CA: Science and Behavior.

Saunders, S. M., & Resnick, M. D. (1992). Predicting formal help-seeking behavior among high school students identifying themselves as learning mental health problems. *Proceedings, 23rd Annual Conference, Society for Psychotherapy Research, Berkeley CA* (p. 69).

Shapiro, D. A., & Shapiro, D. (1982). Meta-analysis of comparative therapy outcome research: A critical appraisal. *Behavior Psychotherapy, 10,* 4–25.

Shorter, F. (1975). *The making of the modern family.* New York: Basic Books.

Simmel, G. (1950a). The metropolis and mental life. In K. Wolff (Ed.), *The sociology of Georg Simmel* (pp. 409–421). New York: Free Press.

Simmel, G. (1950b). Individual and society in eighteenth- and nineteenth-century views of life. In K. Wolff (Ed.), *The sociology of Georg Simmel* (pp. 58–84). New York: Free Press.

Singer, J. L., & Pope, K. S. (Eds). (1978). *The power of human imagination: New methods in psychotherapy.* New York and London: Plenum Press.

Smith, M. L., Glass, G. V., & Miller, T. I. (1980). *The benefits of psychotherapy.* Baltimore: Johns Hopkins University Press.

Sullivan, H. S. (1953). *The interpersonal theory of psychiatry.* New York: Norton.

Taube, C. A., Kessler, L., & Feuerberg, M. (1984). Utilization and expenditures for ambulatory mental health care during 1980. *National medical care utilization and expenditure survey.* Data report 5. Washington, DC: U.S. Department of Health and Human Services.

Taube, C. A., Mechanic, D., & Hohmann, A. A. (Eds.). (1989). *The future of mental health services research.* Washington, DC: U.S. Department of Health and Human Services.

Thomä, H., & Kächele, H. (1985). *Psychoanalytic*

practice: Vol. 1 Principles. Berlin and New York: Springer-Verlag.

Thomä, H., & Kächele, H. (1988). Psychoanalytic practice: Vol. 2. Clinical studies. Berlin and New York: Springer-Verlag.

Tillich, P. (1960). Love, power, and justice: Ontological analyses and ethical applications. New York: Oxford University Press.

Tönnies, F. (1957). Community and society. East Lansing: Michigan State University Press. (Original work published 1887)

Turkle, S. (1978). Psychoanalytic politics: Freud's French revolution. New York: Basic Books.

Turner, V. (1969). The ritual process: Structure and anti-structure. Chicago: Aldine.

Wallace, A. F. C. (1956). Revitalization movements. American Anthropologist, 68, 264–281.

Warner, W. Lloyd (1961). The family of god: A symbolic study of Christian life in America. New Haven, CT: Yale University Press.

Watts, A. W. (1961). Psychotherapy East and West. New York: Ballantine Books.

Watzlawick, P., Beavin, J. H., & Jackson, D. D. (1967). Pragmatics of human communication: A study of interactional patterns, pathologies, and paradoxes. New York: Norton.

Watzlawick, P., Weakland, J. H., & Fisch, R. (1974). Change: Principles of problem formation and problem resolution. New York: Norton.

Weber M. (1958). The Protestant ethic and the rise of capitalism. New York: Scribners. (Original work published 1904)

Weber M. (1952). Ancient Judaism. Glencoe, IL: Free Press. (Original work published 1921)

Weber M. (1963). The sociology of religion. Boston: Beacon Press.

Weber M. (1958). Bureaucracy. In H. H. Gerth & C. W. Mills (Eds.), From Max Weber: Essays in sociology (pp. 196–244). New York: Oxford University Press.

Weber M. (1978). The types of legitimate domination. In G. Roth & C. Wittich (Eds.), Max Weber: Economy and society (pp. 212–301). Berkeley: University of California Press.

Whitaker, C. A., & Malone, T. (1953). The roots of psychotherapy. New York: Blakiston.

Williams, C. (1938). He came down from heaven. London: Heinemann.

Wirth, L. (1938). Urbanism as a way of life. American Journal of sociology, 44, 1–24.

Wolpe, J. (1958). Psychotherapy by reciprocal inhibition. Stanford, CA: Stanford University Press.

Zaretsky, E. (1973). Capitalism, the family, and personal life. New York: Harper & Row.

2

Psychodynamic Therapies in Historical Perspective: "Nothing human do I consider alien to me."

Bertram P. Karon
Anmarie J. Widener

Psychodynamic therapies are based on psychoanalytic theories and techniques. The hallmark of psychoanalysis and psychoanalytic therapy is that they take unconscious processes seriously. Sigmund Freud, the founder of psychoanalysis, attempted to create an integrated theory of the human personality throughout his life; but as he put parts of the theory together, new observations required him to revise it. At no time did Freud have a completed, integrated theory because at no time did he stop observing, thinking, and discovering. In this respect, Freud provided a model of scientific inquiry. Even today, psychoanalysts disagree not only with each other but also with their own earlier formulations. These differences of opinion are confusing, but as the psychoanalyst Jack Novick put it, "The moment we stop questioning everything we believe, it is no longer psychoanalysis."

HISTORICAL DEVELOPMENT

Freud started out as a research neurologist. His early work in neurology would have made him famous even if he had not gone on to make even more important discoveries in psychology. Reluctantly, he left a career in research for private practice because of his awareness of anti-Jewish prejudice in academia. Freud learned that prejudice influenced the evaluation of scientific work (even in physiology, where the observations are easily checked). This lesson served him in good stead: The most important (and sometimes the only) criterion of scientific truth is your own observations; whether or not other scientists accept these observations is irrelevant.

As a neurologist in private practice, Freud noticed that the common set of symptoms diagnosed as *conversion hysteria* did not respond to neurological treatments. The usual symptoms included paralyzed arms, paralyzed legs, anesthesia, blindness, deafness, and so on—or, more specifically, real physical symptoms without real (medically detectable) nerve or muscle damage. The prevailing theory (as is always the case when the cause of a symptom in psychiatry or psychology is not known) was that it was physiological or genetic. Conversion hysteria was thought to be caused by subtle lesions in the central nervous system. But Freud required of physiological as well as psychological theories that they make scientific sense. Since his knowledge of neurology was better than that of his colleagues, he was able to demonstrate that the symptomatic paralyses found in conversion hysterics could not be neurological in origin. He published his findings on the difference between hysterical and organic paralyses in his first important psychological paper (Freud, 1893).

Hypnosis was claimed by the French neurologist Hippolyte Bernheim and Jean Charcot to alleviate hysterical symptoms. Freud studied with both of them in order to investigate this controversial claim. He confirmed that hypnosis in the form of suggestion (e.g., "You will be able to move your hand") indeed alleviated the symptoms. Suggestive hypnosis as a cure, however, was only temporary. After a period of time, the symptoms reappeared or a new set of symptoms appeared to replace the old ones. This problem is called *symptom substitution.*

That is why today psychoanalytic therapists treat patients, not symptoms. A new symptom, or the reappearance of an old symptom, is not considered a new disorder but most likely a transformation of the old disorder, to be evaluated in terms of whether the new symptom is more or less incapacitating than the old one. Later, Freud collaborated with Josef Breuer, who was then using hypnosis differently. Together they developed the use of hypnosis in order to uncover forgotten memories of painful events and feelings. When these memories or feelings were made *conscious* (i.e., when the patient remembered or became aware of them), the conversion hysterical symptoms disappeared. Freud and Breuer discovered that conversion hysterical symptoms were traumatic experiences and feelings transformed, or "converted," into physiological symptoms. Thus, psychoanalysis as a theory began with the publication of *Studies in Hysteria* (1895) by Breuer and Freud.

Breuer soon discontinued his collaboration with Freud because of two issues.

The first issue was the discovery and use of *free association* rather than hypnosis. One of Freud's patients suggested that he stop talking— that if he just listened without interrupting, she would say something important. He followed her advice, and indeed, she remembered something of importance. Freud realized that something extremely significant had happened. The technique of free association consists of asking the patient to verbalize everything that comes into his or her mind, as nearly as possible. The patient is told that "Nothing is bad, nothing is trivial, nothing is irrelevant." The therapist should not interrupt the patient's thought processes unless it will help the process of discovery. This technique allows the patient and the analyst to discover important issues that neither of them knew existed. Further, what is uncovered under hypnosis sometimes is forgotten when the patient comes out of the hypnotic state, whereas anything that the patient recovered by free association is now part of his or her conscious thought processes. These advantages for the scientifically curious Freud were outweighed for Breuer by the fact that he was not in control of the process.

The second issue that led to the split between Breuer and Freud was that patients began to talk about sexual feelings toward Breuer, which upset Breuer. (More recently discovered information suggests that it was not so much Breuer as Breuer's wife who was upset.) Breuer gave up his work with neurosis and confined his later research to the physiology of the inner ear. Freud, on the other hand, felt that this issue was something to be understood. He did not believe that he was so charming that patients could possibly have reason so often to express their love toward him romantically. In his understanding of this dynamic, he discovered the phenomenon of *transference* (discussed below).

The Unconscious, Regression, Transference, and Resistance

According to Freud, there are four concepts so basic that, if one accepted them, one would be practicing psychoanalysis even if one disagreed with Freud in every other respect. These concepts are the unconscious, repression, transference, and resistance. Both the unconscious and repression were discovered by Freud's early work with hypnosis.

Freud frequently defined psychoanalysis as the "psychology of the unconscious." The *unconscious* refers to the fact that there are meaningful mental processes that are outside the awareness of the individual and that have important, powerful influences on conscious experiences. According to Freud, a thought can be *conscious* (you are aware of it at this very moment), or it can be *preconscious* (you are not thinking of it at the moment, but you could if you wanted to), or it can be *unconscious* (you cannot think of it even if you want to, but it still exists outside of awareness, like the memories of early childhood). The unconscious, while not anatomically located, can be clinically detected and experimentally confirmed (e.g., Fisher & Greenberg, 1977). Freud did not like the word *subconscious* because it blurred the important distinction between preconscious and unconscious. Of course, he was also aware that the boundaries between the preconscious and the unconscious altered as forces within the mind varied. Key to Freud's view is the understanding that only what is conscious can be changed. Therefore, psychoanalysis and psychoanalytic therapy are aimed at making what is unconscious conscious—for only then may psychological dynamics be transformed. In Freud's words, one cannot fight an enemy one cannot see.

Freud (1901) pointed out that when people make errors such as slips of the tongue or of the pen (writing errors), there are frequently two contradictory conscious thoughts: a thought the individual intends to say or write and another thought the person intends not to say or not to write. The resulting slip of the tongue or pen is a compromise between the two impulses. For example, what makes mistakes like "it is kisstomary to cuss the bride" funny is that the interfering inhibited thought is not hard to guess.

Sometimes, however, when a person makes a slip of the tongue, the person is not aware of thinking of the contradictory idea, but it is an idea that he or she frequently thinks about. Thus, a thought that is preconscious can have

the same effect as one that is conscious but inhibited. In other cases, said Freud, the person denies ever having the contradictory thought or impulse implied by the error, and yet the subsequent pattern of his or her life indicates that the impulse existed all along. Thus, an unconscious impulse can have an effect similar to that of a conscious thought.

Repression refers to the fact that what is unconscious is not an accident. Repression is an unconscious refusal to recognize certain mental contents. In other words, experiences, memories, feelings, thoughts, fantasies, and motivations are repressed (or pushed out of awareness and kept out) because they are too frightening or guilt-producing or unpleasant to experience or to remember. For example, forgetting, Freud suggested, is often the result of repressing an unpleasant thought or something associated with such a thought.

It is an axiom of Freudian psychoanalysis that one is not morally responsible for one's conscious thoughts, including one's dreams, and certainly not morally responsible (or culpable) for one's unconscious or preconscious thoughts. Only actions (including words) have moral consequences. Moreover, the thoughts and feelings about which human beings usually feel most guilty, ashamed, or scared (and repress) are normal childhood thoughts. Nor are our thoughts and feelings, conscious as well as unconscious, necessarily consistent with each other.

Resistance refers to the observation that, when a therapist attempts to help a patient gain awareness of his or her unconscious processes (by undoing repression), all kinds of difficulties suddenly appear and impede the therapeutic process. Patients are typically unaware of this process but seem (unconsciously, of course) to fight to maintain their repressions so that they may keep what is unconscious in the unconscious. At first, Freud and other psychoanalysts used the concept of resistance as if the patient were misbehaving; they soon realized, however, that resistance was a necessary part of the process of change. Resistances are nothing more than the defense mechanisms that the individual ordinarily uses to cope with his or her impulses and experiences. Rather than a form of misbehavior, resistances are examples of coping mechanisms that are at least as important to understand as the material defended against. The individual is unaware (unconscious) of his or her defense mechanisms.

In addition to repression, a number of other defense mechanisms have been described. *Denial* is a defense mechanism whereby the individual does not perceive an external event (whereas repression is used to refer to keeping an impulse, feeling, or memory out of awareness). *Projection* is seeing in someone else what is unacceptable in oneself. *Isolation* is not connecting things that belong together. *Rationalization* is giving a good reason for something that is motivated by an entirely different impulse. *Reaction formation* is doing the opposite of the original impulse in order to maintain a repression (e.g., being neat to oppose the impulse to be dirty, rescuing to oppose the impulse to hurt, being puritanical to oppose one's own sexual impulses). *Displacement* refers to having or expressing a feeling toward someone or something other than where it belongs (e.g., being angry at the dog when one is really angry at one's spouse). *Identification with the aggressor* refers to the act of mastering the feeling of weakness by identifying with the stronger person who has hurt you. *Regression* is the act of going back to an earlier period or an earlier way of functioning (e.g., throwing a childhood temper tantrum when one is an adult).

Defense mechanisms are essential to normal development and functioning. Nonetheless, they usually represent a limitation on development and on success in coping with reality. There is one defense mechanism, however, that always represents health. *Sublimation* refers to a satisfying, in a socially acceptable way, an impulse that, in its original form, would be socially unacceptable. Thus, a talented artist, whose work was limited by his inability to use colors other than brown and black, discovered in his analysis that he was attempting to overcome a harsh, early toilet training by smearing brown and black substances on a canvas in a way that his mother would accept. This insight freed him to use colors effectively, a true sublimation (Karon, 1994).

This list of defense mechanisms is not exhaustive. Freud's daughter, Anna Freud (1936/1966), provided the best description of the defense mechanisms.

Transference is a phenomenon wherein patients relive experiences, feelings, and memories from the past as if they were occurring in the present. Patients are unaware that their present (transferred) experience is really the product of a past experience. Freud called conversion hysteria, anxiety hysteria, and obsessive-compulsive neuroses the *transference neuroses* because patients with these symptoms formed a therapeutically usable transference, that is, one in which enough positive feelings from childhood were transferred to enable them to tolerate the discomfort of treatment. These positive feelings originated with the patient's experiences of love and gratification from parents in early childhood. The transference of romantic or sexual feelings, however, made the patient want a love relationship with the therapist instead of therapy. The transference of negative feelings (anger, fear) usually made the patient want to leave treatment. Romantic and negative transferences were originally the most difficult forms of resistance.

Freud's interpretations of transference reactions changed transference from the most stubborn of the resistances to the most powerful tool of the psychoanalyst. By interpreting transference reactions as reexperiencing of the repressed past (including fantasies), the therapist and the patient are able to reconstruct forgotten (or repressed) feelings and memories that are so dramatically reenacted. Once interpreted, the immediacy and concreteness of the experience provide the patient with a sense of psychological truth about his or her past.

Freud originally conceptualized transference as something that occurred only in treatment. Sandor Ferenczi (1909/1950) pointed out, and Freud accepted, the fact that transference was not unique to therapy but occurred throughout ordinary life. What was unique to therapy was that the transference was observed and used as a source of information and as a dynamic for change. Like the other resistances, transference is a defense mechanism used in coping with life.

Since psychoanalysis is a theory of human functioning, it is not surprising to discover that therapists have transference feelings toward patients. This is termed *countertransference*. Countertransference needs to be paid careful attention by the therapist so as not to impede treatment. It can often be a valuable source of information about the therapeutic process.

Basic Psychoanalytic Technique

Freud's psychotherapeutic tools were free association, the analysis of dreams, the analysis of defense mechanisms, and the analysis of transference.

In order to provide a *blank screen* that would maximize dramatic transference feelings and projections, Freud sat behind the patient and limited his verbalizations, although never to the extent parodied by some popular accounts of psychoanalysis. It was also the case that Freud was more comfortable when seated behind the patient, where he did not have to justify every gesture or shift in his position.

But what emerges in the descriptions of Freud's analyses given by Bettelheim (1982), Kardiner (1977), Cremerius (1981), and Sterba (personal communication) is an attitude of humanity and kindness that was taken for granted. It was not an element of technique and therefore was not described in Freud's papers on technique. The inventor of the concept of the blank screen, like all Viennese psychoanalysts, shook hands with his patients before and after each hour. The injunctions on "abstention" (from too much activity and therapeutic zeal) were addressed to himself, a very active, kind, and eager psychoanalyst (if one can judge from his writings) who found that he had to curb to some extent his natural activity, therapeutic zeal, and talkativeness because they got in the way. But at no time was he schizoid and detached. According to Richard Sterba (personal communication), Freud's patients felt that he was with them every step of the way and that

this is a goal we should aim for in our psychoanalytic technique, although it is difficult to achieve.

Since Freud did not know what he would discover, he saw patients six days per week. At first he felt it was unfortunate that psychoanalysis took as much as 6 months, but as time went by and as the goals of treatment changed, the length of treatment changed to 2, 3, 4, 5, and in some cases many years. As anthropologists have pointed out, in no other culture does one human being listen to the thoughts of another human being for hundreds of hours.

In listening to patients who suffered from the symptoms of conversion hysteria, anxiety hysteria (or phobia), and obsessive-compulsive disorders, Freud and his students learned about the nature of human mental functioning and the process of treatment.

MAJOR THEORETICAL DEVELOPMENTS AND VARIATIONS

Freud developed a number of theories about the human mind. The best overview is provided by his *Introductory Lectures on Psycho-Analysis* (1917) and *New Introductory Lectures on Psycho-Analysis* (1933). The description of mental contents as conscious, preconscious, or unconscious is usually referred to as Freud's *topological theory*.

Freud's Structural Theory

Freud's structural theory divided the mind into three parts: the *I*, the *it*, and the *over-me*. Freud never used the equivalent Latin words *ego*, *id*, or *superego* because, he said, "our theories must be understood by our patients, who are often very intelligent but not always learned" (Freud, 1926, p. 195). He used ordinary German words. The Latin words *ego*, *id*, and *superego* were substituted in the English translation and have confused the professional world ever since.

The *I* (ego) is what you ordinarily think of when you say "I" in reference to yourself. It is almost entirely conscious. However, there is a part of the *I* that is unconscious, the part that employs defense mechanisms. The defense mechanisms operate most efficiently when you are unaware that you are defending. The *it* (id) is a part of the mind that is experienced as if it were an external force. It is entirely unconscious. Unconscious motives and repressed memories are all part of the *it*. The third part of Freud's structural theory is the *over-me* (superego), those dictates of the conscience to which one bows automatically. The *over-me* consists of those values and moral imperatives that conflict with the individual's unbridled impulses and fantasies. The *over-me* is partly conscious and partly unconscious.

According to Freud, all of us start out as an *it*. Freud felt that the *it* functioned according to the *pleasure principle*—that is, every impulse seeks immediate satisfaction. The pleasure principle dominates the unconscious, the *it*, dreams, and symptoms; it also functions as a basic principle in the conscious rational part of mental life.

The satisfaction of one impulse frequently causes the frustration of a different impulse. For example, the infant cannot urinate and be dry at the same time. The *reality principle* intervenes in mental functioning very early, probably from the beginning of life. The reality principle is the need to balance one impulse against another in terms of reality so as to maximize satisfaction over the long run. This principle impels the development of the *I*, which includes the conscious, rational part of the personality. Most modern psychoanalysts, however, believe that a primitive *I* exists even at birth and continues to develop. Rationality is thus seen as the consequence of frustration. Some psychoanalysts have felt that problems in understanding or dealing with reality are due to a lack of sufficient frustration in infancy. But there is sufficient frustration to trigger the reality principle in even the best infancies because of the biological nature of human beings. Schizophrenics, who suffer from an impaired ability to deal with reality, have had less satisfying—not more satisfying—lives, including less satisfying infancies.

The most important part of reality for any child is, of course, his or her parents. By internalizing parents and parental demands into the conscience (the *over-me* or superego), the child can struggle with his or her conscience rather than with his or her parents. This is a tremendous gain in independence. The conscience is not, according to Freud, the still, small voice of God, nor is it innate. It is the internalization of what real people have actually done plus our fantasies of them. Since the *over-me* is the result of real experiences with real people, it is not surprising that people sometimes feel guilty over things about which no rational person ought to feel guilty and do not feel guilty over things about which any responsible person should feel guilty. There is also a positive part of the *over-me* consisting of the ideals and aspirations that have been internalized. This is usually referred to as the *ego-ideal*. Many individuals seem to have more than one *over-me*, each based on the internalization of a different person with differing standards; and these *over-me*'s may be in conflict with each other. Some psychoanalysts believe that the anger of the child is also projected onto the *over-me* (superego), making it more punitive than the real parents.

The *I* (ego) has the task of mediating between the impulses (the *it*), the *over-me* (the superego), and the demands of reality—sometimes referred to as the ego's three harsh taskmasters.

Drives

In Freud's understanding of human beings, it became clear that one's whole life history was relevant and that (everything else being equal) the earlier an experience occurred, the more pervasive and long-lasting were apt to be its consequences. Therefore, early childhood became more and more significant.

To help conceptualize human development, Freud postulated a theory of drives. Freud's *drives* were mistranslated into English as *instincts*, but Freud never used the word *instinct* since that implied nontransformability. Freud said of his drive theory that it was neither all of his theory nor even the foundation of his theory; rather, it was at most a cornerstone— something needed to help organize and hold together his clinical observations. The foundation of his theories consisted of hundreds of actual observations of the human mind. Freud said that he reserved the right to reshape his drive theory or to replace it entirely as advances in scientific knowledge required.

According to his first drive theory, there are two basic drives: sexual drives and self-preservative drives (*libido* and *ego* drives, respectively). These drives are frequently in conflict with each other, and these conflicts may result in symptoms.

Libido refers to a psychic energy or force that connects with the processes of sexual excitation. Freud argued that the usual ways of defining *sexual* (e.g., having to do with the genitals, or with reproduction, or with the difference between the sexes) excluded phenomena that were commonly understood to be sexual (e.g., kissing, masturbation, homosexuality). He redefined sexuality to include all the commonly understood sexual phenomena but also a great deal more. Freud defined libido as organ pleasure or anything that was based on organ pleasure. Critics attacked Freud as explaining too much of human functioning as the result of sexual impulses, but their criticisms were valid only in terms of their own limited perception of genital sexuality. Once you accept Freud's definition of libido, it is clear that sex does not begin when one first has intercourse or at adolescence; rather, individuals are sexual at birth. Experiences with all zones of the body are sexual and are relevant to understanding later human development, sexual and otherwise.

At no time was Freud or any of his students able to find a substance or energy corresponding to libido. Nonetheless, it was a useful metaphor that predicted many phenomena (such as the feeling of a greater sense of energy after a conflict has been resolved). The concept of libido as a substance or form of energy, however, leads to a number of misunderstandings. For example, the notion that libido is limited in quantity leads to the conclusion that self-love and other-love are opposites (as was true in nineteenth-century romantic love, where the love-struck individual proclaimed that he or she was worthless and the beloved was worth everything). Most current psychoanalysts, however, see love of others and self-love as facilitating each other. In Harry Stack Sullivan's graphic language, "If you think all men are pigs, it does not feel particularly good to be even the best of the pigs."

Freud found his first drive theory to be inadequate because some people seemed to invest their libido in the *I* (ego) in his early theory of narcism. Hence the distinction between ego drives and libido drives was hard to maintain. In his later drive theory, there were two basic drives: *eros*, the life drive, which combined sexual and self-preservative drives; and *thanatos*, the death drive, which was aimed at one's own destruction. This late theory, which Freud referred to as "our psychoanalytic mythology," was never made basic to psychoanalysis, and many of his closest coworkers never accepted it. Today, few psychoanalysts accept the thanatos concept.

The American psychologist Henry Murray explained the late drive theory as Freud's intellectualization of the struggle with his cancer. But the psychoanalyst Richard Sterba, who knew Freud personally, pointed out that Freud developed the idea of the death drive long before he had cancer. Before World War I, there had been an unusual era of peace between the major powers in Central Europe. This had led, particularly in Vienna, to extraordinary progress in the arts, the sciences, and the learned disciplines; one could really believe in the ideal of progress. But unlike World War II, World War I was greeted throughout Europe with celebration. Freud was appalled that one of the great catastrophes of history should be greeted as a cause for celebration. He then decided that there must be something self-destructive about human beings to engender such a reaction.

In this late drive theory, aggression was understood as the death drive turned outward. Critics have mistakenly believed that Freud ignored aggression in his first drive theory. But in his early cases, he described symptoms based on the fear of repressed anger (sadism). Freud's abstractions sometimes were mistaken, but his observations were always accurate. In his first drive theory, aggression was described as sadism, a component of libido. (In this early theory, aggression also represented self-preservation, i.e., ego drive; but in symptom formation, sadism was always the problem.) Today most psychoanalysts talk about sexual (in Freud's global sense) and aggressive drives since both drives have evolutionary advantages and both are, to some extent, inconsistent with social organizations (despite the fact that human beings can survive only in social organizations).

Freud overused simple biological explanations and underestimated cultural factors because those were the prevailing views of his colleagues. It was when he called attention to the importance of childhood experience, and of the inner lives of children and adults, that he was considered controversial, if not outright damnable; but these are the insights that have stood the test of time.

Psychosexual Stages

Using the metaphor of libido, Freud described childhood development in terms of psychosexual stages. The most important were the *oral*, the *anal*, and the *genital*. In all stages, all zones of the body are active. Some zones, however, are more important at each developmental stage. Freud thought of the psychosexual stages as biologically determined; but anthropological data show widely varying patterns of childrearing, with differing consequences for the adult personality (e.g., Kardiner, 1939; Whiting & Child, 1953).

The first stage of development is the oral stage. In the first year of life, the most important kinds of organ pleasure supposedly are those concerning the mouth. The oral is the most clearly biologically determined stage since the *rooting reflex* (turning toward the source of stimulation when the cheek is touched) and

the *sucking reflex* are innate. Hence, the child can find the nipple, suck it, and survive. Karl Abraham (1927) divided the oral stage into two phases: the early oral stage, *oral receptive*, when activities concerning sucking and receiving predominate; and the late oral stage, or *oral sadistic*, when biting becomes important. Teething hurts, but the infant discovers that the pain eases when he or she bites something. By biting his or her thumb, the infant discovers that biting causes pain. The infant also discovers that if he or she bites the mother, the mother will get angry.

We now know that being held and interacted with in the first year of life is as important for the baby's normal development as any oral gratification. Babies who are not mothered and interacted with in the first year of life suffer terrible emotional and intellectual consequences that are often not reversible (Bowlby, 1966; Spitz, 1965). The development of a dependable relationship with a mother figure is critical. Patterns of attachment to the mother in the first year have been found to set up lifelong patterns of relationship (Bowlby, 1969).

In the anal stage, the second developmental stage, conflicts about toilet training predominate. According to Abraham, in the early anal or *anal sadistic* stage, the predominant pleasures concern expelling. In the late anal or *anal retentive* stage, the predominant pleasures concern retaining. The connection between anality and sadism may be understood when it is realized that typically parents first hit children during toilet training. When parents inflict pain on the child, the child wishes to inflict pain on others.

Fixation refers to the idea that some events or experiences may have an unusually strong influence over subsequent mental life, that is, that the individual's mental development is "stuck," to some extent, at that point. This may be due to unusually painful or unusually pleasurable experiences, or to unusual gratification followed by unusual deprivation. The different causes lead to different qualities of fixation (although this has not been described in detail). When regression occurs as a defense, the individual typically returns to a previous state or period to which he or she has a fixation. Freud related the character traits of orderliness, cleanliness, and stubbornness (or their opposites) to fixation at the anal stage.

The third psychosexual stage is the genital stage, in which the most important source of organ pleasure is the genitals (although genital sensations have been found to be important from the beginning). René Spitz (1965) observed that infants in the first year who touched their genitals were healthier and had better relations with their parents. The concept of the genital stage leads directly to Freud's concepts concerning object relations and the Oedipus complex (described below). These ideas are extremely controversial, but they accurately describe the most central problems of many people. What is at issue is how universal and how central these formulations are. Unfortunately psychologists have had a tendency to accept or reject emotionally rather than to reasearch these fundamental issues.

Male and Female Development

The word *object* in psychoanalytic theory refers to the object used to gratify a need, as in the phrase "object of the libido." Most of the time, the word *object* refers to a person. According to Freud, the original object for the child is the mother's breast. Next, the whole mother becomes the object. Between the third and fifth years, the Oedipus complex (one of Freud's most controversial ideas) is supposedly at its height.

For the male child, the *Oedipus complex* refers to the wish to gain sole possession of his mother and to rid himself of his father. He fears retaliation by the father. Since this is a sexual wish, the retaliation that is feared is the castration of the penis. This *castration anxiety* is so overwhelming that it leads to a repression of sexual wishes, referred to as the *latency period*, beginning at approximately age 7 and continuing until puberty. The repression of Oedipal wishes leads to the internalization of the feared father into the superego (*over-me*). Of course, Freud also noted that the boy at

times wants the approval of his father and sees his mother as his rival, or he wants the approval of both parents.

Sexual fantasies about the parent may appear in consciousness in adolescence, frightening the adolescent, but represent simply the return of forgotten Oedipal fantasies. While Freud talked about the sequence of Oedipal and latency phases as if they were biological, his case illustrations showed that he was aware that they were variable, depending on the actual training and experiences the child encountered with respect to sexuality. We now know that latency is largely a myth in our present culture, being at most relative (compared to the greater concern with directly genital sexual matters earlier and in adolescence).

The child develops unrealistic sexual theories based on inadequate knowledge. These theories remain in the unconscious of adults and play a role in their fantasies and symptom formation. A reasonable question is "How can the Oedipal child want sexual intercourse with the parent when the child usually has incomplete or false information about sexuality?" According to Freud, the Oedipal child's desire for the opposite-sex parent is sexually tinged. The aim of the Oedipus complex is not necessarily sexual intercourse as an adult would understand it, but rather depends on the experiences and knowledge of the child.

Even more controversial is the *female Oedipus complex*. It is clear that matters concerning females are more complicated than Freud's initial formulation (which he stated tentatively). The little girl discovers that penises and the kinds of people who have them are more valued by her parents. At this point, she frequently thinks that her mother has a penis. At first the little girl, too, wants her mother and wishes to get rid of her father. In reaction to the belief that the lack of a penis is a defect, she turns from her mother, who she discovers does not have a penis, to her father, who does. The *female castration complex* thus leads to the female Oedipus complex rather than resolves it. Since the female Oedipus complex is not repressed out of fear of castration, it is not as severely repressed. Some have argued that this is why women are more comfortable with an older man than men are with an older woman.

The little girl's conscious Oedipal fantasies more often are to have her father's child or to marry her father than to have sex with him. Freud reports that a woman with particularly strong Oedipal conflicts frequently has had all of her positive sexually tinged feelings and fantasies first about her mother as the desired one and her father as the rival, and has then interchanged these objects of her desires and rivalry. It is important to recognize that the unconscious is not civilized: Oedipal rivalries are fantasized as mother and daughter wishing to get rid of each other permanently.

The two great anxieties in human development, according to Freud, are *separation anxiety* and *castration anxiety*. Both anxieties occur in both sexes, although separation anxiety plays the predominant role in the lives of women and castration anxiety plays the predominant role in the lives of men. It is the avoidance of anxiety that is the motive for the defense mechanisms.

It is worth while to read Freud's papers on female development (e.g., 1931, 1933). Alongside ideas that are no longer tenable are some brilliant insights, and dogmatic acceptance or rejection would be a serious mistake. For example, Freud points out that the Oedipal conflict of the child is often based on the parent's actual behaviors and on whether the parent is seductive, rivalrous, or threatening. A particularly valuable insight is that a woman who has a strong envy of the penis may substitute having a child for a penis. Usually the wish is for a male child, who will represent herself reborn with a penis. When such a woman has a little girl, she reacts to the child as a disappointment, as defective, because she has not solved her mother's problem of lacking a penis. Unfortunately, children are gullible: If the mother acts as if the little girl is defective, the child believes it. If the mother acts as if boys are better than girls, the little girl believes it, and when she discovers the difference between the genitals, she thinks she has discovered the reason.

Does penis envy exist? It depends on what you think it means. If it means an innate envy of the penis, there is no evidence for penis envy. But if it means an envy of the special prerogatives of men—particularly if your parents (and especially your mother, who is a woman herself) act as if men are better and more lovable than women—then penis envy clearly exists. Penis envy is expressed in dreams and symptoms because the penis is a very good symbol for the difference between men and women. For many patients, it is only in psychotherapy that they learn the long-lasting consequences of their parents' sexual biases.

Breast, vagina, and womb envy clearly exist in the unconscious fantasies of men (e.g., Karon & Rosberg, 1958a, 1958b), although it is not discussed as often. As Irene Fast (1984) so aptly puts it, children of both sexes want to be and to have everything, and children accept limitations with difficulty.

Of course, jealousy is not confined to the rivalry with the parent but occurs between children as well. According to Freud, sibling rivalry tends to be maximal with a 2- to 4-year age difference (with smaller differences leading to the feeling that the sibling has always been there and larger differences diminishing the rivalry). If the interval is 7 or more years, the older child is apt to be thought of as being like a second parent of that sex.

Freud's confusion and culture-bound limitations in his understanding of female development are an area that is currently being clarified. Among the current revisions of female development, the insights of Helen Block Lewis, Judith Kestenberg, Joyce McDougall, Nancy Chordorow, and Irene Fast have proved most useful. Jean Baker Miller and her coworkers (Jordan, Kaplan, Miller, Stiver, & Surrey, 1991) have well described the differential importance of relationships in female development. For women, autonomy is gained through and within relationships; this is different from the "normal" (i.e., male) sequence of autonomy preceding the ability to relate, postulated by male psychoanalysts like Erikson. Carol Gilligan (1982, 1988; Brown & Gilligan, 1992) has accurately described the qualitative difference in healthy female and male moral development and the culturally based repression of social and self-awareness.

Seduction

Incestuous experiences and fantasies have played an important role in the history of psychoanalytic theory. Freud originally thought that all conversion hysterics had been sexually seduced as children, and that all obsessive-compulsives had sexually seduced another child, usually after being seduced themselves. After being denounced as dirty-minded (since his contemporaries maintained that child abuse almost never occurred), Freud's views began to be validated by others' observations. However, he himself discovered that many of the childhood seductions were fantasies. He published that discomforting discovery, retracting as wrong his earlier theory of childhood seduction as the *universal* trauma in such cases. What he said was that in the majority of conversion hysterics, the childhood seduction was a fantasy and not a real event. But in many cases of hysteria, it was undoubtedly a real event. Freud said this clearly throughout his career.

Strangely, contemporary critics (Masson, 1984) falsely state that Freud denied that children were ever sexually molested or abused. In Freud's (1917) words: "Phantasies of being seduced are of particular interest, because so often they are not phantasies but real memories. Fortunately, however, they are not real as often as seemed to be shown by the findings of analysis. . . . You must not suppose, however, that sexual abuse of a child by its nearest male relative belongs entirely to the realm of phantasy. Most analysts will have treated cases in which such events were real and could unimpeachably be established" (p. 370). This, of course, means that it is up to the analyst to listen carefully to the material and help the patient winnow through it.

It was the professional world, psychoanalytic as well as nonpsychoanalytic, that breathed a sigh of relief when it was claimed that Freud had said that incest and sexual abuse never

happened. But bad things do happen, although fantasies are also a part of our real lives.

Dreams

Dreams were forced on Freud's attention by patients' associations. The barriers between consciousness and the unconscious are more permeable (although they still exist) during sleep. In Freud's view, the purpose of the dream was to preserve sleep in the face of disturbance. He hypothesized that the memories of the previous day, the *day residue*, were simply building blocks out of which the dream was constructed. Impulses that are preconscious or unconscious are the motive forces for the dream, insofar as they tend to interrupt sleep. (The rapid eye movement (REM) state of current electronic dream research is not, as was first thought, dreaming, but rather a state of electrical activation of the brain that recurs spontaneously throughout the night and during which dreams are more likely to occur because the activation is disturbing.)

Therapeutically, the patient is asked to associate to each detail of his or her dream or to something striking about the dream, or is asked what from the previous day was involved in this dream. In each case, the patient arrives at the same material.

The dream as remembered is a distorted version of the preconscious and unconscious thoughts. The *dream work* refers to the transformation of *latent* content (the dreamer's underlying thoughts, wishes, impulses, childhood memories, feelings, allusions to the transference, etc.) into *manifest* content (the dream as dreamed and as remembered). *Distortions* make the latent content not easily recognizable. The distortions are carried out according to the dictates of the dreamer's conscience (*over-me* or superego). The general rule is: The more unacceptable an impulse is to the conscience of the dreamer, the more distorted will be its expression in the manifest content of the dream.

There are three major types of distortion during dreaming. *Condensation* refers to many different thoughts being expressed by a single element of the manifest dream. *Displacement* refers to detaching a wish or impulse or feeling from its proper place and expressing it somewhere else, such as the dreamer's anger appearing as a stranger killing someone. *Visual representation* refers to an abstract thought represented by a concrete image (e.g., a man digging a trench for the second time representing the idea of "retrenching" his finances). Further distortions, referred to as *secondary elaboration*, are introduced in remembering or telling the dream to make it more coherent or meaningful.

Symbols refer to elements that frequently have a given meaning. Today we do not accept the notion of universal symbols based on a collective unconscious inherited from the experiences of previous generations. The notion of the collective unconscious was based on a Spencerian view of evolution that involved the inheritance of acquired characteristics. That theory is no longer part of biology. The collective unconscious would now have to stand on purely psychological evidence, and it does not. Thus, Freud's European patients, who had studied Latin and Greek, used the origins of words in symbol formation. American patients do not use the origins of words in their symbols. There are symbols that are widely used because of the biological nature of human beings and of consequent widespread personal experience. But there is no symbol that is not used by someone in an idiosyncratic way.

Freud himself recommended using symbolic interpretations only when the patient had no associations. Frequently when a patient does associate to a symbol, the associations yield the classically described meaning. Symbolic interpretations remain good clinical guesses that will be right more often than wrong, but will be wrong sometimes. Dreamers use symbols to express something without being aware of what they are expressing. Anything in the patient's experience may appear in dreams, fantasies, and symptom formation. Certainly, the slang of the individual's culture will appear in his or her symbols.

Freud saw dreams as wish fulfillment.

Therefore, nightmares seemed a theoretical problem that was resolved by overlapping explanatory principles. First, anxiety when dreaming can be a way of saying (to oneself) "This is not my wish." The general rule of dream work is that the more unacceptable an impulse, the more distorted its expression is in the dream. But an unacceptable wish (to the over-me) can be expressed openly in the dream if it is accompanied by anxiety. Second, a lesser fear may replace a greater one: For example, a patient may be terrified of a stranger instead of being terrified of his or her parent. Third, the dream may result from a wish for punishment. Fourth, anxiety may wake the dreamer, thus reassuring him or her that this problem is "only a dream." Fifth, the dream is an attempted wish fulfillment, and the attempt may be unsuccessful. Finally, the wish-fulfillment refers to the latent content (preconscious and unconscious thoughts underlying the dream) and not necessarily to the manifest content of the dream.

Symptom Formation

Dreams are triggered by interacting impulses from early childhood and current life; they involve preconscious and unconscious impulses and memories, frustrations from reality, and distortions by *over-me* (superego) values. The final product—the dream proper—is a complex compromise. This is a good model for the formation of symptoms.

A veteran of World War II had a paralyzed arm years after the war was over. Veterans Administration neurologists eventually decided that it was not neurological, but rather conversion hysteria. He was referred to the psychology service. After 6 months of twice weekly psychoanalytic therapy, he began to recover the repressed memory of a trauma. He had been the tail gunner of a two-man bomber that crashed and caught fire. One arm was broken. The plane was going to explode when the fire hit the gas tank. His friend, the pilot, a much larger man, had broken both legs and was unconscious. Despite the patient's terror, with great difficulty using his one good arm, he dragged his friend inch by inch from the plane while bystanders and ambulance personnel refused to help because of the danger. His friend fully recovered. The patient was given a medal but could not remember anything about his heroism. The broken arm fully recovered, but the other arm was paralyzed.

After the session in which he first remembered the trauma, he began to be able to move his arm a little, and regained full use of it with further therapy.

The patient's unconscious wish was that if he had broken both arms, he would not have had to endure the terror of his heroic act. Despite his strong conscience, he could have run for his life since it would have been impossible to save his friend. His unconscious was thus protecting him against reexperiencing the horror. But the unconscious is stupid. The war was over, and even if he were in a similar crash, the paralysis would save him only if it were exactly the same and he again broke the other arm.

Full recovery also required dealing with what Freud called *secondary gain*. Once you have a symptom, it will be used for purposes other than those involved in the original symptom formation. These other purposes, both conscious and unconscious, have to be dealt with before full recovery occurs. In this case, a paralyzed arm meant that the veteran could not work at his job. In the traditional family of the post–World War II era, the husband was the breadwinner of the family, and not being able to work was a good way to express hostility to his wife.

Anxiety hysteria, or *phobia*, is a fear of something not dangerous, or only mildly dangerous and not sufficient to justify the fear. Phobias usually involve an unacceptable wish, and the thing feared represents unconscious issues, like the manifest content of a dream.

Most of what are called phobias by behavior modifiers are really fears; that is, the anxiety is appropriate to the conscious learning history of the individual and therefore should respond to interventions like desensitization. When behavior modifiers report a peculiarly resistant phobia that does not respond to behavioral techniques, it usually will be apparent to any psychoanalytically sophisticated clinician that this is a real phobia—that is, where the fear is discrepant from the conscious learning history of the individual.

Thus, someone who has an automobile accident and is afraid to drive is probably suffering from a fear and not a phobia. But the psychoanalytic patient who was told that we should discuss the possibility of ending her analysis, and for the first time in her life developed a terror of crossing bridges, was suffering from a true phobia. She had not known anyone who had fallen off a bridge, nor had she. But it would be a very stupid psychoanalyst who did not know what bridge she was afraid to cross. (The analysis of this phobia led to further material about her wishes to separate from, fear of separation from, death wishes toward, and threats made by her parents.) A woman, a very safe driver with many years of experience, who was deeply depressed when her husband left her, also developed a phobia of driving. This symptom came under control when a psychoanalytic therapist, on the basis of her material, interpreted her fear of her unconscious wish to run her ex-husband down.

Freud suggested that all phobics need to be encouraged at the appropriate time to do what they fear. It is not important whether they succeed. The attempt will stir up the relevant conflictual material in the therapy, and eventually they will succeed.

Obsessive-compulsive symptoms have similar dynamics. Obsessions are uncomfortable ideas about which one cannot stop thinking. Compulsions are actions that one must perform in order not to experience anxiety. Both the obsessive idea and the compulsive action have a structure similar to that of dreams. According to Freud, such patients did not repress the experiences related to their symptoms, but instead used the defense mechanism of isolation (i.e., not connecting relevant experiences, memories, and feelings with their symptoms or with each other).

A patient was obsessed with the number 4: thinking it, saying it, and tapping it many times every waking hour (Karon, 1958). The number 3 would come into his mind, and he felt compelled to change it to the number 4. Therapy revealed that he was trying to change a world where he had a penis (symbolized by the number 3) and where there was sexuality into a world (symbolized by the number 4) where his mother could love him because there were no penises or sexuality.

The best description in the psychological or psychiatric literature of the successful treatment of a severe obsessive-compulsive, and Freud's best description of his actual treatment technique (Lipton, 1977), is Freud's case history of the so-called Rat-man. His major obsessive idea was an oriental torture in which rats ate into the body of the victim through the anus. Less than 1 year of treatment for 6 days per week led to full symptomatic recovery without relapse (Freud, 1909).

Let us turn next to the *actual neuroses.* Freud mistakenly thought that these symptoms only needed good advice for the patient to recover. In Freud's original conceptions, *anxiety neurosis* (free-floating anxiety without any specific object of fear) was due to incomplete discharge of libido (which turned into anxiety), as with couples who practiced withdrawal as a technique of contraception; *hypochondria* (believing that you are physically ill despite an absence of symptoms) was due to an inadequate sex life; and *neurasthenia* (a lack of energy, headaches, mild depression) was due to masturbation. All of these are now understood as simply neurotic symptoms to be analyzed. Even Freud noted that anxiety neuroses tended to develop into phobias and that the other actual neuroses were mixed with symptoms requiring analysis; therefore, the patients had to be analyzed. While he never explicitly retracted his early theories of actual neurosis, in his later work he treated such patients with analysis (since they always had mixed symptoms).

Free-floating anxiety is simply the fear of an unconscious impulse. There is no such thing as "spontaneous" panic attacks. Every psychoanalytic therapist has had patients with panic attacks that were described as spontaneous and uncaused. Inevitably, there are consistent conditions that trigger the attack of which the patient is unaware, and these consistent conditions have unconscious meaning. When these are explored in the context of psychoanalysis or psychoanalytic therapy, the spontaneous panic attacks remit. For example, a deeply depressed patient also suffered severe spontaneous panic attacks, according to the psychiatrists who treated him (only partially successfully) with medication for most of his life. At the age of 60, when he finally underwent psychoanalysis, it was discovered that the panic attacks always occurred when he was making a presentation to executives at the same level as he or when he felt good. This led to the discovery of childhood traumas: His older brother had tried to kill him when he was feeling good about being allowed to play with this older brother. When he consciously connected his anxiety to the remembered traumas, the panic attacks disappeared.

Freud erroneously thought that the psychoses were untreatable because he believed that psychotic patients could not form a therapeutically usable transference, but that this was a technical problem for which someone might find a solution. Nonetheless, he did have some insights into certain paranoid dynamics (1911). He also understood manic states as attempted denials of depression and depression as involving the *over-me* (superego) reproaching the self in the way that a lost, but loved, other person had reproached the patient, or as the self would have liked to reproach the lost loved one. Since both manic and depressed patients tend to recover spontaneously, he felt that they could be analyzed between episodes to prevent recurrence. Abraham (1912/1950), however, successfully treated depressives even while psychotic.

MAJOR THEORETICAL DEVELOPMENTS AND VARIATIONS

There are major schools of psychoanalytic theory and technique emphasizing different concepts. But it would be a mistake to get caught up in these differences. Each school has had major new insights, but the intelligent psychoanalysts in each school have taken each other's insights into account. All competent psychoanalysts stay as close to the patient's words as possible and sound more alike in treatment than in treatises. Most psychoanalysts use insights from all of the schools. Indeed, Pine (1988) has argued that to be effective, a psychoanalyst must at least use the insights from the drive psychology, ego psychology, object relations, and self-psychology schools. He should have included the interpersonal school as well. Every school invents new terminology to emphasize its differentness. We will describe these new terms only when they are related to important new ideas.

Ego Psychology

The dominant school in the United States is ego psychology, which is the direct continuation of Freud's work, using his terminology. Ego psychologists emphasize structural theory, conflicts, drives, and defense mechanisms. Anna Freud (in England) described (1936/1966) the defense mechanisms, the psychoanalysis of children (1928), and normal development in psychoanalytic structural terms (1965). Charles Brenner (1987) elaborated the structural theory and described all mental functioning as the result of conflict.

The American ego psychologist Erik Erikson (1950, 1959) recast ego psychology in terms of social development. Erikson described the oral stage as the stage when "basic trust versus mistrust" is learned. He described the anal stage as the stage when "autonomy versus shame and self-doubt" is learned. He saw the Oedipal period as the phase when "initiative versus guilt" is learned. In the latency period, when the child is more concerned with school and with acquiring skills, Erikson believes that "industry versus inferiority" is learned. With the onset of adolescence, "identity versus role confusion" is learned. He has been particularly concerned with the problem of identity. In early adulthood, "intimacy and solidarity versus isolation" are learned. Erikson goes on to define stages not included in Freud: adulthood, where "generativity versus stagnation" is learned, and maturity, where "ego integrity versus despair" is learned.

Interpersonal Theory

In the 1930s, Sullivan and Fromm-Reichmann discarded the concept of libido and replaced it with the analysis of the *self* as a system (the "good me," the "bad me," and the "not me"). Crucial to understanding a human being is an understanding of the nature of his or her relations with others now and in the past, as well as the fantasies, conscious and unconscious, about those relations. They shifted away from an emphasis on the biological notion of drives and focused instead on cultural and relational dynamics. The two basic drives were security and satisfaction. Sullivan (1964) thought that interpersonal processes included either "positive-constructive movements toward intimacy, with the securing of satisfactions and the maintenance of ('personal') security, or negative-destructive movements of hostile avoiding, ostracizing, or dominating of persons more or less clearly identified as the sources of insecurity, and thus barriers to the securing of satisfactions" (p. 27).

The interpersonalists did not discard Freud's insights into development, but they added a new set of stages: infancy, childhood, juvenile period, preadolescence, early adolescence, late adolescence, and maturity. Infancy is the preverbal stage. Consequently, experiences are hard to conceptualize or remember and have an "awe-full" character. Anxiety is based on empathy with an anxious mother and, hence, is uncontrollable. Some of the symptoms of psychoses are related to this period. Childhood, when language has been acquired, allows for clearer relations with others but also clearer conceptualizations of one's own experiences. In the juvenile period, relations with peers become important for normal development. Problems in competition arise. The interpersonalists were the first to point out the importance of the preadolescent period, when one first forms a strong relationship with one particular person of the same sex (a best friend). This makes relating to one person of the opposite sex easier. Individuals who have never had a best friend of the same sex seem to need to go through this stage later in life. The adolescent stages are the periods when one attempts to form sexual relationships and work adjustment. Maturity is the period when these tasks are achieved. Problems at any stage may be corrected by good experiences at the next stage.

As analysts, the interpersonalists focus more on interpersonal reactions within therapy and outside it, and they relate these reaction to the relations with others in reality and fantasy in the present and the past. Insofar as the interpersonalists abandoned the concept of libido, there was no theoretical reason why psychotics could not be treated. The most influential work on the development of successful psychoanalytic therapy for schizophrenia was that of Sullivan and Fromm-Reichmann and their students.

Psychoanalytic Developmental Psychology

A precursor of modern separation-individuation theory was Otto Rank (1952), who thought that the trauma of birth was the key to understanding all anxiety. But after a lifetime of working with that concept, he decided (1941) that the biological experience of birth did not leave sequelae but was a good metaphor for all of the critical conflicts in life (which consist of a conflict between the security of being controlled versus the danger of more independence). Erich Fromm (1941, 1947) recast this same basic conflict in interpersonal terms.

Margaret Mahler, after observing the child's development in the first 3 years of life (in addition to psychoanalytic work), delineated most carefully the stages of the separation-individuation process (Mahler, Pine, & Bergmann, 1975). The infant learns to separate itself from its parental relationships and thereby gain an autonomous ego that can relate healthily to a parental object. The stages of this process occur not only throughout development, but also during the process of analysis. A readable application of separation-individuation theory to normal development is provided by Judith Viorst (1986).

Initially, Mahler conceptualized an autistic stage, but infant observation (Stern, 1985) reveals a complex relationship between infant and mother from birth.

Object Relations

There are three major object-relations schools: the English, the Scottish, and the American.

The English school, represented by Melanie Klein (1930, 1948) and her students, emphasizes the importance of the first year of life, as well as the handling of rage, envy, and projective dynamics. They accept the concept of libido but emphasize the aggressive urges and fantasies. For example, the infant, in reaction to feeling powerless and vulnerable, wishes to devour or destroy the mother or the mother's breast or both parents' genitals. The infant is also afraid of being destroyed or devoured by the mother or the mother's breast (*paranoid position* of early infancy). Klein describes development in terms of *projection* (seeing an intolerable part of the self in the outside world) and *introjection* (taking an intolerable part of the outside world into the self so as to control it). One also introjects good parts of the outside world in order to have a good self. Object-relations theorists are apt to think in terms of conflicts between internalized objects, or internalized objects and the self, rather than between the id, ego, and superego. Klein also emphasizes the controversial concept of *projective identification*. There are three parts to this dynamic: First, an unacceptable part of the self is projected onto another person; second, the other person is induced to feel or act in accordance with this projection; finally, the self identifies with this other person. Particularly useful is Klein's concept of the *depressive position*, beginning toward the end of the first year of life. This refers to the terrible infantile dilemma of discovering that he or she deeply loves and murderously hates the same person, namely, the mother. Kleinians tend to interpret early in treatment and to use "deep" (i.e., oral) interpretations.

Both the interpersonalists and the Kleinians arrived independently at the notion that the child forms two concepts: the good mother (when she is being good to you) and the bad mother (when she is being bad to you). These feel so different that the infant thinks of them as two different people. In the depressive position you realize that they are one person, and if you get rid of the bad mother, you lose the good one; similarly, if you accept the good mother, the bad one hurts you. The child also develops a concept of the good and bad self as different. The defense mechanism of *splitting* refers to being unable ever to integrate the good and bad mother images (or the good and bad self-images, etc.) as opposed to separating what has already been integrated.

Klein and her students have developed somewhat different techniques of child psychoanalysis from Anna Freud and somewhat different techniques for treating psychotic patients from the interpersonalists.

The Scottish school, Ronald Fairbairn (1954) and Harry Guntrip (1969), are the most interesting theoretically. They postulate that the "aim of the libido" is not sexual gratification but rather to form a good object relationship, that is, a good relation with a good object (person). Even the infant is represented as object-seeking. Aggression is the reaction to deprivation or frustration. Moreover, the earliest form of anxiety for the child is separating from the mother, separation anxiety. The two basic fears are *depressive anxiety*, that your anger will destroy the object (destroy it, make it go away, turn it from a good object into a bad object), and, even worse, *schizoid anxiety*, that your love will destroy the object. Guntrip adds the fear that you will separate and never find an object relation again.

Each individual is desperately seeking a relationship with a good object, no matter how destructive that search may seem to an outside observer. The individual is struggling to form a good object relationship and to maintain the fantasy of the good parent at any cost. The psychosexual stages are battlegrounds rather than discrete problems. The patient needs to seduce the therapist into mistreating the patient so as to protect the image of the parent as at least being better than other people. Guilt is frequently a defense against helpless terror. It is better to have done something wrong than to be at the mercy of a truly malevolent object or to have had a malevolent parent. This idea is particularly helpful in dealing with the guilt feelings of rape victims, or other victims, and in dealing with criminal and other malevolent behavior motivated by the need to prove that one deserved the mistreatment of one's childhood ("How could my mother love me? I'm nothing but a goddam criminal," unconsciously reversing the time sequence and causality). Fairbairn and Guntrip's other new ideas (e.g., their structural theory) are less useful therapeutically.

The American school, represented by Otto Kernberg (1980, 1988) and Vamik Volkan (1976), integrates British object-relations theory with American ego psychology. Pre-Oedipal development is understood in object-relations terms, and Oedipal conflicts are understood in ego psychological terms. *Narcism* (pathological concern with the self to the exclusion of the legitimate needs of others) is understood as a defense against rage. Splitting and projective defenses are emphasized in the treatment of narcistic and borderline patients (sicker than neurotics but not psychotic).

Self Psychology

Self psychology refers to the concepts of Hans Kohut (1977) and his students. They were concerned about the facts that the energy and drive concepts of ego psychology do not refer to real physical processes; that the technique of ego psychoanalysis (as they understood it) seemed unduly impersonal and cold; and that even fairly well-functioning narcistic patients were not treatable.

Their most important ideas follow. The development of the self depends on being accepted, understood, and appreciated by the parents, being allowed to develop a temporarily grandiose self, and being allowed to idealize at least one parent and identify with this idealized parent. Narcistic patients are those who never received such growth-promoting parenting in childhood, and who have fragile selves that fragment easily, releasing rage. In therapy these patients must be empathically understood and accepted, allowed to idealize themselves, and allowed to idealize the therapist and identify with the idealized therapist as normal stages of growth. Interpretations should be "experience-near."

Psychoanalysts tend to polarize about whether Kernberg's or Kohut's understanding of narcism is more adequate. Research (Wolowitz, 1991) suggests that the reason psychoanalysts cannot agree on the basis of clinical observations is that there is some truth in both points of view.

Affect Psychology

Probably the most important theoretical development in psychoanalysis today is a greater appreciation of the role and nature of affect. Affect has always been central to psychoanalysis. Freud once said, "Psychoanalysis deals with feelings. What else could it possibly be dealing with?" But this seemed so obvious that it was not emphasized, and many analysts intellectualized. Again and again, constructive critics, like Rogers (1961) and the existential psychoanalysts (e.g., May, 1958) have reemphasized emotions. (The other contribution of the existential psychoanalysts was pointing out the central role of the fear of dying, or *nonbeing*.)

Kohut (e.g., 1977) has emphasized empathy and the importance in development, both in childhood and in the psychoanalytic hour, of the correct appreciation of affect. But Kernberg (1988) also has said that the most important thing to understand in the analytic hour is the affect.

Among important insights are Helen Block Lewis' (1983, 1987) work on the role of shame and guilt in psychopathology, as well as the central role shame plays in the female superego (*over-me*) in contrast to the central role of guilt in the male superego (*over-me*). Henry Krystal (1988) has described affect regression, as well as patients who are unable to recognize affect. In his view, affects develop from undifferentiated to highly differentiated, with regression causing a return to primitive, undifferentiated affect. Patients who are unable to recognize affect include victims of massive trauma (concentration camp victims), psychosomatic patients, and many drug addicts.

Most important, however, is Silvan Tomkin's (1962, 1963, 1991, in press) theory of specific primary affects, including the positive affects of excitement and joy, the distinctions between anxiety and distress, the role of shame-humiliation in maintaining psychopathology, and the centrality of affects in motivation and in mental functioning.

Feelings are an essential part of rational thinking and are never inappropriate. If patients are angry, something is hurting. If they are depressed, there is something to be depressed about. If they are afraid, there is something to be afraid of. If the cause is not in consciousness, then it is in the unconscious. If it is not in the present, it is in the past and something in the present symbolizes it. "Spontaneous" anxiety and "meaningless" depression always make sense, and disappear as symptoms when their unconscious meaning is discovered in therapy.

But isolation as a defense is frequently part of severe depressive symptoms. In answer to the question "What was going on when the symptom started?", the typical depressed patient will answer, "Nothing." If pressed, the patient will answer, "Nothing important." If further pressed, the patient will reveal experiences that would depress anyone. As Viggo Jensen aptly put it (personal communication), "An endogenous depression is a severe depression in someone whom you haven't talked to long enough to find out why they are depressed."

THEORY OF CHANGE

The fundamental theory of change in psychoanalysis and psychoanalytic therapy is that what is unconscious does not change and what is conscious can be changed. Therefore the aim of psychoanalytic therapy is to make what is unconscious conscious. In the words of Richard Sterba, "All I have to offer you is understanding, but that is a very great deal."

Bettelheim (1983) has described well the cognitive experience that is curative: "You try to tell that idiot [the therapist], and he doesn't understand. You tell it more clearly, and that idiot still doesn't understand. You tell it more clearly, and that idiot still doesn't really understand. You tell it even more clearly, and you suddenly realize that for the first time in your life you understand it yourself. So the therapist doesn't have to be right, but just has to be close enough so that it's worth the patient's trouble to try to make the therapist understand."

Therapeutic empathy is usually thought of as correct understanding of the patient. But what is perceived by the patient as understanding is actually the therapist's effort to understand correctly (whether or not it is successful).

Freud (1917) at one point considered that making the unconscious conscious was the equivalent of filling in all the gaps in memory. But, as Franz Alexander and Thomas French (1974) pointed out, this goal is impossible to achieve. However, if one accepts Freud's notion that the *screen memories* (i.e., the available memories of childhood) contain a summary (albeit unconscious and symbolized) of everything that is important, most of what is important can be modifiable without reaching the impossible goal of total recall.

At first, Freud's goal was to uncover repressed affects, memories, fantasies, and impulses. An affectless, intellectual knowledge of the repressed was relatively useless; the patient had to be a part of the process of discovery, using his or her own intellectual and emotional capacities to discover, with the therapist, the unconscious material in a convincing, concrete, and emotionally laden way. The analysis of the resistances led to the discovery that these resistances were the patient's characteristic defense mechanisms being used in the therapy process. Becoming consciously aware of one's defense mechanisms became at least as important as making conscious the impulses, feelings, and memories being defended against, so that the patient could now alter the defenses. It also became clear that understanding (and changing) a defense in one context did not automatically change it in all other contexts.

Even the conflicts, memories, and affects defended against usually had to be rediscovered in many different contexts for each of these contexts to be modifiable. This therapeutic rediscovery is called *working through*.

Because transference is such a dramatic phenomenon, and the information it yields is so specific, emotional, and convincing, Strachey (1934) suggested that only transference interpretations were "mutative," that is, produced real change. This is an oversimplification. Transference interpretations can be very powerful, but they are not the only ones that produce change. Malan (1979) similarly, has suggested that linking interpretations—that is, interpretations that link the transference reactions to the past or to current reactions outside of therapy, or that link current reactions outside therapy to the past, or that link all three (transference reaction, current reaction outside therapy, and childhood)—are most effective. Malan's research (1974) found that in brief psychoanalytic therapy (50 sessions), the more the psychoanalyst talked about transference reactions and related them to the past, the more the patient benefitted. Some supposedly psychoanalytic therapists never linked transference reactions to the past, and their patients did not benefit. (There are other ways of conceptualizing the effective interpretation, and Malan's conclusion has been disputed by some researchers.)

Freud described the process of psychoanalysis as the patient forming a new symptom, a transference so intense that it became the patient's chief symptom. With this *transference neurosis* the patient could give up his or her original symptoms, and when the transference neurosis was resolved, the patient was cured. Unfortunately, this was an oversimplification.

One way of conceptualizing the change in psychoanalytic treatment is that the *over-me* or superego is modified, since it is the irrational conscience that triggers the anxiety and guilt that motivate the defenses, including repression. A kindlier and more rational superego permits conscious awareness of impermissible feelings, memories, impulses, relationships, and defenses; and all of these can then be modified on the basis of current reality into a constantly growing self or *I* or ego. For object-relations theorists who emphasize internalized objects, this same process may be described as internalization of the analyst as a good object to neutralize or replace the internalized bad objects of childhood.

However it is conceptualized, internalization of the therapist is a central change process in psychoanalysis and psychoanalytic therapy. Internalization is automatic and unconscious. The patient clearly begins to replace the conscience (*over-me* or superego) based on parental and other childhood determinants with the more flexible and conscious values of the therapist, including the value of continued growth beyond the capabilities, values, and knowledge of the therapist. Insofar as the patient has an identity confusion, the patient also identifies with the therapist (thus modifying the self, *I*, or ego). Like a normal adolescent's identifications, this is a partial and transitory identification, except for those aspects of the therapist that seem permanently valuable to the patient.

The psychoanalytic therapist must form a therapeutic alliance (Sterba, 1934/1987) with the healthy part of the patient to engage mutually in the work of psychotherapy. It is sometimes explained to the patient that "You have two therapists: me and the healthy part of you. We will both work together until you no longer need me. But you will continue your analysis for the rest of your life."

Hope plays an integrative role in mental functioning (French, 1952; French & Wheeler, 1963). Arousing hope is an important part of developing a therapeutic alliance and sustaining treatment. The moment a therapist listens to a patient carefully as a person to be understood and treats his or her symptoms seriously, hope is aroused. Even depressed patients do not really want to convince their therapist to share their pessimism. For many patients, the therapist is the first person to be realistically hopeful, to see their problems as only requiring hard work. Nor is hope important only to the patient. There is no reason for the patient to feel hopeful if the therapist does not share that feeling. Therapists who do not expect to be helpful tend not to be helpful.

Psychoanalysis, once begun, continues as long as the patient lives. The only thing that ends is the time during which he or she works with a therapist. The task of understanding one's self is never complete.

CURRENT STATUS OF RESEARCH AND PRACTICE

The most important body of empirical data relevant to psychoanalysis remains the hundreds of thousands of hours of clinical observations. While many of Freud's theories have not stood the test of time, many others (e.g., regression, fixation, projection, symbolism, and unconscious processes) have been validated in experiments far removed from the therapeutic hour (Fisher & Greenberg, 1977; Tomkins, 1945). The psychoanalytic process itself has been subjected to intensive scrutiny (Thoma & Kachele, 1987, 1992).

The most pervasive finding in contemporary psychotherapy research is that the quality of the therapeutic alliance is a critical factor in determining whether psychotherapy helps. As first postulated by Sterba (1934/1987), the psychoanalytic therapist must form an alliance with the healthy part of the patient to engage mutually in the work of psychotherapy. Different research groups use different measures of the therapeutic alliance, but the phenomenon is so robust that it seems to work no matter which measure is used.

Meta-analyses (e.g., Smith, Glass, & Miller, 1980) show that psychotherapy is more helpful than no treatment. But most meta-analyses find no clear experimental evidence that one type of psychotherapy is better than another, in part because of the paucity of comparative studies. Most available studies have used very brief psychotherapies in order to minimize the researchers' time, often so that they could finish their Ph.D. theses. Not well known yet is the meta-analysis from the University of Bern (Grauwe, 1987) that shows that in comparative studies of treatments of less than 12 sessions, the nonpsychoanalytic treatments are clearly better than their alternative; predominantly in studies of more than 12 sessions, the psychoanalytic therapies are better.

There are myths that economically poor, uneducated, or minority patients do not respond to psychodynamic therapy, but the truth is that it is not offered to them. When it is, they respond to it.

Freud was pessimistic about treating patients over 40. This was a serious mistake; patients in their 40s, 50s, and even 60s do well in psychoanalysis. Bernard Riess (1988, 1989) has even reported treating patients into their 90s.

Effective psychoanalytic therapies for schizophrenia, severe depression, and mania (Teixeira, 1992) exist. Most of these therapies are the outgrowth of the work of the interpersonalists, Sullivan and Fromm-Reichmann, and of the English and Scottish schools of object relations. While Fromm-Reichmann (1950) is still recommended for the technique of psychoanalytic psychotherapy of schizophrenia, Benedetti (1987) and Karon and VandenBos (1981) are also helpful. (Both of the latter books include empirical data on effectiveness.)

Psychoanalysis went through a period of uncovering and revealing early childhood and infantile experiences, feelings, and fantasies and taking these reconstructions seriously. Then there was a period when it was thought that one ought not to take these reconstructions seriously; that the experiences of infancy and early childhood were so primitive and unelaborated that they did not leave clear sequelae. Recent research on early infant development and the early mother–child relationship (Stern, 1985) clearly reveals complex mental processes, albeit ones that are not experienced in words. The traumatic experiences (including, of course, fantasies) of the first year of life are often forced on therapists' attention, unless they will not hear.

But most of the problems in the relations with one's parents and siblings are not time bound. Instead, problems recur in modified form throughout childhood and even into adulthood.

Psychoanalysis has gone from the analysis of the good symptom neurotic, to include the treatment of borderline and character problems, to the treatment of psychoses, and to delinquents. Of course, the majority of people suffering from these problems will never receive real help. But we must help those we can and spread the knowledge we now have. The typical psychoanalytic patient today has had three to five previous "treatments" that have not helped, some of which are so destructive that it is hard to believe anyone could call them treatment. Before transference from the parents can be dealt with, one usually has to deal with the transference from previous destructive pseudotherapists.

As the goal of psychoanalysis changed from alleviating a symptom to changing defenses and character structure and allowing continued growth, the length of therapy changed from 6 months to several years. In fact, a typical time span is 2 to 5 years. On the other hand, the frequency of sessions decreased from six to five or four per week to three per week (which is most usual in the United States).

Attempts to speed up psychoanalysis occurred from the beginning. Rank and Ferenczi's first attempts were not successful, but Rank (1945, 1952) continued to develop a briefer technique that focused on separation anxiety (birth trauma). Alexander and French (1974) developed and described their technique for *briefer psychoanalysis*, or *psychoanalytic therapy*, the latter term now generally used whenever the frequency is less than three times per week, or the total number of sessions is low, but the treatment is based on psychoanalytic principles.

The most important contemporary developments in brief psychoanalytic therapy are those of Malan (1979), Davanloo (1980), Luborsky (1984), and Strupp and Binder (1984). Interestingly, each of them engendered a body of systematic empirical research that went beyond simple clinical observation. Malan's book is a readable exposition not only of his therapeutic technique but also of psychoanalytic theories of psychopathology. Clearest in its delineation of technique and most grounded in current systematic research is Strupp and Binder (1984).

CONCLUSIONS

Despite specific errors, psychoanalysis is still largely the house that Freud built. Current psychoanalysts tend to pay more attention to countertransference (transference feelings of the analyst toward the patient) and pregenital issues, but the basic ways of thinking and of treating the patient are fundamentally similar. Both long-term and brief psychoanalytic therapies have proved useful.

A patient sought help for panic attacks. A month of psychoanalytic crisis intervention twice per week resolved the attacks. It was discovered that her "spontaneous" panic attacks were fear of her unconscious rage at someone who well deserved her anger. It was recommended that she consider psychoanalysis for longer-enduring but subtler issues if she thought it worthwhile. She was skeptical because she had tried psychotherapy earlier and it had not helped.

A year later, the patient entered psychoanalysis, which lasted for 5 years. She described the result: "I have good friends now, but I always had good friends. I'm good at my job, but I was always good at my job. Maybe I'm more productive, and maybe it's a little easier. An outside observer might not notice any difference. But when I first came here, I was doomed. Now I have problems. And that was well worth five years of work."

But only the patient can make such a decision. It is the role of the therapist to do what is possible in the time available and to help the patient know what is possible.

It was Hedda Bolgar who said that the *Odyssey* was a good metaphor for the process of analysis. Psychodynamic therapy is a frightening voyage of self-discovery that is tolerable because the therapist is there. Freud's final formulation of the aim of analysis is most cogent: "Where *It* was, there *I* shall be."

REFERENCES

Abraham, K. (1950). Notes on the psycho-analytic investigation and treatment of manic-depressive and allied conditions. In *Selected papers* (pp. 137–156). London: Hogarth Press. (Original paper published 1912).

Abraham, K. (1927). The first pregenital stage of the libido. *Selected papers on psycho-analysis* (pp. 248–279). New York: Brunner/Mazel. (Original work published 1916).

Alexander, F., & French, T. (1974). *Psychoanalytic therapy: Principles and application.* Lincoln: University of Nebraska Press.

Benedetti, G. (1987). *Psychotherapy of schizophrenia.* New York: New York University Press.

Bettelheim, B. (1982). *Freud and man's soul.* New York: Knopf.

Bettelheim, B. (1983, April). The treatment of a borderline patient. Case conference presented by the Department of Psychology, University of Detroit, Southfield, MI.

Bowlby, J. (1966). *Maternal care and mental health.* New York: Schocken Books.

Bowlby, J. (1969). *Attachment and loss.* New York: Basic Books.

Brenner, C. (1987). *The mind in conflict.* New York: International Universities Press.

Breuer, J., & Freud, S. (1895). *Studies in hysteria.* In S. Freud, *Standard Edition* (Vol. 2, pp. 1-335). London: Hogarth Press.

Brown, L. M., & Gilligan, C. (1992). *Meeting at the crossroads: Women's psychology and girls' development.* Cambridge, MA: Harvard University Press.

Cremerius, J. (1981). Freud bei der arbeit uber die schulter geschaut: Seine technik im spiegel von schulern und patienten. *Jahrbuch der Psychoanalyse, 6,* 123–158.

Davanloo, H. (1980). *Short-term dynamic psychotherapy.* New York: Jason Aronson.

Erikson, E. H. (1950). *Childhood and society.* New York: Norton.

Erikson, E. H. (1959). *Identity and the life cycle.* New York: International Universities Press.

Fairbairn, W. R. D. (1954). *An object-relations theory of personality: Psychoanalytic studies of the personality.* New York: Basic Books.

Fast, I. (1984). *Gender identity: A differentiation model.* Hillsdale, NJ: Analytic Press.

Ferenczi, S. (1950). Introjection and transference. In E. Jones (Ed. & (Trans.), *Sex in psychoanalysis* (pp. 35–93). New York: Brunner/Mazel. (Original work published 1909).

Fisher, S., & Greenberg, R. (1977). *The scientific credibility of Freud's theories and therapy.* New York: Basic Books.

credibility of Freud's theories and therapy. New York: Basic Books.

French, T. M. (1952). *Integration of behavior: Vol. 1. Basic postulates*. Chicago: University of Chicago Press.

French, T. M., & Wheeler, D. R. (1963). Hope and repudiation of hope in psychoanalytic therapy. In T. M. French (Ed.), *Psychoanalytic interpretations* (pp. 269–292). Chicago: Quadrangle Press.

Freud, A. (1928). *Introduction to the technique of child analysis*. New York: International Universities Press.

Freud, A. (1936). *The ego and the mechanisms of defense*. New York: International Universities Press.

Freud, A. (1965). *Normality and pathology in childhood: Assessment of development*. New York: International Universities Press.

Freud, S. (1893). Some points for a comparative study of organic and hysterical motor paralyses. In *Standard Edition* [hereafter *S. E.*] (Vol. 1, pp. 155–172). London: Hogarth Press.

Freud, S. (1901). *The psychopathology of everyday life*. *S. E.* (Vol. 6).

Freud, S. (1909). Notes upon a case of obsessional neurosis. *S. E.* (Vol. 10, 5–148).

Freud, S. (1911). *Psycho-analytic notes on an autobiographical account of a case of paranoia (dementia paranoides)*. *S. E.* (Vol. 12, pp. 9–80).

Freud, S. (1917). *Introductory lectures on psychoanalysis*. *S. E.* (Vol. 15, pp. 1–239; Vol. 16, pp. 241–496).

Freud, S. (1926). The question of lay analysis. *S. E.* (Vol. 20, pp. 179–258).

Freud, S. (1931). *Female psychology*. *S. E.* (Vol. 21, pp. 223–247).

Freud, S. (1933). *New introductory lectures on psychoanalysis*. *S. E.*, Vol. 22, pp. 1–182.

Freud, S. (1933). Femininity. *New introductory lectures on psycho-analysis*. *S. E.* (Vol. 22, pp. 112–136).

Fromm, E. (1941). *Escape from freedom*. New York: Farrar & Rinehart.

Fromm, E. (1947). *Man for himself*. New York: Rinehart.

Fromm-Reichmann, F. (1950). *Principles of intensive psychotherapy*. Chicago: University of Chicago Press.

Gilligan, C. (1982). *In a different voice: Psychological theory and women's development*. Cambridge, MA: Harvard University Press.

Gilligan, C. (1988). *Making connections: The relational worlds of adolescent girls at Emma Willard School*. Cambridge, MA: Harvard University Press.

Grauwe, K. (1987, June 20). *The Bern meta-analysis of outcome studies: Dynamic vs. non-dynamic therapies*. Paper presented at the meeting of the Society for Psychotherapy Research, Ulm, Germany.

Guntrip, H. (1969). *Schizoid phenomena, object relations, and the self*. New York: International Universities Press.

Jordan, J. V, Kaplan, A. G., Miller, J. B., Stiver, I. P., & Surrey, J. L. (1991). *Women's growth in connection: Writings from the Stone Center*. New York: Guilford Press.

Kardiner, A. (1939). *The individual and his society*. New York: Columbia University Press.

Kardiner, A. (1977). *My analysis with Freud: Reminiscences*. New York: Norton.

Karon, B. P. (1958). Some clinical notes on the significance of the number four. *Psychiatric Quarterly*, 32, 281–288.

Karon, B. P. (1989). On the formation of delusions. *Psychoanalytic Psychology*, 6, 169–185.

Karon, B. P. (1994). Artistic creation as adaptive ego function and not regression in the service of the ego. *Psychoanalysis and Psychotherapy*, 10, 80–85.

Karon, B. P., and Rosberg, J. (1958a). Study of the mother–child relationship in a case of paranoid schizophrenia. *American Journal of Psychotherapy*, 12, 522–533.

Karon, B. P., and Rosberg, J. (1958b). The homosexual urges in schizophrenia. *Psychoanalytic and Psychoanalysis Review*, 45, 50–56.

Karon, B. P., & VandenBos, G. R. (1981). *Psychotherapy of schizophrenia: The treatment of choice*. New York: Jason Aronson.

Kernberg, O. (1980). *Internal world and external reality: Object relations theory applied*. New York: Jason Aronson.

Kernberg, O. (1988). Object relations theory in clinical practice. *Psychoanalytic Quarterly*, 57, 481–504.

Klein, M. (1930). The psychotherapy of the psychoses. *British Journal of Medical Psychology*, 10, 242–244.

Klein, M. (1948). *Contributions to psychoanalysis, 1931–1945*. London: Hogarth Press.

Kohut, H. (1977). *The restoration of the self*. New York: International Universities Press.

Krystal, H. (1988). *Integration and self-healing: Affect, trauma, alexithymia: Psychoanalytic reformulations*. Hillsdale, NJ: Analytic Press.

Lewis, H. B. (1983). *Freud and modern psychology*. New York: Plenum Press.

Lipton, S. (1977). The advantages of Freud's technique as shown in his analysis of the Rat Man. *International Journal of Psychoanalysis, 58,* 255–273.

Luborsky, L. (1984). *Principles of psychoanalytic psychotherapy: A manual for supportive-expressive treatment.* New York: Basic Books.

Mahler, M. S., Pine, F., & Bergmann, A. (1975). *The psychological birth of the infant.* New York: Basic Books.

Malan, D. (1976). *Toward the validation of dynamic psychotherapy.* New York: Plenum Press.

Malan, D. (1979). *Individual psychotherapy and the science of psychodynamics.* Cambridge: Butterworth.

Masson, J. M. (1984). *The assault on truth: Freud's suppression of the seduction theory.* New York: Farrar, Straus & Giroux.

May, R. (1958). *Existence: A new dimension in psychiatry and psychology.* New York: Basic Books.

Pine, F. (1988). The four psychologies of psychoanalysis and their place in clinical work. *Journal of the American Psychoanalytic Association, 36,* 571–596.

Rank, O. (1941). *Beyond Psychology.* New York: Dover.

Rank, O. (1945). *Will therapy.* (Trans. Julia Taft). New York: Knopf.

Rank, O. (1952). *The trauma of birth.* New York: Brunner Mazel.

Riess, B. F. (1988, August 13). *Misunderstanding and mishandling of loss, sadness, and depression in older individuals.* Invited paper delivered at the meeting of Psychologists Interested in the Study of Psychoanalysis, Atlanta, GA.

Riess, B. F. (1989). Differential aspects of psychoanalysis of the aged. *Psychoanalysis and Psychotherapy, 7,* 35–43.

Rogers, C. (1961). *On becoming a person: A therapist's view of psychotherapy.* Boston: Houghton Mifflin.

Smith, J. C., Glass, G. V., & Miller, T. I. (1980). *The benefits of psychotherapy.* Baltimore: Johns Hopkins University Press.

Spitz, R. (1965). *The first year of life: A psychoanalytic study of normal and deviant development of object relations.* New York: International Universities Press.

Sterba, R. (1987). The fate of the ego in analytic therapy. In *The collected papers* (pp. 62–70). Croton-on-Hudson, NY: North River Press. (Original paper published 1934).

Stern, D. (1985). *The interpersonal world of the infant.* New York: Basic Books.

Strachey, J. (1934). On the nature of the psychotherapeutic action of psychoanalysis. *International Journal of Psychoanalysis, 15,* 127–159.

Strupp, H. H., & Binder, J. L. (1984). *Psychotherapy in a new key: A guide to time-limited dynamic psychotherapy.* New York: Basic Books.

Sullivan, H. S. (1953). *Interpersonal theory of psychiatry.* New York: Norton.

Sullivan, H. S. (1962). *Schizophrenia as a human process.* New York: Norton.

Sullivan, H. S. (1964). *The fusion of psychiatry and social science.* New York: Norton.

Teixeira, M. A. (1992). Psychoanalytic theory and therapy in the treatment of manic-depressive disorders. *Psychoanalysis and Psychotherapy, 11,* 162–177.

Thoma, H., & Kachele, H. (1987). *Psychoanalytic practice: Vol. 1. Principles.* Berlin, Heidelberg, and New York: Springer-Verlag.

Thoma, H., & Kachele, H. (1992). *Psychoanalytic practice: Vol. 2. Clinical studies.* Berlin, Heidelberg, and New York: Springer-Verlag.

Tomkins, S. S. (1945). *Contemporary psychopathology.* Cambridge, MA: Harvard University Press.

Tomkins, S. S. (1962). *Affects, imagery, and consciousness: The positive affects* (Vol. I). New York: Springer.

Tomkins, S. S. (1963) *Affects, imagery, and consciousness: The negative affects* (Vol. II). New York: Springer.

Tomkins, S. S. (1991) *Affects, imagery, and consciousness: The negative affects anger and fear* (Vol. III). New York: Springer.

Tomkins, S. S. (in press). *Affects, imagery, and consciousness: Cognition and information processing* (Vol. IV). New York: Springer.

Viorst, Judith. (1986). *Necessary losses: The loves, illusions, dependencies and impossible expectations that all of us have to give up in order to grow.* New York: Fawcett Gold Medal.

Volkan, V. D. (1976). *Primitive internalized object relations: A clinical study of schizophrenic, borderline, and narcissistic patients.* New York: International Universities Press.

Whiting, J. W. M., & Child, I. L. (1953). *Child training and personality: A cross-cultural study.* New York: Yale University Press.

Winicott, D. W. (1965). *The maturational process and the facilitating environment.* New York: International Universities Press.

Wolowitz, L. (1991). *Self-object deficit, anger, and envy in the narcissistic condition.* Unpublished doctoral dissertation, Michigan State University.

3

Psychodynamic Therapies in Practice: Time-Limited Dynamic Psychotherapy

Jeffrey L. Binder
Hans H. Strupp
William P. Henry

In this chapter we will present the theoretical background, as well as fundamental principles and procedures, for a contemporary psychodynamic psychotherapy—time-limited dynamic psychotherapy (TLDP). Although our discussion pertains directly to a form of short-term therapy, the views presented are generally applicable to any psychodynamic treatment, irrespective of its length. We assume that the reader is familiar with basic psychoanalytic concepts (see Chapter 2). We will also cite relevant findings from empirical research that either support or question commonly held views about psychodynamic treatment techniques.

HISTORICAL BACKGROUND OF TIME-LIMITED DYNAMIC PSYCHOTHERAPY

Two of Freud's seminal ideas—the notions of dynamic conflict and transference—guided construction of the fundamental therapeutic strategy for all psychodynamic therapies (Freud, 1895, 1900, 1909, 1912; Sandler, Dare, & Holder, 1992). In order for psychological conflict to be resolved, unconscious material must be allowed access to consciousness. This process requires removal of defenses against the unconscious wishes, feelings, and thoughts that have been prohibited by the superego. In order to remove defenses, the imagined dangers associated with anxiety (and other unpleasant affects) must first be identified. The compromise formations constructed by the ego to deal with unconscious urges and censoring forces are expressed interpersonally in the therapeutic relationship in the form of transference. Accordingly, transference enactments contain both the unacceptable material in disguised form and defenses against this material. Defenses are intrapsychic processes (e.g., repression, denial, reaction formation, intellectualization) that are expressed interpersonally in the therapeutic relationship as "resistances" to the therapeutic work. *Interpretation* is the major technical intervention that facilitates the removal of resistances and subsequent discovery of unconscious material. This technical act involves the elucidation of psychological experiences that have been unconscious (Sandler et al., 1992). Psychological conflicts are presumed to originate in childhood and over time persistently influence many areas of the patient's life. Consequently, during the course of therapy, the expression of conflict must be identified in current relationships outside therapy; in recollections from the past, including childhood; and particularly in the therapeutic relationship as transference.

The simultaneous identification of manifestations of psychological conflict expressed as behavior patterns and maladaptive attitudes in the transference, relationships outside therapy, and recollections from the past is termed *insight* (Menninger & Holzman, 1973). The patient's achievement of insight is assumed to be the most important event during treatment that fosters conflict resolution. In each of the foregoing areas of the patient's life, the strategy for interpreting psychological conflict is first to interpret the defenses and their accompanying imagined dangers, and then to interpret the unconscious wishes, feelings, and thoughts.

Freud always envisioned two parallel purposes for psychoanalysis: (1) a scientific method for retrospective exploration of how personality developed in childhood as the individual strove to cope with conflict-inducing experiences and with sexual and aggressive impulses; and (2) a form of psychological therapy. The merger of these two aims was reflected in an increasingly extensive and time-consuming search for and reconstruction of childhood antecedents of a patient's current psychological conflicts. The interpretation of transference paved the way for uncovering childhood conflict-ridden memories. Freud's early analyses usually lasted for a few months. However, the more analysts learned about personality development and functioning, the more ambitious became the aims of therapeutic exploration. Freud acknowledged the increasing length of psychoanalyses (Freud, 1905), and he grew pessimistic about the therapeutic payoff; however, he never retreated from the scientific goal of discovering all that he could about the origins and functioning of personality (Freud, 1914, 1937).

Some of Freud's followers were not as willing to allow the dual aims of psychoanalysis to produce increasingly lengthy treatments. Ferenczi and Rank (1925) also questioned the assumption that therapeutic change required extensive reconstruction of childhood conflict-ridden experiences. Instead, they believed that all consequences of past experiences that were relevant for therapeutic work were embodied in transference manifestations. Therefore, the essential ingredient in therapeutic change was the patient's realization of the maladaptive nature of her or his current emotional experiences in the patient–therapist relationship. Ferenczi and Rank's technical strategies derived from these postulates. The analyst would act in ways that avoided repeating the inferred behavior of parental figures who had contributed to development of the patient's conflicts. The analyst would also be particularly active in making interpretations in order to keep emotional tension high and promote expression of basic conflicts in the immediacy of the transference. Through these methods, it was presumed that therapeutic results would be enhanced and the duration of treatment decreased.

The ideas of Ferenczi and Rank never became influential during their time. However, several decades later, Alexander and French (1946) provided renewed impetus for this work. They questioned the traditional analytic assumption that the depth and endurance of therapeutic results were proportionate to the prolonged work aimed at reconstruction of childhood conflictual experiences. By contrast, Alexander and French asserted that therapeutic change occurs when a patient relives, in the here-and-now of the transference, chronic conflictual patterns of behavior and experiences a different outcome in her or his relationship with the analyst. These authors termed this occurrence the *corrective emotional experience*. They also saw a serious risk in long analyses in which patients become overly dependent on the therapy and the therapist. Accordingly, they experimented with interruptions of treatment, varied the frequency of sessions, and set termination dates. Alexander and French, while utilizing Freud's basic discoveries, advocated flexibility and experimentation in therapeutic strategies and tactics (Strupp & Binder, 1984). As with Ferenczi and Rank before them, it was a period of time before their ideas had an impact on psychoanalytic clinicians. Eventually Alexander and French's work served as an impetus for the development of the contemporary short-term psychodynamic therapies.

THE FIRST GENERATION OF SHORT-TERM DYNAMIC PSYCHOTHERAPY

In the 1960s several groups of psychoanalytic clinicians—working independently until the 1970s—began to experiment with modifications of therapeutic technique in the context of short-term treatment. The Tavistock group in England (Balint, Ornstein, & Balint, 1972; Malan, 1963, 1976a, 1976b, 1979) undertook systematic studies of time-limited therapy of up to 50 sessions, with termination set by a calendar date. Their approach looked very similar to more traditional long-term psychoanalytic therapy, with the addition of a sharp, systematic focus on a circumscribed problem area that is identified by the therapist. Malan, in particular, emphasized the technical strategy of interpretive links between expressions of the focal conflict in the transference and evidence for the same conflict in recollections of childhood relations with parental figures (the *transference/ parent link*). He adduced evidence for the differential therapeutic efficacy of this strategy in a series of studies (Malan, 1976b); however, his findings have not been supported in subsequent research (Piper, Debbane, Bienvenu, de Carufel, & Garant, 1986). The Tavistock treatments run longer than most other short-term approaches because of the wide range of patients being treated.

In Boston, Sifneos (1972, 1979) initiated his active, didactic approach involving approximately 12–20 sessions. He combines standard exploration of links between transference and recollections of childhood conflict with active, anxiety-provoking questions in order to rapidly overcome resistances and to keep emotional tension high. His didactic aim involves guidance on how to deal with interpersonal difficulties. The focus of Sifneos' model is always defined in terms of an Oedipal conflict; that is, the patient's current difficulty is viewed as the derivative of a childhood conflict involving competition with the same-sexed parent for the affection of the opposite-sexed parent. Sifneos is able to keep his treatments quite short without setting an explicit termination date because his criteria for treatment suitability are stringent, including high intelligence and a high capacity for self-reflection, as well as a problem that can be viewed exclusively or primarily as Oedipal in nature.

Another Boston psychoanalyst who pioneered short-term dynamic treatment is James Mann (Mann, 1973; Mann & Goldman, 1982). This approach was based on the assumption that the psychological meanings of time have universal emotional significance. Accordingly, a 12-session treatment contract is strictly adhered to, and the psychological implications of this inevitable ending are explored throughout the treatment. The focus for each patient is defined in terms of a consciously experienced, "chronically endured pain," and the interpersonal implications of this subjective state are ultimately explored in the transference around the issue of termination. Mann, like Sifneos, is able to conduct successful, very short treatments by using relatively stringent patient selection criteria, particularly the capacity to become involved quickly in the work of treatment and to disengage emotionally with ease when the end of treatment arrives.

Lastly, in Montreal, Davanloo (1978, 1980) initiated a form of short-term dynamic therapy that is the most confrontive of all. Like Malan and Sifneos, Davanloo emphasizes the strategy of transference/patient interpretive links made consistently within a well-defined focal problem. However, the distinctive feature of his approach is an aggressive confrontation of resistance in order to activate unconscious feelings. Davanloo's strategy is aimed at eliciting hostile affects and the habitual defenses deployed against them. These conflicts are expressed in the transference, which Davanloo actively interprets. This model of treatment has no preset termination date but generally lasts for no more than 20 sessions. Davanloo asserts that the brevity is not due to stringent selection criteria. Rather, he believes that treatment is kept relatively short due to his active technique.

The first generation of short-term dynamic therapists combined many of the technical innovations of Freud's followers with Freud's basic model of psychopathology and his reliance on transference interpretation. Following Ferenczi and Rank (1925) and Alexander and French (1946), these short-term therapists emphasize active examination of emotional conflict in the immediacy of the patient–therapist relationship rather than lengthy searches for repressed childhood memories. However, Freud's early innovative followers viewed the primary therapeutic ingredient to be the therapist's active encouragement of emotionally healing experiences in the *interactions* between patient and therapist. The short-term dynamic therapists evidence closer adherence to Freud's original viewpoint in placing their primary reliance on *interpretation* of the patient's emotional experiences with the therapist. While they will follow the patient's lead in examining whichever relationships the patient introduces for discussion, they systematically strive to make interpretive links between transference and childhood conflictual experiences that the patient has described. Insight is implicitly defined as awareness of a pattern of conflict evidenced in the transference and in recollections of childhood relationships.

Another innovation of Freud's early followers that has been adopted by the short-term dynamic therapists is to focus therapeutic work on an accessible conflict. This conflict, however, is defined according to Freud's metapsychological model. The problem evidenced in the transference and in childhood recollections is conceptualized in terms of unconscious wishes, defenses, and associated unpleasant affects.

However, patients do not experience conflicts in these terms. Human beings have internal experiences of relationships, with associated views of themselves and others, along with feelings, wishes, thoughts, attitudes, and fantasies. Accordingly, therapists talk with patients in *these* terms. Therefore, the therapist must make a tacit translation of his or her abstract (metapsychological) conception of the patient's conflict into the language in which he or she converses with the patient. The typical result is a loss of clarity and specificity, particularly in regard to guidelines for defining a focal conflict. Thus, Malan (1976a) describes the process by which a therapist defines a conflict focus as highly intuitive—a gradual "crystallization" in the therapist's mind of an appropriate area of therapeutic work. This process may be accomplished proficiently by very experienced therapists, but there are no explicit guidelines for teaching it to novice therapists.

The first generation of short-term psychodynamic therapies shared certain basic features that distinguished them from open-ended, dynamic treatment: (1) relatively stringent patient selection criteria, (2) selection of a circumscribed problem focus and associated treatment goals, (3) "tracking" of the treatment focus, (4) early interpretation of transference within the focus, and (5) an overall active role assumed by the therapist.

Experience with this form of treatment led the developers of the various approaches to strikingly similar conclusions: "(1) Patients suffering from long-standing neurotic and characterological problems could be treated with a dynamically oriented therapy in a much shorter time than had previously been believed. (2) Basic principles of psychoanalytic therapy—interpretation of transference and resistance—could be applied to time-limited therapy. (3) The results of this form of treatment could produce enduring changes in character structure" (Strupp & Binder, 1984, p. 12).

The therapeutic efficacy of these pioneering models has been empirically demonstrated, although no particular approach has proved superior (Crits-Christoph, 1992; Crits-Christoph & Barber, 1991).

THE SECOND GENERATION OF TIME-LIMITED DYNAMIC PSYCHOTHERAPY

Severe limitations result from utilization by the first generation of short-term dynamic therapies of classical Freudian personality theory and therapeutic technical emphasis on transference/parent interpretations. The classical theory refers to highly abstract, impersonal forces and functions (e.g., id, ego, superego) that are far removed from subjective experience. As mentioned above, the therapist who conceptualizes conflict in terms of this theory must engage in at least tacit translations into language understandable to the patient. The theory provides no guidelines for making these translations. Consequently, as mentioned above, there are no explicit, clear-cut principles for teaching therapists how to conceptualize a specific therapeutic focus. A more serious problem is the lack of reliability among clinicians in formulating a problem focus for a given patient. If each therapist must wait for a focus to crystallize in her or his mind, there is no way to encourage any similarity in the foci that eventually materialize for therapists viewing the same patient.

Primary reliance on the therapeutic strategy of transference/parent interpretive links creates the potential for a serious contradiction in therapeutic aims. On the one hand, the therapist's activity and attention to evidence of a focal conflict in the transference serve to heighten the patient's emotional arousal and appreciation of how the conflict is currently expressed. On the other hand, frequent interpretive links to childhood recollections risk shifting the patient's attention from current emotional experiences to relatively intellectualized discussions of distant formative experiences in childhood. Another limitation created by this strategy involves the diversity of patients who are suitable for the treatment. In order to make transference/parent links from early in the therapy, the patient must enter therapy capable of communicating childhood memories that rapidly coalesce into a coherent conflict theme that is also identified in current relationships and in the transference. This capability is more likely to be possessed by patients with relatively well-organized personality structures and/or good communication skills, regardless of the nature of their symptoms. Consequently, many patients who potentially could benefit from short-term dynamic therapy are excluded (e.g., persons with more severe personality disorders or those who, for whatever reasons, do not have ready access to relevant childhood memories).

Contemporary developments in psychoanalytic personality theory, along with integrations with interpersonal personality theory and relevant perspectives from cognitive psychology, have produced a theoretical framework that reduces or solves many of the problems enumerated above. This new framework is the foundation for *time-limited dynamic psychotherapy* (TLDP), a representative of the second generation of short-term dynamic treatments.

It can be argued that the dominant influence today in psychoanalytic personality theory is *object-relations theory*. From this perspective, personality is composed of internal object relations that consists of self-images, images of others, and sets of transactions that take place between self-images and other-images. Associated with any internal transaction is a variety of feelings, wishes, thoughts, attitudes, and expectancies that characterize the transaction. Internal object relationships are the product of interpersonal experiences with significant others that have been internalized, particularly during the formative infancy and childhood years (Greenberg & Mitchell, 1983; Sandler & Sandler, 1978). Object-relations theory provides a language for describing and explaining personality functions that is much closer to phenomenological experience than is the terminology of classical Freudian theory. Object-relations theory particularly emphasizes the development of personality functions from infancy to adulthood.

Concepts and principles from cognitive psychology are being integrated with those of object-relations theory in order to clarify, specify, and expand understanding of the functioning of internalized object relationships (Horowitz, 1988, 1991). Prominent, enduring internalized object relationships are defined as *person schemas* that represent "structures of meaning that integrate knowledge about self and others. These mental structures operate unconsciously to organize thought, complex mood states, self-appraisal and interpersonal actions" (Horowitz, 1991, p. 1). The personality is composed of a hierarchical organization of these person schemas, which, in trun, influence the form of more readily modifiable internal object relationships (IORs). Certain of these are dominant because they are relatively safe; that is to say, they represent either wished-for interpersonal states or compromises between wished-for states and threatening or dreaded interpersonal states. These latter IORs are unconscious (Horowitz, 1991; Knapp, 1991). A compromise IORs may be relatively free of the influence of emotional conflict and, therefore, flexibly adaptable to interpersonal realities. On the other hand, the compromise IOR may be the product of very influential conflict and, therefore, rigid and maladaptive. It can be seen that this theoretical perspective is consistent with Freud's basic notion of dynamic conflict. A person's internal schemas and IORs include expectancies of the response of others to particular types of self-initiated actions. These expectancies are elaborated into *scripts*, which are sequences of actions between self and others, including communications of ideas and feelings as well as appraisals of self and others (Horowitz, 1991).

Interpersonal theory (Anchin & Kiesler, 1982; Strupp & Binder, 1984) explains the actualization of internal object relations in interpersonal relationships. Internal object relationships are patterned like structured role relationships. The enactment of these structured role relationships in current interpersonal relations results in unconscious assignment of certain roles to oneself and to others. There is, then, an isomorphic relationship between internal object relationships and the characteristic form taken by current relationships, particularly with others who have emotional importance for the individual. To the extent that the person's repertoire of internal object relations is not responsive to current interpersonal realities, they may maladaptively influence her or his experiences and behavior in a variety of interpersonal settings. The persistence and rigidity of maladaptive interpersonal patterns are viewed as resulting from the inadvertent reinforcement provided by the responses of others. The notion of *interpersonal complementarity* is a fundamental principle of interpersonal theory. Person A's actions will predictably tend to evoke (or provoke) certain types of reactions from person B, which in turn reinforce certain self-appraisals and expectations of others in person A (Anchin & Kiesler, 1982; Strupp & Binder, 1984).

The foregoing theoretical framework is couched in a language that tries to stay close to clinical and observable data and to avoid, as much as possible, higher-level inferences and complex theoretical constructions that have no apparent consequences for therapeutic activity. Utilizing this framework, TLDP is broadly applicable irrespective of time limits, but it can be readily applied with time constraints.

In TLDP, the psychotherapeutic process is viewed as a set of interpersonal transactions. It is a process that may become therapeutic because of the patient's unwitting tendency to cast the therapist in the role of a significant other and to enact with her or him maladaptive patterns of behavior rooted in unconscious conflicts. Through participant observation the therapist provides a new model for identification. She or he does so, in part, by limiting personal participation in the attitudes and behaviors (such as hostile or controlling) that the patient's maladaptive behavior tends to provoke. The therapist also attempts to grasp latent meanings in the patient's interpersonal behavior and communicates this understanding to the patient, thereby helping the patient to assimilate aspects of her or his experience that were hitherto unrecognized or disowned (repressed). To this end, the patient's experiences with significant others in her or his current and past lives represent important sources of information that aid the therapist's understanding; however, they are secondary to the contemporary transactions between patient and therapist.

The therapist uses the relationship with the patient as the primary medium for bringing about change. What the patient learns in psychotherapy, what conduces to therapeutic change, is acquired primarily in and through the dynamics of the therapeutic relationship. Identifying the recollected childhood origins of current psychological conflict and the unconscious fantasies and feelings associated with the continued influence of these early experiences probably make an important contribution to therapeutic change. However, in TLDP the most important change process is considered to be the recognition of patterns of interaction with others that continuously reinforce maladaptive attitudes and feelings about oneself and others. The sooner this recognition can be associated with the actual enactment of a maladaptive pattern, the greater is the potential for altering it. This is why identifying the influence of maladaptive patterns in the patient–therapist relationship is the primary strategy in TLDP.

Therapeutic learning, therefore, is considered to be experiential learning. The patient changes as she or he lives through affectively painful and ingrained interpersonal scenarios and as the therapeutic relationship gives rise to outcomes different from those expected, anticipated, feared, and sometimes hoped for. To promote these changes, the therapist first assiduously avoids prolonged engagement in activities that have the effect of perpetuating the conflicts that have resulted in the patient's interpersonal difficulties and, second, actively promotes more satisfying experiences associated with collaborating productively in the solution of interpersonal problems.

With respect to the first aim, the therapist remains constantly attentive to the patient's unconscious attempts to elicit reciprocal behavior that meets the patient's wish for or expectation of domination, control, manipulation, exploitation, punishment, criticism, and the like. Such unwitting invitations may take the form of subtle seductions, requests for advice, special attention, extra hours, and many other maneuvers to which the therapist must be alert. The only way to avoid completely the impact of the patient's transference pressures would be for the therapist to erect barriers against any empathic involvement with the patient. A more therapeutic stance is to maintain a "free-floating responsiveness" (Sandler & Sandler, 1978) to the patient's attempts to draw the therapist into a particular scenario. A therapist who cautiously goes along with the patient while remaining alert to her or his own reactions can

obtain invaluable information about the nature of the self- and object-representational components of the patient's relationship predispositions.

With respect to the second aim, the patient must come to experience the therapist as a reliable and trustworthy ally who is in the patient's corner and who has the patient's best interest at heart. To that end, the patient must become convinced that the therapist has something worthwhile to offer, that she or he has a genuine commitment to the patient as a person. These are the essential ingredients of a good therapeutic alliance, the prime moving force in all forms of psychodynamic therapy. Conversely, unless these conditions are met early in therapy, a good outcome—certainly in time-limited therapy—is seriously in question (Henry, Schacht, & Strupp, 1986).

If the therapist successfully fosters this process, the patient's maladaptive interpersonal patterns will be viewed with increasing clarity. The patient will gain a greater ability to question previously accepted assumptions about her or his self-image and about the attitudes and intentions of others that lend the maladaptive patterns their influence. In turn, as the patient gains confidence in the beneficial effects of collaboratively examining maladaptive patterns, she or he is better able to confront previously repressed emotions and fantasies associated with these patterns. The result is progressively greater freedom to modify conflictual attitudes and behaviors in the direction of more adaptive and flexible responses to changing circumstances and realistic opportunities for satisfying interpersonal needs. These changes typically are associated with improved overall functioning.

Assessment and Selection of Patients

The first generation of short-term dynamic therapists proposed an assortment of selection criteria (Crits-Christoph & Barber, 1991). However, many of these criteria are quite abstract, and clinicians have a difficult time agreeing on their precise meanings and behavioral referents. More important, there is no convincing evidence that clinicians can utilize these criteria to predict usefully what will happen in an individual treatment (Binder, Henry, & Strupp, 1987; Luborsky, Crits-Christoph, Mintz, & Auerbach, 1988). Empirical research has revealed that certain patient characteristics can modestly predict performance during treatment or a positive outcome. These characteristics include pretreatment psychological health; positive expectations for treatment; intelligence; moderate anxiety; and the quality of human relatedness. However, relatively better predictions are based on the quality of the patient's involvement in the early sessions of treatment (Luborsky et al., 1988). Therefore, it seems advisable to offer therapy to all patients who are motivated to accept it and who seem at all suitable for the type of treatment being considered (Luborsky et al., 1988; Wolberg, 1980).

TLDP focuses on maladaptive interpersonal patterns and the associated underlying internal object relationship repertoire. Accordingly, the primary suitability criteria presuppose that these patterns and internal structures are sufficiently developed to be characterized by (1) coherent and identifiable interpersonal themes, (2) appreciation of the distinction between oneself and others, and (3) a capacity for concern and integrity in human relationships. Conversely, patients for whom TLDP would not be beneficial include those who are currently in a disorganized psychotic state and those whose affective experiences and object relationships are chronically incoherent, diffuse, and disorganized. There are also patients whose modes of relating manifest identifiable patterns but who see no value in examining interpersonal relationships (or the therapeutic relationship) or who do not value honesty and integrity in human relationships.

The object relations capacities sought in potential TLDP patients may be detected across a broad range of formal diagnostic syndromes. Therefore, neither a presenting symptom picture nor the diagnosis of a specific personality disorder will itself justify exclusion from this form of treatment. We posit for the range of patients previously defined, attention to correcting maladaptive interpersonal patterns will reduce psychopathology in whatever form it takes.

It can be seen that we view any dividing line between diagnosis and treatment as largely artificial. Data gathering and formulating, as well as intervening, go hand in hand from the first session on. The first generation of short-term dynamic therapists innovated the procedure of using the initial assessment interviews as a "trial run" to determine whether the patient is responsive to the therapeutic tasks required by the particular approach to treatment, as well as to gauge the overall quality of his or her involvement in the therapeutic relationship. We agree with this strategy because it provides the most straightforward evidence for suitability and because it increases the likelihood that the patient will leave each interview feeling that he or she has benefited from collaborative work. This latter aim is critically important for quickly establishing a therapeutic alliance, which is crucial for the success of any short-term treatment (Strupp & Binder, 1984).

In TLDP, problems are conceptualized in a format that avoids the abstract and vague formulations that are characteristic of treatment models that rely on Freud's metapsychological theory (see above). A patient's presenting complaints are translated into interpersonal terms and organized into a format called the *cyclical maladaptive pattern* (CMP). The CMP is used as a heuristic that helps the therapist to generate, recognize, and organize psychotherapeutically relevant information. It is not an absolute or final formulation of the problem; rather, it is used throughout the course of treatment to keep the therapist focused on a remediable problem.

The CMP is a working model (Peterfreund, 1983) of a central or salient pattern of interpersonal roles in which patients unconsciously cast themselves; the complementary roles in which they cast others; and the maladaptive interaction sequences, self-defeating expectations, negative self-appraisals, and unpleasant affects that result. The CMP format specifies four categories of information:

1. *Acts of self.* Included are both private and public actions (such as feeling affectionate as well as displaying affection). Acts of self vary in the degree to which they are accessible to awareness.

2. *Expectation of others' reactions.* These are imagined reactions of others to one's own actions. Such expectations may be conscious, preconscious, or unconscious.

3. *Acts of others toward the self.* These are observed acts of others that are viewed as occurring in specific relation to the acts of the self. Often one unwittingly acts in ways that evoke feared—but anticipated—responses (the principle of *complementarity*). Typically, under the influence of a maladaptive pattern, one also tends to misconstrue the interpersonal meanings of the other's actions in a way that confirms one's wished-for or feared expectations.

4. *Acts of the self toward the self (introject).* This category of actions refers to how one treats oneself (e.g., self-controlling, self-punishing, self-nurturing). These actions should be articulated in specific relation to the other elements of the format. How one treats oneself tends to be a reflection of how one perceives treatment by others.

The CMP is graphically depicted in Figure 3.1.

The following narrative illustrates how an initial CMP might appear. The female patient complains of depression, loneliness, and a lack of friends.

1. *Acts of self:* The patient assumes a passive interpersonal stance in which she refrains from exposing personal thoughts and feelings. She avoids social contact by withdrawal or procrastination, defers and submits to others' wishes, and spends much time in private thinking and won-

FIGURE 3.1 Cyclical maladaptive pattern (CMP)

dering rather than in active communication.

2. *Expectations of others' reactions:* The patient expects that other people will ignore or reject her. She validates this expectation with recollections of being ignored or rejected by her mother and by others of importance to her while she was growing up.

3. *Observed reactions of others:* Others find the patient's passivity unappealing and do not spontaneously recognize her distress and come to her aid. However, the patient does not see this as an understandable reaction to her passivity, but instead interprets it as evidence that others are actively rejecting and ignoring her.

4. *Introject (self-image and self-treatment):* The patient views herself as helpless in a hopeless situation. She views herself as socially unappealing and personally unlovable. She refrains from voicing her desires and complaints, hoping that this interpersonal passivity will make her presence more palatable to others.

Note that this CMP narrative tells a clear story about the patient. The material would come from the patient's actions with the therapist and from verbal reports about other relationships. Inference is kept to a minimum.

Because the story is about recurrent interaction patterns, it provides specific clues to the therapist about transference/countertransference issues to watch out for.

The CMP should ideally encompass a pattern of interpersonal transactions that is both historically significant and a source of current difficulty. However, the focus is on constructing a CMP based on information gathered from observations of the patient's behavior in the interview and from reports of current relationships. As information becomes available about past relationships going back to childhood experiences with parental figures, this historical knowledge aids therapeutic understanding by providing a context in which confusing meanings of present events may be more easily interpreted. But this historical information is not essential for formulating a CMP. Consequently, patients who do not have ready access to childhood recollections that would form the basis of a focal conflict as defined by the first generation of short-term dynamic therapists are still potentially suitable for TLDP. Empirical methods for reliably and precisely defining focal conflicts defined as maladaptive interpersonal patterns are currently being investigated (Luborsky & Crits-Christoph, 1990).

Technique in TLDP

In TLDP it is posited that conflict persists in the form of transference experience and behavior because circular interpersonal patterns confirm the patient's mistrustful expectations of others. This notion reflects a viewpoint on transference that takes into consideration interpersonal dynamics to a greater extent than does the traditional definition. The patient's transference experience and behavior are not simply representations of the past superimposed on the therapist as distorted images. Rather, the patient has certain preexisting sets or fixed expectations with which he or she interprets the meanings of interpersonal events. The therapist proceeds on the working assumption that these plausible (from the patient's point of view) interpretations are always in response to something actually occurring (e.g., conscious or unconscious attitudes and behaviors of the therapist or aspects of the therapeutic arrangements). In other words, the patient's transference experience is based on rigid proclivities to interpret events in a certain way, without the flexibility to consider alternatives (Gill, 1982; Hoffman, 1983). Furthermore, having turned to the therapist for help and being unconsciously prepared to relate to her or him as a significant other, the patient becomes exquisitely sensitive to everything that transpires in the evolving relationship. It follows that any clinical data, whether generated in the form of references to people and events outside the therapeutic relationship, the patient's mood and dreams, or the emotional climate of the interviews, must be viewed as "disguised allusions" to the transference (Gill, 1982). Whatever else they may represent, such data should always be scrutinized for what they might reveal about the patient's experience of the therapeutic relationship.

In TLDP, countertransference is defined as encompassing two types of reactions. The first type is therapist actions and reactions (including attitudes and behavior, as well as thoughts, feelings, and fantasies) that are predictably evoked by behavior of the patient that is part of the enactment of a maladaptive pattern. Here we see another facet of transference that is not encompassed in the traditional definition, namely, an evocative (or provocative) action component. The second type of countertransference refers to reactions of the therapist that express unresolved personal issues. These two types are combined, but in the routine work of the TLDP therapist the former source is always investigated first. Countertransference in TLDP terms may be described as a form of interpersonal empathy in which the therapist, for a time and to a limited degree, is recruited to enact roles assigned to him or her by the patient's preconceived CMP. Thus, at the center of the therapeutic process in TLDP is the therapist's ability to become immersed in the patient's modes of relatedness and to "work his way out" (Gill & Muslin, 1976; Levenson, 1972).

There are times when it is extraordinarily difficult for the therapist to avoid emeshment in the patient's scenarios. The pressures stemming from an enacted CMP may be exceedingly subtle, but they are vastly more pervasive than is commonly realized, particularly around the issue of hostility (Binder & Strupp, 1991). There is evidence that regardless of how much warmth, friendliness, and support may be present, if expressions of hostility (direct or indirect) are not effectively handled, there will be repercussions on the development of a positive therapeutic alliance and on outcome (Henry et al., 1986; Kiesler & Watkins, 1989).

In each therapeutic hour, the TLDP therapist attempts to identify a recurrent theme that in one way or another is related to the defined CMP. The most important facet of a theme in any interview is its interpersonal manifestation in the therapeutic relationship. In order for the therapist to identify the general form of the patient's maladaptive pattern, he or she must maintain constant alertness and curiosity about the state of the therapeutic relationship. At the same time, while attempting to understand the current interpersonal transactions, the therapist attends to other aspects of the patient's communications. Thus, any area of her or his life the patient chooses to discuss should be jointly examined. Much can be gained by clarifying and interpreting conflicts that are manifested in relationships outside of therapy. Simultaneously, however, the therapist maintains a mental set aimed at applying what is learned about conflicts in other relationships to understanding the immediate state of the patient–therapist relationship.

Typically, a patient spontaneously reports an interpersonal experience outside of therapy and her or his reactions associated with it. Patients vary in the extent to which they can spontaneously report their interpersonal experiences. The TLDP therapist, through her or his interventions, seeks to obtain as detailed a picture as possible of the patient's interpersonal transactions and associated internal experiences. The CMP provides the format used

to conceptualize these transactions. Five basic questions, based on the format, may serve as a guide to interventions:

1. How does the patient behave toward the other person, and what is the nature of her or his feelings, wishes, and intentions toward the other?
2. What might be the patient's experience of the other's intentions, attitudes, or feelings toward her or him?
3. What might be the patient's emotional reactions to fantasies about and actions of the other?
4. How does the patient construe the relationship with the other, and how might her or his most recent reactions be a consequence of their previous interactions?
5. How does the patient's experience of the interactions and relationship with the other influence the manner in which the patient views and treats herself or himself?

At the same time, the therapist endeavors to make optimal use of all opportunities for exploring and explicating the patient's experience in the therapeutic relationship. To aid this effort, the five guiding questions can be reframed by substituting the first-person *me* for *the other*. In this form, the questions can be posed directly about conditions in the therapeutic relationship, as well as about implications for the relationship that can be detected in reports of interactions outside therapy. Although most analyses of interpersonal patterns will deal with relationships outside of therapy, whenever possible the line of inquiry should return to examination of the therapeutic relationship, where the affective immediacy of the situation is most conducive to instilling in the patient an appreciation of maladaptive interpersonal patterns (Binder & Strupp, 1991; Strupp & Binder, 1984).

Interpretive connections to current and past outside relationships can be helpful in placing a particular transference enactment in broader perspective *after* the enactment has been carefully explored in the immediacy of the patient–therapist relationship and the patient has gained an appreciation of its impact on his or her experience and behavior. This therapeutic strategy distinguishes TLDP from the first generation of short-term dynamic therapies, which attribute much greater importance to the transference/parent link. We believe that concentrating on the analysis of here-and-now transactions is more consistent with the fundamental notion that experiential learning, regardless of what is to be learned, is the most effective.

The TLDP emphasis on experiential learning through analysis of transactions in the patient–therapist relationship should be thought of as a guiding strategy and as a mind set that the therapist disciplines himself or herself to maintain. The actual extent to which transference interventions are used during any session or phase of treatment is determined by three factors: (1) the therapist's identification of material that can be understood as plausibly related to transference issues (Hoffman, 1983); (2) the patient's current receptiveness to examining his or her experiences in the patient–therapist relationship; and (3) the therapist's attentiveness to overt or disguised patient references to their relationship, as well as his or her attentiveness to countertransference reactions.

Clinical Illustration

We have proposed that detection and examination of a maladaptive interpersonal pattern actively influencing the patient's relationships—especially the therapeutic relationship—is the fundamental therapeutic strategy of TLDP. The clinical situation depicted below illustrates how a therapist trainee initially struggled against being pulled into a salient maladaptive interpersonal pattern of her patient. Then, with coaching from her supervisor, she discovered the outlines of this pattern (details have been altered for confidentiality and to highlight important points).

> The patient was a man in his early forties who for several years had been married to his second wife. Both of his marriages had been turbulent, with many arguments over such issues as fi-

nances, children, and the impact on the family of the patient's emotional problems. These problems included repeated episodes of severe depression with suicidal ideation and several suicide attempts, repeated episodes of rage directed at colleagues from work and at family members, and alcohol abuse. The patient had had several courses of outpatient psychotherapy and several hospital admissions after suicide attempts associated with major depressive episodes. Antidepressant medications had proved only temporarily beneficial. His outpatient therapies had been characterized by initial enthusiasm that the therapist would "fix" him, followed by disillusionment and withdrawal from treatment. His prior therapists, as well as hospital staff who had worked with him, had been prone to become impatient in reaction to the patient's initial effusive enthusiasm, without evidence of any positive change, and his continual pressure on others to fix him. The patient was quick to adopt the technical jargon of whoever was working with him, and he would praise the wondrous healing potential of medications for "biochemical imbalances," psychotherapy for "unconscious conflicts," and "the steps" for substance abuse and "codependency."

After another brief hospitalization for depression and suicidal thoughts, the patient was referred to a public mental health outpatient clinic, where he was assigned to the trainee. The major complaint he voiced was feeling alone and unsupported, even by his wife. After several sessions, the patient expressed high hopes for this treatment because he felt that the trainee was warm, caring, and very empathic compared to his last therapist, a man he described as unempathic and cold. The patient announced to the trainee that she could fix him.

The trainee quickly became uncomfortable with the high expectations being thrust on her by the patient. She also felt increasingly stymied by the patient's long monologues in which he praised his therapy and his Alcoholics Anonymous meetings, and in which he pressured the trainee for reassurance that he was making noticeable progress. With help from her supervisor, the trainee discovered her growing reluctance to question the patient about any facet of his idealized picture of their relationship. She had attempted to justify her passivity with the notion that she was still building rapport and attempting to be supportive. In fact, she felt paralyzed and began to realize that she feared causing damage to the patient, such as precipitating another suicidal depression.

The trainee began to gently encourage the patient to collaboratively examine his attitudes about their work and the nature of their relationship. With this encouragement, the patient expressed a major fear, namely, that the therapist would "burst my bubble," as he had perceived so many others doing before. His perception was that previous therapists and hospital staff had ridiculed and dismissed what he considered to be his healthy optimism about succeeding in treatment and his strenuous efforts to become healthier. The trainee realized that her paralysis was a consequence of, on the one hand, being pulled by the patient's behavior into feeling increasingly impatient and critical and, on the other hand, feeling guilty about her untherapeutic attitudes. Once they began to explore the patient's fearful expectations, it became evident that they had identified a salient maladaptive pattern that influenced all important relationships in the patient's life.

How Therapy Ends

Irrespective of whether therapy is short-term or long-term, termination represents one of the most critical challenges for the therapist. The therapist becomes a significant figure to the patient to the extent that she or he is experienced as understanding and helpful, as well as a replica of past significant figures. Often patients do not want to relinquish this important figure and will often cling to the therapist with considerable tenacity. They will unwittingly employ a gamut of maneuvers for averting painful separation experiences. For example, they may bring up "new" problems that "urgently" require solutions; there may be a recurrence of the symptoms and problems that brought them to therapy; they attempt to cling to the therapist by venting hostility and blame on her or him; and they may attempt to master the problem "actively" by leaving therapy before the actual termination date has been reached.

By the same token, the therapist is not immune to problems with ending a therapeutic relationship. A therapist who may experience strong ambivalence toward a patient may secretly relish the prospect of termination but feel guilty about pursuing a realistic ending. In this case, whether or not treatment ends when planned, the decision may not be based on the patient's best interests. Alternatively, the therapist may derive considerable gratification (perhaps both realistically and neurotically) from work with a patient and may therefore wish to prolong the relationship. If the therapeutic relationship had been a good one, the therapist may be genuinely sorry to lose a patient who has become emotionally meaningful. Thus the therapist may be reluctant to explore the patient's feelings about separation or may be willing to postpone termination beyond a prearranged date. Losing a patient may evoke memories of the therapist's own losses and the manner in which she or he has mastered (or failed to master) them.

The experience of ending the therapeutic relationship presents the last opportunity to identify the influence of salient maladaptive interpersonal patterns. It is expected that the way a patient approaches termination will be influenced by the issues that have been the focus of treatment up to this time. The emotionally powerful impact of impending loss may cause a resurgence of a maladaptive interpersonal pattern. The way in which therapist and patient deal collaboratively with this event will determine whether prior therapeutic work is reinforced or undermined. In particular, successful work related to termination will reinforce the patient's internalization of a representation of the therapist as a supportive person. Mann's (1973) discussion of this issue is particularly relevant:

> It is absolutely incumbent upon the therapist to deal directly with the reaction to termination in all its painful aspects and affects if he expects to help the patient come to some vividly affective understanding of the now inappropriate nature of his early unconscious conflict. More than that, active and appropriate management of the termination will allow the patient to internalize the therapist as a replacement or substitute for the earlier ambivalent object. *This time the internalization will be more positive (never totally*

so), *less anger laden and less guilt laden, thereby making separation a genuine maturational event.* Since anger, rage, guilt, and their accompaniments of frustration and fear are the potent factors that prevent positive internalization and mature separation, it is these that must not be overlooked in this phase of the time-limited therapy.

For those who have had painful or traumatic separations or losses, termination of therapy will evoke memories and associated painful affects (or defenses against them). These emotions, associated with the earlier loss, may include grief, rage, shame, guilt, anxiety, and devaluation of the lost object or of oneself. Traumatic early separations and losses include death of a parent during childhood, divorce of parents, birth of a sibling with one or both parents completely absorbed in the event, severe illness, and other sorts of prolonged separation. Such patients will be particularly susceptible to reenacting old losses in a negative way.

There is little consensus about procedures for terminating open-ended psychodynamic therapy (Firestein, 1978). The literature on short-term dynamic therapy offers more agreement, but notable differences remain. For example, as mentioned earlier, Sifneos (1979) and Davanloo (1978, 1980) do not specify termination dates or specific numbers of sessions. Malan (1976a) and Mann (1973), on the other hand, do set calendar dates for termination. To the best of our knowledge, there is no convincing clinical or empirical evidence that favors one or the other approach. However, there is general agreement among short-term therapists that making the patient aware at the outset of limits to the duration of treatment does heighten the attention of both patient and therapist to the tasks at hand.

We recommend that if a termination date is to be set, this should be done early in treatment but *after* a therapeutic focus has at least begun to be outlined by the participants. The reason is that the introduction of a focus is more likely to provide the patient with a belief that there are circumscribed goals that can be achieved in the available time. Once the treatment is underway, the therapist should assume that the

issue of a finite length is *always* an influence even if it is not the focus at any given moment. Therefore, the therapist should continually remain alert for evidence of the patient's reaction to the time limits and bring it to her or his attention. The therapist always attempts to make sense of the patient's communications in terms of the salient maladaptive interpersonal patterns that constitute the therapeutic focus. This is true as well of references to termination, which the therapist attempts to integrate into work on the focal issues that occupy their attention throughout the treatment.

FUTURE DIRECTIONS

Research has confirmed that psychotherapy is at least modestly beneficial for most people (Crits-Christoph, 1992; Lambert, Shapiro, & Bergin, 1986; Luborsky et al., 1988). By contrast, evidence for the superior effectiveness of any particular psychotherapy has not been forthcoming (Goldfried, Greenberg, & Marmar, 1990; Koss & Butcher, 1986; Lambert, 1989; Orlinsky & Howard, 1986). A prime reason appears to be that therapies have been compared according to differences in their characteristic techniques, without giving due consideration to the skills used to implement these techniques (Binder & Strupp, 1991; Luborsky et al., 1988). Like all therapy models, TLDP posits that its distinctive strategy (in this case, systematic analysis of transference/countertransference patterns) will produce positive therapeutic outcomes.

However, recent research on short-term dynamic therapies suggests that adherence to the *type* of therapeutic strategy or technique is not as predictive of outcome as are other therapeutic skills, such as precise formulation of a focal problem and consistently addressing clinical material relevant to the problem (Crits-Christoph, Cooper, & Luborsky, 1988; Piper, Azim, Joyce, & McCallum, 1991) and avoidance of reciprocally hostile interchanges with the patient (Henry et al., 1986). Future research may determine whether prescribed technical strategies and techniques—such as here-

and-now transference interpretations—that are *skillfully* implemented have a particularly beneficial impact. In the meantime, it would be prudent (and wise) to strive continually to enhance one's skillful use of whichever therapy model is being employed.

REFERENCES

Alexander, F. & French, T. M. (1946). *Psychoanalytic therapy*. New York: Ronald Press.

Anchin, J. C., & Kiesler, D. J. (Eds.). (1982). *Handbook of interpersonal psychotherapy*. New York: Pergamon Press.

Balint, M. P., Ornstein, P., & Balint, E. (1972). *Focal psychotherapy: An example of applied psychoanalysis*. London: Tavistock.

Binder, J. L., Henry, W. P., & Strupp, H. H. (1987). An appraisal of selection criteria for dynamic psychotherapies and implications for setting time limits. *Psychiatry, 50,* 154–166.

Binder, J. L., & Strupp, H. H. (1991). The Vanderbilt approach to time-limited dynamic psychotherapy. In P. Crits-Christoph & J. Barber (Eds.), *Handbook of short-term dynamic therapy* (pp. 137–165). New York: Basic Books.

Crits-Christoph, P. (1992). The efficacy of brief dynamic psychotherapy. A meta-analysis. *American Journal of Psychiatry, 149,* 151–158.

Crits-Christoph, P., & Barber, J. (Eds.). (1991). *Handbook of short-term dynamic therapy*. New York: Basic Books.

Chrits-Christoph, P., Cooper, A., & Luborsky, L. (1988). The accuracy of therapists' interpretations and the outcome of dynamic psychotherapy. *Journal of Consulting and Clinical Psychology, 56,* 490–495.

Davanloo, H. (Ed.). (1978). *Basic principles and techniques in short-term dynamic psychotherapy*. New York: Spectrum.

Davanloo, H. (Ed.). (1980). *Short-term dynamic psychotherapy*. New York: Jason Aronson.

Ferenczi, S., & Rank, O. (1925). *The development of psycho-analysis*. New York and Washington, DC: Nervous and Mental Diseases Publishing Co.

Firestein, S. (1978). *Termination in psychoanalysis*. New York: International Universities Press.

Freud, S. (1895). Studies on hysteria. *Standard Edition* (Vol. 2). London: Hogarth Press.

Freud, S. (1900). The interpretation of dreams. *Standard edition* (Vols. 4, 5). London: Hogarth Press.

Freud, S. (1905). On psychotherapy. *Standard edition* (Vol. 7). London: Hogarth Press.

Freud, S. (1909). Notes upon a case of obsessional neurosis. *Standard Edition* (Vol. 10). London: Hogarth Press.

Freud, S. (1912). The dynamics of transference. *Standard edition*, (Vol. 12). London: Hogarth Press.

Freud, S. (1913). The disposition to obsessional neurosis. *Standard edition* (Vol. 12). London: Hogarth Press.

Freud, S. (1914). Remembering, repeating and working-through (Further recommendations on the technique of psycho-analysis, II). *Standard edition* (Vol. 12). London: Hogarth Press.

Freud, S. (1937). Analysis terminable and interminable. *Standard edition* (Vol. 23). London: Hogarth Press.

Gill, M. M. (1982). *Analysis of transference*: Vol. I. *Theory and technique*. New York: International Universities Press.

Gill, M. M., & Muslin, H. L. (1976). Early interpretation of transference. *Journal of the American Psychoanalytic Association, 24,* 779–794.

Goldfried, M. R., Greenberg, L. S., & Marmar, C. (1990). Individual psychotherapy: Process and outcome. *Annual Review of Psychology, 41,* 659–688.

Greenberg, J. R., & Mitchell, S. A. (1983). *Object relations in psychoanalytic theory*. Cambridge, MA: Harvard University Press.

Greenson, R. R., & Wexler, M. (1969). The non-transference relationship in the psychoanalytic situation. *International Journal of Psycho-Analysis, 50,* 27–39.

Henry, W. P., Schacht, T. E., & Strupp, H. H. (1986). Structural analysis of social behavior: Application to a study of interpersonal process in differential psychotherapeutic outcome. *Journal of Consulting and Clinical Psychology, 54,* 27–31.

Hoffman, I. Z. (1983). The patient as interpreter of the analysis experience. *Contemporary Psychoanalysis, 19,* 389–422.

Horowitz, M. J. (1988). *Introduction to psychodynamics*. New York: Basic Books.

Horowitz, M. J. (Ed.). (1991). *Person schemas and maladaptive interpersonal patterns*. Chicago: University of Chicago Press.

Horowitz, M. J. (1991). Introduction. In M. J. Horowitz (Ed.), *Person schemas and maladaptive interpersonal pattern* (pp. 1–10). Chicago: University of Chicago Press.

Kiesler, D. J., & Watkins, L. M. (1989). Interpersonal complementarity and the therapeutic alliance: A study of relationships in psychotherapy. *Psychotherapy, 26,* 183–194.

Knapp, P. H. (1991). Self–other schemas: Core organizers of human experience. In M. J. Horowitz (Ed.), *Person schemas and maladaptive interpersonal patterns* (pp. 81–102). Chicago: University of Chicago Press.

Koss, M. P., & Butcher, J. N. (1986). Research on brief psychotherapy. In S. L. Garfield & A. E. Bergin (Eds.), *Handbook of psychotherapy and behavior change* (3rd ed.) (pp. 627–670). New York: Wiley.

Lambert, M. J. (1989). The individual therapist's contribution to psychotherapy process and outcome. *Clinical Psychology Review, 9,* 469–485.

Lambert, M. J., Shapiro, D. A., & Bergin, A. S. (1986). The effectiveness of psychotherapy. In S. L. Garfield & A. S. Bergin (Eds.), *Handbook of psychotherapy and behavior change* (3rd ed.) (pp. 157–211). New York: Wiley.

Levenson, E. A. (1972). *The fallacy of understanding: An inquiry into the changing structure of psychoanalysis.* New York: Basic Books.

Luborsky, L., & Crits-Christoph, P. (1990). *Understanding transference.* New York: Basic Books.

Luborsky, L., Crits-Christoph, P., Mintz, J., & Auerbach, A. (1988). *Who will benefit from psychotherapy. Predicting therapeutic outcomes.* New York: Basic Books.

Malan, D. H. (1963). *A study of brief psychotherapy.* New York: Plenum Press.

Malan, D. H. (1976a). *The frontier of brief psychotherapy: An example of the convergence of research and clinical practice.* New York: Plenum Press.

Malan, D. H. (1976b). *Toward the validation of dynamic psychotherapy: A replication.* New York: Plenum Press.

Malan, D. H. (1979). *Individual psychotherapy and the science of psychodynamics.* London: Butterworth.

Mann, J. (1973). *Time-limited psychotherapy.* Cambridge, MA: Harvard University Press.

Mann, J., & Goldman, R. (1982). *A casebook in time-limited psychotherapy.* New York: McGraw-Hill.

Menninger, K., & Holzman, P. S. (1973). *The theory of psychoanalytic technique* (2nd ed.). New York: Basic Books.

Orlinsky, D. E., & Howard, K. I. (1986). Process and outcome in psychotherapy. In S. L. Garfield & A. E. Bergin (Eds.), *Handbook of psychotherapy and behavior change* (3rd ed.) (pp. 311–381). New York: Wiley.

Peterfreund, E. (1983). *The process of psychoanalytic therapy: Models and strategies.* Hillsdale, NJ: Analytic Press.

Piper, W. E., Azim, H. F. A., Joyce, A. S., & McCallum, M. (1991). Transference interpretation, therapeutic alliance, and outcome in short-term individual psychotherapy. *Archives of General Psychiatry, 48,* 946–953.

Piper, W. E., Debbane, E. G., Bienvenu, J., de Carufel, F., & Garant, J. (1986). Relationship between the object focus of therapists' interventions and outcome in short-term individual psychotherapy. *British Journal of Medical Psychology, 59,* 1–11.

Sandler, J., Dare, C., & Holder, A. (1992). *The patient and the analyst. The basis of the psychoanalytic process* (2nd ed.). Madison, CT: International Universities Press.

Sandler, J., & Sandler, A. M. (1978). On the development of object relationships and affects. *International Journal of Psychoanalysis, 59,* 285–296.

Sifneos, P. (1972). *Short-term psychotherapy and emotional crisis.* Cambridge, MA: Harvard University Press.

Sifneos, P. (1979). *Short-term dynamic psychotherapy: Evaluation and technique.* New York: Plenum Press.

Strupp, H. H. & Binder, J. L. (1984). *Psychotherapy in a new key: A guide to time-limited dynamic psychotherapy.* New York: Basic Books.

Wolberg, L. (1980). *Handbook of short-term psychotherapy.* New York: Grune & Stratton.

4

Behavior Therapies in Historical Perspective

W. Edward Craighead
Linda Wilcoxon Craighead
Stephen S. Ilardi

The intellectual climate during the last quarter of the nineteenth century was characterized by the widespread acceptance of empiricism, a philosophical perspective that stresses the acquisition of knowledge by means of objective observation and scientific experimentation. The influence of empiricism extended beyond the field of philosophy (e.g., logical positivism, British empiricism) to such disciplines as Newtonian physics, the animal behavior studies of biology, and the nascent field of psychology. Psychology is usually considered to have begun as a scientific discipline with the studies of perception and psychophysics in Wundt's laboratory, in 1876, in Germany. Psychology was influenced at an early stage by the study of neurophysiology, conditioning, and behavior conducted by empirically oriented Russian physicians, physiologists, and biologists, most notably Sechenov, Pavlov, and Bechterev.

In the late nineteenth and early twentieth centuries in the United States, psychology was principally concerned with the study of human consciousness (or the mind), largely due to the influence of William James (1890, 1909). The two major approaches to the study of consciousness have been labeled *Structuralism* (championed by Titchener), which focused on the components of the mind, and *Functionalism* (championed by Angell and then Dewey), which focused on the processes by which the mind works. Both approaches to the empirical study of consciousness employed a method of subjective *introspection* rather than an external, objective observational methodology. During the first quarter of this century another major school of psychology, Behaviorism, with a markedly different empirical methodology and focus, was developed.

BEHAVIORISM

Behaviorism is the conceptual framework within which behavior therapy approaches were developed. The origins of behaviorism may be traced to a multiplicity of influences from different corners of the world; it resulted from the confluence of numerous contemporaneous experiments and theoretical postulations regarding human behavior in the first quarter of this century. However, in the United States, John B. Watson (1878–1958) is usually credited as the most important person in the development of Behaviorism. He defined psychology as *the science of behavior*, which limited the scope of psychological inquiry to directly observable, objectively verifiable events and behaviors. This approach stood in direct contrast to the introspection of Functionalism and Structuralism.

Watson received his Ph.D. from the University of Chicago in 1903 and took a position on the faculty of Johns Hopkins University in 1908; his first major publication espousing his influential views was a *Psychological Review* paper, "Psychology as the Behaviorist Views it," published in 1913. His other major works included *Behavior: An Introduction to Comparative Psychology* (1914) and *Psychology From the Standpoint of a Behaviorist* (1919). He was the President of the American Psychological Association in 1915.

Watson's work, in tandem with the conditioning research in Russia and the animal behavior research in Europe, especially England, sharply focused early-twentieth-century psychology on the study of behavior. There were, of course, exceptions to this primarily behavioral focus. For example, the assembly in 1927 of many of the world's greatest psychologists at the dedication of the new Psychology/Chemistry building at Wittenburg College predicted that the "battlefield" for the study of psychology in the 1930s would be "emotions" (Reymert, 1928). Nevertheless, with their emphasis on environmental influences, stimuli and responses, and learning, behaviorists ruled in basic psychological research. Consequently, over the next half century, as Kazdin (1978) has noted, "In America, several theories of learning were proposed to explain the acquisition of responses. . . . Generally, these premises adhered to the basic methodological tenets of behaviorism: focus upon stimuli and responses, reliance upon objective evidence, and rejection of consciousness. . . ., several important theorists, notably Thorndike, Hull, Tolman, Guthrie, Mowrer, and Skinner, carved out individual positions within the realm of behaviorism" (pp. 71–72). The reader is referred to Kazdin (1978) for a more detailed and extensive discussion of how these various models of learning influenced later clinical behavioral interventions; only those models having a major, direct impact will be described in the following section.

BEHAVIORISM AND BEHAVIORAL INTERVENTIONS

Early Applications

Although in the broadest sense there are numerous recorded historical examples of behavioral interventions (Franks, 1969a; Stewart, 1961; Yates, 1970), there is no direct genealogy from these early examples to modern behavior therapy, nor is there any reason to believe that behaviorists early in this century appealed to such provenance for the generation of their ideas. Rather, early behavioral interventions were derived directly from the developing behavioral model of human behavior, with its emphasis on learning.

Watson and Rosalie Rayner (1920) (one of his students, whom he later married, thereby in Baltimore creating a scandal that led to Watson's leaving the field of psychology [see Cohen, 1979]) employed principles of classical conditioning to condition fear in an 11-month-old infant who is now known as "Little Albert." They elicited a classical emotional response, including crying, trembling, and so on, by producing a loud noise (hitting a steel bar with a hammer); the loud noise was presented simultaneously (paired) with a white rat. Although the white rat had previously been a neutral stimulus for the child, it came, when presented by itself, to elicit the fear response. This response generalized to other white furry objects, such as a white rabbit and even a Santa Claus mask. This experiment supported Watson's hypothesis that "emotional" behaviors in humans were the result of conditioning and that procedures based on conditioning principles might be used to change emotional reactions to conditioned stimuli.

The first systematic attempt to apply Watson's ideas to the realm of clinical intervention was conducted by Mary Cover Jones (1924b). Jones had been friends with Rayner in college, and even though Watson had left psychology for the advertising profession, Jones was able to persuade Watson to help her design intervention programs (based on his conditioning model) for children in the institution managed by Jones and her husband in New York City. These learning theory-based institutional programs developed with Watson, exemplified by her now-famous case study with a little boy named Peter (1924a), were successful in changing the children's behaviors. The most successful procedures appeared to be classical conditioning and social imitation (similar to what was later labeled *modeling* by Bandura and Walters [1963]). Although there were to be only a few sporadic additional applications of conditioning procedures prior to the 1950s (Craighead, Kazdin, & Mahoney, 1981, Ullmann & Krasner, 1965); it is clear that the seeds for the viability of clinical applications of behaviorism were planted by Watson and his colleagues, Rayner and Jones.

At least one other pre–World War II application of behavioral principles warrants mention: the Mowrers' bell-and-pad procedure for the treatment of enuresis. The husband-and-wife team of O. H. Mowrer, a major learning theorist at Yale, and W. M. Mowrer, a human-development specialist, worked together to devise an effective classical conditioning procedure to decrease enuresis (1938) in children. O. H. Mowrer's concern with human problems and his productive career in conditioning in experimental psychology led to his most significant contribution to later behavior therapy—his two-factor theory of learning (Mowrer, 1947; see also 1960a, 1960b). As something of an aside, it is interesting to note that Mowrer's continuing work with clinical problems, together with the influences of his religious background and his struggles with major depression, led to the development of Integrity Therapy, a clinical model virtually unrelated to his previous work.

There were other isolated examples of applications of behaviorally based interventions during the 1930s and 1940s, but the major applications of behavioral theory and empirically based principles of behavioral change came in the 1950s. These applications occurred in the context of the changes in the mental health field that were catalyzed by World War II.

Impact of World War II on Mental Health

The major impact of World War II on mental health in general and clinical psychology in particular has been widely documented (Brems, Thevenin, & Routh, 1991; Reisman, 1976; Routh, 1994). The most pertinent impact for the purposes of this chapter is the fact that clinical psychologists became more involved in the entire therapeutic process. In mental health work prior to World War II, clinical psychologists had served primarily in the role of clinical assessors; social workers had gathered family histories; but the *therapy*, which was primarily psychodynamic in orientation, had been conducted almost exclusively by psychiatrists. The exigencies of increased wartime needs for intervention, coupled with the clinical sequelae of World War II, including extensive mental health needs, resulted in clinical psychologists assuming a prominent role in the delivery of psychotherapy and related clinical interventions. These events led the U.S. Public Health Service and the Veterans Administration (VA) to ask the American Psychological Association (APA), which had become a united group of scientists and practitioners during World War II, to specify the training requirements for graduate programs in psychology and to identify the programs that met those requirements. The APA appointed a committee, chaired by David Shakow, which produced the report "Recommended Training in Clinical Psychology" (1947). This report was largely supported at the 1949 National Institutes of Mental Health (NIMH)-sponsored conference on training in clinical psychology, which was conducted in Boulder, Colorado. The major tenet of the Boulder Conference, and its primary identifying factor, was its conclusion that clinical psychologists should be trained as scientist-practitioners. Although other models of training have been set forth, the scientist-practitioner model (Boulder model) ensured that psychotherapy, at least within the clinical psychology arena, would be subjected to empirical evaluation regarding its effectiveness. It was in the context of this scientist-practitioner model that behavior therapy was developed on a wide scale. It is probably not accidental that psychiatrists (such as Wolpe, Beck, Liberman, and Agras) and social workers (such as Stewart), who have contributed innovative behavioral and cognitive-behavioral procedures, have historically received quicker and wider acceptance and acclaim in clinical psychology circles than in their parent disciplines, which remained largely psychodynamic in their focus. This situation has changed in recent years as behavior therapy has become more widely accepted, and especially as psychiatry has become more biological in its orientation, and the effectiveness of combined biological and behavioral interventions has been recognized (Craighead & Nemeroff, 1989; Hollon et al., 1992).

It is also noteworthy that numerous experimental psychologists had conducted applied experiments relevant to nonclinical World War II efforts. These included not only Skinner and his colleagues' efforts to train pigeons to guide missiles, but also the use of methodological and research procedures in personnel selection and research on humans' skills in interacting with equipment (e.g., human factors) (Hunter, 1946).

Thus, the stage was set for the widespread emergence of behaviorally based interventions. Psychotherapy was more widely needed, psychologists trained in experimental methodology (which was largely behavioral at the time) became more widely involved in its delivery, and principles of learning were being applied to many practical human problems that, as illustrated in the next section, included mental health problems.

Emergence of Behavior Modification/ Behavior Therapy

Within the scope of this chapter, it is not possible to note all the influences or people who made significant contributions to the wide-spread emergence of behavior modification/behavior therapy as a major treatment approach and theoretical orientation with respect to mental health problems. However, virtually all writers on this topic agree that there were three major groups that made substantial contributions during the 1950s; they were (1) Skinner and others engaged in applied operant conditioning; (2) Wolpe, Lazarus, and others from South Africa and the United States studying anxiety and its treatment by systematic desensitization; and (3) Eysenck and his collaborators at the Institute of Psychiatry in London.

Despite the widespread use of behavioral interventions, there still exists no widely accepted definition of *behavior modification* or *behavior therapy*; thus, we will continue to use these terms interchangeably. While some authors have suggested that *behavior modification* is a narrower term than *behavior therapy* and is, in fact, synonymous with the term *applied behavior analysis* (e.g., Eysenck, 1991), *behavior modification* is still frequently employed in the same general sense as *behavior therapy* (Craighead, Craighead, Kazdin, & Mahoney, 1994). Although data have not been collected on this point, it does appear that in the 1990s the term *behavior therapy* is more widely used than *behavior modification*; certainly, applications of clinical procedures based on operant principles are still labeled *behavior modification*, although the term *applied behavior analysis* has emerged as the preferred label for these procedures. Perhaps the pejorative connotations of the term *behavior modification*, resulting from its inappropriate and unfortunate association with things such as the movie *A Clockwork Orange* and so-called brainwashing techniques, has resulted in the apparently increasing preference for the label *behavior therapy*. Another factor that may have influenced this preference is the synthesis of behavior therapy and cognitive therapy, and the development of the more felicitous label, *cognitive-behavior therapy*, to refer to many of the most effective current therapeutic interventions. Nevertheless, many still use the terms *behavior modification* and *behavior therapy* interchangeably, although the latter is more frequently employed.

Skinner and Applied Behavior Analysis

Although credit for the application of behavioral principles to clinical problems is widely shared, there is little question that the most widely known and most controversial behaviorist has been B. F. Skinner. During the early 1950s, Skinner and his colleagues systematically studied the use of operant conditioning principles with psychotic patients at the Laboratory for Behavior Research at Metropolitan State Hospital in Waltham, Massachusetts. His landmark book, *Science and Human Behavior*, published in 1953, described the background and principles of operant conditioning.

Between the mid-1950s and the 1970s, extensive applications of the principles of operant conditioning in both regular and special education classrooms (Bijou & Baer, 1961; O'Leary & O'Leary, 1977) were developed. Operant procedures have been especially useful in the management and teaching of mentally retarded individuals, chronic mental patients, and individuals with developmental disabilities. Again, not all the major figures in applied behavior analysis can be listed without omitting some specific contributions, but major research programs, including those of the Universities of Washington, Chicago, Illinois, and Kansas, should be noted. Specific clinical applications of applied behavior analysis have been identified in Chapter 5 of this volume and in other general reviews of behavioral interventions (Craighead et al., 1994), especially in Kazdin's 1994 book, *Behavior Modification in Applied Settings*. Operant procedures have proved to be especially important in their application to health problems, exerting a seminal influence on the development of the field of Behavioral Medicine (Keefe & Beckham, 1994; Peterson, Sherman, & Zink, 1994).

In 1968, the Society for the Experimental Analysis of Behavior began publication of the *Journal of Applied Behavior Analysis*, which focused on studies applying operant principles to the process of human behavioral change.

The journal's editors have been M. M. Wolf, D. M. Baer, T. R. Risley, W. S. Agras, K. D. O'Leary, D. H. Barlow, B. A. Iwata, J. S. Bailey, E. S. Geller, and N. A. Neef. The initial volume contained an influential paper by Baer, Wolf, and Risley (1968), which had a major impact on the direction of applied behavior analysis. Applied behavior analysts, influenced especially by leaders at Western Michigan and the University of Kansas, formed the Midwestern Association of Behavior Analysis in 1974; this is now the Association of Behavior Analysis (ABA), which has 2,000-plus members in the United States.[1] It also has national and regional affiliates, with membership numbering upward of 7,000.

Applied behavior analysts have had their major impact in the American Psychological Association through APA Division 25, The Experimental Analysis of Behavior, which has a large overlap in membership with the ABA. Operant procedures have also received extensive applications in Europe (the ABA affiliates in Norway and Germany are large and influential) and in Central and South America.

Wolpe and Reciprocal Inhibition

Joseph Wolpe, who received his M.D. and began his career in South Africa, was one of the major contributors to the development of behavior therapy in the 1950s. He was influenced considerably by J. G. Taylor, a Hullian learning theorist. The general principle he invoked to explain and guide his development of behavior therapy procedures was *reciprocal inhibition*, which he based on both the classical conditioning and the Hull-Spence models of learning theory. Wolpe (1958) described the reciprocal inhibition principle in the following familiar quotation: "If a response antagonistic to anxiety can be made to occur in the presence of anxiety-evoking stimuli so that it is accompanied by a complete or partial suppression of the anxiety response, the bond between these stimuli and the anxiety responses will be weakened" (p. 71).

Wolpe and his colleagues worked primarily with anxiety responses and delineated three categories of behavior antagonistic to anxiety (which he viewed primarily as sympathetic nervous system arousal) that could serve to reciprocally inhibit anxiety. These antagonistic behaviors included a modified (shortened) version of Jacobson's (1938) progressive muscular relaxation training, assertive behaviors, and sexual behaviors. Sexual behaviors were utilized specifically in the treatment of anxiety-based sexual dysfunctions, whereas assertiveness and relaxation training were employed more generally in the treatment of anxiety problems. Eventually, assertive responses were combined with Salter's (1949) use of assertiveness and emerged as part of the general behavioral social skills training area.

Wolpe focused more on the use of progressive muscular relaxation training as a means of inhibiting anxiety. Although actual exposure to the anxiety stimulus was sometimes employed, he eventually moved to the more frequent use of imagined anxiety stimuli. Perhaps his major contribution was the development of a specific clinical procedure, *systematic desensitization*, in which a number of situations that evoke anxiety are listed and arranged in hierarchical order; these situations are then imagined by the patient, who remains extremely relaxed while visualizing the previously anxiety-eliciting situations in a graded fashion. Wolpe claimed great success with this procedure in the treatment of a variety of phobias and other anxiety responses. After the fairly wide application and evaluation of systematic desensitization in the United States in a number of laboratories, Lang (1969) and Paul (1969b) concluded that this procedure had been empirically demonstrated to be an effective treatment for anxiety.

Expansion in the United States

Wolpe had several colleagues and students in both South Africa and the United States, where he moved permanently in 1962. He worked first at the University of Virginia and then at Temple University; he is now retired and teaching at Pepperdine University. Among the most important of Wolpe's behaviorist colleagues were S. J. Rachman, who moved from South

Africa to England and eventually to Canada; A. A. Lazarus, who moved to the United States (going first to Palo Alto, California, and then to Princeton, New Jersey); and Alma Hannon, who stayed in South Africa but influenced several second-generation behavior therapists (e.g., G. T. Wilson) who immigrated to the United States. Lazarus gradually adopted a somewhat less behavioral focus with his model of therapy, referred to as *"technical eclecticism,"* or *multimodal therapy*. In many ways, Lazarus' modifications of his approach to therapeutic intervention (Lazarus, 1967, 1971a, 1971b) mirrored the overall movement of the field from a more narrow focus on applied learning to a broader, more inclusive approach incorporating symbolic, cognitive processes of therapeutic change. Rachman's contributions will be noted later in this chapter.

In a 1965 book, Ullmann and Krasner summarized the status of behavioral interventions by identifying the behavioral procedures that had been demonstrated to be effective, as well as many of the outcome questions that needed to be addressed; those pregnant first 63 pages of that book had a major impact on the direction of behavioral research in the United States over the next decade. By 1969, the field had developed to the point where two major review books appeared (Bandura, 1969; Franks, 1969b). These books were especially important in shaping the areas of behavior therapy research and applications and, along with the Kanfer and Philips book (1970), established behavior therapy as a major model in the expanding arena of psychotherapy. As discussed later in this chapter, Bandura's book (1969) also paved the way for the integration of symbolic, cognitive processes (see chapter 10 of that work) and existing behavior change procedures. It was in the late 1960s and early 1970s that most major clinical psychology training programs began to hire behaviorally oriented professors, and behavioral procedures were incorporated into coursework, research, and clinical training, especially in doctoral programs in clinical psychology.

In November 1966, Cyril Franks, Andrew Salter, Dorothy Susskind, and Joseph Wolpe met in Susskind's apartment in New York and created the Association for Advancement of Behavior Therapy (AABT).[2] This "interest group" focused on *advancing* the quality and breadth of behavior therapy, with its model being the Association for the Advancement of Science. The AABT initiated an annual conference, which was conducted concurrently with the meeting of the APA until 1972; since then, its convention has been conducted independently. The AABT also published a newsletter from 1966 to 1970, when it began publishing its journal, *Behavior Therapy*, which has had the following editors: Cyril Franks, Alan Kazdin, David Barlow, Edward Blanchard, Edward Craighead, and Lizette Peterson. Currently, a newsletter, *The Behavior Therapist*, is also published. The AABT has grown from an interest group of 10 to a professional organization of 4,000-plus members, with its own journal, newsletter, and convention; it has thereby played a major role in the development and expansion of behavior therapy.

Behavior therapy gradually branched out from its initial focus on relaxation and systematic desensitization for the treatment of avoidance responses and phobias. This initial focus on anxiety can best be understood in its historical context, in which anxiety was viewed as the core of "neuroses" within the prevailing psychodynamic model of psychopathology and treatment. The first major clinical applications beyond relaxation training and systematic desensitization were further developments and refinements in the use of assertion training. The focus shifted from assertion, as either an "excitatory" (Salter, 1949) or an antianxiety response (Wolpe, 1958), to an emphasis on assertion as an adaptive coping skill. Assertion training as a specific clinical procedure eventually expanded to include the training of more general social skills, which is now an important component of treatment for many clinical problems, including shyness, social phobia, depression, and schizophrenia (Dow, 1994; Chapter 5, this volume).

Early on, behaviorists took the position that traditional assessment (particularly projective tests) and even diagnoses per se were not very

useful. The behavioral model's emphasis was on identifying specific dysfunctional behaviors (and, later, thoughts and emotions) and then carefully analyzing their antecedents and consequences to determine the functional relationships. The diagnostic system in use at that time was based on psychodynamic concepts of neuroses and was not always acceptably reliable. As the American Psychiatric Association's classification system (DSM II, III, III-R, IV) has been revised, the criteria became more clearly objective and the psychodynamic basis tended to be dropped. The development of structured interviews provided clearly operationalized, reliable selection criteria. These factors, plus the need to identify specific disorders in order to obtain funding to evaluate the efficacy of behavioral treatment, encouraged behavioral researchers to develop and evaluate interventions for virtually all Axis I disorders, including schizophrenia, alcoholism, eating disorders, panic disorder, agoraphobia, obsessive-compulsive disorder, and depression.

Behaviorists have been slower to target the Axis II personality disorders. The poorer reliability and the "trait" connotation of these disorders rendered them even less amenable to a behavioral approach, which focused on situation specificity. Each of a person's multiple, specific problems would have been assessed and then addressed clinically by a behavior therapist, without attaching a particular label to any specific cluster of problematic behaviors, thoughts, or emotions. Again, now that structured interviews have led to improved reliability and the use of subjects selected according to clearly operationalized criteria has encouraged the use of group comparison designs, some researchers have begun to tackle these complex clinical problems. Initial empirical evaluations have been reported for the treatment of avoidant personality disorder (Alden, 1989) and borderline (parasuicidal) personality disorder (Linehan, 1993). As noted later, cognitive therapy is now being applied to personality disorders more generally.

During the 1970s and 1980s, behaviorists developed many interventions that were not designed to address specific Axis I or II disorders; behavioral marital therapy, parent training, and family therapy procedures are notable examples. Early procedures with children in classrooms and institutions, and efforts to effect large-scale community changes, were largely undertaken by applied behavior analysts. As will be seen in the section of this chapter dealing with cognitive-behavior therapy, behaviorists continued to look to basic psychology for guidance in the development and refinement of their clinical procedures. As basic psychology made a cognitive shift, so did behavior therapy; hence the movement of the field to the more appropriate, widely used label *cognitive-behavior therapy.*

Eysenck and the Institute of Psychiatry

Hans Eysenck and his colleagues (e.g., M. B. Shapiro) and students (e.g., S. J. Rachman and C. M. Franks) at the Institute of Psychiatry in London played major roles in the early developments in behavior therapy. After World War II, Eysenck worked at Maudsley Hospital, which became part of the University of London's Institute of Psychiatry in 1955. There his group of psychologists, working with several psychiatrists who were amenable to this approach, developed clinical procedures based on principles of learning. In 1959, Eysenck labeled these procedures *"Behavior Therapy"* (Eysenck, 1991). At about the same time, A. A. Lazarus (1958) also employed the term *behavior therapy* in South Africa.

Eysenck was among the first to challenge seriously the effectiveness of traditional verbal psychotherapy. His first salvo was fired in a significant 1952 paper, "The Effects of Psychotherapy," which was followed by several books, the most important of which were probably *Behaviour Therapy and the Neuroses* (1960) and *Causes and Cures of Neurosis* (Eysenck & Rachman, 1965); the latter was required reading in most courses in behavior therapy in the "old days." Although his major point—that traditional psychotherapy was no more effective than spontaneous recovery—has been challenged on many grounds, it is pertinent today that few data have successfully challenged his

original conclusions. Effective psychosocial treatments have gradually moved toward specifically designed therapies for specific disorders rather than generic psychotherapies applicable to virtually all psychological disorders, or at least those subsumed under the rubric of *neurosis.*

Among the group of behavior therapists at the Institute of Psychiatry, Eysenck served as the overall leader, while M. B. Shapiro (although not himself a behaviorist) was the Director of the educational program and a major player in the training of many early behavior therapists. In 1963, Eysenck began the first exclusively behavioral journal, *Behavior Research and Therapy (BRAT)*. Eysenck's outstanding doctoral student, S. J. Rchman, who had worked with Wolpe in South Africa, became the Associate Editor of the journal and succeeded Eysenck as Editor in 1979. Cyril Franks was another important student at the Institute, receiving his Ph.D. in 1954. He immigrated to the United States and had a major impact on the development of behavior therapy through his edited books, his involvement with the AABT, and as the first Editor of *Behavior Therapy.*

Over the years, major research programs in England have continued to play an important role in the development and evaluation of clinical behavior therapy procedures, particularly in the treatment of panic, generalized anxiety, phobias, obsessive-compulsive disorders, tics, and sexual problems. More recently, work there has also taken a cognitive turn, with major contributions by Teasdale, Clark, Salkovskis, Fairburn, and others, many of whom can trace their professional genealogy to the Institute of Psychiatry and to Eysenck, Shapiro, Rachman, and their colleagues.

Behavior therapy has developed relatively independently in many other countries in Europe and, indeed, throughout the world, and the importance of these developments cannot be minimized. For example, the European Association of Behaviour Therapy recently changed its name to the European Association of Behaviour and Cognitive Therapies (EABCT), a movement designed to maintain the union of behavioral and cognitive approaches to therapy. Undoubtedly, this influenced the AABT to conduct a referendum of its members (after many years of debate) allowing for consideration of a possible name change to the Association for Behavioral and Cognitive Therapies.

Nevertheless, the most important events for behavior therapy in the United States in a historical context were the early writing of Eysenck and Rachman, the publication of *BRAT*, and the broad influence of the training program at the Institute of Psychiatry.

Bandura and Social Learning Theory

As noted earlier, Albert Bandura's *Principles of Behavior Modification* (1969) not only summarized the principles and data relevant to behavioral interventions but it also marked a major turn toward the integration of cognitive, symbolic processes into behavior therapy. Bandura had been trained in the Hull-Spence tradition of experimental psychology at the University of Iowa. He served as APA President during 1974. His early contributions focused on modeling and imitation and came to be called *observational learning*. This work and related theoretical developments were summarized in the influential book *Social Learning and Personality Development* (Bandura & Walters, 1963).

Bandura eventually invoked cognitive explanations for learning via modeling and imitation. His early work was conducted with children, but Bandura and his colleagues and students eventually also studied adult problems. He and his colleagues and students (e.g., Mahoney & Thoresen, 1974) also began to study the processes of self-control. Much of this work was theoretically based and was completed with analogue subjects. Nevertheless, Bandura's concepts of modeling, coping versus mastery, self-control, and self-efficacy proved to be clinically useful; these concepts were clearly espoused in a major *Psychological Review* (1977a) paper and in the book *Social Learning Theory* (1977b)

The way in which these historical developments played out in the development and evaluation of specific clinical behavioral interventions is described in Chapter 5, and in various summaries of the status of behavior therapy procedures (Craighead et al., 1994; Masters, Burish, Hollon, & Rimm, 1987; O'Leary & Wilson, 1987; Turner, Calhoun, & Adams, 1992). We now turn our attention to the way in which behavior therapy developed into *cognitive-behavior therapy*, which is now the most appropriate term for a significant number of behavioral interventions, including many of those formerly referred to as *behavior therapy* (Craighead, 1990).

THE "COGNITIVE REVOLUTION" AND THE EMERGENCE OF COGNITIVE-BEHAVIOR THERAPIES

Psychology's Cognitive Revolution

As observed earlier, John Watson (1913) defined psychology as the science of behavior, a science to be limited to the study of directly observable, objectively verifiable events (i.e., behavior). Cognition, affect, and motivation, since they are not generally amenable to direct observation, were held to be beyond the purview of psychological inquiry. This *behaviorist* perspective came to dominate American experimental psychology by the 1930s and remained the predominant theoretical orientation for about 40 years. However, despite the impressive record of experimental and clinical (behavior modification) advances attributable to behaviorally oriented research efforts, the field experienced a rather dramatic reorientation, or *paradigm shift* (Kuhn, 1962), in the late 1960s and 1970s, during which the role of cognition in mediating human behavior became a subject of intense interest throughout academic psychology, including orthodox behavioral circles. The origins of the "cognitive revolution" may be traced primarily to the confluence of three separate, though related, trends: (1) increasing dissatisfaction with behaviorism's stimulus-response (S-R) learning model, which excludes all cognitive events; (2) the influence of computer analogues to human thought processes and the emergence of information processing metaphors of cognition; and (3) the appearance of behavioral learning theory reformulations that incorporated the cognitive mediation of behavior.

Early behavioral theorists proposed that the acquisition of all behaviors could be accounted for on the basis of the S-R learning model; however, this assertion came under increasing scrutiny by the 1960s as experimental findings from a number of psychological subdisciplines appeared to belie the explanatory efficacy of the S-R model (Breger & McGaugh, 1965). The study of language behavior, highlighted in the now famous debate between Skinner (1957) and Chomsky (1959) over language acquisition, suggested strongly that language cannot be viewed as simply a set of associations acquired according to operant conditioning principles (Dember, 1974). Likewise, findings in the area of human memory indicated that people are not merely passive receptacles of new information, but rather that they engage in active strategies (e.g., *chunking*) in the encoding and retrieval of information—strategies that necessarily occur inside the "black box" of the human being. The field of perception also provided numerous examples of the influence of intrasubject events (e.g., cognition) on perceptual processes. Finally, Bandura's (1969) elegant demonstrations of observational learning, or *modeling*, pointed to yet another set of phenomena that were not easily reconciled with the S-R model.

As Kuhn (1962) has observed, however, paradigm . . . shifts in scientific disciplines do not occur simply by virtue of the appearance of data that do not fit the predictions of the existing scientific paradigm; there must also emerge a rival theoretical model that appears to do a better job of accounting for the existing empirical data. In the case of psychology's cognitive revolution, it has been suggested that the appearance of the computer (another black box), in which may be observed the processing of information according to lawful, linear rules, provided psychology with a compelling metaphor for human cognition and suggested a

model in which human thought might take on an *objective* (or at least scientifically testable), rather than a purely subjective, existence (Craighead et al., 1994, chapter 1). Between 1955 and 1965, the computer metaphor inspired numerous attempted theoretical formulations of human cognition according to principles of linear information processing. In turn, some behaviorally oriented theorists began to concede that thoughts might be amenable to scientific investigation. Homme (1965) suggested that human thoughts could be conceptualized as covert operants, or *coverants*, which are presumably subject to the same laws of S-R learning as are behaviors. Cautela (1966, 1967) then extended this principle by arguing that thoughts, through a process termed *covert conditioning*, could be modified according to the established principles of behavior modification.

While the revisions of Homme and Cautela may best be viewed as modifications of existing behavioral theory, Bandura (1969) proposed what may be considered a revolutionary new paradigm, *social learning theory*, representing an original integration of operant and respondent learning with symbolic cognitive processes. Building on the phenomenon of observational learning (or *modeling*), the theory proposed that behavior acquisition may occur solely as a result of cognitive processes (e.g., attention, retention); in essence, it was proposed that cognitive processes could *mediate* the acquisition of new behavior, though Bandura did not deny that new behaviors could also be learned via conditioning processes. In addition, Bandura distinguished between the *acquisition* of a response and the subsequent *performance* of that response. Bandura (1974, 1977a, 1977b) further proposed that behavior is not simply determined by the individual's environment (the orthodox behaviorist position), but rather that person and environment are interconnected in a relationship of *reciprocal determinism*.

Significantly, Bandura made extensive use of information processing models of cognition in formulating his social learning theory model. For example, he invoked constructs such as attention and retention, drawn from information processing theory, to account for observational learning. So, in a manner of speaking, Bandura himself modeled for behaviorally oriented theorists the method of applying findings from other areas of psychology to the realm of behavior modification (Meyers & Craighead, 1984), and thereby set the stage for the development of a new clinical approach—*cognitive-behavior therapy*. This approach differs from conventional behavior modification in its incorporation of cognition as both a mechanism and a target of clinical change and in its replacement of environmental determinism with an acknowledgment of reciprocal determinism between the individual and the environment.

The Emergence of Cognitive-Behavior Therapies

The influence of psychology's cognitive revolution on behavior modification, though multifaceted, may be summarized succinctly: It suggested a central role for cognitive processes in the mediation of behavior and thereby legitimized cognition as a viable target of clinical intervention. Thus, the cognitive revolution catalyzed the transformation of behavior modification into cognitive behavior modification, or cognitive-behavior therapy in more clinical parlance. However, just as cognitive -behavior therapy is not a monolithic treatment approach (there are at least 20 distinct cognitive-behavior therapies [Mahoney & Lyddon, 1988]), but rather a set of related clinical methods and techniques, it may be seen that the various approaches that fall under the general rubric of *cognitive-behavior therapy* arose from a multiplicity of influences. Specifically, there are three primary factors that led to the emergence of cognitive-behavior clinical interventions: (1) the direct application, by behaviorally oriented theorists, of cognitive psychological constructs in the development of new clinical techniques; (2) the reformulation of an existing set of self-control procedures of behavior modification to include cognitive processes; and (3) the independently derived cognitive therapies of Ellis (1962) and Beck (1964, 1970), which were forged in a clinical rather than an experimental setting.

Applied Cognitive Psychology

As noted above, Bandura (1969) borrowed extensively from information processing models in his formulation of social learning theory and became the forerunner of numerous behavior therapists who incorporated cognitive theory into new models of behavior modification—models that may be said to fall under the general rubric of *cognitive-behavior therapy*. Bandura's construct of observational learning, or modeling, was subsequently applied to numerous areas of behavior modification (e.g., social skills training). Similarly, D'Zurilla and Goldfried (1971) drew on the general problem-solving literature, with roots in the information processing field, to develop a problem-solving approach to behavior modification, with applications in such areas as the treatment of clinical depression (Nezu, 1986), weight control (Black, 1987), and severe social skills deficits (e.g., Allen, Chinsky, Larcen, Lochman, & Selinger, 1976; Bedell, Archer, & Marlow, 1980; Spivack & Shure, 1974). Additionally, Meichenbaum (1974, 1975, 1977) developed his model of self-instruction training by making use of constructs, such as *covert speech*, articulated by Luria (1961) and Vygotsky (1962) in the area of language development. These self-instruction techniques were found to have myriad applications in the clinical setting, including the treatment of anxiety, depression, pain, social skills deficits, and schizophrenia. Finally, another basic area of cognitive psychology, attribution theory, found successful incorporation into the clinical setting, most notably in the treatment of major depression (Abramson, Seligman, & Teasdale, 1978; Rehm, 1977). The eventual widespread interest among behaviorally oriented researchers in cognitive variables is suggested by the appearance of a new journal, *Cognitive Therapy and Research*, in 1977 (M. J. Mahoney, S. D. Hollon, and P. C. Kendall have served as its editors).

Reformulation of Self-control Theory

A second principal factor leading to the emergence of cognitive behavior therapies was the cognitive reformulation of self-control clinical interventions. The phenomenon of self-control was originally described in an operant learning context (Skinner, 1953), and self-control principles derived from an operant learning perspective were applied to such clinical problems as weight control (Ferster, Numberger, & Levitt, 1962) and stuttering (Goldiamond, 1965). However, in the self-control literature there appeared an increasing acknowledgment of the potential role of internal factors (i.e., cognitions) in the self-control process (Kanfer, 1970, 1971; Kanfer & Karoly, 1972; Mahoney & Thoresen, 1974; Thoresen & Mahoney, 1974). Correspondingly, several investigators designed self-control programs that directly incorporated cognitive processes, and they attempted to achieve behavior modification through the modification of cognitions (Mahoney, 1974). Thus, these programs share many affinities with explicitly acknowledged cognitive behavior therapies, and accordingly, many investigators have identified self-control interventions as cognitive-behavioral in nature (Mahoney & Arnkoff, 1978).

Cognitive Therapies

As the previous sections indicate, there was a strong historical connection between behavior modification, with roots in experimental psychology, and the emergence of cognitive-behavior therapies. There was, however, a parallel development in the clinical (as opposed to the experimental) arena that also gave rise to therapeutic approaches that were theoretically compatible with the emerging cognitive-behavior procedures. These approaches advocate the alteration of cognitive processes as a means of achieving behavioral change, and the cognitions on which they focus are relatively accessible to consciousness (i.e., can be self-reported with some training); this is in marked contrast to the focus on unconscious thoughts in traditional psychodynamic therapy. Largely

independent of the influence of behavioral psychology, Albert Ellis (1957, 1962) and Aaron Beck (1964, 1970) articulated treatment approaches known as *cognitive therapies* (a name originally applied to Beck's treatment model but now widely used to describe an entire category of primarily cognitive treatment approaches). In brief, cognitive therapies stress the etiological significance of maladaptive, irrational cognitions in the development of psychological disorders and advocate the treatment of psychopathology through a therapeutic process of cognitive restructuring.

Although Kelly's (1955) *personal construct approach* to therapeutic intervention was broadly cognitive in focus, Ellis (1957, 1962) is usually credited with formulating the first comprehensive theoretical model of cognitive therapy. Ellis' approach, known as *rational-emotive therapy (RET)*, finds its theoretical origins in Stoic philosophy and posits that negative emotions, such as anger, sadness, and anxiety, are the inevitable result of irrational thought processes; for Ellis, it is negative thoughts, not negative events, that lead to problematic negative affect. Similarly, illogical thinking is also held to lead to maladaptive behavior. Therefore, the focus of treatment in RET is the restructuring of maladaptive, irrational cognitions. RET has been applied to a wide variety of clinical problems, ranging from depression (Anderson, 1966; Trexler, 1973) and anxiety disorders (Ellis, 1991; Emmelkamp & Beens, 1991; Emmelkamp, Mersch, Vissia, & Vanderhelm, 1985) to alcohol and drug abuse (Ellis, 1982; Trimpey, 1989) and anger management (Ellis, 1975).

Through the establishment of the Institute for Rational Living in New York City, Ellis has been influential in promoting widespread knowledge about this philosophy and in training large numbers of therapists; the Institute also promotes the empirical study of RET. While extensive clinical material describing this approach is available, and while the general effectiveness of a cognitive approach is supported by the larger literature on cognitive restructuring, there are few rigorous empirical evaluations of RET. However, the approach is amenable to study within the tenets of methodological behaviorism, which suggests that RET will continue to be seen as part of the larger behavioral movement. Although naive observers may see RET as primarily a cognitive therapy, Ellis has stated clearly that RET has a strong behavioral component (e.g. shame-attacking exercises). However, the purpose of behavioral exercises is to bring about changes in irrational beliefs (i.e., to see that the anticipated, "awful" consequences don't happen) that are seen as the basis of the clinical problems.

Beck's (1964, 1970) treatment approach, first known simply as *cognitive therapy*, has had a profound impact on the clinical literature of the past two decades. Although trained as a psychoanalyst, Beck began to notice, in his work with depressed patients, a consistent pattern of *conscious* negative thoughts about the self, world, and future, which he referred to as the "cognitive triad" of depression. He observed that these negative thought patterns often represented a distorted view of reality, and he hypothesized that the restructuring of depressive cognitions in therapy would be an effective means of treating the disorder. Although this treatment approach was derived largely from Beck's own clinical practice, Beck did employ a number of specific behavioral techniques (e.g., pleasant activities scheduling) drawn from behavior modification approaches. As with RET, most of the behavioral assignments in cognitive therapy are conducted to test the client's fundamental beliefs or assumptions. A testable hypothesis based on the client's beliefs is developed, and the client is instructed to gather data with which to evaluate each hypothesis. Beck also employed a methodological rigor characteristic of a behaviorist (e.g., operationalizing of explicit intervention, treatment manualization) in the empirical testing of the efficacy of cognitive therapy.

In recent years, Beck's therapy has been more appropriately labeled *cognitive-behavior therapy* and is now frequently referred to as *CBT*. In a landmark comparative outcome study (Rush, Beck, Kovacs, & Hollon, 1977), CBT was shown to be just as effective as a tricyclic antidepressant in the short-term treatment of unipolar major depression, a finding that has been consistently replicated (see Dobson, 1989, for a comprehensive review). This empirical demonstration of the efficacy of Beck's CBT for the treatment of depression, probably more than any other single influence, has been responsible for the emergence of cognitive-behavior therapy as one of the preeminent treatment perspectives on the contemporary psychotherapy scene. In addition, cognitive-behavior therapies derived from Beck's treatment approach to depression have subsequently been formulated for the treatment of several clinical disorders, including panic and generalized anxiety disorders (Barlow et al., 1984; Barlow & Cerny, 1988; Freeman, Pretzer, Fleming, & Simon, 1990) and personality disorders (Beck et al., 1990).

BEHAVIORAL MEDICINE

Emergence as a Separate Field

The important field of behavioral medicine has developed in a way that clearly reflects its close affiliation with behavior therapy; in fact, numerous clinical applications in behavioral medicine may be subsumed under the rubric of *behavior therapy*. The first formal attempt to define this area as a separate field occurred at the Yale Conference on Behavioral Medicine in 1977 (see the review by Shelton, Anastopoulas, & Elliot, 1991), the same year in which a special interest group on behavioral medicine was formed within the AABT. A number of these AABT members were influential in the subsequent development, in 1979, of a separate group, the Society for Behavioral Medicine (SBM). The SBM's mission has continued to be compatible with that of the AABT, and there is still considerable overlap in membership. Although the field is now defined more broadly, one of its early definitions, proposed by Pomerleau and Brady (1979), illustrates its behavioral roots: "Behavioral medicine is (a) the clinical use of techniques derived from the experimental analysis of behavior therapy and behavior modification—for the evaluation, prevention, management, or treatment of physical disease or physiological dysfunction; and (b) the conduct of research contributing to the functional analysis and understanding of behavior associated with medical disorders and problems in health care" (p. 13).

Behavioral medicine as a field has grown tremendously in a relatively short period of time, establishing its own journals and conventions. In fact, many psychology training programs now offer courses in health psychology at the undergraduate and graduate levels, and an increasing number of doctoral programs have identified specific health psychology tracks. The number of psychologists employed in medical settings has grown exponentially, and such positions have become increasingly attractive to behaviorally trained psychologists, since medical centers, with their easy access to clinical populations, afford ample opportunity for the integration of research and clinical practice.

The more behavioral, empirically based philosophy characteristic of behavioral medicine has enjoyed increasing acceptance within general medicine, which in past years had not been particularly open to the idea that psychosocial variables and traditional psychotherapy had much to offer. The development of specialty areas such as pediatric psychology, behavioral gerontology, and behavioral neurology suggests the extent to which medicine and psychology have become intertwined. An example within gerontology is the application of operant procedures, first developed for use with institutionalized schizophrenics and the mentally retarded, to the behavior problems of the elderly, particularly those in institutions. Likewise, parent training procedures, first developed for use with children, have been adapted to train family caregivers of the elderly.

Areas of Intervention

The range of problems addressed in behavioral medicine has now become so broad that it would be pointless to specify them all. Several interventions, however, that have clear, early roots in behavior therapy can be identified. They have had a substantial impact, inasmuch as their characteristic procedures are now widely accepted and available. The behavioral treatment of obesity, which focused largely on stimulus control within a self-control paradigm, was one of the first areas of application. Operant procedures to enhance patient adherence to exercise, dietary modification (e.g., low-fat), and specific medical regimens, as well as procedures including more cognitive components (e.g., stress management, lifestyle change, and relapse prevention), have also been developed. Stress management programs include procedures designed to reduce physiological arousal—most frequently a form of relaxation training (which was first popularized as part of Wolpe's systematic desensitization) or biofeedback (which developed out of laboratory work to study whether physiological responses were amenable to conditioning procedures). Comprehensive multicomponent packages are typically put together to address specific medical problems, such as reducing Type A behavior, modifying specific cardiovascular risk factors (e.g., smoking cessation, weight loss, controlling blood pressure), and managing chronic diseases such as diabetes. Additionally, larger-scale efforts, often labeled *health promotion*, have now become quite popular particularly in the workplace.

Pain management is a somewhat separate behavioral medicine area that also incorporates variations of many of the procedures just mentioned. Again, multicomponent programs are typically developed and tailored to particular medical problems, most notably tension and migraine headaches, pain associated with invasive medical procedures (e.g., venipuncture) or medical treatments (e.g., skin debridement for burns), and chronic pain (such as back, cancer, and arthritis pain).

The general model of skills training has been adapted to provide better teaching of self-care skills so that patients and/or family members may take more responsibility for their own medical care, particularly with chronic diseases. Such interventions are not only cost-efficient (a major concern in the health field), but they typically enhance patients' quality of life by reducing hospital stays, doctor visits, and dependence on medications.

Role of Cognitions

Perhaps most important, from a historical viewpoint, it is notable that behavioral medicine has provided extensive, objective empirical validation consistent with the early tenets of behaviorism. Cognitive interventions are used in many treatment packages, and the availability of clearly objective outcome measures for most medical applications provides a particularly strong forum for their evaluation. While the separate effects of cognitive components are typically difficult to evaluate, it has been possible in specific instances to substantiate "additive" effects. These additive effects are not always obvious on the primary, health outcome measures, but they may show up on other indices such as patient compliance, satisfaction with treatment, and dropout rates. Thus, while the cognitive therapies discussed earlier use behavioral assignments primarily to test irrational beliefs, which are seen as the core of the problem by the cognitive therapist, cognitive interventions added to more traditional behavioral medicine programs may also be viewed as a way to remove obstacles to patient compliance with behavioral prescriptions (e.g., to eat three small meals a day at regular intervals) designed to remedy behavioral deficits, which may be seen as the core of the problem by the behavior therapist.

The reciprocal nature of the relationship between cognitive and behavioral interventions is illustrated by the example of cognitive-behavioral treatment of bulimia; each component (behavioral and cognitive) appears to enhance the effectiveness of the other. The prescription to eat regularly gradually confronts the irrational beliefs that "any eating will turn into a binge" or that "eating normal amounts of food without gaining weight is impossible." Likewise, the direct challenge to irrational beliefs that weight and shape are important determinants of self-worth, happiness, and others' evaluations appears to enhance clients' willingness to comply with the eating prescriptions and to risk the possibility of a slight weight gain. Thus, whether dieting behaviors or overvalued ideas (or both) were the more important initial determinants of binge eating in a given case, treatment for this problem now reflects the fact that, at this point in the history of behavior therapy, truly integrated cognitive-behavior treatments have been developed that have survived the tests of empirical validation and now enjoy widespread acceptance.

At the same time, other more strictly behavioral interventions are being refined and improved. In some areas, attempts to add cognitive components have not been particularly successful or cost-efficient. In those areas, more traditional behavior therapy remains the treatment of choice, and it is not clear what cognition has to contribute. The present broadening of the scope of the behavioral conceptual framework does not suggest that progress in all areas will take the same path. To go back to the famous Gordon Paul quote: ". . . What treatment, by whom, is most effective for this individual, with that specific problem, under which set of circumstances, and how does it come about?" (Paul, 1969a, p. 62). Accordingly, the job of current behaviorally oriented researchers and change agents is to continue research directed to the discovery of specific treatments for specific problems in specific populations, a goal that makes sense only in light of the behavioral tenet that behavior is situation specific.

INTEGRATION OF BEHAVIORAL AND SOMATIC INTERVENTIONS

The current movement toward integrating behavior therapy with somatic (medically based) interventions (as well as with psychotherapeutic interventions derived from other conceptual models) can be viewed within a similar framework. We should not expect to find that integration is always better (or, for that matter, always worse). Each effort must be evaluated on the basis of its empirical merit. If the current results from combining pharamacological treatments with cognitive-behavioral therapies is any indication, we should expect to find widely variable results. Several different models of possible combined effects have been suggested. Currently, work with depression and hyperactivity suggests that pharmacological and cognitive-behavioral approaches are likely compatible, if not in fact additive. Work with both panic disorder and obsessive-compulsive disorder suggests that pharmacological and cognitive-behavior approaches are about equally effective, and are perhaps best seen as different alternatives, each with its own advantages and disadvantages, such as time and cost considerations, differential relapse rates, and possible long-term effects. There is little evidence of additive effects. As noted in Craighead and Agras (1991), the treatment of bulimia may be an example of a disorder in which the mechanisms of the two approaches may not even be compatible; if so, combined treatment would be contraindicated. In the treatment of obesity, currently available pharmacological treatment alone is minimally helpful (and even then for only a short period of time); thus, attempts to evaluate the potential for effective integration must wait for future, more viable medications.

SUMMARY

Behavior therapy as a clinical enterprise originated with the work of Watson and his colleagues in the 1920s, though it did not receive widespread application until the 1950s. The field of behavior therapy subsequently expanded rapidly during the 1960s and 1970s. At the outset, the primary emphasis was the application of findings from basic experimental psychology, especially principles of learning (conditioning and observational learning), to the modification of behaviors characteristic of mental health problems. The other major focus was methodological behaviorism, with emphases on objective assessment and empirical evaluation of the effectiveness of therapeutic interventions.

Although the multifaceted field of behavior therapy has had numerous seminal theoreti-

cians and researchers in the mental health arena, the preeminent early figures include Skinner, Wolpe, Eysenck, and Bandura together with their colleagues and students. Organizations (e.g., the AABT, ABA, and EABCT) and journals have also played a major role in the development of behavior therapy.

As basic psychological models and research became more cognitive in orientation in the 1970s and 1980s, behavior therapy, drawing on basic psychological work, also became more cognitive. The integration of behavior therapy approaches and cognitive psychological principles, as well as related clinical developments such as Ellis' RET and Beck's cognitive therapy, led to the emergence of numerous treatment approaches known collectively as *cognitive-behavior therapies*. Other major historical developments in behavior therapy include the spawning of behavioral medicine and the recent integration of behavioral and somatic interventions in the treatment of medical and mental health problems.

NOTES

1. Appreciation is expressed to Dr. Judy Favell for information regarding the ABA.

2. The founding members of the AABT were John Paul Brady, Joseph R. Cautela, Edward Dengrove, Cyril M. Franks, Martin Gittelman, Leonard Krasner, Arnold A. Lazarus, Andrew Salter, Dorothy Susskind, and Joseph Wolpe. Appreciation is expressed to Ms. M. J. Eimer for information regarding the AABT.

REFERENCES

Abramson, L. Y., Seligman, M. E. P., & Teasdale, J. (1978). Learned helplessness in humans: Critique and reformulation. *Journal of Abnormal Psychology, 87,* 49–74.

Alden, L. (1989). Short-term structured treatment for avoidant personality disorder. *Journal of Consulting and Clinical Psychology, 57,* 756–764.

Allen, G. J., Chinsky, J. M., Larcen, S. W., Lochman, J. E., & Selinger, H. V. (1976). *Community psychology in the schools.* Hillsdale, NJ: Erlbaum.

American Psychological Association Committee on Training in Clinical Psychology. (1947). Recommended training in clinical psychology. *American Psychologist, 2,* 539–558.

Anderson, C. M. (1966). Depression and suicide reassessed. *Rational Living, 1,* 31–36.

Baer, D. M., Wolf, M. M., & Risley, T. R. (1968). Some current dimensions of applied behavior analysis. *Journal of Applied Behavior Analysis, 1,* 91–97.

Bandura, A. (1969). *Principles of behavior modification.* New York: Holt, Rinehart, & Winston.

Bandura, A. (1974). Behavior theory and the models of man. *American Psychologist, 29,* 859–869.

Bandura, A. (1977a). Self-efficacy: Toward a unifying theory of behavioral change. *Psychological Review, 84,* 191–215.

Bandura, A. (1977b). *Social learning theory.* Englewood Cliffs, NJ: Prentice-Hall.

Bandura, A., & Walters, R. H. (1963). *Social learning and personality development.* New York: Holt, Rinehart, & Winston.

Barlow, D. H., & Cerny, J. A. (1988). *Psychological treatment of panic.* New York: Guilford Press.

Barlow, D. H., Cohen, A. S., Waddell, M., Vermilyea, J. A., Klosko, J. S., Blanchard, E. B., & DiNardo, P. A. (1984). Panic and generalized anxiety disorders: Nature and treatment. *Behavior Therapy, 15,* 431–449.

Beck, A. T. (1964). Thinking and depression: II. Theory and therapy. *Archives of General Psychiatry, 10,* 561–571.

Beck, A. T. (1970). Cognitive therapy: Nature and relation to behavior therapy. *Behavior Therapy, 1,* 184–200.

Beck, A. T., Freeman, A., Pretzer, J., Davis, D. D., Fleming, B., Ottaviani, R., Beck, J., Simon, K. M., Padesky, C., Meyer, J., & Trexler, L. (1990). *Cognitive therapy of personality disorders.* New York: Guilford Press.

Bedell, J. R., Archer, R. P., & Marlow, H. A., Jr. (1980). A description and evaluation of a problem solving skills training program. In D. Upper & S. M. Ross (Eds.), *Behavioral group therapy: An annual review* (pp. 332–345). Champaign, IL: Research Press.

Bijou, S. W., & Baer, D. M. (1961). *Child Development: A systematic and empirical theory,* Vol. 1. New York: Appleton-Century-Crofts.

Black, D. R. (1987). A minimal intervention program and a problem-solving program for weight control. *Cognitive Therapy and Research, 11,* 107–120.

Breger, L., & McGaugh, J. L. (1965). Critique and reformulation of "learning theory" approaches to psychotherapy and neurosis. *Psychological Bulletin, 63,* 338–358.

Brems, C., Thevenin, D. M., & Routh, D. K. (1991). The history of clinical psychology. In C. E. Walker (Ed)., *Clinical psychology: Historical and research foundations* (pp. 3–35). New York: Plenum Press.

Cautela, J. R. (1966). Treatment of compulsive behavior by covert sensitization. *Psychological Record, 16,* 33–41.

Cautela, J. R. (1967). Covert sensitization. *Psychological Reports, 20,* 459–468.

Chomsky, N. (1959). A review of *Verbal behavior* by B. F. Skinner. *Language, 35,* 26–58.

Cohen, D. J. B. (1979). *Watson: The founder of behaviorism.* London: Routledge & Kegan Paul.

Craighead, L. W., & Agras, W. S. (1991). Mechanisms of action in cognitive-behavioral and pharmacological interventions for obesity and bulimia nervosa. *Journal of Consulting and Clinical Psychology, 59,* 115–125.

Craighead, L. W., Craighead, W. E., Kazdin, A. E., & Mahoney, M. J. (1994). *Cognitive and behavioral interventions: An empirical approach to mental health problems.* Needham, MA: Allyn & Bacon.

Craighead, W. E. (1990). There's a place for us: All of us. *Behavior Therapy, 21,* 2–23.

Craighead, W. E., Kazdin, A. E., & Mahoney, M. J. (1981). *Behavior modification: Principles, issues, and applications* (2nd ed.). Boston: Houghton Mifflin.

Craighead, W. E., & Nemeroff, C. B. (1989). Commentary on the neuroscience imperative in psychiatry. *Integrative Psychiatry, 6,* 152–164.

Dember, W. N. (1974). Motivation and the cognitive revolution. *American Psychologist, 29,* 161–168.

Dobson, K. S. (1989). A meta-analysis of the efficacy of cognitive therapy for depression. *Journal of Consulting and Clinical Psychology, 57,* 414–419.

Dow, M. G. (1994). Social inadequacy and social skill. In L. W. Craighead, W. E. Craighead, A. E. Kazdin, & M. J. Mahoney (Eds.), *Cognitive and behavioral interventions: An empirical appraoch to mental health problems* (pp. 123–140). Needham, MA; Allyn & Bacon.

D'Zurilla, T. J., & Goldfried, M. R. (1971). Problem solving and behavior modification. *Journal of Abnormal Psychology, 78,* 107–126.

Ellis, A. (1957). Rational psychotherapy and individual psychology. *Journal of Individual Psychology*, 13, 38–44.

Ellis, A. (1962). *Reason and emotion in psychotherapy*. New York: Lyle Stuart.

Ellis, A. (1975). On the disvalue of "mature" anger. *Rational Living*, 10, 24–27.

Ellis, A. (1982). The treatment of alcohol and drug abuse: A rational-emotive approach. *Rational Living*, 17, 15–24.

Ellis, A. (1991). Rational-emotive treatment of simple phobias. Special section: Prescriptive matching in psychotherapy: Psychoanalysis for simple phobias? *Psychotherapy*, 28, 452–456.

Emmelkamp, P. M., & Beens, H. (1991). Cognitive therapy with obsessive compulsive disorder: A comparative evaluation. *Behavior Research and Therapy*, 29, 293–300.

Emmelkamp, P. M., Mersch, P. P., Vissia, E., & Vanderhelm, M. (1985). Social phobia: A comparative evaluation of cognitive and behavioral interventions. *Behavior Research and Therapy*, 23, 365–369.

Eysenck, H. J. (1952). The effects of psychotherapy: An evaluation. *Journal of Consulting Psychology*, 16, 319–324.

Eysenck, H. J. (1960). *Behaviour therapy and the neuroses*. Oxford: Pergamon Press.

Eysenck, H. J. (1991). Behavioral psychotherapy. In C. E. Walker (Ed.), *Clinical psychology: Historical and research foundations* (pp. 417–442). New York: Plenum Press.

Eysenck, H. J., & Rachman, S. (1965). *Causes and cures of neurosis*. London: Routledge & Kegan Paul.

Ferster, C. B., Nurnberger, J. I., Levitt, E. B. (1962). The control of eating. *Journal of Mathetics*, 1, 87–109.

Franks, C. M. (1969a). Introduction: Behavior therapy and its pavlovian origins: Review and perspectives In C. M. Franks (Ed.), *Behavior therapy: Appraisal and status* (pp. 1–26). New York: McGraw-Hill.

Franks, C. M. (Ed.). (1969b). *Behavior therapy: Appraisal and status*. New York: McGraw-Hill.

Freeman, A., Pretzer, J., Fleming, B., & Simon, K. M. (1990). *Clinical applications of cognitive therapy*. New York: Plenum Press.

Goldiamond, I. (1965). Self-control procedures in personal behavior problems. *Psychological Reports*, 17, 851–868.

Hollon, S. D., DeRubeis, R. J., Evans, M. D., Wiemer, M. J., Garvey, M. J., Grove, W. M., & Tuason, V. B. (1992). Cognitive therapy and pharmacotherapy for depression: Singly and in combination. *Archives of General Psychiatry*, 49, 774–781.

Homme, L. E. (1965). Perspectives in psychology: XXIV. Control of coverants, the operants of the mind. *Psychological Record*, 15, 501–511.

Hunter, W. (1946). Psychology in the war. *American Psychologist*, 1, 479–481.

Jacobson, E. (1938). *Progressive relaxation*. Chicago: University of Chicago Press.

James, W. (1890). *The principles of psychology* (2 vols.). New York: Henry Holt.

James, W. (1909). *Psychology*. New York: Henry Holt.

Jones, M. C. (1924a). A laboratory study of fear: The case of Peter. *Journal of Genetic Psychology*, 31, 308–315.

Jones, M. C. (1924b). The elimination of children's fears. *Journal of Experimental Psychology*, 7, 383–390.

Kanfer, F. H. (1970). Self-regulation: Research, issues, and speculations. In C. Neuringer & J. L. Michael (Eds.), *Behavior modification and clinical psychology* (pp. 178–220). New York: Appleton-Century Crofts.

Kanfer, F. H., & Phillips, J. S. (1970). *Learning foundations of behavior therapy*. New York: Wiley.

Kanfer, F. H. (1971). The maintenance of behavior by self-generated stimuli and reinforcement. In A. Jacobs & L. B. Sachs (Eds.), *The psychology of private events* (pp. 39–59). New York: Academic Press.

Kanfer, F. H., & Karoly, P. (1972). Self-control: A behavioristic excursion into the lion's den. *Behavior Therapy*, 3, 398–416.

Kazdin, A. E. (1978). *History of behavior modification: Experimental foundations of comtemporary research*. Baltimore: University Park Press.

Kazdin, A. E. (1994). *Behavior modification in applied settings* (5th ed.). Pacific Grove, CA: Brooks/Cole.

Keefe, F. I., & Beckham, J. C. (1994). Behavioral medicine. In L. W. Craighead, W. E. Craighead, A. E. Kazdin, & M. J. Mahoney (Eds.), *Cognitive and behavioral interventions: An empirical approach to mental health problems* (pp. 197–213). Needham, MA: Allyn & Bacon.

Kelly, G. (1955). *The psychology of personal constructs*. New York: Norton.

Kuhn, T. S. (1962). *The structure of scientific revolutions*. Chicago: University of Chicago Press.

Lang, P. J. (1969). The mechanics of desensitization and the laboratory study of fear. In C. M. Franks (Ed.), *Behavior Therapy: Appraisal and status* (pp. 160–191). New York: McGraw-Hill.

Lazarus, A. A. (1958). New methods in psychotherapy: A case study. *South African Medical Journal, 32,* 660–664.

Lazarus, A. A. (1967). In support of technical eclecticism. *Psychological Reports, 21,* 415–416.

Lazarus, A. A. (1971a). Reflections on behavior therapy and its development: A point of view. *Behavior Therapy, 2,* 369–374.

Lazarus, A. A. (1971b). *Behavior therapy and beyond.* New York: McGraw-Hill.

Linehan, M. (1993). *Cognitive-behavioral treatment of borderline personality disorder.* New York: Guilford Press.

Luria, A. R. (1961). *The role of speech in the regulation of normal and abnormal behaviors.* New York: Wiley.

Mahoney, M. J. (1974). *Cognition and behavior modification.* Cambridge, MA: Ballinger.

Mahoney, M. J., & Arnkoff, D. B. (1978). Cognitive and self-control therapies. In S. L. Garfield & A. E. Bergin (Eds.), *Handbook of psychotherapy and behavior change: An empirical analysis* (2nd ed.) (pp. 689–722). New York: Wiley.

Mahoney, M. J., & Lyddon, W. J. (1988). Recent developments in cognitive approaches to counseling and psychotherapy. *The Counseling Psychologist, 16,* 190–234.

Mahoney, M. J., & Thoresen, C. E. (Eds.). (1974). *Self-control: Power to the person.* Monterey, CA: Brooks/Cole.

Masters, J. C., Burish, T. G., Hollon, S. D., & Rimm, D. C. (1987). *Behavior therapy: Techniques and empirical findings.* New York: Harcourt Brace Jovanovich.

Meichenbaum, D. (1974). *Cognitive behavior modification.* Morristown, NJ: General Learning Press.

Meichenbaum, D. (1975). Self-instructional methods. In F. H. Kanfer & A. P. Goldstein (Eds.), *Helping people change* (pp. 234–243). New York: Pergamon Press.

Meichenbaum, D. (1977). *Cognitive-behavior modification: An integrative approach.* New York: Plenum Press.

Meyers, A. W., & Craighead, W. E. (1984). Cognitive behavior therapy with children: A historical, conceptual, and organizational overview. In A. W. Meyers & W. E. Craighead (Eds.), *Cognitive behavior therapy with children* (pp. 1–17). New York: Plenum Press.

Mowrer, O. H. (1947). On the dual nature of learning—a reinterpretation of "conditioning" and "problem solving." *Harvard Educational Review, 17,* 102–148.

Mowrer, O. H. (1960a). *Learning theory and behavior.* New York: Wiley.

Mowrer, O. H. (1960b). *Learning theory and the symbolic processes.* New York: Wiley.

Mowrer, O. H., & Mowrer, W. M. (1938). Enuresis—a method for its study and treatment. *American Journal of Orthopsychiatry, 8,* 436–459.

Nezu, A. M. (1986). Efficacy of a social problem solving therapy approach for unipolar depression. *Journal of Consulting and Clinical Psychology, 54,* 196–202.

O'Leary, K. D., & O'Leary, S. G. (1977). *Classroom management: The successful use of behavior modification* (2nd ed.). New York: Pergamon Press.

O'Leary, K. D., & Wilson, G. T. (1987). *Behavior therapy: Application and outcome* (2nd ed.). Englewood Cliffs, NJ: Prentice-Hall.

Paul, G. L. (1969a). Behavior modification research: Design and tactics. In C. M. Franks (Ed.), *Behavior therapy: Appraisal and status* (pp. 29–62). New York: McGraw-Hill.

Paul, G. L. (1969b). Outcome of systematic desensitization II: Controlled investigations of individual treatment, technique variations, and current status. In C. M. Franks (Ed.), *Behavior therapy: Appraisal and status* (pp. 105–159). New York: McGraw-Hill.

Peterson, L., Sherman, D. D., & Zink, M. (1994). Applications to pediatric psychology. In L. W. Craighead, W. E. Craighead, A. E. Kazdin, & M. J. Mahoney (Eds.), *Cognitive and behavioral interventions: An empirical approach to mental health problems* (pp. 359–375). Needham, MA: Allyn & Bacon.

Pomerleau, O. F., & Brady, J. P. (1979). *Behavioral medicine: Theory and practice.* Baltimore: Williams & Wilkins.

Rehm, L. P. (1977). Self-control model of depression. *Behavior Therapy, 8,* 787–804.

Reisman, J. M. (1976). *A history of clinical psychology.* New York: Irvington.

Reymert, M. L. (Ed.). (1928). *Feelings and emotions: The Wittenberg Symposium.* Worcester, MA: Clark University Press.

Routh, D. K. (1994). *Clinical psychology since 1917: Science practice organization.* New York: Plenum Press.

Rush, A. J., Beck, A. T., Kovacs, M., & Hollon, S. D. (1977). Comparative efficacy of cognitive therapy and pharmacotherapy in the treatment of depressed outpatients. *Cognitive Therapy and Research, 1,* 17–37.

Salter, A. (1949). *Conditioned reflex therapy.* New York: Capricorn.

Shelton, T. L., Anastopoulos, A. D., & Elliott, C. H. (1991). Behavioral medicine. In. C. E. Walker (Ed.), *Clinical psychology: Historical and research foundations* (pp. 443–458). New York: Plenum Press.

Skinner, B. F. (1953). *Science and human behavior.* New York: Free Press.

Skinner, B. F. (1957). *Verbal behavior.* New York: Appleton-Century-Crofts.

Spivack, G., & Shure, M. B. (1974). *Social adjustment of young children: A cognitive approach to solving real-life problems.* San Francisco: Jossey-Bass.

Stewart, M. A. (1961). Psychotherapy by reciprocal inhibition. *American Journal of Psychiatry, 118,* 175–177.

Thoresen, C. E., & Mahoney, M. J. (1974). *Behavioral self-control.* New York: Holt, Rinehart, & Winston.

Trexler, L. A. (1973). The suicidal person and the restoration of hope. *Rational Living, 8,* 19–23.

Trimpey, J. (1989). *The small book.* New York: Delacorte Press.

Turner, S. M., Calhoun, K. S., & Adams, H. E. (Eds.). (1992). *Handbood of clinical behavior therapy.* New York: Wiley.

Ullmann, L. P., & Krasner, L. (Eds.). (1965). *Case studies in behavior modification.* New York: Holt, Rinehart, & Winston.

Vygotsky, L. (1962). *Thought and language.* New York: Wiley.

Watson, J. B. (1913). Psychology as the behaviorist views it. *Psychological Review, 20,* 158–177.

Watson, J. B. (1914). *Behavior: An introduction to comparative psychology.* New York: Henry Holt.

Watson, J. B. (1919). *Psychology from the standpoint of a behaviorist.* Philadelphia: Lippincott.

Watson, J. B., & Rayner, R. (1920). Conditioned emotional reactions. *Journal of Experimental Psychology, 3,* 1–14.

Wolpe, J. (1958). *Psychotherapy by reciprocal inhibition.* Stanford, CA: Stanford University Press.

Yates, A. J. (1970). *Behavior therapy.* New York: Wiley.

5
Behavior Therapy in Practice

Kim T. Mueser
Robert P. Liberman

Behavior therapy is first and foremost an empirically based, operational approach to understanding and treating psychological/psychiatric disorders. Intervention is problem focused, goal directed, and oriented toward the future. Psychopathology and associated functional impairments of clients are behaviorally specified, measured, monitored, and analyzed in terms of their environmental determinants. Then operationalized goals are set and interventions are designed to improve the frequency, quality, or context of clients' adaptive functioning. Goal setting in behavior therapy is multimodal (Lazarus, 1976, 1981); that is, therapeutic objectives are formulated in all measurable and relevant spheres of human experience, including affect, sensory experience, imagery, cognition, instrumental skills, interpersonal relationships, and psychophysiology.

Behavior therapy is not a collection of techniques to be followed, like recipes, in a rote manner for designated disorders or problems. Rather, each client requires a behavioral analysis of his or her problems, tailored to the person's assets, deficits, excesses, values, culture, and environmental resources. The analysis of behavior is firmly entrenched in the systematic, objective measurement of clinical variables of interest; in fact, adherence to the specification of problems and goals is the most important

characteristic that distinguishes behavior therapy from other models of psychotherapy. Behavioral analysis provides guidelines for assessing the nature, severity, and frequency of targeted problems, and for teasing apart the functional relationships between the client's behavior and its environmental antecedents and consequences.

The behavior therapist and his or her client mutually agree on ways to arrange the immediate therapeutic and natural environments to bring about favorable changes in the client's functioning. Behavior therapists often attempt to influence behavior by changing the environment, especially the interpersonal milieu of the client, which may require interventions carried out with the mediation of relatives, teachers, friends, and natural support groups. Thus, in many cases, behavior therapy involves "environmental engineering," in which therapeutic gains result as a function of changes in the interaction between the client and a responsive environment.

Behavior therapists encourage their clients to take an active role in modifying their environments and the contingencies of reinforcement that impinge on them. Behavior and the environment influence each other in a reciprocal fashion. For example, aggressive behavior induces hostility in others, which, in turn, evokes increased aggression. A child whose tantrums or whining gain attention and other desired ends from parents will learn to use these behaviors to achieve similar demands in the future. Parents may buy momentary relief by giving in to tantrums or whining, thereby inadvertently reinforcing this behavior and increasing the chances that it will occur again.

Behavior therapy can be best viewed as an empirical strategy for analyzing and treating clinical problems, utilizing principles of human learning. The principles of learning, derived from almost a century of experimental psychology, are covered in Chapter 4. Clinicians who wish to embrace the behavioral approach must answer the four questions posed in Table 5.1, in conjunction with the client, relatives, and other caregivers. These questions are raised repeatedly throughout the course of treatment in recurring cycles, at first tentatively and more definitely later as information accrues and progress occurs. Because biological as well as personal and environmental variables determine clinical problems, and because both somatic and behavior therapies emerge from a

common empirical framework for validating treatments, behavior therapists embrace the broad *biopsychosocial* model of psychopathology.

A major focus of behavior therapy is the systematic provision of learning experiences designed to modify maladaptive behavior patterns. For example, instead of avoiding feared situations, phobic persons learn how to expose themselves gradually, either in imagery or in real life, to these situations, and not to leave until the anxiety abates. Socially withdrawn schizophrenic clients are provided with models who demonstrate, in carefully annotated fashion, how to initiate social contacts and maintain conversations, and these clients are then engaged in practice and real conversations to build up their repertoires of social skills. The parents of a hyperactive child are taught how to use tangible and social reinforcers to increase the attention span of their child in study and play situations. Clients who are treated behaviorally for depression are instructed to carry out graded assignments to achieve goals in their instrumental and social roles, thereby learning how to restructure maladaptive cognitions, ob-

---

TABLE 5.1. Questions to be Answered in the Behavioral Analysis of Clinical Problems

1. *What are the problems and goals for therapy?*
   • Assess the client's assets and deficits of adaptive behavior and excesses of maladaptive behavior.
   • Evaluate whether the client's problems are related to inappropriate timing or context of behavioral responses.
   • Consider the full range of objective, subjective, affective, social, and cognitive responses when assessing problems and establishing goals.
2. *How can progress be measured and monitored?*
   • Specify each problem and goal in terms of behavior so that it can be measured and monitored.
   • Consider the frequency, duration, form, latency, or context in which each behavior occurs.
   • Monitor change in the behaviors over the course of treatment and either terminate treatment or modify the intervention based on changes (or lack of change) in the behaviors.
3. *What environmental contingencies are maintaining the problem?*
   • Evaluate the functional relationship between clinical problems and their environmental antecedents (precipitants or triggering stimuli) and consequences (reinforcers).
   • Determine which (if any) social and instrumental contingencies need to be modified for a successful outcome.
4. *Which interventions are more likely to be effective?*
   • Address this question only after the first three questions have been answered.
   • Consider whether interventions at the level of the individual, group, couple, family, or environmental context have the greatest promise.
   • Select interventions based on (1) empirical support from past research on the treatment, (2) evidence that similar treatments have been efficacious with similar problems, and (3) consideration of which environmental contingencies appear to be maintaining the maladaptive behaviors.

tain reinforcement, and increase environmental mastery. The behavior therapist's task is to optimize the social, emotional, and instrumental learning or relearning of the client in his or her natural environments.

BASIC ASSUMPTIONS

Behavior therapy represents an empirically based and operational approach that harnesses principles of human learning with a sound therapeutic alliance to overcome the impairments and disabilities associated with mental disorders. More often than not, the treatment of signs and symptoms of the disorder is indirect rather than direct. Positive goals are targeted that strengthen the individual's adaptive repertoire, thereby protecting the person from stress-related or biologically induced symptoms. A good example is the behavior modification that has revolutionized the care and treatment of mentally retarded and autism-disordered persons, wherein educational programming of a highly structured type is employed to teach self-care and communication skills that reduce the individual's handicap without changing the underlying central nervous system pathology.

Some of the core assumptions underlying behavior therapy include the following:

1. Abnormal behavior, even that stemming from biological disturbances, can be favorably influenced by therapeutic arrangements of an individual's interaction with his or her environment.
2. The same principles of learning govern the maintenance of abnormal and normal behavior and thus can be utilized for therapeutic gain. Behavior therapy is atheoretical with respect to the origins of abnormal behavior. Abnormal behavior can be either learned or determined by psychobiological vulnerabilities. Regardless of the etiology, however, new and more adaptive behaviors can be taught to minimize or eliminate dysfunctional behaviors.
3. Behavioral assessment focuses on the current determinants of behavior rather than on the post hoc analysis of possible historical antecedents.
4. Specificity is the hallmark of behavioral assessment and treatment. Thus, it is assumed that more useful clinical information is obtained by learning what clients do in a situation rather than what they say about themselves.
5. Treatment strategies are individually tailored to the varied needs, resources, and assets of different clients.
6. Instrumental and interpersonal behaviors are changed more readily than cognitions and affective experiences. Treatment usually aims first at changing overt behavior, with the expectation that cognitive and affective changes will follow.
7. Therapeutic interventions may result in unintended side effects, which are not necessarily adverse or reflective of symptom substitution. Usually, ripple effects of treatment represent positive outcomes.
8. Behavior therapy reflects an applied science approach to clinical problems. Hence, it is constantly developing new techniques, resulting in measurable and replicable methods and outcomes that rest on the experimental evaluation of treatment methods.
9. Behavior therapy focuses on the broad, multimodal phenomenology of human experience, not just on overt, observable behaviors. Hence, affect, cognition, imagery, and biological processes (e.g., heart rate or muscle tension) are all proper targets for intervention.
10. Behavioral interventions are not aimed at creating insight but rather at changing behaviors related to adaptive functioning. Insight is more likely to *follow* behavior change than to precede it.

TREATMENT PLANNING

The basic assumptions outlined above are incorporated into a general framework for conducting a comprehensive assessment and for selecting and using behavior therapy techniques. This framework is summarized in Table 5.2. It is important to note, however, that assessment does not proceed in a linear fashion, nor is it confined to the initial period of evaluation. Behavioral assessment and analysis are overlapping, reciprocal, recurring procedures that continue throughout treatment. Behavioral assessment and therapy are inextricably linked

---

TABLE 5.2. Outline of the Behavioral Approach to History Taking, Assessment, and Therapy

I. Problem identification
   A. Define and translate problems and goals into behavioral terms, using as dimensions the frequency, intensity, duration, form or quality, and appropriateness of the context.
   B. Develop a multimodal inventory of the problems and goals in which all levels of human behavioral expression and experience are covered:
      • Social affiliative behavior
      • Instrumental behavior
      • Activities of daily living
      • Affects
      • Cognitions
   C. Determine behavioral deficits: Which behaviors need to be initiated, increased in frequency, or strengthened in form?
   D. Determine behavioral excesses: Which behaviors need to be terminated, decreased in frequency, or altered in form?
   E. Determine behavioral assets: Consider strengths in multimodal terms.
   F. Determine whether interfering symptoms or side effects can be better controlled through pharmacotherapy.
II. Sources of assessment
   A. Self-report questionnaires and inventories (e.g., Fear Survey, Target Complaint Scale, Beck Depression Inventory, Independent Living Skills Survey)
   B. Interviews (e.g., Social Behavior Assessment Schedule, Reinforcement Survey)
   C. Self-monitoring (e.g., diaries, logs)
   D. Behavioral observation (e.g., naturalistic and role playing)
   E. Permanent products of behavioral outcomes
   F. Biological (e.g., heart rate, biofeedback, physical disabilities, drug–behavior interactions)
   G. Sociocultural (e.g., recent changes in milieu or relationships, values and norms, or social network and social support)
III. Behavior analysis of conditions maintaining the problems in living
   A. Antecedents of problems
      • Where, when, with whom?
      • What life events and stressors, both episodic and ambient, may be triggering or influencing problems and relapse?
      • Are symptoms side effects of drugs or cognitive impairments interfering with functions?
   B. Consequences of problem behaviors
      • What would happen if the problems were ignored? Role of sympathy, nurturance, attention, anger, coercion by others?
      • What reinforcers or benefits would the patient gain or lose if the problems were diminished?
   C. Self-motivation
      • Does the patient acknowledge problems and desire change?
      • Does verbal behavior match follow-through in participation in treatment and homework?
IV. Goal setting
   A. Shift focus from problems to goals as soon as possible.
   B. Make sure that goals are:
      • Specific and clear.
      • Chosen or endorsed by patient and significant others.
      • Short term linked to long term.
      • Frequently occurring.
      • Salient and functional.
      • Attainable.

TABLE 5.2. *Continued*

V. C. Include among goals selection of living, working, and learning environments as well as skills to be acquired for adaptation to environments.
  D. Engage patient actively in goal setting.
    • Offer rationales.
    • Solicit options and pros and cons.
    • Provide visual displays.
    • Check for acceptance and understanding.
V. Resource assessment
  A. What resources are available or mobilizable to assist patient in:
    • Learning skills?
    • Using skills?
    • Compensating for skill deficits?
    • Managing symptoms or preventing relapse?
  B. What are the socioenvironmental strengths and deficits in terms of achieving rehabilitation goals?
  C. What resources can be developed to motivate and maintain progress toward rehabilitation goals?
    • Peoples
    • Transportation
    • Places
    • Activities
    • Telephone and mail
    • Money
    • Reinforcement survey
VI. Planning rehabilitation
  A. Delineate overall and specific goals (e.g., monthly, yearly).
  B. Establish long-term (e.g., monthly, yearly) and short-term (e.g., daily, weekly) goals.
  C. Prioritize skills to be acquired and resources to be mobilized.
  D. Set time lines.
  E. Coordinate agency and natural supports and interventions (e.g., pharmacotherapy, case management).
  F. Identify personnel responsible for interventions and liaison.
VII. Monitoring progress
  A. Track progress toward goals rather than persistence of problems.
  B. Ensure that measures are practical, relevant, and convenient.
  C. Involve patient and significant others in recording and acknowledging progress.
  D. Utilize the following methods of ongoing assessment:
    • Goal attainment
    • Frequency counts
    • Interval ratings
    • Intensity ratings
    • Permanent products
VIII. Behavior therapy tactics
  A. Develop a trusting, caring, warm, and mutually respectful therapeutic alliance that serves as the foundation and lever for many of the behavioral techniques.
  B. Develop a time-limited treatment program.
  C. Use behavioral rehearsal or role playing to simulate real-world problem situations.
  D. Prompt, cue, signal, and coach patient to make improvements.
  E. Give homework assignments.
  F. Reinforce small, discrete steps in adaptive directions.
  G. Use therapeutic instructions and promote favorable expectations of the outcome.
  H. Have patient repeatedly practice the desired behavior.
  I. Feed back information on behavioral changes to patient, and periodically reevaluate progress and reset goals.
  J. Reinforce progress and deemphasize reversals.
  K. Generalize gains to the natural environment by involving family members and other aspects of the real world.

in clinical decision making, intervention, and treatment evaluation.

THE STANCE OF THE BEHAVIOR THERAPIST

The behavior therapist assumes a highly directive stance throughout the course of intervention, taking major responsibility for the planning and structure of treatment sessions. The directive stance of behavior therapy is quite similar to that of cognitive therapy approaches (e.g., Beck, Rush, Shaw, & Emery, 1979; Ellis & Harper, 1975). This stance differs greatly from that of psychodynamic and client-centered approaches, in which the direction of treatment sessions is determined mainly by the client and little planning takes place from one session to the next. Despite the highly directive nature of behavior therapy, the actual goals of treatment are established collaboratively between the therapist and client, with periodic reviews conducted to evaluate progress toward these goals, to set new goals, and to decide when therapy has produced maximum gains.

A critical element of behavior therapy is the importance attached to the client's completion of homework assignments to practice in the real world skills that are taught in the session. In order to teach new behaviors that will facilitate more adaptive functioning, behaviors must be generalized through either practice or prompting in the natural environment. Thus, behavior therapy is directive with respect to both guiding the client in the session and planning and monitoring the generalization of new behaviors outside of the session. Positive expectations for active participation, practice, and change are communicated clearly to the client early in treatment.

As part of the directive stance, the behavior therapist assumes major responsibility for ensuring a positive outcome of treatment, and eschews either blaming the client or interpreting the client's behavior when favorable outcomes are not achieved. Rather than viewing failures to improve as due to client resistance, the behavior therapist returns to the functional analysis of the problem with the new evidence in hand and reformulates a plan of intervention. As clients become increasingly able over the course of treatment to formulate goals and plans for achieving them, the behavior therapist reduces his or her level of direction accordingly, gradually fading out toward the termination of therapy.

ISSUES OF TRAINING AND SUPERVISION

Adequate training in behavior therapy requires that the therapist have a thorough understanding of major theories of learning (e.g., classical conditioning, operant conditioning, social learning), finely honed interpersonal skills, the ability to develop and sustain a therapeutic alliance, and a basic knowledge of psychopathology. Many of the philosophical underpinnings of behavior therapy are reflected in the approach taken to training and supervising therapists. Goals of training are explicitly established, and progress toward these goals is monitored on a routine basis. Training sessions are used initially to review basic principles, then to demonstrate targeted skills, and finally to engage the trainee in rehearsing the skills in simulated situations. The trainee then practices these skills with real clients (often videotaping or audiotaping the session) and receives feedback regarding his or her performance. Therapeutic difficulties are often enacted in role plays in supervisory sessions and not just talked about. This approach provides the supervisor with specific information about the trainee's behavior in the session and gives trainees the opportunity to try out different strategies for managing problems that arise in therapy.

As in behavior therapy proper, training and supervision place a premium on behavioral specificity in goal setting, evaluation, and feedback. In many of the specific areas in which behavior therapy has been successfully applied, behaviorally anchored therapist competency scales have been developed, and are used to teach and monitor therapist competence (e.g., exposure and response prevention methods for treatment of obsessive-compulsive disorder, social skills training, behavioral family therapy).

These scales can be useful both for specifying the critical elements of an intervention and for providing behaviorally specific feedback to therapists about their clinical behavior.

BEHAVIOR THERAPY FOR PSYCHIATRIC DISORDERS

The growth of the behavior therapy field over the past 30 years has been extraordinary. Professional organizations at the state, national, and international levels are devoted to dissemination, training, and research in behavior therapy. In recent decades, there has been an exponential rise in the number of professional journals, articles, and books on behavior therapy. Furthermore, in line with the strong empirical foundations of behavior therapy, numerous research grants have been awarded to examine the efficacy of behavioral interventions. The growth in the application of behavior therapy to a broad range of clinical problems and disorders over the past three decades is illustrated in Table 5.3.

The maturity of the field is reflected in the diversity of its methodological scope and the evolution of new techniques through empirical study. Whereas systematic desensitization, aversion therapy, and token economy were the principal behavior therapies two decades ago, they have now been supplanted by new techniques such as overcorrection, contingency contracting, behavior marital and family therapy, cognitive-behavior methods, habit reversal, in vivo exposure and response prevention, anxiety management training, and social skills training. The scope of behavior therapy has been broadened substantially in the past decade by the incorporation of operationalized methods for self-monitoring of thoughts and other cognitive events, comprising a field termed *cognitive-behavior therapy*. Cognitive-behavior therapy has yielded techniques for measuring and modifying self-evaluations, self-statements, values, standards for behavior, and self-reinforcement. These developments have promoted self-management, self-control procedures, and self-directed behavior change. Advances in cognitive-behavior therapy recognize the ways that affects and cognitions can modulate or influence behavior and vice versa.

One of the most salient indications of the increased impact of this form of treatment is the growth in public knowledge regarding concepts rooted in behavioral analysis and therapy. Numerous self-help books are based on core principles of behavior therapy. A veritable explosion of popular psychology books has appeared, based on such behavioral principles as positive reinforcement and assertion training; for example, *Toilet Training in Less Than a Day* (Azrin, 1976), *Effective Parents, Responsible Children* (Eimers & Aitchison, 1977), *Living with Children: New Methods for Parents and Teachers* (Patterson & Gullian, 1971), *The Assertive Woman* (Phelps & Austin, 1975), *Your Perfect Right* (Alberti & Emmons, 1973), and *The One Minute Manager* (Blanchard & Johnson, 1987) have inseminated behavioral learning principles into the larger society. There is now an almost universal acceptance that a critical determinant of social behavior is the availability of good role models for the child and adolescent, an understanding that is rooted in social learning theory that was explicated by Bandura (1969) and others in the 1960s.

Considering the broad scope of behavior therapy, including its use in the treatment of psychopathology, behavioral medicine, education, and business, it would be impossible to review here its many applications. Therefore, we provide a brief, selective review of the efficacy of behavior therapy for some of the psychiatric disorders for which behavioral treatment is most clearly the psychosocial treatment of choice.

Anxiety Disorders

Morbid anxiety is one of the most ubiquitous psychological symptoms. Much of the earliest work in behavior therapy addressed the problem of anxiety, from studies on experimentally induced phobias to the development of the first effective intervention for anxiety, Wolpe's systematic desensitization. Behavior therapy

TABLE 5.3. Expansion of the Scope of Behavior Therapy to Encompass a Wider Spectrum of Clinical Problems and Disorders, as Shown by the Number of Articles on Behaviorism, Published during Selected Years

	1964	1968	1970	1972	1975	1980	1983	1986	1989	1992
Sexual deviations	2	1	10	6	4	8	3	3	3	1
Phobias	1	2	10	7	13	14	26	28	39	11
Alcoholism	1	3	2	8	3	4	3	4	2	3
Eating disorder	1	1	3	4	5	11	9	12	10	6
Enuresis, encopresis	1	0	4	6	5	1	4	4	8	5
Speech disorder	1	6	1	2	1	1	2	4	5	1
Sleep disorder	1	0	2	1	3	4	5	3	14	3
Childhood autism		3	0	2	3	5	7	5	6	5
Depression		1	2	3	3	6	8	12	4	5
Pain		1	0	0	2	3	7	8	11	1
Drug addiction		1	1	3	2	0	0	1	1	2
Sexual dysfunction		1	1	2	0	3	2	3	1	0
Neurodermatitis		1	0	1	0	0	0	0	0	0
Adult psychosis		1	8	6	7	2	1	3	6	7
Gastrointestinal symptoms		1	3	2	2	1	0	0	5	7
Headache		2	0	2	3	5	2	9	5	
Obsessive-compulsive disorder		3	7	5	7	9	6	10	7	
Giles de la Tourette syndrome		1	0	0	0	1	0	2	2	
Hysterical conversion		1	1	2	2	0	1	0	0	
Asthma		1	1	0	1	0	0	2	5	
Mental retardation				4	0	26	13	9	24	10
Tics				1	0	1	1	1	2	0
Frequency of urination				1	1	1	1	0	4	4
Rage and crying				4	2	0	0	0	2	2
Muscle spasm				1	1	0	1	0	2	0
Vascular symptoms					2	1	0	2	9	4
Coprophagia and pica					1	0	0	1	1	1
Social deficits					2	13	6	6	1	2
Child behavior problems					4	11	15	7	15	27
Marital conflict					4	2	2	3	1	1
Anxiety						6	8	7	10	11
Tobacco dependence						6	7	8	11	4
Diabetes						1	1	1	5	5
Spina bifida						1	1	0	0	0
Myopia						2	0		0	2
Cancer						1	2		2	6
Posttraumatic stress disorder							5		8	4
Panic disorder							8		8	2
Herpes							1		0	0
Tinnitus							1		1	1

publications have focused more on the reduction of anxiety than on any other clinical problem.

The sine qua non of successful behavioral treatment of anxiety disorders is the *exposure* of clients to the feared and avoided situations or stimuli. Consequently, a major expectation of clients receiving behavior therapy for anxiety is that they be willing to participate in exposure-based intervention and to complete homework assignments involving self-exposure. Although such exposure-based treatment may result in some short-term discomfort, the long-term benefits are considerable, and great efforts are made to explain to clients that fear can be *un*learned, just as it was learned. Behavioral treatments for specific anxiety disorders are briefly described below.

Agoraphobia

Behavioral treatment of agoraphobia focuses on exposure of the client that is carried out in vivo or indirectly, as through imagery or by viewing models who are facing the feared situation (Mathews, Gelder, & Johnston, 1981). Intensive exposure carried out in massed practice sessions, termed *flooding*, is more effective in reducing fear quickly, but spaced practice and more deliberate self-pacing of exposure may result in more durable treatment gains.

Studies have demonstrated the superiority of direct, in vivo exposure for the treatment of agoraphobia to indirect forms such as systematic desensitization, in which the client uses deep muscle relaxation while imagining the feared situations. Exposure sessions are optimally applied for 2 to 4 hours, often in crowded, busy shopping malls, with the therapist, spouse, or other facilitator withdrawing contact and support once the person has entered the anxiety-provoking situation. In learning theory, *extinction* of the anxiety takes place as the agoraphobic person fails to encounter the dreaded consequences of being in the feared situation (e.g., loss of control, death). In each successive experience of exposure, the anxiety diminishes more and more. Recent studies have found that self-paced exposure, facilitated by instructional manuals or computer instruction, can be as effective as therapist-mediated exposure. The duration of treatment for agoraphobia varies, depending on the severity of the symptoms and the rate of symptom improvement, but it usually lasts at least for several months and in rare cases can extend to over a year.

Panic Disorder

Traditionally, behavior therapists have utilized relaxation techniques and exposure exercises to treat the anticipatory anxiety and agoraphobic avoidance that often accompany panic disorder.

Recent theoretical advances in the conceptualization of panic disorder from a cognitive-behavioral perspective (Barlow, 1988; Clark, 1986) have spawned the development of interventions directly targeting the panic attacks themselves.

Barlow and Craske (1991) have recently developed a comprehensive cognitive-behavioral treatment program for panic disorder. The program consists of education about the etiology and phenomenology of panic, training in controlling breathing techniques, cognitive restructuring, systematic exposure to somatic cues that trigger panic attacks, and in vivo exposure to situations that produce panic. The treatment program is usually provided over a 15-week period with weekly 1-hour treatment sessions. In one controlled study, Barlow and his colleagues found the cognitive-behavioral treatment to be effective for 85% of clients with panic disorder (Barlow, Craske, Cerny, & Klosko, 1989), with treatment gains maintained at a 2-year follow-up (Craske, Brown, & Barlow, 1991). Furthermore, in another controlled study, this intervention was found to be more effective than alprazolam (Klosko, Barlow, Tassinari, & Cerny, 1990), the most common drug used to treat panic disorder. In addition to the evidence supporting cognitive-behavioral approaches to panic disorder, there is support for the efficacy of more cognitively based treatment approaches (e.g., Beck, Sokol, Clark, Berchick, & Wright, 1992).

Social Phobia

Treatment of the symptoms of social phobia, which is characterized by fear and avoidance of social situations such as eating in front of others or public speaking, has been the focus of extensive research in behavior therapy. Similar to agoraphobia, research points to exposure as a guiding therapeutic principle in the behavioral treatment of social phobia (Biran & Wilson, 1981; Emmelkamp, Mersch, Vissia, & Van der Helm, 1985), although other behavioral or cognitive methods may further enhance the treatment response (Butler, Cullington, Murphy, Amies, & Gelder, 1984; Mattick, Peters, & Clarke, 1989). For example, social skills training—which incorporates exposure in a package that also includes modeling, behavioral rehearsal, social reinforcement, and coaching of improved verbal and nonverbal communication—may be a useful adjunct for socially phobic clients, who often have deficits in conversational and emotional expression (e.g., Falloon, Lloyd, & Harpin, 1981).

Avoidance of public speaking has been effectively treated with systematic desensitization and exposure, in which the anxious individual is encouraged to practice speaking before a supportive audience or with video feedback. Practice dating has also been found to be effective in controlled studies for persons with social anxiety who avoid dating, meeting strangers, or going to parties. As exposure to anxiety-evoking social situations of necessity requires some practice of interpersonal skills and communication, it is almost impossible to separate the relative contributions of exposure per se and skills training to the overall therapeutic impact.

A recent advance in the cognitive-behavioral treatment of social phobia has been the development and validation of a standardized treatment approach. In several studies, Heimberg and his colleagues have shown that a group-based cognitive-behavioral intervention, provided over 12 weeks, substantially improved the symptoms of social phobia clients (Heimberg, Becker, Goldfinger, & Vermilyea, 1985; Heimberg et al., 1990). In sum, most cases of social phobia can be effectively treated by behavior therapy, even without adjunctive psychotropic medication.

Simple Phobia

The psychological literature is replete with controlled studies of clients who have benefited from systematic desensitization, social modeling, and/or in vivo exposure for their fears of snakes, spiders, heights, or closed spaces (Borden, 1992). There is compelling evidence that behavior therapy can cure the vast majority of simple phobias in a relatively short-term course of treatment, usually not exceeding several months.

Obsessive-Compulsive Disorder (OCD)

The same exposure principle applies to patients with OCD as to those with phobias. Clients with unwanted ruminations and rituals that are evoked by stimuli—having concrete or symbolic significance of danger, contamination, or catastrophe—are exposed in behavior therapy to the key stimuli and encouraged to refrain (or prevented) from performing activities aimed at avoiding or escaping from the aversive stimuli (*response prevention*). Compulsive rituals usually succeed, albeit temporarily, in reducing the discomfort cued by the evoking stimuli; hence preventing rituals leads to an initial increase in anxiety. If response prevention and exposure are maintained for extended periods of time (e.g., 2 hours per day for several weeks), habituation occurs and greater comfort ensues.

The key factor in the successful treatment of OCD is engaging the client in a motivated and self-directed therapeutic process. Without substantial, active participation by the client in treatment, good outcomes are unlikely. There are several motivational obstacles facing the therapist and client with OCD: (1) the symptoms, in lesser frequency or severity, may be adaptive and reinforced in work, family, and religious settings; (2) the symptoms often provide the client with safety signals and modulate the intrusion of anxiety into daily life; (3) OCD can provide pseudocompensation for long-standing social skills deficits, enabling clients to maintain social relationships or even to dominate them.

Motivation can be aided by having clients define precisely their evoking stimuli and behavior patterns of avoidance and escape; set specific, constructive goals and time frames for change; articulate the benefits (and disincentives) anticipated from therapeutic improvement; agree to daily practice and determine how their schedules can accommodate the intensive exposure periods required for improvement; and recruit relatives or friends as cotherapists to assist in carrying out treatment and reinforcing progress.

Extensive research over the past two decades supports the short-term and long-term efficacy of exposure and response prevention for OCD (Foa, Steketee, & Ozarow, 1985), with little evidence supporting the efficacy of other psychosocial interventions for the disorder. Despite these positive findings, however, a substantial proportion of OCD clients experience minimal benefit from behavior therapy, and it is difficult to engage many others in the treatment. OCD clients with bizarre delusions or strong beliefs in the reality of their obsessions appear to be less responsive to behavioral intervention. There is some indication that the addition of cognitive therapy may help to improve the outcomes of some cases of OCD (Salkovskis & Warwick, 1985). By initially taking serotonin reuptake inhibitors (e.g., fluoxetine, clomipramine), many clients can obtain enough symptom relief to permit them to embark comfortably on a more definitive course of exposure with response prevention (Munford, Hand, & Liberman, 1993).

Generalized Anxiety Disorder (GAD)

A thorough behavioral analysis, investigating the variations in anxiety associated with time of day, personal contacts, stressors, and other environmental stimuli, will usually suggest specific events or themes that elicit the anxiety in clients thought to have GAD. The evoking stimuli often are symbolic or covert, as in fear of illness, death, desertion, separation, or responsibility. GAD may be associated with advancement in social or work relationships and responsibilities that present challenges not previously encountered by the individual. When a person lacks the adaptive behavior necessary to manage new situations or challenges, "free-floating" anxiety ensues.

Behavioral treatment for GAD requires a combination of anxiety management and social skills training. Anxiety management training provides repeated learning trials wherein the patient switches imagery back and forth between the challenging situation or theme and pleasant scenes, coping scenes, mastery scenes, or relaxation. Practice is extended into the home and other natural settings until the individual is able to cope with the new challenge.

Coping self-talk is also introduced that promotes a more realistic engagement with the life situation. Social skills training enables the person to actively shape the interpersonal challenges that are being faced with increasing experiences of success. A vast literature on behavioral treatments for GAD supports the efficacy of this approach (Barlow, 1988; Rapee, 1991).

Posttraumatic Stress Disorder (PTSD)

Controlled research on the treatment of PTSD has lagged behind the interest in the prevalence and etiology of this disorder. As studies suggested that the extent of exposure to the traumatic experience was causally related to the development of the syndrome, it was reasonable to assess the therapeutic benefit from imagery-based reexposure to the trauma. Exposure was the primary ingredient of abreaction for combat-related disorders that were so frequent during and after the two world wars.

Over the past decade, numerous single case studies and several controlled group studies have documented the efficacy of 2–3 months of imaginal exposure treatment of PTSD following combat, rape, assault, accidents, and natural disasters (Foa, Rothbaum, Riggs, & Murdock, 1991; Keane, Fairbank, Caddell, & Zimering, 1989). An alternative behavioral approach to the treatment of PTSD has been teaching coping strategies for the management of anxiety and the other symptoms of the disorder (e.g., intrusive memories, flashbacks, heightened physiological arousal, avoidance of stimuli that trigger recall of the traumatic event). Two controlled studies of PTSD in rape victims support the efficacy of anxiety management treatment (Foa et al., 1991; Resick, Jordan, Girelli, Hutter, & Marhoefer-Dvorak, 1988).

WHO BENEFITS FROM BEHAVIOR THERAPY? Strong evidence is not available regarding which clients with anxiety disorders are most likely to improve with behavior therapy. Because the core manifestation of anxiety disorders is avoidance, and because the common active ingredient of behavioral treatments is exposure to the feared stimuli, clients whose symptoms are so severe that they refuse any attempts at exposure, including systematic desensitization, may be poor responders to treatment. Clinical folklore suggests that the targeted use of antianxiety drugs, with gradual tapering of the dose, may facilitate the engagement of patients in behavioral treatment, but data on this form of therapy are not available.

A second consideration in predicting who will benefit from behavior therapy for anxiety disorders involves secondary gain. Clients with prominent anxiety often inadvertently receive strong reinforcement from their family and friends, which can maintain the anxiety and the sick role and thwart effective treatment. Any of the anxiety disorders can lead to the avoidance of work, family responsibilities, and the maintenance of independent living skills. For clients whose motivation for treatment and change toward autonomy is enmeshed in family relationships and contingencies of reinforcement, adding behavioral family therapy to the treatment plan may confer benefits (Liberman, 1992).

OVERLAP WITH OTHER TREATMENT APPROACHES. There is strong overlap between behavioral and cognitive treatments for anxiety disorders, and many clinicians do not draw a distinction between the approaches, identifying themselves as having a "cognitive-behavioral" orientation. There appears to be little overlap between behavior therapy and other psychotherapeutic approaches to anxiety disorders, with the exception of the treatment of PTSD. Horowitz (1986), working within a psychodynamic framework, emphasizes the gradual exposure of clients with PTSD to traumatic stimuli, similar to imaginal exposure in behavior therapy.

Affective Disorders

Behavior therapy has not been systematically applied to bipolar disorders or psychotic depression, except for initial promising reports of the effectiveness of behavioral family management. However, a large literature has accumulated on the behavioral treatment of major depression and dysthymia. In most clinical applications of behavior therapy to depression, a multimodal approach is used that combines cognitive procedures with social skills training, graded behavioral assignments and practice, and reinforcement of adaptive behavior (Harpin, Liberman, Marks, & Stern, 1982). Even a clearly demarcated therapeutic procedure, such as cognitive-behavior therapy, comprises various components that make it broad spectrum rather than unidimensional.

Although in clinical practice the behavioral treatment of depression is multimodal, a number of different psychological models of depression have been proposed that have served to guide the development of interventions. Two of the most prominent models of depression are the *cognitive model* and the *social skills model*.

Cognitive-Behavioral Treatment

The cognitive model has been most extensively formulated by Beck and his colleagues (Beck et al., 1979). The model posits that depression arises from the client's inability to draw logical inferences about the world due to cognitive distortions (e.g., the person may overgeneralize based on too little information or selective attention to negative information). Interventions are designed to counteract these cognitive distortions through graded behavioral assignments that will yield success experiences; Socratic-type inquiries that aim to teach clients how to identify and monitor their dysfunctional and automatic thoughts; recognition of the connections among thoughts, emotions, and behavior; and identification and alteration of dysfunctional premises that predispose them to distort and negatively evaluate life events.

Social Skill Training

The social skills model of depression suggests that depression arises when clients are unable to interact successfully with others and achieve their instrumental and affiliative needs (e.g., Becker, Heimberg, & Bellack, 1987). Social skills training proceeds through a series of steps that require an active-directive therapist using

TABLE 5.4. Social Skills Competency Checklist of Therapist-Trainer Behaviors

1. Actively helps the patient in setting and eliciting specific interpersonal goals.
2. Promotes favorable expectations, a therapeutic orientation, and motivation before role playing begins.
3. Assists the patient in building possible scenes in terms of the following questions: "What emotion or communication?" "Who is the interpersonal target?" "Where and when?"
4. Structures the role playing by setting the scene and assigning roles to patient and surrogates.
5. Engages the patient in behavioral rehearsal—getting the patient to role-play with others.
6. Uses self or other group members in modeling more appropriate alternatives for the patient.
7. Prompts and cues the patient during role playing.
8. Uses an active style of training by closely monitoring and supporting the patient.
9. Gives the patient positive feedback on specific verbal and nonverbal behavioral skills.
10. Identifies the patient's specific verbal and nonverbal behavioral deficits or excesses and suggests constructive alternatives.
11. Ignores or suppresses inappropriate and interfering behaviors.
12. Shapes behavioral improvements in small, attainable increments.
13. Solicits from the patient or suggests an alternative behavior for a problem situation that can be used and practiced during behavioral rehearsal or role playing.
14. Evaluates deficits in social perception and problem solving and remedies them.
15. Gives specific attainable and functional homework assignments.

the competencies outlined in Table 5.4. The therapist, in concert with the client, pinpoints problematic interpersonal situations, sets specific goals for improving the outcomes of these situations, instructs and coaches the client in making verbal and nonverbal behavioral improvements, offers modeling of adaptive behaviors, engages the client in behavioral rehearsal; and provides feedback, social reinforcement, and homework assignments.

Skills training often focuses on remedying the interpersonal deficits common to persons who are vulnerable to depression, such as being able to assert one's needs, refuse unreasonable requests, and delegate responsibilities to others. Treatment can be offered in group or individual therapy with weekly sessions for 3 months followed by six to eight booster or reinforcement sessions spread out over a 6-month period. Training is provided in the situation-specific contexts of interactions with strangers, friends, relatives, and coworkers. Social deficiencies are targeted and introduced for training in a stepwise, hierarchical fashion, with easier situations handled first. Training in positive assertion emphasizes giving compliments, expressing affection, offering approval, and making apologies. Negative assertion requires the learning of such skills as expressing displeasure and standing up for one's rights.

Teaching includes coaching and instruction in the appropriate context and timing of communicating with others, as well as accurate social perception. The latter requires clients to learn the social meaning of cues, to be empathic with others, and to be able to predict interpersonal consequences. A key element in social skills training, which is also part of cognitive-behavior therapy, involves teaching clients to evaluate their own social behavior accurately and to use self-reinforcement for effort and improvement.

Other Behavioral Approaches

The *problem-solving model* of depression hypothesizes that depressed persons lack adequate cognitive skills for solving everyday problems and achieving goals (Nezu & Perri, 1989). Treatment focuses on teaching a standardized approach to solving problems. The *reinforcement model* posits that depression results when a person's usual pattern of reinforcement, both social and nonsocial, is interrupted (Lewinsohn, Antonuccio, Steinmetz, & Teri, 1984). Treatment based on this model involves helping the client resume engaging in reinforcing activities on a regular basis.

OVERLAP BETWEEN TREATMENT APPROACHES. In some respects, there are more similarities than differences between the behavioral interventions for depression, which may account for the multimodal approach adopted by most behavior therapists in practice when treating depression. Sessions are usually provided for a time-limited basis, such as for a 3- to 6-month period, with booster sessions scheduled to ensure the maintenance of treatment gains. The therapy is highly directive, with the behavioral assessment guiding the therapist's systematic teaching of new skills and remediation of cognitive distortions using active practice in the session. Homework assignments are routinely given to program the generalization of skills from the session to the client's natural environment.

Of the nonbehavioral treatments for depression, behavioral and cognitive-behavior models are most similar to the *interpersonal model* of depression (Klerman, Weissman, Rounsaville, & Chevron, 1984). This model proposes that depression arises out of maladaptive or problematic interpersonal relationships, and focuses on helping clients identify and resolve these difficulties. The interpersonal model is similar to behavioral methods in the strong directive stance of the therapist, the focus on the here and now, utilizing a pragmatic problem-solving orientation, and the time-limited, circumscribed approach taken to resolving the depressive episode. One important difference between the interpersonal approach and behavior therapy interventions is the expectation that clients will complete homework assignments in the behavioral but not the interpersonal treatments.

TREATMENT EFFICACY. Controlled research on the efficacy of a variety of models of behavioral (or cognitive-behavioral) treatment for depression in outpatients has repeatedly documented beneficial effects, to the point where these modalities have been shown to be as effective as pharmacological interventions (e.g., Craighead, Evans, & Robins, 1992; Hollen, Shelton, & Loosen, 1991). Studies that have compared different psychotherapeutic modalities of treatment for depression have failed to detect consistent differences between approache (Robinson, Berman, & Neimeyer, 1990). This conclusion is in line with the results from a large-scale multicenter psychotherapy outcome study of depression sponsored by the National Institute of Mental Health (Elkin et al., 1989), which failed to find any differences between pharmacotherapy, cognitive therapy, or interpersonal therapy in persons with nonpsychotic major depression.

More work remains to be done to elucidate which types of behavior therapy are effective for specific subtypes and varying severities of depression. For example, are cognitive-behavioral interventions more effective with depressed clients who clearly manifest cognitive distortions, and is social skills training more effective for clients with deficits in these areas, as suggested by McNight, Nelson, Hayes, and Jarrett (1985)? Research examining the predictors of outcome in different treatment approaches to depression has failed to identify consistent predictors (e.g., Rude & Rehm, 1991). Beckham (1990) has suggested that the efficacy of different models of psychotherapy for depression can be explained by two alternative models: (1) the depression is maintained by a homeostatic system such that altering one component of the system influences the other components, or (2) common elements of the therapies (e.g., problem solving) are responsible for clinical change.

A limitation of most of the psychotherapy research on depression is that it has examined treatment effects for nonhospitalized outpatients. Although the vast majority of persons with major depression are not hospitalized, it is not clear how generalizable the results are to more severely depressed persons with a history of psychiatric hospitalization. One promising controlled study found that cognitive-behavioral intervention and pharmacological treatment of major depression initiated in the hospital and followed up after discharge resulted in significantly better outcomes than for patients who received only the pharmacological treatment (Miller, Norman, & Keitner, 1989).

The results of controlled outcome studies on the efficacy of behavior therapy for depression provide strong encouragement. Nevertheless, no single treatment is effective for every treatment setting or every person with depression. Given the relatively equal benefits associated with pharmacological and behavioral interventions, selecting a particular modality may rest on factors other than efficacy. For example, some depressed clients either refuse antidepressant drugs or cannot tolerate them because of side effects, so one of the validated behavioral (or interpersonal) therapies would be the treatment of choice for these persons. Also, social skills training for depression has been associated with lower dropout rates than pharmacological or psychodynamic treatment (Bellack, Hersen, & Himmelhoch, 1983); therefore, in clinics where attrition is a concern, social skills training may confer special benefits. From the perspective of practice guidelines for clinicians, Liberman (1984) developed a decision tree or algorithm to assist therapists in matching the appropriate biobehavioral treatment technique or agent with the unique characteristics of the depressed patient.

Schizophrenia

Behavior therapy occupies an increasingly important position among clinical interventions for modifying characteristic symptoms and signs of schizophrenia and for retraining clients' adaptive skills through structured learning experiences. Behavioral clinicians operationalize psychotic dysfunctions in terms of behavioral excesses (e.g., positive symptoms such as delusional verbalizations and aggression) and behavioral deficits (e.g., negative symptoms such as apathy and inadequate self-care skills). Behavior therapy entails modifying the client's environment so that antecedent and consequent stimuli surrounding the problem behaviors supplant or suppress behavior excesses and teach and strengthen adaptive behaviors.

Persons with schizophrenia may require accentuated prompts, gradual and prolonged shaping of new responses, tangible and social reinforcement, and other socioenvironmental prostheses for rehabilitation. Behavioral interventions are almost always superimposed on optimal types and doses of antipsychotic medi-

cation; for example, client learning in specially structured treatment environments is enhanced by the administration of antipsychotic medications in dosages that do not overly sedate or otherwise interfere with the learning process. There is some evidence, however, that behavioral therapies, as well as antipsychotic maintenance medication, confer protection against relapse or exacerbation of psychotic symptoms.

Negative Symptoms

Because antipsychotic medications have been less successful in treating negative symptoms, behavior therapists have designed and evaluated interventions that aim to improve social and self-care skills, increase engagement of clients in instrumental and vocational tasks, and improve independent functioning. Two behavioral strategies have been used extensively to improve negative symptoms and reduce their associated impairments in social functioning— social skills training and token economy programs.

Many persons with schizophrenia lack fundamental verbal and nonverbal communication skills. Such deficits pervade all areas of social functioning and lessen the chances of making a normal adjustment in society. Social skills training has been shown to be a potent means of teaching appropriate interpersonal behavior in people with schizophrenia and of promoting the generalization and durability of these responses (Liberman, DeRisi, & Mueser, 1989). Most often, social skills training for schizophrenia is provided in a group setting, with multiple sessions conducted on a weekly basis for at least several months. Historically, skills training was provided for a limited period of time (e.g., 2– 6 months), with occasional booster sessions scheduled thereafter. Cumulative research and clinical experience, however, have made it clear that chronically disabled clients may require longer treatment periods (e.g., 2 years or more) and may benefit from skills training on an ongoing or booster session basis. Just as maintenance antipsychotic drugs must be used indefinitely to protect against stress-induced relapse, so do psychosocial treatments like social skills training need to remain available indefinitely as a protective measure for persons with chronic schizophrenia who will, of necessity, have to cope with changing stressors and life events during their lifetime. Three controlled studies have provided support for the efficacy of social skills training in reducing the risk of relapse, reducing symptoms, and improving social functioning (Bellack, Turner, Hersen, & Luber, 1984; Hogarty, et al., 1986, 1991; Liberman, Mueser, & Wallace, 1986).

By utilizing token economy procedures—the engineering of a ward environment for social learning purposes—even chronic, regressed, severely withdrawn schizophrenic clients have been motivated to perform an array of prevocational activities through systematic reinforcement by tokens (Allyon & Azrin, 1968). The tokens are exchangeable by clients for coffee, cigarettes, privileges, and other desired goods and activities. Controlled research on the token economy for chronically ill, hospitalized schizophrenic patients has shown it to be superior to equally intensive milieu treatment, as well as to traditional custodial care, in improving social functioning and symptoms (Glynn & Mueser, 1992; Paul & Lentz, 1977).

Positive Symptoms

The greatest success of behavioral procedures in dealing with positive symptoms has been exhibited with behavioral excesses that might be considered the client's acting out of primary disturbances of thought and perception. Aggression, property destruction, self-injurious behavior, screaming, tantrums, stereotypies, and posturing have all been shown to be controllable by a variety of behavioral interventions, including time out from reinforcement, extinction, reinforcement of incompatible or other behaviors, and overcorrection (Wong, Massel, Mosk, & Liberman, 1986; Wong, Slama, & Liberman, 1986).

A few studies have suggested that reinforcement procedures may be effective in reducing delusional speech, but only rarely have such demonstrations been accompanied by evidence of durable and generalizable changes (Liber-

man, Tiegen, Patterson, & Baker, 1973). One promising approach utilizes repeated, discrete trials of training with small units of coherent speech in an effort to supplant loose associations, circumstantiality, mutism, or tangential speech (Liberman, Massel, Mosk, & Wong, 1985).

Another recent development in the treatment of positive symptoms of schizophrenia has been the systematic teaching of coping strategies to clients with chronic residual psychotic symptoms. A careful behavioral analysis is conducted of the situational antecedents and consequences in which one specific symptom occurs (or in which its severity varies), and clients are taught how to monitor the symptom. Next, the effectiveness of coping strategies in the client's repertoire is assessed. Then a new coping strategy is selected or an existing one is chosen for enhancement, and this strategy is practiced in the session, with homework assignments given to rehearse the skill at home. Additional coping strategies are taught as necessary to manage the primary or other psychotic symptoms. This strategy was found to be effective in decreasing the severity of positive symptoms and the associated distress in one recent controlled study (Tarrier et al., 1993).

Family Therapy

As increasing numbers of persons with schizophrenia have returned home in the wake of deinstitutionalization, behavior therapists have recognized the value of working with family members. Behavioral family interventions for schizophrenia (as well as for other adult psychiatric illnesses) have two main goals: (1) reducing the stress and burden on family members and (2) enhancing the client's functioning through improved monitoring, decreased environmental stress, and reinforcement of socially desired behaviors. Family therapy sessions focus on teaching the relatives and client basic facts about the illness, as well as strategies for improved communication, problem solving, and goal setting and attainment. Social skills training procedures are often used to teach skills to all family members. Behavioral treatment for the family is usually provided over an extended period of time (at least 6–9 months and often longer), with sessions gradually decreasing in frequency for the course of treatment. Controlled studies of behavioral family interventions for schizophrenia have been shown to reduce relapse rates, enhance social functioning, and lower the burden on family members (Falloon et al., 1985; Randolph et al., 1994; Tarrier et al., 1988). The results of these studies show some of the most consistent, positive findings of any psychosocial treatment for schizophrenia.

TREATMENT EFFICACY. The practical and highly structured methods of behavior therapy are clearly effective interventions for schizophrenia. Whereas behavior therapy has been more successful in the remediation of negative symptoms (i.e., strengthening patients' adaptive repertoires) than in the control of positive symptoms, broad-spectrum behavioral programs, such as social skills training and behavioral family therapy embedded in a comprehensive system of aftercare including antipsychotic medication, have resulted in substantial reductions in relapse and rehospitalization. Skills training has been repeatedly shown to improve the verbal and nonverbal components of social interaction, but there is a pressing need for more studies on the impact of these changes on long-term community adjustment and psychopathology.

Individual and group-based behavioral approaches to treating schizophrenia—ranging from skills training, the token economy, and teaching coping strategies to time-out and overcorrection—have little in common with other psychotherapeutic models of treatment. Perhaps these methods derived from behavior therapy differ most from psychodynamic and orthodox psychoanalytic treatments for schizophrenia, which have a poor efficacy profile and may even have deleterious effects on the illness (Mueser & Berenbaum, 1990). In contrast to psychodynamic methods, behavioral treatment is highly focused, directive, concrete, and oriented to the achievement of specific, operationalized goals.

Whereas individual and group behavioral treatments for schizophrenia are unique, behavioral family treatments have many commonalities with broad-based psychoeducational approaches that do not have an explicit behavioral focus (Lam, 1991). Effective family interventions for schizophrenia, whether behavioral or not, include a common set of characteristics: (1) treatment is long-term, at least 9 months; (2) the family is educated about the illness and how to monitor it; (3) realistic expectations among family members concerning the client's behavior are promoted; (4) stress is reduced on everyone in the family; and (5) theories of the psychogenic origins of schizophrenia are discounted in favor of stress-vulnerability models. Because several nonbehavioral family interventions have been found to be effective for the long-term treatment of schizophrenia (Hogarty et al., 1986, 1991; Leff, Kuipers, Berkowitz, & Sturgeon, 1985), future research will need to compare different models of family treatment to disentangle their effective components.

Who Gets Better?

Although research on behavior therapy for schizophrenia has produced more favorable results than any other psychotherapeutic modality, there is considerable variability across people with the illness in their response to treatment. At this time, there are no established predictors of the clinical response to behavioral interventions for schizophrenia. Some studies have suggested that cognitive impairments are associated with a slower rate of skill acquisition in social skills training (Kern et al., 1992; Mueser, Bellack, Douglas, & Wade, 1991), but it remains to be determined whether these deficits preclude a clinical response to training. There is some evidence that chronic psychotic symptoms in schizophrenic persons are associated with poor retention of social skills after skills training (Mueser, Kosmidis, & Sayers, 1992). These findings are not definitive, and they underscore the need to carefully examine the client's characteristics as predictors of the treatment response.

Schizophrenia is a multifaceted disease with probable multiple etiologies and pathophysiologies. Refining the ability to make differential treatment recommendations for schizophrenic clients will be an important goal for future research on behavioral interventions for this disorder. Despite the gaps in present knowledge, behavioral approaches in current use offer empirically validated procedures for management of the symptoms and disabilities of schizophrenia. Moreover, the behavioral techniques are specified and operationalized to the point of high procedural descriptiveness, thereby enabling practitioners and researchers to replicate and adapt the methods to their own settings.

A novel and "user-friendly" means of conducting skills training through "modules" has been developed, field-tested, and validated experimentally by Wallace and Liberman and their colleagues at the UCLA Clinical Research Center for Schizophrenia (Liberman & Evans, 1985; Psychiatric Rehabilitation Consultants, 1986–90; Wallace, Boone, Donahoe & Foy, 1985). Each module covers a different domain of importance for the community adaptation of persons with long-term disabling mental disorders such as schizophrenia—basic conversation skills, recreation for leisure, medication self-management, symptom self-management, job seeking, social problem solving, community reentry, and grooming and self-care.

The module comprises a Trainer's Manual, offering a stepwise, highly prescriptive set of instructions for the curriculum; a Patient's Workbook, which provides exercises for patients to practice in vivo; a video that demonstrates the knowledge and skill to be learned; and a User's Guide. Research has documented the efficacy of the modules in patients' acquisition of skills and the durability of the learned skills over a 12- to 18-month period of follow-up. Moreover, patients with schizophrenia who participate in the modular form of training to acquire social and independent living skills show significantly better social adjustment and an improved quality of life than their counterparts who receive supportive group therapy or psychosocial occupational therapy (Eckman et al., 1992; Eckman, Liberman, Phipps, & Blair,

1990; Wallace, Liberman, MacKain, Blackwell, & Eckman, 1992; Vaccaro, Liberman, Blackwell, & Wallace, 1992).

Childhood Disorders

Some of the earliest applications of behavior therapy were to problems in children, such as aggression, defiance, temper trantrums, sleeping problems, enurisis, shyness, and pervasive developmental disabilities. Common to most effective behavioral approaches to disorders of childhood is the inclusion of the family in treatment, with the primary focus on training family members how to systematically reinforce prosocial behavior and extinguish undesirable behaviors. Because the family often has the most control over shaping the child's environment, parents are important cotherapists or mediators in behavioral treatment. Similarly, other people with whom the child is in regular contact (e.g., teachers), and who therefore determine the reinforcement contingencies under which the child operates, are included in behavioral assessment and intervention. We briefly highlight the three childhood disorders for which there is extensive research supporting the efficacy of behavior therapy.

Conduct Disorder

Behavior therapists have been drawn to the problems displayed by children with conduct disorder because (1) the behavioral abnormalities of aggression, lying, stealing, and truancy are dramatic; (2) the long-term consequences in adult psychopathology are serious; and (3) the problems are pervasive, with two-thirds of all children referred to mental health clinics exhibiting this disorder or the similar problem of oppositional-defiant disorder.

Direct observations of parent–child interactions in natural home settings have consistently shown that parents of conduct-disordered children deliver an inordinately large number of poorly formulated, vague commands in a threatening and angry fashion. They are more critical and negative than are parents of so-called normal children. They do not set clear behavioral limits and permit their children's socially inappropriate and aggressive behaviors. In this environment, it may be assumed that the child learns to be aggressive and insensitive to rules governing socially acceptable behavior. Modification of this maladaptive style of family interaction has been the principal focus of behavioral interventions.

Parent training is the most widely tested and effective behavioral approach with conduct-disordered and oppositional-defiant children. Effective models of parent training all have the following core components: Parents are first taught the principles of behavior modification, which emphasize the importance of identifying and maintaining a record of the frequency of problem behaviors or of desired behavioral alternatives. Next, instruction in communication skills—especially the skills required to give clear, positively stated, direct requests—is provided. Parents are then instructed in the use of positive reinforcement. After these skills are learned, parents are taught how and when to use a structured punishment, such as time-out.

Effective parent training requires that substantial therapy time be allotted to role playing, modeling, and the rehearsal of more direct and less hostile modes of interaction. This educational intervention actively attempts to replace vague, threatening commands and excessive criticism with positive attention, reinforcement, and appropriate limit setting. It has also been suggested that parent training is more effective when the therapist deals directly with family resistance to therapeutic instructions, marital conflict, and parent problems. Comparative research has shown parent training to be more effective than alternative therapy approaches commonly provided to families of conduct-disordered children. Parent training can be conducted in individual or multiple-family group sessions, with treatment usually lasting for at least 3 months but rarely for more than 1 year.

For children and adolescents whose antisocial and aggressive behavior results in actions that bring them into juvenile court, a surrogate and prosthetic family program has been designed and validated within a behavior treatment framework. Termed the *teaching family model*, this approach utilizes a pair of adults—usually a married couple—who are intensively trained in the use of behavioral learning principles and skills building and who provide around-the-clock supervision for up to six youngsters in a group home. This model has evolved over two decades of research and development, with an array of service elements that include teaching interactions, point (token) economy systems, self-government, transition back to natural families, liaison with schools backed by reinforcement contingencies, and citizen involvement for the purposes of program evaluation and social validation. Over 100 controlled, single-subject studies have documented the efficacy of the teaching family model; and comparative group designs and program evaluation have found it to yield better educational outcomes and reduced recidivism at lower costs than more traditional community-based or institutional treatment for predelinquent youth.

Attention-Deficit Hyperactivity Disorder (ADHD)

ADHD, characterized by inattention and impulsivity with hyperactivity, is one of the most common childhood disorders that requires mental health treatment. Moreover, children with ADHD do not typically outgrow it, as was suggested in the past. It is now clear that children with this diagnosis not only are severely handicapped at home and school, but are also at high risk of developing serious psychological disorders in adolescence and adulthood. Traditional psychotherapies do not seem to be effective in improving the outcome of these children.

Behavioral treatments have focused on the use of contingent reinforcement to establish adaptive behaviors such as being on task. Token systems that employ contingent removal of reinforcement, as well as its application, have also been used successfully in the school and at home. In most cases, points (reinforcement) are given for the desired behaviors (e.g., sitting in one's seat for 5 minutes) and taken away (punishment) for failure to meet the target criterion. The tokens earned in this way may be exchanged for other primary (e.g., food) or social (e.g., playtime) rewards. ADHD children are also extremely responsive to social reinforcement from adults. The research clearly shows that training parents and teachers in the use of contingent reinforcement significantly improves the treatment outcome.

Undesirable behaviors can be effectively reduced through a punishment procedure that removes the child from all reinforcement (e.g., time-out), as well as one that removes a specific reward (e.g., loss of points). Thus, the contingent use of time-out, alone or in combination with positive reinforcement, has been successful with hyperactive and inattentive behaviors. Additional behavioral strategies that have received empirical support include *self-control training*, a cognitive-behavioral technique that teaches children to monitor and provide consequences for their own behavior, and *required delay*, a technique designed to reduce impulsivity by presenting the child with a problem but requiring him or her to refrain from verbalizing the answer immediately.

There is strong research support for recommending behavior therapy with psychostimulant medication for ADHD children. Most treatment outcome studies suggest that when these two treatments are used together, the results are superior to those obtained by either type of treatment alone, especially for controlling inattentive and hyperactive behaviors. However, the positive findings associated with combined drug and behavioral treatment apply only while the drug is administered, with little benefit after the drug is withdrawn. Behavioral treatment for ADHD, because it is environmentally based and typically involves a range of persons in contact with the child, is provided over extended periods of time to ensure that effective contingencies continue to reinforce adaptive behavior. Therefore, behavior therapy for children with these disorders is a long-term enterprise that often extends over several years.

Autism

Traditional therapies, including medical and psychodynamic interventions, have been ineffective with autistic children. Initial applications of behavior therapy demonstrated that linguistic and interpersonal functions could be enhanced, albeit with limited generalization to the child's natural environment. Recent advances have provided compelling evidence for the efficacy of a range of behavioral strategies for improving the course of autism. Treatment gains are maximized when massed practice is used with significant persons (e.g., parents and teachers) in multiple environments; clinically relevant targets are treated (e.g., toileting, verbal skills, peer interaction, classroom behavior); and the rewards used to reinforce behavior are functionally related to the behaviors being taught. Behavioral treatments for autism have spanned two broad areas of clinical concern: building adaptive behaviors and reducing aggression, self-injury, and stereotypical behaviors.

The symptoms of enuresis and encopresis can significantly increase the likelihood that an autistic child will be institutionalized. Removal of such difficulties is an important step in the child's overall treatment. Training consists of shaping appropriate toileting behaviors by reinforcing component parts (e.g., approach to the toilet, removing clothing) in successive approximations of the goal behavior. Results may be enhanced by the addition of an aversive procedure, such as overcorrection, in which the child is required to clean his or her clothing repeatedly.

Deficits in verbal behavior lead to enduring social handicaps in autistic children. In mute children, verbal imitation is taught first, preferably by providing functionally relevant positive reinforcement for successive approximations to controlled speech. The process involves the following training sequence: The child is reinforced (1) for any verbalization, then (2) for verbalization within 5 seconds of the therapist's verbal prompt, followed by (3) for verbalizations that sound like what the therapist said, then (4) for verbalization of two sounds, and finally (5) for introduction of a third sound. Once imitation is taught, functional speech can be established. Verbal behavior is prompted (e.g., showing a ball and saying the word *ball*), and successive approximations of the word *ball* are reinforced. The verbal part of the prompt is eventually faded, and the child is reinforced for saying the word *ball* when the object is presented. Combinations and chains of words and sentences are shaped in the same manner, using prompts and reinforcements, and later fading the prompts.

These procedures can help almost all autistic children learn rudimentary speech and functional self-care behaviors. However, intensive and prolonged speech training is required to build conversation skills beyond elementary vocabularies and requests. Landmark controlled research has been published by Lovaas and his associates (Lovaas, 1987) that describes an intensive program of behavioral intervention consisting of more than 40 hours per week of one-to-one treatment that lasted for more than 2 years. Autistic children were identified and began behavior therapy before age 3; parents were trained to serve as mediators of the procedures in their homes. Outcomes included the finding that 47% of the subjects receiving intensive, parent-mediated training achieved normal intellectual and educational functioning, in contrast to 2% of control subjects who received 10 hours or less of behavioral treatment per week.

The most widely demonstrated procedure to control aggressive behavior with autistic children is time-out, which is applied in a fashion similar to that used with other childhood disorders (e.g., ADHD) and aggression in adult psychiatric disorders (e.g., schizophrenia). Self-injurious behavior responds best to behavioral suppression that uses restraint or other aversive procedures combined with differential positive reinforcement of other behaviors. In a review of such interventions with autistic children, it was found that this combination was effective in reducing these behaviors in 90% of the studies (Matson & Taras, 1989). Similarly, self-stimulatory and stereotypical behaviors respond best to a combination of a procedure to decelerate the undesired behavior (e.g., restraint or overcorrection) and differential reinforcement for other behavior or an incompatible behavior (Wong, Slama, & Liberman, 1986).

Generalization of newly learned behaviors to other situations is very problematic for autistic children, as the behavior of these children seems to be particularly situation and stimulus bound. Therefore, new responses must be taught in a number of stimulus situations that simulate the nontreatment environment. Also, everyday environments may need to be modified so that newly learned adaptive behaviors are reinforced and maintained. Training the family and teachers as behavior-change agents is critical to ensuring generalization to the home and school.

TREATMENT EFFICACY. The research literature provides strong evidence for the efficacy of behavioral treatment for disorders of childhood. Behavioral treatments for children, similar to those for adults, tend to be highly specified, and this high level of description facilitates the replication and dissemination of effective techniques to a wide range of treatment settings. There is a paucity of evidence supporting the efficacy of nonbehavioral interventions, with the exception of some cognitive treatments for anxiety in children (Francis, 1992), which overlap with the behavioral approach. Thus, behavior therapy is unique both in the nature of its clinical application to children and in the strong empirical support it enjoys.

Although behavioral interventions for children have beneficial clinical effects, behavior therapy places high expectations on family members for active participation in treatment. In fact, family members who receive training in the behavioral approach end up doing the majority of the work required to restructure the child's environment so that the contingencies at home consistently reinforce desired behavior patterns. From the perspective of predicting the clinical response to behavioral treatment for childhood problems, these considerations suggest that children in families who are difficult to engage, whose resistance to completing homework assignments cannot be overcome, or who experience such high levels of environmental stress that sessions must frequently focus on crisis management, rather than teaching and enforcing child management skills, are poor candidates for behavior therapy. However, there is no evidence suggesting that these children would be better served by other psychotherapeutic modalities.

Other Psychiatric Disorders

Behavior therapy has made substantial inroads in the treatment of a wide range of psychiatric disorders not described in detail here. Behavioral treatments are almost the only approach used in the management of a wide range of psychological disturbances that occur in persons with mental retardation. Behavior therapy is also the principal treatment approach, supported by many research studies, used to treat sexual dysfunctions (e.g., premature ejaculation, functional dyspareunia, inhibited orgasm) and paraphilias. Furthermore, controlled research indicates that behavior therapy is effective in the treatment of eating disorders (e.g., bulimia, anorexia nervosa, obesity) and substance use disorders.

The evidence for the efficacy of behavior therapy for personality disorders, dissociative disorders, and somatoform disorders is less compelling. With the exception of some research indicating that behavioral treatment is moderately effective in improving borderline personality disorder (Liberman & Eckman, 1981; Linehan, Armstrong, Suarez, & Allmon, 1991), little controlled research has been conducted on behavior therapy and specific personality disorders. Nevertheless, there are selected case reports suggesting that behavioral treatment can improve the outcome of these less intensively studied disorders. More controlled research is needed in this area.

BEHAVIOR THERAPY FOR OTHER PROBLEMS

The major focus of this chapter has been on the practice of behavior therapy for the treatment of specific psychiatric disorders, as defined by the DSM-III-R (American Psychiatric Association, 1987). However, there are numerous additional uses of behavior therapy for the treatment of other problems or to enhance quality of life. One growing area has been behavioral medicine, that is, the systematic application of behavior therapy to prevent vulnerability to an illness (e.g., teaching safe sex practices to individuals at risk for AIDS), to reduce the severity and improve the long-term outcome of established medical conditions (e.g., hypertension, cancer, coronary artery disease), and to bolster the individual's ability to cope with an illness (e.g., intractable pain). The variety of behavioral interventions for medical conditions that have received empirical support are too great to enumerate here, but some examples are listed in Table 5.5. Lastly, behavior therapy has proved to be beneficial in other nonmedical, nonpsychiatric areas. Behavioral approaches to marital discord have repeatedly been shown to improve marital adjustment and satisfaction (Liberman, Wheeler, DeVisser, Kuehnel, & Kuehnel, 1980). Numerous people with no major psychopathology have participated in individual and group behavioral interventions based on social skills training to learn how to be more assertive, to make friendships or develop intimate relationships, to resolve conflicts better, to be more effective salespeople or managers, to deepen close relationships with family members or lovers, and to talk more effectively with their children and be better listeners. Behavior therapy is utilized by sports psychologists to help athletes achieve peak performance, in schools to teach children prosocial behavior, and in community settings to teach relaxation and imagery skills. Thus, behavior therapy has been applied to facilitate the functioning of many individuals who are not otherwise mental health consumers.

In sum, behavior therapy is not just a model of psychotherapy, but also an empirically driven approach to resolving human problems and achieving personal goals. As such, psychotherapy is just one of many settings in which the behavioral approach is encountered. While the term *behavior therapy* is not well under-

TABLE 5.5. Examples of Behavior Therapy Applied to Medical (Nonpsychiatric) Disorders

Medical Illness	Behavioral Intervention
Hypertension	Biofeedback and relaxation to lower blood pressure
Headache	Relaxation techniques
	Biofeedback of muscular tension (for tension headaches)
	Biofeedback of peripheral blood flow (for migraine headaches)
Coronary artery disease	Relaxation training
	Social skills training to modify aggressive, "Type A" interpersonal behaviors
	Education and goal-setting for life style changes
Gastrointestinal disorders	Habit training and biofeedback (for fecal incontinence)
	Assertiveness training and stress management (for peptic ulcers)
Chronic pain	Contingency reinforcement of graded activity and exercise
	Stress management (e.g., relaxation)
Raynaud's Syndrome (numbing in fingers and toes)	Relaxation training
Cancer	Relaxation training for nausea from chemotherapy
	Stress management training to improve long-term outcome of illness (e.g., breast cancer)
	Pain management techniques (e.g., relaxation) for intractable pain
AIDS	Education and social skills training to promote "safe sex" and discourage needle sharing

stood by the general public, almost everyone is familiar with at least some of the basic concepts underlying the model.

SUMMARY

Behavior therapy is an empirical approach to psychotherapy, based on principles of learning, that has been applied in a variety of clinical and nonclinical contexts. Controlled research on behavioral interventions for specific psychiatric disorders has documented it to be an efficacious treatment for anxiety disorders, depression, schizophrenia, childhood disorders (including conduct disorder, ADHD, and autism), sexual dysfunction and paraphilias, substance use disorders, eating disorders, and mental retardation. Behavior therapy also has begun to play an increasingly important role in the prevention of medical illness by promoting healthy behavior, as well as by improving the ability to cope with a disease and its long-term outcome. Finally, behavior therapy has numerous nonclinical applications, such as reducing marital discord and improving interpersonal skills. The remarkable, wide-ranging results achieved by behavior therapies over the past several decades suggest that this approach has great promise for further advances in the future and is an exciting psychotherapeutic modality in which to practice.

REFERENCES

Alberti, R. E., & Emmons, M. L. (1974). *Your perfect right.* San Luis Obispo, CA: Impact.

American Psychiatric Association (1987). *Diagnostic and statistical manual of mental disorders* (3rd ed., rev.). Washington, DC: Author.

Ayllon, T., & Azrin, N. (1968). *The token economy: A motivation system for therapy and rehabilitation.* New York: Appleton-Century-Crofts.

Azrin, N. (1976). *Toilet training in less than a day.* New York: McGraw-Hill.

Bandura, A. (1969). *Principles of behavior modification.* New York: Holt, Rinehart, & Winston.

Barlow, D. H. (1988). *Anxiety and its disorders: The nature and treatment of anxiety and panic.* New York: Guilford press.

Barlow, D. H., & Craske, M. G. (1991). *Mastery of your anxiety and panic.* Albany, NY: Graywind.

Barlow, D. H., Craske, M. G., Cerny, J. A., & Klosko, J. S. (1989). Behavioral treatment of panic disorder. *Behavior Therapy, 20,* 261–282.

Beck, A. T., Rush, A. J., Shaw, B. F., & Emery, G. (1979). *Cognitive therapy of depression*. New York: Guilford Press.

Beck, A. T., Sokol, L., Clark, D. A., Berchick, R., & Wright, F. (1992). A crossover study of focused cognitive therapy for panic disorder. *American Journal of Psychiatry, 149*, 778–783.

Becker, R. E., Heimberg, R. G., & Bellack, A. S. (1987). *Social skills training treatment for depression*. New York: Pergamon Press.

Beckham, E. E. (1990). Psychotherapy of depression research at a crossroads: Directions for the 1990s. *Clinical Psychology Review, 10*, 207–228.

Bellack, A. S., Hersen, M., & Himmelhoch, J. M. (1983). A comparison of social skills training, pharmacotherapy and psychotherapy for depression. *Behaviour Research and Therapy, 21*, 101–107.

Bellack, A. S., Turner, S. M., Hersen, M., & Luber, R. F. (1984). An examination of the efficacy of social skills training for chronic schizophrenic patients. *Hospital and Community Psychiatry, 35*, 1023–1028.

Biran, M., & Wilson, G. T. (1981). Cognitive versus behavioral methods in the treatment of phobic disorders: A self-efficacy analysis. *Journal of Consulting and Clinical Psychology, 49*, 886–899.

Blanchard, K., & Johnson, S. (1987). *One-minute manager*. New York: Random House.

Borden, J. W. (1992). Behavioral treatment of simple phobia. In S. M. Turner, K. S. Calhoun, & H. E. Adams (Eds.), *Handbook of clinical behavior therapy* (2nd ed.) (pp. 3–12). New York: Wiley.

Butler, G., Cullington, A., Murphy, M., Amies, P., & Gelder, M. (1984). Exposure and anxiety management in the treatment of social phobia. *Journal of Consulting and Clinical Psychology, 52*, 642–650.

Clark, D. M. (1986). A cognitive approach to panic. *Behaviour Research and Therapy, 24*, 461–470.

Craighead, W. E., Evans, D. D., & Robins, C. J. (1992). Unipolar depression. In S. M. Turner, K. S. Calhoun, & H. E. Adams (Eds.), *Handbook of clinical behavior therapy (2nd ed.)*, (pp. 99–116). New York: Wiley.

Craske, M. G., Brown, T. A., & Barlow, D. H. (1991). Behavioral treatment of panic disorder: A two-year follow-up. *Behavior Therapy, 22*, 289–304.

Eckman, T. A., Liberman, R. P., Phipps, C. C., & Blair, K. (1990) Teaching medication management skills to schizophrenic patients. *Journal of Clinical Psychopharmacology, 10*, 33–38.

Eckman, T. A., Wirshing, W., Marder, S. R., Liberman, R. P., Zimmerman, K., Johnston-Cronk, K., & Mintz, J. (1992) Technique for training schizophrenic patients in illness self-management: A controlled trial. *American Journal of Psychiatry, 149*, 1549–1555.

Eimers, R., & Aitchison, R. (1977). *Effective parents, responsible children*. New York: McGraw-Hill.

Elkin, I., Shea, M. T., Watkins, J. T., Imber, S. D., Sotsky, S. M., Collins, J. F., Glass, D. R., Pilkonis, P. A., Leber, W. R., Doeherty, J. P., Flester, S. J., & Parloff, M. B. (1989). National Institutes of Mental Health Treatment of Depression Collaborative Research Program. *Archives of General Psychiatry, 46*, 971–983.

Ellis, A., & Harper, R. A. (1975). *A new guide to rational living*. Englewood Cliffs, NJ: Prentice-Hall.

Emmelkamp, P. M. G., Mersch, P. P., Vissia, E., & Van der Helm, M. (1985). Social phobia: A comparative evaluation of cognitive and behavioral interventions. *Behaviour Research and Therapy, 23*, 365–369.

Falloon, I. R. H., Boyd, J., McGill, C., Williamson, M., Razanl, J., Moss, H., & Gilderman, A. (1985). Family management in the prevention of morbidity of schizophrenia: Clinical outcome of a two-year longitudinal study. *Archives of General Psychiatry, 42*, 887–896.

Falloon, I. R. H., Lloyd, G. C., & Harpin, R. E. (1981). The treatment of social phobia: Real-life rehearsal with nonprofessional therapists. *Journal of Nervous and Mental Disease, 189*, 180–184.

Foa, E. B., Rothbaum, B. O., Riggs, D. S., & Murdock, T. B. (1991). Treatment of post-traumatic stress disorder in rape victims: A comparison between cognitive-behavioral procedures and counseling. *Journal of Consulting and Clinical Psychology, 59*, 715–723.

Foa, E. B., Steketee, G. S., & Ozarow, B. J. (1985). Behavior therapy with obsessive-compulsives: From theory to treatment. In M. Mavissakalian, S. M. Turner, & L. Michelson (Eds.), *Obsessive-compulsive disorder: Psychological and pharmacological treatment* (pp. 49–129). New York: Plenum Press.

Francis, G. (1992). Behavioral treatment of childhood anxiety disorders. In S. M. Turner, K. S. Calhoun, & H. E. Adams (Eds.), *Handbook of clinical behavior therapy* (2nd ed., pp. 227–244). New York: Wiley.

Glynn, S. & Mueser, K. T. (1992). Social learning. In R. P. Liberman (Ed.), *Handbook of psychiatric rehabilitation* (pp. 127–152). New York: Macmillan.

Harpin, R. E., Liberman, R. P., Marks, I. M., & Stern, R. (1982). Behavior therapy for chronically depressed patients. *Journal of Nervous and Mental Disease, 170,* 295–301.

Heimberg, R. G., Becker, R. E., Goldfinger, K., & Vermilyea, J. A. (1985). Treatment of social phobia by exposure, cognitive restructuring and homework assignments. *Journal of Nervous and Mental Disease, 173,* 236–245.

Heimberg, R. G., Dodge, C. S., Hope, D. A., Kennedy, C. R., Zollo, L. J., & Becker, R. E. (1990). Cognitive behavioral group treatment for social phobia: Comparison with a credible placebo control. *Cognitive Therapy and Research, 14,* 1–23.

Hogarty, G., Anderson, C., Reiss, D., Kornblith, S., Greenwald, D., Javna, C., & Madonia, M. (1986). Family psychoeducation, social skills training, and maintenance chemotherapy in the aftercare treatment of schizophrenia: I. One-year effects of a controlled study on relapse and expressed emotion. *Archives of General Psychiatry, 43,* 633–642.

Hogarty, G., Anderson, C., Reiss, D., Kornblith, S., Greenwald, D., Ulrich, R., & Carter, M. (1991). Family psychoeducation, social skills training, and maintenance chemotherapy in the aftercare treatment of schizophrenia: II. Two-year effects of a controlled study on relapse and adjustment. *Archives of General Psychiatry, 48,* 340–347.

Hollon, S. D., Shelton, R. C., & Loosen, P. T. (1991). Cognitive therapy and pharmacotherapy for depression. *Journal of Consulting and Clinical Psychology, 59,* 88–99.

Horowitz, M. (1986). *Stress response syndromes* (2nd ed.) New York: Jason Aronson.

Keane, T. M., Fairbank, J. A., Caddell, J. M., & Zimering, R. T. (1989). Impulsive (flooding) therapy reduces symptoms of PTSD in Vietnam combat veterans. *Behavior Therapy, 20,* 245–260.

Kern, R. S., Green, M. F., & Satz, P. (1992). Neuropsychological predictors of skills training for chronic psychiatric patients. *Psychiatry Research, 43,* 223–230.

Klerman, G. L., Weissman, M. M., Rounsaville, B. J., & Chevron, E. S. (1984). *Interpersonal psychotherapy of depression.* New York: Basic Books.

Klosko, J. S., Barlow, D. H., Tassinari, R., & Cerny, J. A. (1990). A comparison of alprazolam and behavior therapy in treatment of panic disorder. *Journal of Consulting and Clinical Psychology, 58,* 77–84.

Lam, D. H. (1991). Psychosocial family intervention in schizophrenia: A review of empirical studies. *Psychological Medicine, 21,* 423–441.

LaVigna, G., & Donnellan, A. M. (1986). *Alternatives to punishment.* New York: Irvington Press.

Lazarus, A. A. (1976). *Multimodal behavior therapy.* New York: Springer.

Lazarus, A. A. (1981). *The practice of multi-modal therapy.* New York: McGraw-Hill.

Leff, J., Kuipers, L., Berkowitz, R., & Sturgeon, D. (1985). A controlled trial of social intervention in the families of schizophrenic patients: Two year follow-up. *British Journal of Psychiatry, 146,* 594–600.

Lewinsohn, P. M., Antonuccio, D. O., Steinmetz, J. L., & Teri, L. (1984). *The coping with depression course: A psychoeducational intervention for unipolar depression.* Eugene, OR: Castalia.

Lewinsohn, P. M., Munoz, R. F., Youngren, M. A., & Zeiss, A. M. (1986). *Control your depression.* New York: Prentice Hall.

Liberman, R. P. (1984). Individualizing treatment strategies in depression. In L. P. Rehm (Ed.), *Behavior therapy for depression: Present status and future directions* (pp. 231–253). New York: Academic Press.

Liberman, R. P. (1992). Behavior family therapy is scientific and systemic. In J. Cottraux, P. Legeron, & E. Mollard (Eds.), *European research in behavior therapy* (pp. 203–210). Amsterdam: Swets & Zeitlinger.

Liberman, R. P., Derisi, W. J., & Mueser, K. T. (1989). *Social skills training for psychiatric patients.* New York: Pergamon Press.

Liberman, R. P., & Eckman, T. A. (1981). Behavior therapy vs. insight therapy for repeated suicide attempters. *Archives of General Psychiatry, 38,* 1126–1130.

Liberman, R. P., & Evans, C. C. (1985). Behavioral rehabilitation for chronic mental patients. *Journal of Clinical Psychopharmacology, 5* (Suppl), 8s–14s.

Liberman, R. P., Massel, H. K., Mosk, M. D., &

Wong, S. E. (1985). Social skills training for chronic mental patients. *Hospital and Community Psychiatry, 36,* 396–403.

Liberman, R. P., Mueser, K. T., & Wallace, C. J. (1986). Social skills training for schizophrenic individuals at risk for relapse. *American Journal of Psychiatry, 143,* 523–526.

Liberman, R. P., Mueser, K. T., Wallace, C. J., Jacobs, H. E., & Eckman, T. A. (1986). Training skills in the severely psychiatrically disabled: Learning coping and competence. *Schizophrenia Bulletin, 12,* 631–647.

Liberman, R. P., Tiegen, J., Patterson, R., & Baker, V. (1973). Reducing delusional speech in chronic paranoid schizophrenics. *Journal of Applied Behavior Analysis, 6,* 57–64.

Liberman, R. P., Wheeler, E., DeVisser, L., Kuehnel, T. G., & Kuehnel, J. (1980). *Handbook of marital therapy.* New York: Plenum.

Linehan, M. M., Armstrong, H. E., Suarez, A., & Allmon, D. J. (1991). Cognitive behavioral treatment of chronically parasuicidal borderline patients. *Archives of General Psychiatry, 48,* 1060–1064.

Lovaas, O. I. (1987). Behavioral treatment and normal educational and intellectual functioning in young autistic children. *Journal of Consulting and Clinical Psychology, 55,* 3–9.

Mathews, A. M., Gelder, M. G., & Johnston, D. W. (1981). *Agoraphobia: Nature and treatment* New York: Guilford Press.

Matson, J. L., & DiLorenzo, T. M. (1984). *Punishment and its alternatives.* New York: Springer.

Matson, J. L., & Taras, M. E. (1989). A 10-year review of punishment and alternative methods to treat problem behaviors in developmentally disabled persons. *Research in Developmental Disabilities,* 85–104.

Mattick, R. P., Peters, L., & Clarke, J. C. (1989). Exposure and cognitive restructuring for social phobia: A controlled study. *Behavior Therapy, 20,* 3–23.

McNight, D. L., Nelson, R. O., Hayes, S. C., & Jarrett, R. B. (1984). Importance of treating individually assessed response classes in the amelioration of depression. *Behavior Therapy, 15,* 315–335.

Miller, I. W., Norman, W. H., & Keitner, G. I. (1989). Cognitive-behavioral treatment of depressed inpatients: Six- and twelve-month follow-up. *American Journal of Psychiatry, 146,* 1274–1279.

Mueser, K. T., Bellack, A. S., Douglas, M. S., & Wade, J. H. (1991). Prediction of social skill acquisition in schizophrenic and major affective disorder patients from memory and symptomatology. *Psychiatry Research, 37,* 281–296.

Mueser, K. T., & Berenbaum, H. (1990). Psychodynamic treatment of schizophrenia: Is there a future? *Psychological Medicine, 20,* 253–262.

Mueser, K. T., Kosmidis, M. H., & Sayers, M. D. (1992). Symptomatology and the prediction of social skills acquisition in schizophrenia. *Schizophrenia Research, 8,* 59–68.

Munford, P., Hand, I., & Liberman, R. P. (in press). Behavior therapy for obsessive-compulsive disorders: Psychosocial treatment of choice. *Psychiatry.*

Nezu, A. M., & Perri, M. G. (1989). Social problem-solving therapy for unipolar depression: An initial dismantling investigation. *Journal of Consulting and Clinical Psychology, 57,* 408–413.

Patterson, G. R., & Gullion, M. E. (1971). *Living with children: New methods for parents and teachers (rev. ed.).* Champaign, IL: Research Press.

Paul, G. L., & Lentz, R. J. (1977). *Psychosocial treatment of chronic mental patients: Milieu versus social-learning programs.* Cambridge, MA: Harvard University Press.

Perris, C. (1992). A cognitive-behavioral treatment program for patients with a schizophrenic disorder. In R. P. Liberman (Ed.), *Effective psychiatric rehabilitation: New directions for mental health services (number 53)* (pp. 21–32). San Francisco: Jossey-Bass.

Phelps, S., & Austin, N. (1975). *The assertive woman.* San Luis Obispo, CA: Impact.

Randolph, E. T., Eth, S., Glynn, S., Paz, G. B., Leong, G. B., Shaner, A. L., Strachan, A., Van Vort, W., Escobar, J., & Liberman, R. P. (1994). Behavioral family management in schizophrenia: Outcome from a clinic-based intervention. *British Journal of Psychiatry, 164,* 501–506.

Psychiatric Rehabilitation Consultants. (1986–90). *Modules for training social and independent living skills.* Available from Dissemination Coordinator, Camarillo-UCLA Research Center, P.O. Box 6022, Camarillo, CA 93011-6022.

Rapee, R. M. (1991). Generalized anxiety disorder: A review of clinical features and theoretical concepts. *Clinical Psychology Review, 11,* 419–440.

Resick, P. A., Jordan, C. G., Girelli, S. A., Hutter,

C. K., & Marhoefer-Dvorak, S. (1988). A comparative outcome study of behavioral group therapy for sexual assault victims. *Behavior Therapy, 19,* 385–401.

Robinson, L. A., Berman, J. S., & Neimeyer, R. A. (1990). Psychotherapy for the treatment of depression: A comprehensive review of controlled outcome research. *Psychological Bulletin, 108,* 30–49.

Rude, S. S., & Rehm, L. P. (1991). Response to treatments for depression: The role of initial status on targeted cognitive and behavioral skills. *Clinical Psychology Review, 11,* 493–514.

Salkovskis, P. M., & Warwick, H. M. C. (1985). Cognitive therapy of obsessive-compulsive disorder: Treating treatment failures. *Behavioural Psychotherapy, 13,* 243–255.

Tarrier, N., Barrowclough, C., Vaughn, C., Bamrah, J., Porceddu, K., Watts, S., & Freeman, H. (1988). The community management of schizophrenia: A controlled trial of a behavioral intervention with families to reduce relapse. *British Journal of Psychiatry, 153,* 532–542.

Tarrier, N., Beckett, R., Harwood, S., Baker, A., Yusupoff, L., & Ugarteburu, I. (1993). A trial of two cognitive behavioral methods of treating drug-resistant residual psychotic symptoms in schizophrenic patients. I. Outcome. *British Journal of Psychiatry, 162,* 524–532.

Vaccaro, J., Liberman, R. P., Blackwell, G., & Wallace, C. J. (1992). Combining social skills training and assertive case management: The Social and Independent Living Skills Program. In R. P. Liberman (Ed.), *Effective psychiatric rehabilitation: New directions for mental health services,* (pp. 33–42). San Francisco: Jossey-Bass.

Wallace, C. J., Boone, S. E., Donahue, C. P., & Foy, D. W. (1985). The chronically mentally disabled: Independent living skills training. In D. Barlow (Ed.), *Clinical handbook of psychological disorders: A step-by-step treatment manual* (pp. 462–501). New York: Guilford.

Wallace, C. J., Liberman, R. P., MacKain, S. J., Blackwell, G., & Eckman, T. A. (1992). Effectiveness and replicability of modules for teaching social and instrumental skills to the severely mentally ill. *American Journal of Psychiatry, 149,* 654–658.

Wong, S. E. Massel, H. K., Mosk, M. D., & Liberman, R. P. (1986). Behavioral approaches to the treatment of schizophrenia. In G. D. Burrows, T. R. Norman, & G. Rubinstein (Eds.), *Handbook of studies on schizophrenia* (pp. 79–100). Amsterdam: Elsevier Science.

Wong, S. E., Slama, K., & Liberman, R. P. (1986). Behavioral analysis and therapy for aggressive psychiatric and developmentally disabled patients. In L. Roth (Ed.), *Clinical treatment of the violent person* (pp. 22–56). New York: Guilford Press.

6

Depth Existential Therapy: Evolution Since World War II

James F. T. Bugental
Bruce McBeath

The word *existential* has to do with existence, human existence, human life. All psychology and all psychotherapy necessarily must be existential if they are to have validity. Yet the term *existential* has come to have a more restricted meaning, referring to theories and therapeutic approaches that give a central place to the miracle of existence itself. From that arise two other miracles: human awareness of existence and awareness aware of itself—in a word, *consciousness*.

The term *existential* is acceptably employed by many writers in the fields of philosophy, psychology, and psychotherapy. This broad span evidences its generic quality, but it also makes it necessary for each of us who uses it to clarify just what meanings are intended in our particular approach to the concept of existentialism.

In this chapter, *existential* has three significances. It implies a grounding of our concepts and practice in the immediacy and givenness of direct experience. It connotes an effort to set forth foundation postulates with a high degree of self-evident validity. It identifies the primacy to our understanding of human beings of the phenomenological, the perceived, and the subjective world (Stolorow & Atwood, 1992, esp. p. 4).

Since this chapter is directed to actual practice and its supporting theory, each of these meanings will be more often implicit than explicit in the following pages. That fact, in itself, is a manifestation of our existential orientation, which concerns itself with lived experience more than with abstract belief.

Synopsis of the Evolution of This Viewpoint

World War II, for this country at least, provides a reasonable benchmark for a crucial change in the meaning of psychotherapy for both the professions and the laity. During and after the war, literally millions of service people were provided counseling and psychotherapy (Rogers, 1942; Rogers & Wallen, 1946). Concurrently, as increasing numbers of people without gross mental and emotional abnormalities sought counseling and psychotherapy, this work escaped the obloquy that had previously attended "being in therapy." As a result, a revolution occurred in popular awareness and acceptance of the need for aid with life issues (Bugental & Sterling, 1993). Rather than being a strange and chiefly medical activity far removed from the mainstream of American (especially middle-class) life, psychotherapy became the frequent subject matter of Sunday supplements, popular magazines and cartoons, and the several theater arts—as well as being a commonplace aspect of the experience of a much larger portion of the population than ever before.

This shift in popular consciousness was interactive with and parallel to the transplanting of existential thinking from its chiefly European intellectual roots to a broader U.S. audience of nonmedical, nonphilosophically sophisticated, but practicing counselors and therapists. The seminal book that fostered this transition was May, Angel, and Ellenberger's *Existence: A New Dimension in Psychiatry and Psychology* (1958).

As in that book, the existential perspective was at first brought to bear chiefly on psychoanalysis. However, the enrichment it provided to our understanding of the lives of persons being seen in many contexts resulted in a more pervasive influence. Today existential thinking in various forms and degrees permeates many approaches to the field of psychology-psychotherapy (Boss, 1962; Frey & Hesler, 1975; Friedman, 1967; Greening, 1971; Havens, 1974; Keen, 1970; Maslow, 1967, 1968, 1971; May, 1953, 1961, 1969, 1981; Ofman, 1976; Tillich, 1952; van Duerzen-Smith, 1988; Wheelis, 1958).

In this chapter, we will give major attention to two important expressions of the general existential movement now current in American psychotherapy: the existential-humanistic orientation and, as an important example of the emerging transpersonal dimension, a brief synopsis of the psychosynthesis approach.

AN EXISTENTIAL-HUMANISTIC APPROACH TO PSYCHOTHERAPY[1]

The Core Conception

A newly born infant struggles to survive in a sea of possibilities. It can become nearly anything. It can do almost nothing. It is largely a lump of unformed protoplasm. For it to take form, to become a human person, to have some self-direction, to live its life, it must reduce the range of possibilities. Forming a life is much more a process of eliminating than of adding on.

The Self-and-World Construct System (Kelly, 1955)

To live in the infinite openness of space, astronauts must have space suits. Such suits protect against the danger of the vast emptiness and make it possible for the persons who wear them to do what is needed in this condition of threat and opportunity.

To live in the infinite openness of possibility that the infant enters, one must have a self-and-world construct system (SAWC). Such a way of defining oneself and one's world protects against the disabling openness of possibility and makes it possible for the developing person to do what is needed to live in what is, at least latently, a perilous environment (Bugental, 1987).

The SAWC consists of implicit answers to the crucial questions of life, such as these: What is my essential nature? Am I a good person? What are my strengths? What are my failings? What do I need to change? What is valuable in me and must be protected? How important to me are the people with whom I am in relation? Interacting with these questions are others about the outer world. For example: What is the world? Is it safe or dangerous? What are the good things worth going for or sacrificing for? What are the dangers to be avoided? What defenses have I against the world's demands and indifference? How can I increase my power to defend myself and to enhance my satisfactions in life?

Of course, these questions and their answers are only partially conscious, mostly implicit, and widely varying in the firmness with which they are held. A variety of sources are involved in their development, and one of the earliest roots is *destiny*.

Destiny

Only by reducing or eliminating some possibilities can others become genuinely available. Initially, much of this essential reduction comes about as a consequence of what Rollo May identifies as *destiny* (May, 1981). He uses this term to call attention to external influences that begin to shape the developing person. Destiny, for May, has to do with initial circumstances, not end states. He identifies these influential conditions:

Cosmic— *birth and death*
Genetic— *race, gender, innate talents*
Cultural— *society, family*
Circumstantial— *economic, political, and social conditions in the epoch into which one is born* (1981, pp. 89–91).

Each of these circumstances serves to select a span of potentialities for the infant, and in doing so, each eliminates many times more possibilities. Each sets the stage, but none finally determines the action or the transformations that will occur. Thus the space suit, the SAWC, comes into being—at once enabling and limiting.

It is important to recognize that despite the great power of destiny, its effects are not unalterable. A bushman child becomes a world-class runner and grossly changes the otherwise predictable outcomes of her birth, race, gender, society, and much else. The child of illegal immigrants fleeing poverty and oppression takes part in a revolt of the underprivileged and is elected mayor of his city. The scion of wealth and privilege takes up a career of crime and brutality. As these hypothetical instances portray, fact and fiction frequently find rich inspirations in the contrasts between the life courses that seem most likely and those that are actually lived out.

The SAWC through which one begins to create one's life is initially largely the product of these "destiny" influences, particularly those tied to the culture, the society, and the family into which one is born. Over time, each person—sometimes consciously, sometimes without awareness—makes continual modifications in that pattern, and thus it becomes one's individual creation.

Life means the inexorable necessity of realizing the *design* for an existence which each one of us is. . . . the sense of life . . . is nothing other than each one's acceptance of [this] inexorable circumstance and, on accepting it, converting it into [one's] own creation. (J. Ortega y Gasset, cited by R. May [1981], p. 93; *italics in original source.*)

Each person must create/adopt a personal identity and a conception of the world in order to be alive and, to some degree, self-maintaining. Although we begin to develop these essential structures in childhood, they are, to varying degrees, what we rely on as adults as well. When societies and families were generally stable, continuing from one generation to the next with only minor changes, an inherited SAWC served most people adequately and required only minor adaptations. But, as is acutely familiar today, change is more rapid, pervasive, and central, not only in the developed world but nearly globally. In our own culture, we speak of the 1950s "baby boom," the "flower children" of the 1960s, the "hopeful" 1970s, and the "me generation" of the 1980s expressing the astonishing recognition that a considerable portion of our population manifests a distinguishing SAWC in each decade. It is doubtful that ever in human history has such a rate of change continued for so long.

Indeed, an expectation of change, of tentativeness, of undependability is now an element of the SAWCs of many people. (The implications of this expectation for individuals and for societies are important and evocative but beyond the scope of the present statement.)

In each person's life, inner promptings interact with the contingencies of the environing world to evoke, challenge, suppress, or otherwise influence various potentials within the person.

Mabel defines herself as superior in the academic realm, but on graduating from a small high school and entering a large university, she encounters many persons with similar gifts. She panics, misinterpreting her changed grade level as evidence that her mind is failing.

Helen, born to privilege and affluence, encounters few challenges until her middle thirties, when she loses her beloved first child in an automobile accident. Her depression arises not from the loss of her child alone but also from being shockingly confronted with her own vulnerability to contingency.

Larry grows up cherishing his parents' religious dedication, wins their approbation for his decision to enter the ministry, but discovers his own faith faltering when confronted with the lives of his parishioners. His struggles with his own spiritual crisis are complicated by his feeling that he is failing his family.

Examples could be endlessly added, of course. The point is that the way each person handles the inevitable challenges presented by life will depend on many factors, among which is his or her SAWC. Yet concurrently, and less manifestly, that SAWC may change as well.

Obviously, stress results when the SAWC no longer brings sufficient satisfactions or occasions too many frustrations or hurts. That stress may be incidental and readily overcome, or it may be catastrophic and life-threatening—or even life-ending. Many times it is this stress that brings the person to become a client in psychotherapy.

One way—the way an existential-humanistic view of psychotherapy employs—of conceiving the fundamental task of psychotherapy is that it requires that the SAWC be explored so that it can become more effective in yielding satisfaction and preventing frustration.

Searching

The work of such therapy consists of the client's seeking to become aware of—and, to a lesser extent, to express in words—how the client identifies her or his self and world. This work goes forward as the client is helped to look soberly and deeply into his or her own inner experiencing, to express emotions, strivings, and apprehensions, to be open to changing perceptions, and to modify or relinquish self-defeating self and world percepts.

This process is called *searching*, and it is a way of tapping into less conscious aspects of one's living. As such, it is generally similar to psychoanalytic *free association*, *unfolding* (Buber, 1965; Welwood, 1982), or *focusing* (Gendlin, 1962, 1978).

Searching requires that the client, when

undertaking to work in this manner, be as genuinely *present* to the task as possible. *Presence*, as we employ it here, means much more than physical attendance; it includes emotional investment, focused intention, and genuine openness to internal discovery. Of course, this varies constantly, and that variation is itself important to the work, for it can signal points of threat, evasion, or growing comfort.

Resistance

When a person attempts to be present in this way and to describe what truly matters in life and what conflicts are encountered in living out desires for life, he or she will discover that there are obstacles both to expressing to another person what he or she finds within the self and—even more important—to becoming fully aware of these matters within oneself. These blocks are the *resistances*—to knowing, to openness, to being fully *in* one's living.

Freud recognized the centrality of attention to the resistance when he wrote, "There is no psychoanalysis which is not the analysis of the resistance" (1916/1917). Our view of this importance rests on but goes beyond traditional psychoanalytic understanding. We recognize that the forces within the person that hold off the therapeutic inquiry are the same forces that provide some stability to the client's way of being in the world. Thus the resistance is much more than an obstacle to therapy or an opposition to the therapist; it is an aspect of the SAWC, a part of the client's "space suit."

Understanding resistance teaches the therapist to respect it, to avoid becoming its adversary, and to help the client learn to adapt it to better serve her or his life's needs.

The Course of the Therapeutic Work

Helping a client to be sufficiently and genuinely present is the fundamental task of therapy on which all else depends. A client who cannot risk or maintain at least a measure of such participation is not suitable for this kind of therapy. Major psychoses, neurological pathology, subnormal intelligence, and immaturity of life experience thus become contraindications.

Concern

With a client who can attain a degree of presence, the work takes the form of encouraging the client to seek within for a sense of *concern*, a recognition of what truly matters in his or her life *in this precise moment*. This insistence on immediacy is of pivotal importance. To talk *about* what matters in one's life is very different from talking *out* of that experience as it is being lived even as one speaks.

When the client becomes intimately aware of this difference—and copes with the resistance that that awareness nearly always elicits—then the searching process goes forward. Guided not by logical connections, setting aside considerations of self-image, defense/enhancement, and propriety the client soon learns that there is a literally endless series of awarenesses that becomes available.

Expressing these awarenesses is the sole task of the client, but this is not easily accomplished. The resistance aspects of the SAWC intrude on, distract from, and directly block the exploration. This interference always occurs; *indeed, it is essential that it do so*. What interferes with the searching effort is significant far beyond the immediate therapeutic work. *What interferes with the client's efforts to search freely within oneself is what interferes with the client's efforts to conduct personal life as she or he truly wants.*

For this reason, the therapist's attention to the resistance is a prime element in forwarding the work toward the optimum outcome of a freed living for the client. The therapist facilitates the client's self-discovery by encouraging persistence, supporting confrontation of discovered threats, and fostering expression of whatever can be verbalized. These steps prepare the way for a function that calls for the highest therapeutic artistry: highlighting resistances as they are encountered, continually drawing the client's attention to these interferences with free searching, identifying their underlying repetitive patterns, and doing all this in the immediate moment.

When client and therapist have accomplished these steps effectively, the stage is set for the client to engage in the anxious, difficult, but life-renewing work of discovering the ways in which these resistances have been built into his or her life structures (SAWC) and the ways they also handicap the client's living. This is only partially a conscious or explicit process. It occurs implicitly as the client continues searching, and the changes it produces are more likely to be discovered after they have occurred than to be overtly sought and worked out.

Because the foregoing concise statement is so centrally important, the same understanding will now be repeated in somewhat different words: The work of the therapist and client is to help the latter stay with her or his own inner struggle for greater awareness of the self and world perceptions through which the client conducts his or her life. This is a demanding, lengthy, often threatening and painful task. With continued dedication, in time there will be some opening of awareness, a measure of fresh perception of familiar and previously blocked emotions and perceptions, and, ideally, a new-found feeling of having the power to make changes, to live differently and more in harmony with oneself and with others.

A Reprise

The task of creating and revising one's life design is lifelong. It is not something that, once accomplished, need never be reexamined or revised. One's own growth and maturing; the contingencies of living with others, each having a somewhat different life design; and the unpredictability of life generally combine to demand repeated attention—however unwilling—to one's SAWC. Some seek desperately to allow no changes; others welcome some newness; all find threat in the renewed, if implicit, confrontation with the infinitude of possibility (the emptiness of space).

Life always requires that we create a framework within which to discover the meanings we realize by our living. The growth of our being demands that we repeatedly test and enlarge our frameworks. Not to do so is to drop into thingness, is to become less than we are, is to settle for living in a continually shrinking world.

The reexamination and revision of one's SAWC is a vital but threatening undertaking (Bugental & Bugental, 1986). For anyone who attempts it, there is likely to be a sense of anxiety, a reluctance to advance too quickly or too deeply, and a pull to shield from change key elements of how we see ourselves and our worlds.

This experienced threat is understandable when we recognize that a penetrating inquiry into one's sense of identity and the way one believes the world to be involves more than metaphorically shaking the ground under one's feet, the ground of one's being alive. We are well advised to go slowly in this work, for too rapid a disruption of these life-enabling perceptual structures risks precipitating a major personality disorganization (e.g., a psychotic breakdown or another failure of usual functioning).

The Therapeutic Alliance

One of the most powerful resources to counter the threat of overwhelming distress is the alliance that develops between client and therapist.

> This relationship is not immediately comparable to any other in life. It is a friendship; it is a love affair; it is a partnership; it is a blood bond; it is a duel; it is all of these and none of them and yet something more. It is a *therapeutic alliance*, a bond between what is best and most dedicated in the therapist and what is most health-seeking and courageous in the client. It will have many other elements in it at various points, but this is its essence. Each partner to the alliance will fall short at times of being all that it demands and yet it must endure. (Bugental, 1978, p. 72)

The Therapist

The existential-humanistic psychotherapist undertakes a demanding, exciting, boring, confusing, and personally involving assignment. Not for this therapist is the posture of the detached, clinical scientist appropriate. Empathically working with the raw stuff of another's life results in one's own life being called into question. The therapist's SAWC is on the line again and again. If the professional tries to withdraw behind a protective wall of cognitive or diagnostic objectivity, the alliance is threatened and may be unable to provide the support that will be needed if the work is to be deep enough to yield lasting results.

All this is by no means a warrant for blind spontaneity, therapist license, or dissolving the role differentiation on which the alliance is founded. Indeed, the therapist practicing in the fashion here portrayed must be more than usually alert to her or his own inner promptings and their linkage with the client's presentation and needs.

Process Emphasis

One way in which this balance of perspective is supported is by the therapist's giving primary attention to the client's *process*, rather than to the *content*. The *how* of the client's use of the therapeutic opportunity is a far richer area for therapeutic focus than is the *what* of his or her protocol.

In this way, therapists monitor facial expressions, gestures, breathing patterns, body language, and much else besides the narrative of what the client is saying. These nonverbal expressions arise from the preconscious level of the client's consciousness, that is, from inner impulses, feelings, and needs that are apt to be less evident to the client and thus have not yet been recognized and verbalized. They are thus less vulnerable to calculated dissembling or to surface manipulation.

Transference

Of course, clients bring to the consultation room their SAWC, which is to say their way of being with others, their way of presenting themselves, their way of trying to win approval and avoid censure, and their needs in relationships. Of course, these are inevitably played out with the therapist, even though only a small portion may be fully conscious to the client. This enactment is a great aid to the therapeutic work, as the therapist is enabled to discern these patterns as they are manifested and to identify those that act as resistances to the therapeutic work but, more important, to the client's living more fully.

Some of the most penetrating and powerful therapeutic work takes place when the client's projections (transference) interact with the therapist's own projections (countertransference) in what may initially be an unconscious collusion. When this hidden conjunction is recognized, brought out into the open, and worked through in the immediate situation, the results can be truly life-changing (Levenson, 1983, 1991). And not only for the client.

Working Through

The therapeutic work proceeds as the client follows the thread of concern in the searching process; expressing the thoughts, feelings, impulses, and other material that come into awareness; recognizing (with the therapist's aid) the resistances that interfere with the search and with living; and implicitly displaying her or his SAWC. Gradually, certain repetitive patterns become evident.

> Harry continually complained about the unfair treatment he received at the hands of almost everyone he encountered. He seemed intent to demonstrate that life was dealing with him in a shabby way and content simply to make his protests. His complaints never seemed to lead to any change in Harry's own way of being.
>
> Nancy was extremely skillful in winning the approval of almost everyone she met. She was charming, adaptable, and talented. But Nancy never felt she was valued for herself; so, she continually carried a feeling of shame for having "fooled" everyone.
>
> Michael was a success in everything he undertook. He had risen more quickly than anyone else to a post of responsibility in the company for which he worked. He was much admired for his community service, and his home life was regarded as exemplary. Yet Mi-

chael had no idea whether he liked his work, cared genuinely about the community, or even loved his family. In therapy Michael came to recognize that he always responded to outside expectations and had little or no sense of his own needs or wants.

These are three examples of life patterns (SAWCs) that were uncovered in psychotherapy. But recognizing these patterns was not sufficient in itself to bring about changes that would be lasting and satisfying. The essential further step is called *working through*. It consists in tracing through as many of the client's life venues as possible—the permutations of these patterns and of the losses they occasion. This is not a cognitive task alone. As the search process goes forward, with awareness of this life pattern now part of the perspective of both client and therapist, repeated instances of its being played out will spontaneously surface. These may then be explored, with profit in increased understanding of how the pattern has functioned, of what may be valued and preserved in it, and of what needs to be changed or relinquished.

Existential-Humanistic Psychotherapy in Perspective

Successful intensive, long-term psychotherapy with an existential-humanistic orientation is lengthy, expensive, uncomfortable, and intrusive. Unless the therapeutic enterprise disrupts the client's established life patterns, there is no likelihood of significant and lasting life changes occurring. This simple realization comes as a surprise to many clients and to not a few therapists. Significant therapeutic change cannot be attained if therapy is simply an "add-on" to a full and unchangeable life pattern.

For this reason, many therapists with this orientation insist on more frequent contacts and longer-term commitments than are typical in most other approaches. Additionally, therapists may urge clients to adopt meditation or the regular use of personal journaling. The common denominator is the necessity to call for a major investment and a readiness to relinquish some familiar life patterns. These same considerations make this approach less appropriate for most younger people (roughly, under age 25), for those with poor ego functioning or the inability to tolerate significant challenges to key life structures, and for those who are unable to make a significant commitment to the program.

It is perhaps already obvious, but it is pertinent to note that beyond the considerations just listed, there is generally little use of psychodiagnostic testing, formal diagnosis, extended attention to symptoms, efforts to collect a detailed history and match it to the symptom picture, or the employment of interpretation and argumentation as therapeutic tools (Bugental & Bracke, 1992).

SUMMATION

Existential-humanistic psychotherapy is a form of what Koestenbaum (1978) calls *clinical philosophy*. It is not the treatment of a disease or an injury. It is an effort to offer aid to the life task that each person is already undertaking, whether consciously or not. Its goal is not to address symptoms as such; symptoms may or may not be alleviated, but if the work goes well, they will be experienced differently and less disruptively.

Existential-humanistic psychotherapy is an effort to increase clients' access to their power to guide their lives, to find more of the satisfactions they deeply seek, and to avoid some of the pitfalls lying within themselves. This is a program in which it is centrally important to remember that *the power to bring about change resides in the client* and not in the therapist or the method. While other orientations take a similar stand, existential-humanistic psychotherapy makes it absolutely central to its whole approach and organizes all methodology around that postulate.

A fundamental conviction of our perspective is that all human beings realize only a small part of what is latent within themselves. Observers often comment that humans have evolved relatively little compared to the immense strides of the physical sciences. It is our belief that, at least at this stage, evolution is still an individual matter. Throughout history some persons have transcended their cultures and their origins. We believe that more people are capable, in varying degrees, of doing so. When we help clients to confront their own resistances, we are helping them to discover the greater potentials sleeping within them.

Just as individuals are capable of seemingly infinite emergence and growth, so a conceptual system about individuals is an open-ended undertaking. Thus our vision is far from complete. What we have presented above is a progress report, not a finished statement.

PSYCHOSYNTHESIS: A SPIRITUALLY ORIENTED PSYCHOTHERAPY WITHIN THE EXISTENTIAL TRADITION

Psychosynthesis provides an especially intriguing look at how a spiritually oriented psychological framework has been integrated within the broad perspective of existential psychotherapy. Psychosynthesis is the comprehensive psychological approach to understanding human existence intitially developed by Roberto Assagioli, an Italian psychiatrist (1965, 1973). He had a profound interest in the "higher aspects" of human nature and brought to this his integrative mind, synthesizing the work of Freud, Jung (with whom he collaborated), and American humanistic psychology (notably William James and Abraham Maslow). To these he added the fruits of his studies of Eastern spiritual practices, the Kabbalistic tradition of Judaism, and the mystical tradition within Christianity.

Assagioli presented a number of fresh and fertile observations about human experience. Space here limits our attention to three that are particularly distinguishing and to a synoptic account of psychosynthesis psychotherapy. The three observations are insistence on the transpersonal or spiritual aspect of our nature, recognition and description of higher consciousness, and giving central importance to the distinction between the experiencer and the experienced.

Spiritual Aspect of Human Nature

Central to the model of the human psyche Assagioli developed is the *experience* of the individual. Thus he viewed the psyche as an energy system, and he developed his approach to help it develop, mature, and align increasingly with its higher possibilities. Implicit in this approach is Assagioli's conception of human existence as essentially a spiritual enterprise incorporating purpose, meaning, and values.

Assagioli (1965) was careful to identify his approach as lying within the domain of psychology:

> Psychosynthesis does not attempt in any way to appropriate to itself the fields of religion and of philosophy. It is a scientific conception and, as such, it is neutral towards the various religious forms and the various philosophical doctrines, excepting only those which are materialistic and therefore deny the existence of spiritual realities. Psychosynthesis does not aim nor attempt to give a metaphysical nor a theological explanation of the great Mystery—it leads to the door, but stops there. (pp. 6–7)

We are evolving human beings within an evolving social context, and Assagioli believes that evolution is part of our very nature. Freed of crippling and distorting identifications, we tend toward higher, more expansive, more unitive ways of being in our lives. The contents of our consciousness change as we evolve and emphasize more of the aspects of transcendent experience. Self-awareness, as it becomes less cluttered by distortion, seeks the source of all awareness. This more mystical reflection is argued on the basis of a foundation in experience: As individuals attain an increasingly "purified" self-awareness (i.e., less caught up in the contents of consciousness), they manifest more of the larger or higher Self that Assagioli posited.

Higher Consciousness

In designing his framework for psychosynthesis, Assagioli (1973) depicted an upper tier of personality, a higher level corresponding to Freud's construct of the lower unconscious. This he termed the *higher unconscious* or the *superconscious* realm of the psyche, a source of feelings of love, joy, and ecstasy, as well as of inner wisdom and deep intuitive understanding. Assagioli did not deny the darker side of human nature, but he insisted that it was only a part, not the whole, of our endowment.

Just as the lower unconscious gives rise to needs for survival and security, psychosynthesis sees this higher unconscious as exerting a natural pull toward growth, harmony with others, and planetary wholeness. These expressions of our true human nature reside within each of us.

Within the superconscious realm of our psyches is an enormous range of possibilities for growth—and for discord. As conflicting desires arise from different levels of our being, we find that we must deal with components of our SAWC systems that are blocking access to our higher potentials.

> Robert, a 45-year-old, professionally successful attorney, complains of feeling increasingly dissatisfied and "empty." His energy is lessening even as his practice is growing. Psychotherapy discloses how an extreme preoccupation with material accumulation has led to his loss of inner awareness, with a resulting atrophy of the capacity for joy and relatedness.
>
> Julia presents an instructive contrast. She returned from a week-long spiritual retreat filled with ecstatic wonder and the need to share her experience with family and friends. However, while others listened, they were not transported in the way she hoped. She became discouraged and resentful and then withdrew from others in mourning for the lost spiritual world. Her SAWC was ill-fitting, so that she felt unable to accept her very real and very ordinary struggles.

Distinguishing the Experiencer

The experience of identity can be viewed as having two primary aspects: an experiencer and the contents of experience. The frequent failure to make this distinction is a source of much confusion about the nature of human identity and the mode of aiding change and growth through psychotherapy.

This fundamental distinction between the subjective (the *I*) and the objective *(self* or *me)* facets of our being leads to the somewhat unusual view that psychosynthesis holds of the nature of symptoms. Symptoms are positive indications when they signal an ailing self-connection, a lessening of the bondage to the objective, substantive self, and suggest a movement toward liberation of the higher *Self.*

Human beings tend to "take on identifications" and thus are confused about the real nature of their identities. These accumulated identifications are multiple and often conflicting. When one's sense of who one is is limited to the contents of consciousness, then there is confusion and conflict, for multiplicity within the personality is common. We all have several selves, several available identifications. But these identifications are not *I.* They are attributes of the object self.

Psychosynthesis Psychotherapy

A psychosynthesis-oriented course of psychotherapy is based on the unique existential situation of each patient and has as its purpose to foster the harmonizing and integrating of that person's various qualities and functions.

Speaking of the uniqueness of persons in no way implies a kind of isolationism, the one against all others. Instead, existentially oriented psychotherapies take into account both the tragedy and the suffering of isolated human experience and the ecstasy and fulfillment of deeper union with others and with all life. Psychosynthesis was developed in part as a response to the European view of the human individual as essentially alone in an inhospitable world. In contrast, Assagioli viewed the experience of separation as a distortion of our true nature of essential oneness. In a similar vein, Stolorow and his associates (1987, 1992) are developing a fresh perspective in psychoanalysis that takes the intersubjective field as a fundamental fact of life and as the setting of psychotherapy.

Just as this perspective insists on the sharedness of human experience, so it also sees as a primary task of psychosynthesis therapy the fostering of the client's disengagement of the sense of identity from the contents of consciousness. Only in this way can the client operate out of his or her true identity as the *experiencer* (not the *experienced).* As this shift occurs in therapy, the client becomes reacquainted with the deeper subjective experience of being that is behind the identifications ordinarily thought of as the stuff of personality.

An increasingly vital experience of this higher consciousness is the ultimate goal of this psychotherapy (Vaughan, 1985). The route to that goal may include any approach drawn from the broad psychotherapeutic armamentarium. Gestalt awareness techniques, guided imagery and intuition, meditation practices, and, of course, the concern-guided searching described above are all examples. Indeed, it is the use of this range of approaches within a comprehensive perspective holding human nature to be essentially spiritual that distinguishes this as psychosynthesis.

A CONCLUDING PERSPECTIVE

Existential psychotherapies in general—and psychosynthesis as one example of these—tend to be minority perspectives. This is understandable in view of two main factors: (a) an emphasis on the autonomy and potency of the individual client, in contrast to the more frequent emphasis on the therapist or the therapeutic system, and (b) an unwillingness to accept symptom alleviation or other quasi-objective change as a sufficient outcome for treatment.

Implicit in both of these stances is a view of human life as much larger, more complex and subtle, and more extensive in potential than is typical in conventional psychology and psychiatry today. The current emphasis on short-term, objective, fixed, routine patterns for psychological treatment (to be paid for by third parties and managed by anonymous strangers) is anathema to those who practice in the ways that we have here sketched. It is not that such quick-fix therapy is unavailing (it would be better if that were so); it is that its processes and products are apparent confirmations of this shrunken and distorting vision of what it means to be human and alive. It is the subtle cancer on humankind that grows from such objectification, such demeaning, such repeated demonstrations that individuality, subjectivity, and a spiritual seeking are epiphenomena that need not be taken into account and are, for the most part, either luxuries for the few or hindrances to the work of the many.

It is difficult to maintain a hopeful outlook in light of much that is happening in psychology, psychotherapy, and the broad field of mental health. It is unpopular to insist on the something more that we *know* exists but that cannot be counted, spelled out, touched, or otherwise objectively demonstrated. It is difficult and unpopular, to be sure, but there is no doubt in our minds that is is important to do so, for there are always those who will hear, and there will ultimately be an end to this self-destructive fashion. When that end arrives, there will be a time of renewal and rebirth for the human spirit.

NOTE

1. This section draws chiefly on Bugental (1965, 1978, 1987, 1990a) and on Bugental and Kleiner (1993). Case examples of the method will be found in Bugental (1976, 1986, 1990b). Other existential-humanistic approaches are presented by Boss (1963), Keen (1970), Koestenbaum (1978), Mahrer (1983, 1986), Ofman (1976), van Duerzen-Smith, (1988), and Yalom (1980).

REFERENCES

Assagioli, R. (1965). *Psychosynthesis*. New York: Viking Press.

Assagioli, R. (1973). *The act of will*. New York: Viking Press.

Boss, M. (1962). Anxiety, guilt, and psychotherapeutic liberation. *Review of Existential Psychology and Psychiatry*, 2, 173–207.

Buber, M. (1965). *Between man and man* (R. G. Smith, Trans.). New York: Macmillan.

Bugental, J. F. T. (1965). *The search for authentic-ity: An existential-analytic approach to psychotherapy*. New York: Holt, Rinehart & Winston.

Bugental, J. F. T. (1976). *The search for existential identity*. San Francisco: Jossey-Bass.

Bugental, J. F. T. (1978). *Psychotherapy and process: The fundamentals of an existential-humanistic approach*. New York: McGraw-Hill.

Bugental, J. F. T. (1986). Existential-humanistic psychotherapy. In I. L. Kutash & A. Wolf (Eds.), *Psychotherapist's casebook* (pp. 222–236). San Francisco: Jossey-Bass.

Bugental, J. F. T. (1987). *The art of the psychotherapist*. New York: Norton.

Bugental, J. F. T. (1990a). Existential-humanistic psychotherapy. In J. K. Zeig & W. M. Munion (Eds.), *What is psychotherapy? Contemporary perspectives* (pp. 182–192). San Francisco: Jossey-Bass.

Bugental, J. F. T. (1990b). *Intimate journeys: Stories from life-changing psychotherapy*. San Francisco: Jossey-Bass.

Bugental, J. F. T., & Bracke, P. E. (1992). The future of existential-humanistic psychotherapy. *Psychotherapy*, 29, 28–33.

Bugental, J. F. T., & Bugental, E. K. (1986). Resistance to and fear of change. Reprinted in F. Flach (Ed.) (1989), *Stress and its management* (pp. 58–67). Directions in Psychiatry Series No. 6, Vol. 6. New York: Norton.

Bugental, J. F. T., & Kleiner, R. I. (1993). Existential-humanistic psychotherapy. In F. Stricker & J. Gold (Eds.), *The comprehensive handbook of psychotherapy integration* (pp. 101–112). New York: Plenum.

Bugental, J. F. T., & Sterling, M. M. (1993). Newer perspectives for existential-humanistic psychotherapy. In S. Messer & A. Gurman (Eds.), *Modern psychotherapies: Theory and Practice*. New York: Guilford Press.

Freud, S. (1916/1917). Introductory lectures on psychoanalysis, Part III, General theory of the neuroses. Lecture XIX: Resistance and repression. In *The complete psychological works of Sigmund Freud*, Vol. 15. New York: Norton.

Frey, D. H., & Hesler, F. E. (1975). *Existential theory for counselors*. Boston: Houghton Mifflin.

Friedman, M. (1967). *To deny our nothingness: Contemporary images of man*. New York: Delacorte.

Gendlin, E. T. (1962). *Experiencing and the creation of meaning: A philosophical and psychological approach to the subjective*. Glencoe, IL: Free Press.

Gendlin, E. T. (1978). *Focusing*. New York: Everest House.

Greening, T. C. (1971). *Existential-humanistic psychology*. Belmont, CA: Brooks/Cole.

Havens, L. L. (1974). The existential use of the self. *American Journal of Psychiatry, 131*, 1–10.

Keen, E. (1970). *Three faces of being: Toward an existential clinical psychology*. New York: Appleton-Century-Crofts.

Kelly, G. A. (1955). *The psychology of personal constructs*, Vols. 1, 2. New York: Norton.

Koestenbaum, P. (1978). *The new image of the person: The theory and practice of clinical philosophy*. Westport, CT: Greenwood Press.

Levenson, E. A. (1983). *The ambiguity of change: An inquiry into the nature of psychoanalytic reality*. New York: Basic Books.

Levenson, E. A. (1991). *The purloined self: Interpersonal perspectives in psychoanalysis*. New York: William Alanson White Institute.

Mahrer, A. R. (1983). *Experiential psychotherapy: Basic processes*. New York: Brunner/Mazel.

Mahrer, A. R. (1986). *Therapeutic experiencing: The process of change*. New York: Norton.

Maslow, A. H. (1967). Self-actualization and beyond. In J. F. T. Bugental (Ed.), *Challenges of humanistic psychology* (pp. 279–286). New York: McGraw-Hill.

Maslow, A. H. (1968). *Toward a Psychology of being* (2nd ed.). New York: Van Nostrand Reinhold.

Maslow, A. H. (1971). *The farther reaches of human nature*. New York: Viking Press.

May, R. (1953). *Man's search for himself*. New York: Norton.

May, R. (Ed.). (1961). *Existential psychology*. New York: Random House.

May, R. (1969). *Love and will*. New York: Norton.

May, R. (1981). *Freedom and destiny*. New York: Norton.

May, R., Angel, E., & Ellenberger, H. F. (Eds.). (1958). *Existence: A new dimension in psychiatry and psychology*. New York: Basic Books.

Ofman, W. (1976). *Affirmation and reality: Fundamentals of humanistic existential therapy and counseling*. Los Angeles: Western Psychological Services.

Rogers, C. R. (1942). *Counseling and psychotherapy: Newer concepts in practice*. Boston: Houghton Mifflin.

Rogers, C. R., & Wallen, J. L. (1946). *Counseling returned servicemen*. New York: McGraw-Hill.

Stolorow, R. D., & Atwood, G. E. (1992). *The intersubjective foundations of psychological life*. Hillsdale, NJ: Analytic Press.

Stolorow, R. D., Brandchaft, B., & Atwood, G. E. (1987). *Psychoanalytic treatment: An intersubjective approach*. Hillsdale, NJ: Analytic Press.

Tillich, P. (1952). *The courage to be*. New Haven, CT: Yale University Press.

van Deurzen-Smith, E. (1988). *Existential counseling in practice*. London: Sage.

Vaughan, F. (1985). *The inward arc: Healing and wholeness in psychotherapy and spirituality*. Boston: Shambala.

Welwood, J. (1982). The unfolding of experience: Psychotherapy and beyond. *Journal of Humanistic Psychology, 22*, 91–104.

Wheelis, A. (1958). *The quest for identity*. New York: Norton.

Yalom, I. D. (1980). *Existential psychotherapy*. New York: Basic Books.

7

Experiential Therapy in Practice: The Process-Experiential Approach

Robert Elliott
Leslie S. Greenberg

Central to the practice of humanistic, existential, and experiential therapies is a view of the client as an expert on his or her own experience. Within the phenomenological perspective, clients are viewed as having privileged access to their unique experiences. Client processes of discovery and choice are therefore emphasized over the taking of an interpretive or advisory focus. The therapist focuses on explicating implicit meanings rather than on searching for hidden meanings. Clients are encouraged to identify and symbolize their inner experience for themselves rather than having the therapist offer them interpretive links between present and past experience. The individual is thus seen as an aware, reflective agent and therapy as a process of facilitating choice and action by clients confronting their own experience (May & Yalom, 1989; Rice & Greenberg, 1992).

Experiential therapists focus strongly on clients' present experience and on the current moment-by-moment process of attending to and symbolizing bodily felt referents. They believe in a growth tendency that operates to move the person forward in an adaptive manner if the person learns to trust it. Notwithstanding the focus in therapy on the present, the person

is viewed as future-oriented and goal-directed, and behavior is influenced by a vision of the future rather than being directed primarily by the past.

Experiential therapy is centrally oriented to the creation of new meaning. This involves helping the client to clarify tacit meanings and to carry these forward into new meanings through linguistic symbolization. Unique *emotion schemes*, as well as more universal, existential ultimate concerns (Yalom, 1980), are confronted. Clients are helped to confront their own freedom and to accept responsibility for determining their own lives.

Finally, in most forms of experiential therapy, an authentic relationship between client and therapist is seen as central. The relationship between the participants is not reduced to an unconscious repetition of past attachments. Rather, a real "I–thou" relationship is developed between the participants, and this real relationship provides a context for new interpersonal learning.

The three major foundational schools of humanistic-experiential therapy evolved in the 1950s: client-centered, gestalt, and existential. Rogers' (1961) client-centered therapy emphasized the therapeutic relationship and the client's potential to develop naturally into a fully functioning person in a genuine, accepting, and empathic environment. Perls, Hefferline, and Goodman's (1951) gestalt approach focused in a much more directive manner on the client's becoming aware of immediate experience and on processes such as introjection, which interfere with that their awareness. Existential therapy was introduced from Europe by May and others (e.g., May, Angel, & Ellenberger, 1958) and has attempted to direct attention to fundamental, inescapable aspects of human existence, including death, responsibility, loneliness, and the need to construct personal meaning. Each of these three schools has current representatives (e.g., Bozarth, 1990; Bugental, 1981; Polster & Polster, 1973).

Three current approaches represent further developments from these three traditions. Gendlin's (1973, 1981) experiential therapy grew out of client-centered therapy and emphasizes the focusing method. Mahrer's (1983, 1989) intensive experiential therapy is organized around a central exploratory process. Finally, our own process-experiential approach (Greenberg, Rice, & Elliott, 1993; Rice & Greenberg, 1990) attempts to integrate the client-centered, gestalt, and existential traditions within the conceptual framework of modern emotion theory (Greenberg & Safran, 1987). Because of its integrative nature, we will feature the process-experiential approach here.

In common with other humanistic-experiential approaches, the process-experiential approach takes as its basic assumption the view that there are two sorts of barriers to current healthy functioning: (1) difficulties in finding words or images to symbolize one's experiences and (2) dysfunctional *emotion schemes* through which one interprets one's experiences. Therefore, in this view, the process goal of therapy is to enable clients to access their dysfunctional emotion schemes under therapeutic conditions that will facilitate change in relevant emotion schemes.

In the rest of this chapter, we summarize the process-experiential approach. We begin by outlining the general treatment principles that

guide the treatment. Next, we describe what the therapist does (and does not do) in this treatment. The treatment is organized by a set of key experiential tasks presented by clients; each task has a unique client marker and series of client and therapist steps that will foster client resolution of the task. We present the notion of a marker-guided treatment and a general model of task resolution in the therapy, as well as briefly presenting six process-experiential therapy tasks (e.g., an internal conflict or *split*). Finally, we review the major issues in the practical conduct of the treatment, briefly summarize some of the relevant outcome data and adherence measures, and make some concluding recommendations for the future.

GUIDING PRINCIPLES OF A PROCESS-EXPERIENTIAL APPROACH

The process-experiential approach relies on the provision of a genuinely prizing empathic relationship and on the therapist's being highly responsive to the client's experience. Within this context, however, we suggest that the therapist can also profitably guide the client's experiential processing in certain directions. The balance between relationship responsiveness and task directiveness is the central issue for this treatment.

The optimal situation in the process-experiential approach is a synergistic interaction in which client and therapist work together, with each feeling neither led nor simply followed by the other. Instead, the goal is an easy sense of mutual collaboration and coexploration. There is one caveat, however. At times of disjunction or disagreement, clients are viewed as the experts on their own experience, and it is this experience that is viewed as the ultimate reference point. Therapist interventions are always offered in a *nonimposing, nonauthoritative* manner, as suggestions or offers rather than as instructions or statements of truth.

TABLE 7.1. Treatment Principles in the Process-Experiential Approach

Relationship principles: Facilitate a therapeutic relationship:

1. Empathic attunement: Contact and be empathically attuned to the client's internal frame of reference.
2. Therapeutic bond: Communicate empathy in a genuine, prizing relationship.
3. Task collaboration: Facilitate mutual involvement in the goals and tasks of therapy.

Task Facilitation Principles: Facilitate therapeutic work on specific therapeutic tasks.

4. Experiential processing: Facilitate optimal, differential client processes (modes of engagement).
5. Growth/choice: Foster client growth and self-determination.
6. Task completion: Facilitate completion of specific therapeutic tasks.

Source: *Facilitating emotional change* by L. S. Greenberg, L. N. Rice, and R. Elliott, 1993, New York: Guilford. Copyright 1993 by Guilford Press. Adapted by permission.

The combination of relationship and task-oriented styles of intervening adopted in this approach allows us to combine the benefits of both styles and to ameliorate the disadvantages of each. In adopting this flexible dual style, balance and judgment are the guiding characteristics. The therapist must constantly assess the best combination for this client at this time, judging whether more active stimulation or more responsive attunement would be most helpful, all the while keeping the overall balance of autonomy in favor of client-directed exploration. The therapist may be an expert in some of the therapeutic steps that might be facilitative, but it is made clear that the therapist is a facilitator of the client's discovery, not a provider of "truth."

The balance is reflected in a set of six basic treatment principles presented in Table 7.1. These guiding principles are themselves divided evenly between relationship and task facilitation elements, with the relationship principles coming first and ultimately receiving priority over the task facilitation principles.

1. *Empathic attunement: Contact and be empathically attuned to the client's internal frame of reference.* Consistent with the client-centered tradition, empathic attunement is the basis for everything the process-experiential therapist does, including both relationship and task aspects of treatment. The therapist continually tries to make contact with and to maintain a genuine understanding of the client's internal experience or frame of reference. The therapeutic relationship begins with the therapist's attempt to enter the client's frame of reference and continues as the therapist "tracks" what is most important to the client as it evolves throughout the session. The therapist does not take the client's message as something to be evaluated for truth, appropriateness, or psychopathology; there is no attempt to interpret patterns, drives, or defenses or to challenge irrational beliefs.

From the therapist's point of view, empathic attunement involves a series of internal actions by the therapist, including letting go of previously formed ideas about the client, actively entering the client's world, resonating with the client's experience, and grasping what is most crucial or poignant for the client at a particular moment (Vanaerschot, 1990).

2. *Therapeutic bond: Communicate empathy in a genuine, prizing relationship.* Following Rogers (1957) and others, the therapeutic relationship is seen as a key curative element in a process-experiential approach. For this reason, the therapist responds from an internal attitude characterized by a combination of empathy and acceptance/prizing, both genuinely founded in the therapist's experience and beliefs.

In addition to becoming empathically attuned to the client (Principle 1), the therapist communicates this understanding to the client and attempts at all times to foster a relationship in which the client feels deeply understood. The therapist does this by regularly communicating to the client his or her understanding of what the client is experiencing.

If one really develops a sense of what it is like to be the other person, acceptance and warmth almost always follow automatically. The therapist experiences and communicates warm, unconditional *prizing* (Butler, 1952) of the client; a positive feeling is communicated that the client is a worthwhile person whose value does not depend on performing certain behaviors or having feelings. Prizing includes both acceptance (i.e., unconditionality), a general "baseline" attitude of consistent, genuine, noncritical interest in and tolerance for all aspects of the client (Rogers, 1957, 1959), and warmth, an immediate, active sense of caring for, affirming, and appreciating the client at specific moments in therapy.

The therapist's *genuineness* is also essential, as expressed in the idea that the therapist is appropriately congruent (whole, authentic) and transparent (open) in the relationship (Jourard, 1971; Lietaer, 1991; Rogers, 1961). Consistent with this, the therapeutic relationship is viewed as a real human relationship in which the therapist avoids playing roles or hiding behind the "expert role." The therapist's genuineness models and encourages client openness and risk taking, and helps to break down the client's sense of isolation (May & Yalom, 1989). Genuineness also makes the other two conditions effective. It is important to note that we are referring to *facilitative* genuineness, based on the therapist's *accurate* self-awareness, rather than impulsive therapist openness.

3. *Task collaboration: Facilitate mutual involvement in the goals and tasks of therapy.* An effective therapeutic relationship also entails involvement by both client and therapist in the goals and activities carried out in therapy (Bordin, 1979). To begin with, the therapist works to understand the client's view of his or her goals and problems, and accepts the goals and tasks presented by the client. In addition, the therapist helps the client to engage in the general task of experiencing and exploring feelings related to the presented goals and tasks. The therapist accomplishes this by adopting a nonexpert, collaborative tone, by providing information about therapeutic activities as needed, and by negotiating therapeutic tasks with clients.

The three relationship principles provide a model of the optimal client–therapist relationship in a process-experiential approach. These are matched by three treatment principles that guide the pursuit of therapeutic tasks; these principles are based on the general assumption, discussed earlier, that human beings are active, purposeful organisms with an innate need for exploration and mastery of their environment. These principles are expressed in the therapist's attempts to help the client achieve personal goals and solve internal problems.

4. *Experiential processing: Facilitate optimal, differential client processes (modes of engagement).* The optimal client in-session activities vary between and within therapeutic tasks. Therefore, in helping the client to work on specific therapeutic tasks, the therapist facilitates the kind of client experiential processing that is most likely to be productive for that moment in the session and for that client.

We have delineated four different types of client experiential processes, which we refer to as *modes of engagement*: attending, experiential search, active expression, and interpersonal learning. Each of these is most productive in particular in-session contexts. Consequently, the therapist continually uses "micro-markers" to make momentary "microprocess diagnoses" of what is likely to be optimal at given moments in therapy. The therapist then intervenes differentially to best stimulate the client's experiential processing through one of the modes of engagement.

The focus in the *attending/awareness* mode of engagement is on attending directly to particular elements of sensation rather than symbolizing complex relational feelings and meanings. This includes becoming aware of internal sensations (somesthetic and kinesthetic) and external stimuli (visual and auditory), which are essential parts of making clear contact with reality. Attending is an essential part of the immediate experience-based style of work favored in the process-experiential approach. The therapist may facilitate this process of self-awareness in the present by calling attention to some visible aspect of the client's expression, for example, saying, "Are you aware that you are clenching your fists? What do you experience as you do that?" For example, a number of the depressed clients in our research have reported that the therapy helped them learn how to become aware of their feelings and other experiences and how to make use of this information.

The second mode of client engagement, *experiential search*, involves a deliberate turning inward of attentional energy in an attempt to access one's own complex, idiosyncratic inner experience and to begin to symbolize it in words. The process of experiential search enables the client to access and explore emotion schemes that had not previously been available to self-reflective awareness. For instance, a client reported that while dining with friends, she had suddenly and inexplicably found herself feeling very upset. By carefully going back over the incident and reexperiencing it, she was able to identify and put into words the important unexamined personal needs and values that a casual remark by her friend had implicitly challenged.

Experience is pregnant with meaning that is implicit until it is expressed. Thus, the third mode of engagement is *active expression*, which occurs when clients actively and spontaneously express their own emotional reactions. As they do this, they are provided a unique opportunity to discover and own what it is that they *do* feel. Expression also involves allowing the action tendency to run to completion and brings the feeling into *contact* with its appropriate object. Client active expression can be fostered through various sorts of chair work, as when clients use an empty chair to express anger and sadness toward neglectful or abusive significant others.

The final mode of client engagement in process-experiential therapy occurs in the context of the relationship itself through *interpersonal contact*. Through the therapist's genuine empathic attunement and prizing, clients learn that they themselves can exist in relation to another and that this can be a rewarding experience. They are confirmed in their existence as worthwhile people. At particular times, specific experiences with the therapist can provide important new experiences that disconfirm old, restrictive learnings and beliefs about the difficulties or dangers of being with another. For example, one client felt deeply validated when his therapist was able to accept the "warrior" self that he had kept hidden for fear that others would mock him. The therapist's acceptance helped him to own this hidden aspect as part of himself and to consider applying it in appropriate situations.

5. *Growth/choice: Foster client growth and self-determination.* Working within a humanistic framework with existential roots, this approach emphasizes the importance of the client's internal agency. Thus, the therapist emphasizes and values the client's potential for both development and self-ownership, on the one hand, and for freedom, choice, and mature interdependence, on the other hand. One way for the therapist to encourage client growth and self-determination is by listening carefully for, and encouraging ownership of, the client's "growing edge." Another is to offer the client a choice about the goals and tasks in therapy. For example, the therapist might hear and reflect the assertive anger implicit in a particular client's depressed mood; or the therapist might offer a hesitant client the choice *not* to explore a painful issue. Nevertheless, this principle is not pursued in isolation or imposed on the client and is always balanced by empathic attunement and genuine prizing.

6. *Task completion: Facilitate completion of specific therapeutic tasks.* Even in a task-focused treatment such as the process-experiential approach, many therapeutic tasks are not completed, at least not the first time they are introduced. Thus, the last process-experiential treatment principle is helping the client to finish therapeutic tasks. Task completion is facilitated in a number of ways, including framing therapeutic work in terms of tasks in the first place; helping clients follow natural task resolution sequences established for many key experiential tasks (see below); and gentle persistence on key therapeutic tasks.

On the other hand, rigid adherence to a particular current task is counterproductive, and it is sometimes important for the therapist to be flexible in following the client into an emerging task that is more alive or ready for resolution. In addition, it is important to maintain a balance between task focusedness and the therapeutic relationship. At times, the therapist's efforts to help the client complete a therapeutic task may be experienced by the client as a threatening pressure. Anticipating this possibility, the therapist listens carefully and is prepared to offer the client the choice to back off or move to a different task. For example, it might take a number of sessions for a client to resolve important anger and bitterness toward a neglectful parent. The therapist might therefore help the client return to this task week after week, but might temporarily suspend work on it when something more immediately pressing emerges or when the client's embarrassment at expressing strong feelings begins to interfere with work on the initial task.

EXPERIENTIAL RESPONSE MODES

In carrying out the six treatment principles, the therapist uses a number of basic response modes (Goodman & Dooley, 1976). These include therapist responses that are essential to the process-experiential approach and those that play a more supplementary role. Finally, we will describe several responses that are "out of mode" for a process-experiential treatment.

Essential Experiential Response Modes

These account for most of what the therapist does in the process-experiential approach. They include empathic understanding, empathic exploration, process directing, and experiential presence responses (Greenberg et al., 1993).

An important response mode in the process-experiential approach is *empathic understanding*, conveyed by therapist responses that seek simply to communicate understanding of the client's message. These responses include simple reflections and related responses ("Uh-huh") made famous by Carl Rogers. In addition to communicating empathy, such responses commonly serve to enhance the client–therapist relationship, to offer prizing and support to the client (through understanding), and to underline emerging issues. For example, the client might say:

> C: My mother had high blood pressure and a bad heart, but I think she was a hypochondriac. And once us girls got old enough, she didn't do hardly anything and it was left up to us. I had to do it or else it didn't get done.

In response, the therapist might reflect with:

> T: Uh-huh, so it was either you did it or it didn't get done, just a sense of "I have to do it!"

The most characteristic therapist intervention in this approach, however, is *empathic exploration*. These responses simultaneously communicate understanding and help clients move toward the unclear or emerging edges of their experience. Empathic exploration responses take a number of different forms, including evocative and open-edge reflections, exploratory questions, and empathic conjectures. Examples of empathic exploration responses to the client response cited above include the following:

> T: Almost like she would say, "Oh, my *heart!—You* do it!" and you would just feel this tremendous weight of responsibility being put into your hands. (evocative reflection)
> T: (With a pondering quality:) So I guess it was sort of a sense of being left with all that responsibility . . . or something like that? (open-edge reflection)
> T: So it was having all that put on you. What was that like for you then? (exploratory question)

T: I'm not sure, but as you talk about this right now, it seems almost as if you're feeling some of what that was like. Does that fit? (empathic conjecture)

The process-directive nature of the treatment is achieved by a variety of *process directives*. "Direct process, not content" is the simple slogan that sums up our position on therapists' suggestions and other forms of advisement. It is inconsistent with the principle of client self-determination to tell the client what to do to solve problems outside of the therapy session. However, the therapist can suggest in a nonimposing way that the client try engaging in particular in-session exercises; for example:

T: I wonder if it would be okay with you to imagine your mother sitting in this chair here. Can you tell her about what this was like for you?

Other process directives include suggesting that the client attend to a particular experience or carry out a particular action; experiential "homework" is also occasionally used:

T: See if you can stay with the heavy feeling a bit longer. (attention suggestion)
T: The next thing is take a minute and ask yourself, "What is this feeling all about?" (action suggestion)
T: During the week, it might be useful for you to become aware of when and how you do this to yourself. (homework)

It is not only *what* the therapist does but *how* the therapist does it that is important. Thus, the therapist's *experiential presence* is also essential to this approach. The therapist's attitudes involved in fostering the therapeutic relationship are largely communicated through the therapist's "presence" or manner of being with the client. This can be described concretely in terms of paralinguistic and nonverbal behaviors, including silence, vocal quality, and appropriate posture and expression. Thus, the therapist avoids interrupting the client and waits patiently when the client engages in silent self-exploration. Furthermore, much of the therapist's genuine, empathic, prizing attitude toward the client is communicated through his

or her voice quality (Rice & Kerr, 1986), as well as through a comfortable physical posture and distance, expressive speech gestures, appropriate eye contact or gaze, and empathic facial expressions.

Additional Experiential Responses

A number of other experiential response modes are also used in the process-experiential approach, including experiential teaching (giving orienting information or treatment rationales), process observation, and revealing self. These modes are less common than the essential experiential modes described in the previous section and are typically restricted to special therapeutic contexts or tasks. Examples include the following:

T: So you're saying you have two parts of you. One wants to leave the relationship; another feels too guilty to do this—a kind of conflict. At times like this, it is sometimes helpful to have a dialogue between these two sides of yourself. (experiential teaching).
T: As you say this, you seem sort of slumped over in your chair and looking down. (process observation)
T: As I'm listening to you, I'm aware of feeling really moved by what you've been saying. It really touches something in me. (revealing self)

Out-of-Mode Nonexperiential Responses

Although therapist responses such as interpretation, extratherapy advice, reassurance, or confrontation are important in various psychodynamic or cognitive therapies, these content-directive responses are typically avoided. Such responses violate the treatment principles described earlier, particularly growth/choice and empathic attunement. The therapist does not try to give the client new information about the client's self (interpretation), as in psychodynamic treatment. At the same time, the process-experiential approach differs from behavioral and cognitive treatments in that the therapist does not make suggestions about what the client

TABLE 7.2. Revised List of Process-Experimental Tasks: Markers, Interventions, and End States

Task Marker	Intervention	End State
Problem-relevant experience (e.g. (interesting, troubling, puzzling)	Empathic exploration	Clear marker or new meaning explicated
Vulnerability (painful emotion related to self)	Empathic affirmation	Self-affirmation (feels understood, hopeful, stronger)
Absent or unclear felt sense	Experiential focusing	Symbolization of felt sense; productive experiencing
Problematic reaction point (self-understanding problem)	Systematic evocative unfolding	New view of self-in-the-world functioning
Self-evaluative split (self-criticism, tornness)	Two-chair dialogue	Self-acceptance, integrtion
Self-interruption Split (blocked feelings, resignation)	Two-chair enactment	Self-expression, empowerment
Unfinished business (lingering bad feeling re: specific other)	Empty Chair Work	Forgive other or hold other accountable; affirm self/separate
Meaning crisis	Meaning Work	Revision of cherished belief

Source: *Facilitating emotional change* by L. S. Greenberg, L. N. Rice, and R. Elliott, 1993, New York: Guilford. Copyright 1993 by the Guilford Press. Adapted by permission.

should do to solve problems outside of sessions, nor does the therapist confront the client's irrational or dysfunctional attitudes. Instead, the therapist actively helps the client to develop his or her own self-understandings, emotion scheme changes, and problem solutions. In particular, the therapist does this by using the experiential response modes described, as well as helping the client to pursue and resolve a range of therapeutic tasks to be described in the next section.

THERAPEUTIC TASKS

Process-experiential therapy integrates a number of different experiential tasks drawn from client-centered, gestalt, and existential strands of the larger experiential-humanistic therapy tradition. These tasks all include three elements: a marker signaling the client's immediate state of readiness to work on a particular issue or experiential task; a sequence of therapist and client task-relevant actions *(operations)*; and a desired resolution *(end state)*. Table 7.2 summarizes a number of experiential therapy tasks. These will be summarized here, after a

brief presentation of the common elements in the different tasks.

General Task Model

All the tasks in Table 7-2 share certain general processes (Greenberg et al., 1993); these can be described as follows:

1. *Relationship phase:* The client and therapist develop a working alliance.
2. *Empathic exploration phase:* The client engages in the basic therapeutic task of empathic exploration.
3. *Task initiation phase:* As the client and therapist engage in empathic exploration, the therapist listens for task markers and intervenes accordingly, taking into account issues of client trust or "safety." The therapist begins work on a task by proposing it to the client and obtaining the client's agreement.
4. *Evocation/arousal phase:* There then follows an entry phase during which the client's experience is evoked in a more vivid, immediate, or powerful way and

the client moves from a more intellectual, external focus to a more emotional, internal focus.

5. *Experiential exploration phase:* This is usually followed by one of a variety of processes in which there is an dialectical interplay between two different aspects of the client (e.g., a critic and an experiencing self) or between the client's experience and the therapist's understanding of the nature of that experience. When successful, this dialectical process helps the client deepen his or her exploration of core schemes, which generates some new form of experience in the client.

6. *Scheme change or resolution phase:* This new experience is then explored and broadened, leading to change in the client's emotion schemes in the form of enhanced awareness, understanding, or positive reevaluation of the self or others.

7. *Postresolution or carrying-forward phase:* Finally, the client reflects on and symbolizes what has happened, experiences relief, and begins to consider the practical implications of the altered emotion schemes.

With the presentation of the general task model, the main specific tasks of process-experiential therapy will now be described. (It is important to keep in mind that other tasks exist; these are simply the ones that have been studied and described so far.)

Empathic Exploration for Explication of Meaning

In keeping with its client-centered heritage, the generic or baseline task in the process-experiential approach is to help the client explore his or her experiences within an empathic, prizing context. Empathic exploration is the baseline task because the therapist begins each session with it, because the markers for the other tasks emerge from it, and because client and therapist return to it when they pause or complete their work on one of the other tasks.

In a sense, any experience that captures the client's attention in the session can be empathically explored, that is, reexperienced, illuminated, or differentiated, especially when it is incomplete, fuzzy, or global and even when it is expressed only in external terms. Sachse (1992) and Toukmanian (1992) have described multistep models of the process by which clients explicate relevant parts of their meaning structures in the context of empathic exploration. In these models, clients are helped to put forward self-relevant questions that describe, define, and then increasingly clarify problem-relevant feelings and meanings. The therapist's contribution takes the form of implicit *processing proposals* or empathic exploration responses aimed at facilitating each step.

The client begins by attending to some problem-relevant experience, something that is interesting, troubling, or puzzling. At first, the client's attention may be directed to external or purely conceptual aspects of the experience. As the client proceeds, various exploratory activities are facilitated by the therapist, including reexperiencing, searching the edges of awareness, and differentiating experience. The client moves from intellectualized or situational content, to general and then personal evaluation of this content, to the generation and integration of new personal meaning about the self. This new meaning may take the form of a clear marker for a specific task (which signals a new round of therapeutic work). Throughout this process, the therapist helps the client explore through a balanced mix of empathic understanding and empathic exploration, encouraging the client to reexperience, attend to the edges, and differentiate experience.

Mahrer (1983, 1989) has defined a radical version of this empathic exploration process, consisting of four steps that occur in each session. First, by attaining a level of strong feeling, the client accesses an inner, deeper experience and brings it closer to the surface. Second, the deeper experience is received and appreciated. Third, the client "becomes" the deeper potential by enacting and owning it. Fourth, the client tries out this new way of being in the extratherapy world. The relationship between client and therapist in this radical experiential approach is highly nontraditional in that therapist and patient recline in adjacent chairs. Their eyes are closed throughout the session, and the therapist's task is construed as one of experiencing the same thing that the client experiences.

Empathic Affirmation at Vulnerability

Another critical, basic task in the process-experiential approach occurs when the client experiences a moment of intense vulnerability, typically marked by a reluctant confession by the client of a pervasive painful feeling of being "at the end of the road" (Greenberg et al., 1993; Rice & Greenberg, 1991). In this situation, the client's task is to confront and admit to another person some intense, feared aspect of the self that had been previously kept hidden. The therapist's job is to reply with solid empathic understanding responses combined with genuine caring for the client. The therapist does not push for inner exploration and, indeed, does not try to "do" anything with the client's experience except understand and accept it. When the therapist follows and affirms the client's experience in this way, the client typically expresses the vulnerability until he or she "hits bottom" and then begins spontaneously to turn back toward hope. Resolution consists of enhanced client self-acceptance and wholeness, together with a decreased feeling of isolation.

Affirmation events often have an existential content, with the client confronting death, isolation, or meaninglessness. For example, Miss Munn, the well-known client of Carl Rogers

(1983), expresses her vulnerability as feeling "dreadfully alone" in the face of possibly having cancer. Rogers does not try to reassure her about her situation but instead simply tries to capture as accurately as possible what Miss Munn is experiencing. As he does this, she begins to feel comforted and to imagine what it will feel like to have passed through the crisis.

Focusing for an Unclear or Painful Felt Sense

In focusing (Gendlin, 1981, 1984), the therapist helps the client imagine an internal psychological space in which to experience, explore, and symbolize experiences that are either unclear or painful. The full focusing procedure consists of a number of steps, each with its own markers or indicators; the most common marker is the immediate presence of an unclear internal feeling *(felt sense)*. Focusing is also sometimes used when the client is experiencing immediate painful feelings or is having trouble finding an internal focus. The full focusing process begins with *clearing a space* to help the client find an internal focus; then the client is encouraged to attend to the entire unclear internal sense. Next, the therapist helps the client search for a label or *handle* for his or her feeling, encouraging the client to check this label to make sure that it fits the feeling; the labeled sense is then explored more deeply in order to resolve it. Finally, the client *receives* any emergent new experiences and *carries forward* the new experience into new tasks in or out of therapy.

For example, one of Clark's (1990) clients was puzzled by a persistent, vague sense of fatigue. Applying the focusing method to this sensation helped the client to realize that it was about his trouble getting started on things, and with further focusing he came upon the image of a capacitor to symbolize the difficulty. He reported that this symbol provided him with a specific target for further therapeutic work.

Evocative Unfolding of Problematic Reactions

This task intervention, developed out of client-centered therapy (Rice & Sapiera, 1984), addresses a class of emotional processing difficulties that control interactions with other people and external situations. The problematic reaction point (PRP) marker for this event consists of three identifiable features: a particular incident; an emotional or behavioral reaction on the part of the client; and an indication that the client views his or her own reaction as puzzling, inappropriate, or otherwise problematic. From this perspective, the fact that the client is aware of a discrepancy between his or her expected reaction and the actual reaction indicates a current readiness to examine such interactions. For example, the client Margaret reported by Greenberg et al. (1993) expressed puzzlement over her inability to answer a letter from a close friend.

When the incident is vividly reevoked and reprocessed more slowly and completely, clients recognize that their reaction was a direct response to their subjective construals of some aspect of the situation. This, in turn, stimulates further exploration, which leads to the recognition that the particular problematic reaction was an example of a broader style of functioning that is interfering with the client's meeting his or her own needs and goals. For example, when the client Margaret imagined sitting at her desk to reply to the letter, she became aware that her avoidance had been motivated by her need not to disappoint others. Further exploration led the client to awareness of a more general fear of failing, which she connected to childhood experiences.

Two-Chair Work for Conflict Splits or Self-Interruption

There are two different kinds of two-chair work in the process-experiential approach: two-chair dialogue for conflict splits and two-chair enact-ment for self-interruption. Two-chair dialogue addresses a class of processing difficulties in which two schemes or aspects of the self are in opposition, typically indicated by the verbal presentation of a *split* or a currently experienced conflict between the two aspects of the self (Greenberg, 1979). Thus, the client Margaret (Greenberg et al., 1993) described a split between one part that said she should "buckle down" and another part that liked to putter around.

In this task, the therapist initially helps the client to role-play and explore the "critic" aspect of the self, identifying its harsh, negative evaluations of the "experiencing" aspect of the self. The experiencing part, in turn, expresses its affective reactions to the harsh criticism. As the dialogue continues, the harsh critic moves from general statements to more concrete and specific criticisms of the person or situation. In response to these criticisms, the experiencing chair begins to react in a more differentiated fashion until a new aspect of its experience is expressed. A sense of direction then emerges for the experiencer, which is expressed to the critic as a want or a need. The critic next moves to a statement of standards and values. At this point in the dialogue, the critic softens. This is followed by a negotiation or an integration, or both, between the two parts.

Integration sometimes takes more than one session. For example, in her first two-chair work, Margaret's expression of her harsh self-criticisms led to the experiencing aspect's disclosing an almost tragic sense of being alone and abandoned. She then emerged from this despair and began to stand up to her critic by asking it to stop being so disapproving. The split intensified further in the next session, before beginning to resolve two sessions later. After a total of four sessions of two-chair dialogue on this same split, the client reported that she had overcome the writer's block that was one of her presenting problems.

Two-chair enactment, on the other hand, is used when self-interruption processes are operating, that is, when one aspect of the self is blocking or interrupting emotional experiencing or expression by another aspect of the self. This task is marked by an immediate, observable blocking of emotional expression or by a sense of resignation in the client. Resolution of this overregulation of emotional expression is facilitated by asking the client to enact the process of self-interruption. The goal of the intervention is to bring the interruptive tendency under deliberate control so that the previously interrupted emotion can be allowed into awareness and expressed in an appropriate, adaptive manner. With self-expression, clients often also experience a sense of empowerment. For example, when one depressed client acted out the depression that she was experiencing as weighing her down, she began to identify with its power and its protective desire to "toughen you up." Having done this, she was then able to express and validate her strong need to stay connected to the people she cared about, which the depression seemed to have been blocking.

Empty-Chair Dialogue for Unfinished Business

This task intervention, drawn from gestalt therapy, addresses a class of processing difficulties in which schematic emotion memories of significant others continue to trigger the reexperiencing of unresolved emotional reactions. Thus, when one thinks of the other person, bad feelings ensue. This intervention involves reexperiencing the unresolved feelings in the safety of the therapeutic environment, with the immediacy and intensity of the original situation, in order to allow the emotional expression to run its course and be restructured (Daldrup, Beutler, Greenberg, & Engle, 1988). In addition, the client's present resources and capacities promote schematic restructuring and the achievement of closure. This intervention involves four phases: arousal of emotion; expression of what was previously restricted until the expression is completed; relief and recovery;

and restructuring of the perceptions of self and other.

For example, the turning point in Sharon's treatment (Greenberg et al., 1993) occurred in a session in which she alternated between describing episodes of physical abuse by her ex-spouse and empty-chair work. Speaking to him in the empty chair, she expressed hurt, anger, and puzzlement about why he had left her. Toward the end of the session, speaking as the ex-spouse, she realized that he had left out of a sense of boredom because he could no longer control her. This meant that his leaving was due to his immaturity rather than some fault of hers.

Creation of Meaning in Meaning Crises

Consistent with the interests of existential therapists, meaning creation events occur when a client seeks to understand the meaning of an emotional experience or crisis (Clarke, 1989, 1991). This task involves the linguistic symbolization of emotional experience when high emotional arousal is present. Clarke (1989) described the marker for this event as the expression of strong emotion and confusion or puzzlement in conjunction with a description of a challenged cherished belief. Meaning crises often involve loss, disappointments, or other life crises. Therapist interventions that facilitate this task attempt to clarify and symbolize the client's cherished beliefs, the client's discrepant experience, and the discrepancy between belief and experience. The client and therapist work together to accomplish this, often using metaphor to capture aspects of the meaning crisis in words and images.

Typically, resolution of a meaning crisis passes through three phases. First, there is an initial phase in which emotional arousal increases and the elements of the meaning crisis (event, cherished belief, reaction) are specified. Second, the client and therapist explore the cherished belief, including its basis and continued tenability. Finally, the client modifies some aspect of the cherished belief, symbolizes this change, and considers new behavior. For example, the depressed client described by Labott, Elliott, and Eason (1992) wept intensely as she expressed her disappointment and anger at her alcoholic father for hitting her as a child; in exploring her reaction, she discovered that his behavior had violated her cherished belief that "if someone loves you, they don't hurt you." By examining this belief and her experience, she decided that her father hadn't really loved her and that his behavior was not really her fault. Finally, she realized that she needed to work on issues of trust in her marital relationship.

PRACTICAL APPLICATION OF PROCESS-EXPERIENTIAL THERAPY

Format

The process-experiential approach to therapy is most often carried out in an individual format (Greenberg et al., 1993). However, consistent with its gestalt origins, process-experiential therapy is also widely practiced in group formats (see Daldrup et al., 1988), and there is a version available for marital/couples therapy (Greenberg & Johnson, 1988).

Appropriate Clients

As we envision it, process-experiential therapy is most appropriate for use in an outpatient clinic or private practice setting with clients experiencing mild to moderate clinical distress and symptomatology. Some clients seem to enter therapy with processing styles that allow them to engage almost immediately in the empathic exploration and experiential search processes so critical to experiential treatment. These clients quickly respond to empathic interventions by turning inward and exploring,

suggesting some predisposition on their part. Clinically, such clients may have varying diagnoses and problems, including depression, anxiety, low self-esteem, internal conflicts, and lingering resentments and difficulties with others.

In our experience, however, not all clients enter treatment with this ability to focus on and search out the edges of their own experience. In fact, much of the challenge and art of the process-experiential approach comes in adapting the treatment to meet the needs of a variety of clients with various processing styles. For instance, some clients seem to be persistently focused on external factors such as unsupportive others or financial or medical problems, to which they return repeatedly in the face of the therapist's best efforts to help them focus inwardly. Other clients enter therapy seeking expert guidance or advice. These clients may experience the process-experiential therapist's failure to give advice or interpret the causes of their problems as withholding of help.

Nevertheless, the process-experiential approach can still be used successfully with clients whose styles are generally external or interpersonally dependent. For these clients, the therapist needs to gradually create an internal focus through consistent empathic exploration of their inner experience and by occasional experiential teaching. In addition, treatment with these clients may emphasize the use of the more process-directive tasks such as focusing and empty-chair work.

This treatment is best suited to outpatient problems. It is not suited for clients with major thought disorder or schizophrenia, impulse control or antisocial personality patterns, or for those in need of immediate crisis intervention or case management (e.g., acutely suicidal persons). In addition, we are not inclined to use this treatment with those few clients who develop strong negative reactions to the internal exploration and self-determination foci of the treatment or who find the therapist's nondirective stance of not advising or interpreting to be unacceptable.

Treatment Length

As described here, the process-experiential approach is appropriate as either a brief therapy or a long-term treatment, although the balance between task and relationship elements will probably vary with the treatment length. As a brief therapy, the treatment will usually be more active and emphasize task interventions appropriate to the client. As a long-term (i.e., 50+ sessions) treatment of chronic personality or interpersonal difficulties, a process-experiential approach will tend to emphasize relationship aspects, although task interventions are certainly used where appropriate.

Session Length and Frequency

In process-experiential therapy, a standard session length and frequency of 50–60 minutes once a week is typical. In some contexts, it is desirable to use a flexible session length ranging between 50 and 90 minutes (i.e., by scheduling sessions at 1.5-hour intervals) in order to allow for completion of therapeutic tasks. In order to maintain continuity, sessions generally occur on a weekly basis, particularly in brief treatments. Nevertheless, the therapist is flexible and allows for client self-determination within the limits imposed by scheduling.

Training and Supervision

Training is typically broken down into a series of modules. Initial training in the basic tasks of empathic exploration and empathic affirmation is central. Without this, training in the other treatment tasks will be hampered, as they rely on the ability to attend empathically and on the relational attitudes of prizing and genuineness. Training in each task (evocative unfolding, focusing, meaning creation, and two-chair and empty-chair work) proceeds on a number of levels. Three components of training are emphasized: didactic learning of both the underlying theory and the typical client steps to successful resolution; perceptual training involving practice in recognizing markers, experiential states, and emerging signs of resolution; and training in skills. Training in skills involves exposure to examples of skilled performance (i.e., modeling), training in the microskills (components) of the different interventions, and, most important, experiential learning by engaging in both therapist and client roles as part of a training workshop (Greenberg, 1979; Greenberg & Sarkissian, 1984). Training also requires supervised practice with actual clients.

Summary of Available Outcome Data

The outcome of the process-experiential approach has been the subject of at least 12 separate studies with various clinical populations (Greenberg, Elliott, & Lietaer, 1994), including clients with major depression, anxiety, marital conflict, decisional conflicts, and unresolved relationships with significant others (Beutler et al., 1991; Elliott et al., 1990; Greenberg & Webster, 1982; Johnson & Greenberg, 1985; Paivio & Greenberg, 1992). In a review and meta-analysis of this literature, Greenberg et al. (1994) found large pre-to-post effect sizes (E.S. = 1.82) for process-experiential treatments; these effects compare favorably to those of other types of treatment, including cognitive-behavioral therapy. Some of this work is beginning to examine client pretreatment variables that predict successful outcomes (e.g., Beutler et al., 1991). However, the outcome and predictor studies conducted to date have not employed the full range of process-experiential tasks.

Assessment of Treatment Adherence and Task Resolution

Adherence measures have been constructed for most of the task interventions. These measures, developed by Greenberg and Rice (1991) and Goldman (1991), have been shown to discriminate task interventions from each other and from empathic reflection. Specifically, Goldman (1991) demonstrated that the task interventions predominantly utilize different specific therapist interventions, even though there is a slight overlap; she also showed that raters could discriminate between process-experiential and brief dynamic or cognitive-behavioral approaches, both on specific therapist interventions and on more global experiential relationship skills, such as the therapist's tracking of moment-by-moment experience and empathic attunement to affect. Daldrup et al. (1988) also provide a measure of therapist treatment adherence. Finally, an approach to assessing client task completion has been developed in the form of a set of scales for rating degree of task resolution specific to each therapeutic task (Greenberg et al., 1993).

CONCLUSION

It is our belief that the process-experiential approach shows promise as a model for integrating theory, practice, and research in psychotherapy. The task interventions and resolution processes briefly described in this chapter are based on research and have produced theory development both about emotional functioning in general and about how therapists can help their clients to resolve specific experiential difficulties.

However, there is a clear need for the specification and investigation of additional experiential tasks and their markers, task interventions, and paths to resolution, as well as further research on already described tasks and on process-experiential treatments integrating a range of tasks to focus on particular populations of clients. There is not yet enough data to allow us to make strong claims of effectiveness, especially with regard to specific problems or diagnostic groups.

While experiential therapy in general is not currently endorsed as a primary orientation by large numbers of therapists, there is some evidence that it has been incorporated by integratively oriented therapists and is a common secondary orientation endorsed by many therapists who label themselves as eclectic or integrative (Watkins, Lopez, Campbell, & Himmell, 1986).

Moreover, we suspect that this approach may also be of growing relevance to dynamic therapists, who are becoming increasingly interested in the role of therapist empathic attunement; to cognitive-behavior therapists, many of whom are coming to value emotional processes; and to feminist therapists, who share with the process-experiential approach to advocacy of client empowerment and an egalitarian client–therapist relationship.

REFERENCES

Beutler, L. E., Engle, D., Mohr, D., Daldrup, R. J., Bergan, J., Meredith, K., & Merry, W. (1991). Predictors of differential response to cognitive, experiential, and self-directed psychotherapeutic procedures. *Journal of Consulting and Clinical Psychology, 59,* 333–340.

Bordin, E. S. (1979). The generalizability of the psychoanalytic concept of the working alliance. *Psychotherapy: Theory, Research and Practice, 16,* 252–260.

Bozarth, J. D. (1990). The essence of client-centered therapy. In G. Lietaer, J. Rombauts, & R. Van Balen (Eds.), *Client-centered and experiential psychotherapy in the nineties* (pp. 59–64). Leuven, Belgium: Leuven University Press.

Bugental, J. F. T. (1981). *The search for authenticity* (enlarged ed.). New York: Irvington.

Butler, J. M. (1952). The interaction of client and therapist. *Journal of Abnormal and Social Psychology, 47,* 366–378.

Clark, C. A. (1990). A comprehensive process analysis of focusing events in experiential therapy. *Dissertation Abstracts International, 51,* 6098B.

Clarke, K. M. (1989). Creation of meaning: An emotional processing task in psychotherapy. *Psychotherapy: Theory, Research, and Practice, 26,* 139–148.

Clarke, K. M. (1991). A performance model of the

creation of meaning event. *Psychotherapy, 28*, 395–401.

Daldrup, R., Beutler, L., Greenberg, L., & Engle, D. (1988). *Focused expressive therapy: A treatment for constricted affect*. New York: Guilford Press.

Elliott, R., Clark, C., Wexler, M., Kemeny, V., Brinkerhoff, J., & Mack, C. (1990). The impact of experiential therapy of depression: Initial results. In G. Lietaer, J. Rombauts, & R. Van Balen (Eds.), *Client-centered and experiential psychotherapy in the nineties* (pp. 549–577). Leuven, Belgium: Leuven University Press.

Gendlin, E. T. (1973). Experiential psychotherapy. In R. Corsini (Ed.), *Current psychotherapies* (pp. 317–352). Itasca, IL: F. E. Peacock.

Gendlin, E. T. (1981). *Focusing* (2nd ed.). New York: Bantam Books.

Gendlin, E. T. (1984). The client's client: The edge of awareness. In F. R. Levant & J. M. Shlien (Eds.), *Client-centered therapy and the person-centered approach: New directions in theory, research and practice* (pp. 76–107). New York: Praeger.

Goldman, R. (1991). *The validation of the experiential therapy adherence measure*. Unpublished master's thesis, Department of Psychology, York University.

Goodman, G., & Dooley, D. (1976). A framework for help-intended communication. *Psychotherapy: Theory, Research and Practice, 13*, 106–117.

Greenberg, L. S. (1979). Resolving splits: The two-chair technique. *Psychotherapy: Theory, Research and Practice, 16*, 310–318.

Greenberg, L. S. Elliott, R., & Lietaer, G. (1994). Research on humanistic and experiential psychotherapies. In A. E. Bergin & S. L. Garfield (Eds.), *Handbook of psychotherapy and behavior change* (4th ed., pp. 509–539). New York: Wiley.

Greenberg, L. S., & Johnson, S. M. (1988). *Emotionally focused therapy for couples*. New York: Guilford Press.

Greenberg, L. S., & Rice, L. N. (1991). *Change processes in experiential psychotherapy*. NIMH Grant Proposal No. 1R01MH45040, Washington, DC.

Greenberg, L. S., Rice, L. N., & Elliott, R. (1993). *Facilitating emotional change: The moment-by-moment process*. New York: Guilford Press.

Greenberg, L. S., & Safran, J. D. (1987). *Emotion in psychotherapy: Affect, cognition, and the process of change*. New York: Guilford Press.

Greenberg, L. S., & Sarkissian, M. (1984). Evaluation of counselor training Gestalt methods. *Counselor Education and Supervision, 23*, 328–340.

Greenberg, L. S., & Webster, M. (1982). Resolving decisional conflict by means of two-chair dialogue and empathic reflection at a split in counseling. *Journal of Counseling Psychology, 29*, 468–477.

Johnson, S. M., & Greenberg, L. S. (1985). Differential effects of experiential and problem-solving interventions in resolving marital conflict. *Journal of Consulting and Clinical Psychology, 53*, 175–184.

Jourard, S. M. (1971). *The transparent self*. Princeton, NJ: Van Nostrand Reinhold.

Labott, S., Elliott, R., & Eason, P. (1992). "If you love someone, you don't hurt them": A comprehensive process analysis of a weeping event in psychotherapy. *Psychiatry, 55*, 49–62.

Lietaer, G. (1991, July). *The authenticity of the therapist: Congruence and transparency*. Paper presented at the Second International Conference on Client-Centered and Experiential Psychotherapy, Stirling, Scotland.

Mahrer, A. R. (1983). *Experiential psychotherapy: Basic practices*. New York: Brunner/Mazel.

Mahrer, A. R. (1989). *How to do experiential psychotherapy: A manual for practitioners*. Ottawa: University of Ottawa Press.

May, R., Angel, E., & Ellenberger, H. (Eds.). (1958). *Existence: A new dimension in psychiatry and psychology*. New York: Basic Books.

May, R., & Yalom, I. (1989). Existential psychotherapy. In R. J. Corsini & D. Wedding (Eds.) *Current psychotherapies* (4th ed.) (pp. 363–402). Itasca, IL: Peacock.

Paivio, S., & Greenberg, L. S. (1992, June). *Resolving unfinished business: A study of effects*. Paper presented at the meeting of the Society for Psychotherapy Research, Berkeley, CA.

Perls, F. S., Hefferline, R. F., & Goodman, P. (1951). *Gestalt therapy*. New York: Julian Press.

Polster, E., & Polster, M. (1973). *Gestalt therapy integrated*. New York: Brunner/Mazel.

Rice, L. N., & Greenberg, L. S. (1990). Fundamental dimensions in experiential therapy: New directions in research. In G. Lietaer, J. Rombauts, & R. Van Balen (Eds.), *Client-centered and experiential psychotherapy in the nineties* (pp. 397–414). Leuven, Belgium: Leuven University Press.

Rice, L. N., & Greenberg, L. S. (1991). Two affective change events in client-centered therapy. In J. Safran & L. S. Greenberg (Eds.), *Affective change events in psychotherapy* (pp. 197–226). New York: Academic Press.

Rice, L. N., & Greenberg, L. S. (1992). Humanistic approaches to psychotherapy. In D. Freedheim (Ed.), *History of psychotherapy: A century of change* (pp. 197–224). Washington, DC: American Psychological Association.

Rice, L. N., & Kerr, G. P. (1986). Measures of client and therapist vocal quality. In L. S. Greenberg & W. Pinsof (Eds.), *The psychotherapeutic process: A research handbook* (pp. 73–105). New York: Guilford Press.

Rice, L. N., & Saperia, E. (1984). A task analysis of the resolution of problematic reactions. In L. Rice & L. S. Greenberg (Eds.), *Patterns of change: Intensive analysis of psychotherapeutic process* (pp. 29–66). New York: Guilford Press.

Rogers, C. R. (1957). The necessary and sufficient conditions of therapeutic personality change. *Journal of Consulting Psychology, 21,* 95–103.

Rogers, C. R. (1959). A theory of therapy, personality, and interpersonal relationships as developed in the client-centered framework. In S. Koch (Ed.), *Psychology: The study of a science* (Vol. III, pp. 184–256). New York: McGraw-Hill.

Rogers, C. R. (1961). *On becoming a person.* Boston: Houghton Mifflin.

Rogers, C. R. (1983). *Miss Munn* (AAP Tape Library Catalog, Tape No. 5). Salt Lake City, UT: American Academy of Psychotherapists.

Sachse, R. (1992). Differential effects of processing proposals and content references on the explication process of clients with different starting conditions. *Psychotherapy Research, 2,* 235–251.

Toukmanian, S. G. (1992). Studying the client's perceptual processes and their outcomes in psychotherapy. In S. G. Toukmanian & D. L. Rennie (Eds.), *Psychotherapy process research: Paradigmatic and narrative approaches* (pp. 77–107). Newbury Park, CA: Sage.

Vanaerschot, G. (1990). The process of empathy: Holding and letting go. In G. Lietaer, J. Rombauts, & R. Van Balen (Eds.), *Client-centered and experiential psychotherapy in the nineties* (pp. 269–294). Leuven, Belgium: Leuven University Press.

Watkins, C. E., Lopez, F. G., Campbell, V. L., & Himmell, C. D. (1986). Contemporary counseling psychology: Results of a national survey. *Journal of Counseling Psychology, 33,* 301–309.

Yalom, I. D. (1980). *Existential psychotherapy.* New York: Basic Books.

8

Cognitive-Behavioral Therapy in Historical Perspective

Donald H. Meichenbaum

PROLOGUE

> Written histories are always and necessarily interpretive.
>
> (Mahoney, 1993, p. 187)

Historians are in the business of telling stories. Their stories are often filled with (1) descriptions of episodic periods that are demarcated by so-called landmark events, (2) engaging accounts of selected influential historical figures, and (3) discussions of influences that reflect a specific theme (e.g., the impact of economic factors, a religious movement, demographic changes, intellectual shifts). Each historical account constitutes a constructive process whereby the archivist of the past and the prognosticator of the future provide a personal perspective in order to achieve a narrative objective. The historian holds certain tacit assumptions and implicit beliefs that influence how he or she appraises events and what he or she highlights. Holding a "confirmatory bias", the historian is prone to seek data and report events that are consistent with personal beliefs. In short, the historian takes on the task of constructing a narrative that is likely to be plied with metaphors and filled with prominent characters who play the roles of heroes, adversaries, victims, accomplices, and the like. The historian often provides a post hoc explanatory scheme, as if events had more coherence than they actually did.

Just how different is the business of writing history from what we ask clients to do in psychotherapy? A client is asked by a therapist to tell his or her story. Imagine yourself in the position of the client. Where would you begin? What do you include in and exclude from your narrative account? How will your story "hang together"? Moreover, how will your story change over the course of therapy?

In telling the history of cognitive-behavioral therapy, I have a similar dilemma. What are my options? Should I highlight the long tradition of theorists and therapists, from Greek philosophers to twentieth-century semantic therapists, who have highlighted the role of cognitive and emotional processes in psychopathology and behavior change? Should I trace the convergent influences of cognitive, developmental, and social psychology that have contributed to what Dember (1974) has called a *cognitive revolution* in psychology? (By the way, was it a revolution or merely an evolution?) Note: The metaphors that historians (as well as our clients) use color the way they see things and what is reported and emphasized.

In terms of my options, should I describe how

theorists and therapists became disenchanted and disappointed with classical learning theories and strict behavior therapy interventions and developed innovative cognitive-behavioral treatments? Yet, if the historian wants people to read and discuss his or her account, then there is a need to include colorful personalities who see themselves in impassioned battle with prominent theorists. The history of science is replete with examples that scientific paradigm shifts are *not* due to the "convincingness" of new data; rather, such shifts are due to the "passion" and increased plausibility and hopefulness of a new scientific perspective (Kuhn, 1962; Mahoney 1976). The names of "cognitive types" in the twentieth-century reverberate with individuals who did battle and who were passionate advocates (e.g., among others, Dubois, Bartlett, Adler, Horney, Tolman, Kelly, Ellis, Beck, Arnold and Richard Lazarus, Rotter, Bandura, Walters, Mischel, Kanfer, Mahoney, Meichenbaum, Kendall, Hollon, Goldfried, Wilson, Marlatt, and their students). A cast of hundreds!

But what makes these contributors interesting is not only what they said but who they challenged. They questioned the tenets of classical learning theories and psychoanalytic formulations, and caused the field to question how best to conceptualize the clients' thoughts and feelings. Moreover, they raised questions of how the clients' thoughts influence and, in turn, are influenced by their feelings, behaviors, resultant consequences, and physiological processes. They emphasized that individuals not only respond to their environments but are also the architects of those environments.

These new proposals were *not* warmly received by various factions, especially behavioral types who had their own "catechism" to defend. For example, within the major behavior therapy association (Association for the Advancement of Behavior Therapy, AABT) the cognitive types were brandished as malcontents and as oxymorons who had deviated from the scientific basis of psychotherapy. Attempts were made to have them kicked out of the AABT, and efforts were made to limit their opportunities to present scientific papers. Articles that included the term *cognition* were rejected by some journals.

Yet, some 20 years later, psychotherapists in North America have endorsed cognitive-behavioral interventions as the second most widely used treatment approach (i.e., with an eclectic approach being endorsed as first) (Smith, 1982). Smith's survey of 800 clinical and counseling psychologists also revealed that the 10 most influential psychotherapists of the century included such cognitive-behavioral therapists as Albert Ellis (No. 2), Arnold Lazarus (No. 4), Aaron Beck (No. 7), and Donald Meichenbaum (No. 10). Smith concluded that "these findings suggest quite clearly that cognitive behavior therapy is one of the major trends in counseling and psychotherapy" (p. 808). As further evidence of the widespread influence of cognitive-behavioral therapy, Heesacker, Heppner, and Rogers (1982) analyzed approximately 14,000 references cited in three major counseling psychology journals and discovered that in terms of the frequency of citations, among the top 9 were Ellis, Meichenbaum, Bandura, and Mahoney. As we will see, this popularity is supported by empirical data on the relative efficacy of cognitive-behavioral interventions. As Hollon and Beck (1993) recently observed:

> In summary, although important questions remain, it appears that the cognitive and cognitive-behavioral interventions may be effective in the treatment of a broad range of disorders and problems in living. These approaches are at least as effective as the best available alternatives for a number of disorders. Moreover, there are indications that these sustained improvements are not always shared by other treatment approaches. (p. 95)

The disorders *successfully treated* by cognitive-behavioral methods include depression, anxiety disorders such as panic attacks, generalized anxiety disorder, social phobias and posttraumatic stress disorders, the eating disorder of bulimia nervosa, conduct disorder in children, and schizophrenia, as well as life skills enhancement in individuals with developmental disabilities, relapse prevention in clients with substance abuse, and marital distress. Cognitive-behavioral methods have also been applied in behavioral medicine (Beck, 1993; Goldfried, Greenberg, & Marmar, 1990; Turk, Meichenbaum, & Genest, 1983).

How did the cognitive-behavioral approach gain such prominence? Is this popularity warranted, or is it just one more passing fad in the history of psychotherapy? Moreover, how will the conceptual models underlying cognitive-behavioral interventions change?

Since I have been involved intimately in the development and evaluation of cognitive-behavioral treatment procedures for the last 25 years (Meichenbaum, 1977, 1992a), I have decided to use this occasion to address these questions. There are many other historical accounts of the cognitive behavioral therapies (e.g., Arnkoff & Glass, 1992; Beck, 1993; Dobson & Block, 1988; Ellis, 1989; Ingram, Kendall, & Chen, 1991; Mahoney and Arnkoff, 1978; Meichenbaum, 1992b; Raimy 1975; Vallis, Howes, & Miller, 1991). My objective is not to summarize or paraphrase these scholarly narratives. Rather, I intend to highlight the untold portions of the story and, moreover, propose where the field of cognitive-behavioral interventions is headed.

ORIGINS OF COGNITIVE-BEHAVIOR THERAPY (CBT)

It is difficult to pinpoint a specific person or date as to the origin of any psychotherapeutic approach. Like most forms of psychotherapy, CBT was the result of an evolutionary (not revolutionary) process and was part of a zeitgeist that recognized the important role that cognitive appraisals play in how individuals respond to events. Consider the number of cross-currents that contributed to the evolution of CBT.

1. As documented by Victor Raimy (1975), a long tradition of semantic therapists is evident from the initial writings of Pierre Janet (1893), who believed that hysterics suffered from "fixed ideas," to Paul Dubois (1904/1907), who argued that "incorrect ideas" produced psychological distress, to George Kelly (1955), who discussed the role of individuals' "personal constructs" as being critical to how they construe themselves and their world.

But these semantic theorists were predated by Greek, Roman, and Eastern philosophers. For example, in the fourth century B.C, the Roman Stoic philosopher Epictetus noted that "Men are disturbed not by events, but by the views they take of them." The religious leader Gautama Buddha offered the observation that "We are what we think. All that we are arises with our thoughts. With our thoughts we make the world" (Dhammapada, Buddhist observation). In the same vein, the philosopher Immanuel Kant proposed that mental illness occurs when a person fails to correct his "private sense" with "common sense." More than a generation later, Alfred Adler viewed Kant's private sense as "mistaken opinions" that underlie neurotic behavior. Perhaps the modern philosopher-baseball player Satchel Paige captured the promise of this cognitive orientation best when he noted, "If your stomach disputes you, lie down and pacify it with cool thoughts."

While these quotes imply that an individual's cognitions cause emotional dysfunction and maladaptive behaviors, and may be used to alter behavior, more recent accounts have suggested that cognitions, emotions, behaviors, resultant consequences, and accompanying physiological processes interact in a complex, reciprocally determined manner (Bandura, 1978). Cognitions and emotions are viewed as two sides of the same coin, and emotions and interpersonal processes are seen as affecting cognitions, just as much as cognitions can influence emotional and behavioral processes (Greenberg & Safran, 1986). But I am getting too far ahead in my historical account. Before we examine how CBT has evolved into a more complex explanatory scheme, we need to attend to other historical and developmental influences.

2. As noted, a cognitive-behavioral approach emerged, in part, out of an increasing

dissatisfaction with both the theoretical and empirical bases of a strictly behavior therapy approach. A number of critics questioned the adequacy of learning theory explanations of both psychopathology and behavior change. For instance, Breger and McGaugh (1965) challenged the predominant view of stimulus-response (S-R) theories, highlighted the circulatory nature of the definition of reinforcement, and critiqued prominent behavioral interventions such as Wolpe's systematic desensitization for failing to attend to the important roles of relationships and cognitive factors. They also offered a cognitive-affective alternative explanation for the nature of behavior change. Even more challenging attacks on the adequacy of learning theory explanations were offered by Brewer (1974), who made the provocative claim that "There is no convincing evidence for operant and classical conditioning in adult humans!" This heretical viewpoint, after a generation of idolatry of Pavlov, Thorndike, Watson, and Skinner, gave pause to those who would readily extend the language of learning theory to complex human behavior. Too much research was emerging that highlighted that it was not the so-called stimulus consequences, or reinforcement, that influenced an individual's behavior, but rather how the individual perceived the relationship between his or her behavior and critical events. Moreover, the individual's awareness of the contingency of the consequences was a primary determinant of learning (Dulany, 1968; Spielberger & De-Nike, 1966).

The role that meaning and appraisal processes play in influencing an individual's reactions to stressful events was also being demonstrated in the laboratory of Richard Lazarus (1966). He found that what subjects were told about stressful stimuli (e.g., "scary" films) was critical in influencing their physiological and behavioral reactions. For example, if subjects were told that an industrial accident film was a mere dramatization made for educational purposes, compared to a depiction of an actual accident, entirely different patterns of response were evident. As Epictetus had noted, it is not events per se that are critical, but rather what we make of these events. Stress, like beauty, is in the eye of the beholder. As we will see, the treatment implications of this simple adage are substantial.

What should have acted as a death knell to the learning theory approach to intervention was offered by McKeachie (1974), who traced "the decline and fall of the laws of learning." But the lessons of the history of science remind us that data do *not* cause theorists and practitioners to give up their cherished beliefs. As in our clients, disputations are likely to lead to reactance and the hardening of one's categories. Scientists, like clients, have what the seventeenth-century philosopher Francis Bacon characterized as a "confirmatory bias," namely, the penchant to distort and to attend selectively to experience in order to make it fit their memories and expectations. As Mahoney (1991) observed, it is interesting how often modern cognitive concepts have been predated. In 1620, Francis Bacon observed:

> The human understanding when it has once adopted an opinion . . . draws all things else to support and agree with it. And though there be a greater number and weight of instances to be found on the other side, yet these it either neglects and despises, or else by some distinction sets and rejects, in order that the authority of its former conclusions may remain inviolate. (1960, p. 50, as cited by Mahoney, 1991, p. 50)

The beliefs of those who held a strictly behavioral viewpoint remained "inviolate." The arguments by Breger and McGaugh, Brewer, McKeachie, and many others did not readily lead to change until alternative explanatory models were offered.

3. It was the writings of social learning theorists such as Bandura (1969), Bandura and Walters (1963), Kanfer and Phillips (1970), Mischel (1973), Rotter (1966), and others that provided a needed new direction. These authors emphasized the role of mediated self-regulatory processes in behavior change. How individuals set goals, formulate expectations, problem-solve,

make decisions, self-monitor, assign meaning, offer causal explanations, and make attributions were now seen as operative principles of human behavior and appropriate territory for interventions, both on a treatment and on a preventive basis. The bywords became *reciprocal determinism*, which emphasized the interdependence of cognitive, affective, behavioral, and physiological processes, and *transactional analysis*, which described how individuals elicited reactions from others that confirmed their prior beliefs (views of themselves and of others). Within this new framework, clients were taught how they inadvertently, unwittingly, and perhaps, even unknowingly created the reactions in others that they so feared. For instance, the depressed client who had concerns about loss, rejection, and abandonment may have behaved in a "depressing" fashion that caused others to avoid and reject him. Thus, the depressed client's thoughts became what initially Bacon and, later, George Mead (1934) called *self-fulfilling prophecies*.

But these cognitive activities are *not* viewed as being totally reality-based mechanisms that are designed to process data accurately and veridically; rather, they are seen as self-protective devices designed to help individuals maintain self-esteem, reduce dysphoric emotions, and achieve interpersonal goals. This theoretical message received empirical support in the writings of cognitive psychologists.

4. The 1970s and 1980s were marked by a great deal of creative research activity by cognitive psychologists who studied the inferential and decision-making processes of individuals. The work of such cognitive psychologists as Kahnemann, Slovic, and Tversky (1982), Kruglanski (1980, 1990), Mandler (1975), Nisbett and Ross (1980), Taylor and Crocker (1981), Tversky and Kahnemann (1974), and others highlighted that individuals were biased, inefficient, and often incompetent processors of information, as well as poor decision makers. Their decisions were often influenced by habits of thinking, or mental heuristics, rather than being based on the circumstances of actual events. For example, when appraising events, formulating expectations, and making deci-

sions, our proverbial depressed client is prone to attend selectively to or call on other mood-congruent depressogenic examples from the past, and then take these readily available instances as representative of a class of events that guide present and future behaviors.

In short, cognitive psychologists were now beginning to explicate the psychological mechanisms that Epictetus and Bacon, Kant and Dubois, had intuitively described. Moreover, clinical psychologists such as Hollon and Kriss (1984), Kovacs and Beck (1978), Mahoney (1974), Meichenbaum and Gilmore (1984), and Turk and Salovey (1985) have extended these constructs to the understanding of psychiatric disturbance and dysfunctional behaviors. They have proposed that making clients aware of the bidirectional, transactional, and reciprocally deterministic nature of their behaviors, and of the ways in which they may be biased, can serve therapeutic objectives.

The treatment goal was to develop a therapeutic means of accomplishing this learning process in a nondidactic, user-friendly, collaborative, emotionally meaningful, experientially based fashion. Cognitive-behavior therapists developed ways to teach their clients a methodology or strategy for identifying and exploring the validity of their inferences. Clients are taught to view their thoughts as hypotheses worthy of testing. These treatment objectives called for the development of new therapeutic techniques and served as the impetus for problem-solving and coping skills cognitive behavioral interventions, as reflected in the work of D'Zurilla (1986), D'Zurilla and Goldfried (1971), Lazarus (1981), Meichenbaum (1985), Meichenbaum and Cameron (1974), Spivack and Shure (1974), and others. Moreover, there was an increasing appreciation that such therapeutic efforts must be sensitive to the interpersonal aspects of how the individual's schemas and cognitive processes are formulated (Coyne & Gotlib, 1983; Safran & Segal, 1990).

But such cognitive-behavioral interventions also recognized that under some conditions the client's distortions, illusions, false hopes, denial processes, and cognitive-affective biases may be adaptive. As Taylor and Brown (1988) highlighted, under certain conditions, illusions can foster well-being and mental health. As we will see, this line of thinking has given rise to yet newer constructive narrative versions of CBT.

5. All that we have discussed thus far has focused on the evolution of cognitive-behavioral treatment procedures with adults. But there is another very important clinical population with whom CBT has been employed, namely, children and adolescents. Such developmental problems as conduct disorders, impulsivity, anxiety disorders, depression, learning disability, and parent–adolescent conflict have been successfully treated with cognitive-behavioral approaches (Hollon & Beck, 1993; Kendall, 1991, 1993; Meyers & Craighead, 1984). These developmental interventions were influenced by the work of the Soviet psychologist Lev Vygotsky (1978) and his student A. R. Luria (1976). They proposed that children become socialized by internalizing interpersonal communication into private intrapersonal speech. Thus, out of the social discourse that is carefully calibrated to the needs of the child, the tutor influences the child's cognitive development and self-regulatory skills. These higher-level cognitive skills (also called *metacognitions*) reflect the child's ability to notice, catch, interrupt, self-monitor, elaborate, predict, summarize, self-interrogate, access prior information, and problem-solve—in other words, to become a more self-regulated learner (Flavell, 1979; Meichenbaum & Biemiller, 1992). Cognitive-behavior therapists have been able to teach various child clinical populations to self-instruct and to develop self-control skills (Meichenbaum, 1977). More recently, Loera and Meichenbaum (1993) and Meichenbaum (1993a) have discussed how such cognitive-behavioral techniques can be extended to such populations as deaf children and clients with traumatic brain injury.

Perhaps best illustrative of the cognitive-behavioral approach with children is the work with conduct-disordered children. The 5–10% of children who display clinically significant aggressive behavior have been found to show a variety cognitive deficiencies and distortions, as summarized by Kendall (1993). For example, aggressive children, relative to their nonaggressive peers, have been found to:

1. use fewer environmental cues to mediate their behavior;
2. pay greater attention (or to be hypervigilant) to aggressive environmental cues;
3. recall high rates of hostile cues;
4. attribute others' behavior in ambiguous situations to their hostile intentions;
5. underperceive their own level of aggressiveness and their responsibility, especially during the early stages of dyadic conflict;
6. label generalized arousal as anger;
7. generate fewer verbal assertion solutions while generating more action-oriented aggressive solutions to social problems;
8. behave in an aggressive fashion which elicits counter-aggressive behavior, thus confirming their initial expectations and concerns;
9. believe that aggressive behavior will enhance their self-esteem and will not cause victims to suffer.

Kendall (1993) summarizes work by a number of cognitive-behavior therapists such as Kazdin, Lochman, Feindler, Ecton, and their colleagues, who have taught such conduct-disordered children to alter their behavior, thoughts, and feelings. Similar treatment research is now underway with other child clinical populations, both on a treatment and on a preventive basis. These approaches involve parents, peers, and school personnel in order to increase the likelihood of generalization.

6. All of this research activity with adults and children required a publication outlet. In 1977, the journal *Cognitive Therapy and Research* was established under the editorship of Michael Mahoney. The need for a new journal grew out of the burgeoning research activity and the unresponsiveness of editors of behaviorally oriented journals to the new cognitive emphasis. A second reason for the development of a new journal was to foster integration between therapists with different orientations. From the outset, CBT sought to combine the clinical concerns of psychodynamic and systems-

oriented psychotherapy with the technology of behavior therapy. This move toward integration was evident in the initial founding meeting of the Society for the Exploration of Psychotherapy Integration in 1983, where cognitive-behavior therapists played a prominent role. This shift toward integration was also evident in the changing conceptions of cognition that were offered by cognitive-behavior therapists.

CHANGING CONCEPTIONS OF CBT

In addition to the cross-currents that have contributed to the development of CBT, another way to consider the history of CBT is to trace how the concept of *cognition* has evolved. Three different guiding metaphors have been offered by cognitive-behavior therapists to describe the nature of their clients' cognitions in the therapeutic process, namely, conditioning, information processing, and constructing narratives.

Conditioning as a Metaphor

Initially, cognitive-behavior therapists proposed that a client's cognitions could be viewed as "covert behaviors," subject to the same laws of learning as are overt behaviors. The client's cognitions (self-statements and images) were viewed as discriminative stimuli, self-instructions, and conditioned stimuli that come to guide and control behavior. The focus of treatment was to "decondition" and strengthen new connections and to bolster and rehearse adaptive coping skills. The technology of behavior therapy, such as modeling, covert and behavioral rehearsal, and contingency manipulations, was employed to alter not only the clients' overt behaviors but also their thoughts and feelings.

In the tradition of Skinner and other learning theorists, cognitions were viewed as covert operants, or what Homme (1965) called *coverants*, which were supposedly responsive to both external and internal contingencies. Thus, the meaning and impact of the clients' thoughts and images could be altered by pairing them

contiguously with an aversive or positive event. For example, Cautela (1973) proposed that clients who had addictive disorders could be successfully treated by having them pair the image of smoking (or drinking, or overeating) with the accompanying image of their becoming physically ill (e.g., vomiting all over themselves). In a similar fashion, Solyom and Miller (1967) proposed that therapy can enhance the effectiveness of the client's telling himself to relax if the rehearsal of the self-instruction "relax" was paired previously and systematically with the termination or avoidance of an aversive event, such as an electric shock. Mahoney (1974) encouraged clients to pair the aversive snapping of a rubber band around their wrist with addictive urges or negative thoughts that they experienced. Some clients were also taught how to use thought-stoppage techniques to halt obsessive thoughts, and other clients were taught to rehearse coping responses mentally (i.e., engage in covert modeling) (Kazdin, 1974).

Research soon suggested that the *noncontingent application* of these behavior therapy techniques was equally effective; for example, thought stoppage of nonobsessive thoughts or the noncontingent association of aversive and nonaversive images led to the same positive treatment results (Meichenbaum, 1977). Moreover, as noted previously, researchers questioned the adequacy of strict behavioral concepts to explain complex human behavior, and theorists questioned whether the so-called laws of learning apply to overt behaviors, let alone to covert behaviors. Even the phrase *laws of learning* came into question (McKeachie, 1974). Thus, a new paradigm was needed, a new metaphor was required, to conceptualize clients' cognitions. At this time, the use of computers became widespread and the accompanying terminology of information processing provided a promising framework.

Information Processing as a Metaphor

The "mind as a computer" implied that the client could be viewed as engaging in a number of cognitive processes, including decoding, encoding, storage, retrieval, preattentive and attentive processing, attributional biases, and distortion mechanisms, the last in the form of cognitive errors such as dichotomous thinking, arbitrary inference, magnification, minimization, and the like. It was proposed that clients distorted reality. One of the objectives of therapy was to help clients appreciate how this process came about and, moreover, to help clients learn how to think more realistically, more rationally (Beck, 1970; Ellis, 1962). Clients' cognitive errors were viewed as being a consequence of the cognitive structures, beliefs, schemas, current concerns, and tacit assumptions that they brought to situations. It was proposed that such beliefs were strengthened by the manner in which the clients behaved. As noted, the operable terms used to describe this sequence were *transactional, interactional,* and *bidirectional.* Individuals were now viewed as architects of their experience, influencing the data they were creating and collecting. The information processing model proposed that individuals, rather than being passive, may inadvertently, if not unwittingly and even unknowingly, behave in ways that elicit the very reactions in others (a form of data) that they take as evidence to confirm their views of themselves and of the world. Clients were taught how to become their own scientists (Kelly, 1955; Mahoney, 1974).

A number of investigators have employed an information processing perspective to explain their clients' difficulties and then to formulate a cognitive-behavioral intervention plan. These include Beck (1970) and Hollon, (1990), who studied depression; Barlow (1988) and Clark (1986), who studied anxiety disorders; Dodge and Coie (1987) and Novaco (1979), who studied aggression in children and adults, respectively; Marlatt and Gordon (1985), who studied addiction problems; and Wilson and Fairburn (1993), who studied eating disorders. For example, from an information processing perspective, clients are seen to be depressed because they distort reality as the result of a number of cognitive errors and because they hold irrational beliefs. Depressed clients also hold negative views of themselves, of their past, and of their future, emitting characterological attributions of self-blame when they encounter failures and frustrations (e.g., "I am just gullible"). Anxious clients who have panic attacks are vigilant about bodily cues and often misinterpret them as personal threats, given their preoccupation with physical well-being and their need to maintain a sense of personal control. Such misinterpretations lead to catastrophic anxiety-engendering ideation with accompanying physiological arousal (hyperventilation). For example, a racing heart is seen as a harbinger of a possible heart attack; feeling light-headed as an instance of losing control. Thus, a vicious, self-perpetuating cycle is established and maintained between perceived threat, catastrophic ideation, hyperventilation, and the onset of panic attacks.

Adult clients who have problems with anger and who are aggressive have been found to have hostile attributional styles, to interpret ambiguous interpersonal cues as personal provocations, retrieving from memory other aggressive events and failing to generate and implement socially acceptable alternatives. Moreover, they behave in ways that elicit the very coercive and reciprocal reactions from others that confirm their aggressive outlooks. Thus, their expectations and self-statements become self-fulfilling prophecies.

Cognitive-behavior therapists have developed intervention programs that are designed to help clients become aware of these processes and to teach them how to notice, catch, monitor, and interrupt the cognitive-affect-behavioral chains and to produce more adaptive coping responses. Moreover, cognitive-behavior therapists help clients to identify high-risk situations that they are likely to encounter and to consider ways to prepare, handle, and deal with failures if they do occur (namely, a form of relapse prevention training). When positive results occur, clients are encouraged to make self-attributions for the changes they have been able to bring about. Often clients will require specific skills training to accomplish these objectives. Treatment frequently involves significant others (spouse, family members, teachers, peers) in order to increase the likelihood of generalization and maintenance.

These CBT interventions were guided by the complex ways in which cognitive-behavior therapists conceptualized their clients' cognitions, namely, as consisting of (1) cognitive events, (b) cognitive processes, and (3) cognitive structures. A consideration of each of these concepts further elucidates how CBT evolved.

1. *Cognitive events* refer to conscious, identifiable thoughts and images. They occur in the individual's stream of consciousness or can be readily retrieved upon request. These automatic thoughts, or what Plato called *internal dialogue*, incorporate, among other things, attributions, expectancies, evaluations of the self or task, and task-irrelevant thoughts. Images, symbolic words and gestures, and accompanying affect are frequently present as well.

These cognitive events occur automatically. People tend to talk to themselves when the habitual way they do something breaks down and when they have to make decisions under conditions of uncertainty (i.e., trial-and-error thinking). These cognitive events are highly idiosyncratic and are rarely questioned by the individual. The automatic thoughts are likely to be taken as God-given assertions, rather than as hypotheses worthy of testing. Thus, the client's thought that "I am terrible mother" or that "There is no hope; nothing can be done" is accepted as unquestionably true. These thoughts can influence how one feels and behaves. Also, how one feels can influence how prone one is to have such thoughts, how much one believes such thoughts, and how acts on them.

But cognitive events are seen as only one way to view clients' cognitions. Cognitive processes and cognitive structures constitute two other perspectives.

2. *Cognitive processes* refer to those processes that shape mental representations, transforming them and constructing new schemas of experience and action. These cognitive processes include search and storage mechanisms and inferential and retrieval processes. Under most circumstances, we do not attend to the ways we process information. These processes include, among others, mental heuristics or mental habits (Kahnemann & Tversky, 1973), confirmatory biases (Snyder, 1981), and pseudoconfirmation or self-fulfilling prophecies (Frank, 1974).

3. *Cognitive structures* refer to the schemata, silent or tacit assumptions, beliefs that act like a template, a readiness hypothesis, or a peremptory idea that screens, codes, categorizes, and evaluates information. Cognitive structures are abstract mental processes of experience that influence the way information is processed and behavior is organized.

Going back to the mind-as-computer metaphor, a cognitive structure or schema is like a format in a computer programming language. Formats specify that information must be of a certain sort if it is to be interpreted coherently. As Neisser (1976) reports, schemata are even more than formats. They are plans and can act as executors of plans. They influence the perception, interpretation, transformation, organization, and recall of information. As Taylor and Crocker (1981) observe, cognitive structures enable the receiver to identify stimuli quickly, chunk appropriate units, fill in information missing from the stimulus configuration, select a strategy for obtaining further information, solve a problem, and reach a goal. Thus, cognitive structures serve encoding and representational functions, as well as interpretive and inferential functions. They act as what Meichenbaum and Gilmore (1984) have called *core organizing principles*. Cognitive-behavior therapists help clients become aware of, and learn how to control, the influence of their cognitive structures.

From a historical perspective, it is important to appreciate that the terminology of information processing, and especially the concepts of *cognitive structure* and *schema*, existed well before the introduction of the computer. The philosopher Immanuel Kant (Korner, 1955); the experimental and social psychologists Tolman (1932), Bartlett (1932), Lewin (1935),

Dollard and Miller (1950), Miller, Galanter, and Pribram (1960); the developmental psychologists Baldwin (1894), Piaget (1926/1955); and the personologist George Kelly (1955) each had discussed similar concepts. (See Meichenbaum and Gilmore, 1984, for a more detailed historical account.)

Thus, cognitive-behavior theorists made a significant shift in their conceptualization of their clients' cognitions from the initial conditioning framework to that of information processing; but yet more change is presently underway. Clients soon came to be viewed as narrators, storytellers and makers of meaning.

Constructive Narrative as a Metaphor

The notions that clients are architects and constructors of their environments, and that illusions may be adaptive, have given rise to a third metaphor that is guiding the present development of CBT. The constructivist narrative perspective is founded on the idea that humans actively construct their personal realities and create their own representational models of the world. This constructivist perspective is rooted in the philosophical writings of Giambattista Vico, Immanuel Kant, Hans Vaihinger, Ernst Cassirer, and Nelson Goodman and in the psychological writings of Willhelm Wundt, Alfred Adler, George Kelly, Jean Piaget, Viktor Frankl, and Jerome Frank. More recently, the constructivist perspective has been advocated by Epstein and Erskine (1983), Guidano and Liotti (1983), Harvey, Weber, and Orbach (1990), Mahoney and Lyddon (1988), McCann and Perlman (1990), McNamee and Gergen (1992), Neimeyer (1993), Neimeyer and Feixas (1990), (1993), Meichenbaum and Fitzpatrick and White and Epston (1990). Common to all of these proponents are the tenets that the human mind is a product of constructive symbolic activity and that reality is a product of personal meanings that individuals create. It is not as if there is one reality and our clients distort that reality, thus contributing to their problems. Rather, constructionists believe that

there are multiple realities, and that the task of the therapist is to help clients become aware of how they create their realities and the consequences of such constructions.

Bruner (1990), who writes from a narrative psychology perspective, describes how individuals "make meaning" or "construct stories" and "offer accounts" to explain their behavior and their situations. For instance, clients may use metaphors to describe their emotional experience. One client recently reported that she "always stuffed her feelings" and then exploded; another described how he "built walls between himself and others." The cognitive-behavioral therapist helped these clients to appreciate the nature and impact of using such metaphors. "What is the impact, what is the emotional toll, what is the price she or he pays for behaving in accord with the metaphors of 'stuffing feelings' and 'building walls'?" At this point, the therapist explored, collaboratively and experientially, the price the clients paid. Moreover, "If this is not the way they would like things to be, then what could they do?" It is not a big step for clients to suggest that perhaps they should not stuff feelings or build walls. The therapist then says, "Not stuff feelings, not build walls; that is interesting. What did you have in mind?" In this manner, the therapist enlists the client as a collaborator in engaging in what Shafer (1980) called the psychotherapeutic work of *narrative repair*. Therapy is viewed as a narrative phenomenon, not a fact-finding mission. The therapist helps the client to coauthor a new, more adaptive life story. Clients enter psychotherapy because their stories have "broken down" and their lives seem to have little or no purpose, or they perceive the purpose as being blocked or threatened (Vitz, 1992). Therapy is designed to help clients change their understanding of the past and rescript their lives in healthier and happier ways.

These observations about "restorying" harken back to Freud's early observation that his case histories read more like short stories than like scientific papers (Breuer & Freud, 1893–1895). As Vitz (1992) notes, Freud called his method of healing a "literary method," one that makes the patient a narrator and the therapist a writer or coauthor.

The metaphor of a constructive narrative to explain the client's problems has had a number of important theoretical and practical implications for the development of CBT.

1. The therapist is now viewed as a coconstructivist helping clients to alter their stories, as Spence (1984) had proposed. The therapist must first be an empathic, reflective listener to the initial story lines of clients and must then collaboratively help them to transform their stories. A nurturant, compassionate, nonjudgmental set of conditions is required for distressed clients to tell their stories at their own pace. A number of clinical techniques, including reflective listening, Socratic questioning, sensitive probes, imagery reconstructions of stressful experiences, and client self-monitoring, are employed to help clients relate what happened and why. Thus, the role of relationship variables is critical, as is the role of affect in the therapeutic process.

2. The therapist helps clients to reframe stressful events cognitively and to "normalize" their reactions. From this perspective, it is not the symptoms of depression, anxiety, or anger per se that interfere with functioning, but rather what clients say to themselves and others about these reactions—the stories they construct, the accounts they offer, that are important to the adaptive process. The therapist not only helps to validate the client's reactions but also indicates that the client's symptoms are normal. In fact, the client's emotional distress is viewed as a spontaneous, reconstructive, and natural rehabilitative adaptive process. This reconceptualization process is an attempt to formulate collaboratively a "healing theory" of what happened and why (see Meichenbaum and Fitzpatrick, 1993, for a more in-depth discussion). The therapist also helps clients relate examples of their strengths, resources, and coping abilities in order to convey "the rest of the story" (to use a popular phrase). The cognitive-behavior therapist avoids holding a pathology bias, in-stead looking for and building on those occasions when the clients coped effectively.

3. From a narrative perspective, the therapist not only helps clients to break down or disaggregate global stressors into behaviorally prescriptive, manageable events so that they can use problem-solving and emotionally palliative coping techniques, but also helps them improve their coping skills and build new assumptive worlds and new ways to view themselves and their world (Meichenbaum, 1993b). The cognitive-behavior therapist helps clients to construct narratives that fit their present circumstances, that are coherent, and that prove plausible in capturing and explaining their difficulties. As Shafer (1980) indicates, therapy allows clients to retell their tale "in a way that allows them to understand the origins, meanings and significance of present difficulties, and moreover, to do so in a way that makes change conceivable and attainable" (p. 38). What matters most about this story (re)telling or narrative (re)construction is not its "historical truthfulness" but, as Spence (1984) observes, its "narrative coherence" and "adaptive features."

As Howard (1990) and Neimeyer (1993) observe, people can be construed as seeking therapy at points when their life stories become ineffective, necessitating editing, elaboration, or major "rebiographing." As White and Epston (1990) propose, psychotherapeutic reconstruction becomes necessary when people become identified with their problems and subjected to a narrative that limits, denies, or constrains their behavior.

As cognitive-behavior therapists moved toward a more constructive narrative perspective, the gap between their approach and that of constructivist psychotherapists, on the one hand, and of psychodynamically oriented therapists, on the other hand, substantially narrowed. Once cognitive-behavior therapists introduced the concepts of schemata and cognitive structures, the theoretical and practical differences between their approach and the concepts of brief psychodynamic therapists, (Binder, Hovowitz, Luborsky, Malan, Sifneos, and Strupp) and constructivists therapists

(Efran, Epston, Erickson, Feixas, Guidano, Howard, Kelly, Liotti, Lyddon, the Milan school of therapists, Neimeyers, Viney, Vitz) were sure to become more and more indistinct. This is illustrated in the recent writings of such cognitive-behavior therapists as Mahoney (1991) and Meichenbaum (Meichenbaum & Fitzpatrick, 1993; Meichenbaum & Fong, 1993; Meichenbaum & Gilmore, 1984). As Mahoney (1993) has observed, within less than four decades, CBT has emerged, multiplied, differentiated, and developed, and, most important, is contributing to the integration of psychotherapeutic approaches.

CENTRAL FIGURES IN THE EVOLUTION OF CBT

The historical account of CBT would not be complete if it did not include a discussion of some of the central figures who influenced its development. Two figures who stand out are Albert Ellis and Aaron Beck. Each developed his contributions in a somewhat different fashion, and each holds a different perspective of therapy.

Albert Ellis

Albert Ellis is one of the most provocative and controversial figures in the field of psychotherapy in general and in CBT in particular. My own contact with Ellis has been traced in my 1977 book (Meichenbaum, 1977). Ellis, a psychologist working out of the Institute for Rational Living in New York City, has promoted rational-emotive therapy (RET), which holds that a client's maladjustment and emotional dysfunction are due to acceptance of specific irrational beliefs and the adoption of certain modes of thinking (e.g., "awfulizing," "catastrophizing," "musturbation"). A major treatment goal of RET is to make the client aware of the "ABC" features of his or her behavior— for example, helping the client appreciate that the quality and intensity of his or her emotional arousal and "neurotic" symptoms (characterized as consequences [C] by Ellis) are determined by his or her beliefs (B) regarding a particular activating experience or event (A). It is the client's belief about an event, and not the event per se, that causes the maladaptive behavior. If the belief is irrational, then negative affect is aroused (e.g., anxiety, guilt, shame, depression) (Ellis, 1962).

A second treatment goal of RET is the exposition and disputation of the client's irrational beliefs that take the form of unrealistic and absolutistic expectations. For example, the client may hold the belief that his self-worth depends on what others think of him. The RET therapist may use a broad variety of clinical techniques, including self-monitoring, challenging questioning, debating, role playing, modeling, imagery techniques, shame-attacking exercises, skills training, and bibliotherapy, to challenge the client's beliefs and help him alter his behavior. RET therapists tend to challenge the philosophical underpinnings of the client's beliefs, often in a confrontive, disputational fashion. RET therapists attempt to teach clients to forcefully dispute their irrational beliefs, replacing them with rational ones (Ellis & Bernard, 1985).

While Ellis's RET approach has received a great deal of professional attention, it has not been without its critics on both theoretical and empirical grounds. On theoretical grounds, RET has been challenged for its dependence on a rational-empirical disputation approach to evaluate and challenge the client's beliefs. Critics of RET observe that it is not the validity but rather the viability of an individual's beliefs that is critical for adjustment (Neimeyer & Feixas, 1990). Motivated reasoning (holding false notions, using denial instead of engaging in reality-based problem solving, maintaining illusory beliefs about oneself and the world) may be adaptive under certain conditions (Kunda, 1990; Taylor & Brown, 1988). Thus, the equivalence of so-called rationality and emotional well-being has been challenged. Moreover, characterizing the client's beliefs as irrational is pejorative, judgmental, and potentially counterproductive. It also implies that the therapist holds the axiomatic belief system of what constitutes rationality. Moreover, frontal attacks on the client's beliefs are likely to lead to reactance and defensiveness that make the client more resistant to change (Kruglanski, 1990).

The most telling criticism of RET has come from critics who have questioned the efficacy of RET with clients. As Gossette and O'Brien (1992) note, RET is effective in decreasing clients' scores on scales that measure the acceptance of irrational beliefs and on measures of self-reported emotional distress. Both the Irrational Beliefs scale and the Emotional Distress scale include language that overlaps with the verbal content of RET therapy. Thus, the client's change may be due largely to the fact that RET concepts and terminology are often forcefully and didactically presented in the form of lectures, group discussion, and disputational analyses. However, when investigators studied the critical feature of behavioral changes resulting from RET, they found limited improvement. As Gossette and O'Brien (1992) conclude, "behavior change is *relatively insensitive* to RET interventions" (p. 20; emphasis added). A similar pattern of limited effective results of RET is evident in work with children. Haaga and Davison (1993) observe that RET's "professional impact thus far exceeds its scientific status" (p. 215).

Thus, an interesting paradoxical relationship emerges between the popularity of a particular mode of psychotherapy, namely, RET, and the limited demonstration of its effectiveness. The resolution of this paradox (and this is not limited to RET) is in the charismatic and dominating personality of its founder, Albert Ellis. While Ellis deserves credit for his passionate and prolific call for the important role that cognition and emotion play in behavior change and for his simple (perhaps simplistic) ABC view of psychopathology, there is a need to maintain historical detachment and a sense of critical-mindedness in evaluating RET's place in the development of cognitive-behavior interventions.

Aaron Beck

Aaron Beck, in contrast, has been a pioneer in the theoretical and empirical development of cognitive therapies. As a psychiatrist working out of the Center for Cognitive Therapy in Philadelphia, Beck has developed a structured, active, time-limited, cognitive therapy approach that has yielded positive results for psychiatric patients suffering from unipolar depression anxiety and other disorders (see Barlow, 1992; Beck & Emery, 1985; Beck, Rush, Shaw, & Emery, 1979; Chambless & Gillis, 1993, Clark & Salkovskis, 1991; Hollon, DeRubeis, & Seligman, 1992; Hollon, Shelton, & Davis, 1993; Magraf, Barlow, Clark, & Telch, 1993; Sokol, Beck, Greenberg, Wright, & Berchick, 1989; Thase, Simons, Cahalone, & McGeary, 1991). For instance, in summarizing the results of cognitive therapy with depressives, Hollon et al. (1992) concluded that "Patients treated to remission with cognitive therapy had a relapse rate of 26% versus a relapse rate of 64% for those treated with pharmacotherapy" (p. 90). Thase et al. (1991) reported that the results of a 1-year follow-up indicated that cognitive therapy of depressed clients reduced relapse rates to 30%, compared to 70% for pharmacologically treated patients. The subsequent relapse for clients receiving combined antidepressant medication and cognitive therapy was 25% versus 27% for those receiving cognitive therapy alone. The combined treatment of cognitive therapy and medication has been typically associated with only a modest advantage over either single modality (about only one-quarter of a standard deviation) (Hollon et al, 1992). In short, "there is an *enduring effect* for cognitive therapy (of depressives) with only about 20% of all treatment responders relapsing (or seeking additional treatment) within the first 12–24 months following termination, compared to about 50% relapsing of responders to pharmacotherapy alone" (Hollon & Beck, 1993, p. 15; emphasis added).

While these initial results with depressed clients are encouraging, cognitive-behavior therapists are now experimenting with treatment variations that can be applied to clients whose depression is superimposed on chronic personality disorders, or whose depression is accompanied by marital distress and by interpersonal difficulties (Robins & Hayes, 1993). The future challenge will be to develop effective interventions for these populations.

A similar favorable outcome picture emerges in the treatment of anxiety disorder patients. Barlow (1992), Clark and Salkovokis (1991) and Magraf et al. (1993) concluded that 81–90% of panic-disordered patients who received CBT were panic free at 1- to 2-year follow-up, compared to 50–55% of pharmacologically treated anxious patients and 25% of those receiving supportive therapy. Similar stability of treatment results is evident for patients with generalized anxiety disorder and social phobias (Hollon & Beck, 1993). An overwhelming majority (80%) of anxious patients are symptom free at 1–2 years, often with significant improvement on other dimensions. As Magraf et al. (1993) conclude, "We are no longer dealing with experimental treatments that still have to prove themselves. Instead, cognitive behavioral treatments rest on firm experimental evidence that justifies their application in everyday practice" (p. 6).

Once again, while these conclusions are encouraging, Chambless and Gillis (1993) caution that even more powerful treatment interventions are needed to yield long-term significant change and higher end-state client functioning: "Thus, CBT may be effective, but as practiced in research trials, it is no panacea" (p. 257). Beck's innovative efforts gave rise to a great deal of research and successful clinical application. This is especially important today when insurance companies, government policy makers, and clients are calling for accountability, and for time-efficient and effective treatments. Cognitive-behavior interventions have earned a prominent, highly esteemed, and well-deserved place in the clinician's armamentarium. For the first time, psychotherapists have not only demonstrated an effective treatment approach, relative to other treatments, but a therapy approach that has the prophylac-

tic impact of significantly reducing the likelihood of relapse. Clients are learning coping skills that they can use when they leave therapy. Metaphorically, they are taking their therapist's voice with them. As cognitive-behavior therapists are prone to ask their clients, "Do you ever find yourself, out there, asking yourself questions, that we ask each other here in therapy?" When clients answer "yes," then they have demonstrated the internalization process that Vygotsky (1978) described.

The history of CBT has been marked by a commitment to research, to sound empirical evaluation, and to theoretical development and change. Cognitive-behavior therapists have recently extended their efforts to new and more challenging clinical populations including schizophrenic patients, patients with bipolar disorders, HIV patients with depression, patients with personality disorders, sexual offenders, drug addicts, eating-disordered patients, distressed couples, cancer patients, and other clinical groups (see Beck, 1993, for a description of these new developments).

The next chapter in the history of CBT should prove exciting and productive. Stay tuned; it will make for an interesting narrative. Perhaps you will contribute to this development. CBT is no passing fad. It is a treatment approach that will continue to develop, change, and contribute to the integration of psychotherapy.

EPILOGUE

A final personal footnote to the history of CBT is in order, for it further illustrates how a field can evolve and what a difference one person can make. As a new assistant professor and a budding investigator of cognitive-behavioral interventions, I became aware of a great deal of research activity that was underway at various centers. In order to facilitate communication among these various clinicians and researchers, I decided to put out an annual newsletter that summarized this ongoing activity. The first issue appeared in 1976. In this cognitive-behavioral newsletter, I described what various investigators were doing and what new doctoral dissertations on CBT had been written, and I provided editorial comments on promising new directions. I also included the names and addresses of all investigators. My goal was to foster communication, nurture research, and ensure that cognitive behavioral therapy did not become another passing fad.

The initial newsletter went to a couple of hundred people. By the time the fourth newsletter came out in 1979, I had a mailing list of 3,000 people in some 20 countries. An "invisible college" of like-minded researchers and clinicians was developing. Suddenly, a new Ph.D. student whose work was favorably reviewed in the cognitive-behavioral newsletter was receiving reprint requests from around the world. When investigators who had been cited in the newsletter attended conferences, others began to recognize their names and collaborative work emerged. Faculty advisers gave the newsletter to graduate students who were in search of a doctoral dissertation topic, since the newsletter included a discussion of promising new directions for research.

In time, the field of cognitive-behavioral research became so large that it became impossible to continue the newsletter past the fourth issue. Its success had put it out of business. The mailing list for the newsletter was the foundation for the subscription list for the journal *Cognitive Therapy and Research*. Today an international newsletter on CBT exists, as does an international society, several related journals, conferences, and the like. Whereas the initial response of the officers of the AABT was to restrict papers on the topic of CBT, in July 1995 that same behavior therapy organization will cosponsor its international conference with the International Cognitive Therapy Association in Copenhagen, Denmark, under the (aegis) of the World Congress of Behavioral *and* Cognitive Therapies. As the saying goes, "You've come a long way, baby!"

It is with pride that I am able to share the story of CBT, and with some humility feel that I have contributed to its development. I can only express the hope that you (the reader) will have an opportunity to construct such a rewarding narrative when you look back on 28 years of work.

REFERENCES

Arnkoff, D. B., & Glass, C. R. (1992). Cognitive therapy and psychotherapy integration. In D. K. Freedheim (Ed.), *The history of psychotherapy*. Washington, DC: American Psychological Association.

Baldwin, J. (1894). *Mental development in the child and the race*. New York: Macmillan.

Bandura, A. (1969). *Principles of behavior modification*. New York: Holt, Rinehart, & Winston.

Bandura, A. (1978). The self-system in reciprocal determinism. *American Psychologist, 33*, 344–358.

Bandura, A., & Walters, R. H. (1963). *Social learning and personality development*. New York: Holt, Rinehart, & Winston.

Barlow, D. H. (1988). *Anxiety and its disorders*. New York: Guilford Press.

Barlow, D. H. (1992). Cognitive-behavioral approaches to panic disorder and social phobia. *Bulletin of the Menninger Clinic, 56*, 14–28.

Bartlett, F. (1932). *Remembering*. Cambridge: Cambridge University Press.

Beck, A. T. (1970). Cognitive therapy: Nature and relation to behavior therapy. *Behavior Therapy, 1*, 184–200.

Beck, A. T. (1993). Cognitive therapy: Past, present and future. *Journal of Consulting and Clinical Psychology, 61*, 194–199.

Beck, A. T., & Emery, G. (1985). *Cognitive therapy of anxiety and phobic disorders*. Philadelphia: Center for Cognitive Therapy.

Beck, A. T., Rush, A. J., Shaw, B. F., & Emery, G. (1979). *Cognitive therapy of depression*. New York: Guilford Press.

Breger, L., & McGaugh, J. (1965). Critique and reformulation of "learning theory": Approaches to psychotherapy and neurosis. *Psychological Bulletin, 63*, 338–358.

Breuer, J., & Freud, S. (1893–1895). Studies on hysteria. *Standard Edition, 2*, 1–305.

Brewer, W. (1974). There is no convincing evidence for operant or classical conditioning in adult humans. In W. Weimer & D. Palermo (Eds.), *Cognition and the symbolic processes*. New York: Halsted Press.

Bruner, J. (1990). *Acts of meaning*. Cambridge, MA: Harvard University Press.

Cautela, J. (1973). Covert processes and behavior modification. *Journal of Nervous and Mental Disease, 157*, 27–35.

Chambless, D. L., & Gillis, M. M. (1993). Cognitive therapy of anxiety disorders. *Journal of Consulting and Clinical Psychology, 61*, 248–260.

Clark, D. M. (1986). A cognitive approach to panic. *Behavior Research and Therapy, 24*, 461–470.

Clark, D. M., & Salkovskis, P. M. (1991). *Cognitive therapy with panic and hypochondrosis*. New York: Pergamon Press.

Coyne, J. C., & Gotlib, I. H. (1983). The role of cognition in depression: A critical appraisal. *Psychological Bulletin, 94*, 472–505.

Dember, W. (1974). Motivation and the cognitive revolution. *American Psychologist, 29*, 161–168.

Dobson, K. S., & Block, L. (1988). Historical and philosophical bases of the cognitive-behavioral therapies. In K. S. Dobson (Ed.), *Handbook of cognitive-behavioral therapies*. New York: Guilford Press.

Dodge, K. A., & Coie, J. D. (1987). Social information-processing factors in reactive and proactive aggression in children's peer groups. *Journal of Personality and Social Psychology, 53*, 1146–1158.

Dollard, J., & Miller, N. E. (1950). *Personality and psychotherapy: An analysis in terms of learning, thinking and culture*. New York: McGraw-Hill.

Dubois, P. (1904/1907). *The psychic treatment of nervous disorders*. New York: Funk & Wagnell.

Dulany, D. (1968). Awareness, rules, and propositional control: A confrontation with S-R behavior thery. In T. R. Dixon & D. L. Horton (Eds.), *Verbal behavior and general behavior theory*. Englewood-Cliffs, NJ: Prentice-Hall.

D'Zurilla, T. (1986). *Problem-solving therapy: A social competence approach to clinical intervention*. New York: Springer.

D'Zurilla, T., & Goldfried, M. (1971). Problem solving and behavior modification. *Journal of Abnormal Psychology, 78*, 107–126.

Ellis, A. (1962). *Reason and emotion in psychotherapy*. New York: Lyle Stuart.

Ellis, A. (1980). Rational-emotive therapy and cognitive-behavior therapy. Similarities and differences. *Cognitive Research and Therapy, 4*, 325–340.

Ellis, A. (1989). The history of cognition in psycho-therapy. In A. Freeman, K. M. Simon, L. E. Beutler, & H. Arkowitz (Eds.), *Comprehensive handbook of cognitive therapy*. New York: Plenum.

Ellis, A., & Bernard, M. E. (1985). What is rational-emotive therapy (RET)? In A. Ellis & M. E. Bernard (Eds.), *Clinical applications of rational-emotive therapy*. New York: Plenum Press.

Epstein, S., & Erskine, N. (1983). The development of personal theories of reality. In D. Magnusson & V. Allen (Eds.), *Human development: An interactional perspective*. New York: Academic Press.

Flavell, J. (1979). Metacognition and cognitive monitoring: A new area of cognitive-developmental inquiry. *American Psychologist, 34*, 906–911.

Frank, J. (1974). *Persuasion and healing* (2nd ed.). New York: Schocken Books.

Freeman, A., & Dattilio, F. M. (1993). *Comprehensive casebook of cognitive therapy*. New York: Plenum.

Goldfried, M. R., Greenberg, L. S., & Marmar, C. (1990). Individual psychotherapy: Process and outcomes. *Annual Review of Psychology, 41*, 655–688.

Gossette, R. L., & O'Brien, R. M. (1992). The efficacy of rational-emotive therapy in adults: Clinical facts or psychometric artifact? *Journal of Behavior Therapy and Experimental Psychiatry, 23*, 9–24.

Greenberg, L., & Safran, J. (1986). *Emotion in psychotherapy*. New York: Guilford Press.

Guidano, V. F., & Liotti, G. (1983). *Cognition processes and emotional disorders*. New York: Guilford Press.

Haaga, D. A., & Davison, G. C. (1993). An appraisal of rational-emotive therapy. *Journal of Consulting and Clinical Psychology, 61*, 215–221.

Harvey, J. H., Weber, A. L., & Orbach, T. L. (1990). *Interpersonal accounts: A social-psychological perspective*. Oxford: Basil Blackwell.

Heesacker, M., Heppner, P. P., & Rogers, M. E. (1982). Classics and emerging classics in psychology. *Journal of Counseling Psychology, 29*, 400–405.

Hollon, S. D. (1990). Cognitive therapy and pharmacotherapy for depression. *Psychiatric Annals, 20*, 249–258.

Hollon, S. D., & Beck, A. T. (1993). Cognitive and cognitive-behavioral therapies. In S. L. Garfield & A. E. Bergin (Eds.), *Handbook of psychotherapy and behavior change: An empirical analysis* (4th ed.) New York: Wiley.

Hollon, S. D., DeRubeis, R. J., & Seligman, M. E. (1992). Cognitive therapy and the prevention of depression. *Applied and Preventative Psychology*, 1, 89–95.

Hollon, S. D., & Kriss, M. (1984). Cognitive factors in clinical research and practice. *Clinical Psychology Review*, 4, 35–76.

Hollon, S. D., Shelton, R. C., & Davis, D. D. (1993). Cognitive therapy for depression: Conceptual issues and clinical efficacy. *Journal of Consulting and Clinical Psychology*, 61, 270–275.

Homme, L. (1965). Perspectives in psychology: Control of coverants, the operants of the mind. *Psychological Record*, 15, 501–511.

Howard, G. S. (1990). Narrative psychotherapy. In J. K. Zeig & W. M. Munign (Eds.), *What is psychotherapy?* San Francisco: Jossey-Boss.

Ingram, R. E., Kendall, P. C., & Chen, A. H. (1991). Cognitive-behavioral interventions. In C. R. Snyder, D. R. Forsyth, & R. Donelsen, (Eds.), *Handbook of social and clinical psychology: The health perspective*. New York: Pergamon Press.

Janet, P. (1893). *Nevroses et idee fixes* (2 vols.). Paris: Alcan.

Kahnemann, D., Slovic, P., & Tversky, A. (1982). *Judgment under uncertainty: Heuristics and biases*. Cambridge: Cambridge University Press.

Kahnemann, D., & Tversky, A. (1973). On the psychology of prediction. *Psychological Review*, 80, 237–251.

Kanfer, F., & Phillips, J. (1970). *Learning foundations of behavior therapy*. New York: Wiley.

Kazdin, A. (1974). Covert modeling and the reduction of avoidance behavior. *Journal of Abnormal Psychology*, 81, 87–95.

Kelly, G. (1955). *The psychology of personal constructs* (2 vols.). New York: Brunner/Mazel.

Kendall, P. C. (Ed.) (1991). *Child and adolescent therapy: Cognitive-behavioral procedures*. New York: Guilford Press.

Kendall, P. C. (1993). Cognitive-behavioral therapies with youth: Guiding theory, current status, and emerging developments. *Journal of Consulting and Clinical Psychology*, 61, 235–247.

Kendall, P. C., & Hollon, S. D. (1979). *Cognitive-behavioral interventions: Theory, research, and procedures*. New York: Academic Press.

Korner, S. (1955). *Kant*. Varmondworth, England: Penguin Books.

Kovacs, M., & Beck, A. T., (1978). Maladaptive cognitive structures and depression. *American Journal of Psychiatry*, 135, 525–533.

Kruglanski, A. W. (1980). Lay epistemiology process and contents. *Psychological Review*, 87, 70–87.

Kruglanski, A. W. (1990). Lay epistemic theory in social-cognitive psychology. *Psychological Inquiry*, 1, 181–197.

Kuhn, T. S. (1962). *The structure of scientific revolutions*. Chicago: University of Chicago Press.

Kunda, Z. (1990). The case for motivated reasoning. *Psychological Bulletin*, 18, 480–489.

Lazarus, A. A. (1981). *The practice of multimodal therapy*. New York: McGraw-Hill.

Lazarus, R. (1966). *Psychological stress and the coping process*. New York: McGraw-Hill.

Lewin, K. (1935). *A dynamic theory of personality*. New York: McGraw-Hill.

Loera, P. A., & Meichenbaum, D. (1993). The "potential" contribution of cognitive behavior modification to literacy training for deaf students. *American Annals for the Deaf*, 138, 87–95.

Luria, A. R. (1976). *Cognitive development: Its cultural and social foundations*. Cambridge, MA: Harvard University Press.

Magraf, J., Barlow, D. H., Clark, D. M., & Telch, M. J. (1993). Psychological treatment of panic: Work in progress on outcome, active ingredients, and followup. *Behaviour Research and Therapy*, 31, 108.

Mahoney, M. J. (1974). *Cognition and behavior modification*. Cambridge, MA: Ballinger.

Mahoney, M. J. (1976). *Scientist as subject: The psychological imperative*. Cambridge, MA: Ballinger.

Mahoney, M. J. (1991). *Human change processes*. New York: Basic Books.

Mahoney, M. J. (1993). Introduction to special section: Theoretical developments in the cognitive psychotherapies. *Journal of Consulting and Clinical Psychology*, 61, 187–194.

Mahoney, M. J., & Arnkoff, D. (1978). Cognitive and self-control therapies. In S. Garfield & A. E. Bergin (Eds.), *Handbook of psychotherapy and behavior change: An empirical analysis* (2nd ed.). New York: Wiley.

Mahoney, M. J., & Lyddon, W. J. (1988). Recent developments in cognitive approaches to counseling and psychotherapy. *The Counseling Psychologist*, 16, 190–234.

Mandler, G. (1975). *Mind and emotion*. New York: Wiley.

Marlatt, G. A., & Gordon, J. R. (1985). *Relapse prevention: Maintenance strategies in the treatment of addictive behaviors*. New York: Guilford Press.

McCann, I. L., & Perlman, L. A. (1990). *Psychological trauma and the adult survivor*. New York: Brunner/Mazel.

McKeachie, W. (1974). The decline and fall of the laws of learning. *Educational Researcher, 3,* 7–11.

McNamee, S., & Gergen, K. J. (Eds.). (1992). *Therapy as social construction.* London: Sage.

Mead, G. H. (1934). *Mind, self and society.* Chicago: University of Chicago Press.

Meichenbaum, D. (1977). *Cognitive behavioral modification: An integrative approach.* New York: Plenum.

Meichenbaum, D. (1985). *Stress inoculation training.* Elmsford, NY: Pergamon Press.

Meichenbaum, D. (1992a). The personal journal of a psychotherapist and his mother. In G. G. Brannigan & M. R. Merrins (Eds.), *The undaunted psychologist.* New York: McGraw-Hill.

Meichenbaum, D. (1992b). Evolution of cognitive behavior therapy: Origins, trends and clinical examples. In J. Zeig (Ed.), *The evolution of psychotherapy* (Vol. II). New York: Brunner/Mazel.

Meichenbaum, D. (1993a). The "potential" contributions of cognitive behavior modification to the rehabilitation of individuals with traumatic brain injury. *Seminars in Speech and Language, 14,* 18–31.

Meichenbaum, D. (1993b). Stress inoculation training: A twenty-year update. In R. L. Woolfolk & P. M. Lehrer (Eds.), *Principles and practice of stress management.* New York: Guilford Press.

Meichenbaum, D., & Biemiller, A. (1992). In search of student expertise in the classroom: A metacognitive analysis. In M. Pressley, K. Harris, & J. Guthrie (Eds.), *Promoting academic competence and literacy: Cognitive research and instructional innovation.* New York: Academic Press.

Meichenbaum, D., & Cameron, R. (1974). The clinical potential of modifying what clients say to themselves. *Psychotherapy, 4,* 515–534.

Meichenbaum, D., & Fitzpatrick, D. (1993). A constructivist narrative perspective of stress and coping: Stress inoculation applications. In L. Goldberger & S. Breznitz (Eds.), *Handbook of stress.* New York: Free Press.

Meichenbaum, D., & Fong, G. (1993). How individuals control their mind: A constructive narrative perspective. In D. M. Wegner & J. W. Pennebaker (Eds.), *Handbook of mental control.* New York: Prentice-Hall.

Meichenbaum, D., & Gilmore, J. (1984). The nature of unconscious processes: A cognitive behav-ioral perspective. In K. Bowers & D. Meichenbaum (Eds.), *The unconscious reconsidered.* New York: Wiley.

Meichenbaum, D. H., & Goodman, J. (1971). Training impulsive children to talk to themselves: A means of developing self-control. *Journal of Abnormal Psychology, 77,* 115–126.

Meyers, A. W., & Craighead, W. E. (Eds.). (1984). *Cognitive behavior therapy with children.* New York: Plenum.

Miller, G., Galanter, E., & Pribram, K. (1960). *Plans and structure of behavior.* New York: Holt.

Mischel, W. (1973). Toward a cognitive social learning reconceptualization of personality. *Psychological Review, 80,* 252–283.

Neimeyer, R. A. (1993). An appraisal of constructivist psychotherapies. *Journal of Consulting and Clinical Psychology, 61,* 221–234.

Neimeyer, R. A., & Feixas, G. (1990). Constructivist contributions to psychotherapy integration. *Journal of Integrative and Eclectic Psychotherapy, 9,* 4–20.

Neisser, U. (1976). *Cognition and reality: Principles and implications of cognitive psychology.* San Francisco: Freeman.

Nisbett, R., & Ross, L. (1980). *Human inference: Strategies and shortcomings of social judgment.* Englewood Cliffs, NJ: Prentice-Hall.

Novaco, R. (1979). The cognitive regulation of anger and stress. In P. C. Kendall & D. Hollon (Eds.), *Cognitive behavioral interventions.* New York: Academic.

Piaget, J. (1926/1955). *The language and thought of a child.* New York: New American Library.

Raimy, V. (1975). *Misunderstanding of the self: Cognitive psychotherapy and the misconception hypothesis.* San Francisco: Jossey-Bass.

Robins, C. J., & Hayes, A. M. (1993). An appraisal of cognitive therapy. *Journal of Consulting Clinical Psychology, 61,* 205–215.

Rotter, J. (1966). Generalized expectancies for internal versus external control of reinforcement. *Psychological Monographs, 80.*

Safran, J., & Segal, Z. (1990). *Interpersonal processes in cognitive therapy.* New York: Basic Books.

Shafer, R. (1980). Narration in the psychoanalytic dialogue. *Critical Inquiry, 7,* 29–53.

Smith, D. (1982). Trends in counseling and psychology. *American Psychologist, 37,* 802–809.

Snyder, M. (1981). Seek and ye shall find: Testing hypotheses about other people. In E. Higgins, C. Herman, & M. Zanna (Eds.), *Social cogni-*

tion: The Ontario symposium. Hillsdale, NJ: Erlbaum.

Sokol, L., Beck, A. T., Greenberg, R. L., Wright, F. D., & Bercheck, R. J. (1989). Cognitive therapy of panic disorder: A nonpharmacological alternative. Journal of Nervous and Mental Disease, 12, 711–716.

Solyom, L., & Miller, S. (1967). Reciprocal inhibition by aversion relief in the treatment of phobias. Behavior Research and Therapy, 5, 313–324.

Spence, D. (1984). Narrative truth and historical truth: Meaning and interpretation in psychoanalysis. New York: Norton.

Spielberger, C. D., & DeNike, L. D. (1966). Descriptive behaviorism versus cognitive theory in verbal operant conditioning. Psychological Review, 73, 306–326.

Spivack, G., & Shure, M. B. (1974). Social adjustment of young children: A cognitive approval to solving real-life problems. San Francisco: Jossey-Bass.

Taylor, S. E., & Brown, J. (1988). Illusion and well-being: A social psychological perspective on mental health. Psychological Bulletin, 103, 193–210.

Taylor, S. E., & Crocker, J. (1981). Schematic bias of social information processing. In E. Higgins, C. Herman, & M. Zanna (Eds.), Social cognition: The Ontario symposium. Hillsdale, NY: Erlbaum.

Thase, M. E., Simons, A. D., Cahalone, J. F., & McGeary, J. (1991). Cognitive behavior therapy of endogerous depression. Part 1: An outpatient clinical replication series. Behavior Therapy, 22, 457–467.

Tolman, E. (1932). Purposive behavior in animals and man. New York: Century.

Turk, D. C., Meichenbaum, D., & Genest, N. (1983). Pain and behavioral medicine. New York: Guilford Press.

Turk, D. C., & Salovey, P. (1985). Cognitive structures, cognitive processes and cognitive behavior modification. Cognitive Therapy and Research, 9, 1–35.

Tversky, A., & Kahnemann, D. (1974). Judgment under uncertainty: Heuristics and biases. Science, 185, 1124–1131.

Vallis, T. M., Howes, J. L., & Miller, P. C. (Eds.). (1991). The challenge of cognitive therapy. New York: Plenum.

Vitz, P. C. (1992). Narratives and counselling, Part 1: From analysis of the past to stories about it. Journal of Psychology and Theology, 20, 11–19.

Vygotsky, L. S. (1978). Mind in society: The development of higher psychological processes. Cambridge, MA: Harvard University Press.

White, M., & Epston, D. (1990). Narrative means to therapeutic ends. New York: Norton.

Wilson, G. T., & Fairburn, C. G. (1993). Cognitive treatment for eating disorders. Journal of Consulting and Clinical Psychology, 61, 261–269.

9
Cognitive Therapies in Practice

Keith S. Dobson
Brian F. Shaw

THE DOMAIN OF THE COGNITIVE THERAPIES

One of the exciting developments in the field of psychotherapy has been that of the cognitive therapies. These treatments grew out of the behavioral tradition in treatment and share with behaviorism a focus on empirical demonstration of outcomes, as well as on behavior change as an index of successful therapeutic change. At the same time, cognitive therapies have expanded the theoretical framework for therapy from the behavioral models, and have included explicit reference to cognitive constructs in the etiology and treatment of dysfunctional behavior (Dobson & Block, 1988; Mahoney, 1974). Cognitive therapies are meditational; they share an assumption that it is the perception of events, rather than events themselves, that mediates the response to different circumstances and ultimately determines the quality of adaptation of individuals (Beck, 1976; Ellis, 1980).

A number of specific therapeutic models exist within the broad framework of the cognitive-behavior therapies (Dobson & Block, 1988; Mahoney, 1988, 1991). Depending on the estimate, the number of cognitive therapies ranges from 12 to 17. Although some of these models have attracted more theoretical and research attention than others, each of them has distinguishing feature(s).

In general, cognitive-behavior therapies vary along two major dimensions. One dimension is the extent to which they focus on the behavioral versus the cognitive components of dysfunction and therapy. Some of the cognitive therapies aim at assessing and modifying specific coping behaviors related to problematic functioning. For example, stress inoculation training (Meichenbaum, 1977) teaches the patient how to prepare for, cope with, and overcome different types of environmental stressors through the systematic use of self-talk and coping behaviors related to the stressors. Other therapies focus on cognitive assessment and intervention. For example, Guidano (1987, 1991; Guidano & Liotti, 1983) has developed a constructivistic cognitive therapy that focuses on the underlying structure of cognition and the historical development of cognitive structures, patterns, and processes. Although constructivistic cognitive therapy recognizes the importance of improved behavioral adaptation as a sign of therapeutic success, its emphasis is on assessing and modifying the underlying cognitive processes that lead to behavioral dysfunction.

Related to but distinct from the differentiation of cognitive therapies along the behavioral-cognitive dimension is the distinction between rational and postrational (also called *developmental* [Mahoney, 1988, 1991] or *constructivistic* [Guidano & Liotti, 1985]) forms of cognitive therapy. The distinction between rational and postrational models of cognitive therapy rests on the philosophical difference between these therapies with regard to the nature of reality, the knowability of reality, and the nature of subjective experience. Rational forms of cognitive therapy rest on the assumption that there is an external, stable world that can be known through accurate experience and cognition. According to a rational perspective, an individual will experience symptoms and dysfunction to that his or her perceptions are distorted (e.g., exaggerated, minimized), and this individual has an idiosyncratic, nonverifiable experience. Therapy based on a rational perspective teaches the patient to challenge cognitive distortions and dysfunctional attitudes and attempts to determine the potential causes of these distortions.

In contrast, a postrational approach assumes that an external, permanent reality does not exist, but that reality is the result of subjective and social experience (Neimeyer, 1993). Put otherwise, reality is a constructed entity that rests on the nature of the knower more than on the nature of what is known. From a postrational perspective, individuals are dysfunctional to the extent that their experience is disturbing to them or is inconsistent with social experience. The truth or falsity of experience is of less interest to a postrational theorist than is the viability of that experience. Postrational treatment focuses on the nature of the development of the cognitive constructs the patient employs, their strength, coherence, and viability, and on the use of different therapeutic strategies to explore alternative, more emotionally, behaviorally, and cognitively adaptive functions.

The distinction between rational and postrational forms of cognitive-behavior therapy makes it clear that there are deep philosophical differences within this field. These differences have implications for a large number of issues, not the least of which are the assessment of dysfunction, the conceptualization of patient problems, the nature of the therapeutic relationship, the treatment strategies employed by the therapist, the manner in which therapeutic success and failure are defined, and the potential for integration across the different models of cognitive therapy.

Our purpose in presenting the above ways to conceptualize and differentiate the cognitive therapies is to suggest at once the complexity and the richness of these approaches. Although we cannot do justice to the large and increasing number of cognitive therapies in this chapter, the reader is advised that this field is in a state of growth and maturation; and that while we will present some of the more prominent cognitive therapies, there are many that we will be able to allude to or reference only in passing. Once these models have been presented and discussed, we will discuss how to conceptualize and measure change in cognitive-behavior therapy. The chapter will conclude with some suggestions about future issues for the field.

THE COGNITIVE THERAPIES IN PRACTICE

It is impossible, given the space limitations to describe all of the practice issues in a single chapter (see, e.g., Dobson, 1988; Freeman, Simon, Beutler, & Arkowitz, 1989). First, therefore, we will present the principles and practices of what might be considered the prototypical congitive therapy, which is Beck's approach (Beck, 1976, 1988; Beck & Emery, 1985; Beck, Rush, Shaw, & Emery, 1979). Next, we will present the treatment model, some of the common therapy strategies, and the recent innovations within this approach. We will then consider four other cognitive therapies: Ellis' rational-emotive therapy (Ellis, 1962, 1991; Ellis & Dryden, 1987), self-management therapy (Kanfer, 1977; Rehm, 1984; Rehm & Rokke, 1988), problem-solving therapy (D'Zurilla, 1986, 1988; Nezu, Nezu, & Perri, 1989), and constructivistic cognitive therapy (Guidano, 1987, 1991; Guidano & Liotti, 1985; Mahoney, 1988, 1991). These latter treatment models will be contrasted with Beck's cognitive therapy, and some of the differences in practice among these approaches will be discussed.

Cognitive Therapy

Cognitive therapy is a short-term, problem-oriented therapy that focuses on both behavioral and cognitive change methods as the primary strategies for alleviating personal distress and enhancing the coping ability of the patient. The principles of cognitive therapy were first articulated in the 1970s (Beck, 1970, 1976), and the first published cognitive therapy manual appeared at the end of that decade (Beck et al., 1979). The first manual, directed to the treatment of depression, has since been followed by manuals related to anxiety disorders (Beck & Emery, 1985), marital dysfunction (Beck, 1988), personality disorders (Beck, Freeman, & Associates, 1990), and drug abuse (Beck, Wright, Newman, & Liese, 1993).

The model underlying cognitive therapy is well known in the field and rests on a diathesis-stress conceptualization. Within this framework is the idea that patients who suffer from an emotional disorder have certain dysfunctional, self-defeating cognitive structures that potentiate distorted thoughts and images in specific situations. Inasmuch as a central tenet of cognitive theory deals with the extent to which the person in question has a/an (un)realistic perception of the situations encountered, cognitive therapy is essentially a rational form of psychotherapy. Treatment consists largely of assisting patients to become aware of the biased perceptions and thinking errors they engage in, teaching them methods to perceive external problems more realistically, and assisting them to cope with those realistically perceived situations.

In addition to the rational aspects of cognitive therapy, there are some components of the treatment that imply a constructivistic model of psychopathology. Several authors (e.g., Dobson, 1986; Kovacs & Beck, 1977; Segal, 1988; Young, 1990) have highlighted the role of cognitive schemas as the structures that may potentiate distorted thinking. Cognitive schemas are conceived of as abstract aspects of cognitive functioning, hypothetically based on experience and residing in long-term memory, that affect a number of cognitive processes, including attention, information processing, encoding, and recall (Markus, 1977). The cognitive model of psychopathology predicts that patients who suffer from a given disorder likely have cognitive schemas (often expressed as attitudes towards the self) that serve as vulnerability factors for the negative thinking seen in specific situations. Based on this model, part of cognitive therapy involves the identification and modification of these schemas, as it is only through the modification of such aspects of cognition that long-term treatment success can be assured.

In summary, although cognitive therapy is largely a rational form of treatment, certain aspects of this therapy also look at the construction of personal meaning and the representation of experience. It is notable that although earlier expositions of this treatment highlighted the assessment and modification of automatic thoughts and dysfunctional attitudes (e.g., Beck et al., 1979), more recent writings highlight the role of the self-schema and constructivistic processes (e.g., Beck et al., 1990; Young, 1990). Whether there has been a shift in the field away from a rational and toward a postrational perspective, or whether these changes in theorizing reflect other changes in the application of cognitive therapy to new disorders and the necessity of theoretical modification to fit the disorder, is at present unclear (Robins & Hayes, 1993).

As depression was the disorder that received the earliest detailed attention, we will present the cognitive therapy of depression in detail. Recent innovations in cognitive therapy related to other disorders will be briefly discussed in a later section.

Depression is a complex disorder with cognitive, affective, behavioral, and physiological or vegetative components (American Psychiatric Association, 1987, 1994). Although cognitive therapists attend to the entire range of symptoms related to depression in treatment, the cognitive model of depression focuses on the importance of cognitive and behavioral aspects of the disorder. It is through the modification of these symptoms that overall treatment success may be gained.

In practice, a cognitive therapist begins the treatment of a depressed person with a detailed assessment, including such issues related to depression as suicide potential, marital or family relations, medication usage and history, medical history, and occupational problems. Although the assessment may suggest the need to attend to one of the above issues before focusing on the depression itself, in many instances problems in these arenas are related to the depression. As part of the assessment of the patient's current functioning, the cognitive therapist will determine the depth of depression that is part of the patient's experience. If the patient is seen as having severe, chronic depression, options such as hospitalization or intensive family monitoring and support are considered.

An essential aspect of the assessment process in cognitive therapy for depression involves the formulation of the patient's problem (Beck et al., 1979; Persons, 1989). The case conceptualization will include a sense of the patient's particular cognitive vulnerabilities (i.e., a sense of self-identify in the context of their goals, hopes, and motivation), as well as the life stressors potentiating the current depressive episode. Often the therapist will explore past episodes of depression in order to determine commonalities across these episodes that suggest the nature of the vulnerabilities.

One of the first interventions will be to present the patient with a general description of the treatment approach, as well as a preliminary cognitive conceptualization of the patient's problems. The patient's response to the formulation is diagnostic of his or her willingness to participate actively in the treatment, and as this therapy draws heavily on the collaboration between patient and therapist, any signals from the patient that he or she does not understand or accept the model warrant a more complete assessment of the problem and discussion of the relevance of the model for the depression. If, in the end, the patient cannot see that his or her problems fit the model (or if the therapist cannot develop a sound cognitive conceptualization), referral for another treatment may be appropriate. Of course, cognitive therapists will also consider other selection criteria in deciding to accept or reject a particular patient for therapy (Safran & Segal, 1990).

Once treatment begins, an early technique is to assess the patient's current level of functioning and range of action. An activity schedule may be used for this purpose, or the patient may keep a diary. In additon to simply tracking activities, this schedule may be elaborated to include ratings of the level of depression. These ratings may be compared to the patient's activities, and trends in the depression may be determined. For example, it may be that for a given single young male patient, the depression is worse on weekends, when he does not have the structure of his weekday job and does have the social isolation of time spent alone. Such a pattern of depression may suggest the need to work with the patient to generate some structure for the weekends, particularly activities that involve some degree of pleasurable social contact.

With some patients, it is helpful to have them track not only their activities, but also the sense of mastery (i.e., sense of accomplishment) or pleasure that they derive from these activities. Although a depressed patient may be physically active, he or she may not receive psychological benefit from these activities. A pattern of anhedonia suggests several different possible problems and interventions. It may be, for example, that the patient is actually performing activities poorly, and that the sense of lack of mastery is veridical. In this case, the therapist may help the patient identify those skills that need development and work with the patient to improve them. It may be that the activities the patient is engaged in are necessary (e.g., house cleaning, work) and that there is little that can be built into these activities to make them more enjoyable. This would suggest that the patient needs to expand his or her range of activities, to do things that lead to a sense of mastery or pleasure. Sometimes patients who are ruled by their sense of what is necessary also need to discuss and reexamine their priorities; in particular they sometimes need encouragement and support to be more interested in what they do in order to ensure that their own emotional needs are being met. A third possibility that exists when patients report pursuing activities without mastery or pleasure is that they are engaging in internal dialogue that undermines their actions. For example, a computer programmer who has had difficulty concentrating may undermine his or her attempt to complete a computing task by saying such things as "It took longer than it should have," "I could have done better," or "Anyone could have done this better than me." Such negative automatic thoughts can be explored for distortions, and if distortions are found, they suggest a different approach to the patient's depression than the above two other problems.

Cognitive therapy for depression emphasizes the need to assess and modify cognitive distortions by reappraising automatic thoughts. Beck and his associates have described many common types of distortion seen in depression (Beck et al., 1979; Burns, 1980), including magnification and minimization, dichotomous thinking, labeling, fortune-telling, and the use of "should" statements. Cognitive therapists teach the patient the role of distorted, negative thinking in the maintenance of their depression, and then the systematic recording, challenging, and modification of that distorted thinking. One technique, for example, is to ask the patient to record the actual experiences and carefully compare them with the patient's negative review of those experiences. "Reviewing the evidence" sometimes will demonstrate to patients that their conclusions have been unduly pessimistic and will encourage a more realistic response to their experience. Another technique is to encourage patients to collect new evidence related to their ideas or predictions. Testing negative predictions can be a particularly powerful method to demonstrate that distorted thinking is counterproductive; it is also a means of encouraging patients to become more actively involved in problem solving in their own lives.

Due to the pervasive nature of negative thinking in depression, a good part of the treatment of depressed patients is centered on the techniques of cognitive assessment and modification in this area. At the same time, over the course of sessions, and as the patient begins to cope more adequately with life problems, themes in these problems will begin to emerge. It may be, for example, that a particular female patient has a hard time becoming more socially active because she believes that others will judge her socially unacceptable; she may also recall more negative social experiences than might be perceived by another person. This pattern of predicting and recalling interpersonal problems is suggestive of a cognitive schema in the area of social relations. It may be that the patient believes she is socially flawed in some way, that others are fundamentally critical and unforgiving, or both. At an appropriate time in this patient's treatment, her cognitive therapist will identify this pattern of cognition and may (depending on his or her conviction about which schema may be operative) suggest that there is a cognitive consistency in the way she approaches interpersonal situations. The therapist and patient would then spend some time examining this hypothesis (they may review other situations that could help to prove or disprove which schema is active, or they may develop new "experiments" for the patient to test her own thinking in related situations) and would come to some conclusion about the adequacy of the conceptualization. If they concur that a dysfunctional schema is active, they can then discuss means to modify that schema.

In the example just cited, the therapist and patient may decide that it is the patient's belief that others will judge her harshly that restricts her from being more socially active. In order to challenge this belief, a number of different interventions may be developed, discussed, and then implemented with the patient's consent. For example, the patient may be encouraged to seek some feedback from others about her acceptability. Typically, such an intervention would begin with less risky social relationships (e.g., good friends of the same sex) and then might be expanded to include more challenging types of relationships (e.g., first dates). A more dramatic way to challenge the belief about social unacceptability might be to have the patient behave provocatively with some of her friends—to actually do things that risk negative reactions—and then seek their reactions to her behavior. Assuming that the friends did not criticize her for her conduct, this action might powerfully demonstrate to the patient that it is her own perceptions of what is acceptable, rather than her friends', that limit her actions. This intervention could also be used as a platform to discuss the distinction between friends who reject some aspect of her behavior and friends who reject her as a person.

The cognitive therapy of depression tends to follow a predictable course, with an early focus on behavioral competencies, coping, and activities, followed by an extensive period of cognitive assessment and intervention, focused first on situation-specific cognitive distortions and later on more general self or interpersonal schemata. While many patients will show some reduction of depression early in treatment, the cognitive model predicts that the later work will have a preventative effect with respect to future stressors and will reduce the likelihood of relapse. Given that patients with depression have a high relapse rate (Belsher & Costello, 1988), the work done in cognitive therapy on underlying schemas is seen as a critical component of the therapy.

The cognitive therapy of depression has been applied in a relatively straightforward manner to anxiety problems (Beck & Emery, 1985), with two major differences. One difference is that whereas in depression the cognitive distortions that are dealt with are often related to memories of past events or losses, or negative interpretations *after the fact*, in anxiety the negative cognitions are almost uniformly related to negative *predictions* about future threats. Thus, the work of cognitive therapy for anxiety consists of assessing predictions, structuring therapeutic situations, and then encouraging the patient to disprove his or her own predictions. A common feature of cognitive

therapy for anxiety is to work with the patient to choose progressively more difficult situations, with the end goal being to have the patient expose the self to the most challenging situation. As in depression, there is often an underlying theme in the cognitions of anxiety patients that will be identified and discussed at some point in treatment.

The second difference between the cognitive therapy of anxiety versus depression concerns the content of the patient's cognitions. Whereas in depression the most typical themes are self or interpersonal inadequacy, loss, and failure, in anxiety disorders the themes are related to threat. From the cognitive perspective, the threat is often interpersonal in nature (e.g., seeing others as threatening by virtue of their ability to judge one's self), but it may also be physical or health-related (e.g., fearing certain insects due to their potential for injury). Thus, while the self and interpersonal themes may be highly similar in anxious and depressed patients—and, indeed, some patients who are initially depressed will go through a phase of significant anxiety as their problems shift from being past oriented to dealing with current or future problems (Dobson, 1985)—concern about physical threats is generally found in anxiety disorders.

The application of the cognitive model to marital disorders draws on notions of distorted thinking similar to those seen in anxiety and depression (Beck, 1988; Epstein & Baucom, 1988; Freeman, 1983). One difference, however, is that the cognitive distortions seen in marital dysfunction are not typically related to negative predictions, as seen in anxiety disorders, or to selective negative perceptions, as seen in depression. Rather, the focus of much of the work is on negative attributions made for the partner's behavior. Considerable research has shown that distressed couples make far more negative attributions for their partner's behavior than do nondistressed couples (Jacobson, McDonald, Follete, & Berley, 1985); cognitive therapy in this context examines these negative automatic thoughts.

In addition to the attributional focus, cognitive therapy for marital problems places a high premium on examining and correcting the couple's potentially destructive beliefs (Epstein & Baucom, 1988). Certain beliefs, such as never-ending intimacy, can be severely challenged as a couple moves from the honeymoon to the young parent stage. Often these beliefs need clarification and modification to achieve more permanent marital satisfaction. Finally, research findings suggest that some basic communication problems and problem-solving skills deficits may be present in marital distress. Cognitive therapists will frequently use techniques to improve communication and enhance skills as part of their therapy.

One of the most recent and provocative developments in cognitive therapy has been the growth of the treatment of personality disorders (Beck et al., 1990; Linehan, 1987; Young, 1990). Personality disorders, by their very nature, suggest an enduring interpersonal style of dysfunction marked by disturbances of self-perception and even of self-identity in some forms (American Psychiatric Association, 1987). Consistent with the trait-like nature of these disorders, cognitive models of personality disorders have focused on the stable cognitive schemas that patients with personality disorders manifest, and how to modify these schemas in the context of potentially disturbed situational behavior. Young (1990) focuses on what he terms *early maladaptive schemas (EMSs)*, which he suggests emerge from disturbed early experience, in which the person develops a disturbed self-image which later results in problematic interpersonal behavior. Young and others (Guidano, 1987, 1991; Guidano & Liotti, 1985) suggest that the complete therapy of personality-disordered individuals relies not only on the assessment and modification of situational distorted thinking, but also on changes in EMSs (*tacit beliefs* in Guidano's terminology).

In general, the progression from treatments for depression and anxiety through martial disorder to personality disorders has seen a decreasing focus on problematic behavior, a decreasing focus on skills deficits and their treatment, and a corresponding increasing focus on schemas and early experiences that later result in adolescent or adult psychopathology. Consistent with this shift in focus is the sugges-

tion that cognitive therapy requires more time to be effective; whereas early treatments for depression often involved 12–20 sessions, current cognitive therapies for personality disorders may take years to complete (Beck, 1991; Young, 1990).

In general, the outcome research on cognitive therapy supports its efficacy. There is a large controlled psychotherapy outcome literature in the area of depression, which consistently shows that cognitive therapy for depression is at least as good as other treatments (Dobson, 1989; Dobson & Pusch, 1993; Hollon, Shelton, & Davis, 1993), and the research on cognitive therapies for anxiety disorders also demonstrates treatment success (Chambless & Gillis, 1993). Although there is less research in the areas of marital distress (Baucom, Epstein, Rankin, & Burnett, in press) and a relative dearth of studies on personality disorders, what literature exists again supports the models. To date, what has been more difficult to evaluate is the extent to which gains in cognitive therapy are due to cognitive change processes, as opposed to other affective and/or interpersonal aspects of psychotherapy (Beck, 1993; Hollon et al., 1993; Robins & Hayes, 1993). It is also unclear to what extent the various aspects of the therapy contribute to the outcomes that have been attained. For example, emerging literature in the area of depression suggests that cognitive interventions may contribute little to patient change that cannot be accounted for by behavior change methods (Dobson, 1993). More research is needed to develop a clear sense of the value of cognitive therapy (particularly in the areas of marital and personality disorders), as well as the mechanisms of change.

Rational-Emotive Therapy

Rational-emotive therapy (RET) was developed by Albert Ellis before cognitive therapy emerged (Ellis, 1957, 1962) and has changed relatively little in its theoretical underpinnings or treatment technologies (Ellis & Dryden, 1987; Dryden & Ellis, 1988). RET is based on what Ellis has termed an *ABC* model of distress, where A stands for the activating event, B for the beliefs that moderate the events, and C for the consequences of having certain beliefs. According to Ellis, beliefs can be classified as rational or irrational, and it is the degree of rationality used by the individual in appraising an activating event that results in emotional/behavioral consequences, rather than the event itself. Thus, the impact of being turned down for a date is determined by the degree to which the individual can rationally believe that "it is not the end of the world" and that "there will be other possible dates," versus the extent to which the individual may engage in irrational thinking such as being "unlovable" and "likely to be lonely forever." RET theory suggests that it is the particular nature of irrational thinking that dictates the type of disorder seen. For example, a patient who is always predicting disasters will experience anxiety, while a person who castigates the self for failures will become depressed (Ellis, 1991; Walen, DiGuiseppe, & Dryden, 1992).

According to the RET model, the extent to which a person engages in irrational thinking is largely open to introspection, and to direct challenge and disputation. Ellis has written extensively about the different means that can be used to undermine irrational thinking (e.g., disputation, behavioral experiments, humor, rational role models) and has added immensely to the treatment technology literature. RET involves a rich amalgam of treatment techniques, which is undoubtedly part of the reason Albert Ellis and RET have has such a pronounced influence in psychotherapy in general (Chapter 8, this volume).

Despite the successes of RET, it is clear that challenges to this approach remain. Criticisms have been leveled about the limited amount of outcome research that has been conducted on RET (Haaga & Davidson, 1989, 1993), as well as the methodological rigor employed in that research. Despite the claims by Ellis about RET's success (Dryden & Ellis, 1988), it appears that more systematic research is warranted. One issue that also needs to be considered in future research on RET is the measurement of outcomes. RET theory pro-

poses that irrational beliefs mediate dysfunction; accordingly, not only should changes in patients' problems be correlated with changes in these beliefs, changes in the beliefs should actually predict change in patients' problems. Research on the change processes hypothesized by RET is needed (Haaga & Davidson, 1993).

Problem-Solving Therapies

It has been recognized for some time that certain forms of psychopathology are associated with problem-solving deficits, in particular, social problem-solving deficits (D'Zurilla & Nezu, 1982; Heppner & Anderson, 1985; Nezu & D'Zurilla, 1989; Platt & Spivack, 1972). Within this realm, a distinction has been made between problem-solving processes that may be flawed and potentially inadequate implementation of processes that are sound (i.e., social skills deficits). Some of the process variables that have been examined include the accurate appraisal of life situations and the ability to generate potential solutions to problems.

Due to the recognition of a number of potential problem-solving problems associated with psychopathology, several treatments have been developed to cope with these deficits (D'Zurilla, 1986, 1988; Nezu et al., 1989). Problem-solving therapies employ a standard approach to cognitive and behavioral assessment and modification. Typically, the treatment moves from an examination of the patient's problem(s), to an exploration of potential solutions, to discussion of the relative merits and demerits of different solutions, to choosing a potential solution, implementing it, evaluating the outcome, and, if necessary, repeating the entire process with a redefined problem. During the therapy process, cognitive skills such as the ability to see creative solutions and to evaluate alternative solutions are examined, and the patient is taught more effective strategies if necessary. Social skills are examined to ensure that the patient can implement the intended solution, and if necessary, skills training can be used to assist the patient in solving problems.

Problem-solving therapy is a very adaptable form of treatment and has been employed in a wide range of patient problems, including depression, suicidal behavior, anxiety, marital problems, and adolescent social problems (D'Zurilla, 1986; 1988; Nezu et al., 1989; Robin, 1981). Its versatility also allows problem-solving therapy to be employed as part of an eclectic treatment, in which the focus might be on schematic assessment and change, but where a particular problem emerges that can be addressed with these techniques.

Data on the efficacy of the treatment approach are available (D'Zurilla, 1988) and generally support the use of problem-solving therapies. There continue to be issues that warrant further research, including the best means for assessing problem-solving competence. The most widely employed technique is the Means-Ends Problem Solving Procedures (Platt & Spivack, 1975), in which subjects imagine themselves to be in hypothetical interpersonal situations and develop the means to obtain certain predetermined outcomes to those situations. This measure is correlated with psychopathology but appears to be nonspecific in that regard. As such, the specific nature of social problem-solving deficits in unique forms of psychopathology requires more attention.

Another issue for the field of problem-solving therapies concerns mechanisms of change. As problem-solving therapies are progressive and multidimensional, with each step in the sequence building on the prior ones, it is very difficult to identify the critical steps in the sequence. Dismantling studies would help to clarify the essential mechanisms involved in these treatment strategies.

Self-Management Therapies

Self-management is a term that "refers to certain natural processes by which individuals direct and control their behavior" (Rehm & Rokke, 1988, p. 136). While different theorists have emphasized one or another self-management process, some of the processes that have been associated with this approach include (1) self-monitoring, (2) performance standards, (3) performance expectancies, (4) self-attributions for success and failure, and (5) self-reinforcement (Kanfer, in press; Rehm, 1984; Rehm & Rokke, 1988).

Self-management therapies assess the above potential problem areas and then impose treatments that are appropriate for the specific patient and problem. The self-management model is generic and has been applied to a large number of clinical problems, including anxiety and depression (Fuchs & Rehm, 1977; Rehm & Rokke, 1988), smoking cessation (DiClemente, 1981), and others (Karoly & Kanfer, 1982). In general, this approach seems most applicable where specific behavioral performance is useful as an index of the success of the treatment, since much of the model examines the functional behavior of the individual. For example, because in eating disorders the eating behavior can be assessed to assess its appropriateness in terms of amount and time, self-management strategies seem particularly appropriate. For conditions such as personality disorders, where the problems are typically more in number and more diffuse in nature, these therapeutic strategies are less applicable.

Constructivistic Therapies

Whereas most of the cognitive therapies and all of those discussed to this point rest on an underlying rational epistemology, constructivistic psychotherapies use an approach based on postrationalism. Thus, whereas other cognitive therapies assert that there is a knowable external reality, and that dysfunction can be measured by the lack of concordance between an individual and his or her world, constructivistic therapies assert that reality is subjective, and that dysfunction reflects a lack of viability or adaptiveness of one's self and one's world constructions (Mahoney, 1991; Neimeyer, 1993; Neimeyer & Feixas, 1990). Whereas traditional cognitive therapies focus on identifying distorted or irrational thinking or behavioral deficits, constructivistic therapies emphasize the viability of cognition and the internal consistency of cognitive organization. Constructivistic therapies are less focused than traditional approaches to treatment, which tend to be disorder-specific, and also take a longer period of time.

A number of specific constructivistic therapies have emerged, including personal construct therapy (Gara, Rosenberg, & Meuller, 1989; Kelly, 1955), structural-developmental cognitive therapy (Guidano, 1987, 1991; Guidano & Liotti, 1985), and others (Mahoney, 1988, 1991; Rosen, 1985; Weiner, 1985). To date, outcome research on these approaches is limited (Neimeyer, 1993), as the authors are for the most part interested in exploring therapy processes, and predictors of change, rather than formalizing the outcomes associated with treatment. The reduced focus on the assessment of outcomes is also due to the fact that the traditional logical positivistic research methods associated with psychotherapy research are to some extent repudiated by theorists who employ constructivistic methods. Efforts to establish outcomes based on idiographic and descriptive methodologies are likely to be a focus within this therapy area (Neimeyer, 1993).

FUTURE ISSUES FOR THE COGNITIVE THERAPIES

As this review of the major forms of cognitive therapy attests, several clinically rich interventions have developed within this field in a relatively short time. Cognitive therapies have become a major part of the armamentarium of psychotherapists (Chapter 8, this volume) and are likely to remain so for the foreseeable future. Despite the interest in and development of these approaches, however, there are a number of issues that require attention for the field to grow and mature. In this section, we outline what we perceive as the four major challenges to the field of cognitive therapies: the assessment of outcomes, investigation of the mechanisms and moderators of change, and therapeutic integration, both within the cognitive therapies and between cognitive and other approaches. Each of these issues is addressed in turn.

Outcome Assessment and Limit Testing

Despite the accumulating evidence in favor of the therapeutic value of the cognitive therapies (Beck, 1991, 1993; Robins & Hayes, 1993; Chapter 8, this volume), some of the treatments have been subjected to more outcome research than others. As previously noted, RET has been criticized for the relatively small amount of data that has been collected to support this therapeutic efficacy (Haaga & Davidson, 1993). Sustained efforts to establish the value of cognitive therapies are needed.

Related to the issue of absolute outcome (i.e., how much change can each type of therapy produce?) are the questions of differential change (i.e., which one has the best outcome?) and cost effectiveness (i.e., which one has the best outcome at the lowest cost?). Although to some extent the two latter questions require different research designs and assessment methods than does the first question, it is possible to design research that can address all of these issues within the context of single studies. It is recommended that investigators take these issues into account in their research plans.

One final issue related to the assessment of outcomes is the domains in which the treatments are investigated. As described, Beck's cognitive therapy was first applied to depression, and its applicability to other patient problems was investigated later. One issue that emerges is whether or not the treatment can be adequately applied to other patient problems, and if so, which ones. From the opposite perspective, it is possible that there are patient problems for which cognitive therapy is not appropriate, or where the outcomes associated with its application would not warrant its continued use. It may also be that for these therapies to work with other patient problems, significant modifications of the theory or treatment interventions will be required. Examination of the boundary conditions for the cognitive therapies, as well as modifications based on new applications, will become an important part of theory and treatment development.

Mechanisms and Moderators of Change

As previously stated, the existing data on the cognitive therapies is generally encouraging. Not surprisingly, theorists have attempted to investigate the processes involved in change. From this perspective, one line of research has been the examination of patient variables that moderate change. As the cognitive models of psychopathology stipulate certain cognitive and behavioral dysfunctions, two common strategies have been to examine the amount of change in these variables associated with treatment success and to predict treatment success with these variables (Beck, 1991; Hollon et al., 1993; Robins & Hayes, 1993). More recently, studies have also examined treatment by aptitude (predictor variable) interactions to evaluate whether certain client characteristics predict better success in psychotherapy. This approach also seems appropriate for research in the cognitive therapies.

Although some research has examined the therapy variables most often associated with change in the cognitive therapies (Dobson, 1993; Kornblith, Rehm, O'Hara, & Lamparski, 1983), relatively little dismantling or component research has been conducted to date. It would be valuable to examine which treatment techniques are most often associated with patient change in order to learn more about optimal treatment strategies, as well as about the process of change itself.

Integration of the Cognitive Therapies

Despite the relatively short history of the cognitive therapies, there has been a veritable explosion of treatments, from this perspective (Dobson & Block, 1988; Mahoney, 1988, 1991). However, in spite of the increasing number of identifiable cognitive therapies, an examination of these treatments suggests many similar constructs and intervention techniques. This similarity of constructs and techniques highlights the questions of the extent to which these are actually unique treatment approaches and the extent to which these treatments can be integrated.

From our perspective, some of the cognitive therapies are close to each other and could be integrated. For example, problem-solving and self-management therapies share certain assumptions about the nature of psychopathology—that it is marked by specific identifiable skill and process problems—and it seems possible to generate complete sets of these problems within each type of psychopathology to develop a comprehensive treatment approach. As another example, RET and cognitive therapy have already been identified as cousins (Beck, 1991; Dryden & Ellis, 1988; Ellis, 1991), and many of the constructs and therapy techniques of these two approaches seem to have common characteristics. In both of these instances, integration seems a real possibility.

In contrast, some of the cognitive therapies seem to be more difficult to integrate. Perhaps the most notable example is a therapy based on a rational epistemology and another based on a postrational framework. As these treatments have divergent basic assumptions, true integration is likely less possible than eclecticism in terms of the treatment techniques applied to a specific patient.

Integration with Other Models of Psychotherapy

Considerable theoretical interest has been expressed in integration between the cognitive therapies and other treatment approaches (Greenberg & Safran, 1987; Mahoney, 1991; Safran & Segal, 1990; Segal & Blatt, 1993). For the most part, these attempts at integration share an emphasis on cognitive processing and construction of experience, and then attempt to relate cognitive constructs and processes to some other area of human experience, such as emotional experience or interpersonal relations.

Integration is an extremely complex endeavor (Norcross, 1986). In order to engage in the process, clear constructs are required. The unique and common aspects of the treatments must be elaborated, and it must be made clear to what extent true integration is occurring versus the simple amalgamation of intervention techniques, as happens in eclecticism. Ideally, the emergent integrated model can be contrasted with the two (or more) former intervention models, and it can be demonstrated at both the theoretical and practical levels that the integrated theory is superior to its forebears. These demands are daunting, and it is no doubt partly for these reasons that few truly integrated therapies have emerged. A major future challenge will be for the cognitive therapies to define their position in the overall field of psychotherapy.

CONCLUDING COMMENTS

In this chapter, we have attempted to capture some of the breadth and possibility of the cognitive therapies. As participant observers in the development of these treatments, it has been exciting to see their rapid expansion and widespread adoption. We are impressed by the high degree of theoretical and empirical rigor that characterizes these therapies, and we encourage the continued critical consideration of their strengths and limitations, as it is through such an examination that the field will grow. One of the threats we perceive for the field of cognitive therapies is movement away from empiricism and toward an acceptance of case methods. Although cognitive therapy by definition is applied to individuals, we believe that is has been the demonstration of outcomes on defined *groups* of subjects, using standardized and replicable research tools, that has been largely responsible for the high credibility afforded these treatments. Continued use of these research methods will be important for the continued development of this field.

REFERENCES

American Psychiatric Association. (1987). *Diagnostic and Statistical Manual-III-Revised.* Washington, DC: Author.

American Psychiatric Association. (1994). *DSM-IV Draft Criteria.* Washington, DC: Author.

Baucom, D., Epstein, N., Rankin, L. A., & Burnett, C. K. (in press). Understanding and treating marital distress from a cognitive-behavioral orientation. In K. S. Dobson & K. D. Craig (Eds.), *Progress in Cognitive-behavior therapy.* Newbury Park, CA: Sage.

Beck, A. T. (1970). Cognitive therapy: Nature and relation to behavior therapy. *Behavior Therapy, 1,* 184–200.

Beck, A. T. (1976). *Cognitive therapy and the emotional disorders.* Madison, CT: International Universities Press.

Beck, A. T. (1988). *Love is never enough.* New York: Harper & Row.

Beck, A. T. (1991). Cognitive therapy as the integrative therapy. *Journal of Psychotherapy Integration, 3,* 191–198.

Beck, A. T. (1993). Cognitive therapy: Past, present, and future. *Journal of Consulting and Clinical Psychology, 61,* 194–198.

Beck, A. T., & Emery, G. (1985). *Anxiety disorders and phobias: A cognitive perspective.* New York: Basic Books.

Beck, A. T., Freeman, A., & Associates. (1990). *Cognitive therapy of personality disorders.* New York: Guilford Press.

Beck, A. T., Rush, A. J., Shaw, B. F., & Emery, G. (1979). *The cognitive therapy of depression.* New York: Guilford Press.

Beck, A. T., Wright, F. D., Newman, C. D., & Liese, B. S. (1993). *Cognitive therapy of drug abuse.* New York: Guilford Press.

Belsher, G., & Costello, C. (1988). Relapse after recovery from unipolar depression: A critical review. *Psychological Bulletin, 104,* 84–96.

Burns, D. (1980). *Feeling good.* New York: Signet.

Chambless, D. L., & Gillis, M. M. (1993). Cognitive therapy of anxiety disorders. *Journal of Consulting and Clinical Psychology, 61,* 248–260.

DiClemente, C. C. (1981). Self-efficacy and smoking cessation maintenance. *Cognitive Therapy and Research, 5,* 175–187.

Dobson, K. S. (1985). The relationship between anxiety and depression. *Clinical Psychology Review, 49,* 305–324.

Dobson, K. S. (1986). The self-schema in depression. In L. Hartman & K. Blankstein (Eds.) *Perception of self in emotional disorder and psychotherapy* (pp. 187–218). New York: Plenum Press.

Dobson, K. S. (Eds.). (1988). *Handbook of cognitive-behavioral therapies.* New York: Guilford Press.

Dobson, K. S. (1989). A meta-analysis of the efficacy of cognitive therapy for depression. *Journal of Consulting and Clinical Psychology, 57,* 414–419.

Dobson, K. S. (1993, June). *Comparative outcomes of components of Beck's cognitive therapy for depression.* Paper presented at the meetings of the Society for Psychotherapy Research, Pittsburgh, PA.

Dobson, K. S., & Block, L. (1988). Historical and philosophical bases of the cognitive-behavioral therapies. In K. S. Dobson (Ed.), *Handbook of cognitive-behavioral therapies* (pp. 3–38). New York: Guilford Press.

Dobson, K. S., & Pusch, D. (1993). Towards a definition of the conceptual and empirical boundaries of cognitive therapy. *Australian Psychologist, 28,* 117–134.

Dryden, W., & Ellis, A. (1988). Rational-emotive therapy. In K. S. Dobson (Ed.), *Handbook of Cognitive-behavioral therapies* (pp. 214–272). New York: Guilford Press.

D'Zurilla, T. (1986). *Problem-solving therapy: A social competence approach to clinical intervention.* New York: Springer.

D'Zurilla, T. (1988). Problem-solving therapies. In K. S. Dobson (Ed.), *Handbook of cognitive-behavioral therapies* (pp. 85–135). New York: Guilford Press.

D'Zurilla, T., & Nezu, A. (1982). Social problem-solving in adults. In P. C. Kendall (Ed.), *Advances in cognitive-behavioral research and therapy* (Vol. 1, pp. 172–214). New York: Academic Press.

Ellis, A. (1957). Outcome of employing three techniques of psychotherapy. *Journal of Clinical Psychology, 13,* 344–350.

Ellis, A. (1962). *Reason and emotion in psychotherapy.* New York: Lyle Stuart.

Ellis, A. (1980). Rational-emotive therapy and cognitive behavior therapy: Similarities and differences. *Cognitive Therapy and Research, 4,* 325–340.

Ellis, A. (1988). *How to stubbornly refuse to make yourself miserable about anything—yes, anything!* Secausus, NJ: Citadel.

Ellis, A. (1991). The revised ABCs of rational-emotive therapy. *Journal of Rational-Emotive and Cognitive-Behavioral Therapy, 9,* 139–192.

Ellis, A., & Dryden, W. (1987). *The practice of rational-emotive therapy.* New York: Springer.

Epstein, N., & Baucom, N. (1988). *Cognitive-behavioral marital therapy.* New York: Brunner/Mazel.

Freeman, A. (Ed.). (1983). *Cognitive therapy with couples and groups.* New York: Plenum Press.

Freeman, A., Simon, K., Beutler, L., & Arkowitz, H. (Eds.). (1989). *Comprehensive handbook of cognitive therapy.* New York: Plenum Press.

Fuchs, C. Z., & Rehm, L. (1977). A self-control behavior therapy program for depression. *Journal of Consulting and Clinical Psychology, 45,* 206–215.

Gara, A., Rosenberg, S., & Mueller, D. R. (1989). Perception of self and other in schizophrenia. *International Journal of Personal Construct Psychology, 2,* 253–270.

Guidano, V. (1987). *Complexity of the self.* New York: Guilford Press.

Guidano, V. (1991). *The self in process: Towards a post-rationalist cognitive therapy.* New York: Guilford Press.

Guidano, V., & Liotti, G. (1983). *Cognitive processes and emotional disorders.* New York: Guilford Press.

Greenberg, L., & Safran, J. (1987). *Emotion in psychotherapy: Affect, cognition, and the process of change.* New York: Guilford Press.

Haaga, D., & Davidson, G. C. (1989). Outcome studies in rational-emotive therapy. In M. Bernard & R. DiGuiseppe (Eds.), *Inside rational-emotive therapy: A critical appraisal of the theory and therapy of Albert Ellis* (pp. 287–314). San Diego, CA: Academic Press.

Haaga, D., & Davidson, G. C. (1993). An appraisal of rational-emotive therapy. *Journal of Consulting and Clinical Psychology, 61,* 215–220.

Heppner, P. P., & Anderson, W. P. (1985). The relationship between problem-solving, self-appraisal, and psychological adjustment. *Cognitive Therapy and Research, 9,* 415–427.

Hollon, S. D., Shelton, R. C., & Davis, D. D. (1993). Cognitive therapy for depression: Conceptual issues and clinical efficacy. *Journal of Consulting and Clinical Psychology, 61,* 270–275.

Jacobson, N. S., McDonald, D. W., Follete, W. C., & Berley, R. A. (1985). Attributional process in distressed and nondistressed married couples. *Cognitive Therapy and Research, 9,* 35–50.

Kanfer, F. (1977). Self-regulation and self-control.

In H. Zeir (Ed.), *The psychology of the 20th century* (pp. 194–215). Zurich: Kindler Verlag.

Kanfer, F. (in press). Motivation and emotion in behavior therapy. In K. S. Dobson & K. D. Craig (Eds.), *Advances in the cognitive-behavior therapies*. Newbury Park, CA: Sage.

Karoly, P., & Kanfer, F. (Eds.). (1982). *Self-management and behavior change: From theory to practice*. New York: Pergamon Press.

Kelly, G. (1955). *The psychology of personal constructs*. New York: Norton.

Kornblith, S. J., Rehm, L. P., O'Hara, M. W., & Lamparski, D. M. (1983). The contribution of self-reinforcement training and behavioral assignments to the efficacy of self-control therapy for depression. *Cognitive Therapy and Research, 7*, 499–527.

Kovacs, M., & Beck, A. T. (1977). Cognitive-affective processes in depression. In C. E. Izard (Ed.), *Emotions in personality and psychopathology* (pp. 214–247). New York: Plenum Press.

Linehan, M. (1987). Dialectical behavioral therapy: A cognitive behavioral approach to parasuicide. *Journal of Personality Disorders, 1*, 328–333.

Mahoney, M. (1974). *Cognition and Behavior Modification*. Cambridge, MA: Ballinger.

Mahoney, M. (1988). The cognitive sciences and psychotherapy: Patterns in a developing relationship. In K. S. Dobson (Ed.), *Handbook of cognitive-behavioral therapies* (pp. 357–385). New York: Guilford Press.

Mahoney, M. (1991) *Human change processes*. New York: Basic Books.

Markus, H. (1977) Self-schemata and processing information about the self. *Journal of Personality and Social Psychology, 35*, 63–78.

Meichenbaum, D. (1977). *Cognitive behavior modification: An integrative approach*. New York: Plenum Press.

Neimeyer, R. A. (1993). An appraisal of constructivist psychotherapies. *Journal of Consulting and Clinical Psychology, 61*, 221–234.

Neimeyer, R. A., & Feixas, G. (1990). Constructivist contributions to psychotherapy integration. *Journal of Integrative and Eclectic Psychotherapy, 9*, 4–20.

Nezu, A., & D'Zurilla, T. (1989). Social problem solving and negative affective conditions. In P. C. Kendall & D. Watson (Eds.), *Anxiety and depression: Distinctive and overlapping features* (pp. 285–315). New York: Academic Press.

Nezu, A., Nezu, C., & Perri, M. G. (1989). *Problem-solving therapy for depression: Theory, research and guidelines*. New York: Wiley.

Norcross, J. C. (Ed.). (1986). *Handbook of eclectic psychotherapy*. New York: Brunner/Mazel.

Persons, J. (1989). *Cognitive therapy in practice: A case formulation approach*. New York: Norton.

Platt, J. J., & Spivack, G. (1972). Problem solving thinking of psychiatric patients. *Journal of Consulting and Clinical Psychology, 39*, 148–151.

Platt, J. J., & Spivack, G. (1975). *Manual for the Means-End Problem Solving Procedures (MEPS): A measure of interpersonal cognitive problem-solving skill*. Unpublished manuscript. Philadelphia: Hahnemann Mental Health Centre.

Rehm, L. (1984). Self-management therapy for depression. *Advances in Behavior Research and Therapy, 6*, 83–98.

Rehm, L., & Rokke, P. (1988). Self-management therapies. In K. S. Dobson (Ed.), *Handbook of cognitive-behavioral therapies* (pp. 136–166). New York: Guilford Press.

Robin, A. L. (1981). A controlled evaluation of problem-solving communication training with parent–adolescent conflict. *Behavior Therapy, 12*, 593–609.

Robins, C. J., & Hayes, A. M. (1993). An appraisal of cognitive therapy. *Journal of Consulting and Clinical Psychology, 61*, 205–214.

Rosen, H. (1985). *Piagetian dimensions of clinical relevance*. New York: Columbia University Press.

Safran, J., & Segal. Z. V. (1990). *Interpersonal process in cognitive therapy*. New York: Basic Books.

Segal, Z. V. (1988). Appraisal of the self-schema construct in cognitive models of depression. *Psychological Bulletin, 103*, 147–162.

Segal, Z. V., & Blatt, S. (Eds.), (1993). *The self in emotional distress: Cognitive and psychodynamic perspectives*. New York: Guilford Press.

Walen, S., DiGuiseppe, R., & Dryden, W. (1992). *A practitioner's guide to rational-emotive therapy*. New York: Oxford University Press.

Weiner, M. L. (1985). *Cognitive-experiential therapy: An integrative ego psychotherapy*. New York: Brunner/Mazel.

Young, J. (1990). *Cognitive therapy for personality disorders: A schema-focused approach*. Sarasota, FL: Professional Resource Exchange.

10
Group Psychotherapy in Historical Perspective

Max Rosenbaum
Kathleen M. Patterson

The history of group psychotherapy is as old as the beginning of recorded time. Every religious, social, or political movement that has reached masses of people could be described as a form of group psychotherapy. Ancient Greek drama, medieval morality plays, monastic orders that stressed group confessional, and Anton Mesmer's large groups in the eighteenth century all may be considered forerunners of group therapy.

There are many who claim to have pioneered modern methods of group therapy (Bach & Illing, 1956; Bierer, 1948; Corsini, 1955; Dreikurs, 1952, 1959; Dreikurs & Corsini, 1954; Gifford & Mackenzie, 1948; Hadden, 1955; Klapman, 1946; Kotkov, 1950; Meiers, 1945; Moreno, 1957; Slavson, 1950, 1951; Teirich, 1957; Thomas, 1943). This chapter will review the work of many of these pioneers in both the United States and Europe. Because the first author is a psychologist who was trained as a psychoanalyst, the bias of this chapter is psychodynamic.

GROUP THERAPY IN THE UNITED STATES BEFORE WORLD WAR II

Joseph Hersey Pratt

There is general agreement that the founder of contemporary group psychotherapy (at least in the twentieth-century United States) was Joseph Hersey Pratt, an internist who practiced in Boston, Massachusetts (Mullan & Rosenbaum, 1962). In 1905, Pratt was treating tubercular patients, many of whom were poor Irish immigrants. These patients tended to become discouraged and disheartened during the course of their illness. In order to improve their morale, Pratt lectured to groups of up to 25 patients in weekly classes. Every patient in these groups kept a record book (the invention of a North Carolina physician, C. L. Minor) for recording temperature, diet, rest periods, and other details. Pratt noticed that a "fine spirit of camaraderie had developed" through these "supportive and inspirational" groups. Pratt worked in relative isolation from the neuropsychiatric community of Boston. At that time, editorials in the medical journals criticized clergymen who treated nervous and mental disorders. Although Pratt was a physician, he was criticized because his classes were held in the church that helped finance his project. Opponents of his class method also contended that his good results were due to his strong personality. Pratt denied this allegation.

It is apparent from Pratt's early writings that he had little understanding of his own impact on his patients. In 1913, Pratt met Isadore Coriat, one of the first American psychoanalysts, who also practiced in Boston. Coriat introduced him to the work of Joseph Jules Dejerine, a French physician and pioneer in the treatment of psychoneurosis, whose book, *The Psychoneuroses and Their Treatment* (Dejerine & Gauckler, 1913) had recently appeared in an English translation. This work went almost unnoticed (Pratt, 1953). Dejerine, who had worked with methods of emotional reeducation for more than 15 years before his book was published, stated: "Psychotherapy depends wholly and exclusively upon the beneficial influence of one person on another." It was only after Pratt had worked with the class method for some years that he began to understand the more profound implications of his work. Although at the outset his approach to group psychotherapy was repressive-inspirational, toward the end of his professional life, Pratt indicated an awareness of the more dynamic self-discovery factors involved in his work.

Trigant Burrow

Another pioneer in group therapy approaches was Trigant Burrow, one of the first American psychoanalysts. In the *History of Psychoanalysis in America* (Oberndorf, 1953), Burrow was cited as one of the four most original contributors to the science of psychoanalysis before 1920. Burrow, who had both a medical degree and a doctorate in psychology, began to work as a psychiatrist under the supervision of Adolf Meyer. In 1909, Meyer introduced Burrow to two European psychoanalysts, Freud and Jung, who had come to lecture at Clark University in Massachusetts. With Meyer's encouragement, Burrow began to study psychoanalysis and traveled to Europe to enter his own analysis with Jung. Following his analysis, Burrow returned to the United States, where he became one of the founding members of the American Psychoanalytic Association in 1911. He planned to return to Europe in 1913 to have further analysis with Freud, but World War I disrupted his plans.

From 1912, Burrow became increasingly dissatisfied with the emphasis psychoanalysis placed on the individual, to the exclusion of social forces and the environment (Burrow, 1912–1913, 1914). He believed that behavioral disorders were correlated with social relatedness. In 1918, Burrow accepted a new analytic patient, Clarence Shields, an intuitive and somewhat retiring young man. Shields challenged Burrow to reverse the analytic position in order to test the "honesty" of the relationship. Shields proposed that he become the analyst and sit up, while Burrow was to be the patient and lie down. Although Burrow was fully aware of the resistance mechanisms at work in this suggestion, he consented to the experiment. This arrangement evolved into sessions in which both Burrow and Shields were to sit up, face to face. Through this experiment, Burrow became aware of the authoritarian aspect of the analytic experience in the definition of doctor and patient roles. Years later, Burrow complained that Harry Stack Sullivan, a colleague at the Phipps Clinic in Baltimore, failed to credit him for his seminal contribution to Sullivan's interpersonal theory of psychiatry.

Burrow's work with Shields served as a springboard for his research on group behavior. Burrow kept in contact with Freud, who was very negative about the new direction of Burrow's work, remarking that Burrow "wanted to change the world." Freud actively discouraged Burrow's work, to the extent that he blocked the publication of his papers in analytic journals. When Burrow became president of the American Psychoanalytic Association, Freud, who was critical of the United States in general, stated that this was an example of the American tendency to elevate people of modest accomplishments to major positions.

In the early 1920s, Burrow met with coworkers and patients at a rustic camp on Lake Chateaugay in the Adirondacks mountains to study patterns of social relatedness. This did not sit well with Freud. In 1921, Hans Syz, a Swiss psychiatrist from Zurich, came to the Phipps Clinic, met Burrow, and became deeply interested in Burrow's studies and approach. They worked closely together for the rest of their professional careers.

In 1927, Burrow published two important works: a paper entitled "The Group Method of Analysis" (Burrow, 1927a) and the book *The Social Basis of Consciousness* (Burrow, 1927b). Freud remained negative about Burrow's work, however. The more Burrow studied groups, the more he became intrigued with the possibility of finding a biological basis for group relatedness. He dropped the term *group analysis* in favor of *phyloanalysis*. This work estranged him from the organized psychoanalytic community. In 1933, when the American Psychoanalytic Association was reorganized, he was dropped from membership because his approach was considered too biological. Ironically, years later, the American Psychoanalytic Association invited Burrow to a major celebration as one of the pioneer psychoanalysts, ignoring the fact that they had dropped him from membership. Although Burrow was a prolific writer, with 68 articles and 5 books to his credit, his writing style grew increasingly difficult to understand, discouraging his readers.

Edward Lazell

Prior to World War I, several physicians in the United States had begun using group approaches in psychiatric care; however, the results of their work were not published until after the war. In 1921, Edward Lazell, a psychiatrist who was working with schizophrenic patients in a government hospital in the Washington, D.C., area, published an article describing his work, which consisted mainly of lectures to his patients. This article (Lazell, 1921) noted the advantages of the group method in language that was consistent with the current psychoanalytic literature.

L. C. Marsh

A decade after the appearance of Lazell's article, L. C. Marsh (1931) published an article describing in detail his use of the group method with patients in a mental hospital. Marsh began his career as a minister. In 1909, he worked with patients at Worcester State Hospital in Massachusetts, using diverse techniques: inspirational lectures, dance classes, and art classes. His approach stemmed from his belief that patients could be supportive of one another. In contrast to Lazell's didactic approach, Marsh was active and directive. Marsh later entered

the field of medicine and became a psychiatrist. Although he made no attempt to present a unified theory, he was a conscientious and dedicated clinician.

Jacob L. Moreno

Jacob L. Moreno, the originator of psychodrama, claimed that he used group therapy in 1910 and that he coined the term in 1931 (Moreno, 1911, 1957). As a medical student in Vienna, Moreno organized groups of prostitutes and used group techniques in his practice before coming to the United States in 1925. By 1929, he was publicly demonstrating his methods. He described his approach in detail at the 1932 annual conference of the American Psychiatric Association. In 1931 he founded the first journal on group therapy, *Impromptu*. The journal ceased publication after a few years, and in 1937 he founded a new journal, *Sociometry*. The editorial board of this journal consisted of psychologists, psychiatrists, and sociologists. In 1947 he turned this journal over to the American Sociological Association and founded yet another journal, initially entitled *Sociatry*, which became *Group Psychotherapy*. This publication, now called the *Journal of Group Psychotherapy, Psychodrama and Sociometry*, is published by the American Society of Group Psychotherapy and Psychodrama, the organization founded by Moreno. It is one of two major journals on group therapy in the United States, the other being the *International Journal of Group Psychotherapy*, the official journal of the American Group Psychotherapy Association.

Louis Wender

Beginning in 1929, Louis Wender used psychoanalytic concepts when he practiced group therapy with borderline psychotic patients in Pinewood, a private psychiatric hospital in Westchester County, New York. His article "The Dynamics of Group Psychotherapy and Its Application" (Wender, 1936) was subsequently published as a training manual for the psychiatric services of the U.S. army during World War II. Wender was aware of Burrow's work, which he described as an "extramural . . . psychoanalytic in technique . . . [which] carries large sociological and philosophical implications." In contrast, he described his own mode of group psychotherapy as a "method confined to the intramural treatment of certain types of mild mental disease." His groups were composed of six to eight patients of the same sex that met two or three times a week for 1-hour sessions. Wender described the transference phenomena that occurred in the group as a representation of the family, with the therapist perceived as the parent and other group members perceived as siblings. He believed that a partial reorganization of the patient's personality was possible through treatment with group psychotherapy.

Paul Schilder

In 1934, Paul Schilder, a bold thinker, began using group therapy approaches with outpatients at Bellevue Hospital in New York City. He described his work with 50 patients at the annual meeting of the American Psychiatric Association in 1936. He was quite active in his groups, often directly challenging his patients. Schilder was well versed in the psychoanalytic literature of his time, as well as with earlier writings. He was familiar with Freud's paper on group psychology, in which the group leader was described as primarily a representative of the father. In contrast, Schilder postulated that the group leader could be both a father and a mother image (Schilder, 1940). Schilder (1936, 1939) published two articles on group therapy that are pertinent for today because they discuss the importance of *value systems* and *ideologies* in psychotherapy.

Samuel Slavson

In the early 1930s, Samuel Slavson, a civil engineer who had been involved for years with social group work and progressive education

activities, began working with activity group therapy at the Jewish Board of Guardians, a New York City agency that treated children and their parents. The executive director of the agency was Slavson's brother, John Slawson, a psychologist who had studied juvenile delinquents in the mid 1920s. John Slawson's wife took groups of children and preadolescents on picnics and other socializing experiences as part of the volunteer Big Sisters program. She observed that this activity appeared to be helpful to the clients. When Samuel Slavson began working at the agency, he combined progressive education, group work, and psychoanalytic concepts. Later, he organized more formal groups that met weekly, composed of children up to the age of 15. His activity group therapy emphasized the acting out of conflicts, impulses, and patterns of behavior. As a group leader, Slavson was permissive, observing the interaction of the children in a room that contained games and craft media.

In 1943, Slavson published his first book, *An Introduction to Group Therapy*. In the same year, he presented a paper to the American Orthopsychiatric Association as part of a special symposium on group therapy with children and adults (Lowrey et al., 1943). This presentation summarized his work with approximately 800 children in 63 distinct groups over a period of 9 years. Slavson was aware of the work of Burrow, Wender, Schilder, and others, but he stated that his unique contribution to the field was his work in activity group therapy for children between the ages of 8 and 15. He was reluctant to use the term *psychotherapy*; he preferred to describe his work as *situational therapy*.

Later in his career, Slavson organized programs for adults, as well as for patients in mental hospitals. He was intolerant of what he believed to be superficial approaches and severed ties with any practitioner whom he perceived to be hurtful to patients. He stressed clinical diagnosis and was impatient with philosophical and sociological concepts. A passionate worker, he firmly believed that his job was to ensure the careful and orderly development of the field of group psychotherapy. To this end, he published 194 works and was a prime mover in the formation of the American Group Psychotherapy Association in 1942.

Although his coworkers and students overlooked a good deal of his intemperate behavior, Slavson was known to be brutal in his disagreements. Unfortunately, this led to bitter personal antagonism with Jacob Moreno, the originator of psychodrama.

It is an interesting note that, as with Pratt, it was years after Slavson began his work that he realized the applicability of psychoanalytic concepts. He entered personal psychoanalysis twice, which helped him understand the deeper meaning of the unconscious. In his later writings, Slavson (1979) noted that he came upon activity group psychotherapy

> through pathways other than psychoanalysis namely progressive education and social group work. However, its relation to Freudian formulations became quickly apparent to me and it was not difficult to reinterpret the dynamic phenomena in these groups in the light of Freud's basic principles. . . . (p. 168)

Carl Rogers

Carl Rogers' basic premise throughout his practice and writings was the belief in the client's capacity to deal constructively with personal conflicts. His nondirective, client-centered approach was in marked contrast to the psychoanalytic approach, with its emphasis on intrapsychic and interpersonal exploration. Rogers' original clinical work with children in Rochester, New York, probably oriented him to Slavson's activity group therapy. By 1940, Rogers was a professor at Ohio State University and aware of the forces emerging in the child guidance field. He encouraged his students to use group techniques (Hobbs, 1951). His students were interested in the interactions among group members and the resolution of situational conflicts on a conscious level. In accordance with his dictum of unconditional acceptance, Rogers felt that the group therapist should be permissive and accepting, helping the group members clarify their self-concepts.

THE ADVENT OF WORLD WAR II

Due to the shortage of trained professionals and the need to treat large numbers of psychiatric patients in the armed services, group psychotherapy increased in importance during World War II. The enthusiasm for this practice spread to the civilian population, and every school of psychotherapy became receptive to group therapy. At this time, psychologists became involved in the use of group techniques to resolve labor–management conflicts and other social problems. Much of this work was stimulated by Kurt Lewin's (1948) studies of group dynamics, as well as Sherif's (1948) study of frame of reference and Asch's (1956) studies of group pressure to conform. Sherif was aware of group therapy, and in discussions with the first author, he expressed great enthusiasm for it. Although group dynamics researchers did not offer a theory about the processes of group psychotherapy, their research on group cohesiveness and involvement helped clarify the dynamics at play in therapy groups and highlighted the positive as well as the negative influences on participants in the therapy group.

Nathan Ackerman

Nathan Ackerman (1945, 1947), a pioneer in the field of family therapy, gained experience with groups while working with coal miners and their families during the mid-1930s. He subsequently developed the Ackerman Family Therapy Institute in New York City. This institute continues to provide training and service in family treatment, emphasizing analytic and systemic interventions.

Alexander Wolf

Alexander Wolf (1949, 1950), a psychiatrist and psychoanalyst, made a major contribution to group psychotherapy. He began his work in 1938, stimulated by the work of Wender and Schilder, as well as by his own deep-seated conviction that psychotherapy should be available to people of limited income. By 1940, he was devoting almost his entire practice to group approaches, working with heterogeneous groups of 8 to 10 patients each. During his 4 years of military service in World War II, he continued his work as a psychiatrist with groups from diverse patient populations. After the war, he trained many psychotherapists.

Wolf presented his findings about his work with groups at professional conferences held in 1948 and 1949. These presentations included a carefully formulated theoretical basis for his approach and drew heavily from his clinical experiences. Wolf became increasingly disenchanted with group approaches that emphasized group dynamics rather than the exploration of intrapsychic and interpersonal phenomena. He referred to his work as "psychoanalysis *in* groups" rather than "psychoanalysis *of* groups." He maintained that he did not treat a group, but rather the individual patient interacting with members of the group.

Wolf, who met with his groups twice a week for 1 1/2 hours, found that group members frequently continued to meet after the formally scheduled meetings had ended. Taking advantage of this, he encouraged group members to meet without the therapist in what was called the *alternate session*. In contrast to critics who believed that this procedure encouraged acting out, Wolf felt that it facilitated the separation from the analyst/parent. Instead of encountering the omniscient ego ideal of the single therapist, the patient was presented with a group with whose common aims he had to align himself. Wolf (1959) stated:

> Rather than strengthening the entrepreneurial ideal—typified in the neurotic's mind by the notion of the omnipotent therapist—group analysis helps to destroy the false antithesis of the individual versus the mass by helping the patient to become aware that his fulfillment can only be realized in a social or interpersonal setting. (p. 67)

Wolf worked toward an egalitarian ideal in his therapy, with the goals of diminishing his own leadership role and of redistributing authority, power, and leadership among his group of patients. In contrast to many current prac-

titioners who stress *interaction*, Wolf believed that the *group qua group* cannot become the means by which its members resolve *intrapsychic* difficulty. A survey (Rosenbaum, 1952) determined that Wolf had more influence over his generation of psychoanalytic group therapists than any other person in the field.

Jerome Frank

After he was discharged from military service in 1947, Jerome Frank, a psychologist who had worked with Kurt Lewin, joined Florence Powdermaker, a research-oriented psychoanalyst, in a research project on group psychotherapy. Powdermaker had organized an interdisciplinary study of group psychotherapy for two groups of patients: outpatient neurotics at a Veterans Administration mental hygiene clinic in Washington, D.C., and inpatient chronic schizophrenics who had not responded to shock therapy or routine hospital care at a Veterans Administration hospital in Perry Point, Maryland. This project consisted of largely descriptive but systematic research. The researchers were able to delineate patterns of behavior and recurrent themes in the therapy groups (Powdermaker & Frank, 1953). The approach to group therapy with neurotic patients had

> points in common with that of Foulkes, Ackerman, Slavson and Wolf, and we were influenced in our thinking by Schilder's analytic concept and Trigant Burrow's emphasis on the study of group interaction. We were stimulated by Bion's perception of the group process but avoided his exclusive attention to it. Although our groups were not social clubs, as were Bierer's, the leadership was completely informal. We differed from Schilder, especially in not using questionnaires and set tasks, and from Wender, Klapman, and Lazell in that in no case did the psychiatrist in charge give case histories or systematic presentation of psychiatric concepts. He encouraged interactions among patients. He helped them to examine their attitudes and behavior toward one another (process) as well as the personal material which they presented (content). (Powdermaker & Frank, 1953, p. 4)

The Repressive-Inspirational Approach

Almost five decades after Pratt began his work, his methods were still influential in the group therapy literature. Klapman (1946) used a directive, highly intellectual textbook-mediated therapy in a mental hospital. In 1937, Low (1950) founded a movement that he called Recovery, Incorporated. His original group of 30 patients had all received shock therapy or other physical therapies as psychiatric inpatients. There was a strong repressive-inspirational element to his approach, which emphasized self-help and camaraderie. He rejected psychoanalytic concepts in favor of "will" therapy.

Variations of the repressive-inspirational approach have been used with many different patient populations. In this approach, a supportive subculture is established in which the leader of the group is important because his or her enthusiasm establishes the climate of the group. Many mechanisms are at work in this approach, including group identification, group status, esprit de corps, a friendly environment, communal feeling, unification of the group, group socialization, loss of isolation, emotional acceptance of group members, ego support, social approval, realization that others are in the same boat, the testimony and example of others, sharing of mutual experiences, and reassurance. Weight Watchers and Alcoholics Anonymous are prime examples of repressive-inspirational approach.

GROUP THERAPY IN THE POSTWAR YEARS

After the end of World War II, psychologists and psychiatrists presented many new approaches to psychotherapy. These approaches were incorporated into the practice of group psychotherapy in the 1950s. Fritz and Laura Perls lectured throughout the United States about gestalt therapy. Irvin Polster, one of Perls' students, moved from Cleveland, Ohio, to California and introduced gestalt approaches there. The early theories of Wilhelm Reich, especially

his ideas about character armor and body acceptance, found new adherents such as Charlotte Selver. Her work on body acceptance was incorporated into the work of many group therapists. Abraham Maslow left Brooklyn College and moved to Brandeis University, where he lectured and wrote about self-actualization and a humanistic approach to psychotherapy. Carl Rogers and his students, especially Nicholas Hobbs, introduced a nondirective, humanistic approach to group therapy, which became part of the encounter movement.

T-Groups and the National Training Laboratories

During World War II, Kurt Lewin had been invited by the U.S. government to study the eating habits of the American population in order to find a way to encourage the consumption of seldom used parts of cattle, such as the heart, lungs, and entrails. His students included Leland Bradford, Ronald Lippitt, and Kenneth Benne. In 1945 and 1946, these students held nightly meetings in which they began to object to the interpretations of group behavior that had been presented by the group leaders. Kurt Back has described this time as the "starting point of the T-group movement" (1973, p. 9), which led to the establishment of the National Training Laboratories (NTL) in Bethel, Maine. The NTL, which sponsored thousands of training workshops, was originally concerned with such issues as organizational development and skill training. Over time, some of its leaders became interested in personal growth and use of nonverbal techniques to promote self-actualization and intimacy. Most of these group leaders were based in California. It was there, in the 1960s, that the encounter movement came into full flower.

The Encounter Movement

Encounter groups were quasi-therapeutic sensitivity groups in which authenticity, openness, confrontation, and encounter were encouraged. The emphasis was on facing one another and on honest expression of feelings (Bibout, 1978). Proponents of encounter groups felt that this intense experiential contact led to holistic growth. These groups relied on the techniques of dyadic therapy—expression of feelings, role playing, feedback, and mirroring.

The center of the encounter movement was the Esalen Institute, founded by Michael Murphy on a tract of land that he had inherited at Big Sur, California. He invited humanistic clinical practitioners and advocates of Eastern philosophies, especially Zen Buddhism, to teach at the institute. Alan Watts was the leading teacher in the latter group. Teachers in the former group were Fritz Perls, William Schutz, and Bernard Gunther, and as well as practitioners of psychodrama and NTL techniques.

The advocates of encounter groups were often unaware that their techniques stemmed from Wilhelm Reich's theories about character armor, a well as the techniques of his later students such as Alexander Lowen. The encounter movement flourished from 1962 to 1972 and attracted many adherents. It was also subjected to enormous criticism, including the accusation of using brainwashing techniques. In response to this controversy, Lieberman, Yalom, and Miles (1973) initiated a study of over 250 students who were invited to participate in 1 of 17 different encounter groups. This study largely initiated the use of systematic empirical methods to study group processes and outcomes and produced results that have had wide-ranging implications for the practice of group therapy generally.

Lieberman and colleagues provided the first documentation that group experiences could produce significant psychological injury as well as benefit to participants. They went on to observe that the likelihood that a group member would experience psychological damage or injury was more closely related to the style of leadership employed by the group facilitator than to either the personality of the group participant or the theoretical model employed by the leader. For example, emotionally cathartic and abreactive group models produced both the most casualties and the most beneficiaries,

depending on the leader. Supportive leaders who provided caring interpretations were inclined to produce benefits among group members, while less supportive and more critical leaders tended to have relatively high casualty rates. Leaders who exhibited a controlling style, on the other hand, produced few changes among the participants in either a positive or a negative direction.

The encounter group movement stimulated group psychotherapy, and numerous practitioners of group therapy emerged at this time. While initially used in the encounter group movement, many of the procedures introduced by these clinicians have become accepted and practiced in modern group therapy.

William Schutz

The strongest advocate of the use of physical (especially touching) and nonverbal methods in encounter groups was Will Schutz, who, before his move to Esalen, worked in the Department of Psychiatry at the Albert Einstein Medical School in the Bronx, New York. Schutz had also been involved at the University of California at Berkeley in instituting sensitivity training for the staff at Napa State Hospital, a facility for the chronically mentally ill. The purpose of this training was to facilitate the establishment of a "therapeutic community," as proposed by Maxwell Jones (1953). Jones, who began his work in England, was a prime mover in establishing open wards and innovative approaches in mental hospitals in the United States.

Carl Rogers Revisited

At about the time that Esalen was founded, Carl Rogers left Madison, Wisconsin, to became a resident scholar at the Western Behavioral Sciences Institute in La Jolla, California. He attracted humanistic psychotherapists, many of whom became interested in working with small groups. George Bach, Paul Bindrim, and Fred Stoller developed the idea of marathon groups. Encounter techniques applied to community groups were developed by Jack and

Lorraine Gibb. The concept of self-led encounter groups was developed by Betty Berzon, Larry Solomon, and Jerome Reisel. In his work with groups, Rogers stressed the experiential. Rogers stated that he became more open about expressing *his* feelings as he worked with clients. Toward the end of his life, he stressed the utility of group approaches in the resolution of international as well as ethnic and racial conflicts.

Eric Berne

Another California-based approach to group psychotherapy was based on *transactional analysis*, a method of diagnosis and treatment devised by Eric Berne of San Francisco. Berne at one time was a candidate at the San Francisco Institute of Psychoanalysis. Although there is disagreement as to whether he became disenchanted with the psychoanalytic approach or was asked to leave the institute, Berne stated that he was deeply influenced by Freud. In 1958 he published a paper entitled "Transactional Analysis: A New and Effective Method of Group Therapy," which he later expanded into a book (Berne, 1961). Many therapists who practice transactional analysis incorporate a variety of experiential therapy techniques into their work that are drawn from other approaches.

Berne defined the basic unit of social communication as a *transaction*. *Strokes* are units of recognition that may be physical, nonverbal, or verbal. According to Berne, a person cannot survive without strokes. Behavior consists of strokes that an individual wants to receive, as well as *strikes* that he or she wants to give. The personality of an individual is based on the strokes received during infancy and childhood. Berne described the personality as composed of three *ego states*—parent, adult, and child.

On one occasion, when the first author was to meet with Eric Berne, he arrived to find him in the driveway of his home. Berne had had a martial disagreement and had no access to his home office, so he met with his individual patients in the front seat of his auto, parked in the driveway. Some therapists would find this unusual. Slavson would have been appalled.

Moreno would have been amused. Berne felt that it was reality.

Fritz Perls

Fritz Perls, the originator of gestalt therapy, was a flamboyant character. When he arrived in New York City in 1946, there was a great burst of creative and intellectual expression in the theater, arts, and literature. Perls was stimulated by this ferment and attracted to many of the leaders, especially Paul Goodman. Beginning in 1950, he and his wife, Laura, began organizing training groups. This work was influenced by Zen Buddhist teachings, Moreno's psychodrama, Dianetics, and the sensory awareness techniques of Charlotte Selver. When he first arrived in New York, Perls had felt comfortable with the interpersonal theory of Sullivan. Over time, Perls moved away from a psychoanalytic approach, which he perceived as overly intellectual, with too much emphasis on interpretation. In contrast, Perls' approach emphasized the constant reference to one's immediate experience, which he referred to as the *here and now*.

GROUP PSYCHOTHERAPY IN EUROPE

There was a certain insularity about group psychotherapy in the United States. Group psychotherapy had been practiced in Europe for many years. From 1900 to 1930, during the early period of group psychotherapy, a group method called *collective counseling* was used by German and Austrian psychotherapists to treat patients with a wide range of emotional problems. Danish and Russian psychiatrists also employed group methods. Dreikurs (1952) claimed that Alfred Adler and other European practitioners were pioneers in the field of group therapy whose contributions were not sufficiently recognized because publishing professional papers was easier in the United States. It is probable that Adler, who was deeply committed to socialism and to finding ways to bring psychotherapy to the working classes, was very attracted to group approaches as an alternative to the psychoanalytic approach, which was used with individuals from more affluent backgrounds. Most European psychiatrists who used group approaches worked in relative ignorance of one another. Group approaches, which flourish in a climate of political freedom, did not fare well in a Europe that became more and more conservative before World War II.

After World War II, reports came to the United States about the exciting work that had been carried out in England during the war (Taylor, 1958). A few British psychiatrists had become interested in the therapeutic potential of group processes. They observed that many soldiers became psychiatric casualties because they were placed in the wrong job. Consequently, they devised new selection procedure for choosing suitable candidates for officer training.

Wilfred Bion

Wilfred Bion, a psychiatrist who had been a tank commander during World War I, devised a *leaderless group test* in which candidates for officer training were given a particular task and observations were made about the way in which the task was carried out. Although these groups were initially leaderless and unstructured, it became a clear that a status hierarchy developed. Some candidates chose leadership roles, others preferred to collaborate, and still others chose to obstruct the leader.

In 1943, Bion and John Rickman, a psychiatrist with psychoanalytic training, were sent to the Northfield Military Hospital near Birmingham to help deal with unruly conditions that had developed in several of the wards. Rickman organized discussion groups with the patients. Bion observed that the soldiers were overtly unhappy with military life and wanted to return to civilian life. He decided to challenge the authoritarian setting of the military hospital in an effort to transform the discontented soldiers into responsible, healthy community members. Bion relinquished his authoritarian role as an officer and a physician and challenged the pa-

tients either to continue to live with the discomforts of a chaotic community or to shoulder the responsibility of organizing their communal activities. The patients, who could no longer blame the British army for their misery, had to face the consequences of their own disruptive behavior. Bion remained at the hospital for 6 weeks, and his work, referred to as the *North-field Experiment*, was successful. He repeated this approach in another hospital, again with successful results. This resulted in an examination of the administration of mental hospitals, which at that time were little more than warehouses for segregating patients from society; little effort was being made to encourage patients to accept responsibility for their own lives.

When World War II ended, Bion was placed in charge of group psychotherapy at the Tavistock Clinic in London. He began his formal psychoanalytic training, with Melanie Klein as his analyst. Bion was strongly influenced by Klein's model of human development and subsequently based his theories on Klein's concepts. It is difficult to summarize Klein's wide-ranging theories, which modified the orthodox Freudian theory of personality. She believed that the *ego exists from birth* and that good and bad emotions stem from the infant's contact with the mother, who represents the outside world. Klein and Anna Freud were the primary influences on the contemporary British psychoanalytic community. Each held disparate views about emotional development, and each attracted adherents who identified strongly with their teachers. Their controversies created a good deal of tension in the British psychoanalytic community. To this day, there are Freudians, Kleinians, and those who call themselves the *Middle School*.

Bion observed that massive emotional reactions often occurred when he conducted groups. Bion, as the group leader, did not provide any structure or direction for the group. Patients often became confused or angry at what they perceived as his passivity. Occasionally, patients indicated a desire to leave the group. The group seemed to want more direction from the therapist at these times. Bion occasionally offered an interpretation of the *group's* current emotional state. The emphasis of these interpretations was on group behavior, namely, on whether the group was attempting to resolve a problem or to avoid it.

Bion developed a theory of the group as a series of emotional states, which he called *basic assumption cultures*. Group members contributed to the work of the group, as they reacted to this culture, by either accepting or rejecting it. Bion used the term *valences* to describe the relationship between the group member and the group culture. The patient moved through the valences of pairing, dependency, or fight–flight. In 1949 and 1950, Bion published a series of articles describing his work with groups, which later appeared in book form (Bion, 1961). Bion's speculations attracted the attention of Herbert Thelen, an educator who was conducting research at the University of Chicago. Thelen attempted to validate Bion's ideas about groups (Stock & Thelen, 1958). He encouraged several of his students to become serious researchers in the field of group psychotherapy (Whitaker & Lieberman, 1967).

In the latter part of his life, Bion moved away from work with groups. He lectured widely, especially in Latin America, where Klein's theories are highly regarded, and he found there a receptive audience. His later work with schizophrenics influenced many psychotherapists. When Bion grew disenchanted with the political infighting that took place among the rival schools in the British analytic community, he moved to California, where he lived until his death.

S. H. Foulkes

During the early 1930s, S. H. Foulkes, a classically trained psychiatrist and psychoanalyst from Germany, came to England to escape the Nazi terror. In England, Foulkes developed an institute for the training of groups analysts, founded a journal, *Group Analysis*, and helped inaugurate systematic training on the Continent of Europe. He was knowledgeable about social psychology, including the work of Kurt Lewin, and he had read several of Burrow's articles on group psychotherapy in the mid-1920s.

In 1940, while in private civilian practice in Exeter, Foulkes held his first group session in the waiting room of his office. He recalled that he went home and told his wife that a historical event had taken place in psychiatry but that no one knew about it. Foulkes (1975) wrote that his method of

> group analytic psychotherapy . . . grew out of and [was] inspired by my experience as a psychoanalyst, but is *not* a psychoanalysis of individuals in a group. Nor is it the psychological treatment of a group by a psychoanalyst. It is a form of psychotherapy *by* the group, *of* the group, including its conductor. Hence the name group-analytic psychotherapy. (p. 3)

Foulkes believed in the maturation of the group over time and realized that the group experience is not static but always dynamic. The significance of Foulkes' contribution to group psychotherapy is often overlooked. It took great courage for Foulkes to gather all of his patients together in his waiting room and encourage them to free-associate and begin a dialogue.

At the outset of World War II, Foulkes became a psychiatrist in the British army. His relative isolation gave him the opportunity to rethink his classical psychoanalytic training. During his training in Frankfurt, Germany, he had been influenced by the Institute of Social Research, which was in close contact with the Institute of Psychoanalysis. He had worked as an assistant to Kurt Goldstein, a pioneer in neurology research. This experience contributed to Foulkes' conviction that the total situation in a group determined all of the part processes and their meaning. His thinking was similar to Goldstein's observation that the central nervous system is composed of a communicating network, not of individual neuron functions (Goldstein, 1939). Foulkes was aware of the work of Joshua Bierer, who organized patients in mental hospitals in England into social clubs. He realized that Bierer's approach, which was along the lines of Adlerian theory, was more leader centered, active, and directive than his.

While Foulkes did not elaborate on his experience at the Northfield Military Neurosis Centre during World War II, he described his experimental work in conversations with the first author. In cooperation with Tom Main, Harold Bridger, and, for a short time, Joshua Bierer, he developed a project to change the culture of the hospital through the education and training of the staff. Foulkes emphasized psychoanalytic principles on the ward that he supervised. He and his coworkers discussed their work at the hospital, shared clinical experiences, and exchanged points of view. American psychiatrists who visited the hospital for 2 days were impressed by what they observed. They reported that there was no equivalent work in the United States.

THE INTERNATIONAL CONGRESS OF GROUP PSYCHOTHERAPY

The First International Congress of Group Psychotherapy was held in Toronto, Canada, in 1954. A major effort was made to establish communications between the warring factions, which for the most part consisted of followers of Slavson and Moreno. By the time the Second International Congress of Group Psychotherapy was held in Zurich, Switzerland, in the summer of 1957, Moreno, Slavson, Stokvis from the Netherlands, Hulse from the United States, Foulkes and Bierer from Great Britain, Lebovici from France, and many other practitioners had been involved in setting up an International Council of Group Psychotherapy. This council had a formal constitution and a committee to set up membership qualifications. An effort was made to facilitate communication between local societies of group psychotherapy, each of which had its own standards.

Slavson had set up a system of correspondents throughout the world to keep him informed of activities in the field of group psychotherapy. He publicized these activities in the *International Journal of Group Psychotherapy.* He was not receptive to information about psy-chodrama activities. At the 1957 meeting in Zurich, the antagonism between Slavson and Moreno was obvious to all observers. Slavson, with his extensive knowledge of the literature, could be very authoritarian. Intuitive and empathic, Moreno also could be very grandiose. The two were bound to clash. Moreno, a physician and psychiatrist, was disdainful of Slavson's training. Slavson had attended a public psychodrama meeting that Moreno conducted in New York City in 1930 or 1931. He had been called to the stage by Moreno as part of the demonstration and afterward insisted that Moreno had publicly humiliated him. Other researchers and practitioners were not thrown off track by the antagonism between Moreno and Slavson but continued their plans to develop an International Association of Group Psychotherapy. Moreno served as the first president of the association. Foulkes, who lectured in the United States after World War II, spent part of his summer holidays in Switzerland. This allowed him to meet with and encourage an exchange of ideas among group therapists in many nations. Because of his extensive knowledge of the field and his mature, low-key personality, he was a moderating influence in the resolution of rivalries in the International Association.

The Third International Congress of Group Psychotherapy was held in Milan, Italy, in 1963. The Fourth International Congress, held in Vienna, Austria, in September 1968, was very successful in gathering participants from all over the world. The letterhead of the International Council of Group Psychotherapy in 1968 listed members from 46 nations. The Fifth International Congress was held in Zurich in the summer of 1973. At that time, a formal constitution for the International Association of Group Psychotherapy was proposed and the association was formally incorporated. Later congresses were held in Copenhagen, Zagreb, and Amsterdam. In August 1992 the Eleventh International Congress of Group Psychotherapy was held in Montreal, Canada. The Twelfth Congress will be held in Buenos Aires in 1995. For the most part, tensions in the international proceedings have been minimal. There have been didactic training workshops preceding the last two congresses, and attendees have been able to listen to many points of view.

CURRENT DIRECTIONS IN GROUP THERAPY

As medicine has become increasingly technological, and as the ideal of the compassionate physician is fast disappearing, the use of group approaches has become increasingly important. Support groups are used for all types of patients, from women suffering from breast cancer to terminally ill patients. Because the idea of mutual aid, fundamental to group therapies, also encourages social engineering, some support groups adopt social and political goals.

By 1993, alternative methods of health care had been grudgingly accepted by the National Institutes of Health in Washington, D.C. Many of these alternative methods actively use group counseling approaches. Dean Ornish (1990), an internist, developed a program for reversing heart disease that emphasized the importance of diet. Ornish found, however, that for patients with heart disease, learning techniques of stress management and healthy living was also necessary. To this end, Ornish's patients attend twice-weekly groups led by a psychologist, in which they explore their relationships, values, self-image, and feelings of rejection and anger. Yoga exercises, stretching exercises, and directed visualization are also encouraged.

After the end of World War II, many clinicians published papers describing their experiences in working with group therapy. By 1953, 1,200 papers had been published relating to group psychotherapy. By 1955 the number had swelled to 1,700. The present annual rate is about 300 books, articles, and theses. Articles concerned with group therapy appear in almost every publication devoted to issues of mental health (Liff, 1983). A list of books and papers published on group psychotherapy from 1906 to 1980 totaled 13,186 references; however, this list failed to include many of the British and European writers (Lubin & Lubin, 1987).

The work of Irvin D. Yalom consolidated much of the theoretical diversity that had long existed in the field, especially in North America, and facilitated professional interest in group therapy since the 1970s. Drawing from his research on encounter groups with Lieberman and Miles (Lieberman et al., 1973), Yalom began identifying the ingredients of effective therapy groups and applying them to an integrative model of *interpersonal* therapy. His book, entitled *The Theory and Practice of Group Therapy* (1985), now in its third edition, reports that patients regularly identified 12 characteristic aspects of the group experience that were "curative." These qualities were:

1. Providing and receiving interpersonal input.
2. Experiencing cathartic discharge of emotions.
3. Group cohesiveness.
4. Promotion of self-understanding.
5. Experimenting with interpersonal output or behavior.
6. Confronting existential conflicts and questions.
7. Acquiring a sense of the universality of one's problems.
8. Instillation of hope.
9. Becoming aware of one's own and others' altruism.
10. Reenacting family dynamics.
11. Receiving guidance from others.
12. Identifying with the healthy behaviors of others.

Through careful observations of group processes and systematic interviews with group therapy patients, Yalom concluded that the most helpful factors were interpersonal input, self-understanding, and catharsis (factors 1, 2, and 4), while the least helpful were family reenactment, guidance, and identification (factors 10, 11, and 12).

Yalom (1985) advocates a therapeutic style that is at once active and supportive. This approach has been adapted to inpatient populations and settings (Yalom, 1983), suggesting its breadth and flexibility. Yalom's approach is particularly appealing to clinicians who are seeking more rapid ways of effecting change, although for some, it may be criticized for deemphasizing the importance of intrapsychic and transference phenomena.

With the advent of integrative and consolidating models of therapy, the overeager enthusiasm that characterized the group therapy movement in the 1960s and 1970s has largely evaporated, in favor of the adoption of a more concilitory tone (e.g., Klein, Bernard, & Signer, 1992). Contemporary practitioners appear more eager to listen to one another than to indoctrinate one another. Over the last decade, there has been a rapprochement of group therapy practitioners and groups therapy researchers, who, for the most part, had been rather unfriendly neighbors. There is thoughtful concern about which approach is most helpful to which patients and a strong push toward the use of time-limited interventions, including time-limited group psychotherapy (Rosenbaum, 1983).

The years following World War II saw many imaginative investigations of group interaction. But the study of group dynamics has not clarified the processes at work in therapy groups. Basic questions remain unanswered. Transference, counter-transference, resistance, types of intervention (active, direct, passive), the use of individual or group interpretations, the composition of groups, the selection of patients, time-limited or open-ended groups, and the phases of group development are issues that continue to be researched. The matching of the group therapist and the group of patients appears to be central as well. The possible influence of cultural and social differences on treatment outcome has been given less attention than it deserves.

Although in the past insufficient attention was given to the identification of change elements in the group process, current research efforts focus on elaborating theoretical models. Bloch and Crouch (1985) surveyed theories of group treatment and extracted six factors involved in patient change. They noted that practitioners often assume that one specific theory and its attendant techniques are *the* important change factors. Bloch and Crouch

stressed the importance of developing a taxonomy of well-defined terms, which would allow for the generation of testable hypotheses and methodological investigation.

The future growth of group psychotherapy appears to be assured. Systems theory, object relations theory, Lacan's ideas, and Patrick de Mare's theories about large group treatment all have been absorbed into the practice of group psychotherapy. Yet, the field of group psychotherapy remains in search of a systematic theory. Testimonials, while interesting, are no substitute for theory. Kurt Lewin's maxim, "There is nothing as practical as a good theory," remains central.

REFERENCES

Ackerman, N. W. (1945). Some theoretical aspects of group psychotherapy. In J. L. Moreno (Ed.), *Group therapy: A symposium* (pp. 117–124). New York: Beacon House.

Ackerman, N. W. (1947). Interview group psychotherapy with psychoneurotic adults. In S. R. Slavson (Ed.), *The practice of group therapy* (pp. 135–155). New York: International Universities Press.

Ackerman, N. W. (1958). *The psychodynamics of family life*. New York: Basic Books.

Asch, S. (1956). Studies of independence and conformity: A minority of one against a unanimous majority. *Psychological Monographs*, 70 (whole no. 416).

Bach, G. R., & Illing, M. A. (1956, January). Historische perspektive zur gruppen psychotherapie. *Zeitschrift fur Psycho-somatische Medizin*, 131–147.

Back, K. (1973). *Beyond words: The story of sensitivity training and the encounter movement*. Baltimore: Penguin Books.

Berne, E. (1961). *Transactional analysis in psychotherapy*. New York: Grove Press

Bibout, J. (1978) Basic encounter groups: Their nature, method and brief history. In H. Mullan & M. Rosenbaum, *Group psychotherapy: Theory and practice* (2nd ed., pp. 305–329). New York: Free Press

Bierer, J. (Ed.). (1948). *Therapeutic social clubs*. London: H. K. Lewis.

Bion, W. R. (1961). *Experiences in groups*. New York: Basic Books.

Bloch, S., & Crouch, E. (1985). *Therapeutic factors*

in group psychotherapy. Oxford: Medical Publications.

Burrow, T. (1912–1913). Psychoanalysis and society. *Journal of Abnormal Psychology, 7,* 340–346.

Burrow, T. (1914). The psychoanalyst and the community. *Journal of the American Medical Association, 42,* 1876–1878.

Burrow, T. (1927a). The group method of analysis. *Psychoanalytic Review, 14,* 268–280.

Burrow, T. (1927b). *The social basis of consciousness.* New York: Harcourt, Brace and World.

Burrow, T. (1928). The basis of group analysis, or the reactions of normal and neurotic individuals. *British Journal of Medical Psychology, 8,* 198–206.

Corsini, R. J. (1955). Historic background of group psychotherapy. *Group Psychotherapy, 8,* 219–255.

Dejerine, J., & Gauckler, E. (1913). *The psychoneuroses and their treatment.* Philadelphia: Lippincott.

Dreikurs, R. (1952). Group psychotherapy: General review. In *Proceedings of the First International Congress of Psychiatry* (pp. 223–237). Paris: Hermann & Cie Press.

Dreikurs, R. (1959). Early experiments with group psychotherapy. *American Journal of Psychotherapy, 13,* 882–891.

Dreikurs, R., & Corsini, R. J. (1954). Twenty years of group psychotherapy. *American Journal of Psychiatry, 110,* 567–575.

Foulkes, S. H. (1975). *Group analytic psychotherapy: Methods and principles.* New York and London: Gordon and Breach.

Freud, S. (1922). *Group psychology and the analysis of the ego* (Vol. 18). London: Hogarth Press.

Gifford, S., & Mackenzie, J. (1948). A review of the literature on group treatment of psychoses. *Diseases of the Nervous System, 9,* 19–23.

Goldstein, K. (1939). *The organism.* New York: American Book Company.

Hadden, S. B. (1955). Historic background of group psychotherapy. *International Journal of Group Psychotherapy, 5,* 162–168.

Hobbs, N. (1951). Group centered psychotherapy. In C. Rogers (Ed.), *Client centered therapy* (pp. 278–319). Boston: Houghton Miflin.

Jones, M. (1953). *The therapeutic community: A new treatment method in psychiatry.* New York: Basic Books.

Klapman, J. W. (1946). *Group therapy: Theory and practice.* New York: Grune & Stratton.

Klein, R. H., Bernard, H. S., & Singer, D. L. (Eds.). (1992). *Handbook of contemporary group psychotherapy.* Madison, CT: International Universities Press.

Kotkov, B. (1950). Bibliography of group therapy. *Journal of Clinical Psychology, 6,* 77–91

Lazell, E. W. (1921). The group treatment of dementia praecox. *Psychoanalytic Review, 8,* 168–179.

Lewin, K. (1948). *Resolving social conflicts.* New York: Harper.

Lieberman, M., Yalom, I. D., & Miles, M. (1973). *Encounter groups: First facts.* New York: Basic Books.

Liff, Z. A. (1983). Editorial. *International Journal of Group Psychotherapy, 33,* 412.

Low, A. A. (1950). *Mental health through will-training.* Boston: Christopher.

Lowrey, L. G., Slarson, S. R., Spiker, D., Peck, H.B., Glauber, H. M., & Ackerman, N. W. (1943). Group therapy (special section). *American Journal of Orthopsychiatry, 13,* 648–690.

Lubin, B., & Lubin, A. W. (1987). *Comprehensive index of group psychotherapy writings.* Madison, CT: International Universities Press

Marsh, L. C. (1931). Group therapy of the psychoses by the psychological equivalent of the revival. *Mental Hygiene, 15,* 328–349.

Meiers, J. I. (1945). Origins and developments of group psychotherapy. *Sociometry, 8,* 499–534.

Moreno, J. L. (1911). *Die gottheit als komediart.* Vienna: Anzengruber Verlag.

Moreno, J. L. (1957). *The first book on group psychotherapy.* New York: Deacon House.

Mullan, H., & Rosenbaum, M. (1962). *Group psychotherapy.* New York: Free Press.

Oberndorf, C. B. (1953). *A history of psychoanalysis in America.* New York: Grune & Stratton.

Ornish, D. (1990). *Dr. Dean Ornish's program for reversing heart disease.* New York: Ballantine Books.

Powdermaker, F., & Frank, J. D. (1953). *Group psychotherapy: Studies in methodology of research and practice.* Cambridge, MA: Harvard University Press.

Pratt, J. H. (1953). The use of Dejerine's methods in the treatment of the common neuroses by group psychotherapy. *Bulletin of the New England Medical Center, 15,* 1–9.

Rosenbaum, M. (1952). The challenge of group psychoanalysis. *Psychoanalysis, 1,* 42–58.

Rosenbaum, M. (1983). *Handbook of short-term therapy groups.* New York: McGraw-Hill.

Schilder, P. (1936). The analysis of ideologies as a psychotherapeutic method especially in group treatment. *American Journal of Psychiatry, 93,* 601–617.

Schilder, P. (1939). Results and problems of group psychotherapy in severe neurosis. *Mental Hygiene, 23,* 87–98.

Schilder, P. (1940). Introductory remarks on groups. *Journal of Social Psychology, 12,* 83–100.

Sherif, M. (1948). *An outline of social psychology.* New York: Harper.

Slavson, S. R. (1943). *An introduction to group therapy.* New York: Commonwealth Fund.

Slavson, S. R. (1950). *Analytic group psychotherapy.* New York: Columbia University Press.

Slavson, S. R. (1951). Pioneers in group psychotherapy. *International Journal of Group Psychotherapy, 1,* 95–99.

Slavson, S. R. (1979). *Dynamics of group psychotherapy.* M. Schiffer (Ed.) New York: Jason Aronson.

Stock, D., & Thelen, H. (1958). *Emotional dynamics and group culture.* New York: New York University Press.

Taylor, F. K. (1958). A history of the group and administrative therapy in Great Britain. *British Journal of Medical Psychology, 31* (pts. 3, 4), 153–173.

Teirich, H. R. (1957). Gruppentherapie and dynamische gruppenpsychotherapie in Deutschland. *Heilkunst, 10,* 1–6.

Thomas, G. W. (1943). Group psychotherapy: A review of the recent literature. *Psychosomatic Medicine, 5,* 166–180.

Wender, L. (1936). The dynamics of group psychotherapy and its application. *Psychiatric Quarterly, 14,* 708–718.

Wolf, A. (1949). The psychoanalysis of groups: I. *American Journal of Psychotherapy, 4,* 16–50

Wolf, A. (1950). The psychoanalysis of groups: II. *American Journal of Psychotherapy, 1,* 525–558.

Yalom, I. D. (1983). *Inpatient group psychotherapy.* New York: Basic Books.

Yalom, I. D. (1985). *The theory and practice of group therapy* (3rd ed.). New York: Basic Books.

11
Group Therapy in Practice

Barbara Ballinger
Irvin Yalom

THE FIRST GROUP MEETING

The clock reads 5:10 P.M. Eight people, six group members and two group leaders, face each other silently in a small room, their chairs pushed into an irregular circle. One chair sits empty.

Ms. A, middle-aged and overweight, appears overtly frightened. She sits stiffly, unmoving, except for occasionally biting her fingernails in a distracted manner. Periodically she looks at one of the cotherapists (Dr. E sits next to her), but otherwise her gaze is fixed, focused on no one. Beside her, a poised older man of indeterminate age, Dr. C, scans the others' faces from his comfortable posture in an armchair. His look is direct and calm from intense dark eyes.

Mr. D, a bearded man in a tweed jacket, sits directly across from Dr. C and scowls into the center of the circle. He looks up abruptly to meets Dr. C's passing gaze, stares back unsmilingly, then leans forward to resume his brooding posture.

From her position next to Mr. D, Dr. E, her youthful face offset by a generous frosting of gray hair, also scans the room, looking at each face with quick appraisal. The room remains silent.

Mr. D shifts in his chair with a sharp intake of breath. All eyes turn to him. "Well," he says impatiently, "clearly, someone needs to begin. I will."

He has scarcely spoken when the door abruptly opens wide to admit Ms. H, an elegant woman with a fashionable haircut and a short skirt. She looks quickly around, spots Dr. E, then breezes into the room. "Hello, everyone!" she says cheerfully and folds herself into the available chair. "Whew! I didn't realize I'd have to walk so far. The parking is terrible! These shoes are not made for walking." She glances at Mr. D, then moves her smile to Dr. B and looks steadily at him as she sits back and crosses her legs. Dr. B looks back for a moment before turning again to scan the group.

As you may have assumed, this gathering is a psychotherapy group meeting for its first weekly session. The group will be an intensive, long-term interactional group with the goal of producing characterologic change. We will explore the interactional model in greater detail shortly, but first, let us consider some questions: Who are these people? What motivated them to go to a psychotherapist? And why, given all the options in psychotherapy currently available, did the therapist decide to treat them in a therapy group?

WHY GROUP PSYCHOTHERAPY?

People come to psychotherapists with the primary hope of relieving psychological suffering—perhaps depression, anxiety, or unremitting anger. Often they have come to a point where their social or work functioning is compromised. They may be weary of a persistent pattern of failed relationships or find themselves acutely stressed to a degree that taxes their usual defenses. Generally, they feel alone or believe that they have strained the resources of their personal relationships. They know they need help but generally have no idea what form help may take.

And help is often attainable; comprehensive reviews of the many controlled studies of psychotherapy outcomes confirm that psychotherapy generally helps patients. Powerful evidence exists, as well, for the usefulness of group psychotherapy. One rigorous review of 475 outcome studies concludes that "the average person who receives psychotherapy is better off at the end of it than 80% of the persons who do not" (Smith, Glass, & Miller, 1980, p. 87). This study also found individual and group therapy to be almost identical in effectiveness. Several more recent studies, using meta-analysis and surveys of the outcome literature, support the conclusion that group psychotherapy is a beneficial intervention (Dies, 1992; Orlinsky & Howard, 1986; Tillitski, 1990; Toseland & Siporin, 1986).

Even though we may be confident about the general effectiveness of group therapy, we are still left with the question of therapy selection: How, given the many current modalities of psychotherapy, does the therapist decide on group psychotherapy for a particular patient? Keep in mind that there is conflicting evidence as to whether inappropriate therapy can be harmful. Some reviews suggest that although therapy generally helps patients, it can also make them worse (Bergin & Lambert, 1978; Strupp, Hadley, & Gomes-Schwartz, 1977), while others suggest that there is little risk of a negative outcome from group psychotherapy (Dies, 1992; Dies & Teleska, 1985; Erickson, 1987; Orlinsky & Howard, 1986). Patients do, however, respond differently to the approaches and styles of individual therapists, and some patients are better able than others to benefit from the interpersonal milieu of a group.

So let us review what sorts of problems motivated the people in our group to seek help. We will focus on three patients. Ms. A, 51, a lonely, anxious woman, was divorced by her husband of 30 years 2 years ago. A housewife throughout her marriage, she felt traumatized by the loss of her identity and security. She experiences chronic shame over her long-standing obesity and, though she wishes to remarry, is discouraged by the emphasis on youth and slimness in the singles scene.

Mr. D., 47, an assistant professor in the humanities at a prominent university, describes himself as frustrated by his failure to advance in his career, as well as his inability to sustain intimate relationships. His most recent girlfriend left him several months ago because, he is convinced, of his lack of academic success. Bitter about women's expectations and impotently angry with more successful men, he has found himself unable to control his impulses to attack people verbally, both socially and at work.

Ms. H., 35, who describes herself as a free spirit, takes pride in her lack of inhibition. She finds this attitude helpful in her work as a bodywork therapist. She feels empowered by behaving seductively and enjoys the impact she has on men. She believes she is quite effective at managing women, too. However, despite her skill in affecting people, she is not able to keep them close to her. Most recently, her third husband left her and her best friend cut off their relationship after she had an affair with the friend's husband. Distressed and frustrated, she sought therapy in order to understand why people can't deal with her uninhibited style.

It is apparent that each of these patients experienced distress associated with disturbances in their social relationships. Accordingly, the therapist selected group therapy, because it is particularly effective in addressing interpersonal problems. It is a therapy that derives its power from the compelling importance of social contact.

THE INTERPERSONAL PERSPECTIVE

We humans are a social species. The desire for recognition by our social group and the impact of its loss are profound and profusely acknowledged throughout our creative and professional literatures. William James (1890) described social isolation thus: "No more fiendish punishment could be devised . . . than that one should be turned loose in society and remain absolutely unnoticed by all the members thereof" (p. 293).

Why are interpersonal relationships so important? As a species essentially unarmed with tooth and claw, and characterized by a long, vulnerable infancy, humans depend on membership in social units to survive. This is also true of all primarily ground-dwelling members of the great apes, our closest relatives; only the almost exclusively arboreal orangutan leads a solitary existence. John Bowlby explored the formation of the social bond in the fundamental mother–infant dyad, and the repercussions of its disruption or pathology, in his seminal three-volume series *Attachment and Loss* (Bowlby, 1980). A significant association between the absence of social relationships and the increased risk of mortality is now well established in the epidemiological literature (Berkman & Syme, 1979; House, Landis, & Umberson, 1988; House, Robbins, & Metzner, 1982), and the literature associating quality of life and social connectedness is extensive and growing rapidly.

Few escape the pain of loneliness. Many experience both an attraction to and a fear of social relationships; for those with compromised social development, these conflicts can be intolerably painful. Such people then substitute patterns of behavior that serve as facsimiles of relating and make acceptance by others difficult, sometimes all but impossible. Dysphoria expressed in a wide range of symptoms emerges out of such failures in relationship.

THE INTERPERSONAL FRAME OF REFERENCE IN GROUP PSYCHOTHERAPY

The interpersonal model of group psychotherapy, as posited by Irvin Yalom—the primary approach that will be discussed in this chapter—addresses maladaptive interactional patterns by focusing on these patterns as they emerge between the group members in the here-and-now of the therapy group. The model derives from Harry Stack Sullivan's interpersonal theory of psychiatry. Sullivan viewed psychiatry as essentially concerned with the processes of interaction between people. He defined psychological disorder as "interpersonal processes either inadequate to the situation . . . or excessively complex because of illusionary persons also integrated into the situations" (Sullivan, 1938, p. 126). Psychological cure is the "expanding of the self to such final effect that the patient as known to himself is much the same person as the patient behaving to others" (Sullivan, 1940, p. 237).

Sullivan used the term *parataxic distortions* to describe the tendency to distort one's perceptions of others according to how their characteristics affect one's internal sense of security. A central idea in his theory is that personality is formed in the maturing child almost entirely as a synthesis of interactions with influential human beings (and is also, we now assume, dependent on genetic components). As described briefly above, the need for close affiliation has evolved as protective of physical survival and is experienced as psychological urgent. In the effort to maintain a vital sense of security, the developing child tends to amplify those aspects of the self that are affirmed by significant others and to squelch those that bring rejection. Ultimately, even after the sense of self has solidified, the person is likely to react to others according to how their manifest qualities were once valued in the child's human environment. For example, a quality that has been discarded in the formation of the personality may be highly threatening when encountered in another person, and that person is unconsciously rejected. Thus the individual often responds more to an internal fantasy life than to the actual person of the other.

Parataxic distortions are similar to transference in its broadest definition—that is, when the term *transference* is applied to the distortions inherent in all interpersonal relationships (and not limited to patient–therapist relationships). Because a psychotherapy group provides a vast array of interpersonal relationships, group members are faced with their entire repertoire of distorting tactics. Thus, for patients with overt interpersonal problems, the psychotherapy group is the ideal arena in which to investigate interpersonal distortions; the main task of the group may be seen as helping patients to identify, acknowledge, understand, and change maladaptive ways of experiencing and responding to others.

The small therapy group, provided that it is not too heavily structured, will evolve into a social microcosm. All the patients' interpersonal perceptual distortions, all their pathological interpersonal behavior, will inevitably be exhibited in the here-and-now of the group. Once identified, they become potentially accessible to therapeutic intervention.

The process of pathology display and identification is often more potent in group than in individual therapy: A greater range of interpersonal stimulation is available, and there is a greater number of eyes and ears to assist in the identification of patterns. Other patients are often more effective in socially influencing a patient than are the group therapists, whose behavior is viewed as mandated by their professional role. With the support of other members and the therapists, the patient may then find the courage to experiment with entrenched patterns. The group's support of such efforts is a potent force that strengthens the personal sense of mastery and reinforces the patient's attraction to the group. Continued experimentation with new adaptive behaviors in the safe matrix of a supportive group can lay the foundation for generalizing change outside of the group.

THERAPEUTIC FACTORS: HOW DO GROUPS HELP?

We know from outcome studies that groups are effective agents of change and that the group mobilizes powerful interpersonal forces. But what are the precise mechanisms of change in the group therapeutic process? A series of therapeutic factors are operating in groups. Yalom has identified 10 such factors that appear to be "bare-boned mechanisms of change." They occur and function interdependently. Of these, interpersonal learning and group cohesiveness are particularly important and complex and, accordingly, will be dealt with in somewhat more detail. The 10 therapeutic factors are as follows:

1. Instillation of hope.
2. Universality.
3. Imparting information.
4. Altruism.
5. Corrective recapitulation of the primary family group.
6. Development of socializing techniques.
7. Imitative behavior.
8. Catharsis and cognitive reflection.
9. Interpersonal learning.
10. Group cohesiveness.

Instillation of Hope

As noted earlier, patients often come to a therapist with no clear goal other than relief of their distress. They often feel discouraged and even despairing about the persistence of their discomfort and their inability to help themselves. They have usually failed to fulfill their own or some significant other's expectations. Jerome Frank uses the term *demoralization* to describe the complex of "helplessness, hopelessness, confusion and subjective incompetence" common to patients able to benefit from psychotherapy (Frank & Frank, 1991, p. 14). For such unhappy people, beginning to hope is a powerful change indeed.

Hope—the belief that it is possible to

achieve a goal—may, like social attachment, have evolved as protective of survival (Tiger, 1979). The psychotherapy research literature confirms an association between high expectations of help before beginning therapy and positive outcomes of treatment (Bloch, Bond, Qualls, Yalom, & Zimmerman, 1976). Hope also serves the practical function of keeping the ambivalent patient in treatment long enough to benefit. Religious healing rituals of the shaman or faith healer are generally most effective with illnesses that have important emotional elements (Frank & Frank, 1991). Such practices have endured for ages in many cultures and presumably draw their power from patients' positive expectancies.

The power of the placebo response in medical treatment is well known; Frank believes that there is a parallel between placebos and the effectiveness of psychotherapy (Frank & Frank, 1991). He suggests that both derive their therapeutic power for the patient's willingness to believe, in combination with effective communication of the healer's confidence.

In group psychotherapy, patients are able to benefit by observing the improvement of peers who have problems similar to their own. The use of testimonials by improved participants is a widely used tenet of such successful self-help groups as Alcoholics Anonymous, Compassionate Friends (a group for bereaved parents), and Gamblers Anonymous.

The strength of the therapist's own belief system is also of great importance. Research supports the view that effective therapists are those who believe most strongly in their ability to help (Goldstein, 1962).

Universality

Another very common experience for patients entering therapy is the fear that they are absolutely alone in the nature and depth of their despair; they believe that no one else shares or could understand their problems, impulses, or fantasies. Because many patients are deeply isolated, they have little opportunity to learn about the extent to which others share their experiences.

Over many years of asking members of training groups (non-patients) to reveal anonymously the one thing they would be least willing to share with the group, Yalom found a few recurring themes. The most common secret was a deep conviction of basic inadequacy, a feeling that to be thoroughly known would mean to be revealed as a fraud. Second was a profound sense of interpersonal alienation; each person secretly believed that he or she was unable to love (Yalom, 1985). These persistent findings would seem to confirm the pervasiveness of feelings of inauthenticity and inadequacy even in ostentibly healthy persons. How much worse must they be for people who are demoralized? How much harder to admit? It is always deeply reassuring to hear, in the therapy group, that many others share one's experiences, fears, and impulses—a consoling "welcome to the human race" experience.

Imparting Information

We humans react to the unknown with anxiety; we ease our anxiety with explanation (or myth if the event exceeds our understanding), or take action when we have some idea of what to do. For demoralized psychotherapy patients, already in distress about interpersonal issues, the unknown dimensions of group therapy can be frightening indeed. In the interpersonal group therapy model, the therapist makes particular use of explanation before group therapy even begins, by anticipating this anxiety and systematically addressing patients' misconceptions about the group process. We will say more about this below in the discussion of preparation for group therapy.

Another type of information offered in the psychotherapy group is the advice that is often given by other patients. Advice giving inevitably occurs in all groups, usually early in the life of the group. Though patients usually do not benefit from the actual content of the advice, the process itself—the demonstration of interest and concern—is often deeply gratifying. Also, the mode of the patient's offering or responding often reveals much about his or her interpersonal dynamics and can be used to good purpose in the group.

Altruism

Altruism is widely known to play a role in the recovery from emotional problems. Ritualized service to others is part of the process of helping oneself in primitive cultures (Frank & Frank, 1991), as well as in contemporary self-help groups such as Alcoholics Anonymous, where members who are further advanced in their recovery serve as sponsors of new members.

Demoralized patients often believe that they, unable as they are to help themselves, have nothing to offer anyone else. For such people to be taken seriously in a group, and to be able to give as well as receive, is a powerful boost to self-esteem and hope. Also, by the time they seek treatment, patients are often morbidly self-absorbed; to forget themselves sufficiently to offer support, reassurance, or honest feedback to someone else can be an exhilarating change in their frozen internal process.

Corrective Recapitulation of the Primary Family Group

Patients who enter group therapy invariably experience their families of origin as unsatisfying, even traumatic. The process of a psychotherapy group often reevokes the ambiance, memories, and interactional patterns of the primary family unit. These patterns color the interactions with other group members and the therapists. Everything from ingratiating self-abasement to ruthless efforts to defeat other members in sibling rivalry or dethrone the therapist from parental power is manifest in the group.

The therapist's task is, first, to help patients recognize the old patterns. Next comes pursuit of the understanding that while such patterns may have been adaptive years ago, they are not helpful in the patient's current situation, in the group, and in life. Lastly, the patient must be helped to experiment with new behaviors in the group.

Development of Socializing Techniques

Social skills, the basic building blocks of interaction, are often deficient in patients with interpersonal problems. Patients may be blithely unaware of social habits that are off-putting for others; such habits may lead to rejection that patients perceive as evidence of their basic unworthiness. In the group, they can first become aware of their self-defeating patterns via feedback from other members and then begin to experiment with changes in their group behavior. Such experimentation is by no means trivial; it often serves as the patient's initial efforts at conscious manipulation of deeply engrained habits. Success in the group arena can be enormously emboldening and can encourage the patient to experiment with change in outside relationships.

Imitative Behavior

The social learning literature demonstrates that imitation is an effective therapeutic force (Bandura, Blanchard, & Ritter, 1969). The group therapy milieu is ripe territory for such a learning modality. It is readily apparent in the group that therapists and some patients have more effective coping styles than others; it is not uncommon for group members to try on parts of others' social techniques, shedding aspects that don't fit, as they try to create new social strategies and styles for themselves.

Catharsis and Cognitive Reflection

Strong emotion per se, or catharsis, may seem intuitively to be an important therapeutic factor. Yalom and colleagues found, however, that strong experience and expression of emotion were associated with a successful outcome of group therapy only when they were coupled with cognitive reflection (Lieberman, Yalom, & Miles, 1973).

Interpersonal Learning

Interpersonal learning is a therapeutic factor with a broad range and great complexity. Essential to its power, as discussed earlier in this chapter, is the innate social nature of human beings. This factor is additionally dependent on two other elements: the corrective emotional experience and the group as a social microcosm.

The Corrective Emotional Experience

This therapeutic event is a patient's encounter in the group with emotional sequelae of a past experience that exceeded his or her ability to cope at the time and that traumatized the patient. The corrective experience can occur when a situation elicits such strong emotion; in the supportive here-and-now environment of the group, the patient is able to use feedback and self-reflection to recognize the emotion as inappropriate to the current situation. He or she then is freed to interact in a way less encumbered by this pattern of intense, automatic response and to explore interpersonal relationships more deeply.

The Social Microcosm

Freely interacting psychotherapy groups act as social microcosms in which members, by simply being themselves, display their maladaptive behavior patterns in the here-and-now of the group. Patients who are irritable or ingratiating or arrogant or self-deprecatory will operate in the same manner in the here-and-now of the group. Therefore, a past history or a current description of the patients' outside behavior is less necessary in group therapy than in other therapeutic approaches; much more accurate data become available as patients reenact interpersonal difficulties in the immediate present of the group.

Group Cohesiveness

Group cohesiveness, which is essential for a successful group therapeutic experience, is the group therapy equivalent of the therapeutic alliance in individual psychotherapy. As used here, group cohesiveness is defined as "the resultant of all the forces acting on all the members to remain in the group" (Cartwright & Zander, 1962, p. 74). Most psychiatric patients have a barren history of group allegiance; often they have never before been vital, involved, and valued members of a group, starting with their families of origin (or they were valued only for their distorted selves). For them, a successful group therapy experience can so change fundamental interpersonal patterns as to be termed curative.

The research literature strongly indicates that successful therapy is most likely when the relationship between therapist and patient is characterized by trust, acceptance, warmth, and empathic understanding (Gurman & Razin, 1977; Parloff, Waskow, & Wollfe, 1978; Strupp et al., 1969). Interestingly, this holds whatever the orientation of the therapist; effective therapists from different schools resemble each other more than do good and bad therapists espousing the same theoretical view (Gurman & Razin, 1977; Lambert & Bergin, 1973; Lieberman et al., 1973).

In group therapy, the attraction of the member to the group has a similar therapeutic power. A study of 12 psychotherapy groups that ran for 13 months found that the therapeutic outcome correlated with the members' feeling of involvement in the group and with their perception of total group cohesiveness (Kapp et al., 1964). A study of the outcome at the end of a year for five outpatient groups found positive outcome associated with only two predictor variables: "group cohesiveness" and "general popularity" (Yalom, Houts, Zimerberg, & Rand, 1967). Budman and colleagues, in a particularly well-designed investigation of cohesiveness, found it to be significantly correlated with the outcome (Budman et al., 1989). The results showed clinical improvement to correlate most strongly with cohesiveness measured early in the group's history, suggesting that early cohesiveness is an important element for a successful group.

Cohesive groups provide a broader range of social and emotional experiences; not only do they offer greater support and acceptance than less cohesive groups, they also tolerate more conflict—often a necessary ingredient of the therapeutic process. Such tolerance grows only over time as the group matures; in the group's first meetings, patients are typically leery of each other and of the situation. Therapists must be particularly vigilant at these times; without the therapist's help, patients may react to their initial severe anxiety either by fleeing the group entirely or by so alienating other members that social recovery becomes highly unlikely. Let us look again at the group introduced at the beginning of the chapter, this time from the therapists' points of view, to see how therapists may structure their interventions early in the group. We resume with Ms. H's late arrival.

Ms. H's tardy entrance is immediately recognized by the therapists as her presumption of special status—she either doesn't need to or "can't" arrive on time. They had noted in the pregroup screening interview that she tended to see herself as exempt from social rules, and thus were not surprised to see this attitude manifest in the group.

Ms. H also immediately sexualizes her behavior in the group, ignoring the other women and quickly focusing on Dr. B. He avoids affirming her seductive behavior but is careful not to reject her. He therefore maintains neutral eye contact long enough to acknowledge her arrival before returning his attention to the rest of the group. Predictably, however, the new arrival interrupts the process and becomes the focus of the group's attention. Mr. D again scowls into the center of the circle; Ms. A stares mutely ahead. Dr. B turns back to Ms H.

"Welcome, Ms. H," he says. "We've been expecting you. Glad you could make it. As you know, the group begins promptly at 5, so we've already started. Mr. D was speaking. We can pause for introductions in a bit. Mr. D, you were saying?"

Here let's examine Dr. B's comments and the considerations underlying them. Why does he return the focus to Mr. D? His decision on when and to whom to speak is informed by a variety of sources—pregroup screening, observation in the group, and his own knowledge of therapeutic factors. In this early meeting, he and Dr. E must help amplify the group members' similarities rather than their differences. Dr. B assumes that Ms. H's late arrival will be disruptive for all the patients, some more than others. He knows that Mr. D is prone to verbal attacks and that he is bitter toward women. He has observed that Mr. D feels competitive with him. Thus he assumes that Mr. D's reaction to Ms. H's late arrival is likely to be inflamed by her flaunted sexual power and her focus on Dr. B, and that he is likely to express his distress by a verbal attack. A new group cannot tolerate overt conflict. Dr. B therefore anticipates and diverts such an attack, emphasizing the development of a baseline of trust. The opportunity for confrontations will occur again and will be tolerated better when the group is more cohesive. In addition, Dr. B models adherence to the group's boundaries; it starts on time and will end on time. Late arrival, which disrupts whatever has been happening in the group and is irritating to therapists and patients alike, is a common expression of narcissism in group therapy. If tardiness persists, the group, when it becomes more cohesive, will confront it more forcibly.

CREATING AND SHAPING THE GROUP

Selecting Patients

The groups discussed in this chapter are long-term outpatient groups, existing for a minimum of 6 months, that meet once or twice weekly with ambitious goals of both symptom relief and personality change. Proper selection of members is crucial: Patients must be both self-reflective and willing and able to examine their interactions with others. Inappropriately selected patients are likely to drop out early, deriving no benefit personally and disrupting the process of the group's work.

It is easier to describe what patient populations should be excluded from an interactional group than to list those that could be included. Typically, brain-injured, paranoid, psychotic, addicted, sociopathic, and hypochondriacal patients do not do well in such groups. Patients in the throes of a major affective illness such as major depression or overt mania usually are either too distressed or too distractible to be in a group. The same applies to patients in acute crisis. Patients with chronic interpersonal problems—even severe characterologic disturbance—who are cognitively intact, able to recognize the psychological nature of their distress (as opposed to patients who express distress exclusively with somatic symptoms), and able to recognize self-defeating patterns in their thought and behavior are able to participate in the group task.

Note that the selection process consists of making a match between patient and group. Any patient excluded from a high-functioning, interactional group will likely be a candidate for a special group composed of patients with such recalcitrant problems as psychosis, substance abuse, chronic pain, battering, and compulsive gambling.

Preparing the Group

As we have noted earlier, beginning in a therapy group is a very anxiety-producing event. Some of that anxiety is inevitable, as it derives from the patient's primary interpersonal problems. Some, however, arises from simple fear of the unknown, of entering an ambiguous, potentially threatening situation. This anxiety can be considerably eased if the therapist provides some systematic information about how the group will function and corrects any misconceptions the patient may have. In addition to such obvious essentials as time, duration, and expectations about attendance, explanations should be offered as to how the patient's problems can be understood through interper-

sonal theory. The interactional model of the group as the means of addressing such problems should provide considerable support, though it may occasionally be necessary for the patient to experience stress in the growth process.

One of the hallmarks of the interpersonal group is the use of the current moment, the here-and-now, and patients must be oriented to engage in the here-and-now. The therapist emphasizes that the purpose of the group is to help each member understand as much as possible about his or her relationship with each of the other group members (because that, in turn, will inform the patient about his or her modes of relating to others in the world). Therefore, patients are told, time spent in examining in-group relationships in the here-and-now is the efficient way to work on relationships with significant individuals in their lives. Furthermore, centering interaction on the events that occur among patients in the group here-and-now serves to keep everyone engaged and involved even when they are not actually speaking. Events in the here-and-now are relevant for everyone present, whereas discussion of outside relationships excludes most of the other members of the group.

Shaping the Group

Therapists provide a good foundation for maximizing the group's potential for success by choosing and preparing patients carefully. Once the group begins, therapists must turn their attention to establishing a working culture. They must shape the group into one that is actively interactive; that becomes cohesive and develops the trust necessary for self-disclosure; and that supports full personal and interpersonal exploration.

The therapist must actively keep in mind, from the very first meeting, the therapeutic factors, the optimal procedural mode, the always crucial priority of the group's physical survival, and a treatment plan for each patient in the group. As we noted in our earlier vignette, the therapist must be sensitive to what the group can tolerate at a given time; for example, Dr. B was careful to defuse a potentially conflictual situation in the first meeting, when the risk to the group's survival and eventual effectiveness would have been too great.

The group functions best when patients freely interact with each other, rather than channeling all their comments through the therapist. The therapist can systematically build this norm in a variety of ways. She or he may regularly ask patients to respond to other members, may affirm or discourage selective behavior via facial expression and posture, or may question interactions with the therapist. Similarly, it is important for the therapist to model the tolerance of strong emotion: Free expression of feelings is fundamental to group therapy and typically problematic for patients in their private lives.

Now that we have a better understanding of what a psychotherapy group needs to thrive, let us look again at our group. The next vignette shows it as a mature, cohesive interpersonal psychotherapy group. The interventions the therapists offer now are more nuanced and challenging, in keeping with the greater interpersonal sophistication attained by the group.

The Mature Group

Ms. A leans forward in her chair, tears running down her cheeks. The group listens silently. "It's not fair," she says. "I took care of my husband. He was supposed to take care of me. It's scary being alone. I feel like I'm being punished. But I didn't do anything wrong!" She sobs hard.

Mr. D says fiercely, "You sure didn't do anything wrong! A lot of men would be grateful for a woman who wanted to take care of them. I get so mad that no one will do that for me!" Ms. A smiles gratefully at him. Mr. D. smiles back, looking surprised. "Plus," he says, "You're not alone; you're with us."

"How are you feeling toward each other?" Dr. E asks.

"I feel like you really understand," Ms. A says shyly to Mr. D. "I felt this rage, outrage, it's not fair, and felt terribly alone; but then you were there with me, and I wasn't alone." She begins to cry again. "It's so comforting."

"Well, it was interesting for me," Mr. D says. "I got caught up in feeling mad for you; then I realized how mad I am for myself." He looks down at his folded hands, frowns, and lowers his voice. "And how afraid of ending up alone." He and Ms. A look soberly at each other.

"It looked like something else happened between the two of you as well," Dr. E says.

"Well, after I said I was mad, I felt closer, literally like I had moved physically closer," Mr. D says, glancing at Dr. B. "And I felt . . . connected. It felt good," he says sheepishly. "And you looked different to me somehow. And I thought, like, 'we're in this together.' It's hard to describe." He sat back and folded his arms. "But you can't make people take care of you. I realize that better listening to you."

"But it sounds like you were able to care about each other," says Dr. E.

Ms. H sighs audibly. "Well, of course we care about each other, don't we? I mean, is that some surprise?" She turns to Ms. A. "And you can get people to do things you want them to; I can, anyway. I guess you can too. I mean, you're very sweet. But if you want to attract men, you have to lose some weight. Men really care about how you look. You've got to be sexy or they'll never even see you; it's like you're invisible."

"That's not true," Mr. D says heatedly.

"Oh, yes, it is," Ms. H says levelly.

"What is it about you that Mr. D and I can't see?" asks Dr. B.

This group, now several months into its life span, is spontaneously interactive, though the therapists continue to intervene and expedite communication and reflection. Members self-disclose, and support and confront each other. Ms. A has moved beyond her frightened silence and is able to express her outrage and fear at feeling abandoned and her loneliness. Because the group is able to accept and support her, her needs become less overwhelming, and the possibility of change becomes imaginable.

Mr. D is better able to detect and express his

disappointed hopes and expectations, instead of just erupting in angry outbursts without reflection. He has learned to modulate his anger sufficiently to use it in communication that does not alienate others; for example, his expression of anger was part of his feeling closer to Ms. A. He is also able to access deeper feelings beyond anger and to acknowledge his own dependency needs.

The group is cohesive enough to tolerate conflict between Ms. H and Mr. D, although, as we see, Dr. B must still help them reflect on the process. Ms. H, too, has had insights into her behavior. She understands that sexuality plays a protective function for her and compensates for a need not to feel invisible.

MODIFYING GROUPS TO FIT THE NEEDS OF DIFFERENT CLINICAL SITUATIONS

The interpersonal model, as described above, is most appropriate for a therapy group of at least several months' duration that is composed of patients with specific goals of characterologic change. Patients typically have difficulty with some aspect of their interpersonal relationships, yet are capable of adult self-sufficiency to a significant degree. Obviously, there exist many other situations with different clinical constraints, with vastly different clinical populations, where interactional group therapy can be of benefit if it is appropriately modified.

Basic Steps

There are three basic conceptual steps that are essential to the process of modifying a group to fit a particular setting:

1. The particular clinical situation must be assessed.
2. Appropriate outcome goals must be established.
3. Informed by these two steps, the therapist must make appropriate modifications in technique.

Assessing the Clinical Situation

In every clinical situation there are two kinds of restraints: those that are intrinsic and unchangeable and those that are extrinsic, a matter of habit or tradition, and therefore subject to change. The demands of health maintenance organizations in terms of the number of therapy meetings a patient may attend, for example, are intrinsic and generally unchangeable by the tertiary care therapist, while the tradition of allowing individual therapists to yank their patients out of an inpatient group may be entirely extrinsic and changeable.

Formulating Goals

Once the therapists understand the intrinsic constraints of the clinical situation, they must begin to formulate goals that are appropriate to the setting, the time constraints, and the clinical population. The importance of setting appropriate goals can scarcely be overemphasized; a mismatch between what the therapist strives to achieve and what is possible is a setup for a therapeutic failure that is demoralizing for the patient and discouraging for the therapist. It is well to remember that the goals of the basic outpatient group are ambitious; such ambition must be curtailed in a time-limited group or one with more compromised patients. Care must be taken to make success attainable; the patients do not need another failure.

Modifying Technique

Once appropriate goals are set, therapists must turn their attention to using techniques that can best achieve those goals. The modification of technique may best be depicted in the context of illustrative examples. Consider one very common contemporary group: the acute inpatient group.

Inpatient Groups

ASSESSING CLINICAL CONSTRAINTS. The clinical facts of life for the inpatient group are stark. Patients enter the group with a broad array of psychological difficulties, ranging from those with severe, disabling major psychosis to relatively well-integrated individuals who may have made a suicidal gesture or experienced a drug-induced acute psychotic state. Some patients may be in the group unwillingly. The duration of hospitalization is very brief, generally only a few days. This results, of course, in a rapidly fluctuating group composition; patients leave or new members enter the group at almost every meeting. Leadership varies also; rarely will overburdened professional schedules permit the same two coleaders to be present on a consistent basis.

GOALS. Given this clinical situation, what are appropriate clinical goals for the inpatient group?

1. *Decreasing isolation.* All hospitalized psychiatric patients have experienced a significant disruption of important supportive relationships. Because the interpersonal group helps patients share with one another and allows them to receive feedback from others, it breaks the pattern of isolation and reestablishes them as part of a community.

2. *Talking helps.* Patients commonly have developed habits of hiding or disguising their distress; they may avoid it by talking too much or too little. In a group, they experience the relief that comes from sharing their pain, feeling understood, and realizing that others suffer too. In other words, the inpatient group introduces the patient to the therapeutic factors of cohesiveness and universality.

3. *Helping others.* Psychiatric patients are almost always demoralized. They have experienced themselves as pathologically unique in their inability to help themselves, and as a drain and a burden on the other people in their lives. To be able to offer something to someone else is reassuring to their self-worth in a way that cannot be duplicated by receiving help from others.

4. *Spotting problems.* By helping patients

pinpoint areas in which they can do further work, inpatient groups offer a fresh perspective on the overwhelming problems that resulted in hospitalization. Patients are all too familiar with the global, unyielding nature of their problems, such as chronic depression or suicidal ideation. But the varying viewpoints and feedback in the group may identify specific interpersonal disturbances that can serve as points of access for continued therapy.

5. *Engaging the patient therapeutically.* For patients to benefit from psychiatric hospitalization, it is important that they continue the process of therapy after hospitalization. Aftercare groups are effective in maintaining advances made during hospitalization. The inpatient group can be crucial in creating a good initial experience for the patient so that he or she is motivated to continue care.

MODIFICATION OF TECHNIQUE. Now, having assessed the constraints of the clinical situation and having established a set of attainable goals, we are ready to turn to the implications of these steps for strategy and technique.

1. *Time frame.* Given the fact that group turnover is rapid, that new patients enter the group at almost every meeting, that the therapist cannot count on "culture bearers" to be present at the next meeting, and that it would be futile to think of "working through" issues during a series of meetings, inpatient group therapists must make a radical change in their time frame for therapy. In the inpatient setting, it is appropriate to think of the life of the group as consisting of a single session.

2. *Efficiency and activity.* A time frame of a single meeting demands that the therapist be efficient and active. There is no time to waste, no time to let issues gradually develop; the therapist must offer as much as possible to as many pa-

tients as possible in a single meeting. The therapist must therefore be active; the passive, nondirective therapist is not effective in inpatient group work.

3. *Support.* Since a major goal of the inpatient therapy group is to offer patients a positive therapy experience—one that they will wish to continue after they leave the hospital—it is important that the members experience the group as safe, supportive, and constructive. Thus the therapist must endeavor to be as supportive as possible: be directly encouraging, acknowledge the patient's efforts, be empathic, avoid conflict, and build supportive norms into the group structure.

4. *Structure.* Since the great majority of hospitalized patients are anxious, confused, and disorganized, it is important for the therapist to offer a stabilizing therapy experience: External structure facilitates the reestablishment of an internal structure. Therapists must therefore offer a clearly defined, structured experience. They must be clear about spatial and temporal boundaries, provide a clear orientation to group therapy, and offer a consistent and coherent group procedure.

TRAINING AND SUPERVISION

Group psychotherapy, like individual psychotherapy, requires specialized skills. Yet, even leading psychotherapy training programs commonly make the serious error of assuming that individual therapy skills can be easily extrapolated to therapy group leadership. First-year psychiatry residents, for example, routinely are expected to lead groups on acute inpatient wards with minimal or no supervision.

A basic education in group therapy should include several components: observing experienced group clinicians lead groups, personal psychotherapy, personal participation as a member of a group, and leading supervised groups.

Observing Experienced Clinicians Lead Groups

Observing an experienced group therapist is an invaluable early component of the group therapy training program. It offers inexperienced therapists the opportunity to participate vicariously in group leadership without the anxiety of premature clinical responsibility. If several trainees can observe simultaneously and engage in a postgroup discussion, all can benefit from the questions and comments derived from their varying perspectives.

While observing the group via videotape or through a two-way mirror has the advantage of minimal interference with the group; being physically present in the room provides observers better access to the group's emotional tone. Some groups can tolerate this intrusion and some cannot, but all will be affected. If they observe in the room, trainees should sit outside the circle of the group so that their observer status is clear, and the group leader should state that the observers will be silent. Some leaders make good therapeutic use of the observation process by permitting the group members to observe the postgroup discussion of the cotherapists and observers. Such a discussion permits an unusual opportunity for modeling transparency; furthermore, it alleviates resistance patients have about observation (Yalom, 1985).

Personal Psychotherapy

A personal self-exploratory course of individual psychotherapy is indispensable for any therapist. In addition, a group experience is an invaluable part of the group therapist's educational process. Being a member of a group permits the trainee to experience, in a deep emotional sense, the currents and power of the group. The American Group Psychotherapy Association recommends a minimum of 60 hours of participation in a group. Training or T-groups, designed to help participants increase the breadth and depth of their interactions and their knowledge of the group process, are provided by some training programs. While not specifically therapy groups, they may be therapeutic, depending on the goals individuals set for themselves in being part of such groups. Trainees may experiment with self-disclosure and become more aware of personal strengths and weaknesses; they will experience more richly the sense of "groupness," the group role they assume, and the value and power of feedback. Particularly relevant to their roles as future group leaders are their personal perceptions of the leaders—the power they hand over to the leaders, their dependency on them, their unrealistic expectations of them. If no training group is available, trainees should consider joining a regular outpatient group. Alternatively, together with other mental health professionals, they may seek out expert leadership to form a therapists' therapy group.

Supervision in Leading Groups

The trainee's first group experience should be as part of a cotherapy team—preferably when the coleader is more experienced. The coleader can model appropriate clinical attitudes and interventions, as well as guide and modify those of the trainee.

Supervision of the trainee's therapy groups is absolutely critical. The American Group Psychotherapy Association recommends a minimum of 180 supervised hours for group therapy trainees. Clinical experience alone is not sufficient. In a study of nonprofessional group leaders at a psychiatric hospital, Yalom and colleagues compared leaders who received ongoing supervision and an intensive course in group leadership with those who received neither. At the end of 6 months, they found that the leaders who received no training or supervision had reinforced their errors and were less skilled than they had been at the beginning, while the other group improved (Ebersole, Leiderman, & Yalom, 1969).

Though supervision is generally done by the student presenting clinical material from process notes, supervisors can be far more effective if they observe the entire group or colead

with the trainee. They may also view segments of a videotape of the group or observe the last half hour of the group and meet with the trainee immediately afterward. Generally, at least 1 hour of supervision should be given for each group session.

CONCLUSION

Group psychotherapy is an effective intervention for individuals suffering from problems with interpersonal relationships. It derives its power from the compelling importance of social relationships. Group psychotherapy is based theoretically on the interpersonal perspective of Harry Stack Sullivan, which defines psychopathology in terms of the processes that go on between people. One is mentally healthy to the degree that one is able to participate satisfyingly in such interactions and is known to others as one is known to oneself.

Interpersonal group psychotherapy is an interactional approach in which patients experience others and are experienced by them in the here-and-now of the group. Interpersonal learning and cohesiveness are powerful mechanisms of change in group psychotherapy. Other therapeutic factors include instillation of hope, universality, imparting of information, altruism, corrective recapitulation of the primary family group, development of socializing techniques, imitative behavior, interpersonal learning, group cohesiveness, catharsis, and cognitive reflection.

The effective therapist must thoroughly prepare patients for the group experience: Patients must be educated beforehand about the rationale of group therapy, the proposed structure of the group, and what will be expected of them in the group. The therapist must act to facilitate spontaneous interaction among group members, as this allows for maximum interplay of the therapeutic factors. A series of vignettes illustrates the group process from the initial meeting to the mature group.

Selection of patients is crucial; including patients who are unable to accomplish the group's task sets them up for failure and disrupts the group. Goals must be revised for different populations and clinical situations, although the fundamental interpersonal structure can be maintained.

Group leadership is a skill distinct from individual psychotherapy and requires specialized supervision and training. Observing groups led by experienced clinicians, leading supervised groups, and personal individual therapy and group participation are important components of training.

REFERENCES

Bandura, A., Blanchard, E., & Ritter, B. (1969). The relative efficacy of desensitization and modeling approaches for inducing behavioral, affective, and attitudinal changes. *Journal of Personality and Social Psychology, 13*, 173–179.

Bergin, A. E., & Lambert, M. (1978). The evaluation of therapeutic outcomes. In S. L. Garfield & A. E. Bergin (Eds.), *Handbook of psychotherapy and behavioral change: An empirical analysis* (2nd ed.) (pp. 152–162). New York: Wiley.

Berkman, L., & Syme, L. (1979). Social networks, host resistance, and mortality: A nine-year follow-up study of Alameda County residents. *American Journal of Epidemiology, 109*, 186–204.

Bowlby, J. (1980). *Attachment and loss* (Vols. I–III). New York: Basic Books.

Bloch, M. B., Band, G., Qualls, B., Yalom, I., & Zimmerman, E. (1976). Patients' expectations of therapeutic improvement and their outcomes. *American Journal of Psychiatry, 133*, 1457–1459.

Budman, S., Soldz, S., Demby, A., Feldstein, M., Springer, T., & Davis, S. (1989). Cohesion, alliance and outcome in group psychotherapy. *Psychiatry, 52*, 330–350.

Cartwright, D., & Zander, A. (Eds.). (1962). *Group dynamics: Research and theory.* Evanston, IL: Row, Peterson.

Dies, R. R. (1993). *The efficacy and cost-effectiveness of group treatments.* Unpublished manuscript, University of Maryland, College Park.

Dies, R. R., & Teleska, P. H. (1985). Negative outcome in group psychotherapy. In D. T. Mays & C. M. Franks (Eds.), *Negative outcome in psychotherapy and what to do about it* (pp. 118–141). New York: Springer.

Ebersole, G., Leiderman, P., & Yalom, I. (1969).

Training the nonprofessional group therapist. *Journal of Nervous and Mental Disorders* 149:385.

Erickson, R. C. (1987). The question of casualties in inpatient small group psychotherapy. *Small Group Behavior, 18*, 443–458.

Frank, J. D., & Frank, J. B. (1991). *Persuasion and healing: A comparative study of psychotherapy* (3rd ed.). Baltimore: Johns Hopkins University Press.

Goldstein, A. (1962). *Therapist–patient expectancies in psychotherapy.* New York: Pergamon Press.

Gurman, A., & Razin, A. (1977). *Effective psychotherapy: A handbook for research.* New York: Pergamon Press.

House, J., Landis, K., & Umberson, D. (1988). Social relationships and health. *Science, 241*, 540–545.

House, J., Robbins, C., & Metzner, H. (1982). The association of social relationships and activities with mortality: Prospective evidence from the Tecumseh community health study. *American Journal of Epidemiology, 116*, 123–140.

James, W. (1890). *The principles of psychology* (Vol. I). New York: Henry Holt.

Kapp, F., Gleser, G., Brisserden, A., Emerson, R., Winget, J., & Kashdan, B. (1964). Group participation and self-perceived personality change. *Journal of Nervous and Mental Disorders, 139*, 255–265.

Lambert, M., & Bergin, A. (1973). Psychotherapeutic outcomes and issues related to behavioral and humanisitc approaches. *Cornell Journal of Social Relations, 8*, 47–61.

Lieberman, M., Yalom, I., & Miles, M. (1973). *Encounter groups: First facts.* New York: Basic Books.

Miller, D. (1959). The study of social relationships: Situation, identity, and social interaction. In S. Koch (Ed.), *Psychology: A study of a science* (Vol. III, pp. 639–737). New York: McGraw-Hill.

Orlinsky, D. E., & Howard, K. I. (1986). Process and outcome in psychotherapy. In S. L. Garfield & A. E. Bergin (Eds.), *Handbook of psychotherapy and behavior change* (pp. 283–329). New York: Wiley.

Parloff, M., Waskow, I., & Wolfe, B. (1978). Research on therapist variables in relation to process and outcome. In S. L. Garfield & A. E. Bergin (Eds.), *Handbook of psychotherapy and behavioral change: An empirical analysis,* (2nd ed.). New York: Wiley. pp. 233–82.

Smith, M., Glass, G., & Miller, T. (1980). *The*

benefits of psychotherapy. Baltimore: Johns Hopkins University Press.

Strupp, H., Fox, R., & Lessler, K. (1969). *Patients view their psychotherapy*. Baltimore: Johns Hopkins University Press.

Strupp, H., Hadley, S., & Gomes-Schwartz, B. (1977). *Psychotherapy for better or worse: The problem of negative effects*. New York: Jason Aronson.

Sullivan, H. S. (1938). Psychiatry: Introduction to the study of interpersonal relations. *Psychiatry, 1*, 121–134.

Sullivan, H. S. (1940). *Conceptions of modern psychiatry*. New York: W. W. Norton.

Tiger, L. (1979). *Optimism: The biology of hope*. New York: Simon & Schuster.

Tillitski, C. J. (1990). A meta-analysis of estimated effect sizes for group vs. individual vs. control treatments. *International Journal of Group Psychotherapy, 40*, 215–224.

Toseland, R. W., & Siporin, M. (1986). When to recommend group treatment: A review of the clinical and the research literature. *International Journal of Group Psychotherapy, 36*, 171–201.

Yalom, I. (1985). *The theory and practice of group psychotherapy*. New York: Basic Books.

Yalom, I., Houts, P., Zimerberg, S., & Rand, K. (1967). Prediction of improvement in group therapy. *Archives of General Psychiatry, 17*, 159–168.

12
Family Therapy in Historical Perspective

John F. Clarkin
Daniel Carpenter

Not unlike beauty, family therapy (we will use the term *family therapy* generically to include both family and marital therapy) is in the eye of the beholder. To the theoretician of human systems, family therapy is the only form of intervention, as all difficulties in the individual are an aspect of systems functioning. To those who see pathology as both an individual and an environmental affair, family therapy is one of many treatment weapons in an array of treatment approaches. Others have focused on family systems therapy as a revolutionary epistemology in which the "true" situation is filtered through the family's and the therapist's fallible eyes. To the growing number of feminists in the family field, the focus of family therapy is on challenging the traditional family structure to allow women greater autonomy and control. For the research community, family therapy is a form of treatment that must be evaluated in controlled designs that compare it to other competing treatments. To make things even more complicated, most observers see the development of family therapy as separate from that of marital treatment. In this chapter, we focus on the historical emergence of concepts that have been used to describe family functioning and related treatment interventions. We will strive to achieve some historical perspective.

HISTORY OF THE FAMILY THERAPY MOVEMENT

Family therapy began as a practical response to clinical needs. The seeds that would grow into family and marital therapy were found in the then vastly different fields of social work, gynecological medicine, psychoanalysis, group dynamics, and the child guidance movement. The scope of this historical review is limited, and the interested reader is referred elsewhere for more detail (Broderick & Schrader, 1981; Nichols, 1984).

During the late nineteenth century, the *social work movement* was attempting to address the needs of the poor by working with families to help them find food and housing. The orientation of workers at the time was quite progressive, recognizing the need to assist whole families rather than viewing psychological problems as located in the individual. Although not often explicitly recognized as among the founders of the family therapy movement, social workers were the first to address the problems of the family system as a means of improving life for individuals.

Physicians in Europe and the United States in the 1920s began to work with clients who were reporting *sexual difficulties*. Havelock Ellis in England and Magnus Hirschfeld in Ger many conducted early research on the sexual behavior of their clients and used their data for education and counseling. Although the primary service offered by these early pioneers was education about contraception and family planning, it is very likely that what became known as *marital counseling* was beginning (Broderick & Schrader, 1981).

The *child guidance movement* began as a natural step from Freud's theories about the development of psychopathology. Freud theorized that psychological problems had their genesis in early interaction patterns between child and parents, particularly the mother. Alfred Alder reasoned that intervening in the lives of growing children would be effective in preventing adult neuroses, and he developed clinics where children, parents, and school teachers were counseled (Nichols, 1984). Child guidance centers were established in the United States in the 1920s with a similar orientation and mission. The orientation remained one of protecting the growing child from the pathogenic influences of overprotective or otherwise neurotic mothers. Theories attempting to classify pathogenic parenting styles were developed, including those on maternal overprotectiveness (Levy, 1943) and the schizophrenogenic mother (Fromm-Reichmann, 1948). Although the theoretical importance of the family was recognized, treatment still focused on the individual.

Gradually, the emphasis shifted from the individual to the family as the focus of treatment as clinicians like John Bowlby (1949) began to include family members in evaluations and at times of crisis. However, it was left to later clinicians to actually make the family the focus of treatment.

Another historical foundation for the family and marital therapy movements was the *interpersonal school of psychiatry*, which began to revise psychoanalytic theory to note the influence of the family not only in the development of mental illness but also in its maintenance (e.g., Harry Stack Sullivan and Erich Fromm). The first professionals to meet conjointly with whole families were influenced by the advent of group studies and Lewin's field theory (Lewin, 1951). Clinicians began to write about a group as more than a collection of individuals. The group itself was seen as having a process and an identity separate from the sum of the individual processes and identities of its members (Bion, 1948). One aspect of the group movement was Moreno's psychodrama (Moreno, 1945), in which small groups enact mini-dramas in the lives of the participants to stimulate discussion and insight. The transition to thinking about families as small groups was natural.

The inclusion of both spouses in therapy meetings as a means of addressing marital and sexual problems was a natural progression from counseling individuals about the same problems. *Conjoint marital therapy* formally began during late 1929 and early 1930 when Paul Popenoe and Abraham Stone independently opened separate marriage counseling clinics in Los Angeles and New York City, respectively. A few years later, Emily Mudd opened a marriage counseling center in Philadelphia. Dr. Mudd was a pioneer not only in providing marital counseling but also in its empirical investigation. She conducted studies evaluating the effectiveness of marital counseling (Mudd, 1951) and published the first case book (Mudd, Stone, Karpb, & Nelson, 1958). The latter was the first attempt in this field to provide what we would now call a treatment manual.

A milestone in the development of the marriage counseling field was the establishment in 1945 of the American Association of Marriage Counselors. The solidification of the field progressed steadily, with standards for certification of marriage counselors set in 1948 and standards for counseling centers and training centers following (Broderick & Schrader, 1981). However, the field of marriage counseling has lacked a unifying theory or cohesive force. Always a multidisciplinary profession, its diversity adds to the clinical richness but promotes a lack of cohesion in the field, with, for example, multiple journals and little interconnection.

Long before the first family therapists held conjoint family meetings, a number of authors wrote about the importance of *family issues in the treatment of individual patients*. For example, Flugel (1921) wrote about his separate analysis of family members in *The Psychoanalytic Study of the Family*. During the 1930s and 1940s, Moreno wrote about psychodrama with small groups, including married couples and families. Ackerman proposed that the difficulties of an individual should be viewed in the context of the entire family (Ackerman, 1938). Richardson's (1945) book, *Patients Have Families*, stressed the importance of taking a systems view. At the Tavistock Child Guidance Clinic in England, Bowlby had begun to use joint family meetings as an aid in initial evaluations and an auxiliary to individual treatment (Bowlby, 1949). However, it was not until the 1950s that meetings with the entire family began to be seen as a distinct treatment modality. It is generally recognized that three independent professionals and one group began to meet with families within a period of a few years: John Bell, Nathan Ackerman, Murray Bowen, and the Palo Alto group (Gregory Bateson, Don Jackson, John Weakland, and Jay Haley).

Perhaps the first to hold *conjoint family meetings* was John Bell, a psychology professor at Clark University. On a visit to England, he heard about clinical work at the Tavistock Clinic and had the idea of inviting family members to meetings with patients. Although he reported his experiences, he did not publish them until much alter and was not originally given credit for his contribution.

Nathan Ackerman, a child psychiatrist, followed Bowlby's steps in including family members for meetings when individual treatment was at an impasse. In theory and in practice, he went further than Bowlby in viewing the problems of the individual in the context of the larger family system. He developed systems of family diagnosis and was an early and influential teacher of family therapy.

Murray Bowen, while working at the Menninger Clinic in Topeka, Kansas, with psychotic children, set up a novel treatment approach by having the mothers of the children live with them for a time on the grounds of the hospital. He later joined a large research project at the National Institutes of Mental Health in Bethesda, Maryland, on the interaction of families with a schizophrenic child in which entire families lived on an inpatient unit. Initially, his primary approach consisted of treating the child alone and holding auxiliary meetings with the family. However, after observing problematic interaction patterns within each family, he treated all newly admitted families exclusively with family therapy meetings, with better results.

Another force in the development of family therapy was a group of researchers led by Gregory Bateson, an anthropologist, who in 1952 received a grant to study the different levels of abstraction in communication. In 1954, he obtained an additional grant to study the communication patterns of schizophrenics. At that time, the group consisted of Bateson, Jay Haley, John Weakland, and Don Jackson. This group produced the influential paper "Towards a Theory of Schizophrenia" (1956), in which they proposed that confused patterns of communication in schizophrenic families might account for the bizarre statements and social dysfunction demonstrated by these patients.

In summary, the emergent notion of marital and family therapy was a counterforce to the powerful and dominant individual orientation with which psychological problems and mental illness were approached in the early part of this century. Despite clinical evidence that working with families was effective in addressing the chief complaints of people seeking help, it took decades before individual problems were seen in the context of the family as a system. The early examination of marital and family therapy was typified by case studies. Standardized instruments were not used, and outcome studies were practically nonexistent. One exception might be Mudd's work around 1951. A theme that pervaded the field, exemplified by the child guidance centers and the early sex therapists in Europe and the United States, was that of offering education and support to families and couples faced with difficulties. Marsh (1935) provided lectures to patients, family members, and the community at the Worcester State Hospital in Massachusetts. The topics covered included basic developmental and abnormal psychology, vocational and social issues (e.g., how to look for jobs, how to converse casually), aspects of emotional and religious life, and sexuality. Clearly, this is a forerunner of what is currently known as *psychoeducation*.

RATIONALE AND THEORETICAL ORIENTATION OF FAMILY THERAPIES

There are a multitude of family therapies, and it is often said that they have certain underlying assumptions that unite them. However, the diversification is so extensive that not all the approaches share even the assumption that the focus of intervention is family systems dysfunction. The most they have in common is that the family or marital pair is seen in therapy as a unit (or subunits), but even this practice has exceptions, as some advocate treatment of the family or marital unit through treatment of the individual (e.g., Bowen, 1978; Wachtel & Wachtel, 1986).

The goal in this section is to describe the schools of family therapy in historical perspective. The schools are often identified with certain charismatic leaders who have historical and modeling importance to their followers. Family therapy was begun by pioneer clinicians who were discontented with the individual focus of the day, and they introduced the treatment of the family/couple as a pragmatic attempt to intervene effectively and efficiently. These forays into treatment were accompanied by theoretical constructs describing what the clinicians perceived operating in the families and what the treatments were trying to accomplish.

In describing each of the schools of family therapy, we will mention the historical context and the important leaders in this orientation. We will describe the central foci of intervention, related research on relevant constructs, and the strategies/techniques of this approach.

We will also assess the degree to which the orientation can be taught and detailed in a manual for experimental investigation.

The techniques available to family therapists can be divided into five categories: psychoeducational, cognitive-behavioral, structural, strategic, and insight-oriented. However, much overlap between the diverse schools has developed, both in underlying theory and in overt techniques. For example, some of the most interesting approaches are the behavioral approaches and techniques used in the context of family systems theory (see, e.g., Barton & Alexander, 1981). We believe that the field of psychotherapy in general, and family therapy in particular, must advance beyond a rigid adherence to one particular philosophy, and must continue to integrate the techniques and strategies most efficacious in addressing the presenting problem. An excessive commitment to a single school interferes with the progression of family therapy as a broadly effective and flexible treatment approach. We use the division into schools purely for heuristic purposes to aid in definition of the techniques.

Psychoeducational Approaches

Probably all therapies have an instructional element. The therapist is seen as an expert and conveys information either explicitly or indirectly. While the psychoeducational approach is not a distinct school of family therapy, recently some have brought it to a new level (Clarkin, 1989). This approach should be seen in historical context.

As noted earlier in this chapter, the early family movement was, in part, a reaction against the view that the individual was the locus and cause of pathology. In their enthusiasm for the family movement, some family therapists approached the family as the causative agent of severe psychiatric disorders like schizophrenia and bipolar disorder, and treatment was based on this assumption. As our understanding has advanced, it has become clear that disturbed family interactions themselves do not cause, but rather follow from, severe disorders in a member. However, there are data indicating that the family's interaction with a psychotic patient may be quite dysfunctional, and can have a significant impact on the patient's ability to remain relatively free of symptoms and to function outside a hospital environment. Furthermore, there is growing evidence that the presence of a severely disturbed family member provides a strong chronic stress for the family, producing intense emotional reactions, behavioral disruptions, and at times symptoms in other family members. A coping and adaptation model for the family can be used effectively in place of the earlier etiology-pathology model for certain severe disorders.

Focus of Intervention

This reconceptualization of the role of the family in psychotic disorders has led to an increasing focus on providing explicit information about individual psychiatric disorders to the identified patient and family members. Providing information can be helpful to the families in their understanding of the disorder and in the coping behavior used with the patient.

Strategies/Techniques

Information is communicated to families through written material, lectures, and discussions in family groups or in a workshop format. For example, Anderson and her colleagues (Anderson, Reiss, & Hogarty, 1986) have described a day-long "survival skills workshop" that the family attends without the patient. They provide information on the nature of schizophrenia (or bipolar disorder), including its history and epidemiology, biology, and phenomenology. They also discuss current theories on the causes of the disorder, emphasizing the biochemical and structural organic factors that may play a part. Families are told that they are not to blame for the disorder, any more than they would be to blame for diabetes or heart disease. Finally, the clinicians describe the current state of pharmacologic and psychosocial

treatments, as well as techniques for the family that will facilitate their coping with the burden of a chronic mental illness. The goals of psychoeducational family therapy are straightforward. It is designed to increase the family's knowledge and understanding of the patient's illness and treatment, and to facilitate their management of environmental stressors, emotional responses, and adaptive coping.

The psychoeducational approach is not limited to the treatment of psychotic disorders. For example, many family therapists provide information about child development, spiraling interaction patterns, and age-appropriate normal behavior to parents with dyssocial children as part of a comprehensive program to improve their family management skills (e.g., Patterson, 1982).

Cognitive-Behavioral Approaches

Rather than revolutionary approaches to family therapy led by a few charismatic figures, the cognitive-behavioral approaches have grown naturally from the research on family interactions and cognitive, behavioral, and cognitive-behavioral approaches to individuals. The accumulation of knowledge in the cognitive-behavioral tradition has been impressive, both in the area of marital interaction and intervention (e.g., Baucom & Epstein, 1990) and in family therapy (see the seminal work of Patterson, 1971). Techniques of cognitive-behavioral marital and family therapy draw on the basic principles of learning. Emphasis is placed on methods of intervention utilizing communication training, training in problem-solving skills, operant conditioning techniques, social exchange processes, and reciprocal reinforcement.

Focus of Intervention

The focus of intervention is on the specific cognitions and behaviors that are problematic. These include both the behaviors that call for intervention and prosocial behaviors that are absent.

COGNITIVE PHENOMENA. A number of cognitive phenomena are hypothesized to play important roles in martial communication and maladjustment (Baucom, Epstein, Sayers, & Sher, 1989): selective attention, attributions, expectancies, assumptions, and standards. For example, distressed spouses tend to attribute their partner's undesired communication behavior as global and stable (Camper, Jacobson, Holtzworth-Munroe, & Schmaling, 1988; Fincham & O'Leary, 1983). Positive events are ignored, and the partner is blamed for his or her negative behavior, which is seen as intentional, global, stable, and originating in internal factors. By contrast, nondistressed spouses give each other credit for positive behavior and overlook and/or exonerate their spouses for negative behavior (Holtzworth-Munroe & Jacobson, 1985; Jacobson, McDonald, Folette, & Berley, 1985).

One can only speculate as to the antecedents of these cognitive sets in the relationship between spouses and family members. Since the premarital impact of spouse communication predicts later marital conflict (Markman, 1981), and since a positive set toward the other would be presumed at the time of marriage, it may be that the premarital impact of spouse communication predicts a growing negative cognitive set toward the other.

Distorted assumptions can influence behavior between spouses. Distressed spouses assume that their partners cannot change their relationship and that overt disagreement is destructive (Epstein & Eidelson, 1981). Likewise, unrealistic assumptions and standards about relationships are predictive of general marital distress (Epstein & Eidelson, 1981; Jordan and McCormick, 1987). Spouses' low efficacy expectations regarding their ability to solve their marital problems are associated with marital distress and depression (Pretzer, Epstein, & Fleming, 1985).

COMMUNICATION. Communication skills are essential to healthy family functioning, not only at times of balance and calm but especially at times of crisis and disequilibrium. Functional communication among family members includes the clear articulation of ideas and feelings, consistency between verbal and nonverbal messages, and the reception of the message as intended by the initiator. In contrast, conflicting, ambiguous, and contradictory messages such as double-bind communication are often detrimental to marital and family adjustment (Bateson et al., 1956).

The amount and quality of verbal communication have differentiated distressed and nondistressed couples in empirical studies. Distressed couples exhibit more anger and criticism than nondistressed couples, and, over time, whining, withdrawal, and criticism predict marital distress. There are more inaccuracies in the communication of distressed compared to nondistressed couples, and distressed couples are comparatively less reliable observers of their own interactional behavior (Elwood & Jacobson, 1982, 1988). Dysfunctional families also are less accurate perceivers of communications and are more likely to respond with anger rather than questions or support.

COMMUNICATION DEVIANCE. Communication deviance, a concept developed in a research context, consists of distortions of linguistic-verbal reasoning, such as unfinished phrases, unintelligibility, odd word usage, and difficulty in accurately perceiving, integrating, and describing an object or concept. Marked communication deviance has been found in the families of high-risk children who later become schizophrenic (Miklowitz & Stackman, 1992). The initial level of communication deviance found among parents is the best individual predictor of the onset of "broad" schizophrenia-spectrum disorders (schizophrenia or personality disorders with associated psychotic processes) among disturbed but nonpsychotic adolescents followed into adulthood (Goldstein, 1987).

The causal relationship of family communication deviance to schizophrenia in a family member remains unclear, however. Communication deviance in parents is only modestly correlated with the level of thought disorder in schizophrenic offspring (Goldstein, 1987; Johnston & Holzman, 1979; Wynne, Singer, Bartko, & Toohey, 1976). Levels of communication deviance are uncorrelated with DSM-

III-R diagnoses in parents (current or past) or with parental global adjustment ratings (Goldstein, Talovic, & Nuechterlein, 1990). It may be that communication deviance reflects a subclinical marker of psychopathology that is not always manifested as a diagnosable disorder.

EXPRESSION OF NEGATIVE AFFECT. The communication of both positive feelings and negative affects such as anger, hostility, and resentment is central to effective communication. However, problematic communication of affect involves "character-assassination" remarks (e.g., "You are so incompetent") or generalized criticisms of a person's behavior ("You never try hard at school"). Not surprisingly, the problematic communication of negative affect has been found in distressed families.

Distressed couples and families make more criticisms, attend more to negative or critical statements, give less praise, and are more likely to withdraw from communications. Although some degree of negative communication is to be expected in every family, an excessive number or duration of negatively toned interactions is associated with disturbance in one or more family members. It is common in disturbed families to see "negatively escalating cycles" in which criticism by one family member is countered by a critical retort, which is followed by countercriticism from the first speaker. These cycles become increasingly pejorative and personal and often include negative, defensive, nonverbal behavior (Hahlweg et al., 1989).

Assessed in research settings by the Camberwell Family Interview, expressed emotion (EE) reflects the amount of criticism, devaluation, and anger expressed by the family. High EE relatives are critical in direct interaction, and high EE parents of offspring with schizophrenia show negative escalation cycles in interactions that are mutually generated by the critical parent and target patient (Hahlweg et al., 1989; Strachan, Feingold, Goldstein, Miklowitz, & Nuechterlein, 1989; Strachan, Leff, Goldstein, Doane, & Burtt, 1986).

Excessive EE from relatives is predictive of the course of a number of mental disorders, including schizophrenia (Brown, Birley, & Wing, 1972; Brown, Monck, Carstairs, & Wing, 1962; Nuechterlein et al., 1986; Tarrier, Barrowclough, Vaughn, & Bamrah, 1988; Vaughn & Leff, 1976; Vaughn, Snyder, Jones Freeman, & Falloon, 1984), bipolar disorder (Miklowitz, Goldstein, Nuechterlein, Snyder, & Mintz, 1988), nonpsychotic depression (Hooley, Orley, & Teasdale, 1986; Vaughn & Leff, 1976), and obesity (Fischmann-Havstad & Marston, 1984). Family treatment is most effective in delaying new episodes of schizophrenia if it is successful in reducing the number of critical comments and intrusive, "mind-reading" statements observed among parents during family interaction (Doane, Goldstein, Miklowitz, & Falloon, 1986).

PROBLEM SOLVING AND CONFLICT RESOLUTION. Distressed couples show more negative problem-solving behavior (Vincent, Weiss, & Birchler, 1975) and more problem escalation (Revenstorf, Halweg, Schlinder, & Vogel, 1984) than nondistressed couples. Negative reciprocity is also greater among distressed compared to nondistressed couples (Billings, 1979; Gottman, Notarius, Markman, Bank, Yoppi & Rubin, 1976; Margolin & Wampold, 1981; Raush, Barry, Hertel, & Swain, 1974; Revenstorf et al., 1984). Negative reciprocity may involve mutual fault finding, cross-complaining, and global, negative criticisms. Positive reciprocity is more characteristic of nondistressed couples (Revenstorf te al., 1984), but not in all samples (e.g., Margolin & Wampold, 1981).

Families with deficient problem-solving skills tend to act impulsively, or find solutions that serve only one member, or address only one aspect of the problem. The families of psychiatric patients are more passive and express less confidence in their coping and problem-solving strategies than comparison samples (Powers, Dill, Hauser, Noan, & Jacobson, 1985). Parents whose own parents were divorced may have more trouble solving problems with their children and may initiate more conflict (Forehand, McCombs, Wierson, Brady, & Fauber, 1990). Poor problem solving and increased conflict initiation, in turn, predict adolescent cognitive and social incompetence, conduct disorder, and anxiety-withdrawal. There appears to be a strong relationship between parental problem-solving skills and the cognitive and social abilities of their children (Baumrind, 1975; Bee et al., 1982; Bradley & Caldwell, 1980).

While all couples display conflict, the patterns of behavior when there is disagreement most strongly characterizes distressed couples (Gottman, Markman, & Notarius, 1977; Hahlweg et al., 1984a; Hahlweg, Revenstorf, & Schindler, 1984b; Margolin & Wampold, 1981). In particular, negative behavior begets negative behavior in distressed couples, whereas it elicits positive or neutral behavior in nondistressed couples (Revenstorf et al., 1984; Schaap, 1984). Healthy families tend to use both communication and problem-solving skills to resolve disagreements and conflicts.

COERCIVE FAMILY PROCESSES. A common maladaptive approach to family problem solving is negative coercive cycles. In these cycles, two (or more) individuals within a family control each others' behavior, a pattern of reward/punishment known as *negative reinforcement* (Patterson, 1982). In this model, children first learn to perform mild, relatively innocuous, aversive behaviors (e.g., whining, teasing, running back and forth, negativism) as a way of terminating aversive behaviors that have been manifested by a parent (e.g., scolding, issuing negative commands). The result is that the parent eventually responds in a neutral or positive way in order to terminate the child's aversive behavior. For the child, his or her aversive behavior has terminated the parent's aversive behavior. For the parent, his or her acquiescence has terminated the child's aversive behavior. In this manner, the parent's attempts to discipline the child often have the effect of reinforcing the child's coercive behaviors (Patterson, Capaldi, & Bank, 1991).

The aversive behaviors of the child may escalate as this family interactional pattern continues. Minor coercive behaviors such as whining may escalate to more intense (if less frequent) coercive behaviors such as hitting, temper tantrums, and stealing. Coercive exchanges can be thought of as a series of "rounds" that escalate in severity and increase the probability that one or more family members will react aggressively (Robinson & Jacobson, 1987).

In comparison with normal children, aggressive children are more likely to respond to aversive maternal behavior with an increase in their own aversive behavior (a coercive cycle), acting as if the mother's aversive behavior was a reward. In contrast, aversive maternal behavior tends to suppress prosocial behavior on the part of the aggressive child (Kopfstein, 1972; Patterson & Cobb, 1971; Wahler & Dumas, 1987). This pattern of aversive parental behavior following a prosocial child behavior is less frequently observed in families of nonproblem children (Snyder, 1977). "Bursts" of coercive responding in aggressive children, initially triggered by aversive parental behavior, eventually lead to positive behavior on the part of mothers or at least to a discontinuation of maternal aversive behavior (Patterson, 1976). When mothers and their aggressive children show evidence of bidirectional "coercive entrapment," a lower number of positive interchanges is observed than in families with no entrapment (Burgess & Conger, 1978). Perhaps as a consequence, coercive relationships are frequently associated with depression in one or more family members (Patterson, 1980). Coercive entrapment between a parent and child is believed to reinforce aggressive behavior in the child that may generalize to other settings (Patterson, 1982).

Strategies/Techniques

COMMUNICATION TRAINING. As an expert in communication, the family therapist models and teaches family members to express their thoughts and feelings clearly to one another. Family meetings provide an arena for family discussion in which there is an implied limit on conflict and blame. Family members are taught to listen carefully and to allow others to complete their statements without interruption. By helping families communicate their needs clearly, the therapist teaches them to be specific about what they want. They are taught problem solving, negotiation, the use of compromise, and contingency contracting.

PROBLEM-SOLVING SKILLS. The steps by which an individual or family deals effectively with personal and interpersonal difficulties has been termed *problem solving*. Developed initially to deal with individual behavioral problems, problem solving has been applied extensively to marital dysfunction, child behavioral disorder, and family therapy of severe psychopathology.

Problem solving involves five discrete steps, which are taught as part of a package: problem identification and goal setting, generation of solutions, evaluation of solutions, implementation, and evaluation of the results. Cognitive and behavioral approaches to parental behavior, problem children and adolescents, pathology such as schizophrenia and bipolar disorder, and marital pairs have been manualized and can be reliably taught.

CONTINGENCY CONTRACTING (BEHAVIOR EXCHANGE). Dysfunctional families have a tendency in interpersonal relationships to use excessive amounts of punishment and negative reinforcement, inadvertently rewarding and increasing unwanted behavior. Contingency contracting is used to address these problems by increasing the clarity of target behaviors, providing gratifying and easily obtainable reinforcement, increasing positive reinforcement, and decreasing negative reinforcement and punishment. These techniques have been used with a wide range of family problems (e.g., acting-out problems with children and adolescents and marital therapy). However, they are applicable to a wide range of problems, limited only by the therapist's skill in identifying target behaviors and reinforcers.

POSITIVE REINFORCEMENT AND EXTINCTION. Families that exhibit disturbed interaction patterns have usually changed the patterns of reinforcement and reward and have difficulty extinguishing behaviors that are undesired. People in distressed marriages attend more to negative behavior than positive behavior and respond differentially to negative behavior while ignoring positive behavior. Distressed couples are less self-disclosing, more critical, and more aggressive with each other. The use of negative reinforcement patterns is quite common in both distressed marriages and conduct-disordered families. In these contexts, negative behavior is rewarded because a desired consequence is provided that stops the negative behavior. For example, a child's temper tantrum is reinforced with provision of the demanded thing or is intermittently punished.

Structural Family Therapy

One of the unique contributions of the family orientation has been the recognition of structured (repetitive and predictable) behavioral sequences in family groups that contribute to the etiology and/or maintenance of symptomatic behaviors. Minuchin (1974) and his associates (Minuchin, Montalvo, Guerney, Rosman, & Schumer, 1967) were the first to identify and describe the appropriate and healthy relationship among family members, specifying the strength of boundaries between people and the degree of cohesion within subgroups of the family.

Focus of Intervention

The focus of structural family intervention is on the repetitive family interactions that create the boundaries between individuals and the in-groups and out-groups of family interaction. Effective and maladaptive family functioning are described in terms of family structure, that is, the operational rules that family members use to organize and carry out necessary family functions. The structural elements in the family, and thus the foci of assessment and intervention, are family boundaries, alignment, and power distribution (Aponte & VanDeusen, 1981).

BOUNDARIES. The family is the primary social unit, with a number of individuals and subgroups. The boundaries or divisions among the individuals, the subgroups of the family, and the family and other individuals in the neighborhood, community, and surroundings are important to the functioning of the family (Minuchin, 1974). The boundaries of a subsystem are the rules that define who participates and in what manner. The function of the boundaries is to ensure differentiation and proper functioning. Boundaries must be clear and well defined. When appropriate boundaries exist between family members and the subunits of the family, there is functioning in the context of both warmth and autonomy. When boundaries are too diffuse, overinvolvement and a lack of psychological separation are dangers; when boundaries are too rigid, the family lacks warmth and involvement.

OVERINVOLVEMENT. Unclear boundaries between parents and their children may foster overdependence and overinvolvement and may result in lack of differentiation and separation by the offspring (Minuchin, 1974). In families containing an individual suffering from a psychiatric disorder, it is not unusual to see a pairing of an overprotective, overinvolved parent with a disabled, passive, and withdrawn offspring. Because ill offspring in these families often elicit such responses, however, an overinvolved relationship is best thought of as a dyadic attribute rather than simply as a problem generated by a parent.

The construct of overinvolvement has been operationalized in several ways. As part of the expressed emotion construct and coding system (Leff & Vaughn, 1985), overinvolvement is operationalized as a tendency to be overprotective, overly concerned or overly controlling of, or domineering toward an offspring. In addition, Parker, Tupling, and Brown's (1979) well-validated parental bonding instrument has provided a working definition of overprotection: parental overcontrol, intrusion, excessive contact, and preventing the child from acting independently (Parker, 1983).

In general, overinvolvement is associated with poor social adjustment and chronic symptoms. For example, overinvolvement is common among families of chronic patients (Miklowitz et al., 1986) but is infrequent among parents of recent-onset schizophrenic

patients (Nuechterlein et al., 1986). Patients in emotionally overinvolved families are more likely to have had poor premorbid social adjustment and a high degree of residual symptoms between episodes (Miklowitz, Goldstein, & Falloon, 1983). Emotionally overinvolved parents are more likely than normally involved parents to manifest high levels of communication deviance (Miklowitz et al., 1986). Overinvolvement is a *risk factor* for schizophrenic relapse independent of the level of criticism demonstrated by the family (Brown et al., 1972; Leff & Vaughn, 1985; Vaughn & Leff, 1976; Vaughn et al., 1984).

There is no reason to assume that overinvolvement is limited to families with a schizophrenic member. Patients with neurotic depression are more likely to rate their parents as overprotective and low in caring than are patients with manic-depression and matched controls (Parker, 1983). Similarly, patients with borderline personality disorder rate their parents as more protective and less caring than do nonborderline patients (Zweig-Frank & Paris, 1991).

Strategies/Techniques

The strategies and techniques of structural family therapy emphasize behavioral and organizational changes in the family that restore a more normative hierarchy. These include changes in the marital coalition, as well as in parent–child dyads. Triadic relationships (e.g., mother, daughter, father) are also quite important, as a third person will often be brought into a dyadic relationship to reduce or defuse conflict. Frequently, the goal is to eliminate triangulation and focus on dyadic interactions.

Techniques that enable the structural family therapist to interrupt and change such dysfunctional family structures (Minuchin, 1974; Minuchin & Fishman, 1981) include *enactment*, the technique of eliciting or playing out of interpersonal problems the family describes in the therapeutic setting; *focusing*, in which the therapist selects a focus and develops a theme for the family therapy work; *boundary making*, focusing on and changing the psychological distance between two or more family members (e.g., a mother who speaks for her daughter. To increase the distance between mother and daughter, the therapist can mark a boundary by commenting that the mother is helpful in the way she reads her daughter's mind and speaks for her but that the daughter then doesn't have to do it herself); *unbalancing* in order to change the hierarchical relationship between members of a family system or subsystem by affiliating with certain family members, ignoring family members, or entering into a coalition with some family members against others; and *complementarity*, in which, for example, the family therapist attempts to help the individuals in the family perceive and understand the workings of their mutual interdependence and their membership in an entity larger than themselves (the family).

Many of the behavioral techniques can be used in the context of a structural or strategic intervention program as well. Often the interventions endorsed by structural and strategic therapists reflect a knowledge of behavioral interventions. Conversely, the specifics of a particular behavioral intervention, including who does what aspect of a behavioral intervention, exhibit an implicit understanding of the nature of the family structure and have an impact on the family as a whole. Minuchin's conception of the family and related treatment strategies are well described and can be taught.

Strategic Therapies

Strategic approaches to changing the family are built on the initiation of planned action by the therapist in order to help a family unit solve a problem that they have been unsuccessful in overcoming (Haley, 1973). Clinicians identified with the strategic approach include Milton Erickson and Jay Haley; members of the Mental Research Institute such as John Weakland, Paul Watzlawick, Richard Fisch, Arthur Bodin, and Carlos Sluzki; and Gerald Zuk, Lynn Hoffman, and Mara Palazzoli-Selvini (Stanton, 1981).

Focus of Intervention

The focus of intervention is on the misguided attempt to solve a family problem that has led to symptoms in one or more members of the family. The symptoms are conceptualized as a communication act or sequence of behaviors that has a homeostatic function in the family unit. Strategic therapies are designed to incisively disrupt the homeostatic process, allowing the family to interrupt their current patterns and develop new ones. A most incisive strategic intervention is a task given by the therapist that uses the presenting problem as a way to make a structural change in the family (Haley, 1976). There is no direct recommendation for a better family structure; families are free to reorganize in any way, but it is assumed that the reorganization will be at a more functional level. In strategic family therapy, a special emphasis is placed on overcoming the resistance of the family and introducing new behaviors.

One person's desire to dominate, control, and manipulate others has historically been recognized as a primary motivator of human behavior. During the last two decades, these motives have regained a place of value, particularly in family therapy. Haley, Madanes, and Dell have explored the importance of power and control in family function and dysfunction. As individuals often struggle to control the behavior, feelings, or thoughts of another, a common response to these efforts is an escalation of the conflict by active or passive rejection of the first person's efforts and a complementary effort to exert control.

Strategies/Techniques

Tasks and directives given by the therapist to the family are the major techniques of this therapeutic approach. Strategic family therapists use reframing, positive connotation, symptom prescription, and restraint from change as their main interventions. More specifically, the interventions often take the form of overt behavioral recommendations rather than cognitive formulations. Positive connotation and reframing occur when the therapist perceives and understands the patient's or family's frame and counters this frame with another competing view. This alternative view offers a good reason why such behavior takes place and why it should continue. Symptom prescription has been called the most powerful form of problem resolution. Watzlawick, Weakland, and Fisch (1974) give a number of examples, including prescribing less of the same, making the covert overt, advertising instead of concealing, and utilizing resistance. All strategic therapists repeatedly use this technique to unbalance the system. The assumption underlying symptom prescription, especially if it includes amplification, is that the problematic behavior is not sufficiently problematic to motivate the family's desire for change. In addition, symptom prescription assumes that persisting in the behavior will highlight the particular problematic components. Finally, this technique allows the family to put under conscious control behaviors that have seemed mysterious and uncontrollable.

In using restraint from change, families are instructed to be suspicious of change and to work hard not to change what they are doing. They are told that there is clearly a very strong reasons for them to remain in their current situation and that to change may lead to unforeseen consequences that could be disastrous. Restraint allows the therapist to regulate the pace and tempo of change and, in highly resistant families, fosters the desire to change by supporting avoidance of change.

Strategic family therapy, as described by Haley, is highly individualized, depending on the particular clinical situation, and lends itself to the case method he uses. This makes it much more variable and hard to teach.

Insight-Oriented Techniques

In this country, Nathan Ackerman was a pioneer in applying psychodynamic concepts to the family and in regarding family therapy as a necessity in the assessment and treatment of children (see Bloch & Simon, 1982, for Ackermans' edited papers). In the 1950s, Murray Bowen, another psychiatrist with psychodynamic training, examined the intense emotional relationship between mother and schizophrenic offspring a part of the family emotional system (Kerr, 1981). England has also been a locus for the application of psychdynamic thinking to the marital unit an the family. The psychodynamic understanding of marital conflict, as conceptualized by H. V. Dicks (1967), is still a classic. The writings of Stierlin (1977) and A. C. R. Skynner (1976) have also explicated the psychodynamics of family life.

Focus of Intervention

Insight-oriented family methods are used with the implicit assumption that unverbalized or unconscious cognitive-affective issues are interfering with a family's ability to either function effectively or learn new ways of relating. Unconscious themes may involve marital contracts (Sager, 1976), split representations or projection (Dicks, 1967), or modes of expressing unconscious conflicts (Stierlin, 1977). *Marital contracts* refer to the (largely unconscious) expectations, roles, needs, and sources of gratification that will be provided by the spouse in exchange for the provision of parallel functions. These contracts are rarely verbalized, but are acted on and integrated as if they had been consciously negotiated. At times, discrepancies in each person's contract emerge immediately. More commonly, they are relatively consistent with a given stage in the relationship but become uncongruent when either one person or the nature of the relationship changes.

There are a range of interpersonal methods that individuals use (unwittingly) to manage unconscious impulses and conflicts. Stierlin (1977) described three prominent modes: binding, delegating, and expelling. In the last method, the person projects all conflicts or intolerable affects onto a member of the family and then tries to resolve the conflict by eliminating the object of the projection. This mode is seen in many divorces and in adolescent runaways. The delegating mode involves projection of unconscious wishes or conflicts onto a family member and partial identification with this person, resulting in vicarious gratification of the impulse. For example, a father struggling at midlife with issues of masculinity may unconsciously encourage premature sexuality in his adolescent son as a source of vicarious gratification. The binding mode involves either acting out or projection of fears and fantasies onto a child, who is then drawn closer or prevented from forming a separate identity in supposed efforts to protect the child. For example, a depressed, anxious mother experiences the world as ungratifying and critical. She then uses her child as a source of narcissistic supplies, pulling the child into the family with guilt, helplessness, or pseudopraise for how essential the child is to her.

INTIMACY AND AUTONOMY NEEDS. In any close relationship there are needs and desires for intimacy, closeness, and attachment and, at the same time, needs for autonomy, independence, and privacy. These forces have been articulated in a number of theoretical contexts. Bowlby and colleagues (e.g., Bowlby, 1969) have described the attachment drive, an innate tendency to form and maintain one or a few very strong relationships that provide the potential for the experience of "felt security." Ainsworth (e.g., Ainsworth, 1973) has discussed this drive as complementary with autonomy, the drive to explore, learn, and grow. The more the child feels a secure attachment, the more that child is able to explore and investigate the surrounding environment.

The relative strength and emphasis on these two drives have provided family theorists with a central interpersonal dynamic in families, although the language is somewhat different across theoreticians. Bowen (e.g., Bowen, 1978) has written extensively on the concepts of fusion and isolation, the two extremes of interpersonal relatedness. Minuchin (e.g., Minuchin, 1974) has emphasized proximity and distance within a family in terms of the nature of boundaries between individuals and subunits. Stierlin (1977) has discussed the centripetal (proximity-seeking) and centrifugal (autonomy-seeking) forces in a family. These forces are dynamics not of an individual, but rather of the family as a whole. The family

that can maintain a cohesive entity yet allow individual exploration and development has achieved a balance between these forces. Most families with a disturbed member, however, are tilted toward one or the other of these forces.

Strategies/Techniques

While the experiential and psychodynamic schools of psychotherapy have different goals, both have in common the use of techniques to expand the cognitive-emotional horizons of the family members, with the assumption that such expansion will lead to behavior and character change. In expressive dynamic therapy, the therapist uses the context of therapeutic neutrality to employ such techniques as clarification, confrontation, and interpretation with the individual, marital dyad, or family unit.

The dynamically oriented family and marital therapist uses clarification, confrontation (i..e, identification of contradictory aspects of the patient's behavior or the impact of the behavior of which the patient is unaware), and interpretation (either in the here-and-now interaction or in more generic interpretations) to induce change in the family system. Ackerman (1938) was a pioneer in utilizing dynamic techniques in a family therapy format, and Dicks (1967) described the use of dynamic techniques in the intervention with marital couples.

Common Therapeutic Elements

In practice, there are many common elements and much eclectic usage of strategies and techniques across the various schools of intervention. Family therapy shares many treatment elements with all other forms of psychotherapy. All psychosocial treatments require the development and maintenance of a good patient–therapist relationship, or therapeutic alliance. There is an assumption that most patients experience some degree of corrective emotional experience, or reliving of significant life experiences, in the presence of an empathic therapist who demonstrates new ways of relating. In this context, the patient is able to identify with the therapist and utilizes the behaviors discussed and modeled. In all forms of psychotherapy, there is a certain degree of transmission of new information. The learning can be about methods of behavior, ways of thinking, or increased awareness of complex emotions. Most therapies involve some shaping of people's behavior through implicit and explicit rewards for behaviors considered appropriate and discouragement of behaviors considered harmful. This shaping can occur through advice, suggestion, persuasion, role playing, and practice.

EMPIRICAL BASIS OF FAMILY THERAPY

Our major focus in this section is on the historical development of the empirical investigation of family therapy. This development has not been without its detractors, as there are many family theorists who think that research to describe the family system and to capture intervention is theoretically impossible. Some (e.g., Colapinto, 1979; Tomm, 1983) have argued, for example, that traditional research methods are derived from linear and reductionist paradigms, and are therefore inadequate to contribute to our knowledge of how systems such as families operate and change.

Table 12.1 lists representative research efforts that have occurred in the family therapy field. We have included both early and more recent studies so that the interested reader can examine the developing family therapy research designs and methodologies.

Current state-of-the-art investigations in the individual therapy and family therapy areas involve manualized treatments with a control group or contrasting treatment, with adequate outcome measure of patient and family functioning and assessment of clinical as well as statistical significance. It is clear that the methodology in family therapy research has improved. Manualized treatments have been developed. Randomized designs comparing family treatment to no treatment or alternative treatments are being used. Outcome measures are being developed to capture family interaction as well as patient symptom status (Jacob & Tennenbaum, 1988).

Most important for the growth of the field, the research results are positive in showing the effects of family treatment on certain conditions. The research suggests that family treatment is effective with schizophrenia, phobias, and adolescent and child acting-out difficulties (Clarkin & Carpenter, in press; Gurman, & Kniskern, & Pinsof, 1986). In terms of strategies and techniques used in the family and marital treatment formats, there is substantial evidence for the effectiveness of cognitive and behavioral techniques, with little data on the other approaches. There is very little compari-

TABLE 12.1. Representative Family Therapy Studies

Experimental Groups	Strategies/Techniques	Results
Filial therapy (FT) versus control (Stover & Guerney, 1967) for child behavior problems	Client-centered	FT > control; mothers were more empathic and children less nonverbally aggressive
Family crisis therapy (FCT) versus inpatient hospitalization (Langsley, Machotka, & Flomenhaft, 1971)	Systemic, supportive; medications as needed	FCT > = inpatient hospitalization
Behavioral family therapy (BFT) versus group therapy (Stuart, Jayaratne, & Tripodi, 1976) for child behavioral problems	Cognitive/behavioral	BFT > group therapy
Inpatient individual therapy versus inpatient family therapy (Ro-Trock, Wellisch, & Schoolar, 1977) for child behavioral problems	Structural/systemic	Family therapy > individual therapy; children in family condition were not rehospitalized

Experimental Groups	Strategies/Techniques	Results
Family therapy versus control group (Garrigan & Bambrick, 1977, 1979) for child behavioral problems	Zuk's (Zuk, 1971) go-between method	Family therapy > control; improvement in children's symptoms in therapy group; Some aspects of this continued at follow-up
Client-centered family groups (CFG) versus eclectic-dynamic family therapy versus behavioral family intervention (BFI) versus no-therapy controls (Klein, Alexander, & Parsons, 1977) for delinquent adolescents	Client-centered, cognitive/behavioral, dynamic/eclectic	BFI > CFG > control = eclectic
Crisis family versus medication only (Goldstein, Rodnick, Evans, May, & Steinberg, 1978) for schizophrenia		High medication + family > medication only
Behavioral family therapy (behaviorally focused, social learning approach) versus court-implemented program as usual (Gant, Barnard, Kuehn, Jones, & Christophersen, 1981) for delinquent adolescents	Cognitivebehavioral	BFT > control
Behavioral marital therapy (BMT) versus waitlist (WL) control (Baucom, 1982)	Behavioral	BMT > WL in altering presenting marital complaints
Family psychoeducational intervention versus routine outpatient care (Leff, Kuipers, Berkowitz, Eberlein-Vries, & Sturgeon, 1982) for schizophrenia	Cognitive/behavioral	FPI > control; Relapse rate in control group much higher (50%) than in experimental group (9%); among families in which the stated aims of therapeutic intervention were achieved, none relapsed; all patients received medications, and all were returned to high EE homes.
Individual family reciprocity training versus group-based family reciprocity training versus control group (Raue & Spence, 1985) for child behavioral problems	Cognitive/behavioral	Individual family reciprocity training = group-based family reciprocity training > control
Marital treatment versus individual cognitive treatment for depression and marital conflict (Beach & O'Leary, 1992)	Cognitive/behavioral	Both treatments reduce depression; marital treatment superior in decreasing marital distress
Strategic family therapy (SFT) versus BFT (Szykula, Morris, Sudweeks, & Sayger, 1987) for child behavioral problems.	Structural/systemic, cognitive/behavioral	SFT = BFT
Family therapy (dynamic-eclectic) versus individual therapy (supportive) (Russell, Szmukler, Dare, & Eisler, 1987) for eating disorders	Dynamic/electic	Family therapy > individual therapy for patients <19 years old without chronic illness
Family management versus individual management (Falloon, McGill, Boyd, & Pederson, 1987) for schizophrenia	Cognitive/behavioral	Family > individual management
Problem-solving skills training (PSST) versus parent management training (PMT) versus PSST + PMT (Kazdin, Siegel, & Bass, 1992) for child behavioral problems	Cognitive/behavioral	PSST + PMT > PSST = PMT
Multisystemic therapy (MST) versus "treatment as usual" (incarceration and/or probation) (Henggeler, Melton, & Smith, 1992) for delinquent behavior	Structural/systemic	MST > control; reduction in incarceration for boys in the treatment condition and decrease in criminal behavior

son research, that is, studies in which patients and families are randomized to either family therapy or a competing therapy (e.g., individual or group therapy). When comparison studies are done, it is most usual to compare two forms of family intervention. Only now are family therapy researchers beginning to look at clinical significance as opposed to merely statistical significance, so there will be more attention to *how much* family therapy is helpful.

The relationship between theoretical family constructs, family intervention, and the empirical outcome of family therapy research is tenuous. A striking and serious difficulty in the field is the chasm between those who write about systems theory and the research that is being pursued.

PERSPECTIVES AND FUTURE DIRECTIONS

From the perspective of this chapter, one can discern some emergent themes. We have tracked key family constructs and indicated those with empirical support. We have also examined which of the constructs were the foci of family intervention and which schools of family therapy have had the most validation with particular patient groups.

The family revolution was a reaction against the exclusive focus on the individual as the locus and cause of pathology. Today, in perspective, it would appear that while the family field continues to hold tenaciously to the centrality of family systems concepts, there is some pull of the pendulum back to the center. There are hints that the role of the individual in family systems thinking has been too neglected. It is the individual in families who has the symptoms of chronic illness, such as diabetes, schizophrenia, bipolar disorder, and high blood pressure. We are learning that there are barriers to individual functioning that reside in the individual and that cannot be ignored. In family violence, for example, the perpetrator cannot be shielded by family systems constructs and must be treated as responsible for his or her actions.

The task now is to integrate into a coherent theory and an empirical venture both the individual and the family system. The EE research in the course of schizophrenia in the individual, and Patterson's work with coercive family systems and delinquent adolescents, are models. Attribution theory, as applied to individuals in a marital relationship, is another example. At the systems level, the couple relates with negative reactions, while at the individual level, destructive attributions are operative.

The historical roots of family therapy are multiple and diverse, including the family life movement, sex therapy, family systems thinkers, and social psychiatrists. This diversity lives on in the various facets of the family movement today: behavioral marital and family therapy, systems epistemology, and the research-orientation, to name but a few. This field shows no signs of coalesing, and the diversity remains clinically enriching.

Many of the early systems concepts around which several clinicians in the field have coalesed still lack empirical support (e.g., double bind). Other constructs, such as EE, coercive styles, overinvolvement, negative affective style, and communication deviance, have received empirical phenomenological descriptions and some validation as to their impact on family pathology and its course. It remains to be seen if some of the more creative family constructs can be empirically supported.

Not only must there be more integration of the individual and the family system, there must be recognition of the different ways in which the family operates in reference to difference disorders. Our research must yield specifics about family constructs and patterns in reference to specific illnesses and problem areas. The former reliance on family systems constructs general enough to be applied to any problem condition is no longer sufficient. Ideally, one would have a model of a particular area of pathology, with explicated family variables of known strengths, before articulating a family intervention that addresses that disorder/condition. The history of family therapy, not unlike the history of individual therapy, has not been so rational.

There is also a need for a more standard and accepted way to classify the family unit for treatment planning. A family diagnostic system is probably beyond our current knowledge, but some uniform recognition of family variables in treatment planning would recognize that even if the individual has the disorder, the family unit is a crucial part of the environment.

There will be pressures in this era of managed care for more crisp definition of indications for marital and family treatment. This discussion of necessity fits into the overall topic of differential therapeutics (Clarkin, Frances, & Perry, 1992; Frances, Clarkin, & Perry, 1984) and strategic treatment planning (Beutler & Clarkin, 1990). One approach to this issue is to point to problem areas that have been shown empirically to respond to family treatment, reviewed earlier in this chapter. Another approach is to specify the mediating goals of treatment (e.g., reduce family EE) in the treatment of specific disorders and conditions.

There remains controversy over the family's role in the development, maintenance, and exacerbation of the individual's pathology. Historically, the family therapy field rebelled against attempts to locate the dysfunction and its cause in the individual. In this process, the field often neglected the causal potency and responsibility of the individual. With the advent of groups to advocate the rights of the mentally ill, such as the National Alliance for the Mentally Ill (NAMI), the families of the mentally ill entered the controversy, until then debated only in journals, about the family's role in the etiology of such disorders as schizophrenia. The families of the seriously mentally ill had felt blamed and denigrated by family therapists who apparently used constructs that blamed the family for the illness. The use of psychoeducational approaches has been a recent reaction to the earlier approaches. Psychoeducational approaches to families and their issues have early roots and have reemerged today. Issues of physical and sexual abuse of spouses and children also raise questions about the blanket application of systems thinking to all behaviors.

While diversity of constructs in the understanding of family systems as related to healthy and pathological functioning is enriching, it seems clear that in today's fiscal climate, only those interventions that have proved effective will be reimbursed by the mental health system. Empirical work supporting the effectiveness of various forms of family therapy as applied to specific diagnostic/problem constellations is a current necessity, without which the application of family intervention will disappear.

Family therapy began as a pragmatic attempt to deal with individual and family difficulties effectively and efficiently. The family therapy enterprise still remains pragmatic, with studies on combinations of strategies and techniques from the various schools. The empirical work assessing the efficacy of practical family therapies is making headway. Not only does it appear that family therapy is effective (especially in some areas, such as schizophrenia, marital difficulties, child and adolescent problems), but the empirical methodology in family therapy research is improving substantially.

We salute our students who will determine the course of these matters and add their own historical perspective to the field.

REFERENCES

Ackerman, N. W. (1938). The unity of the family. *Archives of Pediatrics, 55*, 51–62.

Ackerman, N. W. (1958). *The psychodynamics of family life.* New York: Basic Books.

Ainsworth, M. D. S. (1973). The development of infant–mother attachment. In B. M. Caldwell & H. N. Ricciuti (Eds.), *Review of child development research* (Vol. 3, pp. 1–94). Chicago: University of Chicago Press.

Anderson, C. M., Reiss, D. J., & Hogarty, G. E. (1986). *Schizophrenia and the family.* New York: Guilford Press.

Aponte, H. J., & VanDeusen, J. M. (1981). Structural family therapy. In A. S. Gurman & D. P. Kniskern (Eds.), *Handbook of family therapy* (pp. 310–360). New York: Brunner/ Mazel.

Asarnow, J. R., Goldstein, M. J., & Ben-Meir, S. (1988). Parental communication deviance in childhood onset schizophrenia spectrum and depressive disorders. *Journal of Child Psychology and Psychiatry, 29*(6), 825–838.

Barton, C., & Alexander, J. F. (1981). Functional family therapy. In A. S. Gurman & D. P. Kniskern (Eds.), *Handbook of family therapy* (pp. 403–443). New York: Brunner/Mazel.

Bateson, D., Jackson, D. D., Haley, J., & Weakland, J. (1956). Towards a theory of schizophrenia. *Behavioral Science, 1,* 251–264.

Baucom, D. H. (1982). A comparison of behavioral contracting and problem-solving/communications training in behavioral marital therapy. *Behavior Therapy, 13,* 162–174

Baucom, D. H., & Epstein, N. (1990). *Cognitive-behavioral marital therapy.* New York: Brunner/Mazel.

Baucom, D. H., Epstein, N., Sayers, S., & Sher, T. G. (1989). The role of cognitions in marital relationships: Definitional, methodological and conceptual issues. *Journal of Consulting and Clinical Psychology, 57*(1), 31–38.

Baumrind, D. (1975). The contributions of the family to the development of competence in children. *Schizophrenia Bulletin, 14,* 12–37.

Beach, S. R., & O'Leary, K. D. (1992). Treating depression in the context of marital discord: Outcome and predictors of response of marital therapy versus cognitive therapy. *Behavior Therapy, 23,* 507–528.

Bee, H. L., Barnard, K. E., Eyres, S. J., Gray, C. A., Hammond, M. A., Spietz, A. L., Snyder, C., & Clark, B. (1982). Predictions of IQ and language skill from perinatal status, child performance, family characteristics and mother–infant interaction. *Child Development, 53,* 1134–1156.

Beutler, L., & Clarkin, J. F. (1990). *Systematic treatment selection: Toward targeted therapeutic interventions.* New York: Brunner/Mazel.

Billings, A. (1979). Conflict resolution in distressed and nondistressed married couples. *Journal of Consulting and Clinical Psychology, 47*(2), 368–376.

Bion, W. R. (1948). Experience in groups. *Human Relations, 1,* 314–329.

Bloch, D., & Simon, R. (1982). *The strength of family therapy: Selected papers of Nathan W. Ackerman.* New York: Brunner/Mazel.

Bowen, M. (1978). *Family therapy in clinical practice.* New York: Jason Aronson.

Bowlby, J. (1949). The study and reduction of group tension in the family. *Human Relations, 2,* 123–128.

Bowlby, J. (1969). *Attachment and loss. Vol. 2: Attachment.* New York: Basic Books.

Bradley, R. H., & Caldwell, B. M. (1980). The relation of home environment, cognitive competence, and IQ among males and females. *Child Development, 51,* 1140–1148.

Broderick, C. B., & Schrader, S. S. (1981). The history of professional marriage and family therapy. In A. S. Gurman & D. P. Kniskern (Eds.), *Handbook of family therapy* (pp. 5–35). New York: Brunner/Mazel.

Brown, G. W., Birley, J. L. T., & Wing, J. K. (1972). Influence of family life on the course of schizophrenic disorders: A replication. *British Journal of Psychiatry, 121,* 241–258.

Brown, G. W., Monck, E. M., Carstairs, G. M., & Wing, J. K. (1962). Influence of family life on the course of schizophrenic illness. *British Journal of Preventive Social Medicine, 16,* 55–68.

Burgess, R. L., & Conger, R. D. (1978). Family interaction in abusive, neglectful, and normal families. *Child Development, 49,* 1163–1173.

Camper, P. M., Jacobson, N. S., Holtzworth-Munroe, A., & Schmaling, K. B. (1988). Causal attributions for interactional behaviors in married couples. *Cognitive Therapy Research, 12,* 195–209.

Clarkin, J. F. (1989). Family education. In A. Bellack (Ed.), *A clinical guide for the treatment of schizophrenia* (pp. 187–205). New York: Plenum.

Clarkin, J. F., & Carpenter, D. (in press). Family therapy outcome and process research. In G. P. Sholovar (Ed.), *Textbook of Family and Marital Therapy.*

Clarkin, J. F., Frances, A., & Perry, S. (1992). Differential therapeutics: Macro and micro levels of treatment planning. In J. Norcross & M. Goldfried (Eds.), *Handbook of psychotherapy integration* (pp. 463–502). New York: Basic Books.

Colapinto, J. (1979). The relative value of empirical evidence. *Family Process, 18,* 427–441.

Dickinson, R. L. (1949). *Human sex anatomy.* Baltimore: Williams & Wilkins. (Revised and expanded in 1949)

Dicks, H. (1967). *Marital tensions.* London: Tavistock.

Doane, J. A., Falloon, I. R. H., Goldstein, M. J., & Mintz, J. (1985). Parental affective style and the treatment of schizphrenia: Predicting course of illness and social functioning. *Archives of General Psychiatry, 42,* 34–42.

Doane, J. A., Goldstein, M. J., Miklowitz, D. J., & Falloon, I. R. H. (1986). The impact of individual and family treatment on the affective climate of families of schizophrenics. *British Journal of Psychiatry, 148,* 279–287.

Doane, J. A., Jones, J. E., Fisher, L., Ritzler, B., Singer, M. T., & Wynne, L. C. (1982). Parental communication deviance as a predictor of competence in children at risk for adult psychiatric disorder. *Family Process*, 21, 211–223.

Doane, J. A., West, K. L., Goldstein, M. J., Rodnick, E. H., & Jones, J. E. (1981). Parental communication deviance and affective style: Predictors of subsequent schizophrenia-spectrum disorders in vulnerable adolescents. *Archives of General Psychiatry*, 38, 679–685.

Elwood, R. W., & Jacobson, N. S. (1982). Spouse agreement in reporting their behavioral interactions: A clinical replication. *Journal of Consulting and Clinical Psychology*, 50, 783–784.

Elwood, R. W., & Jacobson, N. S. (1988). The effects of observational training on spouse agreement about events in their relationship. *Behavior Research Therapy*, 26, 159–167.

Epstein, N. B., & Eidelson, R. J. (1981). Unrealistic beliefs of clinical couples. Their relationship to expectations, goals, and satisfaction. *American Journal of Family Therapy*, 9, 13–22.

Falloon, I., McGill, C., Boyd, J., & Pederson, J. (1987). Family management in the prevention of morbidity of schizophrenia: Social outcome of a two-year longitudinal study. *Psychological Medicine*, 17, 59–66.

Fincham, F. D., & O'Leary, K. D. (1983). Causal inferences for spouse behavior in maritally distressed and nondistressed couples. *Journal of Social and Clinical Psychology*, 1, 42–57.

Fischmann-Havstad, L, & Marston, A. R. (1984). Weight loss maintenance as an aspect of family emotion and process. *British Journal of Clinical Psychology*, 23, 265–271.

Flugel, J. C. (1921). *The psychoanalytic study of the family*. London: Hogarth Press.

Forehand, R., McCombs, T. A., Wierson, M., Brady, G., & Fauber, R. (1990). Role of maternal functioning and parenting skills in adolescent functioning following parental divorce. *Journal of Abnormal Psychology*, 99, 278–283.

Frances, A., Clarkin, J. F., & Perry, S. (1984). *Differential therapeutics: A guide to the art and science of treatment selection in psychiatry*. New York: Brunner/Mazel.

Fromm-Reichmann, F. (1948). Notes on the development of treatment of schizophrenics by psychoanalytic psychotherapy. *Psychiatry*, 11, 263–274.

Gant, B. L., Barnard, J. D., Kuehn, F. E., Jones, H. H., & Christophersen, E. R. (1981). A behaviorally based approach for improving intrafamilial communication patterns. *Journal of Clinical Child Psychology*, 10(2), 102–106.

Garrigan, J. J., & Bambrick, A. F. (1977). Family therapy for disturbed children: Some experimental results in special education. *Journal of Marriage and Family Counseling*, 3(1), 83–93.

Garrigan, J. J., & Bambrick, A. F. (1979). New findings in research on go-between process. *International Journal of Family Therapy*, 1(1), 76–85.

Goldstein, M. J. (1987). Family interaction patterns that antedate the onset of schizophrenia and related disorders: A further analysis of data from a longitudinal prospective study. In K. Hahlweg & M. Goldstein (Eds.), *Understanding major mental disorder: The contribution of family interaction research* (pp. 11–32). New York: Family Process Press.

Goldstein, M. J., Rodnick, E., Evans, J., May, P., & Steinberg, M. (1978). Drug and family therapy in the aftercare of acute schizophrenics. *Archives of General Psychiatry*, 35, 1169–1177.

Goldstein, M. J., Talovic, S. A., & Nuechterlein, K. H. (1990). *Family interaction vs. individual psychopathology: Do they indicate the same processes in the families of schizophrenics?* Paper presented at the Third International Schizophrenia Symposium, Transactional Processes in Onset and Course of Schizophrenic Disorders, Bern, Switzerland.

Gottman, J., Markman, H., & Notarius, C. (1977). The topography of marital conflict: A sequential analysis of verbal and nonverbal behavior. *Journal of Marriage and Family*, 39, 461–477.

Gottman, J., Notarius, C., Markman, H., Bank, S., Yoppi, B., & Rubin, M. E. (1976). Behavior exchange theory and marital decision making. *Journal of Personality and Social Psychology*, 34, 14–23.

Gurman, A. S., Kniskern, D. P., & Pinsof, W. M. (1986). Research on the process and outcome of marital and family therapy. In S. Garfield & A. Bergin (Eds.), *Handbook of psychotherapy and behavior change* (pp. 565–624). New York: Wiley.

Hahlweg, K., Goldstein, M. J., Nuechterlein, K. H., Magana, A. B., Mintz, J., Doane, J. A., Miklowitz, D. J., & Snyder, K. S. (1989). Expressed emotion and patient–relative interaction in families of recent-onset schizophrenics. *Journal of Consulting and Clinical Psychology*, 57, 11–18.

Hahlweg, K., Reisner, L., Kohli, G., Vollmer, M., Schindler, L., & Revenstorf, D. (1984a).

Development and validity of a new system to analyze interpersonal communication (KPI). In K. Hahlweg & N. S. Jacobson (Eds.), *Marital interaction: Analysis and modification* (pp. 182–198). New York: Guilford Press.

Hahlweg, K., Revenstorf, D., & Schindler, L. (1984b). Effects of behavioral marital therapy on couples' communication and problem-solving skills. *Journal of Consulting and Clinical Psychology*, 52(4), 553–566.

Haley, J. (1973). *Uncommon therapy*. New York: Norton.

Haley, J. (1976). *Problem solving therapy*. San Francisco: Jossey-Bass.

Hautzinger, M., Linden, M., & Hoffman, N. (1982). Distressed couples with and without a depressed partner: An analysis of their verbal interaction. *Journal of Behavioral Therapy and Experimental Psychiatry*, 13, 307–314.

Henggeler, S. W., Melton, G. B., & Smith, L. A. (1992). Family preservation using multisystemic therapy: An effective alternative to incarcerating serious juvenile offenders. *Journal of Consulting and Clinical Psychology*, 60, 6(6), 953–961.

Hinchcliffe, M., Hooper, D., Roberts, F. J., & Vaughn, P. W. (1978). The melancholy marriage: An inquiry into the interaction of depression. IV. Disruption. *British Journal of Medical Psychology*, 51, 15–24.

Hoffman, L. (1981). *Foundations of family therapy: A conceptual framework for systems change*. New York: Basic Books.

Holtzworth-Munroe, A., & Jacobson, N. D. (1985). Causal attributions of married couples: When do they search for causes? What do they conclude when they do? *Journal of Personality and Social Psychology*, 48, 1398–1412.

Hooley, J. M., Orley, J., & Teasdale, J. D. (1986). Levels of expressed emotion and relapse in depressed patients. *British Journal of Psychiatry*, 148, 642–647.

Jacob, T., & Tennenbaum, D. L. (1988). *Family assessment: Rationale, methods, and future directions*. New York: Plenum.

Jacobson, N. S., Follette, W. C., & McDonald, D. W. (1982). Reactivity to positive and negative behavior in distressed and nondistressed married couples. *Journal of Consulting and Clinical Psychology*, 50, 706–714.

Jacobson, N. S., McDonald, D. W., Follette, W. C., & Berley, R. A. (1985). Attributional processes in distressed and nondistressed married couples. *Cognitive Therapy Research*, 9, 35–50.

Jacobson, N. S., Waldron, H., & Moore, D. (1980). Toward a behavioral profile of marital distress. *Journal of Consulting and Clinical Psychology*, 48, 696–703.

Johnston, M. H., & Holzman, P. S. (1979). *Assessing schizophrenic thinking*. San Francisco: Jossey-Bass.

Jordan, T. J., & McCormick, N. B. (1987, April). *The role of sex beliefs in intimate relationships*. Paper presented at the annual meeting of the American Association of Sex Educators, Counselors, and Therapists, New York.

Kazdin, A. E., Siegel, T. C., & Bass, D. (1992). Cognitive problem-solving skills training and parent management training in the treatment of antisocial behavior in children. *Journal of Consulting and Clinical Psychology*, 60, 733–747.

Kerr, M. E. (1981). Family systems theory and therapy. In A. S. Gurman & D. P. Kniskern (Eds.), *Handbook of family therapy* (pp. 226–264). New York: Brunner/Mazel.

Kinsey, A. C., Pomeroy, W. B., & Martin, C. F. (1948). *Sexual behavior in the human male*. Philadelphia: Saunders.

Kinsey, A. C., Pomeroy, W. B., Martin, C. F., & Gebhard, P. H. (1953). *Sexual behavior in the human female*. Philadelphia: Saunders.

Klein, N. C., Alexander, J. F., & Parsons, B. V. (1977). Impact of family systems intervention on recidivism and sibling delinquency: A model of primary prevention and program evaluation. *Journal of Consulting and Clinical Psychology*, 45, 469–474.

Klerman, G. L., Weissman, M. M., Rounsaville, B. J., & Chevron, E. S. (1984). *Interpersonal psychotherapy of depression*. New York: Basic Books.

Kopfstein, D. (1972). The effects of accelerating and decelerating consequences on the social behavior of trainable retarded children. *Child Development*, 43, 800–809.

Langsley, D. G., Machotka, P., & Flomenhaft, K. (1971). Avoiding mental hospital admission: A follow-up study. *American Journal of Psychiatry*, 127(10), 127–130.

Leff, J., Kuipers, L., Berkowitz, R., Eberlein-Vries, R., & Sturgeon, D. (1982). A controlled trial of social intervention in the families of schizophrenic patients. *British Journal of Psychiatry*, 141, 121–134.

Leff, J., & Vaughn, C. (1985). *Expressed emotion in families*. New York: Guilford Press.

Levy, D. (1943). *Maternal overprotection*. New York: Columbia University Press.

Lewin, K. (1951). *Field theory in social science*. New York: Harper.

Margolin, G., & Wampold, B. E. (1981). Sequential analysis of conflict and accord in distressed and nondistressed marital partners. *Journal of Consulting and Clinical Psychology, 49,* 554–567.

Markman, H. J. (1981). The prediction of marital distress: A five year followup. *Journal of Consulting and Clinical Psychology, 49,* 760–762.

Marsh, L. C. (1935). Group therapy and the psychiatric clinic. *Journal of Nervous and Mental Disease, 82,* 381–393.

Miklowitz, D. J., Goldstein, M. J., & Falloon, I. R. H. (1983). Premorbid and symptomatic characteristics of schizophrenics from families with high and low levels of expressed emotion. *Journal of Abnormal Psychology, 92,* 359–367.

Miklowitz, D. J., Goldstein, M. J., Nuechterlein, K. H., Snyder, K. S., & Mintz, J. (1988). Family factors and the course of bipolar affective disorder. *Archives of General Psychiatry, 45,* 225–231.

Miklowitz, D. J., & Stackman, D. (1992). Communication deviance in families of schizophrenia and other psychiatric patients: Current state of the construct. *Progress in Experimental Personality and Psychopathology Research, 15,* 1–46.

Miklowitz, D. J., Strachan, A. M., Goldstein, J. A., Snyder, K. S., Hogarty, G. E., & Falloon, I. R. H. (1986). Expressed emotion and communication deviance in the families of schizophrenics. *Journal of Abnormal Psychology, 95,* 60–66.

Minuchin, S. (1974). *Families and family therapy*. Cambridge, MA: Harvard University Press.

Minuchin, S., & Fishman, H. C. (1981). *Family therapy techniques*. Cambridge, MA: Harvard University Press.

Minuchin, S., Montalvo, B., Guerney, B., Rosman, B., & Shumer, F. (1967). *Families of the slums*. New York: Basic Books.

Moreno, J. L. (1945). *Psychodrama*. New York: Beacon House.

Mudd, E. H. (1951). *The practice of marriage counseling*. New York: Association Press.

Mudd, E. H., Stone, A., Karpf, M. J., & Nelson, J. F. (Eds.) (1958). *Marriage counseling: A casebook*. New York: Association Press.

Nichols, M. (1984). *Family therapy: Concepts and methods*. New York: Gardner Press.

Nuechterlein, K. H., Snyder, K. S., Dawson, M. E., Rappe, S., Gitlin, M., & Fogelson, D.

(1986). Expressed emotion, fixed dose fluphenazine decanoate maintenance, and relapse in recent-onset schizophrenia. *Psychopharmacology Bulletin, 22,* 633–639.

Parker, G. (1983). *Parental overprotection: A risk factor in psychosocial development*. New York: Grune & Stratton.

Parker, G., Tupling, H., & Brown, L. B. (1979). A parental bonding instrument. *British Journal of Medical Psychology, 52,* 1–10.

Patterson, G. R. (1971). *Families: Applications of social learning to family life*. Champaign, IL: Research Press.

Patterson, G. R. (1976). The aggressive child: Victim and architect of a coercive system. In E. J. Nash, L. A. Hamerlynck, & L. C. Handy (Eds.), *Behavioral modification and families: 1. Theory and research* (pp. 267–316). New York: Brunner/Mazel.

Patterson, G. R. (1980). Mothers: The unacknowledged victims. *Monographs of the Society for Research in Child Development, 45*(5), 1–64.

Patterson, G. R. (1982). *A social learning approach to family intervention: III. Coercive family process*. Eugene, OR: Castalia.

Patterson, G. R., Capaldi, D., & Bank, L. (1991). An early starter model for predicting delinquency. In D. J. Pepler & K. H. Rubin (Eds.), *The development and treatment of childhood aggression* (pp. 139–168). Hillsdale, NJ: Erlbaum.

Patterson, G. R., & Cobb, J. A. (1971). A dyadic analysis of "aggressive" behaviors. In J. P. Hill (Ed.), *Minnesota symposia on child psychology* (Vol. 5, pp. 72–129). Minneapolis: University of Minnesota Press.

Powers, S. I., Dill, D., Houser, S. T., Noan, G. G., & Jacobson, A. M. (1985). Coping strategies of families of seriously ill adoelscents. *Journal of Early Adolescence, 5,* 101–113.

Pretzer, J. L., Epstein, N., & Fleming, B. (1985). *The marital attitude survey: A measure of dysfunctional attributions and expectancies*. Unpublished manuscript.

Raue, J., & Spence, S. H. (1985). Group versus individual applications of reciprocity training for parent-youth conflict. *Behavior Research and Therapy, 23*(2). 177–186.

Raush, H. L., Barry, W. A., Hertel, R. K., & Swain, M. A. (1974). *Communication, conflict and marriage*. San Francisco: Jossey-Bass.

Revenstorf, D., Hahlweg, K., Schindler, L., & Vogel, B. (1984). Interactional analysis of marital conflict. In K. Hahlweg & N. S. Jacobson (Eds.),

Marital interaction: Analysis and modification (pp. 159–181). New York: Guilford Press.

Richardson, H. B. (1945). *Patients have families.* New York: Commonwealth Fund.

Robinson, E. A., & Jacobson, N. S. (1987). Social learning theory and family psychopathology: A Kantian model in behaviorism? In T. Jacob (Ed.), *Family interaction and psychopathology* (pp. 117–162). New York: Plenum.

Ro-Trock, G. K., Wellisch, D. K., & Schoolar, J. C. (1977). A family therapy outcome study in an inpatient setting. *American Journal of Orthopsychiatry, 47,* 514–522.

Russell, G. F. M., Szmukler, G. I., Dare, C., & Eisler, I. (1987). An evaluation of family therapy in anorexia nervosa and bulimia nervosa. *Archives of General Psychiatry, 44,* 1047–1056.

Sager, C. J. (1976). *Marriage contracts and couple therapy.* New York: Brunner/Mazel.

Sallows, G. (1972). *Comparative responsiveness of normal and deviant children to naturally occurring consequences.* Unpublished doctoral dissertation, University of Oregon, Eugene.

Schaap, C. (1984). A comparison of the interaction of distressed and nondistressed married couples in a laboratory situation: Literature survey, methodological issues, and an empirical investigation. In K. Hahlweg & N. S. Jacobson (Eds.), *Marital interaction: Analysis and modification* (pp. 133–158). New York: Guilford Press.

Shaw, D. (1971). *Family maintenance schedules for deviant behaviors.* Unpublished doctoral dissertation, University of Oregon, Eugene.

Simon, R. (1992). *One on one: Conversations with the shapers of family therapy.* New York: Guilford Press.

Singer, M., & Wynne, L. (1963). Differentiating characteristics of parents of childhood schizophrenics, childhood neurotics, and young adult schizophrenics. *American Journal of Psychiatry, 120,* 234–243.

Singer, M., & Wynne, L. (1965a). Thought disorder and family relations of schizophrenics. III. Methodology using projective techniques. *Archives of General Psychiatry, 12,* 187–200.

Singer, M., & Wynne, L. (1965b). Thought disorder and family relations of schizophrenics. IV. Results and implications. *Archives of General Psychiatry, 12,* 201–212.

Skynner, A. C. R. (1976). *Systems of family and marital psychotherapy.* New York: Brunner/Mazel.

Snyder, J. J. (1977). Reinforcement analysis of interaction in problem and nonproblem families. *Journal of Abnormal Psychology, 86,* 528–535.

Stanton, M. D. (1981). Strategic approaches to family therapy. In A. S. Gurman & D. P. Kniskern (Eds.), *Handbook of family therapy* (pp. 361–402). New York: Brunner/Mazel.

Stierlin, H. (1977). *Psychoanalysis and family therapy.* New York: Jason Aronson.

Stover, L., & Guerney, J. (1967). The efficacy of training procedures for mothers in filial therapy. *Psychotherapy: Theory, Research and Practice, 4,* 110–115.

Strachan, A. M., Feingold, D., Goldstein, M. J., Miklowitz, D. J., & Nuechterlein, K. H. (1989). Is expressed emotion an index of a transactional process? II. Patient's coping style. *Family Process, 28,* 169–181.

Strachan, A. M., Leff, J. P., Goldstein, M. J., Doane, J. A., & Burtt, C. (1986). Emotional attitudes and direct communication in the families of schizophrenics: A cross-national replication. *British Journal of Psychiatry, 149,* 279–287.

Stuart, R. B., Jayaratne, S., & Tripodi, T. (1976). Changing adolescent deviant behavior through reprogramming the behaviour of parents and teachers: An experimental evaluation. *Canadian Journal of Behavioural Science, 8,* 132–144.

Szykula, S. A., Morris, S. B., Sudweeks, C., & Sayger, T. (1987). Child-focused behavior and strategic therapies: Outcome comparisons. *Psychotherapy, 24,* 546–551.

Taplin, P. (1974). *Changes in parental consequation as a function of intervention.* Unpublished doctoral dissertation, University of Oregon, Eugene.

Tarrier, N., Barrowclough, C., Vaughn, C., & Bamrah, J. S. (1988). The community management of schizophrenia. *British Journal of Psychiatry, 153,* 532–542.

Tomm, K. (1983). The old hat doesn't fit. *Family Therapy Networker, 7,* 39–41.

Vaughn, C. E., & Leff, J. P. (1976). The influence of family and social factors on the course of psychiatric illness. *British Journal of Psychiatry, 129,* 125–137.

Vaughn, C. E, Snyder, K. S., Jones, S., Freeman, W. B., & Falloon, I. R. H. (1984). Family factors in schizophrenic relapse: Replication in California of British research on expressed emotion. *Archives of General Psychiatry, 41,* 1169–1177.

Velligan, D. I., Goldstein, M. J., & Falloon, I. R. H.

(1991, April). *The impact of individual and family treatment on communication deviance in the families of schizophrenic patients.* Paper presented at the International Congress on Schizophrenia Research, Tucson, AZ.

Velligan, D. I., Goldstein, M. J., Nuechterlein, K. H., Miklowitz, D. J., & Ranlett, G. (1990). Can communication deviance be measured in a family problem-solving interaction? *Family Process, 29,* 213–226.

Vincent, J. P., Weiss, R. L., & Birchler, G. R. (1975). A behavioral analysis of problem solving in distressed and nondistressed married and stranger dyads. *Behavior Therapy, 6,* 475–487.

Wachtel, E. F., & Wachtel, P. L. (1986). *Family dynamics in individual psychotherapy.* New York: Guilford Press.

Wahler, R. G., & Dumas, J. E. (1987). Family factors in childhood psychology: Toward a coercion-neglect model. In T. Jacob (Ed.), *Family interaction and psychopathology* (pp. 581–627). New York: Plenum.

Watzlawick, P., Weakland, J., & Fisch, R. (1974).

Change: Principles of problem formation and problem resolution. New York: Norton.

Wynne, L. C., & Singer, M. T. (1963a). Thought disorder and family relations of schizophrenics. I. A research strategy. *Archives of General Psychiatry, 9,* 191–198.

Wynne, L. C., & Singer, M. T. (1963b). Thought disorder and family relations of schizophrenics: II. A classification of forms of thinking. *Archives of General Psychiatry, 9,* 199–206.

Wynne, L. C., Singer, M. T., Bartko, J., & Toohey, M. (1976). Schizophrenics and their families. Recent research on parental communication. In J. M. Tanner (Ed.), *Developments in psychiatric research* (pp. 254–286). London: Hodder and Stoughton.

Zuk, G. H. (1971). *Family therapy: A triadic-based approach.* New York: Behavioral Publications.

Zweig-Frank, H., & Paris, J. (1991). Parents' emotional neglect and overprotection according to recollections of patients with borderline personality disorder. *American Journal of Psychiatry, 148,* 648–651.

13

Family Systems Therapy in Practice: A Systemic Couples Therapy for Problem Drinking

Michael Rohrbaugh
Varda Shoham
Carol Spungen
Peter Steinglass

This chapter describes a systemic couples therapy for problem drinking. The therapy is systemic because it (1) focuses on the relational context of problem drinking, not solely on the individual who drinks; (2) assumes that drinking problems are maintained by ongoing cycles of social interaction; (3) adapts treatment to the client family's world view; and (4) respects reluctance to change. Applying these systemic principles to drinking problems is both promising and difficult. On the one hand, there is growing evidence that working with the drinker's marriage and family relationships yields more durable treatment outcomes (McGrady et al., 1986). On the other hand, problem drinking is a magnet for personal attributions of badness (the moral model) and madness (the disease model) that can easily fog the lens of a systemic perspective.

We have operationalized this systemic couples therapy in the form of a treatment manual that integrates ideas and techniques from a variety of systemic treatment approaches, including the alcoholic family model of Steinglass, Bennett, Wolin, and Reiss (1987); the interactional view of the Mental Research Institute in Palo Alto, California (Fisch, 1986; Fisch, Weakland, & Segal, 1982); coconstruc-

tivist approaches such as solution-focused therapy (Berg & Miller, 1992) and White and Epston's (1990) externalization techniques; contributions of the early Milan group applied to alcohol treatment (Borwick, 1991; Lewis, 1987); and structural/strategic family interventions developed specifically for problem drinking (Bepko & Krestan, 1985; Elkin, 1984; Treadway, 1989).

The manual, which was developed for a federally funded research project,[1] focuses on couples in which the male partner is a problem drinker (Beutler, Patterson, Jacob, Shoham, Yost, & Rohrbaugh, 1993). The research protocol requires that couples receive 20 therapy sessions over a 6- to 9-month period. The first 12 sessions are scheduled fairly close together in a 6- to 9-week acute treatment phase, with the remaining 8 meetings spread out over about 4 months. For a couple to enter the project, the male drinker must meet DSM-III-R criteria for moderate to severe alcohol dependence. The presence of other problems or comorbid conditions—including severe marital dysfunction—does not exclude a couple from participating, but problem drinking must be a primary complaint and the partners must be married or in a committed relationship.

Admittedly, the research context imposes certain constraints on the manual's applicability. First, treatment focuses mainly on couples, while family systems approaches often have a broader focus and involve other family members in treatment. Second, we have so far used this approach only with identified male drinkers and not at all with females who may face different issues in recovery (see Treadway, 1989).[2] Third, the 20-session format limits treatment to a shorter time frame than many clinicians consider ideal. Finally, although the model is now undergoing a fairly rigorous clinical trial and appears to show promise, the number of complete cases to date is too small to allow us to report meaningful outcome results.

After an introductory section on systemic views of problem drinking, the main body of this chapter describes the phases of the model itself: consultation, treatment, and restabilization. A subsequent section touches on some implementation issues that have arisen in the first year and a half of our work with the model; another uses data from a recent Q-sort study to review what practitioners of our approach find most distinctive about it, highlighting points of convergence with and divergence from the widely used 12-step (disease) model. A final section considers the model's general applicability.

SYSTEMIC MODELS OF PROBLEM DRINKING

From a systemic perspective, alcohol problems are inextricably interwoven with the family and social context in which they occur. While not discounting the individual's history, systems models assume that drinking problems, like other problems, persist primarily as an aspect of current, ongoing interaction between the drinker and his or her significant others (Weakland, Watzlawick, Fisch, & Bodin, 1974). The origin of a problem is less relevant than how it persists, since the system both maintains and is maintained by the symptom (Minuchin, 1974). The boundaries of the person are somewhat muted in this approach, because the variables crucial to treatment reside not so much within people as between them. Accordingly, the focus of alcohol treatment from a systemic perspective is not the individual drinker but the system of relationships in which drinking is embedded.

Like individual models of alcoholism, systemic models vary on several important dimensions. In their formulations of problem maintenance, some systemic approaches take into account broad cultural influences and family dynamics extending back several generations, while others focus narrowly on the presenting problem and how those most concerned try to solve it. Some models are primarily concerned with behavior (doing) and others with what behavior means (viewing), and some approaches define family pathology, while others (non-normative) do not. A major issue dividing systemic models of alcoholism is the extent to which they assume that drinking serves an adaptive function in family relationships: While some systems therapists embrace the idea that symptoms serve functions for families (Steinglass, 1980; Steinglass et al., 1987), others reject this notion altogether (Fisch et al., 1982; Berg & Miller, 1992).

Systemic models also offer diverse approaches to intervention. In some, the therapist intervenes directly, on the basis of a specific strategy or plan, to interrupt problem patterns as quickly and efficiently as possible (Haley, 1976; Weakland & Fisch, 1992), while in others, he or she stays neutral or curious about the problem and avoids any attempt to influence clients deliberately (Hoffman, 1981). Some educate family members about dysfunctional family patterns, alternative coping skills, or even the nature of disorders such as alcoholism, while others work within the clients' own belief system with the goal of helping them construct a more workable reality. Despite their many variations, systemic therapies do have in common the idea that the locus of a problem transcends the individual and that the focus of treatment should therefore be relational—it should address the context of drinking.

Both functional and descriptive formulations of problem maintenance inform our systemic approach to problem drinking. Toward the functional end of the spectrum is Steinglass et al.'s (1987; Steinglass, Tislenko, & Reiss, 1985) *alcoholic family* model, which grew from clinical observations that problem drinking often has adaptive consequences in family relationships. These investigators noted apparent benefits of "wet" family interaction, compared to "dry" (sober) interaction, that varied from family to family (e.g., increased or decreased intimacy or affect). According to Steinglass et al., alcohol maintains a kind of stability in these families, even though such stability is ultimately dysfunctional. The defining characteristic of an alcoholic family is that drinking becomes the central organizing principle governing family routines, rituals, and problem-solving strategies. Treatment therefore requires a *family detoxification* process that redefines alcohol as a foreign invader and removes it from the household and family system. Because cessation of drinking is potentially disruptive to the family, successful treatment often requires a realignment of family processes.

Descriptive variants of the systemic approach include the problem-focused interactional therapy developed at Palo Alto's Mental Research Institute (Fisch et al., 1982) and the solution-focused therapy developed at the Milwaukee Brief Family Therapy Center (de Shazer, 1988; O'Hanlon & Weiner-Davis, 1989). The latter has been applied to drinking problems by Berg and Miller (1992). The two models have common theoretical roots and focus both on interaction patterns that inadvertently maintain problem drinking and on exceptions to these patterns that imply resources for change. Neither assumes that drinking is necessarily functional or adaptive for the people involved, yet both aim to change the interaction sequences in which drinking is embedded. To oversimplify, the main difference is that problem-focused (Palo Alto) therapists intervene by asking clients to do what constitutes "less of the same," while solution-focused (Milwaukee) therapists ask them to do "more of what's different."

Our integrative systemic therapy for drinking problems incorporates elements of these diverse systemic approaches. Thus, from Steinglass and

colleagues, we draw the concepts of family-level detoxification, family identity, and alcohol as an invader of family life; from the problem-focused therapy of Weakland et al. comes the idea of problem–solution loops and the techniques of using clients' world view or *position* and restraining them from precipitous change or celebration; and from the solution-focused approach of de Shazer, Berg, and colleagues we draw techniques that call attention to clients' strengths and resources. Also important are contributions of the early Milan team, especially the key concept of neutrality, applied to alcohol treatment by Lewis (1987) and Borwick (1991), and the technique of circular questioning (Flueridas, Nelson, & Rosenthal, 1986; Penn, 1985). Finally, we borrow White and Epston's (1990) externalization tactics to build collaboration against alcohol as an external invader, and we rely heavily on structural and strategic family therapy techniques in the restabilization phase and to counter resistance (Bepko & Krestan, 1985; Berenson, 1979; Elkin, 1984; Treadway, 1989). Our goal in putting together diverse ideas and techniques was to construct an internally consistent, integrative therapy that includes leading systemic contributions to treating alcohol problems. To avoid procedural confusion (given the theoretical incompatibilities of some of the models from which we were drawing), we attempted to specify guidelines for what to do when, and rationales for emphasizing some principles and procedures while deemphasizing others.[3] The resulting integration undoubtedly reflects our own theoretical preferences and biases. Not surprisingly, some of the issues and rough spots we have encountered in implementing the manual involve "tensions of integration"; several of these will be noted in a later section.

Another consideration in framing a systemic treatment for problem drinking was how this would differ from more established treatment approaches such as the 12-step model of Alcoholics Anonymous. Our initial thinking was that, compared to traditional (12-step) alcohol treatment, our systemic approach would emphasize (1) current interactional determinants of drinking problems rather than personality deficits and co-pathologies resulting from past experience in a dysfunctional family; (2) understanding and using clients' own language or reality rather than teaching a new belief system; (3) not confronting denial directly, but using neutrality to build collaboration, shift responsibility to the client, and avoid a more-of-the-same solution; and (4) family therapy as collaborative and joint rather than separate and equal. Most of these differences were borne out in a Q-sort study summarized at the end of the chapter.

CLINICAL PRINCIPLES AND PROCEDURES

Overview

Ideally, therapy proceeds according to the three sequential phases schematized in Figure 13-1: the consultation phase (sessions 1–6), the treatment phase (sessions 6–12), and the restabilization phase (sessions 13–20). During the initial consultation phase the therapist and

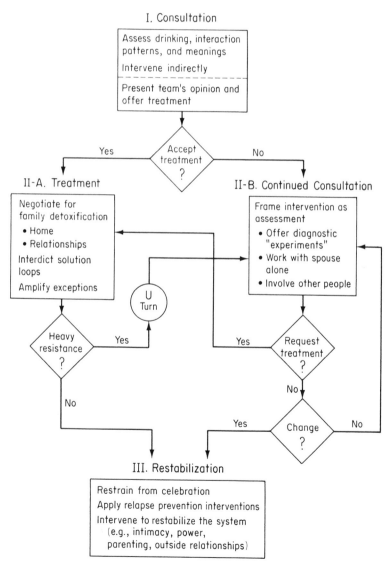

FIGURE 13.1. A systemic therapy for problem drinking.

team conduct a systemic assessment, begin to intervene indirectly with circular and solution-focused questions intended to introduce the possibility of change, and offer the couple "treatment" while remaining neutral about whether they should choose it. The therapist makes a thorough assessment of the extent and consequences of drinking and (especially) of the family interaction patterns in which drinking is embedded, since these are assumed to play a critical role in problem maintenance. He or she solicits details about exceptions to problems, such as how the couple manages to make things go well or keep them from getting worse. The goal is to understand not only what clients *do* but also how they *view* themselves and their situation (e.g., what drinking means in their relationship and in the broader familial/cultural context). Throughout this phase, the therapist attempts to establish an empathic, collaborative relationship with the clients *as a couple*; he or she also maintains a posture of neutrality by not aligning with either partner against the other and not directly advocating sobriety or change.

In the sixth session, the therapist presents the consultation team's opinion and offers treatment. This opinion (1) compliments the couple for dealing with a difficult situation, (2) highlights the specific and serious ways in which alcohol has invaded their family life, and (3) acknowledges that change will be difficult and may have some unexpected negative effects. To proceed, the couple must actively *choose* treatment—which means choosing to change their relationship with alcohol. If one or both spouses are ambivalent about treatment or unwilling to make a clear commitment, the therapist is careful not to push or sell recovery. Instead, he or she respects the clients' ambivalence and proposes further study of the issue, thus setting the stage for indirect intervention framed as continued consultation.

If the couple does choose treatment, the therapist shifts from a neutral stance to align with them against alcohol as an external invader of family life. The main component of treatment is *family detoxification*, through which the therapist helps the couple negotiate a series of agreements about dealing with alcohol. For most couples, this requires establishing an official quitting date, and then making their home, and often their social contacts, alcohol free. Family detoxification usually involves rehearsing difficult social situations, meeting with other family members, using meanings and metaphors identified in the assessment phase, and encouraging the couple to notify key relatives and friends of their commitment to change. Other, more strategic treatment components involve interdicting interaction patterns that inadvertently support drinking: The therapist frames specific tasks and suggestions in terms compatible with clients' own position (Fisch et al., 1982) and amplifies exceptions to the problem using solution-focused interview techniques (Berg & Miller, 1992). These strategic and solution-focused tactics serve to supplement the more formal process of family detoxification. They are applied *along with* family detoxification and put to good use in later phases of therapy as well.

A key principle in the systems manual is to avoid confronting resistance or denial directly. Thus, in the consultation phase, maintaining neutrality helps to build collaboration and gives clients the responsibility for choosing change. If resistance arises in the treatment phase (e.g., if clients don't keep an agreement), the therapist's first approach is to reframe noncompliance positively, as partial success or as understandable reluctance to change too quickly; the therapist may also take a "one-down" position by accepting blame for going too fast or not being clear. If resistance continues, the therapist is likely to announce a U-turn (after consulting with the clinical team) and recommend further consultation to explore whether change is, after all, a good idea. At this point—or if the couple does not choose treatment in the first place—intervention shifts to strategic and structural tactics such as prescribing a controlled drinking experiment, intensifying the restraint-from-change stance, seeing the spouse alone, or involving other family members or friends. While the main goal of these tactics is to lead couples back to family detoxification, it is also possible—though less likely—that positive outcomes will occur without the couple's ever choosing to participate in treatment per se.

The final phase of therapy—restabilization and relapse prevention—is designed to help the couple deal with the predictably difficult consequences of sobriety and change. Understanding how wet interaction may have been adaptive for the couple sometimes suggests ways of helping them stay dry. Here the therapeutic focus is on intrafamilial issues such as intimacy, sexuality, parenting, extended family relationships, and the marital power balance, as well as finding or creating outside relationships not organized around drinking. The therapeutic stance remains one of gentle restraint, emphasizing low expectations while experimenting with new ways of relating. Special attention is given to reframing and rehearsal interventions designed to make relapse not only less likely but also less catastrophic.

Phase I: Consultation

The main goals of the consultation phase are (1) to obtain assessment information necessary to develop an effective opinion and intervention plan, (2) to begin to intervene indirectly with solution-focused and circular questions intended to introduce the possibility of change, and (3) to offer the couple treatment aimed at helping them change their relationship with alcohol. Guidelines for this phase are more specific than those for the later treatment and restabilization phases and can be summarized on a session-to-session basis.[4]

Session 1: Problems and Solutions

After a brief social stage, the therapist makes the transition to business by explaining the format of therapy and telling the couple in general terms what to expect. He or she explains the team format (wherein other project therapists and the supervisor discuss each case in detail), the scheduling of sessions, the distinction between consultation and treatment, confidentiality, and missed-appointment policies—answering questions, balancing attention

to each spouse, and working to establish an empathic stance that will continue throughout therapy.

The first assessment task is to define the problem and clarify the clients' complaints. The therapist begins by asking in a general way what brought the clients to therapy at this particular time, and then queries each spouse specifically about how he or she sees the problem—and whether, in his or her view, there *is* a problem. The therapist does not expect or press the spouses to agree. The next step is to explore more systematically each of the stated complaints, beginning with what the couple considers most pressing. (Ideally, this is the husband's drinking, but couples often have other agendas related to problems in their marriage; hence, we make clear to clients that, while our primary focus will be problems related to alcohol, we will try to address other problems too.) To understand complaints in behavioral terms, the therapist asks for specific examples and seeks to understand where, when, and how long complaint behaviors occur. For example, a complaining but defensive husband might be asked, "What did your wife *do* when she criticized your drinking last week?", "What happened then?", "How did you get her to stop?" An important guideline is for the therapist to have enough details to know what the problem might look like on film: "If we had a video of this, what would I see?" A related approach to clarifying a complaint is to ask what improvement will look like. For example, "What would he (or she, or the two of you) be doing differently that would let you know that this (the complaint) is taking a turn for the better?"

Whether or not drinking is the couple's primary complaint, the therapist explores their experience with alcohol and other substances in some detail. We clarify what, where, when, how much, and with whom each spouse drinks, inquiring about the wife's drinking habits as well as the husband's. Included are questions about the severity of drinking (e.g., blackouts, morning drinking, job problems) and use of other substances such as marijuana and cocaine. We also ask about history: When did drinking become a problem for them? Who was the first to notice? How have the drinking patterns changed over time?—although the history is generally less important than what the clients are doing now. In this phase, the therapist pays close attention to the specific ways alcohol has invaded or disrupted the couple's marriage and family life, yet is careful to maintain neutrality: His or her task is not to educate the clients about their dysfunctional behavior but to gather evidence to support the alcohol-as-external-invader metaphor that will be presented with the team's opinion in session 6.

A special problem arises when the drinker (or couple) states at the beginning of therapy that the drinking has stopped or implied that it is no longer a problem. Here we want to acknowledge the clients' optimism but at the same time express concern about premature celebration: "I'm pleased about this positive sign, but in our experience, such changes are often temporary; in fact, some couples find that quitting is only the beginning of their problems." This is a variant of the "two voices" or "restraint from celebration" intervention often used later, in the restabilization phase (see Treadway, 1989).

With a clear picture of the couple's major complaints, the therapist's next task is to understand the patterns of interaction that surround—and help to maintain—those complaints. This follows from the systemic assumption that, regardless of how problems originate, they persist as an aspect of current, ongoing social interaction (Weakland et al., 1974). We further assume that the most relevant interaction sequences revolve around well-intentioned attempts by the people involved to solve the problem. Thus, an important strategic goal is for the therapist to identify—and ultimately interrupt—problem-maintaining solutions applied by the couple and sometimes by others with whom they interact. The most direct way to investigate problem–solution loops is to ask what each spouse has been doing to deal with various complaints, especially those related to drinking. If there are multiple complaints, it may be necessary to track solution patterns for each one separately, although there will often

be a common theme or basic thrust to what people are doing (e.g., nagging, attempting to control, talking or not talking about the problem). Following the Palo Alto Brief Therapy model, the therapist's task is to identify specific interaction sequences in which a more-of-the-same solution leads to more of the problem, leading to more of the solution, and so on. The most relevant problem-maintaining solutions are current, but solutions tried and discarded in the past should be investigated as well, since these may give hints about what has worked before (and may again). For example, a wife who in the past had taken a hard line with her husband about not drinking at the dinner table later reversed this stance because she did not want to be controlling. As his drinking problem worsened, she dealt with it less and less directly by busying herself in other activities or retreating to her study to meditate. Careful inquiry revealed that the former hard-line approach, though distasteful, had actually worked; when the wife set limits, the husband controlled his drinking. By relabeling her former stance as "caring" and "reassuring" to the husband, the therapist was later able to help the wife reverse her stance in a way that broke the problem cycle. This example also makes another point: Although problem-maintaining solutions usually involve someone doing something, what someone *doesn't* do (e.g., comment on a loved one's drinking) can also be important. in any case, the therapist's objective here is simply to recognize problem-maintaining solution patterns; it is neither necessary nor helpful at this stage to point them out to the couple.

Although marital interaction is our main focus, it is also relevant to inquire about the solution efforts of other family members (parents, siblings, children) and friends. For example, how does the husband's mother (son, brother, boss, best friend, etc.) handle his drinking? What does he or she say and do? What happens then? Although intervention will focus primarily on the couple, interaction sequences involving other people may become targets for intervention as well. Thus, it is important to know about solution patterns in the broader system, though these will generally not need to be tracked as closely as sequences involving just the couple.

If the spouses' interaction in the session mirrors what happens or might happen at home, a useful tactic is to shift the focus from "here and now" to "there and then." For example, if the wife pursues or accuses and the husband distances or denies, the therapist comments on the pattern and asks if the dance is familiar: Is this what happens at home? Do they do this often? In what situations? How does the dance develop and how does it end? The goal at this point is not to provoke intensity or restructure the marital relationship directly, but rather to understand as specifically as possible what the spouses are doing (and how they view what they are doing). Thus, while the therapist does not encourage enactment of problem sequences in the session, he or she uses their occurrence to explore what happens in the couple's natural environment.

Although the main reason for tracking sequences and solution loops is to arrive at a descriptive formulation of problem maintenance, information relevant to a functional formulation can also be obtained. Comparing wet interaction sequences when someone has been drinking to dry sequences when people are sober (Leipman, Silvia, & Nirenberg, 1989) often suggests hypotheses about possible adaptive consequences of drinking for the family—for example, increasing or decreasing intimacy or affect (Steinglass, 1980, 1981). This material may be useful in constructing the balanced team opinion and in planning for the restabilization phase, when the couple will be working to establish a satisfactory alcohol-free relationship. We hasten to add, however, that hypothesizing about the function of symptoms requires more inference and speculation than tracking sequences and problem–solution loops and should not distract the therapist from being clear about what the clients are actually *doing*.

In addition to what clients are doing, it is important to understand how they are *viewing* themselves, each other, the problem, and therapy. Clients' views are used in several ways. First, their views of the advantages—and especially the disadvantages—of giving up alcohol

will be important in preparing the team's opinion for session 6. Since most clients prefer to emphasize the advantages of giving up alcohol, the therapist questions them closely about possible difficulties and unforeseen disadvantages. What will be most difficult about being sober? What implications will this have for their relationships with friends, family, and—most important—each other? Second, intervening to change problem-maintaining interaction patterns will depend on framing therapeutic tasks and suggestions in terms compatible with clients' own position (Fisch et al., 1982; Weakland & Fisch, 1992). Assessing client position depends mainly on paying careful attention to what they say (e.g., "How do they see themselves and want to be seen by others?", "What do they hold near and dear?"); it is also illuminating to ask for their best guess about *why* the various problems are happening, including why they think the husband drinks and why they handle the problem the way they do. Third, meanings and metaphors are key ingredients in reinforcing the clients' identity as a couple and in helping them join together against alcohol as an external invader of their relationship. To lay the groundwork for this central therapeutic metaphor, the therapist asks early on about the couple's view of the extent to which they *control* alcohol's intrusion into their lives, using questions of the form "What percent of the time do you control drinking and what percent of the time does drinking control you as a couple?"

The most important client views concern their *customership* for therapy and their readiness for change. Although much about customership will be known from the way the clients have presented themselves so far, direct questions about who is more motivated to change and who is more optimistic that this therapy will help should make this crucial aspect of the clients' position clearer. It is also important to understand how (if at all) the clients sought help in the past, what they found helpful or unhelpful, how the helper(s) viewed their problems, and how the therapy ended. We are especially interested in their experiences with alcohol treatment programs, including Alcoholics Anonymous and Alanon.

In the last 15–20 minutes of session 1, the therapist explores *exceptions* to problems. The objective in this solution-focused phase of the interview is to ask questions in a way that highlights for the couple possible resources and solutions to their dilemma (Berg & Miller, 1992; de Shazer, 1985, 1988; Lipchik & de Shazer, 1986; O'Hanlon & Weiner-Davis, 1989). For example:

- What is different about the times when the two of you enjoy life without alcohol? How do you get that to happen?
- What was your longest period of sobriety? How did you accomplish that?
- What is an example of time that usually would have been a drinking time but wasn't? How did you do that?
- Tell me about a problem that the two of you as a couple handled well in the past. How did you do that?

We also ask de Shazer et al.'s "miracle question" to orient clients toward a time in the future when the problem no longer exists:

> Suppose that one night, while you are asleep, there is a miracle and the problem that brought you into therapy is solved. However, because you are asleep you don't know that the miracle has already happened. When you wake up in the morning, what will be different that will tell you that this miracle has taken place? What else? (Berg & Miller, 1992, p. 13)

To make the prospect of a healthy, alcohol-free future more vivid, the therapist presses for details, asking, for example, "What will you be doing that is different?", "What else?" (see Berg & Miller, 1992, pp. 77–82, for examples). How clients answer such solution-focused questions is often less important than how the questions are asked, since the purpose is less to gather information than to seed ideas about possible change. This style of interviewing is an important vehicle for change in later phases of therapy as well.

The session closes with the following solution-focused homework assignment: "Between now and our next meeting, pay attention to what it is about your relationship you would like to continue or preserve. In other words, what would you like *not* to change?" The couple may discuss or not discuss this with each other, as they wish. They may also make notes or not make notes, but the therapist will want to know what they came up with at the next session.

Session 2: The Clients as a Couple

Parts of session 2 are used to follow up on the homework assignment, clarify unfinished business from session 1, and extend solution-focused, indirect intervention. The main purpose of this session is to understand, explore, and reinforce the clients' relationship *as a couple*. A simple, specific guideline underscoring this point is that the therapist uses the phrase "you as a couple" as much as possible.

At this point, the therapist pursues one or more of the following options: He or she may conduct a semistructured *oral history interview*, tracing the evolution of the couple's relationship. A second option is a *couple identity exercise* that builds on the positive set established by the solution-focused homework task and brings into focus how the clients view themselves as a couple. Briefly, the therapist asks each spouse to "think of two or three words, images, or phrases that capture the *strength* of your relationship—its values, flavor, and unique style," and then asks them each to recount an incident or story that illustrates what they mean. Depending on the role of alcohol, the therapist asks how the story would have been different if the husband had or had not been drinking. A third option is an experiential *sculpting exercise* that further illuminates the couple's problem-maintaining solution patterns at a symbolic or metaphorical level (Papp, 1983) and sets the stage for later interventions aimed at externalizing alcohol as an unwelcome third party in the couple's relationship.

Session 3: Individual Sessions with Each Partner

In session 3 the therapist meets with the spouses (or partners) separately, taking care to spend about the same amount of time with each of them. The main goals are to assess (1) each partner's commitment to the marriage (or relationship), (2) whether one spouse feels intimidated by the other, and (3) whether there is actual or potential physical abuse. These meetings can also be used to clarify complaints, patterns of problem maintenance, and each client's position on issues relevant to therapy. The therapist begins by asking if there is anything that spouse would like to add to what has been discussed, or if there is anything the therapist should know that might be easier to talk about alone. If either spouse asks that a disclosure be treated confidentially, the therapist explains that, while he or she prefers not to share confidences, it is necessary to preserve the freedom to do what he or she feels is in the best interest of the couple and each spouse. If clients cannot trust the therapist in this way, they are advised not to make sensitive disclosures.

We address commitment to the marriage directly with questions such as "Do you love this person?", "Do you want your marriage to continue and thrive?", "Are you optimistic that this will happen?" Although the therapist does not ask specifically about extramarital affairs, he or she is attuned to the possibility that there may be one. If a spouse is ambivalent about staying in the marriage, the therapist asks if he or she will agree to give the marriage an honest try, at least for the duration of therapy. If the spouse is unwilling to do this, the therapist consults with the supervisory team about whether to offer the usual treatment.

It is crucial to assess intimidation and possible physical abuse, especially with the wife. Here, too, we are direct: "Is your husband ever violent or abusive when he drinks or at other times?", "Do you ever fear for your safety?", "For the safety of the children?", "Do you often feel you can't say what you feel because of how he might react?" The same kinds of questions are asked of the husband. Ideally, concerns about intimidation and potential violence can be deferred until the treatment phase, when the couple begins to negotiate for change. If this seems indicated, the therapist expresses

concern about the wife's safety and discusses with her the possibility of raising these issues later in therapy. If a pattern of intimidation is present, individual sessions may also be indicated later to protect or empower the spouse. On the other hand, if the husband is still actively drinking in the consultation phase and there is evidence of clear and present danger to the wife or someone else, the therapist acts much sooner (after consulting with the supervisory team).

Session 4: The Broader System

This session broadens the consultation lens to encompass the couple's family and social networks. The main goal is to understand how the couple's drinking and relationship problems fit the broader system. A secondary goal is further indirect intervention through circular questioning.

The couple and therapist first construct a family genogram covering at least three generations, from the couple's grandparents to their own children and grandchildren (McGoldrick & Gerson, 1985). The genogram includes information about (1) the cast of characters (family members' bio-legal relationships, demographic and personality characteristics); (2) family relational patterns (closeness, distance, conflict, influence, etc.); (3) family member functioning (medical, emotional, and behavior problems, especially drinking problems); (4) the nature and timing of important family events; and (5) information about significant friends, coworkers, and helpers. After defining the cast of characters, the therapist asks a series of questions about family relationships and family member functioning. For example:

Of all the people we've talked about
• Are any people especially close or not on speaking terms?
• Whose opinions do you most respect? Who do family members most often turn to for advice?
• Who in the family would you say is having the most problems these days?

- Who are the drinkers in the family? Who are the teetotalers? Has anyone had a problem with drinking? What did they do about it? Who was most concerned? How was the problem resolved?
  - Who outside the family is most influential in your lives? With whom do you spend most time? Where do they stand on drinking?

This information has specific applications in later phases of treatment. For example, knowing who is influential in the broader network will have implications for whom the couple should later notify of their commitment to change. Understanding family beliefs and coalition patterns will often be useful in the restabilization phase of treatment, or earlier, when strategic or structural interventions are required to deal with heavy resistance.

The transition to circular questions is a natural extension of the preceding genogram questions, the goals being (1) to explore systemic hypotheses about how the couple's difficulties with drinking fit the larger system; (2) to examine possible consequences of change that will be useful in developing the team's balanced (neutral) opinion; and (3) to challenge indirectly the couple's problem-supporting premises and, by implication, suggest avenues to change (Flueridas et al., 1986; Lipchik & de Shazer, 1986; Penn, 1985). While some circular questions may be asked of all couples (e.g., "How would your relationship be different if John stopped drinking?", "If the drinking continues or gets worse, what will life be like for your family five years from now?"), most of the questions in this section are guided by hypotheses or issues unique to each case (e.g., "Will your parents see more or less of the kids if John stops drinking?"). A crucial guideline for circular questioning is that the therapist remain neutral by not taking sides on any issue, balancing questions to both partners, and not directly advocating sobriety or change. He or she avoids declarative statements and expresses no direct opinions on the matters being discussed.

Session 5: Loose Ends and Clarification

In session 5 the therapist continues circular questioning, investigates the couple's daily routines and family rituals, and clarifies whatever may still be unclear in preparation for session 6. He or she reviews the couple's activities on a typical day, from the time they get up until the time they go to bed, and inquires about how they get together with family and friends to socialize and to celebrate special occasions and holidays. Information about how alcohol disrupts or invades these routines and rituals will be useful in the team's opinion and will highlight patterns to address in working toward family detoxification (Steinglass, 1992; Steinglass et al., 1987).

Case Planning

Before session 6—the pivotal session in which the therapist presents the team's opinion, offers treatment, and (if all goes well) begins negotiating for family detoxification—the therapist and supervisor, with input from the team, have three interrelated tasks: (1) evaluating the assessment data; (2) outlining a carefully constructed message (opinion) from the team; and (3) planning tentative strategies for the treatment phase.

Session 6: Presenting the Opinion and Offering Treatment

In the sixth and final consultation session, the therapist presents the team's opinion and offers treatment. The opinion is carefully balanced, documenting specific ways in which alcohol has invaded the couple's family life while acknowledging the many difficulties likely to be associated with sobriety and change. Above all, the therapist avoids taking sides about whether the couple should change. The team can (and will) offer treatment, but whether the couple should choose to participate can only be decided by them. If both spouses do choose treatment, family detoxification in the form of negotiating to change their relationship with alcohol begins right away, in this same session.

In most cases, the opinion begins with a compliment from the team, acknowledging some specific way(s) the couple has coped with their difficult situation. The main body of the opinion then consists of two interwoven messages: (1) *alcohol appears to be a major player invading your family life in ways that are causing serious difficulties* and (2) *changing this situation will be very difficult for you as a couple and may have unforeseen negative consequences.* Each of these messages is carefully documented with information the clients have provided and is framed in ways that make use of their own language. In presenting the first message, the therapist develops and extends the metaphor of alcohol as an external invader that seems more in control of the couple's life than vice versa. He or she documents the invasion with specific examples and portrays this as a problem for the clients as a couple, not as a problem only for the drinker.

> What I mean when I say that alcohol is a major player in your life is, for example, the time that you said you wanted to spend a certain kind of vacation together and it turned out very differently because of the drinking . . . or that the two of you never seem to be able to have sex together unless Joe has been drinking . . . or that you are in hot water at work because you don't seem to be able to concentrate after you've been drinking.

Because the second message—that change will be difficult and may entail certain hazards—concerns the future, it need not (and cannot) be documented as specifically as the first (invasion) message. Assessment information usually provides some basis for commenting on what is likely to be especially difficult for the couple—and we know from other couples that giving up alcohol can be very difficult, if for no other reason than the unpredictability involved. While negative consequences of change may involve the spouses as individuals (e.g., what will they do with their time?), the most important repercussions will concern their *relationships*—with family, friends, and, of course, each other.

How the therapist presents the opinion is as important as the specific content. Ideally, there is a certain drama or hypnotic quality to the presentation, and the main points of the two messages should come across clearly and succinctly. If it is apparent that the couple is preoccupied or unable to attend to the opinion (e.g., due to a fight, crisis, or some other difficulty), the therapist postpones it until the next session. If the clients question or challenge the opinion, he or she explains again the key points but is not argumentative or defensive.

Immediately following the opinion, the therapist offers treatment. He or she explains that our method is usually effective in helping couples take charge of problems related to drinking, but that it makes sense only for people who genuinely want to do that. In presenting the possibility of treatment, we emphasize *goals* rather than the specific methods to be employed. The main goal of treatment is for the couple to change their relationship with alcohol (or substances generally) in order to gain control over this invader on a long-term basis, and we believe that abstinence is usually the best way to achieve this goal. Another goal is to help the couple deal with difficulties in their relationship that either contribute to the drinking problem or arise after drinking stops. Accepting treatment means that the couple chooses to work toward these goals with our help. How this happens—the specific methods—will be decided collaboratively and will depend on what they feel is best for them as a couple. The therapist also stresses that treatment will require the active participation of both spouses—as well as the cooperation of others in their household—and that many of the tasks will not be easy. Only the couple can decide whether they are ready for something like this—and they may want time to think about it or talk it over.

If one or both spouses are ambivalent about treatment or unwilling to make a clear commitment, the therapist avoids taking sides and does not push or sell recovery. Instead, he or she maintains a posture of nonblaming curiosity, trying to understand what the clients themselves are proposing to do about the drinking and why. If they persist in their ambivalence or opposition to treatment, the therapist respects their position and proposes further study of the issue. At this point therapy moves to phase II-B—covert intervention framed as continued consultation.

Phase II-A: Treatment

As noted above, the goal of treatment is to help the couple change their relationship with alcohol on a long-term basis. Treatment usually consists of *family detoxification* (a term for therapists, not clients) supplemented by strategic interdiction of problem–solution loops and solution-focused amplification of exceptions to problems. When the couple chooses treatment, the therapist shifts from a neutral stance to align with the clients against alcohol (the invader) and begins helping them negotiate a series of agreements aimed at detoxifying their home environment and, ultimately, their outside social relationships. To this end, we usually recommend that the problem drinker abstain completely from alcohol and that the family establish a completely alcohol-free home. We are willing to be flexible, however, and entertain certain exceptions if the spouses are united in believing that such an arrangement is best for them and willing to demonstrate that they can handle it responsibly. In any case, our minimum requirement for treatment is that the clients, as a couple, have a clear and meaningful goal for change. Ideally, they leave session 6 with an agreed-on quitting date (if the husband is still drinking) and a clear plan for beginning the family detoxification process.

Because our systems therapy places so much emphasis on clients explicitly choosing (or not choosing) treatment, it is important to be clear with them that being in treatment means that they, as a couple, have the goal of changing their relationship with alcohol. It also means that they are actively working toward that goal. Being clear about this definition—and whether or not the therapist and clients are engaged in treatment at a given point in therapy—helps to keep change goals more sharply in focus. This is why we are careful to distinguish *consultation* from *treatment* and why we continue or return to consultation when customership is lacking. Another semantic distinction we sometimes make is between *therapy*—a general term covering all client–therapist contact—and *treatment*—a term we reserve for working toward change. In this terminology *therapy* subsumes *consultation* and *treatment*.

Family Detoxification

The term *family detoxification* (Steinglass, 1992; Steinglass et al., 1987) refers to a process through which the problem drinker in the family stops drinking and his or her environment becomes alcohol-free. This does not necessarily mean that the drinker will show withdrawal symptoms or other signs of physiological addiction—though he may. When medical complications are likely to arise, we seek consultation from a physician. In theory, family detoxification need not preclude a brief period of inpatient detoxification for the (individual) drinker, but in practice, we have rarely had to recommend this. The important point is to define detoxification as a process that will affect, and be affected by, the drinker's family. Because both spouses have a vital stake in the outcome, they should plan and negotiate as a couple how this process will unfold.

Family detoxification involves both doing and viewing. On the doing side, the therapist helps the couple negotiate a series of detailed agreements about how they will deal with alcohol. At the same time, he or she works to help the clients revise the meaning drinking holds for them as a couple. Important concepts here are collaboration and externalization. The therapist collaborates with the couple in order to help them collaborate with each other in a coalition against alcohol. *Externalization* refers to interventions designed to help the couple redefine drinking as alien to their relationship and join together against alcohol as an external invader of family life.

Family detoxification occurs in two conceptually distinct stages. The first involves arranging for an alcohol-free husband and home and the second for alcohol-free social situations and relationships. In other words, the objective is first to detoxify the family's daily routines and then to ensure that the family's external boundaries are protected from any new invasion by alcohol. In this way, the couple moves into the outside world with a clear plan that, like a protective bubble, helps them stay alcohol-free (Steinglass, 1992). Ideally, couples undergo the second level of family detoxification only after drinking has stopped and the home is alcohol-free, but in practice, the two stages often overlap. When one's social life is heavily loaded with drinking, for example, making the home alcohol-free usually requires changes in relationships with family, friends, or coworkers.

In each stage, the process of negotiating for change involves developing, implementing, and revising a plan until the details and loopholes are worked out well enough for the couple to succeed. When clients are amenable, the therapist writes out the agreements the couple makes in the form of a contract and asks both spouses to sign the contract before they leave the session. Because some clients are put off by this, we present contracting as one way—not the only way, but in our experience a good way—to work toward change. Either way, the therapist helps the spouses formulate specific steps they will take in dealing with alcohol, including who will do what and when. As the plan develops, the therapist encourages them to anticipate what might go wrong and anticipates that what they propose to do will be difficult. At the next session, he or she inquires in detail about how the plan was implemented, framing noncompliance as partial success and/ or understandable reluctance to change. Since family detoxification is a multistep process, a more or less complete plan will usually take a number of sessions to develop and implement. By that time, it is likely that the couple will be struggling to adjust to fundamental—and potentially very difficult—changes in their relationship. For this reason, the therapist cautions the couple to go slow. It is usually better to achieve change slowly and steadily than to promote rapid change that may not last.

During the first stage of family detoxification, questions inevitably arise about what exactly an alcohol-free home entails. What about cooking wine? Dinner guests? Lunches out with colleagues? A relative's occasional nightcap? The car or boat where beer is stashed? While the therapist's goal is to move the couple toward *total* removal of alcohol from both their physical space and their daily routines, they should not feel coerced into making agreements about family detoxification, and both should believe that what they agree to do is in their best interst as a couple. In one case, a couple accepted the idea of an alcohol-free household but worried that this would be disconcerting for the wife's 85-year-old mother, who lived with them and enjoyed a glass of brandy at bedtime. The couple was confident that they could handle this exception and, in consultation with the therapist, excluded the mother's brandy from their detoxification agreement, with no apparent ill effect on the progress of therapy.

An important principle is that the steps clients take toward family detoxification not be more of the same in the sense of recapitulating problem–solution loops. A better aim is to block or reverse interaction sequences centering on well-intended spousal "solutions" to the problem, especially the specific ways the spouse has attempted to get the drinker to quit (Weakland & Fisch, 1992). Thus, if the wife tries actively to prevent the drinking (e.g., by hiding bottles), we would prefer that the husband—not the wife—physically remove the alcohol from the home. Conversely, if the wife typically avoids dealing with the alcohol, having her take an active role in removing it would make sense as less of the same. The point here is simply that family detoxification should be done in a way that alters rather than reinforces typical interaction sequences. In presenting suggestions for change, it is also important to avoid the implication that the drinking is somehow the wife's fault and to frame suggestions in a manner consistent with her (or his) own views or position (Fisch et al., 1982).

If other people (children, family, friends) live in the couple's household or are frequently present there, we pay attention to how they will accommodate to the changes the couple is making. It is useful for the therapist to meet these people and, with the couple, seek their collaboration. Planning for such a meeting usually begins in the second session of the treatment phase, with the meeting itself occurring in the third or fourth session. Ideally, the couple will have had some success and will know how other family members are reacting to the changes. But even if little has changed, the household-meeting session can still focus on how to make further family detoxification agreements more successful.

The second stage of family detoxification deals with alcohol as it impinges on the couple's extended family, their social network, and their work environment. One task at this stage is to help the couple plan how they will handle difficult situations and relationships where alcohol is likely to intrude. For example, the therapist might ask the couple to role-play how they would interact with a waiter at a restaurant when they are out with friends who have ordered drinks. Because it is impossible to anticipate all difficult situations the clients may face, planning usually focuses on at least two or three situations that in the past have been high-risk for drinking. The therapist helps the couple rehearse alternative ways of handling these situations in order to protect their alcohol-free identity.

The couple's willingness to notify key family members and associates of their commitment to change is a crucial step in solidifying therapeutic gains, and we intervene specifically to promote this. In addition to its motivating effects on the clients, this intervention has the potential of altering interpersonal systems in ways that can help changes last. If social patterns and pressures in the drinker's larger system do not change, the drinker may soon become involved in situations that tax his willpower. And if the notification includes a request for a significant other's help in making changes last (e.g., by helping the drinker avoid certain high-risk situations or giving feedback if a slip seems imminent), relapse may be less likely. Because problem drinkers are often reluctant to let other people know that they have a problem, even

when they are doing something about it, the therapist does not push the idea of notification but presents it from a position of restraint, that is, as an important but very difficult step the couple might want to consider if and when they are ready. He or she anticipates and accepts reluctance at this point, gently reframing it as reflecting the couple's understandable apprehension about change.

To go forward with the intervention, the therapist helps the couple decide whom they should notify; what the specific content of the message should be; and how, when, and by whom the notification should be given. The "who" question has important structural implications, both for neutralizing high-risk drinking situations and relationships and for changing family alliance and coalition patterns. A general guideline is to notify any friends, family members, or work associates who either drank with the husband or have reason to be concerned about the couple's welfare—and geographic distance should not be an obstacle. Whether given orally or in writing, the notification itself should be clear and succinct. As for content, the key points are that (1) the couple (not just the husband) recognizes that alcohol has invaded their relationship and (2) they have decided to do something about it. For example:

> Dear Joe and Susan: Carol and I want you to know that we have been having some problems related to my drinking. Because of this, we have decided to remove alcohol from our lives, at least for the time being. We trust this won't affect our friendship with you, and we look forward to seeing you both Saturday night.
>
> Love, Tom

Responding to Reluctance and Noncompliance

Despite our best efforts, family detoxification sometimes does not go smoothly. This can happen as early as session 6 if the clients are reluctant to accept the offer of treatment or unable to agree on suitable change goals. It can also happen later if family detoxification begins but falters because the clients do not follow through.

When clients are reluctant to choose treatment, the therapist is careful not to push or sell the idea of change, maintaining neutrality, as discussed above. And when the couple cannot agree about treatment, the therapist must be even more careful not to side with the spouse who is a customer for change. If the treatment question remains unresolved after a session or two—and the clients have had ample time to think about it—therapy moves to phase II-B: intervention framed as continued consultation. Here the therapist begins to work more strategically, attempting to address one or both spouse's complaints in the framework of further consultation about whether changing their relationship with alcohol would indeed be worthwhile.

A common but difficult situation arises when the couple is interested in treatment—that is, working toward some change goal—but resistant to the idea of complete abstinence. In this case, the therapist points out that, in our experience, establishing abstinence and an alcohol-free environment is usually a crucial first step in getting a handle on problems like the ones they are having. If clients remain skeptical about the goal of an alcohol-free environment, a useful externalization strategy is to develop the analogy of a situation in which someone has an allergy, and the nature and location of the allergen are unclear (Steinglass, 1992). It is as if the family is allergic to something, with alcohol high on the list of suspects. A logical first step is to get rid of the suspect and see what happens, just as a first step after consulting an allergist might be to make the house pet-free or dust-free.

Another problem arises when the couple or one spouse (usually the drinker) wants to work on a relationship problem, minimizing the alcohol problem or defining it as secondary or under control. In this case, the therapist acknowledges and assesses the relational complaint and agrees to make it a focus of therapy *after* we are (all) reassured that the drinking is under control. (This is defined simply as program *policy* based on lessons learned from long experience.) Whether or not formal contracting occurs, the goals that the couple has agreed on can then be used as criteria for whether the drinking is under control. Work on identified relationship problems can begin or proceed to the extent that the therapist and couple are confident that progress is being made toward family detoxification. The guiding principles are that the therapist (1) not be distracted from alcohol by other complaints and (2) check on whether drinking is under control before taking up other issues.

Other guidelines concern what to do when work on family detoxification begins but falters due to noncompliance or partial compliance with the terms of an agreement. A principle applicable to *all* negotiations for change is to address reluctance and noncompliance in a nonadversarial, nonblaming way. While the therapist should make clear when what the couple does (or does not do) is incompatible with the goal of an alcohol-free home (e.g., the basement is still a part of the house, and cooking sherry is still alcohol), it is equally important that he or she acknowledge whatever happened as understandable and, without reprimanding the couple, work toward keeping family detoxification on track. Thus, if the couple follows through on only *some* of an agreement, the therapist might frame this as partial success or take the solution-focused tack of asking how they managed to do what they did do. He or she may also take a one-down position—for example, by taking the blame for going too fast or not being clear. And if an agreement collapses altogether, the therapist may frame this as an understandable response to the couple's frustrating situation. The goal of these reframing-support tactics is to encourage the couple to try again.

Interdicting Problem-Solution Loops and Finding Exceptions

The second major component of the treatment phase involves interrupting problem-maintaining interaction patterns and amplifying exceptions to problem drinking. To do this, the therapist uses strategies and techniques from both problem-focused brief therapy

(Weakland & Fisch, 1992) and solution-focused brief therapy (Berg & Miller, 1992). These tactics supplement the process of family detoxification and often provide a vehicle for addressing problem patterns more directly, albeit by less direct means.

As noted above, an important assessment goal is to identify problem–solution loops in which more of one's well-intentioned solution leads to more of the complaint, which leads to more of the solution, and so on. As problem-maintaining solution patterns become clear, the therapist and the team can begin to formulate what less of the same might look like. The key question is this: What behavior, by whom, in what situation would suffice to reverse the problem-maintaining solution? Pursuing such a *strategic objective* (a term for therapists, not clients) and thus promoting less of the same is central to our therapy, regardless of whether the couple formally chooses treatment.

Identifying specific situations in which a problem–solution sequence typically occurs is especially relevant to planning an intervention. In one case, for example, a couple's complaints concerned both the unemployed husband's urge to drink while the wife was at work and a general lack of trust in the couple's relationship. The therapist learned that a predictable interaction sequence ensued when the wife arrived home from work: As she kissed him hello, the husband appeared despondent and sometimes smelled of alcohol; the wife asked what was wrong, got little response, but continued to repeat the question in one form or another until the husband said he didn't think she really loved him and she probably found the men at work more attractive than him. The wife denied this, but the denial seemed only to confirm the husband's suspicions, and an accusation–denial cycle escalated until one of the spouses became angry and left the room. An important series of interventions in this case focused on changing what happened when the wife arrived home from work. The therapist was able to interdict two of her well-intentioned solutions in this situation with carefully framed suggestions to do things *other* than asking the husband what was wrong and defending herself in the face of his accusations, especially when he had been drinking.

The most direct way to interrupt a problem–solution loop is to suggest some specific action in some specific situation that will require someone to do less of the same (Fisch et al., 1982). It is crucial that the suggestion be framed in terms compatible with the clients' position—especially with how they prefer to see themselves. Some spouses, for example, will be attracted to the idea of making a loving sacrifice, but others may want to teach the partner a lesson. Another, less direct way to promote a less-of-the-same solution is to redefine what someone is doing in a way that stops short of prescribing change, yet makes it difficult for them to continue (e.g., "I've noticed that your reminding and watching him so closely might seem to give him an excuse to keep drinking without feeling guilty—he can justify it to himself simply by blaming you").

While problem-focused brief therapy attends primarily to what people *do* about their complaints, solution-focused brief therapy attempts to shift how people *view* their situation in order to mobilize resources for change. To accentuate exceptions to complaints, the therapist asks questions such as "How did you manage to do that?", "What did you do differently?", and "What will have to happen for her to do that more often?" The therapist highlights interactional exceptions with questions such as "What do you suppose you do differently when he doesn't drink?" and "What do you imagine she notices different about you when you don't drink?" Also, because the miracle question introduced in session 1 provides a useful jumping-off point for exploring exceptions, we often reintroduce it in the treatment phase. (Berg & Miller [1992] describe these and other useful solution-focused strategies for problem drinkers in detail.) While the purpose of solution-focused questioning is to accentuate the positive, we are careful to avoid premature celebration of change; cautious optimism is more characteristic of our general stance.

Whether and how to use problem- and/or solution-focused tactics in the treatment of a particular case depends mainly on the therapist's (and team's) intuitions about what will be most likely to work. While the two strategies—interrupting solutions that don't work and promoting those that do—have common theoretical roots and can potentially be integrated, we nevertheless recommend that the therapist be clear about which he or she is pursuing at any given time.

Phase II-B: Intervention Framed as Continued Consultation

If the couple does not choose treatment, or if treatment reaches the point of a U-turn, therapy continues in the form of strategic and structural interventions framed as further consultation about the advisability of change (see Figure 13-1). The goal of such continued consultation is to return the couple to the treatment (family detoxification) track or, failing that, to provoke change less directly. Activities in this phase usually involve one or several of the following: (1) diagnostic "experiments" designed to challenge the drinker to show that he can control drinking or the couple to show that they can tolerate change; (2) seeing the wife alone, especially when she is a customer for change and the drinker is not; or (3) involving other people beyond the couple, such as family members, friends, or other helpers.

U-Turns

When family detoxification falters and reframing interventions fail to encourage the clients to try again, therapy moves to phase II-B with the announcement of a U-turn. After consulting with the team, the therapist presents the U-turn decision dramatically and apologetically: "We now recognize that we failed to appreciate sufficiently the possible dangers of change, though in retrospect the clues were there; let us slow down and consider again the choices you have as a couple, including the choice of living with the drinking." Reframes that cast the choice not to change in terms of loyalty to a (distasteful) family tradition are

sometimes very powerful here. In any case, the therapist usually stays in a restraint-from-change position unless or until the clients actively request treatment.

Controlled Drinking Experiments

Intervention in the form of a controlled drinking experiment (Treadway, 1989) may be useful when one or both spouses indicate, either directly or indirectly, that they believe drinking is not a problem and is really under control. The main objective of this intervention is to create a situation that challenges the drinker (and couple) to either demonstrate control or request help. The therapist takes the position that, while the drinking may indeed be controllable (and not a problem), it is important to find out just how controllable it is. He or she asks the drinker how many drinks a day he can handle responsibly and seeks to define a level of consumption beyond which both spouses would agree that there is a problem. The therapist then challenges the drinker to observe that limit. We also try to set up the experiment in a way that interdicts the spouse's problem-maintaining solutions. Thus, the wife may be asked to help by carefully but unobtrusively observing the drinker's behavior; and most important, she should suspend her usual ways of trying to prevent or stop the drinking (e.g., pleading, lecturing, investigating) so as not to contaminate our observations.

The therapist follows up the controlled drinking experiment by framing failure or noncompliance with the task as evidence that there probably is a problem with controlling drinking; the couple may then be more amenable to treatment. If the clients disagree with this assessment, the therapist can prescribe the task again and up the ante. If the client succeeds in limiting his drinking, it is even more important to repeat the experiment again (and again), since "one swallow doesn't make a summer." And if the drinker continues to demonstrate control—which is possible but unlikely—the next challenge is whether the couple can have a stable and satisfactory relationship with this level of alcohol consumption.

Seeing the Spouse Alone

Many of our continued consultation strategies involve seeing the wife alone. This format is most indicated when she is a customer and the drinker is not, or when there is evidence of a coercive relationship in which the spouse is in some way intimidated by the drinker, that is, when she is reluctant to assert herself or take a stand about the drinker's behavior for fear that he may be violent, hurt himself, or abandon her.

Individual meetings are helpful because they afford a better opportunity to help the wife take a stand or reverse her usual stance in relation to the drinking. For example, a straightforward coaching strategy might aim to help her detach herself from the problem and avoid the "responsibility trap" (Bepko & Krestan, 1985); structural empowerment strategies might be used to build or reinforce coalitions that would help the spouse take a stand (e.g., "Who best understands your predicament?," "How about bringing her in next time?"); rehearsal of specific responses (e.g., leaving home, asking the drinker's friends or relatives to look in on him) may be necessary when there is a possibility of violence or self-destructive behavior. Referral to a support group helps in some cases, but this should supplement, not supplant, direct intervention by the therapist.

The therapist can also use individual sessions for brief therapy interventions aimed at interdicting specific problem-maintaining solutions. Here we usually frame suggestions in terms of assessment (e.g., "Let's try this to 'see what we're up against' " or " 'how being less reactive fits you' ") rather than as interventions intended to change things. Another indirect strategy is to ask circular questions about the consequences of the wife's acting or not acting in various ways, not only for her but also for various family relationships (e.g., "What would your mother think about you putting your foot down with John? Has she ever done that with your dad?").

Individual meetings with the spouse are framed as nonthreateningly as possible to the drinker (e.g., "I want to try to help her with the problem *she* is having with this"), but resistance should be expected and the therapist must not be intimidated. In some cases, individual sessions with the spouse can be interspersed with joint and/or individual sessions with the drinker; in other cases, it makes sense to exclude him from the therapy (at least temporarily) and work with the spouse alone.

Involving Other People

We follow Treadway's (1989) maxim, "When stuck, add people." The therapist can begin to work in this direction by calling one or more influential people in the clients' lives—for example, a relative, friend, employer, or Alcoholics Anonymous sponsor—to ask, first, their opinion of the problem and, second, if they would be willing to cooperate in the future if there is something we think they can do to help. This sets the stage for inviting important others to attend a session with one or both spouses. Depending on the dynamics of a case, such *convening* interventions might be used to mobilize influence, build cotherapeutic coalitions, mark generation boundaries, or detriangulate other family members from the couple's relationship. This works best when the therapist contacts the other people directly, rather than sending a message through the clients, but this is done only with the clients' prior consent.

Phase III: Restabilization and Relapse Prevention

When drinking stops and the couple's household and social relationships become alcohol-free, the therapist acts to help them deal with the predictably difficult consequences of sobriety and change. Because the couple's relationship will probably have been organized around alcohol—and because the drinking probably had adaptive, stabilizing consequences for them, in addition to the more obvious negative effects—they are likely to experience alcohol-free family life as *de*stabilizing, at least initially. Our goals for the restabilization phase of therapy are purposefully modest. We do not attempt to resolve deep underlying issues or create fundamental changes in family relationships. In the few sessions available, we aim only to identify possible areas of difficulty and address *some* of them with structural or strategic interventions. (It is reassuring to know that, with alcohol removed, some couples and families will *naturally* restabilize in a more satisfactory way, without our help or intervention.) We also employ specific reframing and rehearsal interventions designed to make relapse less likely and less catastrophic.

The boundaries and procedures of phase III are necessarily less precise than those of phases I and II due to the great variability in how couples progress to this point. Although phase III ideally begins around session 13 (following the acute treatment phase), with drinking stopped and family detoxification complete, some couples are well ahead of this schedule and others are well behind it. Phase boundaries are further clouded by the fact that both restabilization and relapse prevention interventions are likely to have been introduced much earlier in therapy; for example, restraint from celebration is applied whenever clients suggest that the drinking is behind them and the battle over (which can be as early as the first session), and the relapse-prevention technique of anticipating and planning for high-risk situations is an important element of family detoxification.

The therapist's main task in this phase is to intervene in a limited way to help the couple (re)stabilize their relationship without alcohol. He or she uses structural and strategic family therapy techniques to "resolve the past" and address issues such as intimacy and sexuality, the marital power balance, parenting, extended family relationships, and having satisfactory outside relationships without alcohol. To resolve the past, for example, the therapist normalizes past hurts while restraining clients from giving them up too quickly (Treadway, 1989); he or she may also help the couple plan a symbolic act or ritual to put the past behind them (Imber-Black, Roberts, & Whiting, 1988) or prescribe the symptom (Shoham & Rohrbaugh, in press). In general, we find that the best way to promote sexual intimacy is to re-

strain people from pursuing it. The therapist may also normalize sexual dysfunction by pointing out that most couples have sexual difficulties either prior to or after sobriety and that the physiological effects of alcohol will eventually wash out of the system. Control experiments, in which the spouses alternate in terms of who is in charge, serve to make control issues explicit and provide a basis for renegotiating the marital power balance (Bepko & Krestan, 1985). The therapist might also prescribe experiments in over- and underresponsibility, again as a prelude to rebalancing the relationship. If child and parenting difficulties commonly arise (or become apparent) when a "new" (sober) parent reappears on the scene, we use structural interventions to block problematic parent–child coalitions, move children out of parental roles, and (re)establish an effective co-parental alliance (Elkin, 1984; Minuchin, 1974; Treadway, 1989). One way to do this is to identify a child problem and focus the parents on working together to solve it. Finally, some clients will have difficulty restructuring relationships with family and friends where drinking was an important shared activity. Here the therapist coaches the couple on renegotiating these relationships or, if necessary, making the difficult decision to shelve them for a while. Another challenge is to help the couple establish and maintain new alcohol-free relationships if they have not yet done so on their own. Alcoholics Anonymous can be very helpful in this regard if the 12-step approach fits the couple's style and world view.

Throughout phase III, the therapist maintains a stance of gentle restraint in order to help the couple avoid utopian expectations as they experiment with new ways of relating. *Restraint from celebration* is the name we give to this stance, as well as to the specific intervention the therapist makes whenever one or both spouses appear overly optimistic about establishing or adjusting to an alcohol-free family life: "One part of me is happy for you and says 'go for it,' but the more sensible part reminds me of all the couples I've seen in your situation and how difficult working out an alcohol-free lifestyle can be" (Treadway, 1989). Other relapse prevention strategies involve (1) distinguishing lapses from relapses to normalize slips and make them less catastrophic; (2) making explicit the interactional circumstances in which the husband will be most tempted to drink; (3) externalizing the urge to drink; and (4) establishing an early warning system to help the couple recognize when the urge may be about to "sneak up on them." If the husband does begin drinking again, the main strategy for dealing with the lapse is to define it as such, calmly and understandingly, and reaffirm with the couple that they are still working toward changing their relationship with alcohol. The therapist acknowledges their disappointment but helps them view the lapse as another learning opportunity.

The structure of our project requires that therapy terminate after 20 sessions, regardless of how much (or how little) progress has been made with the drinking problem. The usual termination strategy is solution focused, accentuating what the couple has accomplished. We are careful to emphasize, however, that maintaining gains will be difficult and that the threat of alcohol (re)invading their relationship may never be completely behind them. Many couples are reassured by knowing that they will have some kind of ongoing support, and we help them plan what to do (and who to call) should the need arise. If more intensive therapeutic work remains to be done, we refer couples to a program or therapist likely to continue with strategies that have been successful, and if little progress has been made, we encourage the clients to try something entirely different.

ISSUES IN IMPLEMENTATION

Integrating ideas and techniques from different systemic therapies has been an interesting challenge. The models we draw on call the therapist's attention to different clinical phenomena (e.g., hypotheses about adaptive consequences of drinking vs. descriptions of problem–solution loops) and prescribe different therapeutic actions (e.g., neutrality vs. strategic intervention), often for the same clinical situation. To resolve these tensions of integration, we have tried to specify rules governing which concepts and techniques to invoke in which circumstances (Colapinto, 1979). One rule, for example, is that the therapist maintains neutrality until the clients, as a couple, make a clear choice to change their relationship with alcohol; only then does the therapist begin to intervene directly with family detoxification and strategic solution-interdiction techniques. Another rule, however, allows strategic techniques to be used *later* in therapy, without a clear commitment to change, but here they are framed as continued consultation. To deal with differing formulations of the relevant problem unit (e.g., problem–solution loops vs. the alcohol-invaded household vs. multigenerational drinking patterns), we follow the *rule of expanding context*. Here the integrative principle is to begin by working on the couple's interaction and broaden the focus only when intervention at the couple level appears insufficient (Treadway, 1989). Assessment of broader system patterns in the consultation phase sets the stage for wider-angle intervention but does not require that it happen.

Because our treatment manual is fairly complicated and offers decreasing structure as therapy progresses, another interesting challenge has been to monitor the extent to which therapists actually follow the guidelines provided. Furthermore, the fact that a therapist adheres to manualized treatment does not necessarily mean that he or she does so competently (Waltz, Addis, Koerner, & Jacobson, 1993). We monitor adherence and competence in several ways. Project therapists participate in a weekly supervision group (the meeting of the clinical team), and the supervisor regularly reviews selected videotapes of key sessions. Therapists also record assessment and intervention information on a standard Treatment Record form organized according to the various phases of therapy. A more formal, research-based approach involves a Systems Manual Adherence Scale developed for use by outside (expert) raters. The scale has five sections (structuring, joining, tactics and interventions, proscriptions, and overall evaluation) designed for use with video segments from any phase of therapy and a special section for rating implementation in session 6 (presenting the opinion, offering/ beginning treatment), with a follow-up at the beginning of session 7. Pairs of experts familiar with the model were able to rate segments from the first seven sessions completed, with a high degree of inter-rater reliability. Three of our therapists received high adherence and competence ratings, but two did not. The outside feedback was useful in supervision and helped us make necessary personnel changes with some degree of diplomacy. The same experts are now using revised scales to rate video segments from the early, middle, and late phases of therapy for all cases. These data will eventually provide a basis for studying the relationship between adherence/competence and overall outcome. We should also be able to determine how the therapist's presentation of the team's opinion in session 6 relates to the couple's readiness to begin family detoxification.

A Q-SORT STUDY OF CONCEPTUAL ADHERENCE

In addition to studying how our therapists actually *do* systemic therapy, we have been interested in how they *view* the treatment of alcohol problems and whether this conforms to the model as we conceived it. To investigate this *conceptual adherence*, we devised a Q-sort instrument consisting of 50 statements intended to sample diverse opinions about the nature of alcoholism and approaches to alcohol treatment (Rohrbaugh, Shoham, & Grencavage, 1994). The item sample included statements representing family-systems, 12-step, and cognitive-behavioral viewpoints, as well as other issues in the field. Respondents were asked to rank the 50 statements by sorting them into eight categories along a continuum from "least agree" (category 1) to "most agree" (category 8).[5]

Not surprisingly, independent Q-sorts by the authors were highly intercorrelated and had the highest loadings on the family systems factor that emerged when 40 Q-sorts obtained from various sources were factor-analyzed. Four of

our five therapists and the expert raters also had moderately high loading on this factor (indicating that they sorted the 50 statements in roughly the same way we did). Interestingly, the therapist with the lowest behavioral adherence scores also showed low conceptual adherence; her Q-sort was essentially uncorrelated with our sorts and had a primary loading on another factor.

The Q-sort method was also useful in identifying therapeutic beliefs most and least associated with different viewpoints, including our own, and in studying similarities and differences among these viewpoints. In addition to the family-systems therapists associated with our project, we obtained over 30 Q-sorts from alcohol-treatment professionals in California, Arizona, and Virginia who professed other viewpoints (especially 12-step and cognitive-behavioral models). When this sample of Q-sorts was factor-analyzed, three main factors emerged. As expected, they corresponded to the family-systems, 12-step, and cognitive-behavioral viewpoints.

The items with the highest scores on the family-systems factor pertain to the two major foci of our model: the locus of the problem and the therapist's stance. Highly ranked statements locating the problem in relationships rather than in individuals included the following:

- The locus of a drinking problem transcends the individual drinker; treatment should therefore focus on the relationships in which drinking is embedded.
- The drinker's current relationships and life situation are more relevant to treatment than are personality deficits and pathologies resulting from past experience in a dysfunctional family.
- Treatment of alcohol abuse should aim to change the interaction sequences surrounding problem drinking.

Other highly ranked items pertained to the therapeutic stance:

- The therapist should attempt to understand and use the client's own language or reality rather than teaching a new belief system.

• If the drinker or other family members are ambivalent about treatment, the therapist should not attempt to push or sell sobriety.

Q-sort comparisons of the family-systems and 12-step viewpoints revealed areas of both convergence and divergence. Proponents of both models, for example, tended to agree that alcoholism should not be an excuse for irresponsible or illegal behavior. The most pervasive differences concern basic assumptions of the disease model. For example, beliefs such as "Alcoholics are powerless against alcohol" and "Once an alcoholic, always an alcoholic" received much higher endorsements on the 12-step factor than on the family-systems factor, while the opposite was true for "*Problem drinking* is a better term than *alcoholism*."

More intriguing comparisons emerged for items about the locus of the problem, the target of intervention, and the therapeutic stance. Three items ranked moderately high on *both* factors suggest that attention to the family context is not the sole province of family-systems therapists:

• The member of the family who exhibits alcoholic symptoms is the *identified patient*; the real patient is the entire family.
• Spouses of alcoholics engage in a variety of dysfunctional behaviors related to their partner's drinking (e.g., nagging, attempting to control, providing alcohol, drinking in the presence of the alcoholic, reinforcing drinking with attention).
• Because cessation of drinking is potentially disruptive to the family, successful treatment often requires realignment of family relationships.

On the other hand, items implying that treatment should focus on current family relationships *more* than on the individual drinker elicited sharp disagreement (i.e., high scores on the family-systems factor and moderate to low scores on the 12-step factor):

• The locus of a drinking problem transcends the individual drinker; treatment should therefore focus on the relationships in which drinking is embedded.
• The drinker's current relationships and life situation are more relevant to treatment than personality deficits and pathologies resulting from past experience in a dysfunctional family.

Finally, differences in the therapist's stance were reflected in higher family-systems rankings for the following:

• The therapist should attempt to understand and use the client's own language or reality rather than teaching a new belief system.
• It is best for the therapist to avoid confronting denial directly.

The Q-sort results are consistent with the conceptual and technical differences we had envisioned. They also underscore the main principles of the systemic model presented in this chapter. The therapist (1) locates the drinking problem in current, ongoing relationships and identifies interactional sequences that maintain it; (2) takes seriously the clients' views of the problem, speaks their language, and avoids selling sobriety or confronting denial; (3) joins the couple in their battle with the bottle only when they clearly and jointly choose to change; and (4) responds to reluctance in a strategic, nonconfrontational manner.

APPLICABILITY

What can be said about indications and contraindications for this systemic approach to drinking problems? Because systematic outcome data are not yet available, we cannot answer this question with great confidence. On the basis of work with project couples to date, we would speculate that neither the severity nor the chronicity of either drinking or relationship problems limits the model's applicability. What does appear important, however, is that the clients have some degree of commitment to their relationship as a couple, and that at least one of them is concerned about the drinking.

Our most difficult and least successful cases have involved clients who enter therapy with their coupleness in doubt, either because it has not been established or because one or both partners contemplate leaving the relationship. Under these circumstances, an approach based on empowering clients *as a couple* may not be indicated.

Another possible basis for evaluating the applicability of a systemic approach—the fit between symptom and system—is being evaluated in the research project for which our manual was developed (Beutler et al, 1993). The main hypothesis is that *internalizing* alcoholics, whose drinking tends to be steady and interwoven with family dynamics, will benefit more from family-systems treatment than from symptom-focused cognitive and behavioral treatment, while the opposite should be true for *externalizing* alcoholics who lack impulse control and tend to drink episodically. One rationale for this hypothesis comes from Beutler's work on the relevance of patient coping style to psychotherapy treatment selection (e.g., Beutler, 1983; Beutler et al., 1991). Another comes from models of the alcoholic family (Steinglass et al., 1987) and from intriguing evidence that (1) spouses of steady (but not) episodic drinkers often report *decreased* marital satisfaction when drinking stops (Dunn, Jacob, Hummon, & Seilhamer, 1987) and that (2) these couples actually show improved problem solving when intoxicated (Jacob & Leonard, 1988). In order to examine the overlap between coping styles, drinking styles, and the marital contexts in which problem drinking occurs, we are now attempting to distinguish *relationship-syntonic* and *relationship-dystonic* alcohol problems based on client reports and ratings of videotaped interactions. At this point, however, the potential relevance of patient coping style and/or symptom-system fit to differential treatment selection is a hypothesis that remains to be tested.

Finally, although we have so far used systemic couples therapy almost exclusively with identified male drinkers, the clinical literature on female alcoholism gives reason to suspect that this approach may also be applicable to women. Compared with the alcoholic husband-father, for example, the alcoholic wife-mother appears more likely to drink at home on a regular basis; more likely to hide her drinking; and more likely to seek help for marital, family, and emotional problems she does not associate with alcohol abuse per se (Beckman & Amaro, 1986; Blume, 1986; Wilsnack & Beckman, 1984). In general, her drinking appears more closely tied to family dynamics than does that of male drinkers and more likely to escalate in response to familial stress. It therefore seems plausible that women with alcohol problems will be attracted to—and benefit from—a treatment that emphasizes changes in family relations together with cessation of drinking (see note 2).

Acknowledgment

This work was supported by National Institute of Alcoholism and Alcohol Abuse Grant RO1-AA08970 awarded to Larry Beutler (PI), Theodore Jacob, and Varda Shoham (co-PIs).

We are indebted to Lisa Grencavage, who did background research for the treatment manual; to Andres Consoli, Tracey St. Johns, and the other project therapists who helped refine our therapeutic guidelines; and to Chuck Walsh, Carol Dolan, and other outside experts who provided valuable critiques of videotaped therapy sessions.

NOTES

1. The Couples Alcoholism Treatment (CAT) project compares family-systems with cognitive-behavioral treatments for two subtypes of married male alcoholics. The project is in progress.

2. An adaptation of this systemic couples therapy for female problem drinkers is currently under pilot investigation.

3. Due to space limitations, we cannot review here all of the specific clinical situations for which the manual provides guidelines on what to do and when.

4. Consultation sessions are typically 90 minutes long; other sessions are 60 minutes long.

5. A virtue of Q-methodology is that the statistical correlation between any two Q-sorts provides a convenient index of the relationship between the viewpoints those Q-sorts represent. When correlations among multiple Q-sorts are then factor-

analyzed, the emergent Q-factors serve to define a typology of views (Brown, 1980). Factor loadings in this framework reflect the affiliation of Q-sorts with factors, and factor scores indicate which items contribute most and least to each factor. This is in contrast to the more familiar R-factor analysis, in which items or tests are correlated over people (Kerlinger, 1986; Nunnally, 1978).

REFERENCES

Beckman, L., & Amaro, H. (1986). Personal and social difficulties faced by women and men entering alcohol treatment. *Journal of Studies on Alcohol, 47,* 135–145.

Bepko, C., & Krestan, J. (1985). *The responsibility trap: A blueprint for treating the alcoholic family.* New York: Free Press.

Berenson, D. (1979). The therapist's relationship with couples with an alcoholic member. In E. Kaufman & P. Kaufmann (Eds.), *Family therapy of drug and alcohol abuse* (pp. 233–242). New York: Gardner Press.

Berg, I. K., & Miller, S. D. (1992). *Working with the problem drinker: A solution-focused approach.* New York: Norton.

Beutler, L. E. (1983). *Eclectic psychotherapy: A systematic approach.* New York: Pergamon Press.

Beutler, L. E., Engle, D., Mohr, D. C., Daldrup, R. J., Bergan, J., Meredith, K., & Merry, W. (1991). Predictors of differential response to cognitive, experiential, and self directed psychotherapeutic procedures. *Journal of Consulting and Clinical Psychology, 59,* 333–340.

Beutler, L. E., Patterson, K., Jacob, T., Shoham, V., Yost, L., & Rohrbaugh, M. J. (1993). Matching treatment to alcoholism subtypes. *Psychotherapy, 30,* 463–472.

Blume, S. (1986). Women and alcohol: A review. *Journal of the American Medical Association, 256,* 1467–1476.

Borwick, B. (1991). The co-created world of alcoholism. *Journal of Strategic and Systemic Therapies, 10,* 3–19.

Brown, S. R. (1980). *Political subjectivity: Applications of Q methodology in political science.* New Haven, CT: Yale University Press.

Colapinto, J. (1979). The relative value of empirical evidence. *Family Process, 18,* 427–441.

de Shazer, S. (1985). *Keys to solution in brief therapy.* New York: Norton.

de Shazer, S. (1988). *Clues: Investigating solutions in brief therapy.* New York: Norton.

Dunn, N. J., Jacob, T., Hummon, N., & Seilhamer, R. A. (1987). *Journal of Abnormal Psychology, 96,* 99–107.

Elkin, M. (1984). *Families under the influence.* New York: Norton.

Fisch, R. (1986). The brief treatment of alcoholism. *Journal of Strategic and Systemic Therapies, 5,* 40–49.

Fisch, R., Weakland, J. H., & Segal, L. (1982). *The tactics of change.* San Francisco: Jossey-Bass.

Fleuridas, C., Nelson, T. I., & Rosenthal, D. (1986). The evolution of circular questions: Training family therapists. *Journal of Marital and Family Therapy, 12,* 113–127.

Haley, J. (1976). *Problem-solving therapy: New strategies for effective family therapy.* San Francisco: Jossey-Bass.

Hoffman, L. (1981). *Foundations of family therapy: A conceptual framework for systems change.* New York: Basic Books.

Imber-Black, E., Roberts, J., & Whiting, R. (1988). *Rituals in families and family therapy.* New York: Norton.

Kerlinger, F. N. (1986). *Foundations of behavioral research.* New York: Holt, Rinehart & Winston.

Leipman, M., Silvia, L., & Nirenberg, T. (1989). The use of behavior loop mapping for substance abuse. *Family Relations, 38,* 282–287.

Lewis, B. (1987). Cybernetics and the treatment of alcoholism: Thoughts on a model. *Alcoholism Treatment Quarterly, 4,* 127–139.

Lipchik, E., & de Shazer, S. (1986). The purposeful interview. *Journal of Strategic and Systemic Therapies, 5,* 88–99.

McCrady, B. S., Noel, N. E., Abrams, D. B., Stout, R. L., Nelson, H. F., & Hay, W. M. (1986). Comparative effectiveness of three types of spouse involvement in outpatient behavioral alcoholism treatment. *Journal of Studies on Alcohol, 47,* 459–467.

McGoldrick, M., & Gerson, R. (1985). *Genograms in family assessment.* New York: Norton.

Minuchin, S. (1974). *Families and family therapy.* Cambridge, MA: Harvard University Press.

Nunnally, J. C. (1978). *Psychometric theory.* New York: McGraw-Hill.

O'Hanlon, W., & Weiner-Davis, M. (1989). *In search of solutions: A new direction in psychotherapy.* New York: Norton.

Papp, P. (1983). *The process of change.* New York: Guilford Press.

Penn, P., (1985). Feed forward: Future questions, future maps. *Family Process, 24,* 299–311.

Rohrbaugh, M., Shoham, V., & Grencavage, L. (1994, February). *A Q-sort study of conceptual adherence to a systemic treatment manual.* Paper presented at the meeting of the North American Society for Psychotherapy Research, Santa Fe, NM.

Shoham, V., & Rohrbaugh, M. J. (in press). Paradoxical Interventions. In R. J. Corsini (Ed.), *Encyclopedia of psychology.* New York: Wiley.

Steinglass, P. (1980). A life history model of the alcoholic family. *Family Process, 19,* 211–225.

Steinglass, P. (1981). The alcoholic family at home: Patterns of interaction in dry, wet and transitional stages of alcoholism. *Archives of General Psychiatry, 38,* 578–584.

Steinglass, P. (1992, October). *Family-level detoxification: What it is and why it works.* Workshop presented at the meeting of the American Association of Marital and Family Therapy, Miami, FL.

Steinglass, P., Bennett, L., Wolin, S., & Reiss, D. (1987). *The alcoholic family.* New York: Basic Books.

Steinglass, P., Tislenko, L., & Reiss, D. (1985). Stability/instability in the alcoholic marriage: The interrelationship between course of alcoholism, family process, and marital outcome. *Family Process, 24,* 365–376.

Treadway, D. C. (1989). *Before it's too late: Working with substance abuse in the family.* New York: Norton.

Waltz, J., Addis, M. E., Koerner, K., & Jacobson, N. S. (1993). Testing the integrity of a psychotherapy protocol: Assessment of adherence and competence. *Journal of Consulting and Clinical Psychology, 61,* 620–630.

Weakland, J. H., & Fisch, R. (1992). Brief therapy—MRI style. In S. H. Budman, M. F. Hoyt, & S. Friedman (Eds.), *The first session in brief therapy* (pp. 306–323). New York: Guilford Press.

Weakland, J. H., Watzlawick, P., Fisch, R., & Bodin, A. (1974). Brief therapy: Focused problem resolution. *Family Process, 13,* 141–168.

White, M., & Epston, D. (1990). *Narrative means to therapeutic ends.* New York: Norton.

Wilsnack, S., & Beckman, L. (1984). *Alcohol problems for women.* New York: Guilford Press.

14

Integrative and Eclectic Therapies in Historical Perspective

Marvin R. Goldfried
John C. Norcross

Rivalry among theoretical orientations has a long and undistinguished history in psychotherapy, dating back to Freud. In the infancy of the field, therapy systems, like battling siblings, competed for attention and affections in a "dogma eat dogma" environment (Larson, 1980). Clinicians traditionally operated from within their own particular theoretical framework, often to the point of being blind to alternative conceptualizations and potentially superior interventions (Goldfried, 1980). Mutual antipathy and exchange of puerile insults between adherents of rival orientations were very much the order of the day (Norcross & Newman, 1992).

Since the 1980s the field has witnessed both a general decline in ideological struggle and the stirrings of rapprochement. The debates across theoretical systems appear to be less polemical, or at least more issue-specific, than they had been in the past. The theoretical substrate of each system is undergoing intensive reappraisal as psychotherapists acknowledge the inadequacies of any one system and the potential value of others (Norcross, 1986).

Psychotherapy integration is characterized by a dissatisfaction with single-school approaches and by a concomitant desire to look across theoretical boundaries to see what can be learned from other ways of conducting psychotherapy. While various labels are applied to this movement—*eclecticism*, *integration*, *convergence*, and *rapprochement*—the goals are similar. The ultimate outcome of integration and eclecticism, not yet fully realized, is to enhance the efficacy, efficiency, and applicability of psychotherapy.

This chapter will explicate the influential historical developments, major theoretical variations, and current directions in psychotherapy integration, and thereby set the stage for the subsequent chapter on integrative and eclectic psychotherapies in practice. We begin by describing the historical development of integrative and eclectic therapies from their early stirrings in the 1930s to their full manifestation in the early 1980s. This segues into a brief consideration of the principal varieties of psychotherapy integration, namely, theoretical integration, technical eclecticism, and common factors. The next section, on theory of change, focuses on the mechanisms of change and the theoretical rationale that is used in describing these changes. Thereafter, we examine the current status of psychotherapy integration in terms of practice, training, and research. The chapter concludes with a summary of integration's critical elements and a few final observations.

HISTORICAL DEVELOPMENT

Until recently, little had been written about the history of integrative and eclectic approaches to psychotherapy. Though interest in this issue dates back to the 1930s, it consisted primarily of a latent theme rather than a more clearly delineated field of study. Consequently, it was not until the 1980s, when the field of psychotherapy integration became an actual movement, that historical reviews were published (Arkowitz & Messer, 1984; Goldfried & Newman, 1986). Given the limitations of space, we will only touch on some of the highlights of the historical trend toward psychotherapy integration and eclecticism. A more thorough description and analysis may be found elsewhere (Arkowitz, 1992; Goldfried & Newman, 1992).

The Early Stirrings

One of the earliest attempts to integrate the psychotherapies was made by French, who delivered an address at the American Psychiatric Association meeting in 1932. In his talk, which was somewhat heretical at the time, he attempted to link psychoanalysis and Pavlovian conditioning. His presentation was published the following year (French, 1933), together with comments from members of the audience. The publication included not only his conceptual links between two orientations (e.g., repression and extinction), but also the very mixed reactions of members of the audience. While some applauded French's stance, others were outraged by his attempt to cross such diverse theoretical boundaries.

A few years later, Rosenzweig (1936) outlined what was to be the first commentary on common elements across the different theoretical schools of thought. Rosenzweig argued that the effectiveness of all forms of therapy could be explained by (1) the ability of therapists to instill a sense of hope in their patients; (2)

the ability of interpretations, regardless of their accuracy, to make the poorly understood nature of the problem more understandable; and (3) the synergistic nature of the change process, whereby a differential focus on a given aspect of human functioning can have positive effects on other aspects of the patient's functioning.

Little was written on the topic until 1950, when Dollard and Miller published their classic work *Personality and Psychotherapy*. In a book dedicated to "Freud and Pavlov and their students," Dollard and Miller, like French before them, described how various psychoanalytic concepts could best be understood in a framework of learning theory. Although this translation of one orientation into another did relatively little to create any innovative interventions, the book was a seminal contribution and remained continuously in print for some 30 years.

Dealing with the same issue as Rosenzweig, Garfield (1957) included in his introductory clinical psychology text what he concluded to be common factors across the psychotherapies. Included among these were the therapist's understanding and support, and the patient's opportunity to experience an emotional catharsis and gain self-understanding.

In general, only a handful of writers addressed the issue of therapeutic rapprochement from the 1930s through the 1950s. During this period, there was relatively little diversity of orientations, a preoccupying economic depression, a devastating world war, and a period of social and political conservatism that no doubt discouraged psychotherapists from undertaking this process of self-examination. All this changed in the 1960s, when the field witnessed a marked shift in interest in psychotherapy integration.

The 1960s

In his landmark book *Persuasion and Healing*, Frank (1961) picked up on the theme of common ingredients that seemed to be associated with psychological change and other forms of healing. He argued that a variety of different healing methods—primitive shamanism, religious conversion, brainwashing, the placebo effect in medicine—all served to instill an expectation for change or improvement. According to Frank, this establishment of hope dealt directly with patients' demoralization and set in motion a process of change.

Three decades after French published his presentation that drew parallels between Freud and Pavlov, Alexander (1963) reaffirmed the notion that psychodynamic therapy might best be understood in learning theory terms. A respected psychoanalyst, Alexander observed that "we are witnessing the beginnings of a most promising integration of psychoanalytic theory with learning theory, which may lead to unpredictable advances in the theory and practice of the psychotherapies" (p. 48). In the same year, Carl Rogers (1963) observed that therapists were becoming increasingly less tied to their own particular theoretical orientations, and that the field was becoming better able to observe more directly what was actually going on during the change process.

In his book *The Modes and Morals of Psychotherapy*, London (1964) highlighted both the strengths and the limitations associated with psychodynamic and behavioral orientations. Challenging the constraints associated with each of these orientations, London stated: "There is a quiet blending of techniques by artful therapists of either school: A blending that takes account of the fact that people are considerably simpler than the Insight schools give them credit for, but that they are also more complicated than the Action therapists would like to believe" (p. 39).

In England, Marks and Gelder (1966) similarly acknowledged that there was probably common ground as well as differences between psychodynamic and behavioral approaches. They suggested that the two approaches might best be viewed as complementary rather than antagonistic. This point was echoed by another British professional, Wolf (1966), who suggested that "Their integration is sooner or later inevitable, however passionately some or many of us may choose to resist it" (p. 535).

In 1967, Lazarus stepped out of the constraints of his behavioral roots by maintaining that clinicians could fruitfully be "technically eclectic" without necessarily subscribing to the theoretical superstructure associated with any given intervention procedure. Very much the pragmatic clinician, Lazarus urged others to use the criterion of clinical effectiveness, rather than of theoretical school, to determine how they intervene. His more recent statement on this issue is included within his multimodal therapeutic approach (Lazarus, 1992).

Acknowledging that behavioral procedures, such as systematic desensitization, were beginning to have demonstrated clinical effectiveness, Bergin (1968) suggested that such interventions could be more effective if employed within a therapeutic context involving warmth, empathy, and a certain amount of interpretation. This comprehensive approach was seen as being particularly relevant in the most complex clinical cases.

Following the tradition of French and Alexander, Marmor (1969) argued that all forms of therapy, whether the theory acknowledges it or not, involve principles of learning. Such learning, however, probably went beyond a simple stimulus-response (S-R) model and involved cognitive factors as well. He also concluded that neither the behavioral nor psychodynamic approaches were sufficient in themselves to implement change, and like others before him (Bergin, 1968; Lazarus, 1967; London, 1964; Marks & Gelder, 1966), Marmor concluded that the two forms of therapy might best be viewed as complementary.

The 1970s

Writing in the newly founded journal *Behavior Therapy*, Bergin (1970) noted that the introduction of cognitive methods (e.g., reappraisal of life events) into behavior therapy might very well lead to the investigation of problems that traditional behavior therapy failed to consider. His prophecy turned out to be quite accurate, as many behavior therapists involved in the creation of cognitive interventions (e.g., Davison, Goldfried, Lazarus, Mahoney, and Meichenbaum) later developed an interest in psycho-therapy integration. Lazarus' (1971a) *Behavior Therapy and Beyond* provided a detailed intro-duction of nonbehavioral methods into the behavioral repertoire. Lazarus' thesis was un-derscored by London (1972), who called for an end to ideology within behavior therapy circles.

The ways that behavioral and psychody-namic therapies may be integrated, both clini-cally and conceptually, were dealt with in a series of papers by Feather and Rhoads (1972a, 1972b). Birk (1973) followed up on this point, noting that the behavioral approach helped to provide a focus on external stimuli (e.g., work deadlines), whereas the psychodynamic inter-ventions dealt more with internal phenomena (e.g., thoughts, feelings). The sequencing of these two forms of intervention was also consid-ered in a later paper by Birk and Brinkley-Birk (1974), and just how these two same orienta-tions might be used to treat sexual disorders was outlined in Kaplan's (1974) *The New Sex Therapy*.

In 1975, a number of important books and articles on integration were published. In *Mis-understandings of the Self*, Raimy (1975) sug-gested that a common factor across therapeutic orientations was their ability to alter the pa-tients' misconceptions of themselves and oth-ers. In the first of a series of articles on psy-chotherapy integration written by the German psychologist Bastine (1975), common strategies together with specific procedures by which they might be implemented were similarly outlined. Also, in the first of many contributions, Wach-tel (1975) suggested how psychodynamic and behavioral approaches might complement each other, such as the former helping to identify problematic interpersonal themes and the latter supplying methods to encourage new behavior patterns. This thesis was expanded into what has since become a classic work, namely, *Psy-choanalysis and Behavior Therapy* (Wachtel, 1977). Also in 1975, Egan expanded an experi-ential orientation to therapy to acknowledge the potential contributions of the behavioral ap-proach.

Based on his empirical orientation, Strupp (1976) called psychoanalytic therapy to task for

continuing its use of procedures based on faith and tradition rather than on data that deal with clinical effectiveness. At the same time, Goldfried and Davison (1976) published *Clini-cal Behavior Therapy*, in which they suggested that "It is time for behavior therapists to stop regarding themselves as an outgroup and in-stead to enter into serious and hopefully mutu-ally fruitful dialogues with their nonbehavioral colleagues" (p. 15). The fact that clinicians of varying orientations were already doing so was reflected in a survey by Garfield and Kurtz (1976), in which they found that more than half of the clinical psychologists in the United States considered themselves eclectic.

After having practiced behavior therapy for approximately two decades, Lazarus (1971a) raised the question of whether or not behavior therapy—indeed, any specific school of ther-apy—had "outlived its usefulness." Interestingly enough, the editor of the *Journal of Humanistic Psychology* (Greening, 1978) agreed with Laza-rus' thesis and urged his experiential colleagues to remain open to efforts at rapprochement. Davison (1978) similarly urged his behavioral colleagues at a meeting of the Association for the Advancement of Behavior Therapy (AABT) to consider incorporating experiential methods into their behavioral practice. As it turned out, some behavior therapists were already involved in expanding the scope of permissible behav-ioral practice, particularly when confronted with complicated clinical issues such as agora-phobia (Goldstein & Chambless, 1978). As revealed in a survey by Mahoney (1979), lead-ing behavior therapists confessed that they were dissatisfied with their current understanding of human behavior.

In a textbook reviewing leading systems of psychotherapy, Prochaska (1979) ended with the presentation of a transtheoretical orienta-tion that could encompass various schools of thought, one that took into consideration the stages of the change process and the problem areas in need of consideration. As a potential language system for communicating across the different orientations, several authors (e.g., Goldfried, 1979; Ryle, 1978; Sarason, 1979) independently suggested that experimental cognitive psychology might conceivably appeal to clinicians of both psychodynamic and behavioral orientations. Thus, psychodynamic therapists could respond to the phenomena studied (e.g., distortions and misinterpretations), while behavior therapists could relate to the idea of incorporating basic research findings into clinical work.

The 1980s

During the 1980s, psychotherapy integration moved from a latent theme to a clearly defined area of interest—indeed, a movement. In this decade numerous books, journals, articles, chapters, and conferences appeared on the subject, and a professional society dedicated to the advancement of psychotherapy integration was formed.

In 1980, Goldfried reviewed the movement toward psychotherapy integration and suggested that fruitful comparison across different orientations might be based on clinical strategies. These strategies—for example, corrective experiences and feedback—occupy a level of abstraction somewhere between specific techniques and global theories. A special issue of *Cognitive Therapy and Research* contained responses of therapists from different orientations to questions about what might constitute the psychotherapy change process (Brady et al., 1980). Mahoney (1980) noted that not only had behavior therapists begun to look at cognitive variables, but that some of these cognitions were in fact "implicit" or "unconscious." In the same year, Marmor and Woods published a book specifically concerning integration, as did Garfield.

Also at the beginning of this decade, the fact that psychotherapy integration was more international in scope became increasingly evident. In England, Dryen (1980) dealt with the difference in therapeutic style across theoretical orientations. In Germany, Bastine and his colleagues (Bastine, 1980; Linsenhoff, Bastine, & Kommer, 1980) discussed the methods for accomplishing an integration of the psychothera-

pies, as well as its theoretical and practical benefits.

In the early 1980s there was a dramatic increase in the number of books written from an integrative perspective, such as Goldfried's (1982) *Converging Themes in Psychotherapy*, Wachtel's (1982) *Resistance*, Ryle's (1982) *Psychotherapy*, and Segraves' (1982) *Marital Therapy*. This was but the beginning, as a continual stream of volumes appeared over the next few years (e.g., Arkowitz & Messer, 1984; Beutler, 1983; Driscoll, 1984; Dryden, 1984; Fensterheim & Glazer, 1983; Hart, 1983; Prochaska & DiClemente, 1984; Textor, 1983). Moreover, journals began to feature special discussions on the topic of psychotherapy integration, such as a 1982 issue of *Behavior Therapy* and a 1983 issue of the *British Journal of Clinical Psychology*.

Recognizing the need for an organization to bring together these separate voices and foster the growing integration movement, the Society for the Exploration of Psychotherapy Integration (SEPI) was founded in 1983. SEPI is interdisciplinary in nature and has grown to be international in its scope. The purpose of SEPI was to provide a community in which dialogue across orientations, and also between researchers and clinicians, might take place. SEPI not only reflected but also provided great impetus for the psychotherapy integration movement.[1]

As more authors became interested in the topic of psychotherapy integration, there developed a need for more outlets for their ideas. Consequently, several journals appeared, such as the *Journal of Integrative and Eclectic Psychotherapy*, *Integrative Psychiatry*, and the *Journal of Psychotherapy Integration*, the last serving as the official publication of SEPI.

Toward the end of the 1980s, many of the major books on psychotherapy integration reflected the fact that interest in this topic had grown to be international in scope. For example, from English-speaking Canada, Greenberg and Safran (1987) published *Emotion in Psychotherapy*; from French-speaking Canada, Lacomte and Castonguay (1987) edited *Rapprochement et Integration en Psychotherapie*.

From Italy, Guidano (1987) contributed *Complexity of the Self*. From the United States came volumes by Beitman (1987), Norcross (1986, 1987), and Wachtel (1987).

With the growth of the integration movement came a predictable focus on specific issues. Cases in point were special sections on the possibilities of common language in psychotherapy (Norcross, 1987) and recommendations on integrative training (Beutler et al., 1987; Norcross et al., 1986); in the *Journal of Integrative and Eclectic Psychotherapy*. The integration of different therapeutic modalities, such as individual and family therapy, was also the focus of attention (e.g., Allen, 1988; Feldman, 1989; Wachtel & Wachtel, 1986). The growing interest in psychotherapy integration within psychiatry was reflected in a 1988 special issue of *Psychiatric Annals*, as well as in the Beitman, Goldfried, and Norcross (1989) review in *American Journal of Psychiatry*.

Toward the end of the 1980s, there was a call for empirical work on psychotherapy integration (e.g., Goldfried & Safran, 1986; Norcross & Grencavage, 1989). Both the need and possible directions for future work in this area were described by Wolfe and Goldfried (1988), who summarized a special National Institute of Mental Health research conference dealing with this topic; more will be said about this conference later in this chapter.

Why the Trend Toward Psychotherapy Integration?

Given the fact that psychotherapy integration can be traced to the early 1930s, the question may be raised as to why it has only been in more recent years that it has captured the interest of mental health professionals. In an attempt to answer this question, Norcross and Newman (1992) have identified eight interacting and mutually reinforcing factors.

1. The first is the proliferation of different schools of psychotherapy over the years, causing fragmentation and confusion.

2. Related to this "hyperinflation of brand-name therapies" is the growing awareness that no one approach to therapy has been found to be totally applicable to all clinical cases.

3. The concurrent interest of the federal government and insurance companies in psychotherapeutic services has brought with it growing pressure for accountability, consensus, and pragmatism; there is something to be said for the differing schools "hanging together" rather than "hanging separately" under such intense scrutiny.

4. As psychotherapy has become short-term in nature, and as it has begun to focus on specific clinical problems, therapists of disparate orientations have started to share a more common focus. Dealing with clinical realities within time constraints has promoted the tendency to use whatever works, regardless of orientation.

5. Therapists have had increased opportunities to observe and experiment with different therapeutic interventions. This has occurred with the advent of therapy manuals reflecting different theoretical traditions and with the growth of problem-oriented specialty clinics that are staffed by professionals of various orientations and disciplines.

6. As a result of considerable psychotherapy outcome research, a typical conclusion has been drawn that for many (but not all) disorders, no one theoretical approach has been shown to be consistently more effective than any other.

7. Partly as a consequence of this failure to find consistent differential effectiveness, there is a growing awareness and appreciation of the common factors that exist in all forms of therapy.

8. A final and critical impetus to psychotherapy integration has been the formation of a professional network—SEPI—that has provided an invaluable context within which integration-minded professionals can work.

It is difficult to determine which of these separate factors has been most instrumental in engendering the current interest in psychotherapy integration. What is clear, however, is that forces operating both inside and outside the field of psychotherapy have contributed to this trend. Whatever the relative contributions of these factors, all have operated in forming a new *Zeitgeist*, a hospitable atmosphere in which to explore psychotherapy integration.

VARIETIES OF INTEGRATION

There are numerous pathways toward the integration of the psychotherapies (Arkowitz, 1989; Mahrer, 1989; Schacht, 1984). The three principal varieties are (1) technical eclecticism, (2) theoretical integration, and (3) common factors (Norcross & Grencavage, 1989). All three share a desire to increase therapeutic effectiveness by looking beyond the confines of single-school perspectives, but they do so in rather different ways and at different levels (see Norcross & Newman, 1992, for review).

Technical Eclecticism

Eclecticism is the least theoretical of the three, but it should not be construed as either atheoretical or antitheoretical (Lazarus, Beutler, & Norcross, 1992). Technical eclectics seek to improve our ability to select the best treatment for the person and the problem. This search is guided primarily by data on what has worked best for other patients in the past with similar disorders and similar characteristics. In this sense, eclecticism predicts for whom interventions will work: The foundation is empirical rather than theoretical. The eclectic models of Beutler (1983; Beutler & Clarkin, 1990; Beutler & Consoli, 1992; Chapter 15, this volume) and Lazarus (1971b, 1976, 1989a, 1992) exemplify this form of integration.

Proponents of technical eclecticism use procedures drawn from different sources without necessarily subscribing to the theories that spawn them. That is, no necessary connection exists between metabeliefs and techniques. In the words of Lazarus (1967): "To attempt a theoretical rapprochement is as futile as trying to picture the edge of the universe. But to read through the vast array of literature on psychotherapy, *in search of techniques*, can be clinically enriching and therapeutically rewarding" (p. 416).

Theoretical Integration

In this form of synthesis, two or more therapies are integrated in the hope that the result will be better than that resulting from the constituent therapies alone. As the name implies, the emphasis is on combining the underlying theories of psychotherapies—what London (1986) eloquently labeled *theory smushing*. This is done along with the blending of therapy techniques from each—what London called *technique melding*. Various proposals to integrate psychoanalytic and behavioral theories illustrate this direction, most notably the work of Wachtel (1977, 1987; Wachtel & McKinney, 1992), as well as grander schemes to meld all the major systems of psychotherapy, as in the transtheoretical model of Prochaska and DiClemente (1982, 1984, 1992).

Thus, theoretical integration entails a commitment to a conceptual synthesis beyond the technical blend of methods. The goal is to create a conceptual framework that synthesizes the best elements of two or more approaches of therapy. However, it aspires to more than a simple combination; it seeks an emergent theory that is more than the sum of its parts and that leads to new directions for practice and research (Norcross & Newman, 1992).

The primary distinction between technical eclecticism and theoretical integration, then, is that between empirical pragmatism and theoretical flexibility.[2] *Integration* refers to a commitment to a conceptual creation beyond eclecticism's pragmatic blending of procedures. A corollary to this distinction, rooted in theoretical integration's early stage of development, is that current practice is largely eclectic. Integration represents a promissory note for the future. In the words of Wachtel (1991, p. 44):

> The habits and boundaries associated with the various schools are hard to eclipse, and for most of us integration remains more a goal than a constant daily reality. Eclecticism in practice and integration in aspiration is an accurate description of what most of us in the integrative movement do much of the time.

Common Factors

In this variation of psychotherapy integration, we attempt to determine the core ingredients that different therapies share, toward the eventual goal of developing more parsimonious and efficacious treatments based on those commonalities. This search is predicated on the widespread belief and accumulating research that commonalities are more important in accounting for psychotherapy outcome than the unique factors that differentiate among them. In specifying what is common across disparate orientations, we may also be selecting what works best among them (Goldfried, 1980; Norcross & Newman, 1992). The works of Jerome Frank (1973, 1982; Frank & Frank, 1991) and Sol Garfield (1980, 1986, 1992) have been among the most influential contributors to the common factors approach.

The energetic debate in the field between those emphasizing the power of therapeutic commonalities and those stressing the unique or specific factors attributed to different therapies has gradually given way to a consensus that is not a dichotomy. Indeed, it has been suggested that the field of psychotherapy can gradually integrate by combining the fundamental similarities *and* the useful differences across the schools (Beitman, 1992). In this way, we can maximize effectiveness by employing those factors common across therapies highlighted in research while capitalizing on contributions of specific techniques found to be differentially effective for selected circumstances (Garfield, 1992; Lambert, 1992).

THEORY OF CHANGE

One means of conceptualizing the theory of change is to focus on a level of abstraction between theory and technique. We will probably never reach common ground in the theoretical or philosophical realm of psychotherapy, and searching for commonalities across approaches in terms of specific procedures will probably not reveal much more than minor points of similarity (Goldfried, 1980). By contrast, an intermediate level of abstraction, known as a *principle of change* or a *clinical strategy*, fits between global theories (e.g., psychoanalysis, behaviorism, systemic analysis) and specific techniques (e.g., dream analysis, progressive muscle relaxation, family sculpting).

Change principles, we believe, are the level at which meaningful points of convergence can be found among the psychotherapies. Preliminary research on proposed therapeutic commonalities (Grencavage & Norcross, 1990) and agreement on treatment recommendations (Giunta, Saltzman, & Norcross, 1991) have supported this view of change principles as the level of abstraction most amenable to theoretical convergence. Figure 14.1 illustrates this intermediate level of abstraction occupied by the principle of change.

	Level	Example
High	Theoretical frameworks	Psychodynamic, experimental, behavioral
	Change principle	Increasing client awareness
Low	Clinical techniques	Interpretation, reflection, self-monitoring

FIGURE 14.1. Levels of abstraction. (Adapted from Goldfried & Safran, 1986.)

Transtheoretical Model

Although there are reportedly over 400 different psychological therapies (Karasu, 1986) based on divergent theoretical assumptions, the transtheoretical model, developed by Prochaska and his colleagues, has been able to identify only 10 different processes of change (Prochaska, Velicer, DiClemente, & Fava, 1988). Similarly, over 200 distinct techniques have been advanced, but these techniques can be summarized by a much smaller set of processes. The processes of change were initially identified in a comparative analysis of the leading psychotherapy systems (Prochaska, 1979) and were subsequently confirmed and refined in a series of research studies on self-initiated and treatment-facilitated change (Prochaska, DiClemente, & Norcross, 1992). The transtheoretical model was designed to be complex enough to do justice to the complexities of behavior change, yet simple enough to reduce confusion on the field.

Table 14.1 presents these 10 change processes, along with their definitions and representative examples of specific interventions. As seen there, several processes of change are primarily used by the verbal or insight therapies, such as psychoanalytic and experiential approaches. Several other processes are used primarily, if not exclusively, by the directive or action therapies, notably behavior therapy and some forms of family systems therapy. Comparative studies of psychotherapy further indicate that certain therapies, principally gestalt and cognitive approaches, employ processes traditionally associated with both insight and action therapies. All therapies employ the therapeutic relationship and self-liberation in treatment, although they vary in the emphasis and label applied to them.

One method for examining the theory of

TABLE 14.1. Titles, Definitions, and Representative Interventions of the Processes of Change

Process	Definitions: Representative Interventions
Verbal/Insight Therapies	
Consciousness raising	Increasing information about self and problem: observations, confrontations, interpretations, bibliotherapy.
Self-reevaluation	Assessing how one feels and thinks about oneself with respect to a problem: value clarification, reflections, imagery, corrective emotional experience.
Dramatic relief	Experiencing and expressing feelings about one's problems and solutions: catharsis/abreaction, psychodrama, grieving for losses, role playing.
Environmental reevaluation	Assessing how one's problem affects the social environment: perspective taking, empathy training, documentaries.
Behavioral/Action Therapies	
Counterconditioning	Substituting alternatives for problem behaviors: relaxation, desensitization, assertion, cognitive disputation.
Stimulus control	Avoiding or countering stimuli that elicit problem behaviors: restructuring one's environmnent (e.g., removing alcohol), avoiding high-risk cues, fading techniques.
Contingency management	Rewarding or punishing oneself or others for making changes: contingency contracts, overt and covert reinforcement, self-reward, punishment.
All Therapies	
Helping relationships	Being open and trusting about problems with someone who cares: therapeutic alliance, social support, nonpossessive warmth.
Self-liberation	Choosing and committing to change: decision making, encouragement, logotherapy techniques, commitment-enhancing techniques.
Few Therapies	
Social liberation	Increasing alternatives for nonproblem behaviors available in society: advocating for rights of the repressed, empowering, policy interventions.

Source: Adapted from Prochaska, DiClemente, & Norcross (1992).

change and organizing the change processes is to consider the stages of change. Individuals modifying problem behaviors progress through an invariant series of stages, from contemplation to maintenance. *Contemplation* is the stage in which individuals are aware that a problem exists and are seriously thinking about overcoming it but have not yet made a commitment to take action. Gradually, individuals move into *preparation*, the stage that combines intention and behavioral criteria. Here they are committed to taking action in the near future and may have already taken a few small or tentative steps toward eliminating the problem. *Action* is the next stage in which individuals modify their behavior, experiences, or environments in order to overcome their problem. Action requires the most overt behavioral change and requires a considerable commitment of time and energy. And last, *maintenance* is the stage in which individuals work to prevent relapse and consolidate the gains obtained during action (see Prochaska et al., 1992, for review).

Accumulating clinical and research experience indicates that the change processes are differentially employed and effective, depending on the stage of change. Individuals in the contemplation stage are most open to consciousness-raising techniques, such as observation, confrontation, and interpretation. Contemplators are also open to dramatic relief, which raises emotions and lowers negative affect. Contemplators, in and outside of therapy, are most likely to engage in self-reevaluation and environmental reevaluation: As they become more conscious of themselves and the nature of their conflicts, they affectively and cognitively reevaluate their values, problems, and the effects of their problems on other people.

As people enter the preparation stage and approach action, they increasingly believe that they possess the autonomy and ability to modify their lives in key ways, and thus begin to profit from self-liberation or willpower. Successful action entails effective use of behavioral processes: counterconditioning to develop healthy alternative behaviors, stimulus control to make

their environments work for them rather than against them, and contingency management to reward themselves for attempting to change and for maintaining progress. Throughout the cycle of change, helping relationships in various guises prove to be invaluable.

Competing systems of psychotherapy have promulgated apparently rival processes of change. However, ostensibly contradictory processes of change become complementary when embedded in the stages of change. Specifically, change processes traditionally associated with the experiential, humanistic, and psychoanalytic persuasions are most useful during the contemplation stage. Change processes traditionally associated with the behavioral tradition are most useful during the action and maintenance stages.

In this respect, efficient behavior change depends on doing the right things (processes) at the right time (stages). Two mismatches are common. First, some psychotherapists tend to rely on change processes most indicated for the contemplation stage—consciousness raising, self-reevaluation—while their patients are moving into the action stage. These clinicians try to modify behavior by becoming more aware, a common criticism of classical psychoanalysis: Insight alone does not necessarily bring about behavior change. Second, other psychotherapists rely primarily on change processes most indicated for the action phase—contingency management, stimulus control, counterconditioning—without the requisite awareness and decision making provided by a period of contemplation and preparation. These therapists try to modify behavior without awareness, a common criticism of radical behaviorism: Overt action without insight is likely to lead to temporary change (Prochaska et al., 1992).

A number of other organizing heuristics have been advanced to demonstrate the complementary, not contradictory, nature of change processes in psychotherapy. Different goals for the psychological treatment of the identical clinical problems, for example, will probably generate different change processes and psychotherapy systems. A goal of expanded awareness of a problem's origins would lead one to employ primarily verbal or insight processes, while patients desiring overt behavior change with little historical or intrapersonal awareness would lead to action and behavioral process. A person's personality style, to take another example, may also dictate preferential use of some change processes over others. As Beutler and colleagues discuss in the following chapter, highly resistant and externalizing patients respond better to less directive, insight-oriented therapies than to highly structured, directive interventions.

Theoretical complementarity and integration are the keys to synthesizing the major systems of psychotherapy. Each theoretical tradition has a place, often a differential place, in the "big picture" of behavior change. Depending on the client's stage of change, treatment goals, personality style, and other key matching variables, different therapy systems will play more or less of a prominent role.

The insight and verbal therapies focus primarily on the subjective aspects of the individual, the processes occurring within the organism. This perspective of the individual sees greater potential for inner-directed changes that can counteract some of the external pressures from the environment. By contrast, the behavioral and family systems therapies focus primarily on the external and environmental forces that set limits on the individual potential for inner-directed change. These are what the existentialists would call the more *objective* level of the organism (Prochaska & Norcross, 1994).

Psychotherapy integration in general, and the transtheoretical model in particular, maintain that to rely only on the awareness processes and to ignore the genuine limits the environment can place on individual change is to act as if inner-directedness is the whole picture. On the other hand, the action emphasis on the more objective environmental processes selectively ignores the potential for inner, subjective change that individuals possess. An integrative model posits that a synthesis of both awareness and action processes provides a more balanced view that moves along the continuous dimensions from inner to outer control, subjective to objective functioning, and self-initiated to

environmentally induced changes. These continuous dimensions afford a more complete picture of humans by accepting their potential for inner change while recognizing the limits that environments and contingencies place on such change (Prochaska & Norcross, 1994).

CURRENT STATUS

Having considered the various processes of change associated with an integrative approach to psychotherapy, we now turn to the current status of practice, training, and research.

Practice

Psychotherapy integration, as is now evident, comes in many guises and manifestations. It is clearly neither a monolithic entity nor a single operationalized system. In this sense, referring to *the* integrative or eclectic psychotherapy causes one to fall prey to the *uniformity myth*, a pervasive misconception that all psychological treatments sharing the same brand name are conceptualized and conducted identically (Kiesler, 1966).

This caution notwithstanding, most of contemporary psychotherapy now practiced goes by the label of *eclectic* or *integrative*. Approximately one-third to one-half of American mental health professionals disavow any affiliation with a particular school of therapy and, instead, endorse a variation of psychotherapy integration (Norcross, 1986). Reviewing 25 studies performed on various health professionals between 1953 and 1990, Jensen and associates (1990) reported that the incidence varied from 19% to 68%, the latter figure being their own finding. The consistent finding is that eclecticism/integration is routinely the modal orientation of responding psychotherapists. Similar results are also found in both European and non-European countries (Norcross & Newman, 1992).

In an early attempt to examine the practices of self-described eclectic psychotherapists, Garfield and Kurtz (1977) surveyed 145 eclectics and discerned 32 different theoretical orientations in use. The most popular hybrid of theoretical orientations were psychoanalytic and learning, psychoanalytic and client-centered, and learning and humanistic. Most combinations, however, were blended and employed in an idiosyncratic fashion. Norcross and Prochaska (1988) updated these 1977 results by studying 113 eclectic clinicians. The prototypical combinations of theoretical orientations, in contrast to those of the earlier Garfield and Kurtz study, were cognitive and behavioral, humanistic and cognitive, and psychoanalytic and cognitive. A particularly interesting finding was that one or more psychotherapists reported using each of the possible combinations of theories presented to them.

This study and other research also demonstrates an emerging preference for both the term *integration* and the practice of theoretical integration, as opposed to *eclecticism*. Clinicians now prefer the self-identification of *integrative* over *eclectic* by an almost 2 to 1 margin. This preference probably represents a historical shift analogous to social progression: one that proceeds from segregation to desegregation to integration. Eclecticism has represented desegregation, in which ideas, methods, and people from diverse theoretical backgrounds intermingle. Currently, we appear to be in a transition from desegregation to integration, with increasing efforts directed at discovering viable integrative principles for assimilating and accommodating the best that different systems have to offer (Norcross & Prochaska, 1988).

Integrative practice is obviously more complex than the self-reported prevalence that these survey glimpses provide. It is much more difficult to determine precisely what eclectic or integrative practice entails. Far more process research is needed on the conduct of these psychotherapies, and such investigation will probably rely on audio, video, and transcript recordings of the therapy offered in order to clarify the nature of therapeutic interventions (Goldfried, 1991). Until precision is attained in description and practice, the crucial question of whether outcomes are enhanced by psychotherapy integration will remain unanswered.

Training

Training therapists in psychotherapy integration presents somewhat of a dilemma. As noted by Andrews, Norcross, and Halgin (1992) in their extensive discussion of the issue, many of the long-standing difficulties in clinical training are compounded by the fact that there is no single, agreed-on form of psychotherapy integration. Moreover, those interested in integrated training must decide whether to educate beginning therapists to competence in a single orientation, being mindful of appropriate referrals to clinicians of other orientations when necessary, or to provide training in a multitude of orientations.

Andrews et al. (1992) lean more toward the integrated model, which may be approached in several steps. To begin with, trainees require a fundamental grounding in relationship formation and communications skills, particularly since therapy outcome research has found these areas to account for a very large proportion of the variance across orientations (Lambert, 1992). Following this, trainees should be exposed to a variety of conceptual models of human behavior, each of which should be presented in a nonjudgmental, descriptive manner. This training model then focuses on the implications of these different models of human functioning for actual intervention. In the fourth step of the training sequence, beginning therapists become competent in the use of at least two intervention models. In the final phase of training, attempts are made to integrate the different perspectives and to offer guidelines for the selection of different procedures, depending on particular issues inherent in the case at hand. It is acknowledged, however, that this provides only the beginning of thorough training in psychotherapy integration, as both time and experience are required to bring the therapist to the point of being able to function integratively in actual practice. Thus, additional training beyond the usual internship or residency is in order.

In discussing some of the particular dilemmas associated with integrative training, Andrews and his colleagues (1992) acknowledge that at our current stage in the development of the field, most integrative clinicians have probably received their own training within a single orientation. As a result, trainers and supervisors may at times revert to the model on which their own training was originally based, even while still approaching cases with an integrative stance. This may very well be confusing to the trainees, particularly since they are confronted with a wide array of possible formulations and methods of intervention. It is therefore important for trainers and supervisors to acknowledge the difficulty experienced by trainees, perhaps by disclosing the complexities that they themselves may experience in the decision-making process.

In the final analysis, training therapists in psychotherapy integration is much like teaching jazz piano: "The student must acquire factual knowledge, master technical skills, and appreciate musical principles. Then—and only then—the disciplined improviser must learn to combine these elements in unique, improvisational, and yet coherently integrated performances" (Andrews et al., 1992, p. 587; also see Schacht, 1991).

Research

For the most part, interest in psychotherapy integration over the years received most of its impetus from clinical practice. Mental health professionals of different orientations, in attempting to apply their theories clinically, encountered clear limitations along with their successes. This led to a dialogue among therapists in which conceptual and clinical issues pointed to the need for more integrative approaches to intervention. Only very recently has the field begun to shift its attention to research into this new orientation to therapy.

In 1986, the National Institute of Mental Health (NIMH) held a workshop to discuss potential research directions in the field of psychotherapy integration (Wolfe & Goldfried, 1988). One of the recommendations was to encourage the comparative analysis of "pure-form" therapies to identify both the common and unique processes that appear to contribute to change. It was also noted that there exists a need to find neutral languages that would allow for communication across orientations, as well as for retrieving basic research findings from the literature. In essence, it was suggested that work on "desegregation" was needed to inform the development of "integration," in which results of psychotherapeutic change processes could be used to formulate an integrative intervention for various kinds of clinical cases. The workshop also concluded that there exists a need for controlled outcome studies to determine whether integrative approaches to therapy are more effective clinically than those that follow a single orientation.

Although research relevant to psychotherapy integration is still in its very early stages, work on a number of these dimensions is currently underway. Lambert (1992), in a review of psychotherapy outcome research in general, has suggested that to the extent that integrative approaches overlap with more traditional methods, it is likely that they will be shown to be at least as effective. He suggests that in light of the findings that point to the effectiveness of some commonalities across orientations (e.g., the therapeutic relationship), it is essential that these be highlighted in integrative attempts. At the same time, it is important not to overlook the empirically demonstrated unique contributions of certain interventions (e.g., exposure methods with anxiety disorders).

Researchers studying the psychotherapy process as it exists in different orientations provide an example of current work being done on the desegregation of the therapies (e.g., Beutler & Consoli, 1992; Goldfried, 1991). Findings are also beginning to appear that indicate an interaction between patient characteristics and particular interventions, such as the finding reported by Beutler and Consoli (1992) that cognitive interventions were more effective than insight-oriented treatment with externalizing patients, and that defensive or reactive individuals responded better to nondirective than directive treatments. Also relevant is the work of Prochaska and DiClemente (1992), which suggests that an intervention that takes into account where a patient exists within the general phase of the change process can be more effective than treatment procedures that do not.[3]

The prescriptive matching done in clinical research (and in practice) has largely entailed tailoring specific techniques in individual psychotherapy to a client's disorder or presenting problem. While we fully expect that there will be a continued movement toward the development of specific treatments for different diagnostic groupings, the traditional emphasis on prescriptive matching will be redirected in at least three ways. First, psychological therapies will be increasingly matched to client variables beyond diagnosis. Patient objectives, coping behaviors, resistance levels, and situational context, among others, will be systematized as means of applying tailored interventions (Lazarus, Beutler, & Norcross, 1992; Norcross, 1991). As the following chapter by Beutler and collaborators attests, research has begun to support the value of designing psychotherapeutic interventions to fit these and other patient characteristics.

Second, prescriptive matching will be broadened to denote not only specific clinical procedures but also therapist relationship stances (Norcross, 1993). One way to conceptualize this issue, paralleling the notion of *treatment of choice* in terms of techniques, is how the clinician determines the *relationship of choice* in terms of interpersonal stances for individual clients. Under which circumstances or with which clients, for example, should a therapist be loud, active, and directive versus relatively quiet, passive, and nondirective? The challenge will be to articulate and operationalize the grounds on which to tailor interpersonal styles and stimulus values to meet the needs of diverse clients (see Norcross, 1993, for examples).

Third and finally, prescriptive matching has now graduated beyond psychological interventions within the narrow context of psychosocial therapies. The 1990s will witness strong efforts to combine psychotherapy and pharmacother-apy (Beitman & Klerman, 1991), as well as individual, family, and group therapies (Feldman, 1992), if for no reason other than pressure for cost efficiency in mental health care.

SOME CRITICAL ELEMENTS

In comparison to leading systems of psychotherapy, integrative and eclectic models are distinctive in at least two ways. First, psychotherapy integration posits that a large number and wide range of mechanisms constitute the active ingredients of change. Psychoanalysts may believe that interpretations, analysis of resistance, and resolution of transference are the active mechanisms of change, while behaviorists may attribute change to skill training, desensitization, and contingency management. By contrast, integrative and eclectic therapists believe that both the awareness-enhancing processes of psychoanalysis and the action-producing processes of behaviorism—plus many others—are the curative factors in psychotherapy. In sum, psychotherapy integration embraces an inclusive and broad epistemology of change.

Second, integrative and eclectic psychotherapies are comparatively unique in that they typically emphasize process over content. This distinction between process and content in psychotherapy is a critical one (Held, 1991). Psychotherapy systems without formal theories of personality, such as eclectic and integrative approaches, are primarily process theories and have few predetermined concepts about the content of therapy. Therefore, they attempt to capitalize on the unique aspect of each case by restricting the imposition of formal content. By contrast, most systems of psychotherapy focus on the content to be changed as a carryover from that system's theory of personality and psychopathology. Many books purportedly focusing on psychotherapy frequently confuse content and process and, as a consequence, examine the content of therapy, with little explanation about the processes (Prochaska & Norcross, 1994). Put differently, theories of personality and psychopathology tell us *what* needs to be changed, while theories of process tell us *how* change occurs (Arkowitz, 1989).

A comparative analysis reveals how much psychotherapy systems agree on the processes producing change (the how) while disagreeing on the content to be changed (the what). In other words, different theories do not dictate the specific interventions to use as much as they determine the therapeutic goals or content to pursue (Beutler, 1983; Prochaska & Norcross, 1994).

As an illustration, consider the psychological treatment of specific phobias. Freud (1919), the intrapsychic master, stressed that if the psychoanalyst actively induced patients to expose themselves to the feared stimuli "a considerable moderation" of the phobia would be achieved. This observation predates the contemporary consensus on the importance of the behavioral methods of exposure and response prevention in alleviating specific phobic behaviors. Freud, then, early and readily understood the process of reducing phobic behavior, but he decided that the desirable content or goal of psychoanalysis was to make the unconscious conscious. He opted to disregard the behavioral process of change in pursuit of other content to be changed (Norcross, 1991).

As noted earlier, a tripartite distinction is found in psychotherapy integration among common factors, technical eclecticism, and theoretical integration. These are not three separate or distinct ways of approaching the task of integrating the therapies; rather, they are clearly interrelated. For example, common factors inform us about what different theoretical models have in common and, as a result, highlight the areas in which more detailed empirical and clinical examination is required. In looking for greater specificity in our clinical and research efforts, we thus move into clarification of the parameters of these general principles. This represents the technical eclecticism thread of the movement, in which we examine which techniques are effective in which clinical situations. Once we have obtained information on the effectiveness of several techniques, it is possible to engage in a bottom-up approach to theory construction. Thus, while theoretical

constructs associated with a given school of thought may have generated specific interventions, the existence of a technically eclectic array of effective methods requires us to regroup what we have found to be effective into a new conceptual model involving a form of theoretical integration.

CONCLUDING OBSERVATIONS

The growth of interest in eclectic and integrative psychotherapies has crystallized into a formal movement during the last decade. At its most dramatic, this movement has been termed a "revolution" or a "metamorphosis" in mental health (London, 1988; Moultrup, 1986). This transformation has begun to shift our attention from *who* is correct to *what* is correct in psychotherapy. Probably for the first time since the birth of psychotherapy a mere 100 years ago, the majority of mental health professionals are overtly expressing dissatisfaction with any single-school approach and publicly acknowledging their interest in learning from other ways of thinking about psychotherapy and behavior change. Whether we call it a gradual evolution or an abrupt revolution, psychotherapy integration in its many forms will certainly represent the therapeutic zeitgeist of the twenty-first century (Goldfried & Castonguay, 1992; Norcross, Alford, & DeMichele, 1992).

Conspicuously absent from this chapter has been acknowledgment of the contributions of conventional, pure-form systems of psychotherapy, such as psychodynamic, behavioral, existential, cognitive, and systemic. While perhaps not immediately apparent, pure-form therapies are part and parcel of the integration movement. In fact, integration could not occur without the constituent elements provided by these therapies—their theoretical systems and their clinical methods. In a very real sense, these preexisting therapies add to our therapeutic armamentarium, enrich our understanding of the clinical process, and generate the process and outcome research from which integration draws (Norcross & Newman, 1992).

The ultimate objective of the integration

movement is to improve the efficacy of psychotherapy. To achieve this end, integration needs to promote a welcoming attitude on the part of school-based psychotherapies and to build on the documented successes of pure-form therapies. What we seek, then, is to forge a productive relationship between integration and these brand-name therapies: something akin to what the psychoanalyst calls the *working alliance*, what the behavior therapist might term a *relational precondition*, the experientialist an *I-Thou relationship*, the cognitive therapist a *collaborative empiricism*, and the family therapist an *open system*. Psychotherapy integration seeks to cultivate an inclusive and empirical approach in which the valuable contributions of pure-form therapies are collegially acknowledged and their respective strengths collaboratively enlisted.

Integrative and eclectic therapies, as presented in this and the next chapter, constitute a vibrant and promising movement that has been catalytic in the search for new ways of conceptualizing and conducting psychotherapy, ways that go beyond the confines of a single school. Integrative perspectives have encouraged practitioners and researchers to examine what other theories and therapies have to offer them and, more important, their clients. Open inquiry, transtheoretical dialogue, and cross-fertilization have fostered new ways of thinking about psychotherapy and change.

The early successes of the integration movement, however, raise a critical question for its future: Will there be competition and proliferation of various schools of psychotherapy integration, just as there has been intense competition among the pure-form schools? We and others (e.g., Arkowitz, 1992; Arnkoff & Glass, 1992; Goldfried & Safran, 1986; Lazarus, Beutler, & Norcross, 1992; Norcross & Newman, 1992; Wachtel & McKinney, 1992) are convinced that partisanship and competition among developing integrative models will simply repeat the same old historic mistakes of psychotherapy. Psychotherapy integration will then, ironically, become the rigid and institutionalized perspective that integration attempted to counter in the first place. Rather, our view

of—indeed, our hope for—the integration movement is that it will engender an open system of informed pluralism, deepening rapprochement, and empirically grounded practice that leads, in the final analysis, to enhanced efficacy of psychotherapy.

Acknowledgment

Preparation of this chapter was supported in part by Grant No. MH40196 awarded to the first author from the National Institute of Mental Health.

NOTES

1. For further information about SEPI, contact Dr. George Stricker, The Derner Institute, Adelphi University, Garden City, NY 11530.

2. Detailed debates on the relative merits of technical eclecticism versus theoretical integration can be found in Goldfried and Wachtel (1987), Beutler (1989) and Arkowitz (1989), as well as Lazarus (1989b) and Beitman (1989).

3. Further consideration of research issues in psychotherapy integration is provided by Goldfried (1991), Lambert (1992), Norcross (1993), and Wolfe and Goldfried (1988).

REFERENCES

Alexander, F. (1963). The dynamics of psychotherapy in light of learning theory. *American Journal of Psychiatry, 120,* 440–448.

Allen, D. M. (1988). *Unifying individual and family therapies.* San Francisco: Jossey-Bass.

Andrews, J. D., Norcross, J. C., & Halgin, R. P. (1992). Training in psychotherapy integration. In J. C. Novcross & M.R. Goldfried (Eds.), *Handbook oh psychotherapy integration.* (pp. 563–592). New York: Basic Books.

Arkowitz, H. (1989). The role of theory in psychotherapy integration. *Journal of Integrative and Eclectic Psychotherapy, 8,* 8–16.

Arkowitz, H. (1992). Integrative theories of therapy. In D. K. Freedheim (Ed.), *History of psychotherapy: A century of change* (pp. 261–303). Washington, DC: American Psychological Association.

Arkowitz, H., & Messer, S. B. (Eds.). (1984). *Psychoanalytic and behavior therapy: Is integration possible?* New York: Plenum Press.

Arnkoff, D. B., & Glass, C. R. (1992). Cognitive therapy and psychotherapy integration. In D. K. Freedheim (Ed.), *History of psychotherapy: A century of change* (pp. 657–694). Washington, DC: American Psychological Association.

Bastine, R. (1975). Auf dem Wege zu einer integrierten Psychtherapie [Towards an integrated psychotherapy].*Psychologie Heute*, *53–58*.

Bastine, R. (1980). Ausbildungen in psychotherapeutischen Methoden und Strategien [Training in psychotherapeutic methods and strategies]. In V. Birtsche & D. Tscheulin (Eds.), *Ausbildung in klinischer Psychologie und Psychotherapie*. Weinheim: Beltz.

Beitman, B. D. (1987). *The structure of individual psychotherapy*. New York: Guilford Press.

Beitman, B. D. (1989). Why am I an integrationist (not an eclectic). *British Journal of Guidance and Counselling*, *17*, 259–273.

Beitman, B. D. (1992). Integration through fundamental similarities and useful differences among the schools. In J. C. Norcross & M. R. Goldfried (Eds.), *Handbook of psychotherapy integration* (pp. 202–230). New York: Basic Books.

Beitman, B. D., Goldfried, M. R., & Norcross, J. C. (1989). The movement toward integrating the psychotherapies: An overview. *American Journal of Psychiatry*, *146*, 138–147.

Beitman, B. D., & Klerman, G. L. (Eds.). (1991). *Integrating pharmacotherapy and psychotherapy*. Washington, DC: American Psychiatric Press.

Bergin, A. E. (1968). Technique for improving desensitization via warmth, empathy, and emotional re-experiencing of hierarchy events. In R. Rubin & C. M. Franks (Eds.), *Advances in behavior therapy*. New York: Academic Press.

Bergin, A. E. (1970). Cognitive therapy and behavior therapy: Foci for a multidimensional approach to treatment. *Behavior Therapy*, *1*, 206–212.

Beutler, L. E. (1983). *Eclectic psychotherapy: A systematic approach*. New York: Pergamon Press.

Beutler, L. E. (1989). The misplaced role of theory in psychotherapy integration. *Journal of Integrative and Eclectic Psychotherapy*, *8*, 17–22.

Beutler, L. E., & Clarkin, J. (1990). *Systematic treatment selection: Toward targeted therapeutic interventions*. New York: Brunner/Mazel.

Beutler, L. E., & Consoli, A. J. (1992). Systematic eclectic psychotherapy. In J. C. Norcross & M. R. Goldfried (Eds.), *Handbook of psychotherapy integration* (pp. 264–299.) New York: Basic Books.

Beutler, L. E., Mahoney, M. J. Norcross, J. C., Prochaska, J. O., Sollod, R. M., & Robertson, M. (1987). Training integrative/eclectic psychotherapists II. *Journal of Integrative and Eclectic Psychotherapy*, *6*, 296–332.

Birk, L. (1973). Psychoanalysis and behavioral analysis: Natural resonance and complementarity. *International Journal of Psychiatry*, *11*, 160–166.

Birk, L., & Brinkley-Birk, A. (1974). Psychoanalysis and behavior therapy. *American Journal of Psychiatry*, *131*, 499–510.

Brady, J. P., Davison, G. C., Dewald, P. A., Egan, G., Fadiman, J., Frank, J. D., Gill, M. M., Hoffman, I., Kempler, W., Lazarus, A. A., Raimy, V., Rotter, J. B., & Strupp, H. H. (1980). Some views on effective principles of psychotherapy. *Cognitive Therapy and Research*, *4*, 271–306.

Davison, G. C. (1978). *Theory and practice in behavior therapy: An unconsummated marriage* (audiocassette). New York: BMA Audio Cassettes.

Dollard, J., & Miller, N. (1950). *Personality and psychotherapy: An analysis in terms of learning, thinking, and culture*. New York: McGraw-Hill.

Driscoll, R. (1984). *Pragmatic psychotherapy*. New York: Van Nostrand Reinhold.

Dryden, W. (1980). "Eclectic" approaches in individual counselling: Some pertinent issues. *The Counsellor*, *3*, 24–30.

Dryden, W. (Ed.). (1984). *Individual therapy in Britain*. London: Harper & Row.

Egan, G. (1975). *The skilled helper*. Monterey, CA: Brooks/Cole.

Feather, B. W., & Rhodes, J. M. (1972a). Psychodynamic behavior therapy: 1. Theory and rationale. *Archives of General Psychiatry*, *26*, 496–502.

Feather, B. W., & Rhodes, J. M. (1972b). Psychodynamic behavior therapy: 2. Clinical aspects. *Archives of General Psychiatry*, *26*, 503–511.

Feldman, L. B. (1989). Integrating individual and family therapy. *Journal of Integrative and Eclectic Psychotherapy*, *8*, 41–52.

Feldman, L. B. (1992). *Integrating individual and family therapy*. New York: Brunner/Mazel.

Fensterheim, H., & Glazer, H. I. (Eds.). (1983). *Behavioral psychotherapy*. New York: Brunner/Mazel.

Frank, J. D. (1961). *Persuasion and healing: A comparative study of psychotherapy*. New York: Schocken Books.

Frank, J. D. (1973). *Persuasion and healing* (2nd

ed.). Baltimore: Johns Hopkins University Press.

Frank, J. D. (1982). Therapeutic components shared by all psychotherapies. In J. H. Harvey & M. M. Parks (Eds.), *The Master Lecture Series: Psychotherapy research and behavior change*. Washington, DC: American Psychological Association.

Frank, J. D., Frank, J. (1991). *Persuasion and healing* (3rd ed.). Baltimore: Johns Hopkins University Press.

French, T. M. (1933). Interrelations between psychoanalysis and the experimental work of Pavlov. *American Journal of Psychiatry, 89*, 1165–1203.

Freud, S. (1919). Turnings in the ways of psychoanalytic therapy. *Collected Papers* (Vol. 2, pp. 392–402). London: Hogarth Press.

Garfield, S. L. (1957). *Introductory clinical psychology*. New York: Macmillan.

Garfield, S. L. (1980). *Psychotherapy: An eclectic approach*. New York: Wiley.

Garfield, S. L. (1986). An eclectic psychotherapy. In J. C. Norcross (Ed.), *Handbook of eclectic psychotherapy* (pp. 132–162). New York: Brunner/Mazel.

Garfield, S. L. (1992). Eclectic psychotherapy: A common factors approach. In J. C. Norcross and M. R. Goldfried (Eds.), *Handbook of psychotherapy integration* (pp. 169–201). New York: Basic Books.

Garfield, S. L., & Kurtz, R. (1976). Clinical psychologists in the 1970s. *American Psychologist, 31*, 1–9.

Garfield, S. L., & Kurtz, R. (1977). A study of eclectic views. *Journal of Clinical and Consulting Psychology, 45*, 78–83.

Giunta, L. C., Saltzman, N., & Norcross, J. C. (1991). Whither integration? An exploratory study of contention and convergence in the Clinical Exchange. *Journal of Integrative and Eclectic Psychotherapy, 10*, 117–129.

Goldfried, M. R. (1979). Anxiety reduction through cognitive-behavioral intervention. In P. C. Kendall & S. D. Hollon (Eds.), *Cognitive-behavioral interventions: Theory, research, procedures* (pp. 117–152). New York: Academic Press.

Goldfried, M. R. (1980). Toward the delineation of therapeutic change principles. *American Psychologist, 35*, 991–999.

Goldfried, M. R. (Ed.). (1982). *Converging themes in psychotherapy: Trends in psychodynamic, humanistic, and behavioral practice*. New York: Springer.

Goldfried, M. R. (1991). Research issues in psychotherapy integration. *Journal of Psychotherapy Integration, 1*, 5–25.

Goldfried, M. R., & Castonguay, L. G. (1992). The future of psychotherapy integration. *Psychotherapy, 29*, 4–10.

Goldfried, M. R., & Davison, G. (1976). *Clinical behavior therapy*. New York: Holt, Rinehart & Winston.

Goldfried, M. R., & Newman, C. (1986). Psychotherapy integration: An historical perspective. In J. C. Norcross (Ed.), *Handbook of eclectic psychotherapy* (pp. 25–61). New York: Brunner/Mazel.

Goldfried, M. R., & Newman, C. (1992). A history of psychotherapy integration. In J. C. Norcross & M. R. Goldfried (Eds.), *Handbook of psychotherapy integration* (pp. 46–93). New York: Basic Books.

Goldfried, M. R., & Safran, J. D. (1986). Future directions in psychotherapy integration. In J. C. Norcross (Ed.), *Handbook of eclectic psychotherapy* (pp. 463–483). New York: Brunner/Mazel.

Goldfried, M. R., & Wachtel, P. L. (1987). Clinical and conceptual issues in psychotherapy integration: A dialogue. *Journal of Integrative and Eclectic Psychotherapy, 6*, 131–144.

Goldstein, A. J., & Chambless, D. L. (1978). A reanalysis of agoraphobia. *Behavior Therapy, 9*, 47–59.

Greenberg, L. S., & Safran, J. D. (1987). *Emotion in psychotherapy*. New York: Guilford Press.

Greening, T. C. (1978). Commentary. *Journal of Humanistic Psychology, 18*, 1–4.

Grencavage, L. M., & Norcross, J. C. (1990). Where are the commonalities among the therapeutic common factors? *Professional Psychology: Research and Practice, 21*, 372–378.

Guidano, V. F. (1987). *Complexity of the self: A developmental approach to psychotherapy and theory*. New York: Guilford Press.

Hart, J. (1983). *Modern eclectic therapy*. New York: Plenum Press.

Held, B. (1991). The process/content distinction in psychotherapy revisited. *Psychotherapy, 28*, 207–217.

Jensen, J. P., Bergin, A. E., & Greaves, D. W. (1990). The meaning of eclecticism: New survey and analysis of components. *Professional Psychology: Research and Practice, 21*, 124–130.

Kaplan, H. (1974). *The new sex therapy*. New York: Brunner/Mazel.

Karasu, T. B. (1986). The specificity versus nonspecificity dilemma: Toward identifying therapeutic change agents. *American Journal of Psychiatry,* 143, 687–695.

Kiesler, D. J. (1966). Some myths of psychotherapy research and the search for a paradigm. *Psychological Bulletin,* 65, 110–136.

Lacomte, C., &. Castonguay, L. G. (Eds.). (1987). *Rapprochement et integration en psychotherapie.* Montreal: Gaetan Morin Editeur.

Lambert, M. J. (1992). Psychotherapy outcome research: Implications for integrative and eclectic therapists. In J. C. Norcross & M. R. Goldfried (Eds.), *Handbook of psychotherapy integration* (pp. 94–129). New York: Basic Books.

Larson, D. (1980). Therapeutic schools, styles, and schoolism: A national survey. *Journal of Humanistic Psychology,* 20, 3–20.

Lazarus, A. A. (1967). In support of technical eclecticism. *Psychological Reports,* 21, 415–416.

Lazarus, A. A. (1971a). *Behavior therapy and beyond.* New York: McGraw-Hill.

Lazarus, A. A. (1971b). Has behavior therapy outlived its usefulness? *American Psychologist,* 32, 550–555.

Lazarus, A. A. (1976). *Multimodal behavior therapy.* New York: Springer.

Lazarus, A. A. (1989a). *The practice of multimodal therapy.* Baltimore: Johns Hopkins University Press.

Lazarus, A. A. (1989b). Why I am an eclectic (not an integrationist). *British Journal of Guidance and Counselling,* 19, 248–258.

Lazarus, A. A. (1992). Multimodal therapy: Technical eclecticism with minimal integration. In J. C. Norcross & M. R. Goldfried (Eds.), *Handbook of psychotherapy integration* (pp. 231–263). New York: Basic Books.

Lazarus, A. A., Beutler, L. E., & Norcross, J. C. (1992). The future of technical eclecticism. *Psychotherapy,* 29, 11–20.

Linsenhoff, A., Bastine, R., & Kommer, D. (1980). Schulenubergreifende Perspektiven in der Psychotherapie [Transtheoretical perspectives in psychotherapy]. *Integrative Psychotherapie,* 4, 302–322.

London, P. (1964). *The modes and morals of psychotherapy.* New York: Holt, Rinehart & Winston.

London, P. (1972). The end of ideology in behavior modification. *American Psychologist,* 27, 913–920.

London, P. (1986). *The modes and morals of psychotherapy* (2nd ed.). New York: Hemisphere.

London, P. (1988). Metamorphosis in psychother-apy: Slouching toward integration. *Journal of Integrative and Eclectic Psychotherapy,* 7, 3–12.

Mahoney, M. J. (1979). Cognitive and noncognitive views in behavior modification. In P. O. Sjoden & S. Bates (Eds.), *Trends in behavior therapy.* New York: Plenum Press.

Mahoney, M. J. (1980). Psychotherapy and the structure of personal revolutions. In M. Mahoney (Ed.), *Psychotherapy process* (pp. 157–180). New York: Plenum Press.

Mahrer, A. R. (1989). *The integration of psychotherapies.* New York: Human Sciences Press.

Marks, I. M., & Gelder, M. G. (1966). Common ground between behavior therapy and psychodynamic methods. *British Journal of Medical Psychology,* 39, 11–23.

Marmor, J. (1969). Neurosis and the psychotherapeutic process: Similarities and differences in the behavioral and psychodynamic conceptions. *International Journal of Psychiatry,* 7, 514–519.

Marmor, J., & Woods, S. M. (Eds.). (1980). *The interface between psychodynamic and behavioral therapies.* New York: Plenum Press.

Moultrup, D. (1986). Integration: A coming of age. *Contemporary Family Therapy,* 8, 157–167.

Norcross, J. C. (Ed.). (1986). *Handbook of eclectic psychotherapy.* New York: Brunner/ Mazel.

Norcross, J. C. (Ed.). (1987). *Casebook of eclectic psychotherapy.* New York: Brunner/Mazel.

Norcross, J. C. (1991). (Special section editor). Prescriptive matching in psychotherapy: Psychoanalysis for simple phobias? *Psychotherapy,* 28, 439–472.

Norcross, J. E. (Ed). (1993). Research directions for psychotherapy integration: A roundtable. *Journal of Psychotherapy Integration,* 3, 91–131.

Norcross, J. C. (Special Section Ed.). (1993). The relationship of choice: Matching the therapist's stance to individual clients. *Psychotherapy,* 30, 402–426.

Norcross, J. C., Alford, B. A., & DeMichele, J. T. (1992). The future of psychotherapy: Delphi data and concluding observations. *Psychotherapy,* 29, 150–158.

Norcross, J. C., Beutler, L. E., Clarkin, J. F., DiClemente, C. C., Halgin, R. P., Frances, A., Prochaska, J. O., Robertson, M., & Suedfeld, P. (1986). Training integrative/eclectic psychotherapists. *International Journal of Eclectic Psychotherapy,* 5, 71–94.

Norcross, J. C., & Grencavage, L. M. (1989).

Eclecticism and integration in psychotherapy: Major themes and obstacles. *British Journal of Guidance and Counselling, 17,* 227–247.

Norcross, J. C., & Newman, C. F. (1992). Psychotherapy integration: Setting the context. In J. C. Norcross & M. R. Goldfried (Eds.), *Handbook of psychotherapy integration* (pp. 3–45). New York: Basic Books.

Norcross, J. C., & Prochaska, J. O. (1988). A study of eclectic (and integrative) views revisited. *Professional Psychology: Research and Practice, 19,* 170–174.

Prochaska, J. O. (1979). Systems of psychotherapy: A transtheoretical analysis. Homewood, IL: Dorsey Press.

Prochaska, J. O., & DiClemente, C. C. (1982). Transtheoretical therapy: Toward a more integrative model of change. *Psychotherapy: Theory, Research and Practice, 19,* 276–288.

Prochaska, J. O., & DiClemente, C. C. (1984). *The transtheoretical approach: Crossing the traditional boundaries of therapy.* Homewood, IL: Dow Jones-Irwin.

Prochaska, J. O., & DiClemente, C. C. (1992). The transtheoretical approach. In J. C. Norcross & M. R. Goldfried (Eds.), *Handbook of psychotherapy integration* (pp. 300–304). New York: Basic Books.

Prochaska, J. O., DiClemente, C. C., & Norcross, J. C. (1992). In search of how people change: Applications to addictive behaviors. *American Psychologist, 47,* 1102–1114.

Prochaska, J. O., & Norcross, J. C. (1994). *Systems of psychotherapy: A transtheoretical analysis* (3rd ed.). Pacific Grove, CA: Brooks/Cole.

Prochaska, J. O., Velicer, W. F., DiClemente, C. C., & Fava, J. S. (1988). Measuring processes of change: Applications to the cessation of smoking. *Journal of Consulting and Clinical Psychology, 56,* 520–528.

Raimy, V. (1975). *Misunderstandings of the self.* San Francisco: Jossey-Bass.

Rogers, C. R. (1963). Psychotherapy today or where do we go from here? *American Journal of Psychotherapy, 17,* 5–15.

Rosenzweig, S. (1936). Some implicit common factors in diverse methods in psychotherapy. *American Journal of Orthopsychiatry, 6,* 412–415.

Ryle, A. (1978). A common language for the psychotherapies? *British Journal of Psychiatry, 132,* 585–594.

Ryle, A. (1982). *Psychotherapy: A cognitive integration of theory and practice.* London: Academic Press.

Sarason, I. G. (1979). Three lacunae of cognitive therapy. *Cognitive Therapy and Research, 3,* 223–235.

Schacht, T. E. (1984). The varieties of integrative experience. In H. Arkowitz & S. B. Messer (Eds.), *Psychoanalytic therapy and behavior therapy: Is integration possible?* (pp. 107–131). New York: Plenum Press.

Schacht, T. E. (1991). Can psychotherapy education advance psychotherapy integration? *Journal of Psychotherapy Integration, 1,* 305–319.

Segraves, R. T. (1982). *Marital therapy: A combined psychodynamic-behavioral approach.* New York: Plenum Press.

Strupp, H. H. (1976). Some critical comments on the future of psychoanalytic therapy. *Bulletin of the Menninger Clinic, 40,* 238–254.

Textor, M. R. (Ed.). (1983). *Integrative psychotherapie.* Munich: Schobert.

Wachtel, P. L. (1975). Behavior therapy and the facilitation of psychoanalytic exploration. *Psychotherapy: Theory, Research, and Practice, 12,* 68–72.

Wachtel, P. L. (1977). *Psychoanalysis and behavior therapy: Toward an integration.* New York: Basic Books.

Wachtel, P. L. (Ed.). (1982). *Resistance: Psychodynamic and behavioral approaches.* New York: Plenum Press.

Wachtel, P. L. (1987). *Action and insight.* New York: Guilford Press.

Wachtel, P. L. (1991). From eclecticism to synthesis: Toward a more seamless psychotherapeutic integration. *Journal of Psychotherapy Integration, 1,* 43–54.

Wachtel, P. L., & McKinney, M. K. (1992). Cyclical psychodynamics and integrative psychodynamic therapy. In J. C. Norcross & M. R. Goldfried (Eds.), *Handbook of psychotherapy integration* (pp. 335–370). New York: Basic Books.

Wachtel, E. F., & Wachtel, P. L. (1986). *Family dynamics in individual psychotherapy.* New York: Guilford Press.

Wolf, E. (1966). Learning theory and psychoanalysis. *British Journal of Medical Psychology, 39,* 1–10.

Wolfe, B. E., & Goldfried, M. R. (1988). Research on psychotherapy integration: Recommendations and conclusions from an NIMH workshop. *Journal of Consulting and Clinical Psychology, 56,* 448–451.

15

Integrative and Eclectic Therapies in Practice

Larry E. Beutler
Andrés J. Consoli
Rebecca E. Williams

This chapter provides a brief illustration of integrative and eclectic psychotherapies in practice. As the preceding chapter explains, technical eclecticism is one thrust of the psychotherapy integration movement and represents a class of comprehensive treatment approaches that empower the clinician to select specific therapeutic strategies, techniques, and relationships to match the needs of each unique patient.

The first author and his colleagues (Beutler, 1979, 1983, 1986; Beutler & Clarkin, 1990; Beutler & Consoli, 1992) have developed, and are attempting to validate, a brand of technical eclecticism called *systematic eclectic psychotherapy (s.e.p.)*.[1] In this chapter, the reader will be introduced to the characteristics of treatment in the s.e.p. model. We will navigate through the four central levels of psychotherapy within the s.e.p. model and outline the decisions made at each level. These levels are patient characteristics, treatment context, patient–therapist relationship qualities, and selection of strategies and techniques. Decisional guides and case examples will be provided throughout the chapter to aid the reader in conceptualizing clinical material and in developing an effective treatment plan from the vantage point of s.e.p. At the close of the chapter, we will discuss future directions and trends with respect to the practice of technical eclecticism.

BACKGROUND

It is helpful to differentiate among three major thrusts or forms of psychotherapy integration: *theoretical integration* (integration of current approaches at the level of developing a new theory that embodies key elements of other theories); the *common factors approach* (the belief that all psychotherapies exert their effects through the same underlying principles and factors); and *technical eclecticism* (an empirical integration of strategies in order to select specific treatment procedures for given individuals) (Arkowitz, 1992; Chapter 14, this volume). Some (e.g. Norcross, 1986) suggest the terms *haphazard eclecticism* or *syncretism* (the unsystematic but well-intentioned effort to "do what's best for the patient") as a point of contrast to these more systematic approaches.

Technical eclecticism (Lazarus, 1989a; Norcross, 1986), the approach illustrated by s.e.p., rests on two cardinal assumptions: (1) not all therapeutic interventions are equally effective for all individuals (i.e., "different folks benefit from different strokes") and (2) therapeutic procedures can be applied independently of the theories from which they were derived. If these assumptions are true, it follows that the empirical value of various procedures may usefully guide the selection and use of different strategies with different patients, without the necessity of accepting or validating the theories from which these procedures are drawn. It further follows that with this approach it may be possible to circumvent much useless controversy about the "truth" of different theories.

Technical eclecticism proposes that treatment procedures from a variety of theoretical frameworks can be integrated and systematically applied in therapy. This is achieved by relying on scientific evidence not only of the clinical efficacy of the interventions, but also of the types of patients with whom the interventions work best. Technical eclecticism is distinguished from theoretical integration by its focus on clinical operations rather than on theory; from the common factors approach by its focus on the distinguishing and specific procedures; and from syncretism by its advocacy of systematic decision guidelines for application of these procedures.

We will discuss s.e.p. at length and only briefly mention another form of technical eclecticism, the multimodal therapy, developed by Arnold A. Lazarus (1989a, 1989b). Both approaches highlight the importance of tailoring specific treatments to given patients, and both attempt to answer Gordon Paul's (1969) famous question: "What treatment, by whom, is most effective for this individual with that specific problem, under which set of circumstances, and how does it come about?" (p. 44). Also, both approaches emphasize the importance of tailoring therapeutic relationship styles to given patients: formal and somewhat distant with some patients, less formal and more empathic with others (Beutler & Consoli, 1993; Lazarus, Beutler, & Norcross, 1992).

Multimodal therapy is characterized by a multimodal assessment of a person through what it is known as the BASIC I.D. The acronym stands for Behavior, Affect, Sensation, Imagery, Cognition, Interpersonal Relationships, and Drugs/Biology. The multimodal therapist creates a modality profile for each patient that outlines the excesses and deficits in each area of the BASIC I.D. and then customizes a treatment plan based on those problematic areas. The assessment also establishes a probable "firing order" of the modalities (e.g., I.BSCA) through a process termed *tracking*. The multimodal therapist addresses the needs of the patient by tuning in to the patient's preferred or dominant modality and then slowly moving the patient into more productive modes, a procedure called *bridging*.

Although an influential and early form of technical eclecticism, multimodal therapy does have some limitations. Two of the criticisms raised against it are its scarcity of empirical research and its relatively unchanged nature since its formulation in 1976. The claim that the BASIC I.D. construct encompasses "human temperament and personality" and accounts for "everything from anger, disappointment, disgust, greed, fear, grief, awe, contempt, and boredom to love, hope, faith, ecstasy, optimism, and joy" seems a bit too optimistic and does not account fully for "sociocultural, political, and other macroenvironmental events" (Lazarus, 1989b, p. 504). Finally, and perhaps most important for our purposes, multimodal therapy does not provide explicit guidelines for determining the treatments of choice and does not generate specific client markers for different treatments.

SYSTEMATIC ECLECTIC PSYCHOTHERAPY

The s.e.p. psychotherapy approach is a psychosocial intervention that emphasizes the therapeutic alliance between therapist and patient and that remains skeptical of the role of diagnosis in the planning of specific psychotherapy strategies (Beutler, 1989). It is systematic because it strives to develop specific, research-based guidelines to determine which procedures are selected and implemented with a given patient and which ones are contraindicated (Beutler & Clarkin, 1990). It is eclectic because it attempts to bring together therapeutic strategies, techniques, and relationship stances from different schools that are occasionally and erroneously viewed as incompatible. Psychotherapy in this model is defined as a social-influence or persuasion process. The content of the persuasive message is specified by the therapist's operational theory (an explanation of change and a formulation of treatment objectives), while the techniques are the means of conveying this message and exerting an influence over its acceptance (Beutler & Consoli, 1992).

The s.e.p. approach follows a sequence of not necessarily linear, but increasingly specific, decisions to arrive at and to carry out a treatment plan. First, the s.e.p. therapist considers the patient's predisposing qualities, including personal characteristics, stressors, and resources. Second, the therapist decides the context in which to carry out treatment (setting, mode, format, frequency, and duration), considering the patient's diagnosis and social support. Third, the therapist selects the therapist–patient relationship patterns that will be likely to enhance the therapeutic alliance (role induction, in-therapy environmental management), taking into account the patient's demographic background and interpersonal needs. Finally, the therapist chooses the psychotherapeutic strategies and techniques to be implemented, based primarily on the patient's predisposing qualities. It is at this last level that the therapist defines the focal target(s) of change and the specific strategies and procedures to be used.

One of the limitations of the s.e.p. approach is that it has been primarily utilized with individual patients and groups in outpatient settings. While it has been studied on some inpatient populations, its applicability to couples and families has not yet been assessed. One of the strengths of the model is the ample research conducted with individual patients, which has shown promising, if not confirming, results of the major constructs of s.e.p. (Beutler, Engle, Shoham-Salomon, et al., 1991; Beutler &

Mitchell, 1981; Calvert, Beutler, & Crago, 1988). Cross-cultural studies have also been conducted with the s.e.p. model, which have determined significant refinements and have outlined plans for prospective tests (Beutler & Consoli, 1992; Beutler, Mohr, Grawe, Engle, & MacDonald, 1991).

Characteristics of Treatment

Among the various models of psychotherapy, s.e.p. is distinguished by its emphasis on establishing the empirical value of specific strategies of change and their accompanying procedures. This emphasis contrasts with that of most approaches to psychotherapy, which derive treatment recommendations from theories of psychotherapy rather than from specific techniques. Put another way, most systems of psychotherapy are theories of psychopathology; *s.e.p. is a technology of behavior change*. Additionally, s.e.p. endeavors to discover specific rather than common contributors to treatment efficacy among available therapeutic strategies and techniques.

The foregoing is not meant to devalue or minimize the role of theory in therapeutic applications. Nor is it meant to suggest that relationship qualities that are common to all schools of intervention are unimportant. We acknowledge how valuable it would be to have a commonly accepted and verified theory that would provide a basis for treatment selection. Yet, we do not believe that therapists will, can, or should agree on a common theory of psychopathology and change. To do so would signal that growth of new knowledge and creativity of thought had been stifled.

Thus, as applied to psychotherapy, we believe that theories of two different types have importance, but for very different reasons (Beutler & Clarkin, 1990). The type of theory that would be of greatest value if held in common among therapists would be at the level of application. This would not be a theory of change or of pathology, but one of decisional processes. Ideally, this theory would be one that is closely tied to empirically established relationships between patient–therapy matching dimensions and outcomes of treatment. It would be expressed as a theory-drive decisional process, and would consist of a set of indicators and contraindicators for different treatment components. This level of theory is a "theory" only to the degree that the proposed relationships have not yet been consensually accepted or empirically demonstrated.

The more abstract theories of psychotherapy, which therapists have such a prolific propensity to develop, are also important, but from a different frame of reference. These theories provide a value-laden view of what is socially good, bad, and adaptive, and thus may be transmitted from the therapist to the patient as life-guiding views and values.

Because life-guiding philosophies cannot be evaluated for absolute truth, s.e.p. focuses on defining the relationships that can be used at the first level of theory application. This first level is the matching of therapist strategies and patient characteristics in a way that will most efficiently result in the transmission of pragmatic theories of life. Because their effects can be verified, for the task of selecting effective interventions, theories of interpersonal influence are considered to be of more value than are theories of the etiology of pathology.

In a similar way, s.e.p. acknowledges that inherently helpful therapist behaviors account for the preponderance of psychotherapeutic benefit. Rather than stopping with this recognition, as do the proponents of common factor approaches (e.g., Frank & Frank, 1991; Garfield, 1980; Orlinsky & Howard, 1986; Parloff, 1986), s.e.p. maintains that therapist support, empathy, caring, acceptance, and respect form the foundation to which the more selective effects of specific procedures can be *added* (Beutler & Consoli, 1993). The therapist-facilitative qualities exert their effects by enhancing the therapist's role as a benevolent agent of influence, and thus increase the power of specific procedures when used selectively with different patients. In this way, s.e.p. combines the power of so-called common and spe-

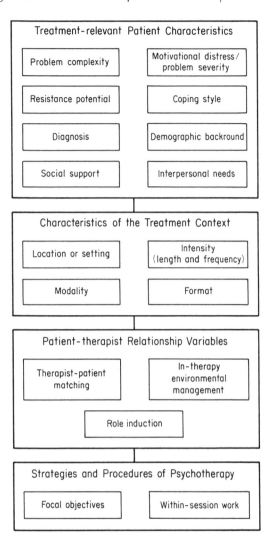

FIGURE 15.1. The four central dimensions of psychotherapy: patient characteristics, treatment context, patient–therapist relationship, and psychotherapy strategies.

cific factors in psychotherapy (Chapter 4, this volume).

In integrating these various principles, s.e.p. emphasizes that effective treatment planning entails the matching of four related sets of variables: (1) patient characteristics, (2) treatment context, (3) patient–therapist relationship, and (4) strategies of psychotherapy. These variables are described in the following pages and are graphically displayed in Figure 15.1.

TREATMENT-RELEVANT PATIENT CHARACTERISTICS

The therapist is first called on to select, from among the hundreds of patient characteristics discussed in the literature, those that will most enhance the predictive efficacy of psychotherapy. While Beutler and Clarkin (1990) outline a large number of potentially important characteristics, the need for brevity and simplicity will allow us to illustrate the decisions that follow from only a few of them. Four variables, *problem complexity, motivational distress/problem severity, resistance potential,* and *coping style,*[2] will be considered in terms of the selection of specific strategies and procedures of psychotherapy. Since this chapter focuses largely on the selection of psychotherapeutic procedures, much of our subsequent discussion will be on the role of these variables in psychotherapy practice. However, other patient variables will also be mentioned because they are important at earlier levels in the decision process. We will draw the reader's attention to the roles of *patient diagnosis* and *social support* availability in decisions regarding the context of treatment, and to *patient demographic background* and dominant *interpersonal needs* in decisions about selecting a therapist and developing a therapeutic relationship. Rather than taking space at this point to define each of these constructs, only to repeat the definitions later, we will introduce and define each of these patient qualities when their role in treatment planning is discussed.

CHARACTERISTICS OF THE TREATMENT CONTEXT

Four basic aspects of treatment context are considered by s.e.p.: (1) the treatment location of setting—"where"; (2) the intensity of treatment (including the recommendation of no treatment)—"how much"; (3) the modality (i.e., medical, psychosocial, or some combination) through which treatment is delivered— "what kind"; and (4) the format (e.g., the implementation of couple, family, group, or individual therapy) in which this modality is transmitted—"with whom." These contextual variables are involved in the first level of treatment matching: Patient predisposing characteristics are matched with, and to the optimal level of *intensity* (length and frequency of treatment), the least restrictive *setting*, and the most efficient *modality* and *format.*

Formal psychiatric diagnosis, as well as assessments of problem severity and the availability of environmental and social support, are the patient qualities that are most directly linked to decisions about treatment context. At a minimum, the clinician must address questions about the degree of environmental restriction that is required to ensure the patient's and others' safety, the prescription of medical and pharmacological interventions, and the frequency or duration of intervention initially needed.

Beyond these decisions, the patient's available support and diagnosis should be used to help the clinician determine the nature of the treatment format (e.g., use of combinations of group, individual, and family intervention) that is likely to be most helpful. These decisions are reevaluated throughout treatment as a function of the changes made by the patient, including symptomatic severity, and in response to changing social supports.

In mental health, diagnoses are shorthand descriptions of symptomatic behaviors. Diagnosis has its greatest value for assigning treatment in two areas: (1) assignment of treatment setting and (2) assignment of medical treatment modalities. Of secondary importance, diagnosis provides a description of symptoms that must be considered in evaluating the effectiveness of treatment. Diagnoses that reflect serious, debilitating, or life-threatening conditions require the recommendation of treatment settings that are restrictive and protective (inpatient or partial-care settings). Serious conditions such as these also suggest the need for more intensive or long-term treatment. Among the diagnoses for which restrictive treatments must be given consideration are psychotic conditions, bipolar mood disorders, major depression with suicidal intentions, some organic disorders in which serious decompensation is observed, and acute substance abuse in which detoxification is required.

Diagnostic conditions may also serve as indicators for the use of specific medications. Antipsychotics (neuroleptics), antianxiety drugs (anxiolytics), stimulants, antidepressants, antimanics, and various combinations of these drugs have specific effects on the nature of the symptoms that are reflected in these diagnostic groupings. Formal diagnosis has little to suggest in the way of planning and implementing psychotherapy, however, at least beyond providing an indication of what symptoms are sufficiently debilitating to require a change in the course of treatment.

While diagnosis is a primary variable in determining the treatment context, patient access to a supportive social environment should also be considered. The role of social support is somewhat broader than that of diagnosis. For example, the patient's social support is a principal variable in determining whether improvement will persist after treatment (e.g., relapse) and is implicated in decisions about the use of family and group therapies. In using social support to make discriminating treatment decisions, it is often helpful to know how many (and what) individuals are geographically available to the patient, as well as the degree to which the patient feels supported by these people. Formal measures of social support are available to assist this decisional process (e.g., Sarason, Levine, Basham, & Sarason, 1983). Those patients whose initial evaluation and personal history suggest a relative absence of individuals from whom support can be obtained may benefit from social therapies such as group therapies. These therapy formats can often build and enhance the patient's access to other people. Homework tasks that involve the improvement and extension of social contacts may also be indicated.

By the same token, those patients whose families or spouses are available but are not experienced at being supportive may be candidates for therapies designed to improve family relationships. Family and marital therapies may be indicated at some time in the treatment. The point at which these therapies occur, however, must be determined in conjunction with an assessment of problem severity since this variable is helpful in determining the intensity of needed treatment.

In the initial evaluation, patients offer pressing reasons to explain why they have come to therapy at this time. The therapist listens, questions, collects data, and formulates hypotheses. Ultimately, an agreement regarding treatment objectives must be reached in order to establish a common ground for working together. The evaluation process, while focused on making initial decisions regarding the maximal protection of the patient, provides the foundation for the relationship that supports these treatment decisions.

PATIENT–THERAPIST RELATIONSHIP VARIABLES

Relationship variables comprise the third set of variables that establish the efficacy of systematic treatment. The patient–therapist relationship is the foundation of psychotherapy: Only through a strong relationship can the therapist induce and maintain receptivity to the treatment to be used and adjust the treatment to meet the patient's expectations. Hence, it is important that the evaluation make specific efforts both to select the therapist, from among those available, who will work most effectively with the patient, and to take steps to counter any factors that might impede forging a working unit of patient and therapist. By knowing the nature of relationship variables, the therapist sets the stage for and establishes a therapeutic stance that will be beneficial for the achievement of a successful treatment outcome.

S.e.p. identifies three ways to enhance the development of a therapeutic relationship: (1) therapist–patient matching, (2) role induction, and (3) in-therapy environmental management (Beutler & Clarkin, 1990).

Therapist–Patient Matching

Patients look for many things in the therapist's role—a new and different perspective on problems, permission to express feelings and behaviors, an authoritative informant on life's dilemmas, and a model of mastering conflicts with which the patient has struggled unsuccessfully, among other expectations and fantasies. The well-matched therapist must be enough like the patient to be seen as someone who understands the patient's experience and, at the same time, must be sufficiently different from the patient to provide an alternative and meaningful view of the situation. Within the limits of availability, the selection of therapists for specific patients relies on finding this optimal match between similarity and complementarity.

Beutler and Bergan (1991) suggest that effective matching of at least two key dimensions is necessary for a productive therapist assignment: (1) demographic similarity and (2) the dominant wish or need that one seeks to fulfill or achieve by engaging in interpersonal relationships. Interpersonal needs characteristically exist on a continuum between being oriented toward nurturance, dependence, and attachment on one end and being oriented toward self-sufficiency, autonomy, and independence on the other.

Patient–therapist similarity in background characteristics such as gender, age, ethnic background, and socioeconomic status may precipitate a sense of trust and twinship that is therapeutically beneficial. Similarity of age and gender may be particularly helpful in order to keep the patient in therapy long enough for work to begin, a factor that is especially important when the patient has not been in therapy before and does not know what to expect (Beutler, Crago, & Arizmendi, 1986). However, assigning a therapist who is demographically similar to the patient is not always possible in either public or private clinics. Development of the necessary trust may be facilitated, when patient and therapist backgrounds are dissimilar, by using empathic listening skills, by reinforcing areas of perceived similarity, and by

placing relatively less emphasis on the use of directive and instructional interventions.

In addition, the selection of a therapist should take into account the nature of the patient's interpersonal needs. On this dimension, however, differences between patient and therapist are often facilitative of improvement. Patients benefit from seeing a different and even contrasting model of needs and ways of satisfying needs. Hence, a patient who is dependent and nurture-seeking may benefit from seeing a therapist who is self-sufficient and independent. One who is independent and isolated may benefit from a therapist who is yielding and people-oriented. Thus, a review of research literature by Beutler and Clarkin (1990) revealed that the patient–therapist dissimilarity along the dimension of valuing closeness versus autonomy is associated with the likelihood and magnitude of therapeutic change.

In order to emphasize therapeutic differences in interpersonal needs, therapists who are working with dependent patients may elect to remain somewhat formal, nondisclosing of personal information, and autonomous, especially if patients are not confident in their ability to retain distance. This stance, if also supportive and caring, provides reassurance for failing self-assurance and conveys an alternative value system to one that is prone to sacrifice personal wants and freedoms in order to retain the love and support of others. Conversely, therapists whose patients are assertively independent and loudly self-sufficient can afford to be somewhat self-disclosing and informal, conveying that there is little danger in such vulnerability and openness.

Role Induction

Role induction refers to the conveyance of attitudes designed to ensure that the prospective patient's expectations are realistic representations of what will transpire in therapy. Additionally, role induction prepares the patient for assuming a productive and collaborative role on entering therapy. It thereby invokes, either implicitly or explicitly, a therapeutic contract by concretizing the parts that are assumed by both therapist and patient.

Therapeutic contracting is a technique that allows the therapist and patient to mutually specify responsibilities and the nature of the relationship. Contracting is specifically designed to bring the patient's expectations about therapy into line with what can be provided. Hence, it is important that the clinician know what the patient's expectations and previous experiences are and tailor the role induction process accordingly. This is particularly true since role specification may have an important impact on the patient's motivation and goals. Written or verbal descriptions of what therapy is designed to do, along with instructions about what constitutes productive therapeutic activity on the part of the patient, can facilitate symptomatic change, foster role-appropriate attitudes, and nurture positive feelings about treatment. Observational and participatory learning methods, such as videotapes or role plays, can provide modeling and skill development.

The contract includes the delineation of time limits and treatment goals, as well as the consequences for noncompliance with it. While the contract addresses some of the patient's expectations, it is always re-negotiable and subject to change as one proceeds through the phases (within sessions) and stages (across sessions) of treatment.

In-Therapy Environmental Management

In-therapy environmental management is comprised of those therapist acts designed to foster the development of a productive treatment relationship once it has begun. Two characteristics distinguish between role induction and environmental management techniques. First, while role induction attempts to prepare the patient for therapy *before* therapy begins, environmental management describes the acts of the therapist *during* therapy. Second, while role induction seeks to change the patient's attitudes and expectations, environmental management seeks to direct the therapist to accommodate to the attitudes and expectations of the patient.

Characteristics of the therapist's practice environment—such as the physical layout, the attitude and appearance of the support staff, and the nature of office procedures—can support (or impede) the in-therapy environmental influences. Supportive environmental characteristics can decrease premature termination while increasing therapeutic benefit. Likewise, the therapist's verbal style, voice tone, vocabulary, and expressed emotion can be managed in ways that strengthen (or weaken) the therapeutic relationship.

SPECIFIC STRATEGIES AND PROCEDURES

Most approaches to psychotherapy would accept the wisdom of the guidelines just presented. That is, they are likely to embrace the rationale for determining treatment contexts and relationships. These concerns are often similar across the psychotherapies. It is in the moment-to-moment and week-to-week workings of psychotherapy itself that the distinctiveness and explicitness of technical eclecticism generally, and s.e.p. specifically, are best seen. Accordingly, the remainder of this chapter will focus on the specific practice guidelines and decisional criteria on which technical eclecticism rests.

The last step in treatment planning is the selection of general strategies, along with the specific procedures by which the therapist implements these strategies.

Figure 15.2 presents the Summary Sheet that accompanies our Prescriptive Therapy Planning Form. The lower portion of this sheet is used to summarize the ratings and treatment decisions that derive from the initial assessment. This form directs the therapist to the selection of treatment strategies and techniques that will tailor the interventions to the individual patient. The patient's status on four dimensions is rated: motivational distress/problem

---

Subject I.D. #:_____   Therapist:_____   Rater:_____

Session #:_____   Intake Date:_____   Tape #:_____

Identify assessment devices used and record the scores   ☑ Check the appropriate box under each heading

Assessment - Indicators

I.   State Anxiety Score:_____

    Assessment Device:_____

Judged Motivational Distress
☐ Low
☐ Adequate
☐ High

II.   Problem Complexity

Problem Complexity
☐ Symptomatic
☐ Thematic

III.   Reactance Score:_____

    Assessment Device:_____

Reactance Level
☐ Low
☐ Medium
☐ High

IV.   Coping Style Score:_____

    Assessment Device:_____

Coping Style
☐ Externalizer
☐ Internalizer

Treatment Plan

Recommend:

I.   ☐ (a) Arousal Induction Procedures **or**
    ☐ (b) Arousal Reduction Procedures

II.   ☐ (a) Symptom Change Outcome Goals **or**
    ☐ (b) Thematic Change Outcome Goals

III.   ☐ (a) Therapist-directed Interventions **or**
    ☐ (b) Self-directed, Nondirective, or Paradoxical Interventions

IV.   ☐ (a) Behavior and/or Skillbuilding Focus **or**
    ☐ (b) Insight or Emotional Awareness Focus

FIGURE 15.2. Summary sheet.

severity, problem complexity, resistance/reactance potential, and coping style. Treatment strategies are selected by combining several sources of information. Clinical impressions are supplemented by formal tests. We use the Symptom Checklist (SCL-90R), the State-Trait Anxiety Inventory (STAI), the Minnesota Multiphasic Personality Inventory (MMPI and MMPI-II), and the Therapeutic Reactance Scale (TRS) to establish the patient's standing on these four dimensions.

Some of the decisions required of the therapist are made at the beginning of treatment and remain constant throughout. Other decisions are made on a session-by-session basis, and still others are implemented after blocks of several sessions. The focus of these decisions in s.e.p. is on the identification of *therapeutic strategies* rather than on the application of specific techniques. However, menus of techniques are suggested for implementing the strategic decisions. Specifically, the overall psychotherapy plan is based on the integration of the following strategic decisions:

1. Select treatment outcome objectives that coincide with the patient's level of problem complexity. Complex problems signal the need to change interpersonal patterns and ongoing conflicts, while noncomplex problems indicate that symptomatic relief alone is the goal of treatment.
2. Adapt the immediate, moment-to-moment goals of treatment to the patient's level of distress. The goal with highly distressed individuals is to lower distress; with less distressed individuals, the goal is to raise distress.
3. Focus the intervention on the level of the patient's major defenses. Among those who rely on external coping styles, the focus is on changing thoughts and behaviors; among those with low externalizing tendencies, the focus is to foster insight and emotional awareness.
4. Apply a level of directive guidance that can be tolerated by the patient, based on estimates of resistance potential. Among those with high resistance potential, the strategy is to introduce homework assignments and in-therapy interventions through relatively benign, nondirective, or paradoxical suggestions; among those with low resistance potential, the strategy is to assign specific, directed, and active therapy tasks both within and outside of the session.

In s.e.p., treatment is initially contracted to take place over a 15- to 20-week period, with a renewable contract if the problem's complexity and severity indicate the need for longer treatment. By this point, symptomatic improvement should be noted, and the therapist and patient can then decide, in a flexible fashion, whether or not to continue with adjusted treatment goals.

Problem Complexity

Problem complexity is defined by the degree to which the presentation of symptoms is situation or event specific. Problems that are recurrent, that are not directly related to situational cues and events, and that reflect symbolic expressions of recurrent life themes are considered to be complex. Problems and symptoms that are situational, that are evoked by identifiable and infrequent external events, and that lack a high degree of symbolic significance (e.g., situational disturbances, many marital problems, uncomplicated bereavement, simple phobias) are considered to be noncomplex.

Figure 15.3 identifies the types of decisions and clinical judgments that determine problem complexity. Formal tests are used to supplement this clinical information. For example, the SCL-90R is a checklist that yields information on the number and spread of symptoms. The presence of several different types of moderate to severe symptoms on this checklist is one index of a complex problem. The rated complexity of the patient's problem leads to a decision to focus either on symptomatic change, in the case of noncomplex problems, or on the alteration of life patterns and the interpersonal contexts in which behavior occurs, in the case of complex problems.

Research (Lambert & DeJulio, 1978; Stein & Lambert, 1984) suggests that a caring, supportive atmosphere may be sufficient to produce improvement in patients with noncomplex problems. Neither lengthy therapist experience nor specific therapy procedures are necessary for patient improvement in these instances. Thus, for problems that are situational and single occurrences, the focus of treatment can legitimately be restricted to removal of the symptomatic presentations through support and reassurance. Complex problems require a different kind of treatment, however, as illustrated by the following example.

Isabel, a 33-year-old Mexican-American woman and mother of three teenagers, came into treatment asking for help in finding ways to discipline and get along with her 15-year-old daughter, Marina. In the course of psycho-

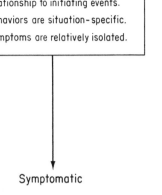

- Chronic habits and transient responses.
- Behavior repetition is maintained by inadequate knowledge or by ongoing situational rewards (positive reinforcement).
- Behaviors have a direct relationship to initiating events.
- Behaviors are situation-specific.
- Symptoms are relatively isolated.

- Behaviors are repeated as themes across unrelated and dissimilar situations.
- Behaviors are ritualized (yet self-defeating) attempts to resolve dynamic and/or interpersonal conflicts.
- Current conflicts are expressions of the patient's past rather than present relationships.
- Repetitive behavior results in suffering (rather than gratification).
- Symptoms have a symbolic relationship to initiating events.
- Problems are enduring, repetitive, and symbolic manifestations of characterological conflicts.

Symptomatic   Thematic

FIGURE 15.3. Problem complexity.

therapy, Marina ran away from home and was picked up by the police. At her request, and with her parents' consent, she was taken to a youth shelter. During her brief stay there, Marina disclosed that her uncle, Roberto, her mother's brother, had been sexually abusing her since the age of 7, most of the time in her own bedroom. Roberto was detained immediately. Marina had approached her mother 2 years ago and had told her about Roberto's abuses. Isabel demanded that Roberto cease the abuse but at the same time decided to keep it secret from José, her husband, out of fear that José would kill Roberto. Roberto's abuse of Marina did not stop, and Isabel found herself unable to keep Roberto out of the house. Immediately after Marina publicly disclosed Roberto's abuse, Isabel became extremely agitated and depressed, self-blaming and desperate. At this point, Isabel states that she herself had been abused as a child by her uncle, and that she had reported it to her mother, who denied the events and ordered her to forget about them. Some of Isabel's current fear was related to not wanting her husband to find out about her own sexual abuse as a child. During a session, Isabel recalled her mother saying, "Don't tell anybody or you will never marry."

From this description, it is clear that Isabel's own problem is complex, representing a history of intrapsychically repressed and interpersonally hidden themes that severely limits her ability to function in ways that would provide a safe environment for her daughter. Both treatment techniques and therapist skill and training are important in treating patients whose problems are complex and recurrent. In these instances, therapy must focus beyond the adaptation to a singular event and beyond the provision of comfort and support. For these complex problems, a treatment focused on the recurrent patterns, life themes, and social systems in which the problems occur is more useful than a symptom-focused treatment. *It is in regard to these complex problems that the description of the other three dimensions is most relevant.*

Motivational Distress/Problem Severity

The level of patient distress has frequently been observed in the clinical literature to be a motivating force that enhances the effects of psychotherapy. Clinicians and researchers alike (e.g., Frank & Frank, 1991; Orlinsky & Howard, 1986) suggest that procedures that induce the unaroused patient to experience discomfort are likely to produce greater benefit than procedures that fail to induce emotional arousal. This generalization is likely to be accurate for problems of low complexity, as well as for those that are quite complex. Our own work demonstrates that patients who are subjectively distressed and who are experiencing complex problems are both less likely to deteriorate during treatment and more likely to experience increased change as a result of psychotherapy than those whose distress is low. The experiential procedures used by gestalt and humanistic therapists are particularly adept at raising patient distress to therapy-enhancing levels.

Motivational distress/problem severity is assessed as a state that is expected to vary from session to session. Prior to each s.e.p. session, patients may be asked to complete a measure of motivational distress. Procedures designed either to increase or decrease arousal will be implemented as a function of patient scores. Our previous work has used the SCL-90R GSI (Global Severity Index) subscale as an indicator for the use of arousal versus supportive and coping techniques.

Severe distress is manifest in the impairment of the patient's capacity to relate to the social, occupational, or interpersonal demands of daily life. When the problem is also complex, many of these areas may be impaired by intense and overwhelming anxiety, with the number of impaired areas being an indication of the degree of complexity.

For example, Dolores, a successful Hispanic-Latina businesswoman who was able to cope with a long history of *ataques de nervios* (literally, nerve attacks), sought treatment after finding herself unable to return to work following her mother's death almost a year earlier. Although she had managed to maintain her job through telephone contact, her income was diminishing substantially, and the *ataques* had increased dramatically. Dolores, an only daughter, did not have much of a support system beyond that offered by her mother and a distant relative. The sudden death of her mother taxed Dolores' limited interpersonal resources, plunged her into depression, and exacerbated her *ataques*.

The STAI (Spielberger, Gorsuch, & Lushene, 1970) is a 40-item, self-report inventory

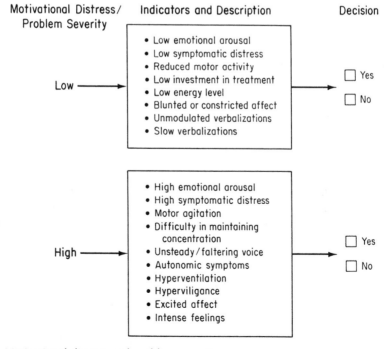

Motivational Distress/ Problem Severity	Indicators and Description	Decision
Low	• Low emotional arousal • Low symptomatic distress • Reduced motor activity • Low investment in treatment • Low energy level • Blunted or constricted affect • Unmodulated verbalizations • Slow verbalizations	☐ Yes ☐ No
High	• High emotional arousal • High symptomatic distress • Motor agitation • Difficulty in maintaining concentration • Unsteady/faltering voice • Autonomic symptoms • Hyperventilation • Hyperviligance • Excited affect • Intense feelings	☐ Yes ☐ No

FIGURE 15.4. Motivational distress and problem severity.

that assesses the patient's level of discomfort. The State Anxiety portion reflects the patient's stress level in current situations. It complements another observational measure that the trained s.e.p. therapist uses, the Client Emotional Arousal Scale (CEAS) (Daldrup, Beutler, Engle, & Greenberg, 1988). This scale, a 7-point anchored continuum from "none" to "intense emotional (voice, body, or language) arousal," helps the therapist identify the nature of emotions and decide whether they are strong enough to serve as an impetus to change. The STAI and the CEAS can be used to assess motivational distress levels. Clinical aids and observations are also helpful following the descriptors presented in Figure 15.4.

Patients with extremely high and dysfunctional levels of distress are candidates for procedures that reduce distress, while those with low levels of distress are candidates for experiential procedures whose objective is to help patients confront and "own" their problems. High distress is an indicator for implementing supportive, structuring, and relaxation procedures. Low distress is treated with confrontation, interpretation, and arousal induction procedures (e.g., experiential role plays or guided imagery).

Coping Style

Emerging evidence suggests that, with the possible exception of anxiety disorders, patient diagnosis is a poor predictor of the differential efficacy of different procedures (Beutler, 1989). The ways patients cope with personal and interpersonal threats bear a relatively strong relationship to how well they respond to different psychotherapy strategies. Patients who cope with problems by externalizing blame, by acting out impulsively, and by directly avoiding problems have been repeatedly shown to be more responsive to treatments that focus directly on changing behaviors than to those that foster insight and awareness (Beutler, 1979; Beutler, Engle, Mohr, et al., 1991; Beutler & Mitchell, 1981; Beutler, Mohr, Grawe, et al. 1991; Sloane, Staples, Cristol, Yorkston, & Whipple, 1975). Alternatively, patients who cope with stress by

internalizing responsibility, self-blame, and heightened self-consciousness tend to respond better to insight-oriented treatments than to behavioral change ones (Beutler, Engle, Mohr, et al., 1991; Beutler, Mohr, Grawe, et al., 1991; Kadden, Cooney, Getter, & Litt, 1992; Sloane et al., 1975).

An illustration of a patient with an externalizing coping style may provide clarification. Frank, a 42-year-old, twice-divorced Vietnam veteran, presented for treatment with intense anger and problems in relating to others. He had a history of polysubstance abuse and had been jailed for assault on two occasions. At intake, Frank was clean, sober, and living alone. He was afraid of losing his job and his apartment due to violent verbal outbursts. Throughout therapy, Frank alternated between blaming his boss, his ex-wife, and the government for his inability to get along with people. Frank can be said to utilize externalizing coping patterns to handle his daily difficulties.

An externalizing coping style is considered to be an enduring trait and has been most widely measured by various combinations of MMPI scales (Dahlstrom, Welsh, & Dahlstrom, 1972). In various stages of our research program, we have relied on measures from the MMPI, coupled with clinical impressions from the patient's history, in assessing coping style.

Elevations on scales 6 (paranoia) and 4 (psychopathic deviance) that exceed those on scales 7 (psychasthenia) and 2 (depression) are taken as indicators of externalization. Indeed, among depressed patients, a cumulative sum of the T scores from these two scales that exceeds 140 is a predictive indicator for the application of cognitive-behavioral change procedures. Scores below this value indicate the use of insight-oriented procedures. Relative elevations of scales 2, 7, 4, and 6 suggest that acting out, distrust, and projection are more frequently occurring patterns than self-blame and introspection.

Figure 15.5 presents the Prescriptive Therapy Planning Form on which we employ the clinician's judgments of the patient's defensive patterns to evaluate coping style and to determine if the treatment techniques selected

Coping Style   Typical Defenses and Description   Decision

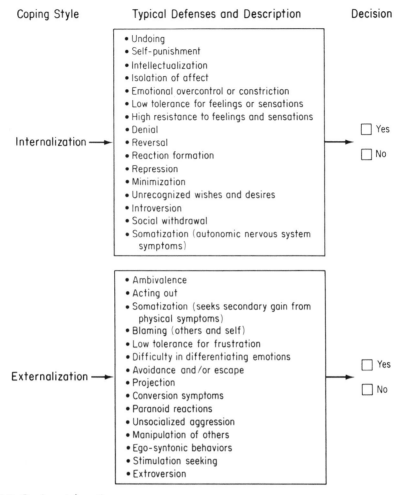

- Undoing
- Self-punishment
- Intellectualization
- Isolation of affect
- Emotional overcontrol or constriction
- Low tolerance for feelings or sensations
- High resistance to feelings and sensations
- Denial
- Reversal
- Reaction formation
- Repression
- Minimization
- Unrecognized wishes and desires
- Introversion
- Social withdrawal
- Somatization (autonomic nervous system symptoms)

Internalization ⟶   ☐ Yes   ☐ No

- Ambivalence
- Acting out
- Somatization (seeks secondary gain from physical symptoms)
- Blaming (others and self)
- Low tolerance for frustration
- Difficulty in differentiating emotions
- Avoidance and/or escape
- Projection
- Conversion symptoms
- Paranoid reactions
- Unsocialized aggression
- Manipulation of others
- Ego-syntonic behaviors
- Stimulation seeking
- Extroversion

Externalization ⟶   ☐ Yes   ☐ No

FIGURE 15.5. Coping style rating.

should be those that address behavior change or enhance awareness and insight.

Resistance Potential

The final dimension to be presented here is that of resistance potential—the likelihood that a patient will resist the therapist's suggestions and interpretations. Research evidence from several sources suggests that those who are so prone do not benefit from directive interventions, while those who are less resistant do, in fact, benefit from the therapist's directives and guidance (Beutler, Engle, Mohr, et al., 1991; Beutler, Engle, Shoham-Salomon, et al.,

1991; Beutler, Mohr, Grawe, et al., 1991; Shoham-Salomon, 1991).

An illustration of the reactions of a patient with high resistance potential may help clarify the concept. Jonathan, a 38-year-old married Caucasian man, came to therapy with myriad physical complaints (migraine headaches, sinus problems, gastrointestinal difficulty). He had made innumerable visits to physicians and had undergone a number of operations since the age of 21. As an only child born to old parents, his early years were experienced as isolating and sad, with episodes of extreme punishment and neglect from his mother. As an adult, Jonathan had suffered from depression and poor interpersonal skills, which were manifested in

Resistance
Potential   Indicators and Description   Decision

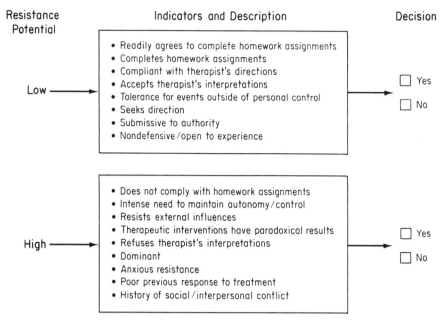

Low

- Readily agrees to complete homework assignments
- Completes homework assignments
- Compliant with therapist's directions
- Accepts therapist's interpretations
- Tolerance for events outside of personal control
- Seeks direction
- Submissive to authority
- Nondefensive/open to experience

☐ Yes

☐ No

High

- Does not comply with homework assignments
- Intense need to maintain autonomy/control
- Resists external influences
- Therapeutic interventions have paradoxical results
- Refuses therapist's interpretations
- Dominant
- Anxious resistance
- Poor previous response to treatment
- History of social/interpersonal conflict

☐ Yes

☐ No

FIGURE 15.6. Resistance rating.

an unsatisfying marriage and a hostile, unrewarding work environment. Jonathan had been seen by 15 therapists in as many years and was highly critical of all of them. He was especially critical of his current therapist, who attempted to help him reconceptualize his physical experience of pain as "emotional pain." This patient's high resistance potential was expressed in his low tolerance both for the therapist's interventions and for accessing painful internal material.

Resistance potential does not have a formally derived measurement procedure well developed on a clinical population. While some research has determined that a combination of special MMPI scales may predict the treatment response to directive and nondirective interventions, there are other instruments that appear to be promising predictors of patient resistance to therapist directives. The Therapeutic Reactance Scale (TRS) was recently revised by Dowd, Milne, and Wise (1991) specifically for predicting resistance to therapist directives. However, clinical indicators from the patient's history and presentation in the assessment interview are also helpful.

Figure 15.6 presents the page from the Pre-scriptive Therapy Planning Form that defines some of the indicators that may identify high resistance potential in patients. Once again, these descriptions are derived from clinical impressions and the patient's history, supplemented by the TRS. Technical procedures indicated for those with high resistance potential include nondirective interventions, self-directive techniques, and paradoxical interventions—those that prescribe "no change," the symptoms themselves, or the exaggeration of symptoms. Patients with high resistance potential do poorly when therapists impose structure or suggest behaviors, intepretations, or guided experiments. In contrast, those who are more cooperative are likely to benefit from therapist instruction, guidance, interpretation, and structuring.

FUTURE TRENDS IN INTEGRATIVE AND ECLECTIC THERAPIES

Integrative and eclectic therapies represent the most popular theoretical orientation (Norcross & Freedheim, 1992), and it is anticipated that their popularity will increase in the future.

There is now greater tolerance for and assimilation of diverse therapeutic formulations (Arkowitz, 1992; Liff, 1992). Thus, the need to validate integrative and eclectic therapies in research, practice, and training is essential.

With the changing economic, social, and political forces shaping the boundaries of psychotherapy, "we must create and apply more responsive models of mental health delivery that fit into, not fight against, the rapidly changing conditions of American culture" (Austad & Hoyt, 1992). It is our belief that s.e.p. is a model that is responsive to the future demands of the mental health delivery system.

Specifically, technical eclecticism in the form of s.e.p. addresses the needs of diverse clients, from diverse situational contexts, with diverse psychological difficulties. Utilizing only one type of treatment and engaging in only one type of therapeutic relationship will no longer satisfy the needs of diverse clients. There is more demand for therapists to tailor their interpersonal stances and styles to fit the unique needs of each client (Beutler & Consoli, 1993; Norcross & Freedheim, 1992).

Norcross and Freedheim (1992) recently conducted a poll of psychotherapy experts in order to "extract and amplify salient trends" that are expected to hold our attention into the next decade. For our purposes, their results can be categorized into three areas: (1) interventions, (2) procedures, and (3) modalities.

It is expected that *interventions* will be increasingly present-centered, structured, and directive. This expectation matches the current technical strategies of s.e.p. The s.e.p. practitioner believes that cross-diagnostic assessments of patient objectives, coping styles, resistances, situational contexts, emotional experiences, and beliefs will, of necessity, be systematized. Once these cross-diagnostic assessments have been understood in relation to one another, they will be used to choose specific interventions. Structured assessment will generate specifically indicated psychological therapies for each client.

Of all the *procedures* employed in psychotherapy, it is expected that audio/video feedback, problem-solving techniques, cognitive restructuring, self-change techniques, *in vivo* exposure, and communication skills will be increasingly employed. In addition, homework assignments, self-control training, expressing support/warmth, imagery and fantasy, social skills training, accurate empathy, behavioral contracting, teaching/advising, relaxation, and computerized therapies are predicted to increase in the coming years. Procedures that are aversive, unstructured, and relatively passive are expected to decline.

The procedures anticipated to be increasingly utilized in psychotherapy are those that are currently used in the systematic approach to psychotherapy. Further, selection from among this vast array of procedures is "specifically dependent on a logical decisional process that takes into account the client, the setting, the problem, and the nature of the counselor's skills" (Lazarus & Beutler, 1993, p. 384).

With regard to the *modalities* or formats of therapy, all indicators show that short-term psychotherapy will be in the ascendancy. This, together with the strong decline predicted for long-term work, produces optimism for s.e.p. and other brief, structured treatments. Marmor (1990), a highly respected member of the psychoanalytic guild, has underscored that psychotherapies of the future will favor short-term techniques "together with an emphasis on flexibly adapting the therapeutic techniques multimodally to the specific needs of each patient."

The expert forecast on the future of psychotherapy posits that clinical work will increasingly harmonize the client's ability to activate information between sessions with the therapist's interpersonal skills within sessions (Norcross & Freedheim, 1992). That is to say, effective clinical work is a balance between the patient's facility to generalize what is learned within sessions to life between sessions and the clinician's ability to accommodate to the patient's changing needs within therapy.

The Future of Technical Eclecticism

The predictions outlined above bode well for technical eclectic approaches such as s.e.p.

S.e.p. is directive in nature, brief in duration, and systematic in choosing from among an armamentarium of techniques in response to each client's problem complexity, motivational distress, resistance level, and coping style.

Lazarus, Beutler, and Norcross (1992) have presented the following 10 predictions on the clinical, research, and training directions of technical eclecticism:

1. Technical eclecticism will represent the psychotherapeutic *Zeitgeist* well into the 21st century.
2. Limitations of theoretical integration will be more fully realized.
3. Treatments of choice for selected clinical disorders will become standard practice.
4. Psychological therapies will be increasingly matched to client variables beyond diagnosis.
5. The meaning of technical eclecticism will be broadened to denote not only specific clinical procedures but also therapist relationship stances.
6. Common therapeutic factors will be concretely operationalized and prescriptively employed.
7. Technical eclecticism will facilitate the ongoing shift to more clinically relevant psychotherapy research.
8. The knowledge base of technical eclecticism will require methodological improvements in clinical research, as well as in programmatic research.
9. Explicitly eclectic training processes and programs will be developed.
10. Technical eclecticism, as one thrust of the psychotherapy integration movement, will become institutionalized.

These predictions, comprehensive in scope, lay the foundation for the future of s.e.p.

CONCLUDING COMMENTS

In s.e.p., the therapist is a tool of persuasive mastery empowered in the therapeutic environment to help the patient change. For some patients, change may occur via symptom reduction; for others, it may occur through insight and emotional integration. Because of the vast array of strategies, techniques, and interpersonal dimensions in this approach, the s.e.p. therapist will need extensive training in clinical decision making and treatment planning.

No doubt contemporary therapists have a lot to think about; for instance, practicing clinicians must be aware of third-party reimbursers (e.g., health insurance brokers). Clinicians today, practicing within the confines of insurance guidelines and short-term treatment, must think and act efficiently in providing a treatment rationale and selecting efficacious therapies. An accurate diagnosis must be provided, along with a justification for treatment based on a comprehensive treatment plan. We believe that the s.e.p. model is a comprehensive, systematic model both for providing the means to make a treatment-relevant diagnosis, and for developing and implementing a viable treatment plan. This treatment plan will address the specific technical interventions and relationship stances indicated for the particular patient—and will do so based on a solid empirical base. In this manner, we may eventually achieve the promise of determining "What treatment, by whom, is most effective for this individual with that specific problem" (Paul, 1969, p. 44).

Acknowledgments

Work on this chapter was supported by Grant No AA 08970 from the National Institute of Alcohol Abuse and Alcoholism, with the first author as Principal Investigator. Correspondence regarding this chapter should be sent to Larry E. Beutler, Graduate School of Education, University of California, Santa Barbara, California 93106.

The authors gratefully acknowledge the contribution of Kevin Gaw, who designed the chapter's graphics.

NOTES

1. It is not our intention to introduce a new acronym or a new therapy. For this reason, our abbreviation appears in lowercase letters.
2. The reader will notice some variability in the way these dimensions have been titled and defined in various publications (e.g., Beutler & Clarkin,

1990; Beutler & Consoli, 1992; Wakefield & Williams, in press). These variations reflect refinements arising from an evolving body of literature. The present descriptions represent the current status of research and theory, and they, too, are expected to change.

REFERENCES

American Psychiatric Association. (1994). *Diagnostic and treatment manual of mental disorders* (4th rev.). Washington, DC: Author.

Arkowitz, H. (1992). Integrative theories of therapy. In D. K. Freedheim (Ed.), *The history of psychotherapy: A century of change* (pp. 261–303). Washington, DC: American Psychological Association.

Austad, C. S., & Hoyt, M. F. (1992). The managed care movement and the future of psychotherapy. *Psychotherapy, 29,* 109–118.

Beitman, B. D. (1987). *The structure of individual psychotherapy.* New York: Guilford Press.

Beutler, L. E. (1979). Toward specific psychological therapies for specific conditions. *Journal of Consulting and Clinical Psychology, 47,* 882–897.

Beutler, L. E. (1983). *Eclectic psychotherapy: A systematic approach.* Elmsford, NY: Pergamon Press.

Beutler, L. E. (1986). Systematic eclectic psychotherapy. In J. C. Norcross (Ed.), *Handbook of eclectic psychotherapy* (pp. 94–131). New York: Brunner/Mazel.

Beutler, L. E. (1989). Differential treatment selection: The role of diagnosis in psychotherapy. *Psychotherapy, 26,* 271–281.

Beutler, L. E., & Bergan, J. (1991). Value change in counseling and psychotherapy: A search for scientific credibility. *Journal of Counseling Psychology, 38,* 16–24.

Beutler, L. E., & Clarkin, J. (1990). *Systematic treatment selection: Toward targeted therapeutic interventions.* New York: Brunner/Mazel.

Beutler, L. E., & Consoli, A. J. (1992). Systematic eclectic psychotherapy. In J. C. Norcross & M. Goldfried (Eds.), *Handbook of psychotherapy integration* (pp. 264–299). New York: Basic Books.

Beutler, L. E., & Consoli, A. J. (1993). Matching the therapist's interpersonal style to client's characteristics. *Psychotherapy, 30,* 417–422.

Beutler, L. E., Crago, M., & Arizmendi, T. G. (1986). Therapist variables in psychotherapy process and outcome. In S. L. Garfield & A. E.

Bergin (Eds.), *Handbook of psychotherapy and behavior change* (3rd ed.) (pp. 257–310). New York: Wiley.

Beutler, L. E., Engle, D., Mohr, D., Daldrup, R. J. Bergan, J., Meredith, K., & Merry, W. (1991). Predictors of differential and self directed psychotherapeutic procedures. *Journal of Consulting and Clinical Psychology, 59,* 333–340.

Beutler, L. E., Engle, D., Shoham-Salomon, V., Mohr, D. C., Dean, J. C., & Bernat, E. M. (1991). University of Arizona: Searching for differential treatments. In L. E. Beutler & M. Crago (Eds.) *Psychotherapy research: An international review of programmatic studies* (pp. 90–97). Washington, DC: American Psychological Association.

Beutler, L. E., & Mitchell, R. (1981). Differential psychotherapy outcome among depressed and impulsive patients as a function of analytic and experiential treatment procedures. *Psychiatry, 44,* 297–306.

Beutler, L. E., Mohr, D. C. Grawe, K., Engle, D., & MacDonald, R. (1991). Looking for differential treatment effects: Cross-cultural predictors of differential psychotherapy efficacy. *Journal of Psychotherapy Integration, 1,* 121–141.

Beutler, L. E., Wakefield, P., & Williams, R. E. (in press). Use of psychological tests/instruments for treatment planning. In M. Maruish (Ed.), *Use of psychological testing for treatment planning and outcome assessment.* Chicago: Erlbaum.

Beutler, L. E., Williams, R. E., & Wakefield, P. J. (1993). Obstacles to disseminating applied psychological science. *Journal of Applied and Preventive Psychology, 2,* 53–58.

Calvert, S. J., Beutler, L. E., & Crago, M. (1988). Psychotherapy outcome as a function of therapist–patient matching on selected variables. *Journal of Social and Clinical Psychology, 6,* 104–117.

Dahlstrom, W. G., Welsh, G. S., & Dahlstrom, L. E. (1972). *An MMPI handbook: Vol. I. Clinical interpretations.* Minneapolis: University of Minnesota Press.

Daldrup, R. J., Beutler, L. E., Engle, D., & Greenberg, L. S. (1988). *Focused expressive psychotherapy: Freeing the overcontrolled patient.* New York: Guilford Press.

Dowd, E. T., Milne, C. R., & Wise, S. L. (1991). The Therapeutic Reactance Scale: A measure of psychological reactance. *Journal of Counseling and Development, 69,* 541–545.

Frank, J. D., & Frank, J. B. (1991). *Persuasion and healing: A comparative study of psychotherapy*

(3rd ed.). Baltimore: Johns Hopkins University Press.

Garfield, S. L. (1980). *Psychotherapy: An eclectic approach.* New York: Wiley.

Kadden, R. M., Cooney, N. L., Getter, H., & Litt, M. D. (1990). Matching alcoholics to coping skills or interactional therapies: Posttreatment results. *Journal of Consulting and Clinical Psychology, 57,* 698–704.

Lambert, M. J., & DeJulio, S. S. (1978, March). *The relative importance of client, therapist and technique variables as predictors of psychotherapy outcome: The place of "Nonspecific" factors.* Paper presented at the midwinter meeting of the Division of Psychotherapy, American Psychological Association, Scottsdale, AZ.

Lazarus, A. A. (1989a). *The practice of multimodal therapy.* Baltimore: Johns Hopkins University Press.

Lazarus, A. A. (1989b). Multimodal therapy. In R. J. Corsini & D. Wedding (Eds.), *Current psychotherapies* (4th ed) (pp. 502–544). Itasca, IL: Peacock.

Lazarus, A. A., & Beutler, L. E. (1993). On technical eclecticism. *Journal of Counseling and Development, 71,* 381–385.

Lazarus, A. A., Beutler, L. E., & Norcross, J. C. (1992). The future of technical eclecticism. *Psychotherapy, 29,* 11–20.

Liff, Z. A. (1992). Psychoanalysis and dynamic techniques. In D. K. Freedheim (Ed.), *History of psychotherapy: A century of change* (pp. 571–586). Washington, DC: American Psychological Association.

Marmor, J. (1990, December). *The essence of dynamic psychotherapy.* Invited address delivered at the second Evolution of Psychotherapy Conference, Anaheim, CA.

Norcross, J. C. (Ed.). (1986). *Handbook of eclectic psychotherapy.* New York: Brunner/Mazel.

Norcross, J. C., & Freedheim, D. K. (1992). Into the future: Retrospect and prospect in psychotherapy. In D. K. Freedheim (Ed.), *History of psychotherapy: A century of change* (pp. 881–900). Washington, DC: American Psychological Association.

Orlinsky, D. E., & Howard, K. I. (1986). Process and outcome in psychotherapy. In S. L. Garfield & A. E. Bergin (Eds.), *Handbook of psychotherapy and behavior change* (3rd ed.) (pp. 311–384). New York: Wiley.

Parloff, M. B. (1986). Frank's "common elements" in psychotherapy: Nonspecific factors and placebos. *American Journal of Orthopsychiatry, 56,* 521–530.

Paul, G. L. (1969). Behavior modification research: Design and tactics. In C. M. Franks (Ed.), *Behavior therapy: Appraisal and status* (pp. 29–62). New York: McGraw-Hill.

Sarason, I. G., Levine, H. M., Basham, R. B., & Sarason, B. R. (1983). Assessing social support: The Social Support Questionnaire. *Journal of Personality and Social Psychology, 44,* 127–139.

Shoham-Salomon, V. (1991). Introduction to special section on client–therapy interaction research. *Journal of Consulting and Clinical Psychology, 59,* 203–204.

Sloane, R. B., Staples, F. R., Cristol, A. H., Yorkston, N. J., & Whipple, K. (1975). *Psychotherapy versus behavior therapy.* Cambridge, MA: Harvard University Press.

Spielberger, C., Gorsuch, R., & Lushene, R. (1970). *The State-Trait Anxiety Inventory (STAI) test manual.* Palo Alto, CA: Consulting Psychology Press.

Stein, D. M., & Lambert, M. J. (1984). On the relationship between therapist experience and psychotherapy outcome. *Clinical Psychology Review, 4,* 127–142.

II
PSYCHOTHERAPY FOR SPECIAL POPULATIONS AND CIRCUMSTANCES

16
Psychotherapy with Women in Theory and Practice

Annette M. Brodsky
Susan L. Steinberg

PSYCHOTHERAPY WITH WOMEN AS A SPECIAL POPULATION

Psychotherapy applied to women is psychotherapy in its modal form. In addition to women being more than 50% of the population, the majority of patients have been women (Chesler, 1972, Gove, 1979; Kessler, Reuter, & Greenley, 1979). Previously, however, generic male norms of behavior were seen as the desired outcome for the mentally healthy adult, and the goals for women in psychotherapy were more tied to a less mentally healthy, stereotyped feminine ideal (Broverman, Vogel, Broverman, Clarkson, & Rosenkrantz, 1972). Thus, psychotherapy in the 1950s and 1960s helped women adapt to their role as homemakers, their sexual role as submissive, compliant partners of a stronger male figure, and their nurturing role as caretaker of children, the sick, the elderly, and the less fortunate.

Women are more likely to be diagnosed as having a mental disorder, whereas men are more likely to have criminal or substance abuse records (Gove & Tudor, 1973; Robins et al., 1984). Epidemiological research in the 1960s and 1970s revealed that women experienced higher rates of psychological distress and depression (Gove, 1972; Radloff, 1975; Weissman & Klerman, 1977). While most of this early research was conducted with white populations, later studies with minority populations have found similar sex differences (Baskin, Blueston, & Nelson, 1981; Williams, 1986).

Certainly, women are not the norm if one considers what is thought of as a person. When patients are asked to draw a person, most men will draw a man and a majority of women will draw a man. Most research studies cannot generalize to people if most of the subjects are women, but they do so when most of the subjects are men. Yet, there are women among all ethnic minorities. Women are children and elderly and homosexual. Women are among all other groups and thus are affected by whatever problems those groups experience. But even though they outnumber men, women are often considered the other, rather than the norm, even within their own minority cultures. Stereotypes of specific cultural groups conjure generic images of blacks, Asians and Jews as acting in certain ways, but one has to add "black women," "Asian women," and so on to get an image of the other half of the generic group image.

The issue of identity within a culture is

important in understanding women as therapy patients. Theoretical positions on psychotherapy with women of color, lesbians, ethnic minority women, and women as members of religious groups have been proliferating in the last few years. In a review of three such books, Hall (1993) points out that while most therapists often confuse pathology with culture-bound behavior, feminist theorists explain, normalize, and validate women's experience that varies from the white male-sanctioned norms. Thus, self concept for women will vary according to their identity within their culture versus their identity as women. As Morales (1993) has shown, one's self-concept is higher when a person from a group-oriented culture (particularly with a strong family orientation) uses the group as a reference to build self-esteem.

Thus, where conflict between the cultural group and the newer identified group (gender or occupational aspirations) exists, self-concept may be lower and may provide a reason for psychotherapy.

In American society, norms regarding women's roles have changed. In 1940, only 8.6% of white mothers with dependent children worked, although the rates for blacks and Hispanics were much higher (Blau, 1984). Before 1970, the norm was for women with small children to be full-time homemakers. In 1970 it shifted, so that for the first time, more women with small children were in the work force than not (Bernard, 1972). In 1985, 47% of the work force was female (BNA, 1986). By 1985, 60% of married women with dependent children and 80% of divorced mothers with children under 18 worked outside the home. Eighty percent of women work in female-dominated jobs, which almost always pay lower wages than male-dominated ones. Women earn only 68 cents for every dollar men earn (*New York Times*, July 1987), and two-thirds of all persons 16 years and over classified below the poverty level are women.

The direct impact of work and social situations in producing multiple stresses on women in the American culture was not built into the awareness training of psychotherapists. The statistics on the higher poverty level of single mothers (Belle, 1990), stress from assuming multiple roles (McBride, 1990), and higher victimization from violence (Koss, 1990) have only recently been acknowledged as factors in etiology, prevention (Russo, 1990), and treatability with psychotherapeutic techniques.

Previously, violence against women was hidden by women's isolation from others and by financial dependence on their batterers (Koss, 1990). Low reported rates of rape and sexual harassment were due, at least in part, to the shame of public exposure of the victim (Burgess & Holstrom, 1973). These issues of victimization of women were known in the subcultures of poor and minority women, but the power of these women to be heard was minimal then and is still so now (Reid, 1993). Even those women who did enter psychotherapy did not necessarily find solutions to their environmental problems. Therapists did not deal with the violence, submissive behavior, or thwarted career aspirations of their women patients because they were not aware of these problems as fixable by psychotherapy. They were more likely to be seen as the woman patient's problems that needed adjustment on her part (American Psychological Association, 1975). Psychotherapy was the rational adaptation to a world that existed, for better or worse. Emotional, behavioral, or even existential change was the corrective procedure for a woman experiencing problems in her life.

THE SOCIAL CONTEXT OF WOMEN AS PATIENTS

Prior to the 1970s, women were expected to have different development, different needs, and different roles in society. Most personality and developmental theorists did not see the process of normal development of men and women resulting in the same type of person. Freud was outspoken about the differences, but others did not address the difference between men and women in describing their route toward appropriate goals. The popularity of the concept of special psychotherapeutic treatment for women, separate from treatment for men, paralleled the demand for equality for women and men in their social roles in the home, family, and workplace.

Betty Friedan's book *The Feminine Mystique* (1963) described women's distress as the "problem with no name." Women in enviable upper-middle-class situations—a loving husband, bright and healthy children, a large home in the suburbs—were flocking to psychotherapists with complaints of fatigue, depression, anger, and anxiety. The psychasthenias of the 1950s became the "tired housewife syndrome" of the 1960s, and melancholia became the "empty nest syndrome." By the early 1970s, "hysterical" and "frigid" women were being newly classified as exhibiting the overlearning of the classical feminine sex-role stereotypes.

Wolowitz (1972) described women who had been raised in genteel society for marriage and the housewife role consistent with the classical feminine sex role of the 1950s. The small girl was taught to display her beauty and to strive to be an object of desire for a future husband. Her identity was that of the beautiful and adaptable physical being ready to be modified to whatever station in life and occupation her male partner brought to their marriage. Her "occupational" role would be defined based on the career of her husband. Her sexuality was part of the offering of the physical object to her dominant partner. Primarily, sex was for her husband's enjoyment, and for reproduction. These traditional women were not to *choose* male partners based on sexual attraction since sex was not an appropriate motivator in choosing a husband. However, when these proper wives developed dysfunctions of sexual desire, therapists were inclined to seek psychodynamic reasons for their problems, not lack of sexual attraction to their partners. The *Los Angeles Times* (1994) presented the story of a civil judgment for fraud against a wife who admitted that she never felt attracted to her "short, fat, bald" husband. If holding a woman accountable for her lack of attraction to her husband becomes a new legal standard it might change some child-rearing practices for girls.

Depression was always predominantly a woman's disorder, even cross-culturally (Weissman, 1991). Whether it was a reporting phenomenon or another artifact because women were more likely to admit feeling depressed, or whether it was a bona fide physiological difference of vulnerability, or whether it was related to hormonal shifts or role restrictions, depression has remained a woman's problem by a 3:1 or 4:1 ratio (Weissman, 1980), and still no single variable can explain the continuing sex difference (Koss, 1990).

In the 1970s, other mental disorders prevalent in women were recognized as related to the social restrictions of women and their adaptation to these roles. Agoraphobia, with a prevalence rate of 85–95% in married women (Chambless & Goldstein, 1980), was seen as reinforced by the ease of women's ability to avoid anxious situations by remaining at home. The acceptance of dependency in women by therapists compounded the problem in agoraphobics as well as alcoholics. Hidden alcoholism of women was enabled by their ease of remaining out of the work force, where their solo drinking was less likely to be discovered.

In the 1980s, controversies over the possible inclusion of new sex-role-related disorders in the Diagnostic and Statistical Manuals III-R and IV were fraught with political issues for feminist therapists. The media publicized symposia wherein feminist therapists argued that the inclusion of post–luteal phase disorder in DSM-III-R would encourage physicians to blame women's depression and anxieties on hormonal cycles; that rapists could be exonerated by a diagnosis of paraphilic rapism; and that women would be blamed for their victimization and oppression by the diagnosis of self-defeating personality disorder. Thus, the concern was that diagnostic nomenclature would be used as a form of social control, to maintain gender inequality, rather than as a description that would lead to therapeutic usefulness (*Los Angeles Times*, 1986).

THE WOMEN'S MOVEMENT AS A GUIDING FORCE FOR CHANGE

The woman's movement of the late 1960s and 1970s helped generate the idea that psychotherapy could be specifically tailored to women struggling with a changing social context. Feminist therapy arose as a grass-roots movement in this country. Some of the early work came out of the consciousness-raising groups in colleges and the informal groups of women who were not in the work force. It began primarily as a middle-class movement of women who felt discrimination in the workplace and home but were not particularly lacking in the tools for basic physical survival. They identified with Betty Friedan's "problem with no name." They were the era's prime consumers of psychotherapy. They could afford the time and the money for therapy. They brought the ills of their cohorts—the empty nest syndrome (middle-aged depression), frigidity (sexual dysfunctions), the tired housewife syndrome (psychasthenia), and premenstrual syndrome.

The women's movement encouraged the review of the empirical basis for differential treatment for women in the health care professions. Feminists in the 1970s (Maccoby & Jacklin, 1974; Sherman, 1971) analyzed sex roles in adults and children from perspectives that challenged, rather than supported, traditional views. For example, bona fide differences in infants consisted of more activity in males, not more alertness; more eye contact with verbalization to faces by females, not more emotionality or dependence.

Later, these new interpretations and new studies of sex roles had an impact on the way psychotherapists viewed their patients and their roles as therapists. It was no longer a theoretical given that women were morally inferior, as Kohlberg (1981) had posited. Some theorists, such as Gilligan (1982), were proposing that women were morally different from men. Assessment measures changed as the basis for norms was adapted to comparable cohorts, rather than to the white male middle-class standard (e.g., MMPI2). Nevertheless, a series of studies using analogues of treatment vignettes demonstrated the pervasiveness of stereotyping of women by psychotherapists. But these analogues, revealing stereotypes of women perceived as inferior to men, were criticized for their artificial laboratory situations. Therapists could report how they would act, but they might perform differently in an actual therapy situation (Sherman, 1980). By the 1980s, therapists had become less naive about analogue situations, and because subjects might suspect sex roles as the dependent variable, analogue studies on sex bias gradually dropped out of the literature.

DEVELOPMENT OF WOMEN-RELATED THERAPY APPROACHES

The term *feminist therapy* has been used since the late 1960s, beginning with the first national roster of feminist therapists in 1970 (Brodsky, 1970), which used self-defined statements of therapists who wished to be identified as feminist therapists, and later in the publications that defined and differentiated feminist therapy from nonsexist therapy (Brodsky, 1975; Rawlings & Carter, 1977). The commonalities among those who considered themselves feminist therapists became apparent as including the concepts of an egalitarian relationship between therapist and patient; a belief in the strong impact of external realities (including sex discrimination) as restrictions on the behavior of women; a belief in the need to develop independence and assertiveness as a goal for adult women; an awareness of power differentials; and a belief that changes in the external environment were necessary for many of the problems presented by female therapy patients.

Feminist therapy became the term coined for treatment offered by feminists who specialized in disorders prevalent in women but trivialized by the professions. Feminist therapists had a political agenda, as well as a psychotherapeutic agenda. Their world view included the effect of the social/economic context of their patients' lives. In relating patients' symptoms to their restricted career options, or conflict about acceptance of their deviation from social standards, or lack of economic resources to become independent, feminist therapists became politically active in correcting the social context that bound their patients to the cages in which they felt confined.

Feminist therapists also discovered that they were sought out by women who saw their problems as stemming from abuse by males. Rape victims, victims of sexual harassment on the job, and survivors of childhood sexual abuse became a large part of their case loads. Lesbian therapists played a vocal role in focusing women's issues in a new model of therapy for women—particularly in addressing the relationship of women therapists to their clients.

New concepts were explored concerning women's reactions to normal phenomena such as achievement motivation. Matina Horner's *fear of success* paradigm (Horner, 1969, 1972) was based on the traditional concept of McClelland et al. (1953) that showed (in Thematic Apperception Test [TAT] stories) a need for achievement in successful individuals. Horner demonstrated the different reactions of women and men to achievement. Women showed much less need to achieve than did men. Indeed, she found a fear-of-success phenomenon whereby women avoided the appearance of success in a male achievement context, creating stories in response to TAT-type cards in which the female characters suffered as a consequence of success or were found to have been mistaken about the reality of their seeming success (Horner, 1969). Pauline Clance (Clance & Imes, 1978) developed the concept of the *imposter phenomenon* for high-achieving women who either do not acknowledge their success or negate the reality that they achieved it legitimately by attributing their success to either luck or error. This "fear" was later related to the expectation of social disapproval or ostracism experienced by competent, successful women who attained positions of power. Feminist therapy development utilized such empirical data to bolster the clinical evidence that women not only had different experiences than men in the work and home situation, but also that they aspired to different goals and reacted differently when they achieved them.

Chesler (1971) noted the parallel of the roles of the therapist and patient in traditional psychotherapies with the roles of the husband and wife in traditional marriages. An expert male therapist (or husband) played the role of adviser and protector of the client (wife), who was appropriately suppliant, dependent, and needy.

This recapitulation of the male therapist–female client as husband–wife encouraged therapies that fostered dependency in women, and may have had an impact on the confusion of professional boundaries that has led to the proliferation of cases of improper sexual intimacy in psychotherapy.

The problem of sexual misconduct of mostly male therapists with female patients was known and exposed to the professions even before the study by Chesler (1971), who interviewed New York women for her doctoral dissertation and presented the results at the meeting of the American Psychological Association (APA). Surveys in the 1960s were not published because they were too controversial (Brodsky, 1989, p. 16). A long political struggle ensued over the next several years to expose the problem more publicly. In 1973, only four cases were presented to the APA Ethics Committee, and no consequences greater than dropping one psychologist for non-payment of dues resulted (APA, 1975). By the 1980s, however, the mental health professions had recognized the impact of the growing number of reports of such cases on insurance premiums, ethics violations, malpractice judgments, and delicensure. Currently, sexual relationships between therapists and patients account for over one-half of malpractice claims against psychologists and a majority of ethics cases, as well as complaints to licensing boards. No particular theoretical approach was related to the behavior (Holroyd & Brodsky, 1977), but the problem is frequently associated with the lack of training or understanding by therapists of the impact of their power in the therapeutic relationship (Bates & Brodsky, 1989).

THE APA SURVEY ON SEXISM IN PSYCHOTHERAPEUTIC PRACTICE

Many of the clients of feminist therapists complained about the therapy they received in the past. Their complaints focused on certain themes, some of which concerned attitudes of their therapists that they regarded as demeaning, trivializing, condescending, and dominating—in a word, sexist. These clients also complained about the actions of their therapists—unprofessional, including sexualized.

In 1973, the APA, in response to various complaints including those of the Association for Women in Psychology, individuals like Hannah Lerman, and the new Committee on Women in Psychology (CWP), appointed a task force on sex bias and sex role stereotyping in psychotherapeutic practice. That group identified, through a literature review and a survey, the areas of sex bias and formulated a resultant set of guidelines for therapy with women (APA, 1975). Several other groups followed suit in the next decade to reinforce and add to the findings and guidelines (Canadian Psychological Association, Counseling Psychologists, Gay and Lesbian Division).

The APA Task Force Report on Sex Bias and Sex Role Stereotyping in psychotherapeutic practice spelled out the areas of concern of the psychologists in the clinical and women's divisions that it surveyed. The following themes arose from the respondents surveyed in 1975:

1. The therapist assumes that problem resolution and self-actualization for women come from marriage or from perfecting the role of wife.
2. The therapist lacks awareness and sensitivity to the woman client's career, work, and role diversity.
3. The female client's attitude toward childbearing and child rearing is viewed as a necessary index of her emotional maturity.
4. In family therapy or treatment of children, the therapist supports the idea that child rearing and thus the child's problems are solely the responsibility of the mother.
5. The therapist defers to the husband's needs in the conduct of the wife's treatment.
6. The therapist or colleague denies the adaptive and self-actualizing potential or assertiveness of female clients and fosters the concepts of women as passive and dependent.

7. The therapist uses theoretical concepts (e.g., masochism) to ignore or condone violence toward and victimization of women.
8. Sexist jokes and offhand comments by the therapist have the effect of demeaning women.
9. The therapist employs inaccurate or demeaning labels (*seductive, manipulative, histrionic,* etc.) when describing female clients.
10. The therapist insists on making Freudian interpretations.
11. The therapist maintains that vaginal orgasm is a prerequisite for emotional maturity and thus a goal of therapy.
12. The therapist labels assertiveness and ambition with the Freudian concept of *penis envy*.
13. The therapist seduces the client.
14. The therapist has a double standard for male and female sexual activities.
15. The therapist heavily weights physical appearance in the selection of patients or in setting therapeutic goals.

GUIDELINES FOR TREATMENT OF WOMEN IN PSYCHOTHERAPY

These themes of complaints regarding therapy with women were then translated into 13 guidelines for the treatment of women in therapy (APA, 1978):

1. The conduct of therapy should be free of constrictions based on gender-defined roles, and the options explored between client and practitioner should be free of sex role stereotypes.
2. Psychologists should recognize the reality, variety, and implications of sex-discriminatory practices in society and should facilitate client examination of options in dealing with such practices.
3. The therapist should be knowledgeable about current empirical findings on sex roles, sexism, and individual differences

resulting from the client's gender-defined identity.

4. The theoretical concepts employed by the therapist should be free of sex bias and sex role stereotypes.

5. The psychologist should demonstrate acceptance of women as equal to men by using language free of derogatory labels.

6. The psychologist should avoid establishing the source of personal problems within the client when they are more properly attributable to situational or cultural factors.

7. The psychologist and a fully informed client mutually should agree upon aspects of the therapy relationship such as treatment modality, time factors, and fee arrangements.

8. While the importance of the availability of accurate information to a client's family is recognized, the privilege of communication about diagnosis, prognosis, and progress ultimately resides with the client, not with the therapist.

9. If authoritarian processes are employed as a technique, the therapy should not have the effect of maintaining or reinforcing sterotypic dependency of women.

10. The client's assertive behaviors should be respected.

11. The psychologist whose female client is subjected to violence in the form of physical abuse or rape should recognize and acknowledge that the client is the victim of a crime.

12. The psychologist should recognize and encourage exploration of a woman client's sexuality and should recognize her right to define her own sexual preferences.

13. The psychologist should not have sexual relations with a woman client or treat her as a sex object.

The major points supported by respondents to the survey include both content and process issues. To summarize: Women in psychother-apy needed to have therapists who would not use sexist language; would not assume that they should prepare for a particular "woman's role" in life; would not expect them to defer to male bosses, therapists, or husbands; would not treat them as sex objects; would not relate all their problems to their gender; and would not keep them in a dependent relationship so that they could not grow beyond therapy.

Other issues that the guidelines addressed included recognition that rape, incest, and sexual misconduct by professionals are abusive and may be criminal; that the client needs to identify such incidents and take action, if so desired; that the social context does not always permit the client to take otherwise appropriate actions (like asserting oneself with an abusing boss, husband, or rapist); and that discrimination on the job keeps qualified women from achieving according to their level of competency. The guidelines represented a document that asserted conditions for therapy with women, and it became apparent that further work would be needed by women's groups to keep the issues in the forefront of practice, research, and clinical training.

ORGANIZATIONS OF FEMINIST THERAPISTS TO PROMOTE GUIDELINES AND DEVELOP THEORY

Armed with this knowledge and the expertise of working with women who bring these issues to their therapy, feminist therapists began to organize more formally, starting with the Feminist Therapist Committee of the Association of Women in Psychology in 1970. Gradually, feminist therapists proceeded to found or influence other organizations, such as the Feminist Therapy Institute. Also, divisions of the APA, including Psychology of Women, Clinical Psychology, Counseling Psychology, and Psychotherapy, as well as both the Canadian Psychological Association and the American Psychiatric Association, developed sections or committees on women. They moved toward consensus on techniques, ethics, and emergence of theory.

These groups were the nuclei of theory development for specific psychotherapies for women clients. It had become clear that most traditional therapies were informed by theories and techniques that reflected cultural and societal biases toward women. The existing models of therapy highlighted, exaggerated, and dichotomized gender differences, or they ignored or minimized differences that clearly existed. The more predominant traditional psychotherapy models—psychoanalysis, behavior therapy, cognitive therapy, and family systems therapy—were criticized for their limited perspectives and applications to women.

In addition to the studies on sex bias, discrimination, and stereotyping of women and their expected roles, research and development of treatment modalities for high-prevalence disorders among women was a further impetus for the development of the feminist therapies. In 1978, a National Conference sponsored by the National Institutes of Mental Health and APA's Division on the Psychology of Women (Division 35) brought together researchers on the various aspects of women's treatment in psychotherapy (Brodsky & Hare-Mustin, 1980). The book resulting from the work of that conference gave testimony to the extensive research literature that had accumulated over the previous decade. There was specific scientific evidence on which to base psychotherapeutic treatment for women's depression, eating disorders, hysterical and phobic disorders, posttraumatic stress disorders (in reaction to rape and domestic violence), and adjustment disorders (women in transition), as well as specific modes of treatment for women such as consciousness-raising groups.

THEORY

Currently, there is no single theory to guide psychotherapy with women. Instead, there are adaptations of existing theoretical approaches to include feminist aspects in treating women and, more recently, emerging theoretical positions that have in common an awareness of gender inequality and discrimination in viewing women's psychological symptoms and treatment. Major issues regarding existing nonfeminist therapy theories were raised and debated in the literature. The following represent some of the predominant foci of those issues.

Psychoanalysis

A major issue was that Freud's basic position on psychosexual development (1905–1938) was founded on the experience of the male child in his shifts of attachment of sexual energy to various bodily zones. Female development, in contrast, became organized around the girl's recognition that she possesses inferior anatomy, and consequently experiences shame and envy of males, which result in inferior moral development. The normal adult woman thus cannot avoid pathological traits such as narcissism, masochism, and passivity.

The sex bias in orthodox psychoanalysis is obvious and has been a target of criticism first by women analysts (Horney, 1926, 1932, 1934; Thompson, 1942, 1950) and later by the feminist psychologists (Albee, 1981; Brodsky, 1980; Chesler, 1972; Hare-Mustin, 1983; Lerman, 1986). Psychoanalytic therapy, they noted, adheres to and promotes a stereotyped image of women. It sets as an ideal passivity and submissiveness in the role of wife and mother. In so doing, therapy may serve to diminish women's lifestyle choices regarding relationships, sexuality, and career, thus constricting their growth and diversity. In addition, psychoanalysis encourages frequent mother blaming (Caplan & Hall-McCorquodale, 1985; Hare-Mustin, 1987) for a patient's inner conflicts or disorders.

Newer generations of psychoanalytic theory and treatment such as object relations (Kernberg, 1984; Kohut, 1977; Mahler, Pine, & Bergman, 1975; Masterson, 1981; Stolorow, 1983; Winnicott, 1965) and ego psychology, (Blank & Blanck, 1979; Hartmann, 1964) focus more specifically on a client's early relationships with parental figures important in fulfilling early needs. Feminist approaches to object relations theory (Chodorow, 1978; Dinnerstein, 1976; Eichenbaum & Orbach, 1983; Miller,

1976; Surrey, 1985) similarly rely on experiences during infancy to explain women's distress, but they address the contributing sociopolitical factors as well.

Feminist therapists challenge the view that disorders of the self result exclusively from inappropriate responses from the primary caregiver (usually the mother) to the child's evolving emotional states and needs. Instead, they teach their clients that because of their subordinate position in society, women form themselves according to the wishes and needs of men. Thus, their sense of self is more malleable and fluid than that of men. In addition, emphasis is placed on the self defined in relationships, which is seen as a normal asset.

Behavior Therapy

Behavior therapies attempt to apply experimentally derived principles of learning in a systematic manner to help individuals change maladaptive behaviors. Often therapy is aimed at changing the interaction between the patient and the environment as the patient learns a repertoire of behavior that is most likely to produce desirable consequences in specific situations.

Behavior modification, unlike psychoanalysis, is not considered inherently harmful to the treatment of women. In fact, the techniques appear to offer greater potential neutrality with regard to social values and can be adapted to social system change (Blechman, 1980, p. 217). Feminists criticized behaviorists for focusing on individual behaviors of women because therapy aimed at individual women (1) does not change the sociopolitical conditions that damage all women; (2) contributes to women's sense of being deficient and in need of an expert to "fix" them, or (3) produces superficial changes in behavior because the real problems are not addressed (Chesler, 1971, 1972, Rossi, 1964; Williams, 1977). In behavior therapy, women are vulnerable due to the power of the therapist to select or encourage behaviors that need modification. Thus, changing one's weight or one's style of dress, as

opposed to one's career or level of assertiveness, are critical goal decisions that clients do not make in a vacuum of guidance from their therapists.

Behavior therapists may ignore gender differences essential to the effectiveness of treatment (Fodor & Epstein, 1983; Kahn, 1981; Linehan & Egan, 1979). For example, one common application of behavioral therapy is assertiveness training, in which individuals are taught skills in order to be more effective in their interpersonal relationships at work. However, when this formula is applied to women, it may backfire given that a direct, assertive, and successful woman is not readily tolerated in some sectors of society (Monahan, Kuhn, & Shaver, 1974). In one study, expert and peer judges of both sexes identified comparable noncoercive behaviors as assertive when enacted by men but aggressive when displayed by women (Rich & Schroeder, 1976).

Feminist therapists adopt behavioral interventions that avoid sex bias by using a thorough functional analysis of behavior to determine the degree to which prevailing environmental conditions, general problem-solving inadequacies, or specific skill deficiencies promote the problematic behavior (Blechman, 1980). The decision that the deficit resides in the woman, rather than in the environment, is made cautiously. *Discrimination training* (Kahn, 1981) uses role playing and discussion to enable women to discern and anticipate the situations and settings in which assertive behavior will be successful and when it will not.

Cognitive Therapy

Criticism of the potential misuse of behavior therapies is readily applicable to the cognitive approaches as well. Cognitive therapy attempts to help clients by teaching them to recognize their misconceived self-statements and the impact of these statements on their behavior, to challenge the validity of these thoughts, and to substitute more reality-based self-statements. Cognitive therapy fails to address the influence of societal devaluation of women. It assumes that a negative self-statement is a distortion of feedback from others, rather than an accurate reading of the devaluation by others due to a sexist stereotype. Internalizing this devaluation is likely to lead to inferior self-concepts and lowered self-esteem (Marecek & Kravetz, 1977). Thus, women's cognitions are likely to be more self-derogatory than men's and require an approach that acknowledges social inequality and its effects.

When cognitive-behavioral models are used to address women's negative self-statements and low self-esteem reinforced by society's devaluation of women, practices include self-awareness training, countering of negative self-statements, and relaxation training combined with a exploration of internalized belief systems that may devalue women. The work focuses on exploring, through discussion, exercises, and reflection, each woman's view of herself and the potential consequences of both positive and negative changes (Jakubowski, 1977; Osborn & Harris, 1975; Phelps & Austin, 1975; Stere, 1985).

Family Systems Therapy

Family systems therapy defines emotional symptoms in terms of interactions and behavioral sequences involving all family members. In systems theory, women and men are treated as if they have equal power within the family. While family therapists do not deny that women are in an inferior political and economic situation relative to men, they maintain the illusion that men and women are equal at home and in the family (Goldner, 1988). Recognition of gender inequality is blatantly absent from the theory, although the theory acknowledges a generational hierarchy with inequality of age differences (Hare-Mustin, 1987).

Family therapists may incorrectly view women and men as equally responsible for dysfunctional dynamics even when one is being victimized or abused (Bograd, 1984, 1986; Wheeler, Avis, Miller, & Chaney, 1985). Oppression is viewed by family systems therapists as "a mutually regulated dance between oppressor and oppressed, a dance maintained by the cyclical interaction sequences between participants" (Libow, Raskin, & Caust, 1982, p. 8). This view neglects the historical factors responsible for shaping this type of interaction, as well as the social and political factors outside the family that keep it in place. This circular form of causality proposed by family systems theory can be a form of blaming the victim. The National Alliance for the Mentally Ill (NAMI) has become a powerful political presence that takes issue with the assumption of family therapists that the control of the behavior of an individual family member is readily changed by "correct" interactions of the rest of the system.

Feminist family therapists (Libow et al., 1982; Luepnitz, 1988; McColdrick, Anderson, & Walsh, 1989) function as advocates for women in families by recognizing and attempting to equalize power imbalances within the marital and family structures, attending to women's issues in the family, and watching for potential victimization of women in the family. They educate family members about the historical and political factors effecting and maintaining family pathology. The wife's view of the family's readiness for termination of therapy is considered, as is the family's option to adopt alternative lifestyles and the wife's life cycle changes. In addition to retirement for the man, transitional crises for the woman (such as pregnancy and postpartum depression or children leaving home) may be explored by the therapist.

Women-in-Relation Therapy

Theorists in the 1970s and 1980s began to challenge the traditional male traits of autonomy and independence as the goals for psychotherapy with women, as well as for men. There developed a respect for and celebration of traditionally female-linked traits such as emotionality and relatedness. Consequently, theorists looked to a conceptual background for understanding these traits and for comprehending why women seemed to develop in opposite directions from men with regard to them.

Nancy Chodorow (1978) utilized an object relations framework to understand the origins of gender differences in styles of relatedness. Her theory follows the logic that by the nature of their early experiences of relationship to a female caretaker, women develop an identity that is grounded in relationships, while men develop autonomous, independent selves. Because women are predominantly the caretakers of young children, children of both sexes form their identity, including their gender definition, through their day-to-day encounters with a female role model. The different ways that girls and boys react to an ongoing relationship with a female caretaker result in differences not only in gender identity but also in interpersonal functioning. These different patterns develop into enduring personality traits and adult interpersonal styles. For the female child, identity formation takes place alongside a role model with which she can identify. Male gender definition, in the presence of a continuous female role model but in the absence of a male model, is achieved by separating oneself from the female caregiver and rejecting what is female. Thus, feminine personality develops "in relation and connection to other people" (Chodorow, 1974, pp. 43–44), whereas male development entails "a more empathic individuation and defensive firming of experienced ego boundaries" (Chodorow, 1978, pp. 166–167).

Chodorow (1978) affirmed the value of female-socialized traits but was careful to point out the limitations for both women and men of having gender-defined traits. She called for the end to traditional family structures that maintain a sexist division of labor defining caretaking as a woman's function. She believed that as men begin to be equally responsible for child care, gendered personality dichotomies will lessen.

Chodorow's theory was popularized and adapted by both theorists and therapists. The theory was modified such that connectedness was considered inherent in female development and autonomy in male development (Chodorow, 1978; Gibbs, 1984; Pollack & Gilligan, 1982; Rubin, 1983). Early life social arrangements were not necessarily the cause of this differentiation. Some supporters viewed women as better than men. Women's abilities to affiliate, empathize, and cooperate were offered as superior to men's abilities to compete, dominate, and aggress. Female-linked traits were invoked as a rationale for why women appear to be more capable of intimate relationships and may be better psychotherapists.

The Stone Center

The theme of woman as better than man also emerged from the work of Jean Baker Miller (1976) and her colleagues at the Wellesley Stone Center. Miller's relational psychology was based on developmental theory combined with a sociopolitical perspective. Traditional models described development as movement through symbiosis (enmeshed relationships) via separation and individuation to independence and autonomy (Mahler Pine, & Bergman, 1975). Self-in-relation theory asserted that development proceeds from more primitive relationships to more sophisticated ones based on reciprocal relations and interdependence. Because of the value they place on relationships and their attunement to others, women are thought to exert (when allowed) a better, more altruistic and benevolent form of power. That is, women find ways to simultaneously increase one's own as well as another's power.

In her critique of a male standard for morality (Kohlberg, 1976), Carol Gilligan (1982) proposed the superiority of a female morality. Analyzing girls' and boys' responses to hypothetical moral dilemmas, Gilligan found that boys (who received higher scores on moral judgment on Kohlberg's scale) use abstract and logical principles, while girls analyze the needs and feelings of the characters involved. In justifying the sophistication of female morality, Gilligan implied that abstract principles of justice actually interfere with empathy, care, and concern.

These theories, which emphasized the ignored and undervalued traits of relatedness, caring, and emotionality, provided a boost to women clients and their therapists, making them feel better understood. However, criticism of these theories focused on the dichoto-mization of gender traits and on efforts to relate these traits to universal, essential, and/or bio-logical factors.

Some feminists argue that dichotomizing sex roles is erroneous and a caricature of human experience (Hare-Mustin & Marecek, 1986). The view of the exclusively autonomous male ignores men's reliance on their wives to manage their households and their secretaries to man-age their offices. Similarly, viewing women as exclusively nurturing, self-sacrificing, and other-directed ignores the complexity of their decision making and leadership in raising chil-dren and maintaining single-parent house-holds.

Hare-Mustin and Maracek (1986) also point out the failure of sex role dichotomizing theo-ries to understand behavior within context. It is not necessarily that men invoke logic and rules, while women invoke caring and feelings. Rather, the individual with more power in the situation tends to use reason, rather than emotion, to achieve results (Zuk, 1972). This can be seen in women as readily as in men. While women use appeals for caring from au-thoritative males as boss, leader, or husband, women simultaneously use rules and rationality in disciplining their children. It is their chil-dren, both male and female, who appeal to love, empathy, and sympathy from both par-ents. Thus, in the end, it appears that power, or its lack, governs behavior in relationships, not gender.

Finally, women are not homogeneous, as appears to be the conclusion of a dichotomous theory. Class, race, ethnicity, age, and other differences among women are ignored, when white middle-class women become the standard for all women (Reid, 1993). One of the princi-ples that is central to all feminist approaches to the treatment of women is a multicultural perspective. The feminist concern is that thera-pists not repeat with minority women the mis-takes that ignoring the diversity of majority women has brought. An attempt to establish a research database to gain greater knowledge about women in different racial, class, re-ligious, age, ethnic, and sexual orientation groups is now underway (Brown & Root, 1990; Reid & Comas-Diaz, 1990). By respecting the diverse experiences of women, feminist thera-pists can avoid using the primacy of gender as the only organizing, central issue of every woman who enters therapy (Brown, 1990).

ETHICS IN THE TREATMENT OF WOMEN

While all psychotherapists are bound by the ethical codes of their respective professions (no matter what the sex, race, or ethnicity of the client), there are specific issues of importance with regard to the ethical treatment of women. The Feminist Therapy Institute has provided the first major document that represents a con-sensus of a large group of feminist therapists as to what constitutes ethical therapy with women (Lerman & Porter, 1990). The work on the Feminist Therapy Code of Ethics is based on years of discussion among therapists at confer-ences of the Feminist Therapy Institute. Bear-ing in mind that feminist methodology includes the long, arduous process of consensus, with an equal voice among all participants, the prin-ciples that survived the process represent com-mon agreement.

The Feminist Therapy Ethics Code is an aspirational document for the guidance of femi-nist therapists that promotes sensitivity and training to achieve and maintain an unbiased perspective of cultural diversities; awareness and avoidance of exploitation of the power advan-tage of the therapist; responsibility for monitor-ing any overlapping relationships of the client and therapist; therapist accountability for self-evaluation and competence; and proactive in-tervention outside therapy for social change.

While these guidelines specifically relate to feminist therapists, the principles are all gener-alizable to any therapist working with women. Only the guidelines regarding overlapping rela-tionships are controversial in that feminist ther-apists (particularly in small or conservative communities) tend to see themselves as a mi-nority population, so that they experience dif-ficulty in maintaining exclusively professional relationships with the clients in their particular local groups. This is especially true of lesbian therapists who find themselves at social events and in professional groups with their patients. Hence, controversies regarding dual roles that could lead to therapist influences of power are unresolved among feminist therapists.

WOMEN AND PSYCHOTHERAPY TODAY

Changes in the perspectives of therapists on women in the last two decades can be seen in the increased respect for expression of emotions by both sexes, as well as in awareness of the contribution of external forces limiting the development of women as full partners in the home, work force, and leadership roles. Agreement on certain issues exists among feminist therapists of all theoretical positions. The APA Task Force Guidelines for Therapy with Women presented above still applies. Respecting women as equal to men in intelligence and competence, and as having the same needs for power and achievement as men, will cover much of the prescriptions for nonsexist treatment in therapy. The focus on more specific treatment paradigms for disorders prevalent in women continues through the convening of conferences to encourage research on women's mental health (Keita, 1993; Russo, 1990) and through more focused research projects such as the APA Task Force on Depression. As with the awakening of the National Institute of Health to the need to find out if and how women fit the male-derived profiles on heart disease and other major diseases, mental health studies can be expected to look more closely at women as the missing subjects to validate their male-centered theories and research about psychotherapy practices and outcome.

Finally, new approaches to training therapists in interventions based on feminist processes and theories are becoming more sophisticated and more specific. This can be seen in publications such as that of Worell and Remer (1992), which leads the trainee through the steps of evaluating theories and practices and then developing a feminist transformation of them. Documents can also be anticipated from conferences such as the APA Division on Psychology of Women's Boston Conference on Education and Training in Feminist Practice (1993), which has begun, by convening a national group of experts, the development of training guidelines, with the eventual recognition of feminist practice as a specialization, perhaps to be accredited or diplomated. Meanwhile, the development of theories and special techniques for disorders prevalent in women continues to flourish in the current feminist-friendly climate of the mental health professions, whose practitioners are now considerably more than 50% female.

REFERENCES

Albee, G. (1981). The prevention of sexism. *Professional Psychology, 12,* 20–28.

American Psychological Association. (1975). Report of the Task Force on Sex Bias and Sex Role Stereotyping in Psychotherapeutic Practice. *American Psychologist, 30,* 1169–1175.

American Psychological Association. (1978). Task force on sex bias and sex role stereotyping in psychotherapeutic practice. Guidelines for therapy with women. *American Psychologist, 33,* 1122–1123.

Baskin, D., Blueston, H., & Nelson, M. (1981). Mental illness in minority women. *Journal of Clinical Psychology, 3,* 491–498.

Bates, C., & Brodsky, A. M. (1989). *Sex in the therapy hour: A case of professional incest.* New York: Guilford Press.

Belle, D. (1990). Poverty and women's mental health. *American Psychologist, 45,* 385–389.

Bernard, J. (1972). *The future of marriage.* Hollywood, CA: World Press.

Blanck, G., & Blanck, R. (1979). *Ego psychology: II. Psychoanalytic developmental psychology.* New York: Columbia University Press.

Blau, F. (1984). Women in the labor force: An overview. In J. Freeman (Ed.), *Women and feminist perspective* (pp. 265–289). Mayfield.

Blechman, E. (1980). Behavior therapies. In A. M. Brodsky & R. Hare-Mustin (Eds.), *Women and psychotherapy* (pp. 217–244). New York: Guilford Press.

Bograd, M. (1984). Family systems approaches to wife battering: A feminist critique. *American Journal of Orthopsychiatry, 54*, 558–568.

Bograd M. (1986). A feminist examination of family systems models of violence against women in the family. In M. Ault-Riche (Ed.), *Women and family therapy* (pp. 34–50). Rockville, MD: Aspen Systems Corp.

Brodsky, A. M. (1970). *Feminist Therapy Roster.* Unpublished document, Association for Women in Psychology.

Brodsky A. M. (1975, March). *Is there a feminist therapy?* Paper presented at the Convention of the Southeastern Psychological Association, Atlanta, GA.

Brodsky, A. M. (1980). A decade of feminist influence on psychotherapy. *Psychology of Women Quarterly, 4*, 331–344.

Brodsky, A. M. (1989). Sex between patient and therapist: Psychology's data and response. In G. Gabbard (Ed.), *Sexual exploitation in professional relationships* (pp. 15–26). Washington, DC: American Psychiatric Press.

Brodsky, A. M., & Hare-Mustin, R. (Eds.), (1980). *Women and psychotherapy.* New York: Guilford Press.

Broverman, I., Vogel, S., Broverman, D., Clarkson, F., & Rosenkrantz, P. (1972). Sex role stereotypes: A current appraisal. *Journal of Social Issues, 28*, 59–78.

Brown, L. S. (1990). The meaning of a multicultural perspective for theory building in feminist therapy. In L. S. Brown & M. P. P. Root (Eds.), *Diversity and complexity in feminist therapy* (pp. 1–22). New York: Haworth Press.

Brown, L. S., & Root, M. P. P. (Eds). (1990). *Diversity and complexity in feminist therapy.* New York: Haworth Press.

Bureau of National Affairs (BNA). (1986). *Work and family: A changing dynamic.* Washington, DC: Author.

Burgess, A., & Holstrom L. (1973). Rape trauma syndrome. *American Journal of Psychiatry, 13*, 981–996.

Caplan, P. J., & Hall-McCorquodale, I. (1985). Mother-blaming in major clinical journals. *American Journal of Orthopsychiatry, 55*, 345–353.

Chambless, D. L., & Goldstein, A. L. (1980). Anxieties: Agoraphobia and hysteria. In A. M. Brodsky & R. Hare-Mustin (Eds.), *Women and psychotherapy* (pp. 113–134). New York: Guilford Press.

Chesler, P. (1971). Patient and patriarch: Woman in the psychotherapeutic relationship. In V. Gornick & B. K. Moran (Eds.), *Women in sexist society* (pp. 362–392). New York: Basic Books.

Chesler, P. (1972). *Women and madness.* Garden City, NY: Doubleday.

Chodorow, N. (1974). Family structure and feminine personality. In M. Z. Rosaldo & L. Lamphere (Eds.), *Woman, culture and society* (pp. 46–66). Stanford, CA: Stanford University Press.

Chodorow, N. (1978). *The reproduction of mothering.* Berkeley: University of California Press.

Clance, P. R., & Imes, S. (1978). The imposter phenomenon in high achieving women: Dynamic and therapeutic intervention. *Psychotherapy: Theory, research, and practice, 15*, 241–247.

Dinnerstein, D. (1976). *The mermaid and the minotaur: Sexual arrangements and the human malaise.* New York: Harper & Row.

Eichenbaum L., & Orbach, S. (1983). *Understanding women: A feminist psychoanalytic view.* New York: Basic Books.

Fodor, I. G., & Epstein, R. C. (1983). Assertiveness training for women: Where are we failing? In P. Emmelkamp & E. Foa (Eds.), *Failure in behavior therapy* (pp. 132–154). New York: Wiley.

Freud, S. (1938). Three contributions to the theory of sexuality. In A. A. Brill (Ed.), *The basic writings of Sigmund Freud* (pp. 553–629). New York: Modern Library. (Originally published, 1905).

Friedan, B. (1963). *The feminine mystique.* New York: Dell.

Gibbs, M. S. (1984). The therapist as imposter. In C. M. Brody (Ed.), *Women therapists working with women* (pp. 22–33). New York: Springer.

Gilligan, C. (1982). *In a different voice.* Cambridge, MA: Harvard University Press.

Goldner, V. (1988). Generation and gender: Normative and covert hierarchies. *Family Process, 27*, 17–31.

Gove, W. R. (1972). The relationship between sex roles, mental illness, and marital status. *Social Forces, 51*, 34–44.

Gove, W. R. (1979). Sex differences in the epidemiology of mental disorder: Evidence and explanations. In E. J. Gomberg & V. Franks (Eds.), *Gender and disordered behavior: Sex differences in psychopathology* (pp. 23–68). New York: Brunner/Mazel.

Gove, W. R., & Tudor, J. (1973). Adult sex roles and mental illness. *American Journal of Sociology, 78*, 812–835.

Hall, R. (1993). Reviews. *Psychology of Women Quarterly*, 17, 127–131.

Hare-Mustin, R. (1983). An appraisal of the relationship between women and psychotherapy: 80 years after the case of Dora. *American Psychologist*, 38, 594–601.

Hare-Mustin, R. (1987). The problem of gender in family therapy theory. *Family Process*, 26, 15–33.

Hare-Mustin, R., & Maracek, J. (1986). Autonomy and gender: Some questions for therapists. *Psychotherapy* 23, 205–212.

Hartmann, H. (1964). *Essays on ego psychology: Selected problems in psychoanalytic theory*. New York: International Universities Press.

Holroyd, J. C., & Brodsky, A. M. (1977). Psychologists' attitudes and practices regarding erotic and non-erotic physical contact with patients. *American Psychologist*, 34, 843–849.

Horner, M. S. (1969). Fail bright women. *Psychology Today*, 3, 36–38.

Horner, M. S. (1972). Toward an understanding of achievement-related conflict in women. *Journal of Social Issues*, 28, 157–175.

Horney, K. (1967). The dread of women. In *Feminine psychology* (pp. 133–146). New York: Norton. (Originally published 1926).

Horney, K. (1967). On the genesis of the castration complex in women. In *Feminine psychology* (pp. 37–53). New York: Norton. (Originally published 1932)

Horney, K. (1967). The overvaluation of love: A study of a common present-day feminine type. In *Feminine psychology* (pp. 182–213). New York: Norton. (Originally published 1934).

Jakubowski, P. A. (1977). Assertive behavior and clinical problems of women. In E. I. Rawlings & D. K. Carter (Eds.), *Psychotherapy for women: Treatment toward equality* (pp. 147–167). Springfield, IL: Charles C. Thomas.

Kahn, S. E. (1981). Issues in the assessment and training of assertiveness with women. In J. D. Wine & M. D. Smye (Eds.), *Social competence* (pp. 346–367). New York: Guilford Press.

Keita, G. P. (1994, May). National Conference on psychosocial and behavioral factors in women's health, Washington, DC.

Kernberg, O. (1984). *Object relations theory and clinical psycho-analysis*. New York: Jason Aronson.

Kessler, R. C., Reuter, J. A., & Greenley, J. R. (1979). Sex differences in the use of psychiatric outpatient facilities. *Social Forces*, 58, 557–571.

Kohlberg, L. (1976). Moral stages and moralization: The cognitive-developmental approach. In T. Lickona (Ed.), *Moral development and behavior: Theory, research, and social issues* (pp. 31–53). New York: Holt, Rinehart, & Winston.

Kohlberg, L. (1981). *The philosophy of moral development*. San Francisco: Harper & Row.

Kohut, H. (1977). *The restoration of the self*. New York: International Universities Press.

Koss, M. (1990). The women's mental health research agenda: Violence against women. *American Psychologist*, 45, 374–380.

Lerman, H. (1986). *A mote in Freud's eye: From psychoanalysis to the psychology of women*. New York: Springer.

Lerman, H., & Porter, N. (1990). *Feminist ethics in psychotherapy*. New York: Springer.

Libow, J., A., Raskin, P. A., & Caust, B. L. (1982). Feminist and family systems therapy: Are they irreconcilable? *American Journal of Family Therapy*, 10, 3–12.

Linehan, M., & Egan, K. (1979). *Assertion training for women: Square peg in a round hole?* Paper presented at Symposium on Behavior Therapy for Women, Association for Advanced Behavior Therapy, San Francisco.

Los Angeles Times. (1986, 22 August). Proposed psychiatry changes drawing fire: Addition of three new diagnostic categories stigmatize women psychologists fear, p. E1.

Los Angeles Times (1994, February 18). Marital fraud damage award voided, pp. A3, A28.

Luepnitz, D. A. (1988). *The family interpreted: Feminist theory in clinical practice*. New York: Basic Books.

Maccoby, E. E., & Jacklin, C. N. (1974). *The psychology of sex differences*. Stanford, CA: Stanford University Press.

Mahler, M. S., Pine, F., & Bergman, A. (1975). *The psychological birth of the human infant*. New York: Basic Books.

Marecek, J., & Kravetz, D. (1977). Women and mental health: A review of feminist change efforts. *Psychiatry*, 40, 323–329.

Masterson, J. F. (1981). *The narcissistic and borderline disorders: An integrated developmental approach*. New York: Brunner/Mazel.

McBride, A. B. (1990). Mental health effects of women's multiple roles. *American Psychologist*, 45, 381–385.

McClelland, D. C., Atkinson, J. W., Clark, R. A., & Lowell, E. L. (1953). *The achievement motive*. New York: Irvington.

McColdrick, M., Anderson, C. M., & Walsh, F. (1989). *Women in families: A framework for family therapy.* New York: Norton.

Miller, J. B. (1976). *Toward a new psychology of women.* Boston: Beacon Press.

Monahan, L., Kuhn, D., & Shaver, P. (1974). Intrapsychic versus cultural explanations of the "fear of success" motive. *Journal of Personality and Social Psychology, 29,* 667–674.

Morales, I. (1993). *Acculturation processes in Hispanics.* Unpublished masters' thesis, California State University, Dominguez Hills.

New York Times. (1987, February 23). p. E6.

Osborn, S. M., & Harris, G. G. (1975). *Assertive training for women.* Springfield, IL: Charles C Thomas.

Phelps, S., & Austin, N. (1975). *The assertive woman.* San Luis Obispo, CA: Impact.

Pollack, S., & Gilligan, C. (1982). Images of violence in Thematic Apperception Test stories. *Journal of Personality and Social Psychology, 42,* 159–167.

Radloff, L. (1975). Sex differences in depression: The effects of occupation and marital status. *Sex Roles, 1,* 249–265.

Rawlings, E., & Carter, D. (1977). *Psychotherapy for women: Treatment toward equality.* Springfield, IL: Charles C Thomas.

Reid, P. T. (1993). Poor women in psychological research. *Psychology of Women Quarterly, 17,* 133–150.

Reid, P. T., & Comas-Diaz, L. (Eds.). (1990). Special issue on women of color. *Sex Roles, 22.*

Rich, A. R., & Schroeder, H. E. (1976). Research issues in assertiveness training. *Psychological Bulletin, 83,* 1081–1096.

Robins, L. N., Helzer, J. E., Weissman, M., Gruenberg, H. O., Burke, J., & Regier, D. (1984). Lifetime prevalence of specific psychiatric disorders in three sites. *Archives of General Psychiatry, 41,* 949–958.

Rossi, A. S. (1964). Equality between the sexes: An immodest proposal. In R. J. Lifton (Ed.), *The woman in America* (pp. 98–143). Boston: Beacon Press.

Rubin, L. (1983). *Intimate strangers.* New York: Harper & Row.

Russo, N. F. (1990). Overview: Forging research priorities for women's mental health. *American Psychologist, 45,* 368–373.

Sherman, J. A. (1971). *On the psychology of women.* Springfield, IL: Charles C Thomas.

Sherman, J. A. (1980). Therapist attitudes and sex-role stereotyping. In A. M. Brodsky & R. Hare-Mustin (Eds.), *Women and psychotherapy* (pp. 35–60). New York: Guilford Press.

Stere, L. K. (1985). Feminist assertiveness training: Self-esteem groups as skill training for women. In L. B. Rosewater & L. E. A. Walker (Eds.), *Handbook of feminist therapy: Women's issues in psychotherapy* (pp. 51–61). New York: Springer.

Stolorow, R. (1983). Self-psychology—a structural psychology. In J. Lichtenberg & S. Kaplan (Eds.), *Reflections on self-psychology* (pp. 121–143). Hillsdale, NJ: Analytic Press.

Surrey, J. (1985). Self in relation: A theory of women's development. In *Works in progress.* Wellesley, MA: Stone Center Works in Progress Series.

Thompson, C. (1942). Cultural pressures in the psychology of women. *Psychiatry, 5,* 331–339.

Thompson, C. (1950). Some effects of the derogatory attitude towards female sexuality. *Psychiatry, 13,* 349–354.

Weissman, M. (1980). Depression. In A. M. Brodsky & R. Hare-Mustin (Eds.), *Women and psychotherapy* (pp. 97–112). New York: Guilford Press.

Weissman, M. (1991). Personal communication from Dolores Parron, National Institutes of Mental Health.

Weissman, M., & Klerman, G. (1977). Sex differences in the epidemiology of depression. *Archives of General Psychiatry, 34,* 98–111.

Wheeler, D., Avis, J. M., Miller, L. A., & Chaney, S. (1985). Rethinking family therapy training and supervision: A feminist model. *Journal of Psychotherapy and the Family, 1,* 53–71.

Williams, D. H. (1986). The epidemiology of mental illness in Afro-Americans. *Hospital and Community Psychiatry, 37,* 42–49.

Williams, J. H. (1977). *Psychology of women.* New York: Norton.

Winnicott, D. (1965). *The maturational processes and the facilitating environment.* New York: International Universities Press.

Wolowitz, H. M. (1972). Hysterical character and feminine identity. In J. Bardwick (Ed.), *Readings on the psychology of women* (pp. 307–314). New York: Harper & Row.

Worrell, J., & Remer, P. (1992). *Feminist perspectives in therapy: An empowerment model for women.* Chichester, England: Wiley.

Zuk, G. R. (1972). Family therapy: Clinical hodgepodge or clinical science? *Journal of Marriage and Family Counseling, 2,* 229–304.

17

Counseling and Psychotherapy with Racial/Ethnic Minority Groups in Theory and Practice

J. Manuel Casas

CURRENT STATUS OF RACIAL/ETHNIC MINORITY COUNSELING AND PSYCHOTHERAPY

In the last two decades the counseling and clinical psychology professions have demonstrated an increased interest in the mental health status and needs of the major U.S. racial/ethnic minority populations: African-American, American Indian, Asian-American/Pacific Islander, and Hispanic/Latino (Casas, 1984; Ponterotto & Sabnani, 1989). Nevertheless, many scholars believe that the two professions have not done enough to meet the growing needs of these rapidly expanding populations (Ponterotto & Casas, 1991). In fact, according to Myers, Echemendia, and Trimble (1991), given the present state of professional training, the average new Ph.D. in psychology is only slightly more competent to meet the mental health needs of our culturally diverse population than are psychologists who completed their training 20 years ago. Thus, it is not surprising that numerous writers in the counseling/clinical field (e.g., Casas, 1984, 1985; Pedersen, 1985, 1988; D. W. Sue, 1981; D. W. Sue & D. Sue, 1990) strongly assert that much remains to be done before racial/ethnic minority clients receive the quality of counseling and clinical services currently available to the Euro-American white majority group in the United States.

Acknowledging the urgent need to improve training and services vis-à-vis racial/ethnic minorities, national agencies and professional organizations like the National Institute of Mental Health, the American Psychological Association, and the American Association for Counseling and Development have stated that it is essential to ensure that *all* psychologists are trained to meet the needs of clients from a variety of cultural backgrounds. Although this position has been part of the professional lore in psychology since the Vail conference in 1973, according to Myers et al. (1991), except for a few cosmetic changes, Guthrie's observation (1976) that "even the rat was white" is still true of the modern psychology curriculum.

Working from the perspective that training—didactic and practicum—does fall short of preparing psychologists to meet the counseling and therapeutic needs of many racial/ethnic minority persons, this chapter considers the diversity of theories that underlie much of the counseling/clinical curriculum. More specifically, the objectives of this chapter are to (1) identify and describe selective psychosocial variables and processes that differentiate racial/

ethnic minority groups from the majority Euro-American white group, and that may influence and possibly limit the applicability of the major counseling/psychotherapy theories to these groups; (2) provide an overview of the major traditional counseling/psychotherapy theories, emphasizing the constructs and/or practices of these theories that may limit their applicability to and/or effectiveness with many racial/ethnic minority persons (for more detailed coverage of the theories, the reader is referred to the other chapters in this book); and (3) present some theories that take the above-noted variables and processes into consideration, which may make them more applicable for use with racial/ethnic minorities.

First, however, it is necessary to define the major terms that are used throughout the chapter. Then, to ensure that readers have a common understanding of the racial/ethnic minority populations in question, an overview of relevant demographic information is provided. I am very much aware of the tendency to use what Trimble (1990–1991) has called *ethnic glosses*, or overgeneralized labels, to identify and/or discuss specific racial/ethnic minority groups. Consequently, I alert the reader to the fact that many of the comments in this chapter are generic in nature. Thus, while they may apply to many racial/ethnic minority persons who are more traditional in their adherence to their respective cultures, they may not apply to all. Furthermore, while this chapter focuses on racial/ethnic minority cultures, this focus should not be interpreted as downplaying the importance of understanding other groups that could be considered as distinct and diverse cultures, including, but not limited to, the physically handicapped, the hearing impaired, and lesbians and gays. Finally, while I am well aware of the differences in the respective areas of counseling and psychotherapy (e.g., therapeutic objectives, targeted populations and problems, and therapeutic practices), given the focus of this chapter, the two areas are addressed as one, since they have both generally drawn from the same pool of theories in their work.

DEFINITION OF TERMS

RACIAL/ETHNIC MINORITY: The term *racial/ethnic minority* is here used to refer collectively to the four population groups that are the focus of this chapter. The rationale for using this term is that it captures the essence of those variables that differentiate persons from these groups from the Euro-American white majority. For the sake of clarity, brief definitions of each of the words comprising the term, as well as those of other related words, are provided.

RACE: A biological classification system determined by physical characteristics (e.g., skin pigmentation, head form, nasal index, color distribution and texture of body hair) that are of genetic origin, the combination of which helps to distinguish one human subgroup from other subgroups (Krogman, 1945); it incorporates the following major population groups: Mongoloid (Asian-American/Pacific Islander and Native Americans), Negroid (black Americans), and Caucasoid (white Americans).

ETHNICITY: As defined by Rose (1964), a group classification of individuals who share a unique social and *cultural* heritage (e.g., language, religion, customs) that is passed on from generation to generation. Race should not be confused with ethnicity, which has no biological or genetic foundation. Furthermore, within any ethnic group (e.g., Puerto Ricans), any and all racial groups may be found; similarly, within any racial group, any and all ethnic groups may be found.

CULTURE: According to Linton (1945), "the configuration of learned behavior whose components and elements are shared and transmitted by the members of a particular society" (p. 32).

MINORITY: According to Wirth (1945), "A group of people who, because of physical or cultural characteristics, are singled out from others in society in which they live for differential and unequal treatment, and who therefore regard themselves as objects of collective discrimination. . . . Minority status carries with it the exclusion from full participation in the life of the society" (p. 347).

Majority: In the United States, the group that holds the balance of economic and political power; also, the group whose cultural value system is deemed by its members to be the model value system, the one to be emulated.

Racial/ethnic minority counseling and psychotherapy: In line with the term *cross-cultural counseling*, often the preferred term in the counseling literature. The latter term, however, is open to numerous interpretations; according to Casas (1984) and Pedersen (1978), it can include any dyadic encounter in which the counselor and client are culturally different. It may also encompass counseling and research that is cross-national or international in focus (Casas, 1984). Given the focus on the four racial/ethnic groups noted above, *racial/ethnic minority counseling* is the most precise and descriptive term to use in understanding the counseling issues addressed in this chapter.

RACIAL/ETHNIC MINORITY GROUP PROFILES

Native Americans/American Indians

It is appropriate to begin this presentation of racial/ethnic group profiles with Native Americans—the original Americans. Native American groups include American Indians, Eskimos, and Aleuts (Alaska natives). Since most of the counseling literature on Native Americans has focused on the American Indian, attention here is directed solely to this culturally diverse and heterogeneous group. The reader interested in specific information on Alaska Natives is referred to Dinges, Trimble, Manson, and Pasquale (1981) and Manson (1982).

The 1990 national census reported the American Indian population as numbering roughly 1.9 million (U.S. Department of Commerce, 1990). According to Ponterotto and Casas (1991), due to numerous weaknesses in the census-gathering procedures, this number is very likely a gross underestimate of this population. American Indians are becoming increasingly urbanized, moving to cities for both subsistence and gainful employment. According to LaFromboise (1988), only 24% of the American Indian population live on reservations.

Though highly concentrated in certain states (e.g., California, Oklahoma, Arizona, New Mexico, and North Carolina), American Indians are geographically dispersed throughout the United States. LaFromboise (1988) emphasizes the heterogeneity of this population. There are some 511 federally recognized native entities and an additional 365 state-recognized American Indian tribes. Further, approximately 200 distinct tribal languages are spoken today among the American Indian population. To categorize or stereotype a typical American Indian is neither possible nor desirable. Counseling/clinical practitioners and researchers must acknowledge and be sensitive to the tremendous heterogeneity of the American Indian people (see Herring, 1989, 1990).

The American Indian population is remarkably young, with a median age of 20.4 years (Alaska Natives' median age = 17.9 years). This figure stands in significant contrast to the U.S. population median age, of 30.3 years (LaFromboise, 1988). For more detailed information on this population, refer to Ponterotto and Casas (1991).

The mental health research and service needs of American Indians and other Native American groups are great. The historical and continuing mistreatment of American Indians need not be discussed here. Suffice it to say that this group has been the object of continued oppression, discrimination, prejudice, violence, misunderstanding, and stereotyping (Banks, 1984; Markides & Mindel, 1987). In terms of educational, economic, and political power, American Indians are at the low end of the spectrum; more often than not, they have little influence over what happens in America or in their own lives. American Indian poverty levels, unemployment, malnutrition, inadequate health care, shortened life expectancy, and high substance abuse and suicide rate (among some tribes) are important factors that need to be understood from the therapeutic perspective (Ponterotto & Casas, 1991).

African-Americans

African-Americans constitute the nation's largest racial/ethnic minority group. Currently numbering close to 30 million, African-Americans represent 12.1% of the U.S. population. During the 1980s, this population grew by 14.2% (U.S. Department of Commerce, 1990). Further, the African-American population is growing at a faster pace than the white majority, with an annual growth rate of 1.8% compared to 0.06% for whites (the Hispanic annual growth rate is the highest at 6.1%) (Malgady, Rogler, & Costantino, 1987).

The African-American experience in America is unique. This group first arrived in the 1600s, and unlike all immigrant groups who followed, they came involuntarily as slaves. Stripped of their land, families, languages, and cultural heritage, Americans of African descent have shown remarkable strength and resilience in striving to become fully valued, appreciated, and accepted Americans.

Like the other racial/ethnic groups discussed in this chapter, African-Americans are a heterogeneous group. They are represented by diverse ethnic and cultural groups, including Spanish-speaking blacks from Cuba, Puerto Rico, and Panama, among others; blacks from the various Caribbean islands and Northern Europe; and American Indian blacks (Allen, 1988; Baker, 1988; McKenzie, 1986). It is important for counselors to acknowledge and understand the tremendous diversity within the black population in the United States. As will be made evident later in this chapter, the client's view of his or her blackness and racial identity commitment are important variables that need to be understood and taken into consideration in the counseling and psychotherapeutic processes (Helms, 1990; Parham, 1989; White & Parham, 1990).

Despite many within-group (intracultural) differences among the African-American population, the group as a whole, because of their darker skin, has been subjected to continuing majority-group oppression. In no case have the sheer brutality and evil of racism, prejudice, and penetrating hate been so evident and salient as in the white majority's treatment of African-Americans throughout U.S. history. The long-term effects of historical oppression coupled with present life circumstances, which generally include lower educational and economic achievement, predispose many African-Americans to high levels of psychological stress. All counseling and mental health agencies and organizations emphasize that the counseling and psychotherapy professions must devote increased attention and provide improved services to this group (Ponterotto & Casas, 1991).

Hispanics/Latinos

Over time, given both a high birth rate and a high immigration rate, Hispanics/Latinos have become the fastest-growing racial/ethnic group in the United States. Currently, Hispanics are the second largest minority group after African-Americans. According to the 1990 census, there are 22.4 million Hispanics/Latinos in the United States (9% of the total population). This figure represents a 53% growth rate during the 1980s (U.S. Department of Commerce, 1990). Again, as with Native Americans, these statistics represent a gross underestimate of this population. Hispanics/Latinos are a tremendously diverse group, including Mexican-Americans, Puerto Ricans, Cuban-Americans, and South and Central Americans, among others. In addition to the marked cultural diversity of these subgroups, there is a great deal of heterogeneity within each subgroup. For instance, as a result of the acculturation process, Mexican-Americans who have recently arrived may be quite different in values, behaviors, attitudes, and counseling/psychotherapeutic needs from third-generation Mexican Americans. Further within-group diversity among the Hispanic/Latino subgroups is attributable to geographical region and socioeconomic status.

Demographic studies indicate that while there is great intragroup diversity, the Hispanic/Latino population overall is younger, less educated, poorer, and more likely to live in inner-city neighborhoods than the general population (Rogler, Malgady, Costantino, & Blumenthal, 1987). Their numerous life stressors, coupled with their linguistic minority status (Malgady, Rogler, & Costantino, 1987), make Hispanics/Latinos particularly vulnerable to psychological problems requiring counseling and/or psychotherapy.

Asian-Americans/Pacific Islanders

Like Hispanics, Asian-Americans/Pacific Islanders are represented by a number of major subgroups, including Japanese, Chinese, Filipinos, Koreans, Guamians, Malays, Samoans, and Southeast Asians. An umbrella term used to identify these groups collectively is *Asian/American/Pacific Islander*. At present, it is the third largest racial/ethnic minority group in the United States. As a result of a high rate of immigration, the Asian-American population grew at the astonishing rate of 200% during the 1980s. According to the 1990 census, this group now numbers approximately 7.2 million and represents 3% of the U.S. population (U.S. Department of Commerce, 1990).

Asian-American/Pacific Islander groups are extremely diverse. Like the Hispanics/Latinos in America, Asian-American/Pacific Islander subgroups differ markedly. Further, within a particular subgroup, varying levels of acculturation attest to marked within-group heterogeneity. For instance, a third-generation Japanese-American youth may be more similar to a Euro-American white friend in terms of values, attitudes, and cultural behaviors than to his or her grandfather or same-age cousin who has just arrived from Japan. The great heterogeneity both between and within various Asian-American/Pacific Islander groups defies categorization and stereotypic description.

As immigrant people of color who spoke and continue to speak languages other than English, all Asian-American/Pacific Islander groups have faced major challenges in adjusting to life and work in the United States. All have been objects of past and continued racism and prejudice. Although some Asian-American/Pacific Islander groups have been portrayed as "model minorities" in terms of significant educational and economic success, large percentages of persons who comprise these groups live in poverty and suffer high levels of psychological stress (Banks, 1984; D. W. Sue & D. Sue, 1985) and could benefit greatly from culturally relevant, effective counseling and psychotherapy services.

PSYCHOSOCIAL VARIABLES AND PROCESSES THAT INFLUENCE THE APPLICABILITY OF THEORIES WITH RACIAL/ETHNIC MINORITY GROUPS

Until recently, the major criticisms of existing counseling and psychotherapeutic theories in terms of their applicability to the racial/ethnic minorities described above were limited. The criticisms tended to address the cultural and psychosocial factors inherent in the theories that seemed to limit their use with racial/ethnic minorities. Unfortunately, these variables were usually addressed from a very general perspective (e.g., world views, family orientation); consequently, it was difficult to make the theories more applicable to racial/ethnic minority groups. In the last 10 years, however, efforts have been made to identify and examine such variables with greater specificity (Ivey, Ivey, & Simek-Morgan, 1993). This section summarizes such efforts. However, before discussing them, it seems appropriate to identify some of the general factors that limit the applicability of existing theories to racial/ethnic minority groups.

General Factors That Limit the Applicability of Theories

Historically, the limiting factors tend to be endemic in both the tenets and practices of counseling and psychotherapy. Some of the major factors are the following:

- The persistent belief that most problems are solely intrapsychic (Cushman, 1992).
- The tendency to ignore the fact that many problems may be tied to social, political, and/or economic conditions (D. W. Sue & D. Sue, 1990).
- The fact that the prevailing views of what causes psychological problems and how such problems should be treated have "been derived largely from theories of human behavior developed by middle-class males and tested largely on the same population—the most educated segment of American society during the first three hundred years of its history" (Gelso & Fretz, 1992, p. 335).
- According to Katz (1985), white culture has served as a foundation for counselor training, research and practice. "Therefore, since the goal of counseling has typically been seen as helping persons adjust and adapt, the strategies of counseling have been typically oriented, regardless of the counselor's background, to helping persons choose behaviors that adapt to 'white cultural values' and role definitions rather than develop individual identities that may or may not fit those values" (Gelso & Fretz, 1992, p. 335).
- The profession's use of an etic perspective, which believes that all that is inherent in counseling has universal value (D. W. Sue & D. Sue, 1990).
- The continued existence of racism—personal and institutional, as well as personal and professional biases and stereotypes—and limited life experiences with persons from diverse racial/ethnic minority groups (Casas & Vasquez, 1989).

For additional limited factors identified in the literature, the reader is referred to Ponterotto and Casas (1991).

Culturally Rooted Cognitive and Personality Attributes and Characteristics

It is also important to identify and describe selective culturally rooted psychosocial variables and processes that differentiate persons from racial/ethnic minority groups from persons who are part of the Euro-American white majority. Attention is given to certain variables that help to determine the applicability of major counseling and psychotherapeutic theories to racial/ethnic minority persons.

First, however, it should be noted that while attention is here given solely to psychosocial variables, numerous other historical (e.g., slavery), social (e.g., racism, prejudice, discrimination), economic (e.g., poverty, unemployment), political (e.g., oppression, segregation), and educational factors, as well as unique personal life experiences, can have a significant impact on both the acceptability and applicability of counseling/psychotherapy in general and of theories in particular to racial/ethnic minority persons. For more details on these other factors, refer to Pedersen, Draguns, Lonner, and Trimble (1989).

According to Price-Williams (1985), social scientists, while cognizant of intragroup variability, have found that cultural groups in general often exhibit different personality characteristics because of cultural influences. This is not a recent finding. In the early 1970s, Ramirez and Castañeda (1974) proposed that cultures, communities, and families can be classified on a traditionalism–modernism dimension or continuum with respect to their cultural styles. These researchers also identified specific beliefs, attitudes, and behaviors that may differentiate groups and persons at different points along the continuum. According to them, the traditional end of the continuum is typical of rural communities, conservative religions, and Third World cultures. People with traditional values have a spiritual orientation to life, emphasizing spiritual explanations of the mysteries of life; they are strongly identified with their families and communities of origin; they usually believe in separation of gender and age roles; and they usually believe in strict, autocratic approaches to child rearing. In contrast, the modern end of the continuum is more typical of urban communities, liberal religions, and North American and Western European cultures. People with a modern value system usually emphasize science when explaining the mysteries of life; they have a strongly individualistic orientation; they deemphasize differences in gender and age roles; and they emphasize egalitarianism in child rearing (Ramirez, 1991).

In addition, empirical studies demonstrate significant relationships between cultural factors and specific psychosocial constructs that need to be understood in any cross-cultural therapeutic interaction. Such constructs include the following: cognitive styles (i.e., field dependent/independent—Ramirez & Price-Williams, 1974; divergent thinking—Price-Williams & Ramirez, 1977); achievement motivation (family achievement vs. personal achievement—Ramirez & Price-Williams, 1976); learning and problem-solving styles (modeling vs. trial and error—Ramirez, 1991; cooperative vs. competitive learning—Knight & Kagan, 1977). Other psychosocial characteristics that have been found to differ across cultures include self-disclosure, assertiveness, cooperativeness, shyness, individualism, interpersonal styles, and introversion.

Another important dimension is the impact of culture on the cognitive structure of illness—specifically, its impact on the perception of physical and emotional states, on their interpretations, and on help seeking (e.g., Kleinman, 1982; Mechanic, 1980, Nichter, 1981; Velimirovic, 1978). The literature documents that culture constrains the perceptual, explanatory, and behavioral options that individuals use in understanding and responding to illness. For example, with respect to mental health, Hispanics in general rely primarily on the family and may seek professional assistance only as a last resort. For African-Americans, the church is frequently the only extrafamilial institution that many of them trust and feel safe with when in need of help (Cheatham & Stewart, 1990; Hines & Boyd-Franklin, 1982). According to Ivey, Ivey, and Simek-Morgan (1993), many Puerto Ricans and Chinese with psychological stress often report experiencing physical symptoms and seek medical rather than mental health services. There is evidence that African-Americans often blame themselves for their problems, whereas Puerto Ricans often blame others (McGoldrick, Pearce, & Giordano, 1982).

CULTURAL AND ETHNIC/RACIAL DEVELOPMENTAL PROCESSES

Attention is now directed to two major developmental processes—acculturation and racial identity—that have strong and differential impacts on persons from racial/ethnic minority groups. The purpose of this discussion is to stimulate thought on how these processes may influence the applicability and effectiveness of prevailing counseling theories when used with persons from such groups.

Acculturation: A General Overview

From a sociopsychological perspective, acculturation is a multidimensional process of culture learning that occurs as a result of contact between members of two or more groups (Redfield, Linton, & Herskovits, 1936). Thus, acculturation is a process of attitudinal and behavioral change undergone, willingly or unwillingly, by individuals who reside in multicultural societies or who come in contact with a new culture due to colonization, invasion, or other political changes (Marín, 1992). The psychological and social changes that may occur during acculturation also depend on the characteristics of the individual (e.g., level of initial identification with the values of the culture of origin), the intensity of and importance given to the contact between the various cultural groups, and the numerical balance between individuals representing the original culture and those representing the new. Finally, of utmost importance in understanding acculturation from a sociopsychological perspective is the fact that it is perceived as an open-ended process.

According to Marín (1992), the attitudinal and behavioral learning that occurs during acculturation occurs at three levels:

1. Superficial: This involves learning (and forgetting) the facts that are part of one's cultural history or tradition (e.g., forgetting the names of important historical figures or other facts related to the country of origin while learning prominent

historical facts of the new country's culture).

2. Intermediate: This learning involves the more central behaviors at the core of the individual's social life (e.g., language preferences and use; ethnicity of friends, neighbors, and co-workers; ethnicity of spouse; names given to children; and preference for ethnic media in multicultural environments).

3. Significant: This learning focuses on the beliefs, values, attitudes and norms that comprise the individual's world view and, in turn, all of the personality characteristics exhibited by the individual. The changes that occur at this level tend to be more permanent and are reflected in the day-to-day activities of the acculturated individual.

Psychologists, sociologists, and anthropologists have sought to understand the acculturation process from a general perspective. In addition, they have proposed sociopsychological and environmental models that attempt to explain the evolution of the process itself (see Casas & Casas, 1994). One model that is presently receiving a great deal of attention is the orthogonal acculturation model (Oetting & Beauvais, 1990–1991). This model is based on the orthogonal cultural identification theory, which states that identification with any culture is independent of identification with any other culture. In other words, identifying with one culture in no way diminishes one's ability to identify with any other culture. In contrast, all preceding models of acculturation have viewed the individual along a continuum or continuums between cultures. A benefit of the orthogonal model is the fact that it helps reduce the tendency to use ethnic glosses to identify persons from specific racial/ethnic groups. This model emphasizes the identification of important cultural dimensions and variables of the individual rather than simply his or her racial/ethnic group.

What are the implications of acculturation for mental health? Acculturation is usually seen as an exogenous force shaping psychological distress. According to Rogler, Cortes, and Mal-

gady (1991), "changes in acculturation entail changes in the person's relationship to the effective environment, which impinges in new ways upon his or her psychological well-being" (p. 588). While researchers agree that acculturation influences psychological functioning, the exact and absolute nature of its impact is still to be determined. The reader is referred to Rogler et al. (1991) for a description of studies that have demonstrated a relationship between levels of acculturation and such factors as gang membership (Vigil, 1988), delinquency (Buriel, Calzada, & Vasquez, 1982), alcohol and drug abuse (Boles, Casas, Furlong, Gonzalez, & Morrison, in press), prevalence scores of major depression, phobia, and dysthymia (Burnham, Hough, Karno, Escobar, & Telles, 1987), eating disorders (Pumariega, 1986), and psychological distress (Kaplan & Marks, 1990). From an overall mental health perspective, Gaw (1982) concluded that acculturation level is an important variable that affects presenting complaints, the patient's understanding of the origins of the symptoms, and the family's overall reactions to therapy.

Various measures to assess acculturation level do exist (Garcia & Lega, 1979; Olmedo, Martinez, & Martinez, 1978; Olmedo & Padilla, 1978; Ramirez, Cox, & Castañeda, 1977; Suinn, Rickard-Figueroa, Lew, & Vigil, 1987). Furthermore, various researchers have developed separate measures for use with distinct racial/ethnic groups. For instance, researchers working with the Hispanic/Latino population have devised separate measures for distinct ethnic/national subgroups, such as Cuban-Americans and Mexican-Americans (Cuellar, Harris, & Jasso, 1980; Garcia & Lega, 1979). Likewise, Suinn et al. (1987) saw the need to develop a generic scale for use with Asian-Americans, but they contend that other measures may be necessary for the subgroups comprising this group.

Racial Identity Development Model

Early efforts to identify, define, and understand the racial identity developmental process were made mainly by black social scientists and educators (e.g., Cross, 1971; Jackson, 1975; Thomas, 1971); consequently, it is not surprising that the first racial identity models focused solely on the African-American experience. A major purpose of these models was to assess the attitudinal impact of this process on the psychological development of African-Americans.

More recent models (Atkinson, Morten, & Sue, 1993) are much more broader in scope, addressing the racial/ethnic and cultural development of persons from diverse groups, including Chinese-Americans, Japanese-Americans, Hispanics/Latinos, gays, and lesbians. The major impetus for these models is the fact that these minority groups have shared similar patterns of adjustment to racial, ethnic, and/or cultural oppression. Sue (1990) contends that "in the past several decades, Asian-Americans, Hispanics, and American Indians have experienced sociopolitical identity transformations so that a 'Third World consciousness' has emerged

with cultural oppression as the common unifying force" (p. 95). A more generic identity model developed by Atkinson et al. (1993) is called the *racial cultural identity development model (R/CID)*.

According to Atkinson et al. (1993), the R/CID model provides a framework to help counselors understand the attitudes and behaviors of persons from diverse racial and ethnic backgrounds. The model identifies and defines five stages of development that oppressed people experience as they struggle to understand themselves in terms of their own culture, the dominant culture, and the oppressive relationship between the two cultures: conformity, dissonance, resistance and immersion, introspection, and integrative awareness (Table 17.1). Each stage contains four corresponding beliefs and attitudes that may help counselors to better understand their minority clients. These attitudes/beliefs are believed to be an integral part of the minority person's identity and are mani-

TABLE 17.1. Summary of the Minority Identity Development Model

Stages of Minority Development Model	Attitude Toward Self	Attitude Toward Others of the Same Minority	Attitude Toward Others of Different Minority	Attitude Toward Dominant Group
Stage: 1: Conformity	Self-depreciating	Group-depreciating	Discriminatory	Group-appreciating
Stage: 2: Dissonance	Conflict between self-depreciating and appreciating	Conflict between group-depreciating and group-appreciating	Conflict between dominant-held views of minority hierarchy and feelings of shared experience	Conflict between group-appreciating and group-depreciating
Stage: 3: Resistance and Immersion	Self-appreciating	Group-appreciating	Conflict between feelings of empathy for other minority experiences and feelings of culturocentrism	Group-depreciating
Stage: 4: Introspection	Concern with basis of self-appreciation	Concern with nature of unequivocal appreciation	Concern with ethnocentric basis for judging others	Concern with the basis of group depreciation
Stage: 5: Synergetic Articulation and Awareness	Self-appreciating	Group-appreciation	Group-appreciating	Selective appreciation

Source: Donald R. Atkinson, George Morten, and Derald Wing Sue, *Counseling American Minorities: A Cross-Cultural Perspective*, 4th ed. Copyright © 1993 Wm. C. Brown Communications, Inc., Dubuque, Iowa. All Rights Reserved. Reprinted by permission.

fest in how he or she views the self, others of the same minority, others of another minority, and majority/dominant individuals (Sue, 1990, p. 96).

Certain aspects of this model need to be understood by individuals who may want to use it when working with racial/ethnic minorities:

1. Any and all persons from racial/ethnic groups that differ from the dominant Euro-American group can be identified at any point of their personal history to be at any stage in the model.
2. A person's life experiences and, in particular, the nature of the early contact (i.e., positive or negative) with dominant Euro-American cultural groups will determine the stage at which an individual may enter the developmental process.
3. Given the ever-changing cross-racial/ethnic interactions that can be experienced, it is possible for an individual to stay at one stage, move forward, or even move backward.
4. Within any family, members may find themselves at totally different stages. Needless to say, this can contribute to a variety of family problems (Szapocznik & Kurtines, 1980).

According to many researchers, racial identity development models have three purposes: (1) they can help therapists avoid responding to culturally different clients from a stereotypic perspective by emphasizing within-group differences; (2) implementation of these models has potential psychodiagnostic value (Helms, 1985); and (3) the models give emphasis and credence to the historical and sociopolitical influences that shape racial/ethnic minority identity

TRADITIONAL THEORIES: OVERVIEW, LIMITATIONS, AND STRENGTHS

This final section of the chapter identifies and describes variables and constructs in the targeted theories that may impede (i.e., criticism) or facilitate (i.e., strengths) their applicability to persons from the respective racial/ethnic mi-

nority groups. While more than 400 separate "schools" of psychotherapy have been identified (Karasu, 1986), primary attention here is given to those theories encompassed by the three traditional forces of counseling and therapy; psychodynamic, existential-humanistic, and behavioral, with special attention given to the cognitive behavioral. In addition, attention is directed to family therapies and specific therapies that have been developed for use with particular racial/ethnic groups.

Psychodynamic Theories

Overview

Psychodynamic theories originating in psychoanalytic theory, as developed by Freud (1920/1966), emphasize early life experiences and the role of unconscious forces in determining and directing an individual's mental life. Psychodynamic theories that are distinct from each other include those of Adler (1927), Jung (1954), and Horney (1939). These theories extend the rationalist spirit of Greek philosophy in its command to "know thyself." In the psychodynamic conception, individual problems are viewed as residing within the self and as rooted in early childhood experiences with significant others. Psychodynamic therapy stresses the uncovering, processing, and working through of unconscious mental forces and early life experiences that may serve as the basis for problematic thoughts and behaviors.

Criticism

Psychodynamic theories as a whole have received a great deal of criticism from women and racial/ethnic minority groups. Many persons from these groups still think of psychoanalytic theory as a monolith, with orthodox interpretations based on libido theory and unconscious sexuality. Furthermore, this theory has been perceived as being male and elitist in origin. The perception of its strong male orientation is based on such constructs as penis envy; its elitist perception is based on its highly verbal intellectual orientation and a reputation for long, costly periods of treatment (Ivey et al., 1993, p. 164).

The emphasis of psychodynamic theories on insight is also a point of contention for many persons from racial/ethnic minority groups. D. W. Sue and D. Sue (1990) believe that insight is not highly valued by many culturally different clients; in fact, many Asian elders believe that thinking too much about something can cause problems. "Think about the family and not about yourself" is advice given to many Asians as a way of dealing with problems. This is totally contradictory to Western individualistic notions of mental health—that it is best to examine oneself and then get problems out in the open in order to deal with them (pp. 38–39). Such required self-disclosure and interpersonal openness are sometimes seen as immaturity by Asian cultures. Many African-Americans, American Indians, and other minority group members strongly endorse this view.

There are major class differences as well. People from lower socioeconomic classes frequently do not perceive insight as appropriate to their life situations and circumstances. From their perspective, seeking insight assumes that one has the time and the resources to sit back, reflect on, and contemplate nontangible motivation and behavior.

According to some critics, the developmental stages inherent in psychodynamic theories and the key tasks associated with each stage are Eurocentric in origin and therefore do not address variations in gender and culture (Ivey, 1992). Relative to this criticism, what is needed is a generic framework that considers the role of culture in the developmental process and acknowledges that different cultures may have different needs at different times and that can best be met in the cultural context.

Another major problem in applying psychodynamic theories to racial/ethnic minorities is their emphasis on individuation, separation, and autonomy. Focusing on such processes with family or other/interdependent directed cultures can undermine the therapeutic process. The analysis of dreams, life issues, and traumas is open to interpretation. Unfortunately, historically such interpretations have focused solely on the individual, with minimal attention given to family and cultural issues.

Finally, psychodynamic theories fail to give any action-oriented attention to environmental/contextual variables that many racial/ethnic minority persons believe to be at the heart of their psychosocial problems. According to Cheatham (1990), therapists need to help the family deal with the broader culture and, even more important, to work to change a culture that often is more responsible for the existing psychosocial problems and pathology than are individuals or families (Ivey et al., 1993, p. 178).

Strengths

According to Ivey et al. (1993), several research/practitioners have sought to increase the attention given to culture by psychodynamic theory and, in turn, to increase the theory's acceptance by and applicability to diverse groups. Comas-Diaz and Minrath (1985), for example, state that ethnicity and race need to become part of the psychodynamic treatment process itself. According to these theorists, the modern psychodynamic approach needs to include multicultural issues and variables in therapy. Ivey et al. (1993) contend that "the limitation of traditional psychodynamic practice is that it has not gone far enough, nor has it focused on positive cultural dimensions and issues that can help clients face their lives more courageously and with greater sense of pride" (p. 179).

Bowlby (1988), working from an object relations perspective, an offshoot of psychoanalytic theory that also emphasizes early life experiences, states that each individual develops in relation to the environment (e.g., child–parent interactions). Thus, environmental factors help to shape the nature of individual uniqueness. Taking it one step further, Ivey (1992) contends that object relations could be considered "people relations." For Ivey, object relations theory focuses on the relations between and among people and how the history of interpersonal relationships is transferred from past to present behavior within a specific cultural context.

Taub-Bynum (1984, 1992) believes that we learn about ourselves and our culture in the family and proposes that we need to focus on the family unconscious—an innovative and controversial concept. From this perspective, each individual is a specific focus of experience in the family and the culture, but much of that experience is shared with others. Family experience is implicated in the inner landscape of each person who shares the same family both unconsciously and consciously. Needless to say, further work to validate such a belief is greatly needed.

Another recent psychoanalytic perspective that seeks to give family and culture a primary role in therapy is presented by the French psychoanalyst Jacques Lacan (1966/1977). In contrast to traditionalists, Lacan argues for interdependence as the goal of psychotherapy rather than the traditional autonomy so often associated with ego psychology. According to Ivey et al. (1993), the Lacanian view of development and ego psychology stresses that influences of the family and the culture are so profound that the ego itself is "very feeble." Complementing the "other person" orientation of most racial/ethnic minority groups, a major goal of Lacanian psychoanalysis is to help the client discover how much of the so-called self is the result of a lifetime of interactions in the family and the culture (Ivey et al., 1993, p. 177).

Existential-Humanistic and Person-Centered Theories

Overview

Existential-humanistic theories focus on individuals as empowered to act on the world and, in so doing, to determine their own destiny. According to these theories, the locus of control and decision lies within the individual rather than in past history or environmental/contextual determinants. At the same time, the humanistic aspect of this tradition focuses on people in relation one to another. It is this combination of individual respect and the importance of relationship that gives this framework its long-lasting strength.

Counseling/psychotherapeutic theories that fall under the existential-humanistic rubric include Carl Roger's person-centered approach (1961), Frederick Perls' gestalt approach (Perls, Hefferline, & Goodman, 1951), and Viktor Frankl's logotherapeutic system (Frankl, 1959). Connecting links between these models of counseling and psychotherapy are (1) a focus on present as opposed to past experiences; (2) the importance of a counseling relationship in which the counselor is empathic, caring, genuine, and nonjudgmental; and (3) central goals of counseling that include increased individual autonomy, independence, and self-actualization.

Criticisms

From a racial/ethnic minority perspective, evaluation of existential-humanistic theories is mixed. Some theorists, like Vontress (1988), contend that these theories have value across cultures; others find them too individualistic, too focused on the present, and too limited in their perception of the presenting problems. Like Vontress, Lerner (1992) believes that the positive view of human nature and the desire for an egalitarian approach should make existential-humanistic theory and practice appealing to women and other multicultural groups.

A major criticism of humanistic theories is their tendency to place almost total responsibility for development, growth, and change on the individual, paying little or no attention to the environment. Lerner (1992) maintains that, for women and other minority groups, Rogerian and other humanistic practices are potentially harmful: "No person constructs their own reality without external influences. The theories did not take into account exactly how influential external forces really are" (p. 13). Many minority persons who have suffered oppression may find it difficult to let go of the past and focus on the present. To many of these persons, the present is nothing more than the continuation of the past.

The concept of self-actualization, as addressed in client-centered counseling, has been criticized from a multicultural frame of reference (Lerner, 1992; Rigney, 1981). This criticism is largely based on the belief that, if carried too far, self-actualization can become self-centeredness (Ivey et al., 1993). In North America, the emphasis on self-actualization at times obscures the idea of the person in relation to others (i.e., the interdependent self). As noted above, such an emphasis may be unacceptable to many individuals from racial/ethnic minority groups.

Like psychoanalytic theories, humanistic theories are criticized for their focus on the individuation and separation of the individual from the family or significant others. Such criticism focuses on fusion and boundaries in relationships. According to Ivey et al. (1993), fusion (enmeshment) represents deep closeness between two individuals, so that at times the two feel as one. Traditional theories focused on the self hold that fusion is pathological and something to be avoided; what is important is to maintain firm interpersonal boundaries. Unfortunately, what is considered fusion in some cultures may be normal closeness of relationship in others. Consequently, a therapist who focuses on the primarily North American male values of individuation, self-actualization, and autonomy will view things in terms of boundary and distancing issues and may miss relational issues of interpersonal closeness that are important to the minority client (Ivey et al., 1993).

Humanistic theories, in general, emphasize a highly verbal approach and may require complex cognitive skills on the part of the client; consequently, these theories may be less effective for less verbal clients and in particular for clients from cultures in which talking about emotions and feelings is not accepted as the norm (D. W. Sue & D. Sue, 1990). For such clients, other theoretical approaches may be more appropriate, including behavioral, family systems, consciousness-raising, community organization, and developmental methods and techniques.

Finally, a major thrust of humanistic theories, and person-centered therapy in particular, is to see the world empathically from the client's perspective. Unfortunately, for those counselors and therapists who do not have a strong understanding of and sensitivity to racial/ethnic minority cultures and life experiences, this may not be possible; thus, the therapeutic process is bound to be greatly impeded (Casas & Vasquez, 1989).

Strengths

These criticisms aside, there are two existential-humanistic theories, logotherapy and gestalt therapy, that some theorists believe have substantial promise for use with racial/ethnic minorities. With respect to logotherapy, Frankl's powerful approach, Ivey et al. (1993) contend that since it appeals to the human spirit, it is particular adaptable to multicultural and gender issues that can arise in counseling and psychotherapy. Racial/ethnic minority groups may find Frankl's philosophy and methods particularly applicable because they represent a response to personal and cultural oppression. Furthermore, logotherapy allows clients to generate their own culturally relevant integration of theory and practice. Ivey et al. (1993) further believe that Frankl would endorse efforts to draw traditional and meaningful helping techniques from each culture (p. 320–321).

Relative to gestalt theory, Enns (1987) gives special attention to the exercises in the therapy, which she feels have direct implications for women. Given their shared minority status, it is possible to extrapolate these implications vis-à-vis women to persons from racial/ethnic minority groups. Enns suggests that gestalt exercises can be helpful for women in three ways: (1) helping them become aware of themselves as distinct individuals with power to set personal goals and objectives (particularly in that "I" statements are used); (2) providing for the expression of anger that has built up as a result of being treated as second-class citizens through a variety of gestalt exercises; and (3) enabling more choice regarding what they want out of life. In the end, gestalt therapy stresses the need for individuals to make their own choices. As such, it can be very helpful to women and minorities who have been culturally and/or socially and politically discouraged from making their own choices (Ivey et al., 1993).

Behavioral Theories

Overview

Behavioral theories are based on the belief that maladaptive behavior patterns are learned and therefore can be unlearned. These therapeutic approaches incorporate operant and classical learning paradigms to modify inappropriate and maladaptive behavior and thought patterns. The counselor–client relationship parallels that of teacher–learner, and the approach is basically psychoeducational. While behavioral counseling focuses on the present and future of the client's life, the past may be used to understand the client's presenting problem. Behavioral theories are oriented to action and short-term treatment. Relaxation training, parent education, and stress management are three of its many techniques and strategies. The behavioral counselor/therapist focuses on short-term observable change while keeping an eye on the future and working with the client for long-term maintenance of behavioral change.

Strengths and Criticisms

Of the three general orientations to counseling, the behavioral approach appears to have the greatest racial/ethnic minority appropriateness (Casas 1976). A major reason is that over the years there has been a shift of behavioral theory from a strictly individual orientation to awareness of how the social context affects development (Ivey et al., 1993). For example, if a Hispanic has a behavioral difficulty, no longer is it possible to find fault solely with the person. Therapists are more likely to consider the environmental variables that affect behaviors and thoughts. In summarizing the behavioral approaches with Mexican-Americans, Ponterotto (1987) comments: "This action-oriented, problem-solving approach has been deemed more appropriate for [racial/ethnic minorities] because it involves activating one's role in the environment and, when possible, activating the environment itself" (p. 308).

From another perspective, behavioral techniques tend to be successful in producing change and, owing to their clarity of direction and purpose, are often understandable by and acceptable to minority populations. However, some minority theorists caution therapists not to seek to control clients but instead to allow them to learn self-control in terms of their own behaviors.

A criticism of behavioral approaches is that they subscribe to the Euro-American white middle-class emphasis on a future goal orientation (e.g., setting time limits in which to reach agreed-on goals). According to Ponterotto and Casas (1991), this emphasis on a future time perspective, a linear view, is at odds with clients who may have a cultural trait of time that is circular. Many American Indians who are culturally traditional may find a futuristic counseling/psychotherapeutic emphasis somewhat confusing and culturally alien (p. 61).

Within the behavioral realm, one theory that has received much attention in the last 15 years is cognitive-behavioral theory. This individualistic theory, not surprisingly, locates the majority of presenting problems within the client. To this point, while there has been a shift toward recognizing how the social context affects development, Kantrowitz and Ballou (1992) point out that individuals are still generally expected to change their subjective experience of reality and improve their ability to adapt to the existing environmental conditions. According to these theorists, this expectation serves to reinforce the dominant (male) social standards (p. 79). Underscoring this perspective, Sampson (1981) states that cognitive therapy strategies privilege the internal, subjective experience of the client and base behavior on the way in which the client thinks about the world (Prilleltensky, 1990). The overall effect, Sampson explains, is that the current concept of self, and of the political arrangements of power and privilege, are accepted as given and remain unchallenged by cognitive therapists (p. 735).

Working from a change agent perspective

(Atkinson, Thompson, & Grant, 1993), Kantrowitz and Ballou (1992) state that community action and challenges to standard social norms must be considered part of the therapeutic process. From another perspective, however, challenging beliefs and thoughts may not fit well with many cultural and gender socialization patterns. For instance, as previously mentioned, Asian-Americans, adhering to an interdependent concept of self, have generally been taught to create emotional harmony and avoid conflict. From the gender perspective, women's perceptions have generally been minimized and misunderstood (Kantrowitz & Ballou, 1992, p. 81).

It has also been stated that nothing in cognitive-behavioral therapy enhances sensitivity to gender, race, and class issues. More specifically, the failure to consider gender, class, race, and ethnic factors, as well as the context, antecedents, and consequences of specific beliefs and behaviors, is a problem in cognitive-behavioral conceptualizations of pathology. Also problematic is its attribution of responsibility, implied by the goal of changing the individual client (Kantrowitz & Ballou, 1992, pp. 82–83). From a positive perspective, cognitive therapists like Ellis (1971), Beck (1972), and Glasser (1965) report having used their techniques successfully with culturally different clients. Ivey et al. (1993) suggest that to surmount discrimination, prejudice, and unfairness, we must generate a new cognitive view of the self and the ability to change situations. Unfortunately, although cognitive techniques have potential and value in multicultural counseling, a weakness of the theory is its emphasis on individual change, with minimal attention given to broader systemic issues.

Meichenbaum (1985), a leading proponent of cognitive-behavioral psychology, especially in relation to stress and anger, believes that reactions to stressful events vary greatly across groups thus, stress training programs should consider cultural differences in determining adaptive coping mechanisms. In some cultures, people tend to cope with stressors passively, by trying to endure them rather than by viewing them as problems to be solved. Stress management training must reflect these cultural preferences. Meichenbaum goes one step further: He suggests that attempting to train clients to cope in ways that may violate cultural norms could actually aggravate stress-related problems (p. 17). In addition, by deemphasizing the individual and becoming more applicable to family-oriented cultures, cognitive-behavior therapists are now recognizing the benefits of adapting the theory for use with couples and families (Meichenbaum, 1990).

Relative to practice, the relaxation training and the visual/auditory aspect of biofeedback that are often used with cognitive-behavioral therapy may be a plus for persons from cultures that expect the therapist to do something tangible with or to them, not just sit back and listen. According to Ivey et al. (1993), a special feature of anxiety hierarchies that are often used in relaxation training and biofeedback is that they concretize anxiety specifically and in small units. This could be important for persons from cultures that are used to dealing with concrete, tangible variables in their lives. To this end, if a counselor works with an African-American woman who suffers from considerable stress due to harassment or discrimination on her job, in a situation where legal action is impossible, the use of stress management with an anxiety hierarchy might be very fruitful. However, if stress management is only a bandage and assertive action is necessary to change the situation, then modeling and rehearsal techniques, extremely positive interventions for those cultures whose principal mode of learning is based on seeing and doing (e.g., the Hispanic culture; see Ramirez & Castañeda, 1974), might be most appropriate.

Finally, while not normally grouped under behavioral therapies, given its strong social learning basis, multimodal therapy is here considered briefly. Ponterotto (1987) believes that multimodal therapy, with its comprehensive and systematic format, provides a maximum opportunity to develop culturally relevant clinical case conceptualizations for Mexican-Americans. According to this researcher, once such conceptualizations are achieved, the probability of providing effective counseling/psychotherapeutic services to these clients increases greatly. However, Ponterotto is quick to point out that a multimodal framework alone is not enough. Also necessary is a counselor with multicultural values. With such a therapist, the multimodal framework can improve service delivery to Mexican-American clients (p. 311).

Family Counseling

Overview

In recent years, family-centered approaches (e.g., Haley, 1976; Hoffman, 1981; Minuchin, 1974) to problem solving and treatment of emotional disturbances, including marital stress and difficulties of children, have gained wide acceptance in the helping professions (Ho, 1987). Believing that many of these disturbances develop in a family or another relational context, family-centered theories state that it is more effective to work with a family or another relational system than with an isolated individual.

These theories redirect the focus from the isolated, deeper, individual self to a larger group (i.e., the family). A growing number of theorists believe that family-oriented therapy may provide the most appropriate and efficacious intervention framework for persons from racial/ethnic minority groups who have a more family-oriented or other/interdependent psychological orientation of the self.

Cautious Criticisms

McGoldrick, Pearce, and Giordano (1982) note that until recently, race, ethnicity, and culture as they apply to families have been largely ignored by family therapists. For example, the definition of family, while quite diverse even in the United States, differs significantly across cultures. For instance, while the so-called intact nuclear family (which is rapidly disappearing in the United States) is associated with Northern European cultures, other cultures have a much broader definition of family. Hispanics, in general, define the family as including three to four generations, and may consider godparents and close friends as family. According to Ivey et al. (1993), the Chinese take this extended view of family one step further, including all living or deceased ancestors and descendants as members. African-Americans also view the family from a multigenerational perspective. Perhaps most broadly, some Native Americans consider the entire tribe as their family (Attneave, 1969). Until recently, these diverse definitions have largely been ignored by family therapists and as such, family-oriented interventions have too frequently failed when applied to persons from racial/ethnic minority groups.

Unfortunately, family therapy has focused on the problems of the Euro-American white middle-class American family. According to Ho (1987), "family problems of ethnic minorities often are treated by using the same white middle-class American family as a frame of reference. Consequently, cultural and ethnic insensitivity of family therapists and the agencies employing them has emerged as a primary factor contributing to the overall ineffectiveness and underutilization of social services and family therapy by ethnic minority families" (p. 8). Moreover, until recently, the literature on the day-to-day living problems of racial/ethnic minority families has been vague and scattered (Pedersen, 1985). Few publications provide organized, systematic, theory-based data that family-oriented counselors and therapists can access to help racial/ethnic minority families (Ho, 1987, p. 8).

A major problem with family theories is their tendency to treat families as if they were removed from the larger social context. These theories fail to consider the realms of history and culture. By limiting their analyses, family theories fall short of a thorough social critique and thus provide a basis for protecting the status quo (Cushman, 1992, p. 56).

Another criticism is that family therapeutic models reflect the Euro-American white, male-oriented status quo of U.S. culture. Luepnitz (1988) and others (Goldner, 1988; Hare-Mustin, 1978; Lerner, 1986) stress that if family therapy is to be viewed as ultimately bringing about real change for families, then larger social and cultural forces, as well as power distribution within the family, must be addressed.

Furthermore, all members of the family must be empowered to deal with these issues. According to Ivey et al. (1993), "both concerns, feminism and ethnicity, are forcing family therapists to stop and reevaluate their world view in order to reduce cultural and gender bias. It will be a long struggle, but in the future, the quality of effective therapy will be measured not merely by the removal of family symptomatic behavior, but also by the demonstration of consideration for cultural diversity and gender equity" (p. 356).

SELECTIVE THEORIES OR APPROACHES PROPOSED OR DEVELOPED FOR USE WITH RACIAL/ETHNIC MINORITY GROUPS

Many efforts are now being made to revise traditional theories or to develop approaches and practices that may be more effective with racial/ethnic minority groups. Unfortunately, most of this work is based on clinical approaches and interventions that frequently are not strongly tied to any theory (for detailed information, see Ponterotto & Casas, 1991) and have not been subjected to controlled experiment. What these efforts have in commons is the belief that therapeutic theories and practices must be sensitive to the psychosocial and cultural attributes and constructs (e.g., world views, cultural assumptions, historical/life experiences, psychological schemas, acculturation level) of the client, the sociocultural perception of the nature and/or origin of the presenting problem (e.g., internal vs. external to the self), and the desired, socioculturally acceptable outcomes expressed by the client (Atkinson, Thompson, & Grant, 1993; Ponterotto & Casas, 1991).

Identifying New Approaches

Asian Psychotherapies

Some theorists believe that the traditional theories are beyond redemption and have sought to identify non Euro-Western approaches—especially Asian psychotherapies—that may be more congruent with the cultural reality of persons from different racial/ethnic minority groups. In general, these approaches focus on existential and transpersonal levels, giving little attention to the pathological. They contain detailed "maps" of states of consciousness, developmental levels, and stages of enlightenment that extend beyond traditional Western psychologies (Walsh, 1989, p. 547). According to Walsh, some experimental studies demonstrate that certain Asian therapeutic approaches can produce psychological, physiological, and psychotherapeutic effects.

While the two classic Asian psychotherapies are meditation and yoga, two recent innovations, Morita (Ishiyama, 1987) and Naikan (Reynolds, 1981), are receiving greater attention from the therapeutic community. Ishiyama contends that Morita therapy, a Japanese approach to behavior change and personal growth (Morita 1928/1960), has practical application not only for Asian-Americans but also for other racial/ethnic groups and for Euro-American whites. This therapy can be described as an "outcome-oriented, 'doing' therapy with an existential, taoistic philosophy that is presented through a psychoeducational model" (Ishiyama, 1987, p. 547).

Morita therapy helps clients to relinquish emotional self-control and redirect their attention to taking action for what is perceived to be practical and constructive purposes. According to Ishiyama (1987), this therapy contrasts with traditional process-oriented "talking" therapies in which clients' anxieties are treated from a psychopathological viewpoint (p. 548). Interestingly, Morita therapy is becoming appreciated for its technical similarities to modern Western therapies (Ishiyama, 1976) in its use of reattribution, attentional refocusing, modifying dysfunctional beliefs and untested assumptions, paradoxical intention, and reduced environmental stimulation (p. 548).

Naikan therapy, adapted from Buddhism, consists simply of intensive reflection on past relationships. Working from an interdependent perspective of existence, the aim of this therapy is to have clients reflect on how much they have received from others, how much gratitude is due them, and how little this gratitude is demonstrated. According to Walsh (1989), "along with a confrontation with guilt and unworthiness comes the recognition that one has been loved and appreciated in spite of weaknesses and failings. The result is usually an upwelling of gratitude and a desire to contribute more" (p. 554). While there is little empirical research on Naikan therapy, Reynolds (1981) reports that case reports document successful outcomes in treating a variety of neuroses and personality disorders.

Feminist Theory

One theory that is receiving a good deal of attention is feminist theory. The constructs that underlie feminist theory consider the similar historical and life experiences shared by women and by persons from specific racial/ethnic minority groups (e.g., minority status), as well as shared common social attitudes and values (e.g., emphasizing "we" rather than "I," giving greater value to sharing and caring) (Brown & Brodsky, 1992). The extension of feminist theory to racial/ethnic minority groups may appear to be a step in the right direction. However, feminist theorists caution that, while they have successfully extended the therapy model outside of the mainstream (e.g., inclusion of the realities of white lesbians), they are only beginning to do so relative to issues of colors, class, and culture. (Brown & Brodsky, 1992).

Network Therapy

From a family perspective, Attneave has developed an action-oriented form of extended family therapy. This therapy focuses on interdependence within the natural support systems of families, tribes, clans, and other community groups, such as schools, religious congregations, and service organizations (Speck & Attneave, 1973). Attneave's original work was done primarily with American Indians, but it was later adapted to treat inner-city families when she worked with Minuchin, Haley, and Speck at the Philadelphia Child Guidance Clinic.

The primary goal of network therapy is to empower people to access the support of their natural social relationships to help them cope with life crises. Treatment may involve convening groups of relatives, friends, neighbors, coworkers, and often personnel from other human service agencies. According to LaFromboise and Fleming (1990), network interventions with American Indians provide a better understanding of the issue, as well as facilitating more open and creative problem solving, more efficient coordination of the use of community resources, and an increased likelihood that the benefits of the intervention will accrue to more than just the identified client.

Multicultural Model of Counseling and Psychotherapy

Ramirez (1991) developed an eclectic and comprehensive multicultural model that he believes will be more effective in working with people who are different in myriad ways. The model seeks to help people who feel different and alienated to accept and understand their uniqueness. It also seeks to develop cultural (values) and coping (cognitive styles) flexibility to enable individuals to function more effectively with diverse racial/ethnic or cultural groups.

The theoretical base of the multicultural model has its origins in cross-cultural mental health, as well as in the psychology of liberation that evolved from developments in the psychologies of ethnic minorities, the colonized, and women. The cross-cultural emphasis evolved from the application of psychoanalytic and behavioristic theories and intervention approaches in different cultures throughout the world (Ramirez, 1991).

The multicultural model is eclectic with respect to techniques and strategies. From the dynamic approaches and theories, the model focuses on collecting a detailed life history. From the humanistic perspective, the model borrows unconditional positive regard, that is, uncritical acceptance, to allow clients to accept their unique selves. Also from the humanistic approach comes the use of phenomenology, or the therapist's attempt to see the world through the eyes of the client. From the cognitive and behavioristic approaches and theories, the model emphasizes stress reduction, establishing behavioral goals, doing homework, and the client's active participation through role playing. Finally, from the cross-cultural, ethnopsychological, and community schools, the model has adopted an emphasis on values and on the assumption that each cultural and environmental set of circumstances or conditions produces a unique set of coping techniques, or cognitive styles, crucial to personality development and functioning.

Finally, the goals of multicultural therapy and counseling are different from those of the traditional schools of personality change. The model has two categories of goals: individual and institutional, or societal, goals. The individual goals emphasize self-understanding and self-acceptance, as well as understanding the effects of the environment on personality development and adjustment. Multicultural therapy seeks to empower the client to produce significant environmental changes. Institutional and societal goals focus on the identification and elimination of barriers to multicultural development, and on replacing those barriers with positive politics of diversity in families, institutions, and society as a whole (Ramirez, 1991).

Eclecticism

It is now recognized that no one true path to understanding and correcting problems exists for any racial, ethnic, or cultural group (Garfield & Kurtz, 1975; Patterson, 1980). In recent years, an ever-growing number of counselors/ psychotherapists have come to believe that eclecticism is perhaps the most effective approach to take with persons from all groups. According to Lazarus and Beutler (1991), this movement has encompassed eclectic thinkers who differ greatly in both theory and technique, as well as those who focus on the technical aspects of therapy. In recent years, eclectic

thinkers have been placed into three distinct categories: unsystematic eclecticism (Lazarus & Beutler, 1993), theoretical eclecticism, and technical eclecticism (Norcross, 1986).

After a careful review, Lazarus and Beutler (1993) have strong positions relative to these three views. These theorists are very critical of unsystematic eclecticism, stating that "this smorgasbord conception of eclecticism, in which one selects concepts and procedures according to an unstated and largely unreplicable process, is both regrettable and misguided" (p. 381). Furthermore, they contend that "at the very least, a quest for improved therapeutic efficacy argues that counselors require particular organizing principles to guide them in determining under what circumstance a given procedure should be applied or withheld. The haphazard mishmash of divergent bits and pieces, and the syncretistic muddle of idiosyncratic and ineffable clinical creations, are the antithesis of what effective and efficient counseling represents" (p. 381).

With respect to theoretical eclecticism, Lazarus and Beutler are very critical of the integrationists who would take bits and pieces from both psychoanalytical and behavioral approaches, since at present there are no criteria to determine what aspects of each theory to preserve or expunge (pp. 382–383). These authors conclude that theoretical eclecticism "inevitably results in a gallimaufry of methods and ideas that have no consistent rationale and cannot be evaluated" (p. 383).

In contrast, Lazarus and Beutler (1993) have a very positive view of technical eclecticism. They contend that "an effective program of counseling can be based on a systematic process for selecting therapeutic procedures if this decision-making system is, itself, built on empirical demonstrations of the conditions, problems and clients with whom different procedures are effective" (p. 383). More specifically, technical eclectics, while working from a preferred theoretical orientation (Dryden, 1987), recognize that most techniques are not wedded to any theory. Consequently, they feel free to borrow techniques from any theoretical orientation that have been proven to be effective. As quoted by Lazarus and Beutler (1993), this perspective goes along with London's (1964) observation that "However interesting, plausible, and appealing a theory may be, it is techniques, not theories, that are actually used on people. Study of the effects of psychotherapy, therefore, is always the study of the effectiveness of techniques" (p. 33).

From a cross-cultural perspective, one could easily agree with Lazarus and Beutler (1993) that, of the three eclectic perspectives described above, the technical one may be most applicable to racial/ethnic minority clients for the following reasons: (1) it allows the counselor to work from any theoretical orientation and, more specifically, from those orientations that may be more in line with the world views of clients from diverse cultural backgrounds; (2) it directs attention to the use of techniques with demonstrated effectiveness across diverse conditions, problems, and clients. However, it should be noted that while technical eclectics may talk about "conditions," they never directly address culture. Once more, they appear to be working from the ethnocentric perspective of the white Anglo culture, with its receptivity to counseling. As such, so-called diverse conditions appear to refer to variables that serve to differentiate persons within that culture (e.g., socioeconomic status, educational level).

For a culture in which counseling and all that it connotes is totally unacceptable, even technical eclecticism, with all its promises, will fail to reach its potential. From another perspective, technical eclecticism strongly emphasizes the use of techniques and procedures that have been proved to be effective across clients. Unfortunately, as has been amply demonstrated by a variety of researchers (e.g., Casas, 1988), the efficacy of most of the techniques (e.g., cognitive restructuring, interpersonal exploration, self-monitoring) that are presently used in counseling, regardless of theoretical orientation, has not been proved across most racial/ethnic minority groups. Thus, the technical eclectic counselor, working from an ethical perspective, must take care to select and/or test the use of any and all techniques with persons from such groups. Failure to do so puts the

technical eclectic in the realm of the unsystematic eclectic, who Beutler and Lazarus (1993) colorfully describe as using a "ragtag, shotgun collection of miscellaneous" and unproven methods.

CONCLUSION

In agreeing to write a chapter on counseling and psychotherapy theories in relation to racial/ethnic minorities, I knew that I was taking on an overwhelming task. I decided that, if I could not do a thorough assessment of each major theory relative to its applicability and/or limitations vis-à-vis racial/ethnic minorities, I would opt to illustrate an approach that could be used to evaluate the applicability of all theories for individuals from diverse racial/ethnic minority groups. To this end, I decided to identify and describe selective psychosocial variables that serve to differentiate racial/ethnic minority groups from the majority of Euro-American white group and that many researchers believe may influence and limit the applicability of the major counseling/psychotherapy theories to these groups. I then provided an overview of the major traditional counseling/psychotherapy theories, giving special emphasis to those constructs and/or practices that might conflict with the aforementioned psychosocial variables and limit the applicability or effectiveness of the theories with racial/ethnic minorities. Finally, to encourage readers to broaden their theoretical perspectives, I presented selective theories that have been developed, taking the above-noted variables into consideration, which may make them more applicable for use with racial/ethnic minorities.

I believe it is necessary to provide the following concluding remark regarding the use of this approach: Many of the positions taken regarding the applicability or limitations of specific theories relative to racial/ethnic minorities are not based on empirical findings. Instead, they are based on limited clinical endeavors that are most frequently reported in anecdotal thought pieces. Given this fact, I here underscore the pressing need for empirical research

of prosocial and competitive behaviors in Anglo-American and Mexican-American children. *Child Development*, 48, 1385–1394.

Krogman, W. M. (1945). The concept of race. In R. Linton (Ed.), *The science of man in world crisis* (pp. 38–61). New York: Columbia University Press.

Lacan, J. (1977). *Ecrits: A selection*. New York: Norton. (Original work published 1966).

LaFromboise, T. D. (1988). American Indian mental health policy. *American Psychologist*, 3, 388–397.

LaFromboise, T. D., & Fleming, C. (1990). Keeper of the fire: A profile of Carolyn Attneave. *Journal of Counseling and Development*, 68, 537–547.

Lazarus, A. A., & Beutler, L. E. (1993). On technical eclecticism. *Journal of Counseling and Development*, 71, 381–385.

Lerner, G. (1986). *The creation of patriarchy*. New York: Oxford University Press.

Lerner, H. (1992). The limits of phenomenology: A feminist critique of the humanistic personality theories. In L. Brown & M. Ballou (Eds.), *Theories of personality and psychopathology* (pp. 8–129). New York: Guilford Press.

Linton, R. (Ed.) (1945). *The science of man in the world crisis*. New York: Columbia University Press.

London, P. (1964). *The modes and morals of psychotherapy*. New York: Holt, Rinehart & Winston.

Luepnitz, D. (1988). *The family interpreted: Feminist theory in clinical practtice*. New York: Basic Books.

Malgady, R. G., Rogler, L. H., & Costantino, G. (1987). Ethnocultural and linguistic bias in mental health evaluation of Hispanics. *American Psychologist*, 42, 228–234.

Manson, S. M. (Ed.). (1982). *New directions in prevention among American Indian and Alaska Native communities*. Portland: Oregon Health Sciences University.

Marin, G. (1992). Issues in the measurement of acculturation among Hispanics. In K. F. Geisinger (Ed.), *Psychological testing of Hispanics* (pp. 235–251). Washington, DC: American Psychological Association.

Markides, K. S., & Mindel, C. H. (1987). *Aging and ethnicity*. Newbury Park, CA: Sage.

McGoldrick M., Pearce, J., & Giordano, J. (1982). *Ethnicity and family therapy*. New York: Guilford Press.

McKenzie, V. M. (1986). Ethnographic findings on West Indian-American clients. *Journal of Counseling and Development*, 65, 40–44.

Mechanic, D. (1980). The experience and reporting of common physical complaints. *Journal of Health and Social Behavior*, 21, 146–155.

Meichenbaum, D. (1985). *Stress inoculation training*. New York: Pergamon Press.

Meichenbaum, D. (1990, December). *Evolution of cognitive behavior therapy: Origins, tenets and clinical examples*. Paper presented at the second conference on the evolution of psychotherapy, Anaheim, CA.

Minuchin, S. (1974). *Families and family therapy*. Cambridge, MA: Harvard University Press.

Morita, S. (1960). *Shinkeishitsu-no hontai-to ryoho* [Nature and treatment of nervosity]. Tokyo: Hakuyosha. (Original work published 1928).

Myers, H. F., Echemendia, R. J., & Trimble, J. E. (1991). The need for training ethnic minority psychologists. In H. F. Meyers, P. Wohlford, L. P. Guzman, & R. J. Echemendia (Eds.), *Ethnic minority perspectives on clinical training and services in psychology* (pp. 3–11). Washington, DC: American Psychological Association.

Nichter, M. (1981). Idioms of distress: Alternatives in the expression of psychological distress: A case study from South India. *Culture, Medicine, and Psychiatry*, 5, 397–408.

Norcross, J. C. (Ed.). (1986). *Handbook of eclectic psychotherapy*. New York: Brunner/Mazel.

Oetting, E. R., & Beauvais, F. (1990–1991). Orthogonal cultural identification theory: The cultural identification of minority adolescents. *The International Journal of the Addictions*, 25 (5A, 6A), 655–685.

Olmedo, E., Martinez, J., Jr., & Martinez, S. (1978). Measure of acculturation for Chicano adolescents. *Psychological Reports*, 42, 159–170.

Olmedo, E., & Padilla, A. (1978). Empirical and construct validation of a measure of acculturation for Mexican Americans. *Journal of Social Psychology*, 105, 179–187.

Parham, T. A. (1989). Cycles of psychological nigresence. *The Counseling Psychologist*, 17, 187–226.

Patterson, C. H. (1980). *Theories of counseling and psychotherapy* (3rd ed.). New York: Harper & Row.

Pedersen, P. B. (1978). Four dimensions of cross-cultural skill in counselor training. *Personnel and Guidance Journal*, 56, 480–483.

Pedersen, P. B. (Ed.). (1985). *Handbook of cross-cultural counseling and therapy*. Westport, CT: Greenwood Press.

Pedersen, P. B. (1988). *A handbook for developing multicultural awareness*. Alexandria, VA: American Association for Counseling and Development.

Pedersen, P. B., Draguns, J. G., Lonner, W. L., & Trimble, J. E. (Eds.). (1989). *Counseling across cultures* (3rd ed.). Honolulu: University of Hawaii Press.

Perls, F., Hefferline, R., & Goodman, P. (1951). *Gestalt therapy: Excitement and growth in human personality*. New York: Dell.

Ponterotto, J. G. (1987). Counseling Mexican-Amerians: A multimodal approach. *Journal of Counseling and Development, 65*, 308–312.

Ponterotto, J. G., & Casas, J. M. (1991). *Handbook of racial/ethnic minority counseling research*. Springfield, IL: Charles C. Thomas.

Ponterotto, J. G., & Sabnani, H. B. (1989). "Classics" in multicultural counseling: A systematic five-year content analysis. *Journal of Multicultural Counseling and Development, 17*, 23–37.

Price-Williams, D. (1985). Cultural psychology. In G. Lindzay & E. Aronnson (Eds.), *Handbook of social psychology* (3rd ed., Vol. III, 993–1042). New York: Random House.

Price-Williams, D., & Ramirez, M. (1977). Divergent thinking, cultural differences, and bilingualism. *Journal of Social Psychology, 103*, 3–11.

Prilleltensky, I. (1990). On the social and political implications of cognitive psychology. *Journal of Mind and Behavior, 11*, 127–136.

Pumariega, A. J. (1986). Acculturation and eating attitudes in adolescent girls: A comparative correlational study. *Journal of the American Academy of Child Psychiatry, 25*, 276–279.

Ramirez, M. (1991). *Psychotherapy and counseling with minorities: A cognitive approach to individual and cultural differences*. New York: Pergamon Press.

Ramirez, M., & Castañeda, A. (1974). *Cultural democracy, bicognitive development and education*. New York: Academic Press.

Ramirez, M., Cox, B., & Castañeda, A. (1977, June). *The psychodynamics of biculturalism*. Study prepared for the Organizational Research Programs, Office of Naval Research, Arlington, VA. Santa Cruz, CA: Systems and Evaluations in Education.

Ramirez, M., & Price-Williams, D. (1974). Cognitive styles in children: Two Mexican communities. *Revista Interamericana de Psicologia, 8* (1–2), 93–101.

Ramirez, M., & Price-Williams, D. (1976). Achievement motivation in children of three ethnic groups in the United States. *Journal of Cross Cultural Psychology, 7*, 49–60.

Redfield, R., Linton, R., & Herskovitz, M. J. (1936). Memorandum on the study of acculturation. *American Anthropologist, 38*, 149–152.

Reynolds, D. (1981). Naikan psychotherapy. In R. J. Corsini (Ed.), *Handbook of innovative psychotherapies* (pp. 544–553). New York: Wiley.

Rigney, M. (1981, April). *A critique of Maslow's self-actualization theory: The "highest good" for the aboriginal is relationship* (videotape). Adelaide, Australia: Aboriginal Open College.

Rogers, C. (1961). *On becoming a person*. Boston: Houghton Mifflin.

Rogler, L. H., Cortes, D. E., & Malgady, R. G. (1991). Acculturation and mental health status among Hispanics. *American Psychologist, 46*, 585–597.

Rogler, L. H., Malgady, R. G., Costantino, G., & Blumenthal, R. (1987). What do culturally sensitive mental health services mean? The case of Hispanics. *American Psychologist, 42*, 565–570.

Rose, P. I. (1964). *They and we: Racial and ethnic relations in the United States*. New York: Random House.

Sampson, E. E. (1981). Cognitive psychology as ideology. *American Psychologist, 36*, 730–743.

Speck, R., & Attneave, C. (1973). *Family networks*. New York: Random House.

Sue, D. (1990). Culture-specific strategies in counseling; A conceptual framework. *Professional Psychology, 21*, 424–433.

Sue, D. W. (1981). *Counseling the culturally different: Theory and practice*. New York: Wiley.

Sue, D. W., & Sue, D. (1985). In P. B. Pedersen (Ed.), *Handbook of cross-cultural counseling and therapy* (pp. 141–146). Westport, CT: Greenwood Press.

Sue, D. W., & Sue, D. (1990). *Counseling the culturally different: Theory and practice* (2nd ed). New York: Wiley.

Suinn, R. M., Rickard-Figueroa, K., Lew, S., & Vigil, P. (1987). The Suinn-Lew Asian Self-Identity Acculturation Scale: An initial report. *Educational and Psychological Measurement, 47*, 401–407.

Szapocznik, J., & Kurtines, W. (1980). Acculturation, biculturalism, and adjustment among Cuban Americans. In A. M. Padilla (Ed.), *Acculturation: Theory, models, and some new findings*. (pp. 139–160). Boulder, CO: Westview Press.

Taub-Bynum, E. B. (1984). *The family unconscious*. Wheaton, IL: Quest.

Taub-Bynum, E. B. (1992). *Family dreams: The intimate web*. Ithaca, NY: Haworth Press.

Thomas, C. W. (1971). *Boys no more*. Beverly Hills, CA: Glencoe Press.

Trimble, J. (1990–1991). Ethnic specification, validation prospects, and the future of drug use research. *International Journal of the Addictions, 25* (2A), 149–170.

U.S. Department of Commerce (1990). *1990 Census of the population: General population characteristics*. Washington, DC: U.S. Government Printing Office.

Velimirovic, B. (Ed.). (1978). *Modern medicine and medical anthropology in the United States–Mexico border population*. Pan American Health Organization Scientific Publication No. 359. Washington, DC: World Health Organization.

Vigil, J. D. (1988). *Barrio gangs: Street life and identity in Southern California*. Austin: University of Texas Press.

Vontress, C. E. (1988). An existential approach to cross-cultural counseling. *Journal of Multicultural Counseling and Development, 16*, 73–83.

Walsh, R. (1989). Asian psychotherapies. In R. J. Corsini & D. Wedding (Eds.), *Current Psychotherapies* (4th ed., pp. 547–559). Itasca, IL: Peacock.

White, T. J., & Parham, T. A. (1990). *Black psychology: An African-American perspective* (2nd ed.). Englewood Cliffs, NJ: Prentice-Hall.

Wirth, L. (1945). The problem of minority groups. In R. Linton (Ed.), *The science of man (woman) in the world crisis* (pp. 347–372). New York: Columbia University Press.

18
Therapy with Children and Adolescents

Susan M. Panichelli
Philip C. Kendall

Psychological maladjustment in youth is a major problem confronting today's society. Data suggest that 15–22% of youth in America have mental health problems severe enough to warrant treatment (Costello, 1990; National Advisory Mental Health Council, 1990). While it has been recognized that children suffer from psychological disorders, it is only recently that researchers have begun to conduct proper studies to assess the efficacy of various psychological treatments with children and adolescents.

Over 35 years ago, Levitt (1957) provided an initial review and evaluation of 18 papers describing the effectiveness of child psychotherapy and concluded that its efficacy was not demonstrated. Levitt's review paralleled Eysenck's (1952) review of adult psychotherapy, which also argued that the results of therapy were no better than the results obtained over time without treatment. There were many methodological limitations in the studies reviewed by Levitt. In the early studies, the control groups were composed of children who had dropped out of treatment. Therefore, the control groups were not true controls, nor were they randomly assigned to a treatment condition or to a therapist. The evaluation of treatment efficacy was based solely on therapists' evaluations. The reports were composed of a wide age range of subjects (3–21 years old) with a variety of disorders. Today, developmental influences and the nature of specific psychopathologies are important factors that direct treatment programs (Kendall, 1993). The early studies suffered also because parents, teachers, and the children themselves were not involved in the evaluation of treatment effects. The many criticisms (Eisenberg & Gruenberg, 1961; Heinicke & Goldman, 1960; Hood-Williams, 1960) prompted Levitt (1963) to conduct a subsequent review using 22 additional studies. Once again, he concluded that psychotherapy did not foster improvement in children compared to those who did not receive treatment. Since 1963, however, psychotherapy research methods have been improved (Kendall & Norton-Ford, 1982) and there has been greater research attention to child and adolescent disorders (Kendall, 1991a).

Recently, meta-analyses have been conducted to evaluate the efficacy of psychotherapy with children. These reports employ "effect sizes" calculated for published therapy-outcome studies. For example, Casey and Berman (1985) reviewed 75 research studies and concluded that child psychotherapy is indeed effective. The reported analyses demonstrated a significant effect size (.71) due to treatment. A separate meta-analysis led Weisz, Weiss, Alicke, and Klotz (1987) to conclude that child psychotherapy is more effective than no treatment. Apparently, as research methods and clinical services are improved, the data can be said to indicate that psychotherapy is an effective treatment for children with psychological difficulties. The specific question now being addressed is what intervention is most effective for which individual with what specific problem under what set of circumstances and administered by which therapist (Kiesler, 1966; Paul, 1967). Current research looks beyond the general effectiveness of psychotherapy and investigates the efficacy of specific treatments for specific childhood disorders.

DISTINCTIVENESS OF CHILD THERAPY

Child psychotherapy differs from adult psychotherapy. Children do not usually refer themselves to treatment; rather, it is typically the parent or teacher who makes the referral. Children often do not view themselves as having difficulties, frequently attributing any problems to external forces such as the environment, family, or social groups (Compas, Friedland-Bandes, Bastien, & Adelman, 1981; Kazdin, 1988). Children do not readily see the need for or benefits of therapy, leaving the therapist to have to work to maintain the child's interest (Adelman, Kaser-Boyd, & Taylor, 1984; Kazdin, 1988). Additionally, some research has questioned the validity of parental reports, particularly of depressed mothers (Breslau, Davis, & Prabucki, 1988). Parental referrals may be based on parental perceptions that are not necessarily accurate. The parents' perceptions may be related to their own problems such as marital discord, low self-esteem, and stressful circumstances (Forehand, Lautenschlager, Faust, & Graziano, 1986; Freud, 1980, Mash & Johnson, 1983). However, a recent review of the literature on maternal distortions in reporting children's difficulties (Richters, 1992) concluded that there is an absence of conclusive

evidence. Before conclusions can be drawn, there is a need for research to evaluate the validity of depressed mothers' reports on their children. In conducting psychotherapy with children, it is important for the therapist to remember these differences from adult psychotherapy.

OVERVIEW OF THE CHAPTER

This chapter provides an overview of a variety of approaches to psychotherapy with children and adolescents. Psychoanalysis and psychodynamic therapies will be mentioned, with an emphasis on the theories of the prominent figures in each field. A general summary of the theory, research, and techniques of behavior therapy is presented, along with special note of the treatment of attention-deficit hyperactivity disorder. A theoretical discussion of cognitive-behavioral therapy is provided, as well as a review of the research, attention to the treatment of anxiety disorders, and a case study. Family therapy is divided into three main orientations: strategic family therapy, structural family therapy, and parent training. All three are briefly discussed in terms of their theory and are illustrated by examples. The description and discussion of parent training also include research studies and a case example.

PSYCHOANALYSIS AND PSYCHODYNAMIC PSYCHOTHERAPY

Melanie Klein (1932) and Anna Freud (1927, 1946) are best known for the development of child psychoanalysis. Psychoanalytic psychotherapy focuses on the past in order to try to help resolve conflicts interfering with the client's present and future functioning. The goal of analysis is to allow the child to recognize unconscious anxiety defenses to resolve difficulties and conflicts. Anna Freud believed that psychoanalysis should be used sparingly with children who are not developing appropriately because of unresolved conflict. In contrast,

Melanie Klein believes that every child can benefit from therapy.

Distinctiveness of Child Psychodynamic Therapy

Anna Freud (Sandler, Kennedy, & Tyson, 1980) described the advantages of child analysis over adult analysis, along with the factors that aid in the improvement and recovery of children. First, the therapeutic process can produce more profound alterations in the child's character than in the adults'. These alterations do not shatter a child's life as devastatingly as they do that of an adult who has built a life based on abnormality. Second, the therapist can address the child's current relationship with his or her parents rather than relying on the enshrined parental memories of adults. Third, the therapist can transform the environment in some ways to meet the simple needs of the child. By slightly adapting the environment to the child, the burden of adaptation is lightened, whereas adults need to adapt themselves fully to their surroundings.

A child cannot contribute much in terms of the history of his or her difficulties. Children are more focused on and too absorbed in the present to think back to their short-lived past. A child does not know when maladjustment began or how it differs from the behavior of other children. Parents are the ones who must supply the history of the child's development, and therapists must allow for possible inaccuracies that may occur in parental reports. Therapy relies on parents to keep their children in treatment. Children do not decide on their own accord to come to analysis, nor are they asked to consent to treatment. Children do not perceive problems within themselves; rather, others are caused to suffer from their symptoms and acting-out behaviors. It is the parents or people around the child who decide if therapy is deemed appropriate. If the parents decide to pull their child out of treatment, the analyst cannot continue therapy. Therefore, the therapist must decide how to maintain a good alliance with the child's parents so that they will continue to support therapy (Sandler et al., 1980).

Play Therapy and Free Association

Aspects of coming to treatment indispensable for adults (e.g., insight, voluntary decision, a desire to be cured) do not exist for children. Melanie Klein comes to terms with this difference through the creation of play therapy. In contrast, Anna Freud believes that the therapist is capable of inducing treatment willingness in the child. She works to get the child to want to come to therapy by demonstrating skills or powers that can be valuable to the child. She lets them discover how worthwhile it would be for them to come to therapy. Free association, a fundamental tool in psychoanalysis with adults to understand the unconscious, is said to be outside the nature of the child (Freud, 1946). Because verbal expression in children was seen as underdeveloped, Klein tried to substitute play techniques for free association—intending to use play to establish contact with the child's unconscious. Play therapy is used to understand the child's various reactions, strengths, aggressive impulses, sympathies, and attitudes about things and people, all through representations with toys (Wolman, 1972). Toys are considered good analytical tools because they allow the child to carry out actions, thoughts, or images that are only fantasies in the real world. Through play, the therapist observes and can learn the concerns of the child. The analyst interprets the child's actions out loud to the child, often connecting the past to the present, to maintain the child's interest and cooperation and to resolve internal conflicts.

Object Relations

While psychoanalysis focuses on discovering unconscious anxiety and conflict, object relations theory takes on a more interpersonal approach. Object relations theory is a psychodynamic perspective on psychopathology that focuses on the relationships and emotional bonds between people (Cashdan, 1988). *Objects* refer to the significant others in people's lives. Therapy examines the role primary relationships play in regard to the child's perception of interpersonal relations and current relationships. Its purpose is to understand significant childhood interpersonal relationships and how these patterns of relating are repeated in other relationships. Margaret Mahler, a forerunner in object relations, believes that the interactions between mother and child are the determinants of the child's psychological functioning (Mahler, Pine, & Bergman, 1975). She describes the development of the child in relation to its mother as going through a process of *separation-individuation*. If a mother inhibits or rushes this process, the child will have psychological difficulties that will be reflected later in other close relationships.

Therapist's Role

Both psychoanalytic and psychodynamic therapies involve long-term treatment. In working with children, play is most often used as the primary mode of expression because the ability to verbalize feelings is difficult for a child. The therapist is not directive in therapy, but rather allows the child to play and explore on his or her own. The therapist offers interpretations of the symbolic play that can be discussed on the initiation of the child.

Evaluation

One difficulty in determining the efficacy of psychoanalytically oriented therapy is the dearth of research validating its efficacy. Its foundation has been based on theory and case studies rather than scientific experiments. Contemporary psychodynamic therapies are concerned with interpersonal issues rather than unconscious conflict that may be more conducive to empirical validation. Future studies need to address the efficacy of this approach to treatment by conducting experiments using contemporary methodologies. Creating manualized treatment protocols is an option for researchers interested in reliably validating treatment effects. The current trend is to use therapy manuals flexibly (Dobson & Shaw, 1989). In this way, the treatment can be scientifically tested and studied, yet still maintain the individualization required in therapy. Research is needed before an evaluation can be made concerning psychoanalytically oriented approaches to psychotherapy with children.

BEHAVIOR THERAPY

Behavior therapy is derived from principles of learning and is a well-researched approach to treatment for the psychological adjustment of children and adolescents (Ollendick, 1986). A basic assumption in behavior therapy is that all behavior is acquired through the learning process. Behavior therapy does not follow one particular methodology of treatment; rather, it consists of a series of techniques based on empirically tested principles, such as classical conditioning, operant conditioning, and modeling.

Therapist's Role

Interventions focus on changing behavior. Unobservable constructs are reconceptualized into operational definitions that can be measured, treated, and evaluated (McBurnett, Hobbs, & Lahey, 1989). Behavior itself is the focus of change as well as the measure of change. Behavior therapists are directive in an attempt to help alleviate clients' difficulties. Therapists understand and use the factors that influence learning (e.g., reward, punishment, the environment) and provide opportunities for guided practice. The therapist assigns tasks and evaluates the progress toward change. The therapist also serves as an educator who teaches the client new ways of behaving through example and practice. Behavior therapy has been used to treat a variety of disorders, including hyperactivity (Rapport, 1987), conduct disorder (Kazdin, 1987a), depression (Frame, Matson, Sonis, Fialkov, & Kazdin, 1982; Stark, Reynolds, & Kaslow, 1987), and anxiety (King, Hamilton, & Ollendick, 1988).

Behavioral Techniques

Bell and Pad Treatment

One of the pioneering examples of effective behavioral treatment for children is the bell and pad treatment for bed-wetting (Mowrer & Mowrer, 1938). This technique can involve many other behavioral approaches, such as cleanliness training, but it consists essentially of an alarm that buzzes when the child urinates in bed. A current review of the studies of treatments for nocturnal enuresis (Houts, Berman, & Abramson, in press) concluded that children treated with alarms were more likely to cease bed-wetting than those treated with medication or other variations of psychological treatment without the alarm.[1]

Systematic Desensitization

Systematic desensitization (Wolpe, 1958) is the gradual presentation of anxiety-provoking stimuli in a relaxed state. The child is first taught relaxation training (Ollendick, 1986) to help him or her feel calm in a frightening situation and to provide an activity that can be substituted later for a fear response. Once adept at relaxation, the child or adolescent is exposed to a low-anxiety-provoking situation through imagery or a live experience. Live (in vivo) experiences are more effective than imagery for younger children because these children often do not have the cognitive capacity necessary for effective imaging (Hughes, 1993; Ultee, Griffiaen, & Schellekens, 1982). This pairing of an activity—relaxation—with an anxiety-provoking stimulus provides a new way for the child to experience the stimulus. In effect, the fear is replaced with feelings of serenity and relaxation. A hierarchy is constructed to introduce gradually to the individual stimuli that

foster intense fear. With each successful experience, the client ascends the hierarchy to new situations with higher levels of provocation. Research suggests that exposure to the once feared object or situation is an active component of treatment (Barlow, 1988). Systematic desensitization is most often used in treating fears and phobias in children (King et al., 1988; Morris & Kratochwill, 1991) and in treating test anxiety and school phobia in adolescents (Morris, Kratochwill, & Aldridge, 1988).

Modeling

Modeling is a behavioral technique used to change behavior through observation. Numerous studies of modeling report that exposing someone to a model who demonstrates desired behaviors increases the likelihood that observers will perform similarly in the future (Masters, Brush, Hollon, & Rimm, 1987). An individual's behavior is modified as a result of observing someone engage in a behavior and then recognizing its consequences (Bandura, 1969). New responses can be learned and old responses can be inhibited by modeling. The child observes the model, imitates the model's behavior, and receives feedback and reinforcement for the performance.

The therapist may serve as a mastery model in which ideal or fearless behavior is demonstrated. The therapist may also use a coping model in which the therapist demonstrates fear but then uses strategies to overcome it. A coping model appears to be more effective than a mastery model in helping clients overcome avoidance (Ginther & Roberts, 1982; Kazdin, 1974), perhaps because the observer can relate better to the coping model. In terms of the types of modeling observed, participant modeling, in which the therapist guides the client through the fearful situation, was found to be more effective than watching a filmed model or observing a live model (Ollendick, 1986). Modeling has been used to treat fearful (Morris & Kratochwill, 1983), socially withdrawn (La-Greca & Santogrossi, 1980), and aggressive (Bornstein, Bellack, & Hersen, 1980) children and adolescents. Typically it is not the sole intervention, but rather is used in combination with other behavioral techniques.

Operant Conditioning

Operant conditioning involves the modification of behaviors based on their consequences. Experiments have shown that reinforced behaviors are more likely to occur again (Skinner, 1969) and that reinforced adaptive behaviors can come to replace maladaptive ones. By applying positive and negative reinforcements, behaviors can be shaped, maintained, or altered. Specific elements of operant conditioning include token economies, response cost procedures, contingency contracting, and punishment. These behavioral interventions have been used with a variety of childhood difficulties (Kratochwill & Morris, 1991).

Token economy is an operant procedure in which tokens are used like money to buy rewards. Appropriate prosocial and desirable behaviors are delineated and reinforced through token rewards. The child is awarded tokens for appropriate behaviors, which are traded in for rewards such as special classroom privileges, snacks, or special events. Target behaviors can be modified or changed, and new ones can be added periodically to the program. Additionally, response costs, in which the child loses tokens for inappropriate behavior, can be implemented to alter the child's behavior (DuPaul, Guevremont, & Barkley, 1991). Token economies have been found to be effective, particularly in classroom settings, for controlling and altering behavior and improving overall levels of client functioning (McLaughlin & Williams, 1988). It was particularly well implemented and researched throughout the 1970s but later declined in popularity.

Contingency management involves a similar type of intervention in that children are rewarded for appropriate behaviors and receive consequences for maladaptive ones. Together the child and parent or teacher design a behavior contract containing rules to be followed, along with the specific rewards and consequences for following or breaking the rules, respectively. The allotment of rewards is contingent on maintenance of the contractual rules. Specific punishments (e.g., time-out, loss of privileges) are defined in the contract and result from disregard of the contractual limitations (DuPaul et al., 1991). Today operant procedures are not used alone as a method of treatment; rather, they are combined with other forms of therapy.

Evaluation

Overall, behavior therapy has been found to be an effective intervention in treating psychological maladjustment of childhood. The various approaches have undergone numerous scientific evaluations and research examinations. However, behavior therapy has been criticized as reducing and limiting the benefits of therapy to changes in observable behavior. Additionally, there are limited generalizations of the effects once the program is no longer implemented. Contemporary behavior therapists use effective behavioral techniques, but only as one facet of intervention. For example, there is increasing concern for the therapeutic relationships, the client's interpersonal relationships, and the cognitive activities of the client. This move away from strict adherence to purely behavioral techniques has helped to rebuke some critics. Although there is much research investigating the efficacy of behavior therapy, there is a need for studies to support the conclusion that behavior therapy is more efficacious than other approaches to treatment (Casey & Berman, 1985; Ollendick, 1986). One reason why it is difficult to assess its effectiveness comparatively may be due to the many different techniques encompassed in behavior therapy (Mash, 1989).

Treatment of Attention Deficit Hyperactivity Disorder (ADHD)

ADHD is a childhood disorder associated with short attention span, easy distractibility, and poor impulse control. Medication, specifically methylphenidate, is most often used as an effective treatment. Of the alternative treatments, behavioral approaches to the treatment of ADHD have been researched and applied. For example, Pelham et al. (1988) investigated the efficacy of a combination of behavior therapy and methylphenidate. The subjects, aged 5 to 10, met DSM III criteria for ADHD and were divided into five groups. Four groups received behavior therapy, along with either medication or a placebo, and possible social skills training. The fifth group, which received social skills training alone, was used as a contrast treatment group. Efficacy of treatment was assessed using an academic achievement test, positive and negative peer nominations, teacher and parent ratings, and direct behavioral observations before and after treatment.

The results of the Pelham et al. (1988) study demonstrated that the children who received behavior therapy showed clinically and statistically significant improvements in comparison to the contrast treatment group and normal classmate controls. The combination of medication and/or social skills training did not significantly affect the improvement produced by behavior therapy; however, those who received medication were rated higher by teachers in terms of improved behavior than those who received placebos. Overall, although there was significant improvement, very few of the subjects fell within the normal range of functioning on dependent measures after treatment (Kendall & Grove, 1988). The results led Pelham et al. to conclude that behavior therapy is an effective technique in treating ADHD, but that when used alone, it may not be sufficient. Behavior therapy has a clinical impact on ADHD, but a more intensive treatment that continues longer than the 5 months used in this study is likely to improve the overall treatment outcome.

Other behavior therapy approaches have been applied to classroom behavior—techniques such as token economies, contingent teacher attention, response costs, and time-out (Carlson & Lahey, 1988; Carlson, Pelham, Milich, & Dixon, 1992). A study by Carlson et al. (1992) investigated the effects of behavior therapy, stimulant treatment, and a combina-

tion of the two on the classroom behavior of children suffering from ADHD. All subjects were primarily diagnosed with ADHD, although a few also had oppositional disorder or conduct disorder.

Response costs and rewards were the behavioral interventions used in the classroom to manage behavior. Each child began the day with 100 points. Points were earned for accurate completion of assignments and for breaking one or no rules, and were taken away for violations of classroom rules. When a rule was broken, the teacher identified the inappropriate behavior for which points were lost. At the end of the day, children were informed of their total point count, and at the end of the week the children exchanged their points for privileges and rewards to reinforce appropriate behavior. Time-out was used as a punishment when a child became unmanageable or had already lost the daily 100 points. Reports from the teachers were sent home to allow the parents to reinforce appropriate school behavior. Subjects involved in the behavior therapy condition received this classroom structure and a contingency management program, while those in the pure stimulant condition did not.

The measures used to assess treatment effects were observations of classroom behavior, academic work performance, and self-rating questionnaires. Like the Pelham et al. (1988) study, the Carlson et al. (1990) study demonstrates the efficacy of a combination of medication and behavior therapy in improving the classroom behavior of children with ADHD. The results of the two treatments combined were more effective than that of either treatment condition alone. Children who received behavior therapy were more able to stay on task in the classroom and were less disruptive. For some children, behavior therapy without medication was sufficient to improve their behavior; however, pure behavior therapy did not appear to affect the child's level of academic performance. The authors note and possibly attribute this lack of improvement to the reward system used for academic performance. While the children were rewarded for their performance, response costs were not implemented. Research has indicated the necessity of using both rewards and response cost to change behavior patterns (Rosen, O'Leary, Joyce, Conway, & Pfiffner, 1984). The absence of change in academic performance for those in the behavioral therapy condition may be due to the lack of response costs. In summary, the best results were gained by the combination of therapies.

COGNITIVE-BEHAVIORAL THERAPY

Cognitive-behavioral therapy combines performance-based strategies and cognitive interventions to produce changes in cognition, behavior, and emotions (Kendall, 1991b). This approach is concerned with both the external environment and the individual's internal style of processing. Treatment focuses on how people respond to their cognitive interpretations of experiences, rather than on the environment or the experience itself, and how these thoughts and behaviors are related.

Therapist's Role

A cognitive-behavioral therapist acts as a consultant, diagnostician, and educator (Kendall, 1991b). As a consultant, the therapist provides ideas for experimentation, helps sort through experiences, and promotes problem solving. The consultant does not give specific solutions, but rather strives to develop skills in the client, including independent thinking. The therapist facilitates the interaction between the child and the therapist in a collaborative problem-solving effort.

As a diagnostician, the therapist makes decisions by going beyond the verbal report and behavior of both the client and his or her significant others. Decisions are made by integrating data and judging from a background of knowledge of psychopathology and normal development. For instance, the therapist does not decide what a child's difficulties are or what needs to be changed based on parent reports alone. The fact that a parent or teacher refers to a child as being anxious is helpful, but it is

not sufficient to conclude that the child has an anxiety disorder. It is possible that the child is reacting in a way that is appropriate for the child's age and circumstances. The problem may lie in the fact that the parent has unreasonable expectations of or demands on the child. The therapist acts as a diagnostician by assessing the child's difficulties from various sources of information, including the therapist's background of knowledge and expertise.

Lastly, the therapist as an educator encourages the child or adolescent to think independently. The therapist maximizes the strengths of the learner, accepts that individuals do things differently, and pays attention to the internal dialogue of the child, which often affects performance. The educator is involved in the process of learning and communicates behavior control, cognitive skills, and emotional development to the child.

Elements of Cognition

Content, Processes, Products, and Structures

Cognition refers to a complex system that can be reduced to four components: content, processes, products, and structures (Ingram & Kendall, 1986). Cognitive *structures* can be understood as memory and the manner in which information is represented in memory. Cognitive *content* is defined as the information that is stored in memory. Cognitive *processes* refer to how we perceive and interpret our experiences. Cognitive *products* are the result of the interaction of content, structures, and processes.

As an illustration of this complex system, imagine a child walking into a classroom and tripping on a banana peel lying next to the trash can. The child begins to process this experience. The way the event is processed will affect the child's behavioral and emotional consequences. The child may think about the embarrassment of the event, or may enter the classroom without thinking much about tripping. After the experience, conclusions are drawn regarding the tripping—cognitive products. Some children may attribute their fall to their own stupidity and carelessness ("I can't do anything right; I'm so stupid and clumsy that I can't even walk through a doorway"); this often characterizes the cognitions of depressed individuals (Abramson, Seligman, & Teasdale, 1978). An aggressive child may attribute the fall to someone else's purposeful act ("Who put this banana peel here so that I would trip?") (Dodge, 1985). Cognitive structures screen new experiences and incorporate past events to influence current processing. An anxious child would think about the situation through an anxious processing structure and might focus on the embarrassment and future difficulties ("No one will want to be friends with me after I made such a fool of myself," "I hope I didn't break my leg when I fell") (Kendall et al., 1991). The role of the cognitive-behavioral therapist is to pay attention to the child's cognitive activities before, during, and after imperfect interpersonal events.

Individuals perceive and make sense of the world through their personally developed cognitive structures (or *schemas*, as Beck [1976] called them). Cognitive-behavioral treatment works to create experiences that will help build a more functional structure—a coping template (Kendall, 1991b). The child is guided by the therapist through multiple new experiences to help develop a new cognitive structure through which the child can identify and solve problems. The goal is for the child, with the help of the therapist, to acquire a coping cognitive structure for future events.

Distortions and Deficiencies

All cognitive dysfunctions are not the same, and particularly with children, a distinction can be made between cognitive distortions and cognitive deficiencies (Kendall, 1985; Kendall & MacDonald, 1993). *Cognitive distortions* refer to dysfunctional thinking processes in which the child actively processes information in a misguided way. Distorted processing and misperceiving of the social/interpersonal environment are linked to and often seen in children with internalizing disorders such as anxiety and

depression (Kendall, Stark, & Adam, 1990). *Cognitive deficiencies* refer to the absence of information processing. The child acts without thinking, and lacks forethought and planning. Children who are hyperactive or impulsive and suffer from externalizing disorders often demonstrate this type of cognitive dysfunction. Aggressive children demonstrate both cognitive distortions and deficiencies (Kendall, Ronan, & Epps, 1990). They have deficiencies in interpersonal problem solving, yet they also show distortions in their processing of information (Dodge, 1985). Differential treatment should be implemented, depending on the specific cognitive dysfunctions of the child. Those with cognitive distortions require the faulty thinking to be identified and the distorted processing corrected. Those with cognitive deficiencies need to develop the skills of thoughtful problem solving and the skills to help them think before acting.

Applications

Cognitive-behavioral interventions for children and adolescents have been applied to a wide variety of difficulties (Kendall, 1993).[2] Treatment strategies have been implemented for depression (Stark, Rouse, & Livingston, 1991), attention-deficit hyperactivity disorder (Braswell & Bloomquist, 1991), impulsivity (Kendall & Braswell, 1993), antisocial behavior (Kazdin, Esveldt-Dawson, French, & Unis, 1987), and chronic illness (Walco & Varni, 1991). Recently, the approach has been applied in the treatment of anxiety disorders (Kendall et al., 1991). As an illustration, the rest of this section will be devoted to discussing cognitive-behavioral therapy for children anxiety.

Cognitive-Behavioral Treatment for Anxiety

All children feel anxiety to some extent, but excessive anxiety can prevent some children from exploring their world and becoming independent. In a preliminary study on the efficacy of cognitive-behavioral therapy in treating anxiety (Kane & Kendall, 1989), four children diagnosed with overanxious disorder received 16–20 individual hour-long treatment sessions. The sessions focused on getting the child to recognize feelings and cognitions associated with an anxiety-provoking situation, and to develop and evaluate a plan to help cope with the situation. Behavioral training techniques (e.g., modeling, role play, relaxation training, contingent reinforcement) aided in the acquisition of these skills. Once the new skills were learned, they were practiced in vivo and encouraged through social reinforcement by the therapist.

The results suggested that cognitive-behavioral therapy was effective in the treatment of anxiety disorders. Changes in the level of anxiety were demonstrated on parent reports, independent clinicians' ratings, and child self-reports. In addition, negative target behaviors identified before treatment were improved, and follow-up reports provided evidence of reasonable maintenance and treatment effects.

In a recent randomized clinical trial, subjects diagnosed with an anxiety disorder received 16–20 hour-long, individual cognitive-behavioral treatment sessions (Kendall, 1994). Subjects were assigned to immediate treatment or to an 8-week wait-list condition preceding treatment. The treatment program worked to identify cognitive processes associated with excessive anxiety arousal, train the children in the use of cognitive strategies for anxiety management and behavioral relaxation techniques, and provide practice opportunities (in vivos) to help build skills.

The children in treatment were taught new coping strategies through modeling, to recognize self-talk and to use relaxation, imagery, and problem solving. In this way, the children were shown how to change their threatening and anxiety-provoking thoughts into more manageable ones. With exposure to the anxiety-provoking experiences, the children had the opportunity to practice their adaptive self-talk, problem-solve, evaluate their coping strategies, and reward themselves. The in vivo experiences were placed in a hierarchy so that the child could cope successfully with each threatening situation and build on these successful experiences with higher levels of provocation.

Treatment Protocol

The first eight sessions of the manualized treatment protocol were training sessions in which each of the basic concepts was introduced individually. The topics (by session) included (1) building rapport and gathering information about anxiety-provoking situations for the child; (2) identification of different types of feelings; (3) recognition of somatic responses to anxiety (after this session, a meeting with the parents was held to open communication about the program and the child's particular difficulties); (4) relaxation training; (5) recognition of self-talk; (6) coping strategies such as coping self-talk and appropriate actions to ease anxiety; (7) self-evaluation and self-reward; and (8) review of skills learned.

During the second eight sessions, the child was given the opportunity to practice, through in vivo experiences, the newly learned skills in coping with anxiety. The in vivos were experienced in a hierarchy of difficulty to promote success and confidence within the child. "Show That I Can (STIC)" homework tasks provided children the chance to review and practice their newly learned skills in a nonclinical environment. At the end of treatment, the child created a "commercial" to illustrate and inform others how to cope with distressing situations.

Outcomes

Results demonstrated the efficacy of a cognitive-behavioral model for treating anxiety disorders. Across self-reports, parent reports, and behavioral observations, statistical texts provided support for the therapeutic utility of the intervention. In terms of clinical significance, many treated subjects were without a diagnosis at posttreatment and at follow-up, and were found to be within normal limits on several measures. For example, parent reports on the Child Behavior Checklist (CBCL)

(Achenbach & Edelbrock, 1983) revealed a clinically significant improvement for 14 of 17 subjects whose initial internalizing T scores fell in the clinical range. Using parent-structured interview data, 64% of the treated subjects did not have a diagnosis at the completion of treatment, while only 7% of the wait-list subjects demonstrated any change. Concerning self-report, a significantly greater number of treated subjects, compared to wait-list subjects, were found to be within normal limits on the measures on which they once reported clinical levels of distress. Behavioral observation data indicated a visible reduction in anxious behavior. At 1-year follow-up, the reductions in anxiety were maintained. Overall, the outcomes of this randomized clinical trial provided support for cognitive-behavioral therapy as a method of treating anxiety disorders in childhood.

Case Study

Heidi, a 10-year-old girl was referred for treatment because of her avoidance behavior and extreme social concerns. Her apprehension and fear that others would make fun of her and laugh at her prevented her from doing things that she wanted to do, such as playing on the neighborhood softball team or telephoning a friend to get together. During the first sessions, Heidi was extremely shy and fearful. She did not look at the therapist, answered questions in an inaudible whisper, if at all, and maintained an obviously tense body posture. As the sessions progressed, Heidi was able to recognize when she was feeling anxious and to use problem-solving techniques to create coping self-talk and coping actions for specific situations to ease her anxiety. She was educated in new ways of looking at and thinking about future experiences.

Once these skills were developed, a hierarchy of anxiety-provoking situations was created. The proposed experiences were tailored to Heidi's needs, which meant being centered on social concerns. The lower-level situations involved experiences such as buying a soda or asking someone the time. Before each of these experiences, Heidi went through the coping steps she had learned for dealing with anxiety. She first decided how nervous she was, using physiological signs, and tried to get her body to relax. She then acknowledged what she was thinking or what she was expecting to happen; in her case, the concerns were usually about others laughing and making fun of her, and about her doing something like tripping or making a fool of herself. Once she figured out what was worrying her, she and the therapist came up with ideas to help cope with the situation—things she could do or say to herself to help her feel less anxious. For example, how likely was it that others would laugh at her when she asked the time? Had she ever seen anyone trip, and if so, how did others react? Did they refuse to ever be seen with this person? After a plan was set and Heidi felt ready, she then did whatever was decided on (e.g., ask for the time). Once she completed the task, Heidi met with the therapist again to review how she felt, how she coped with the situation, and if it was comparable to what she had anticipated. With each in vivo experience, Heidi gained competence and confidence in her ability to get through these anxiety-provoking situations. She felt a sense of achievement and was ready to tackle the next situation, which would elevate her to a higher level of anxiety. Some of the later in vivos involved playing a game with a peer and giving a speech in front of a small audience. Heidi and her therapist processed each experience before and after it occurred. Afterward, she rated herself as to how she handled the situation and rewarded herself for coping, even if she was not entirely successful.

Heidi was initially diagnosed with both overanxious disorder and avoidant disorder, according to DSM-III-R criteria using standardized interviews with both parents and Heidi before treatment began. At posttreatment, she was without a diagnosis on the same structured interviews as reported by her parents and herself. Her scores on the CBCL (mother's report) demonstrated clinically significant levels on both the Anxiety/Withdrawn scale and the Internalizing Disorders scale before treatment. At posttreatment, both scores were well within the normal range of functioning. On a child report scale, the Coping Questionnaire, she reported extreme difficulties in coping with specific situations she viewed as stressful before treatment, but reported herself to be much better able to handle these same situations after treatment.

On completion of treatment, Heidi became involved in the extracurricular activities that she had wanted to pursue but was afraid to out of fear that she would be teased. She initiated new friendships and was more vocal about her opinions. Her family, teachers, and neighbors noticed the changes in her, which further encouraged her to explore new friendships and activities.

FAMILY THERAPY

Family therapy views psychopathology as resulting from dysfunctional family systems rather than from difficulties within the individual (Haley, 1987; Minuchin, 1974). Each family has its own set of rules, communication patterns, and expectations for its members, and these combine to form the interpersonal system. When there is evidence of psychopathology, the family therapist's interventions focus on changing the interaction patterns that sustain the family's difficulties.

Symptom Bearer

In dysfunctional family systems, there is usually an individual who is seen as the *symptom bearer* (Minuchin & Fishman, 1981). The individual, often a child, identified as the problem helps to balance the dysfunctionality of the system. The behavior of one member in the family will have an influence on other members, and the way the system responds will influence the individual. The individual bears the pain and distress of the family system (Everett & Volgy, 1993). The child who is seen as having difficulties often serves a purpose in the family system. Therefore, the system is defended against change.

As an illustration, Frank was brought to therapy because of his school refusal behavior.

He suffered from asthma and frequently missed school because of his report of frequent attacks. His parents constantly fought over this issue of sending him to school, with his mother wanting to force him and his father considering him too sick to go. During one meeting with his father, it became apparent that Frank's school refusal served a major role in the family system. As reported by his father, whenever Frank's asthma began to subside, Frank's father fell into a depression because of his unhappiness in his marriage. He had thought about leaving his wife many times but remained for his children's sake. Once his father was depressed, Frank suddenly became ill again, and his father's depression lifted to care for his son. There was no talk of divorce or unhappiness because Frank's parents' main concern was Frank's health. Although, with individual therapy, Frank began to go to school more frequently and his asthma became far less severe, the family remained dysfunctional. To demonstrate the system's intense need for a symptom bearer to balance the system and hold it together, a younger sibling took over the job of symptom bearer with complaints of severe headaches.

Strategic Family Therapy

One theoretical framework of family therapy techniques is strategic family therapy. The strategic family therapist is active in directing the therapy (Haley, 1973). The therapist conceptualizes the family's problem and sets clear goals to allow the problem to be solved. Specific therapeutic interventions are created for each defined problem to make changes in the system. Alleviation of the target problem involves the modification of the entire family system. The family does not adapt easily to new ways of interacting; therefore, the therapist uses subtle techniques and interventions to help the family change (Fruzzetti & Jacobson, 1991).

Paradox is a technique of strategic family therapy. In paradox, the therapist directs the client to complete tasks that appear to be in opposition to the goal of therapy. The reasoning behind paradox is the belief that the family will resist change. For example, a therapist instructs a school-refusing child not to go to school and the parents not to allow him to go to school. It is assumed that the family will resist the therapist's influence and do exactly the opposite of the instructions—in this case, send the child to school. If the family is extremely invested in the therapy and follows the therapist's instructions, this is also positive because the therapist has been able to influence and control the problem behavior. Paradox can be a risky procedure if the family does follow the instructions. It is not desirable to have children miss school, and truant behavior may cause more problems for the child in school.

Reframing is another strategic therapy technique enabling the family to view a behavior or situation in an alternative way. Restructuring the behavior in a context will allow it to be understood more positively. An adolescent who refuses to talk to his mother may be described by the family as cold and uncaring. The therapist can reframe the family's understanding of the teenager's behavior as his desire to reach out to them but not to know how.

Structural Family Therapy

One popular method uses the techniques of structural family therapy. Structural theory states that to alleviate disorder or to change the individual, the structure of the family must be changed. Structural therapy addresses the relationships between people in the family. It works to change the family structure, such as by reorganizing hierarchies and maintaining boundaries within subsystems of the family (e.g., parents, siblings).

Minuchin and Fishman (1981), prominent structural family therapists, describe the relationships of members in a dysfunctional family system as being *enmeshed* or *disengaged*. In disengaged families, the boundaries among its members are inflexible and the people are emotionally distant. These families can be distinguished from enmeshed families, whose boundaries are weak, with excessive closeness among members. The therapist helps to make the relationships more balanced by distancing enmeshed members and increasing the involvement of disengaged members. The therapist uses the session to unbalance the system to make changes in the family structure. For example, the therapist may sit between two enmeshed people to prevent them physically from colluding with each other, or may ask two members who do not communicate well with each other to discuss an issue together.

Family structures change continually throughout different phases of life. When these changes occur, the family is most vulnerable to dysfunction and psychopathology. The ability of the family to adapt to these developments determines the course of the family's adjustment. Changes in family structure are produced as individuals change each other. As one member develops, the structure alters to accommodate the new system. When the system is resistant to change, psychopathology can result.

Families form patterns of interactions, which, in turn, dictate rules of behavior in the family. These rules are generalized by individual family members to the outside world. A person functions with only part of his or her capabilities in relation to specific contexts. Although the individual has many abilities, he or she tends to function according to the rules set by the family structure. The therapist uses all the resources and capabilities of the individual to change the family structure (Colapinto, 1991).

Therapist's Role

The therapist's behavior is the catalyst of change in family therapy. The therapist acknowledges and directs the family system to help change its structure. Joining the family enables the therapist to direct the interactions between family members. Becoming part of the family and joining the system also allows the therapist to support and ally with family members, or to be critical of the system or of individuals, and to unbalance the system while still maintaining trust. The therapist tries to restructure the way the family thinks about things and focuses on issues that may be controversial. Joining, unbalancing, focusing, and restructuring are all techniques used by structural family therapists to alter the family structure.

Multisystematic Therapy (MST)

Henggeler and colleagues (Henggeler & Borduin, 1990; Henggeler, Melton, & Smith, 1992) have applied and evaluated MST with serious juvenile offenders. MST is a combination of family therapy and behavior therapy. The approach to treatment follows the assumption that people are involved in many complex systems (e.g., family, peer relationships, school activities). Dysfunctional interactions in any of these arenas may cause and maintain behavior problems. Treatment works to change these interactions, yet also emphasizes the individual's needs and particular circumstances.

An examination of the effectiveness of MST (Henggeler et al., 1992) showed promising results across multiple measurements. Results included significant decreases on measures of criminal behavior and peer aggression, as well as increased family cohesion in the families receiving MST. The authors also reported equal success with adolescents of both genders, different ethnic backgrounds, and different levels of family cohesion. Though MST is promising, evaluations of follow-up are needed. In addition, it would be informative to compare MST to other treatments.

Evaluation

There are few methodologically sound research studies assessing the efficacy of systems family therapy. Nevertheless, reviews of this therapy (e.g., Hazelrigg, Cooper, & Borduin, 1987) often conclude that family therapy is as effective as other approaches (e.g., individual therapy, other modes of family therapy). More specifically, the hypotheses constructed by Haley and Minuchin have not been subjected to rigorous evaluations; hence, their efficacy has not yet been demonstrated. However, behavioral sys-

tems approaches have been evaluated scientifically and show encouraging results (e.g., Alexander & Parsons, 1973; Henggeler et al., 1992). Two solid studies by Alexander and colleagues (Alexander, Barton, Schiavo, & Parsons, 1976; Alexander & Parsons, 1973), though dated, assessed the efficacy of a behavioral family therapy in treating delinquent adolescents. The results were positive, demonstrating more adaptive family functioning and less recurrence of delinquent behavior in the treated families. Although this study supports a systems family therapy, it also includes cognitive and behavioral treatment components: demonstrating the effectiveness of an integrative family therapy and not testing a purely systems hypothesis. Overall, more research is needed to determine the efficacy of structural and systems family therapies.

Parent Training

Parent training is one type of family therapy that has been evaluated through empirical research. Parent training is based on the assumption that children's difficulties arise from dysfunctional interaction patterns between parent and child. The maladaptive behaviors demonstrated by the child are thought to be learned and reinforced by the parents (Fruzzetti & Jacobson, 1991). Parent training is used to alter the familial interaction patterns and to encourage prosocial behaviors rather than negative or inappropriate behaviors (Kazdin, 1991). Parents are taught new ways of interacting and behavior management skills that they can apply to correct or maintain simple and appropriate child behaviors. Positive reinforcement and mild punishment are often used to manage the chosen behaviors. Once the parents have mastered these skills, they can be implemented with more serious behaviors. For example, parents may first implement these strategies regarding a chore they would like their child to complete (e.g., set the dinner table). They are taught appropriate ways of interacting with the child regarding the completion of the task. When the parents have mastered these skills, they can begin to address more problematic behaviors.

Patterson (1982) discussed parent–child interaction patterns in more detail by defining "coercive family processes" as the cause of children's problem behavior. According to Patterson, this process begins when the child behaves in an aversive way and the parent responds to the child in an equally aversive, negative manner. The parent and child get caught up in a cycle of coercion and negative behavior. The responses and behaviors of both parent and child continue to escalate aversively until one of them ends the interaction. This, in turn, negatively reinforces the other person's behavior. Additionally, the child learns from the parent that coercion is an effective way to cope with interpersonal conflict (McBurnett, Hobbs, & Lahey, 1989). By ending this cycle and changing the interactional patterns, deviant behavior can be reduced (Gurman, Kniskern, & Pinsoff, 1986; Kazdin, 1984).

Parent Training Programs

Patterson and his colleagues have conducted research in the area of parent training with antisocial boys (Patterson, 1986). Patterson's (1974) program begins by giving the parents a text to read about learning theory and child management techniques. The parents are asked to pinpoint problem behaviors and are taught to track and monitor a series of target behaviors for a short period of time every day. They are called daily during this stage of treatment to encourage recording of observations of their child's behavior. The next phase involves creating a reinforcement system in which the child can earn points for appropriate behaviors that can be exchanged for daily rewards of their own choosing. Points are given for prosocial behaviors and taken away for negative behaviors. Additionally, the parents are taught to use positive social reinforcement (e.g., smiles, encouraging comments) for appropriate behaviors and mild punishment (e.g., time-out, loss of privileges) for noncompliance and inappropriate behaviors. Parents learn how to problem-solve and negotiate with their children in areas of disagreement.

This program has also been modified for adolescents (Bank, Marlowe, Reid, Patterson, & Weinrott, 1988). In addition to the program described, parents supervise and monitor their adolescent's behavior, punish for delinquency through the loss of privileges and assigning of chores rather than through time-out, and are instructed to report deviant behavior to the authorities. The adolescent is more involved in the parent training sessions and has some input in the process.

Forehand and McMahon (1983) have used and evaluated a variation of parent training. Parents are taught to give more attention to their children for appropriate behaviors and to decrease the number of criticisms and commands. They are instructed in using positive verbal reinforcement and physical contact for prosocial behaviors while ignoring inappropriate behaviors. The second phase teaches parents to give clear, appropriate commands. Parents learn to praise children for compliance and to administer punishment for noncompliance (e.g., time-out). When a child is given a command, the parent is told to allow the child some time to comply and to reward the child for compliance. If the child does not comply, a time-out is instituted and the command is given again. Parenting skills are taught, using behavioral techniques such as modeling, role play, behavioral rehearsal and feedback, and homework assignments.

Robin and Foster (1989) described a parent training program geared to adolescents in which they participate in the treatment. The therapist works with the family to change the familial and communication patterns that led to difficulties in the past. Family members are taught to problem-solve together in an effective, democratic way and to communicate more positively with each other. The therapist accomplishes this through examples, role play, and feedback, as well as practice assignments at home.

The therapy itself usually consists of 7–20 sessions, depending on the severity of the case. First, a therapeutic contract is established between the family and the therapist. Therapeutic goals are set, a trusting relationship is formed between the therapist and the family, and problem-solving techniques are introduced. During the next phase of treatment, the family learns skills such as problem solving and better methods of communication to help deal with conflict. The therapist identifies negative sequences of interaction and models more appropriate and effective means of communicating. Once these skills have been mastered, the next stage involves solving the most conflict-ridden problems. During the last phase, the therapist withdraws from the family's attempts to implement their newly learned skills and effective ways of communicating, problem solving, and negotiating.

Evaluation

Parent training has been implemented in treating children with ADHD (Barkley, 1990; Braswell & Bloomquist, 1991), but it is most often used and well researched in changing the behaviors of aggressive, conduct-disordered, and antisocial children (Forehand & McMahon, 1983; Kazdin, 1987; Patterson, 1974). Overall, it has been found to be an effective means of treatment (McBurnett, Hobbs, & Lahey, 1989; McMahon & Forehand, 1984; Patterson, 1974). For example, studies have demonstrated parent training's efficacy in reducing aggression and changing children's behavior at home and school to normative levels (Patterson, 1974; Wells, Forehand, & Griest, 1980), compared to other family-based treatments, attention-placebo, and no-treatment conditions (Patterson, Chamberlain, & Reid, 1982; Wiltz & Patterson, 1974). Effects have been found to be maintained at a 4.5-year follow-up (Baum & Forehand, 1981).

In terms of adolescent behavior, the results are a bit more mixed. Results of the Patterson treatment designed for adolescents (Marlow et al., 1988) demonstrated a decrease in inappropriate behaviors; however, the adolescents reverted back to delinquency at 1-year follow-up. Additionally, there did not appear to be a change in family interaction patterns. After parent training for delinquent adolescents, the families showed improvement on two measures of familial conflict, but not on audiotapes of familial interactions. Robin (1981) reported differences in familial interactions. However, when changes in conflict levels were compared to those resulting from other treatments, there were no significant differences; all treatments reduced the conflict in the family. Research shows that direct, skill-oriented treatments are effective in dealing with parent–adolescent conflict (Foster & Robin, 1988); however, there is a strong need for more empirical testing.

Wells and Forehand (1985) suggest that parent training is most effective when the treatment is not time limited and when the therapist is experienced. Parent training has been found to be most effective when the parent and child do not engage in an excessive number of aversive responses and behaviors (Dumas, 1984) and when the parents are involved in a social support network (Dumas & Wahler, 1985). It is less effective when the family is isolated or of lower socioeconomic status (Webster-Stratton, 1985). Wells and Egan (1988) have found parent training to be more efficacious than a family systems approach, according to behavioral observations of parent and child.

Some research has asserted that parent training is often not sufficient as the sole mode of treatment in treating aggression (Patterson et al., 1982). Therefore, a recent study (Kazdin, Siegel, & Bass, 1992) evaluated the effects of parent management training, problem-solving skills training (a cognitive-behavioral approach), and a combination of the two in the treatment of antisocial youth. Results demonstrated that all three were found to be effective in improving children's overall functioning and behavior, which was evidenced both at home and at school immediately after treatment and at 1-year follow-up. However, more of the children who received a combination of parent training and problem solving fell into the normative range of functioning than did children in the other groups. Additionally, the children and parents with the combination of treatments demonstrated decreases in aggressive behavior and in parental stress and depression. However, although parent training is one of the few types of family therapy that has been empirically tested, more research is needed to assess its efficacy as the sole mode of treatment.

Case Example

As an illustration of the methods and efficacy of parent training, consider a case discussed by Kazdin (1991). Shawn, a 7-year-old boy, was referred for aggressive outbursts at home and in school. He was described as fighting in school with his peers, being disruptive in class, arguing and throwing tantrums at home, coming home late at night, and stealing from his stepfather. Parent training was provided to Shawn's mother during 16 two-hour weekly sessions. This time frame is typical for parent training, which usually includes 16–20 weekly sessions with the parents.

The goal of treatment with Shawn's mother, and with parent training in general, is to change the interaction patterns between the child and the parents. The parents are taught to behave differently in regard to their children. The sessions aimed at helping Shawn's mother identify and observe concrete behaviors that were problematic. She was trained in using positive reinforcement regularly for desired behaviors and mild punishment for undesired behaviors. Shawn and his mother met to discuss and negotiate the program and to formulate a contractual agreement. The therapist called twice a week to see how the program was working and to correct any problems or difficulties immediately. During the session, Shawn's mother role-played with the therapist to practice effective ways of responding to her child.

In parent training, the parent and therapist together design a program to address small behaviors, which allows the parents the opportunity to implement and practice the skills they have learned in treatment. In Shawn's case, they decided to request of him small household chores. They also implemented 5-minute time-out for fighting; however, if Shawn accepted the time-out without difficulty, it was reduced to 2 minutes.

As the parent training progressed, other behaviors were added to the program in which

Shawn could earn points to be exchanged for rewards and special privileges. A home-based reinforcement program was implemented to help change Shawn's aggressive behaviors in school. Teachers identified target behaviors and evaluated his performance daily in terms of those behaviors. He earned additional points at home for good teacher evaluations.

Kazdin reported that after 5 months, Shawn's behavior at home and at school improved. His parents felt more confident in their ability to manage him, and there was much less arguing at home. At school, although Shawn occasionally got into fights with peers or the teacher, his overall behavior improved and he demonstrated less aggression than before treatment.

SUMMARY AND CONCLUSIONS

Various types of psychotherapy are used in treating children and adolescents with psychological difficulties. Of the different treatments available, behavioral approaches, cognitive-behavioral techniques, and parent management training are the most well researched and empirically tested as efficacious methods of treatment. Nevertheless, psychology is a continually growing field, and additional research on the effectiveness of other treatment approaches (especially when developed for specific disorders of children and adolescents) is warranted. Modern versions of psychodynamic treatments for children require research examination. Systemic family therapy is a promising avenue of treatment, again requiring rigorous research evaluation. Overall, although some studies lend support and validation for particular modes of therapy for certain disorders, there are many more research questions in need of proper attention.

Acknowledgement

Preparation of this chapter was facilitated by a grant from the National Institutes of Mental Health (44042) awarded to Philip C. Kendall.

NOTES

1. Pharmacological treatments were included in this review and were found to be less effective than psychological treatment for enuresis (Houts et al., in press). In general, psychopharmacology has not proved to be as effective in the treatment of childhood disorders such as depression (Geller, Cooper, McCombs, Graham, & Wells, 1989) and schizophrenia (Gadow, 1991). This conclusion is contrary to the adult literature, which demonstrates the efficacy of medications for depression and schizophrenia. Attention is given to the pharmacological treatment of attention deficit hyperactivity disorder in the following pages.

2. Rational-emotive therapy (Ellis, 1962) is a variant of cognitive-behavioral treatment that has been used with children and adolescents (Bernard & Joyce, in press). Its basic goal is to reduce the intensity of negative emotions which are making the client unhappy and making it harder to solve problems and achieve goals (Bernard & Joyce, 1993). The way in which the client views his or her circumstances, through distorted and irrational cognitions, leads to an exacerbation of negative feelings. The therapist's task is to modify the client's irrational assumptions, evaluations, expectations, and beliefs. Together the therapist and client dispute these irrational beliefs and reformulate them into more rational ideas (Bernard & Joyce, 1984). Rational-emotive therapy has been implemented as a treatment for many childhood difficulties, including depression (DiGiuseppe, 1990), anxiety and phobias (Grieger & Boyd, 1983), conduct disorder (DiGiuseppe, 1988), and social isolation (Halford, 1983).

REFERENCES

Abramson, L. Y., Seligman, M. E. P., & Teasdale, J. D. (1978). Learned helplessness in humans: Critique and reformulation. *Journal of Abnormal Psychology, 87,* 49–74.

Achenbach, T. M., & Edelbrock, C. S. (1983). *Manual for the Child Behavior Checklist profile.* Burlington: University of Vermont Press.

Adelman, H. S., Kaser-Boyd, N., & Taylor, L. (1984). Children's participation in consent for psychotherapy and their subsequent response to treatment. *Journal of Clinical Child Psychology, 13,* 170–178.

Alexander, J. F., Barton, C., Schiavo, R. S., & Parsons, B. V. (1976). Systems-behavioral intervention with families of delinquents: Therapist characteristics, family behavior, and outcome. *Journal of Consulting and Clinical Psychology, 44,* 656–664.

Alexander, J. F., & Parsons, B. V. (1973). Short-term behavioral intervention with delinquent families: Impact on family process and recidivism. *Journal of Abnormal Child Psychology, 81,* 219–225.

Bandura, A. (1969). *Principles of behavior modification.* New York: Holt, Rinehart & Winston.

Bank, L., Marlowe, J. H., Reid, J. B., Patterson, G. R., & Weinrott, M. R. (1991). A comparative evaluation of parent training interventions for families of chronic delinquents. *Journal of Abnormal Child Psychology, 19,* 15–33.

Barkley, R. A. (1990). *Attention deficit hyperactivity disorder: A handbook for diagnosis and treatment.* New York: Guilford Press.

Barlow, D. H. (1988). *Anxiety and its disorders: The nature and treatment of anxiety and panic.* New York: Guilford Press.

Baum, C. G., & Forehand, R. (1981). Long-term follow-up assessment of parent training by use of multiple outcome measures. *Behavior Therapy, 12,* 643–652.

Beck, A. T. (1976). *Cognitive therapy and emotional disorders.* New York: International Universities Press.

Bernard, M. E., & DiGiuseppe, R. D. (Eds.). (1990). Rational-emotive therapy and school psychology. *School Psychology Review* (Mini Series), *19,* 287–293.

Bernard, M. E., & Joyce, M. R. (1984). *Rational-emotive therapy with children and adolescents: Theory, treatment strategies, preventative methods.* New York: Wiley.

Bernard, M. E., & Joyce, M. R. (1993). Rational-emotive therapy with children and adolescents. In T. R. Kratochwill & R. Morris (Eds.), *Handbook of psychotherapy with children and adolescents* (pp. 221–246). Boston: Allyn & Bacon.

Bloomingdale, L. M. (Ed.). (1988). *Attention deficit disorder: New research in attention, treatment, and psychopharmacology* (Vol. 3). New York: Pergamon Press.

Bornstein, M. R., Bellack, A. S., & Hersen, M. (1980). Social skills training for highly aggressive children. *Behavior Modification, 4,* 173–186.

Bornstein, P. H., & Kazdin, A. E. (Eds.). (1985).

Handbook of clinical behavior therapy with children. Homewood, IL: Dorsey Press.

Braswell, L., & Bloomquist, M. (1991). *Cognitive-behavioral therapy with ADHD children: Child, family, and school intervention.* New York: Guilford Press.

Breslau, N., Davis, G., & Prabucki, K. (1988). Depressed mothers as informants in family history research—Are they accurate? *Psychiatry Research, 24,* 345–359.

Carlson, C. L., & Lahey, B. B. (1988). Behavior classroom interventions with children exhibiting conduct disorders or attention deficit disorders with hyperactivity. In J. C. Witt, S. M. Elliott, & F. M. Gresham (Eds.), *The handbook of behavior therapy in education,* (pp. 653–677). New York: Plenum Press.

Carlson, C. L., Pelham, W. E., Milich, R., & Dixon, J. (1991). Single and combined effects of methylphenidate and behavior therapy on the classroom performance of children with attention-deficit hyperactivity disorder. *Journal of Abnormal Child Psychology, 20,* 213–232.

Casey, R. J., & Berman, J. S. (1985). The outcome of psychotherapy with children. *Psychological Bulletin, 98,* 388–400.

Cashdan, S. (1988). *Object relations therapy: Using the relationship.* New York: Norton.

Colapinto, J. (1991). Structural family therapy. In A. S. Gurman & D. P. Kniskern (Eds.), *Handbook of family therapy* (Vol. 2, pp. 417–443). New York: Brunner/Mazel.

Compas, B. E., Friedland-Bandes, R., Bastien, R., & Adelman, H. S. (1981). Parent and causal attributions related to the child's clinical picture. *Journal of Abnormal Child Psychology, 9,* 389–397.

Costello, E. J. (1990). Child psychiatric epidemiology: Implications for clinical research and practice. In B. B. Lahey & A. E. Kazdin (Eds.), *Advances in clinical child psychology* (Vol. 13, pp. 53–90). New York: Plenum Press.

DiGiuseppe, R. D. (1988). Cognitive-behavior therapy with families of conduct-disordered children. In N. Epstein, S. Schnebinger, & W. Dryden (Eds.), *Cognitive behavior therapy with families,* (pp. 183–214). New York: Brunner/Mazel.

DiGiuseppe, R. D. (1990). Rational-emotive assessment of school-age children. In M. E. Bernard & R. D. DiGiuseppe (Eds.), Rational-emotive therapy and school psychology, *School Psychology Review* (Mini Series), *19,* 287–293.

Dobson, K. S., & Shaw, B. F. (1989). The use of treatment manuals in cognitive therapy: Experiences and issues. *Journal of Consulting and Clinical Psychology, 56,* 673–681.

Dodge, K. A. (1985). Attributional bias in aggressive children. In P. C. Kendall (Ed.), *Advances in cognitive-behavioral research and therapy* (Vol. 4, pp. 75–111). New York: Academic Press.

Dumas, J. E. (1984). Interactional correlates of treatment outcome in behavioral parent training. *Journal of Consulting and Clinical Psychology, 52,* 946–954.

Dumas, J. E., & Wahler, R. G. (1985). Indiscriminate mothering as a contextual factor in aggressive-oppositional child behavior: "Damned if you do and damned if you don't." *Journal of Abnormal Child Psychology, 13,* 1–17.

DuPaul, G. J., Guevremont, D. C., & Barkley, R. A. (1991). Attention-deficit hyperactivity disorder. In T. R. Kratochwill & R. J. Morris (Eds.), *The practice of child therapy* 2nd ed., (pp. 115–144). New York: Pergamon Press.

Eisenberg, L., & Gruenberg, E. M. (1961). The current status of secondary prevention in child psychiatry. *American Journal of Orthopsychiatry, 31,* 355–367.

Ellis, A. (1962). *Reason and emotion in psychotherapy.* New York: Stuart.

Ellis, A., & Bernard, M. E. (Eds.). (1983). *Rational-emotive approaches to the problems of childhood.* New York: Plenum Press.

Epstein, N., Schnebinger, S., & Dryden, W. (Eds.). (1988). *Cognitive behavior therapy with families.* New York: Brunner/Mazel.

Everett, C., & Volgy, S. S. (1993). Treating the child in systemic family therapy. In T. R. Kratochwill & R. J. Morris (Eds.), *Handbook of psychotherapy with children and adolescents* (pp. 247–257). Boston: Allyn & Bacon.

Eysenck, H. J. (1952). The effects of psychotherapy: An evaluation. *Journal of Consulting Psychology, 16,* 319–324.

Forehand, R., Lautenschlager, G. J., Faust, J., & Graziano, W. G. (1986). Parent perceptions and parent–child interactions in clinic-referred children: A preliminary investigation of the effects of maternal depressive moods. *Behaviour Research and Therapy, 24,* 73–75.

Forehand, R., & McMahon, R, J. (1983). *Helping the noncompliant child: A clinician's guide to parent training.* New York: Guilford Press.

Foster, S. L., & Robin, A. L. (1988). Family conflict and communication in adolescence. In E. J. Mash & L. G. Terdal (Eds.), *Behavioral assessment of childhood disorders* (2nd ed., pp. 717–755). New York: Guilford Press.

Frame, C., Matson, J. L., Sonis, W. A., Fialkov, M. J., & Kazdin, A. E. (1982). Behavioral treatment of depression in a prepubertal child. *Journal of Behavior Therapy and Experimental Psychiatry, 3,* 239–243.

Freud, A. (1927). *Introduction to the technique of child analysis.* New York: Nervous and Mental Disease Publishing Co.

Freud, A. (1946). *The psychological treatment of children: Technical lectures and essays.* New York: International Universities Press.

Freud, A. (1980). *Normality and pathology in childhood: Assessments of development.* London: Hogarth Press.

Fruzzetti, A. E., & Jacobson, N. S. (1991). Marital and family therapy. In M. Hersen, A. E. Kazdin, & A. S. Bellack, (Eds.), *The clinical psychology handbook* (2nd ed., pp. 643–666). New York: Pergamon Press.

Gadow, K. D. (1991). Clinical issues in child and adolescent psychopharmacology. *Journal of Consulting and Clinical Psychology, 59,* 842–852.

Garfield, S. L., & Bergin, A. E. (Eds.). (1986). *Handbook of psychotherapy and behavior change* (3rd ed.). New York: Wiley.

Geller, B., Cooper, T. B., McCombs, H. G., Graham, D., & Wells, J. (1989). Double-blind placebo-controlled study of nortriptyline in depressed children using a "fixed plasma level" design. *Psychopharmacology Bulletin, 25,* 101–108.

Ginther, L. J., & Roberts, M. C. (1982). A test of mastery versus coping modeling in the reduction of children's dental fears. *Child and Family Behavior Therapy, 4,* 41–52.

Grieger, R. M., & Boyd, J. D. (1983). Childhood anxieties, fears, and phobias. In A. Ellis & M. E. Bernard (Eds.), *Rational-emotive approaches to the problems of childhood,* (pp. 211–240). New York: Plenum Press.

Gurman, A. S., & Kniskern, D. P. (1991). *Handbook of family therapy* (Vol. 2). New York: Brunner/Mazel.

Gurman, A. S., Kniskern, D. P., & Pinsoff, W. M. (1986). Research on the process and outcome of marital and family therapy. In S. L. Garfield & A. E. Bergin (Eds.), *Handbook of psychotherapy and behavior change* (3rd ed., pp. 565–626). New York: Wiley.

Haley, J. (1973). *Uncommon therapy.* New York: Norton.

Haley, J. (1987). *Problem-solving therapy* (3rd ed.). San Francisco: Jossey-Bass.

Halford, K. (1983). Teaching rational self-talk to help socially isolated children and youth. In A. Ellis & M. E. Bernard (Eds.), *Rational-emotive approaches to the problems of childhood* (pp. 241–265). New York: Plenum Press.

Hazelrigg, M. D., Cooper, H. M., & Borduin, C. (1987). Evaluating the effectiveness of family therapies: An integrative review and analysis. *Psychological Bulletin, 101,* 428–442.

Heinicke, C. M., & Goldman, A. (1960). Research on psychotherapy with children: A review and suggestions for further study. *American Journal of Orthopsychiatry, 30,* 483–494.

Henggeler, S. W., & Borduin, C. M. (1990). *Family therapy and beyond: A multisystematic approach to treating the behavior problems of children and adolescents.* Pacific Grove, CA: Brooks/Cole.

Henggeler, S. W., Melton, G. B., & Smith, L. A. (1992). Family preservation using multisystematic therapy: An effective alternative to incarcerating serious juvenile offenders. *Journal of Consulting and Clinical Psychology, 60,* 953–961.

Hersen, M., Kazdin, A. E., & Bellack, A. S. (Eds.). (1991). *The clinical psychology handbook* (2nd ed.). New York: Pergamon Press.

Hersen, M., & Van Hasselt, V. B. (Eds.). (1987). *Behavior therapy with children and adolescents: A clinical approach.* New York: Wiley.

Hood-Williams, J. (1960). The results of psychotherapy with children: A reevaluation. *Journal of Consulting Psychology, 24,* 84–88.

Houts, A. C., Berman, J. S., & Abramson, H. (in press). The effectiveness of psychological and pharmacological treatments for nocturnal enuresis. *Journal of Consulting and Clinical Psychology.*

Hughes, J. (1993). Behavior therapy. In T. R. Kratochwill & R. J. Morris (Eds.), *Handbook of psychotherapy with children and adolescents,* (pp. 185–220). Boston: Allyn & Bacon.

Ingram, R., & Kendall, P. C. (1986). Cognitive clinical psychology: Implications of an information processing perspective. In R. Ingram (Ed.), *Information processing approaches to clinical psychology,* (pp. 3–21). New York: Academic Press.

Kane, M. T., & Kendall, P. C. (1989). Anxiety disorders in children: A multiple-baseline evaluation of cognitive-behavioral treatment. *Behavior Therapy, 20,* 499–508.

Kaslow, N. J., & Rehm, L. P. (1991). Childhood

depression. In T. R. Kratochwill & R. J. Morris (Eds.), *The practice of child therapy* (2nd ed., pp. 43–75). New York: Pergamon Press.

Kazdin, A. E. (1974). Comparative effects of some variations of covert modeling. *Journal of Behavior Therapy and Experimental Psychiatry, 5*, 224–231.

Kazdin, A. E. (1984). Treatment of conduct disorders. In J. Williams & R. Spitzer (Eds.), *Psychotherapy research: Where are we and where should we go?* (pp. 3–28). New York: Guilford Press.

Kazdin, A. E. (1987b). Treatment of antisocial behavior in children: Current status and future directions. *Psychological Bulletin, 102*, 187–203.

Kazdin, A. E. (1987a). *Conduct disorders in childhood and adolescence.* Newbury Park, CA: Sage.

Kazdin, A. E. (1988). *Child psychotherapy: Developing and identifying effective treatments.* New York: Pergamon Press.

Kazdin, A. E. (1991). Aggressive behavior and conduct disorder. In T. R. Kratochwill & R. J. Morris (Eds.), *The practice of child therapy* (2nd ed., (pp. 174–221). New York: Pergamon Press.

Kazdin, A. E., Esveldt-Dawson, K., French, N. H., & Unis, A. S. (1987). Problem-solving skills training and relationship therapy in the treatment of antisocial child behavior. *Journal of Consulting and Clinical Psychology, 55*, 76–85.

Kazdin, A. E., Siegel, T. C., & Bass, D. (1992). Cognitive problem-solving skills training and parent management training in the treatment of antisocial behavior in children. *Journal of Consulting and Clinical Psychology, 60*, 733–747.

Kendall, P. C. (1985). Toward a cognitive-behavioral model of child psychopathology and a critique of related interventions. *Journal of Abnormal Child Psychology, 13*, 357–372.

Kendall, P. C. (Ed.). (1991a). *Child and adolescent therapy: Cognitive-behavioral procedures.* New York: Guilford Press.

Kendall, P. C. (1991b). Guiding theory for treating children and adolescents. In P. C. Kendall (Ed.), *Child and adolescent therapy: Cognitive-behavioral procedures* (pp. 3–24). New York: Guilford Press.

Kendall, P. C. (1993). Cognitive-behavioral therapies with youth: Guiding theory, current status, and emerging developments. *Journal of Consulting and Clinical Psychology,61*, 235–247.

Kendall, P. C. (1994). Treating anxiety disorders in youth: Results of a randomized clinical trial. *Journal of Consulting and Clinical Psychology, 62, 100–110.*

Kendall, P. C., & Braswell, L. (1985). *Cognitive-behavioral therapy for impulsive children.* New York: Guilford Press.

Kendall, P. C., & Braswell, L. (1993). *Cognitive-behavioral therapy for impulsive children* (2nd ed.). New York: Guilford Press.

Kendall, P. C., Chansky, T., Freidman, M., Kim, R., Kortlander, E., Sessa, F., & Siqueland, L. (1991). Treating anxiety disorders in children and adolescents. In P. C. Kendall (Ed.), *Child and adolescent therapy: Cognitive-behavioral procedures* (pp. 131–164). New York: Guilford Press.

Kendall, P. C., & Grove, W. (1988). Normative comparisons in therapy outcome. *Behavioral Assessment, 10*, 147–158.

Kendall, P. C., Kane, M., Howard, B., & Siqueland, L. (1989). *Cognitive-behavioral therapy for anxious children: Treatment manual.* Available from the first author, Department of Psychology, Temple University, Philadelphia, PA 19122.

Kendall, P. C., & MacDonald, J. P. (1993). Cognition in the psychopathology of youth and implications for treatment. In K. S. Dobson & P. C. Kendall (Eds.), *Psychopathology and cognition,* (pp. 387–432). San Diego, CA: Academic Press.

Kendall, P. C., & Norton-Ford, J. D. (1982). Therapy outcome research methods. In P. C. Kendall & J. N. Butcher (Eds.), *Handbook of research methods in clinical psychology* (pp. 429–460). New York: Wiley.

Kendall, P. C., Ronan, K., & Epps, J. (1990). Aggression in children/adolescents: Cognitive-behavioral treatment perspective. In D. Pepler & K. Rubin (Eds.), *Development and treatment of childhood aggression* (pp. 341–360). Hilsdale, NJ: Erlbaum.

Kendall, P. C., Stark, K. D., & Adam, T. (1990). Cognitive deficit or cognitive distortion in childhood depression. *Journal of Abnormal Child Psychology, 18*, 255–270.

Kiesler, D. J. (1966). Some myths of psychotherapy research and the search for a paradigm. *Psychological Bulletin, 65*, 110–136.

King, N. J., Hamilton, D. I., & Ollendick, T. H. (1988). *Children's phobia: A behavioral perspective.* New York: Wiley.

Klein, M. (1932). *The psychoanalysis of children.* London: Hogarth Press.

Klein, M. (1975). *Narrative of child analysis: The conduct of psychoanalysis of children.* New York: Delacorte Press.

Kratochwill, T. R., & Morris, R. J. (Eds.). (1991).

Pelham, W. E. (1990). Behavior therapy, behavioral assessment, and psychostimulant medication in treatment of attention deficit disorders: An interactive approach. In J. Swanson & L. M. Bloomingdale (Eds.), *Attention deficit disorders: IV. Current concepts and emerging trends in attentional and behavioral disorders of childhood.* London: Pergamon Press.

Pelham, W. E., Schnedler, R. W., Bender, M. E., Nilsson, D. E., Miller, J., Budrow, M. S., Ronnei, M., Paluchowski, C., & Marks, D. A. (1988). The combination of behavioral therapy and methylphenidate in the treatment of attention deficit disorders: A therapy outcome study. In L. M. Bloomingdale (Ed.), *Attention deficit disorder: New research in attention treatment, and psychopharmacology* (Vol. 3, pp. 29–48). New York: Pergamon Press.

Rapport, M. D. (1987). Attention deficit disorder with hyperactivity. In M. Hersen & V. B. Van Hasselt (Eds.), *Behavior therapy with children and adolescents: A clinical approach* (pp. 325–361). New York: Wiley.

Richters, J. E. (1992). Depressed mothers as informants about their children: A critical review of the evidence for distortion. *Psychological Bulletin, 112,* 485–499.

Robin, A. L. (1981). A controlled evaluation of problem solving communication training with parent–adolescent conflict. *Behavior Therapy, 12,* 593–609.

Robin, S. L., & Foster, A. L. (1989). *Negotiating parent–adolescent conflict: A behavioral-family systems approach.* New York: Guilford Press.

Rosen, L. A., O'Leary, S. G., Joyce, S. A., Conway, G., & Pfiffner, L. J. (1984). The importance of prudent negative consequences for maintaining appropriate behavior of hyperactive students. *Journal of Abnormal Child Psychology, 12,* 581–604.

Sandler, J., Kennedy, H., & Tyson, R. (1980). *The technique of child analysis: Discussions with Anna Freud.* Cambridge, MA: Harvard University Press.

Skinner, B. F. (1969). *Contingencies of reinforcement.* New York: Appleton-Century-Crofts.

Stark, K. D., Reynolds, W. M., & Kaslow, N. (1987). A comparison of the relative efficacy of self-control therapy and a behavioral problem-solving therapy for depression in children. *Journal of Abnormal Child Psychology, 15,* 91–113.

Stark, K. D., Rouse, L. W., & Livingston, R. (1991). Treatment of depression during childhood and adolescence: Cognitive-behavioral procedures for the individual and family. In P. C. Kendall (Ed.), *Child and adolescent therapy: Cognitive-behavioral procedures* (pp. 165–208).

Ultee, C. A., Griffiaen, D., & Schellekens, J. (1982). The reduction of anxiety in children: A comparison of the effects of systematic desensitization in vitro and systematic desensitization in vivo. *Behavior Therapy and Research, 20,* 61–67.

Walco, G. A., & Varni, J. W. (1991). Cognitive-behavioral interventions for children with chronic illness. In P. C. Kendall (Ed.), *Child and adolescent therapy: Cognitive-behavioral procedures* (pp. 209–306). New York: Guilford Press.

Webster-Stratton, C. (1985). Predictors of treatment outcome in parent training for conduct disordered children. *Behavior Therapy, 16,* 223–243.

Weisz, J. R., Weiss, B., Alicke, M. D., & Klotz, M. L. (1987). Effectiveness of psychotherapy with children and adolescents: A meta-analysis for clinicians. *Journal of Consulting and Clinical Psychology, 55,* 542–549.

Wells, K. C., & Egan, J. (1988). Social learning and systems family therapy for childhood oppositional disorder: Comparative treatment outcome. *Comprehensive Psychiatry, 29,* 138–146.

Wells, K. C., & Forehand, R. (1985). Conduct and oppositional disorders. In P. H. Bornstein & A. E. Kazdin (Eds.), *Handbook of clinical behavior therapy with children* (pp. 218–265). Homewood, IL: Dorsey Press.

Wells, K. C., Forehand, R., & Griest, D. L. (1980). Generality to treatment effects from treatment to untreated behaviors resulting from a parent training program. *Journal of Clinical Child Psychology, 9,* 217–219.

Wiltz, N. A., & Patterson, G. R. (1974). An evaluation of parent training procedures designed to alter inappropriate aggressive behavior of boys. *Behavior Therapy, 5,* 215–221.

Witt, J. C., Elliott, S. N., & Gresham, F. M. (Eds.). (1988). *Handbook of behavior therapy in education.* New York: Plenum Press.

Wolman, B. B. (1972). *Handbook of psychoanalysis: Research, theory, and practice.* New York: Van Nostrand Reinhold.

Wolpe, J. (1958). *Psychotherapy by reciprocal inhibition.* Stanford, CA: Stanford University Press.

The practice of child therapy (2nd ed.). New York: Pergamon Press.

Kratochwill, T. R., & Morris, R. J. (Eds.). (1993). *Handbook of psychotherapy with children and adolescents*. Boston: Allyn & Bacon.

LaGreca, A. M., & Santogrossi, D. A. (1980). Social skills training with elementary school students: A behavioral group approach. *Journal of Consulting and Clinical Psychology, 48,* 220–227.

Levitt, E. E. (1957). The results of psychotherapy with children: An evaluation. *Journal of Consulting Psychology, 21,* 189–196.

Levitt, E. E. (1963). Psychotherapy with children: A further evaluation. *Behavior Research and Therapy, 60,* 326–329.

Mahler, M., Pine, F., & Bergman, A. (1975). *The psychological birth of the human infant*. New York: Basic Books.

Mash, E. J. (1989). Treatment of child and family disturbance: A behavioral-systems perspective. In E. J. Mash & R. A. Barkley (Eds.), *Treatment of childhood disorders* (pp. 3–36). New York: Guilford Press.

Mash, E. J., & Barkley, R. A. (Eds.). (1989). *Treatment of childhood disorders*. New York: Guilford Press.

Mash, E. J., & Johnson, C. (1983). Parental perceptions of child behavior problems, parenting self-esteem, and mothers' reported stress in younger and older hyperactive and normal children. *Journal of Consulting and Clinical Psychology, 51,* 86–99.

Mash, E. J., & Terdal, L. G. (1988). *Behavioral assessment of childhood disorders* (2nd ed.). New York: Guilford Press.

Masters, J. C., Brush, T. G., Hollon, S. D., & Rimm, D. C. (1987). *Behavior therapy* (3rd ed.). New York: Harcourt Brace Jovanovich.

McBurnett, K., Hobbs, S. A., & Lahey, B. B. (1989). Behavioral treatments. In T. H. Ollendick & M. Hersen (Eds.), *Handbook of child psychopathology* (2nd ed., pp. 439–471). New York: Plenum Press.

McLaughlin, T. F., & Williams, R. L. (1988). The token economy. In J. C. Witt, S. N. Elliott, & F. M. Gresham (Eds.), *Handbook of behavior therapy in education* (pp. 469–487). New York: Plenum Press.

McMahon, R. J., & Forehand, R. (1984). Parent training for the noncompliant child: Treatment outcome, generalization, and adjunctive therapy procedures. In R. F. Dangel & R. A. Polster

(Eds.), *Parent training: Foundations of research and practice* (pp. 298–328). New York: Guilford Press).

McMahon, R. J., & Wells, K. C. (1989). Conduct disorders. In E. J. Mash & R. A. Barkley (Eds.), *Treatment of childhood disorders* (pp. 73–102). New York: Guilford Press.

Minuchin, S. (1974). *Families and family therapy*. Cambridge, MA: Harvard University Press.

Minuchin, S., & Fishman, H. C. (1981). *Family therapy techniques*. Cambridge, MA: Harvard University Press.

Morris, R. J., & Kratochwill, T. R. (1991). Childhood fears and phobias. In T. R. Kratochwill & R. J. Morris (Eds.), *The practice of child therapy* (2nd ed., pp. 76–114). New York: Pergamon Press.

Morris, R. J., & Kratochwill, T. R. (1983). *Treating children's fears and phobias: A behavioral approach*. Elmsford, NY: Pergamon Press.

Morris, R. J., Kratochwill, T. R., & Aldridge, K. (1988). Fears and phobias. In J. C. Witt, S. N. Elliott, & F. M. Gresham (Eds.), *Handbook of behavior therapy in education* (pp. 679–717). New York: Plenum Press.

Mowrer, O. H., & Mowrer, W. M. (1938). Enuresis: A method for its study and treatment. *American Journal of Orthopsychiatry, 8,* 436–459.

National Advisory Mental Health Council. (1990). *National plan for research on child and adolescent mental disorders*. Washington, DC: National Institutes of Mental Health.

Ollendick, T. H. (1986). Child and adolescent behavior therapy. In S. L. Garfield & A. E. Bergin (Eds.), *Handbook of psychotherapy and behavior change* (3rd ed., pp. 525–564). New York: Wiley.

Patterson, G. R. (1986). Performance models for antisocial boys. *American Psychologist, 41,* 432–444.

Patterson, G. R. (1982). *Coercive family process*. Eugene, OR: Castalia Press.

Patterson, G. R. (1974). Interventions for boys with conduct problems: Multiple settings, treatments, and criteria. *Journal of Consulting and Clinical Psychology, 42,* 471–481.

Patterson, G. R., Chamberlain, P., & Reid, J. B. (1982). A comparative evaluation of a parent-training program. *Behavior Therapy, 13,* 638–650.

Paul, G. L. (1967). Outcome research in psychotherapy. *Journal of Consulting Psychology, 31,* 109–118.

19
Psychotherapy with Older Adults in Theory and Practice

Dolores Gallagher-Thompson
Larry W. Thompson

As early as 1959, Rechtschaffen published a review of the state of the art of psychotherapy with older adults at that time. It focused primarily on the various forms of psychodynamic treatment that had been used, and presented a good deal of both anecdotal and case report data on their effectiveness. It was a landmark work, since it clearly challenged the myth that older adults were somehow "over the hill" and too old to benefit from psychotherapeutic interventions. This myth has continued to be challenged during the past 10 years, which have seen a veritable explosion of theories and therapies (to treat adults in general). Now the gerontologically oriented scientist-practitioner has many approaches from which to choose. Unfortunately, these approaches generally tend to be well described clinically but not necessarily supported by extensive empirical research findings. One of our aims in this chapter is to present both types of information about each of the theoretical positions to be discussed so that the reader may be maximally informed about what is available and how well it has been researched to date. Other comprehensive (though less current) reviews of the general topic of psychotherapy and aging can be found in Brink (1986), Fry (1986), Knight (1986), and Smyer, Zarit, and Qualls (1990).

We will use the arbitrary cutoff of 60 to define the older adult, though there is a serious debate in the gerontological literature as to whether aging would be better defined in functional (rather than chronological) terms. That is, there are persons like Pablo Casals who still play the cello in their 80s, and there are persons who develop multiple strokes or a dementing illness and so function quite poorly even in their 50s and 60s. Thus, chronological age is not always an informative variable. According to the U.S. Census Bureau (1988), old age is defined as 65 and above; in those terms, about 13% of the U.S. population in 1989 was elderly. This proportion is expected to rise to about 20% in the year 2030. Within this group, the fastest-growing segment is the *oldest old*— persons above age 85, who are living longer and who are generally concerned about their quality of life. A more widely agreed-on definition of aging may soon be available. particularly after changes in national health care, Medicare, and Social Security have been finalized.

DEMOGRAPHICALLY, WHO ARE THE ELDERLY?

According to data from the American Association of Retired Persons (1990), the elderly are primarily Caucasian (about 90%), with about

8% being African-American and about 2% from other races. Persons of Hispanic origin (irrespective of race) comprise about 3% of the older population at present. However, the proportion of minority persons who survive to old age is steadily increasing: It is estimated that by the year 2030, about 20% of the total elderly population will be non-Caucasian. This proportion will be higher in states such as California, New York, and Florida, which have both the highest percentages of elders now and high proportions of minorities. Most older adults (about two-thirds) live with their families, though this may mean a child or sibling rather than a spouse; only 42% of older women are married compared to about 77% of older men. Of the current generation of persons over 65, more than half have earned a high school diploma but only about 11% have graduated from college or have an advanced degree. Most are retired or were never in a career track. Only about 12% are now in the labor force, and about half of these are employed part time.

Some other relevant demographics concern health and cognitive functioning. In general, older people have more physical health problems than younger people. About 85% report at least one chronic medical condition (commonly, arthritis, heart disease, hypertension, diabetes, and vision and hearing impairments), yet 95% live in the community, and only about 5% require permanent institutional (nursing home) placement (Butler & Lewis, 1986). There is considerable debate about whether or not intellectual decline (including memory impairment) is part of normal aging. Most cross-sectional investigations support this view, but longitudinal studies (of the same subjects over lengthy time intervals) do not. While the subtleties of this controversy are beyond the scope of this chapter, the reader is referred to Schaie (1989, 1990) for excellent commentaries on this issue. A final point to note is that the prevalence of severe cognitive impairment (as is found in a dementing disorder such as Alzheimer's disease) is prevalent in only about 5% of persons around the age of 65; prevalence does, however, increase to about 30% in persons over the age of 80 (Schoenberg, Kokmen, & Okazaki, 1987).

What are the implications of these demographic data for the psychotherapeutic treatment of older adults? We will attempt to address these issues as we proceed; however, at this point, it may be sufficient to note that persons with health problems, insecurity about their economic future, some slippage in cognitive function and other impairments should probably not be treated in exactly the same manner in therapy as their younger counterparts, who generally have few real deficits to adapt to. It is also important to acknowledge that older adults are an extremely heterogeneous group, and one must be careful not to stereotype them. It is essential to learn about the uniqueness of each older patient so that maximal benefits from therapy can accrue.

EPIDEMIOLOGICAL INFORMATION

A very detailed review chapter, covering most of the spectrum of psychiatric/psychological disorders and including such information as gender differences, risk factors, and prognostic data for each disorder, has been written by Bliwise, McCall, and Swan (1987). It includes a wide range of studies from both Europe and North America and should be consulted by anyone who wishes to obtain in-depth knowledge about the epidemiology of mental illness in later life.

Here we will present a summary of the available information. The most common psychological or psychiatric disorders of later life, as determined by recent Epidemiological Catchment Area (ECA) studies, are certain specific affective disorders: phobic disorder (standardized 1-month prevalence of 4.8% for those 65+ at all five ECA sites combined); dysthymic disorder (or chronic depression, 1.8%); and major depression (under 1%; 0.4% in men and 1.4% in women). The rate of major depression, in particular, was surprisingly below the expectations of many practitioners; it is only about a quarter of that reported in adults aged 18 to 44 (Regier et al., 1988). When depressive symptoms rather than disorders are examined, the prevalence in older adults increases substantially but is still less than in younger persons. As reported by Koenig and Blazer (1992), the proportion of elders scoring above established symptom scale cutoffs has been consistently around 15% in a dozen studies conducted between 1980 and 1990. Blazer and colleagues generally view the counterintuitive ECA results as occurring due to methodological errors, including such factors as the following: older adults are less likely to admit having psychiatric symptoms (preferring a somatic presentation); they are less likely to recall symptom onset and intensity with accuracy; and they are more likely to have depressive symptoms that do not fit into the currently available diagnostic categories (Tweed, Blazer, & Ciarlo, 1991). A caution about these and other difficulties in recognizing depression in older adults has also been included in the recently published consensus statement about diagnosis and treatment of late-life depression prepared by the National Institutes of Health (NIH, 1992). In fact, the whole question of the diagnostic equivalence of late-life depression with depression in younger or middle age has not been adequately addressed to date. There are some who argue, for example, that late-life depression is qualitatively distinct from depression earlier in life, thus calling for a new diagnostic nomenclature that is specific for this age group. Others believe that while the specific symptoms that characterize late-life depression may be somewhat different for older versus younger persons, they are essentially the same set, regardless of age. Since no definitive research has yet been done to clarify these points, it is not known whether our current system of diagnosis over- or underrepresents depression among older individuals. However, the weight of the information collected to date suggests that the available ECA data probably significantly underrepresent the true prevalence of clinical depression in the elderly (for some of the reasons given above).

Additionally, Blazer and colleagues have pointed out that there are specific subgroups within the elderly as a whole who are more at risk for a major clinical depression (Koenig & Blazer, 1992). These include the chronically physically ill (in whom prevalence rates vary from 30% to 50% in different samples), institutionalized elders (about 15%), family members caring for a chronically disabled relative (about 40%; see Gallagher, Rose, Rivera, Lovett, & Thompson, 1989), and the recently bereaved (about 15%; Gilewski, Farberow, Gallagher, & Thompson, 1991). Thus, it appears that certain demographic characteristics (such as health status and living arrangements), as well as certain psychosocial processes (such as being a caregiver or being recently bereaved), are associated with a higher likelihood of major depression, at least compared to elders who are not in these circumstances. Unfortunately, the relationship of these risk factors to the outcome of psychotherapeutic treatment has not been carefully addressed in the literature to date and should be the subject of further research.

Still less is known about the prevalence and risk factors associated with anxiety disorders in the elderly, since these have only recently been the subject of independent study. In a review and critique of the ECA data on this topic, Blazer, George, and Hughes (1991) indicate that the lower prevalence reported for all types of anxiety disorder among those aged 65+ (compared to the middle aged sample, 45 to 64) was possibly due to such factors as recall problems (e.g., older persons being much more likely to not report past episodes of anxiety); confusion as to whether classic symptoms of anxiety (e.g., insomnia, pounding heart, trembling) are related to medical illnesses rather than to psychological complaints; and their speculation that "A higher threshold of discomfort may be required for reporting these symptoms in later life" (p. 26). At any rate, their more in-depth analysis of the older adult data indicated 6-month prevalence rates of about 9% for simple phobia, 5% for agoraphobia, 2% for generalized anxiety disorder, 1.5% for obsessive-compulsive syndrome, about 1% for social phobia, and under 1% for panic disorder. They argue that taken together, these data suggest that anxiety is a significant problem in later life that requires recognition and treatment in its own right.

A related issue concerns the tendency of depressive and anxiety disorders to appear comorbidly. Although no large-scale epidemiological data are available on this topic, smaller studies and clinical experience strongly suggest that this is frequently the case. In a review chapter on this issue, Alexopoulos (1991) concludes that on average, about 40% of elders with major depressive disorder also meet criteria for an anxiety disorder. He also suggests that since there is considerable overlap between these two affective states, independent diagnostic categories make little sense; possibly for the elderly, new diagnostic categories need to be developed that take this reality into account. In terms of implications for treatment, it is suggested that those experiencing comorbid depressive and anxiety disorders require either different types of intervention or modifications of existing methods to best address their situation.

Even less is known about the prevalence of Axis II personality disorders in the elderly. Krossler (1990) reviewed the literature on this topic and reported prevalence rates of between 2.2% and 12.5% in seven separate studies that included both community and psychiatric samples in four different countries. Most recently, an empirical study has been conducted by Ames and Molinari (in press) to address this issue more specifically. In their study of 200 community-living elderly, using a carefully designed structured interview to detect personality disorders, they found that 13% of the sample met criteria for a diagnosis. Also, prevalence of between 1% and 2% for each of the 11 DSM-III-R categories was reported, with no one dominant diagnosis or cluster and no observable gender differences. Other studies, using psychiatric in- or outpatient samples, reported much higher prevalence rates. For example, Thompson, Gallagher, and Czirr (1988), in their study of major depressives presenting for psychotherapeutic treatment, found that two-thirds of their sample of 79 outpatients met criteria for an Axis II disorder while in their current depressive episode. Avoidant and dependent personality disorders were by far the most common. However, only one-third of the sample met criteria when ratings were based on their recollections of their "usual self" throughout their lifetimes (using the same structured interview as in the Ames and Molinari study). Nevertheless, this figure is still more than twice that found in the Ames and Molinari study and so needs to be explored further. The Thompson et al. (1988)

data suggest that help-seeking depressed elders may be considerably more troubled than their Axis I diagnosis alone indicates, with a notable comorbidity of avoidant and dependent features (which may, of course, complicate the provision of psychotherapeutic services—particularly if the therapist is not aware of the Axis II features that may accompany the primary diagnosis). Alternatively, since there was such a discrepancy between their current status and their report of their usual selves, it may be that elders, when depressed, have difficulty giving reliable information about their lifelong symptoms and behavior patterns. Or it may be that the dependent and avoidant features often observed during a state of clinical depression in the elderly may in fact reflect the depressive process rather than specific personality characteristics. Considerably more research is needed to address these and other issues related to personality disorders and their treatment in the elderly and to understand their relationship to psychotherapeutic outcomes.

MAJOR RELEVANT THEORETICAL PERSPECTIVES

For the most part, the current psychotherapy research literature consists of the application of existing theories and techniques (which were mostly developed for the general adult population) to late-life problems. The two predominant approaches have been those featuring cognitive and behavioral theoretical perspectives and techniques and those featuring psychodynamic views and methods. Within the former category, the development of psychoeducational interventions will also be covered (along with individual and group modalities of cognitive/behavioral work). Within the latter category, Erik Erikson's psychosocial developmental theory is the only one that contains a major focus on aging (1959, 1982). It has spawned a therapeutic approach uniquely suited to the elderly, called the *life review* process, which will be covered in some depth.

In this section, we will begin by describing

these theories and how they have been applied to the most common presenting problems of later life (namely, the affective disorders). We will discuss their use in both individual and group formats, including such information as the length and structure of treatment, how the therapeutic relationship is utilized, and some of the unique methods or techniques that characterize that particular system. Finally, we will review the available clinical and empirical evidence in support of the efficacy of each approach.

Cognitive/Behavioral (c/b) Theories and Therapies

Description of the Approach

As is well known, this category includes a variety of interventions ranging from the classic cognitively focused work of Beck and colleagues (Beck, Rush, Shaw, & Emery, 1979) to the strongly behaviorally oriented work of Lewinsohn (Lewinsohn, Biglan, & Zeiss, 1976). A comprehensive review of many modalities along this continuum can be found in two recent books (Bloom, 1992; Dobson, 1988). There are also several publications that describe one or more of the c/b theories and therapies as applied to the elderly, including books by Hussian (1981) and Pinkston and Linsk (1984) on behavioral gerontology; and reviews of behavioral treatments for anxiety (Hersen & Van Hasselt, 1992), behavioral problems associated with the dementias (Fisher & Carstensen, 1990), and cognitive interventions (Fry, 1986; Thompson, Davies, Gallagher, & Krantz, 1986). The perspective in most common use at present blends behavioral and cognitive aspects (in different proportions according to individual needs). A particular variant of it that we developed and modified, and that has perhaps been most thoroughly described and researched by our group in a series of papers based on four different controlled clinical trials (and numerous published case studies) conducted over the past 10 years, has been used with about 300 outpatients—primarily over age 60 and diag-

nosed with major depressive disorder. Our results, along with those of others who have conducted similar research, will be presented below, following a description of the type of c/b therapy to which we are referring.

Conceptually, our approach took as its starting point a model presented about 10 years ago by Lewinsohn that integrated predisposing personality characteristics with the impact of events on current cognitive appraisals, reinforcement contingencies, and affective and behavioral responses to explain the development and maintenance of depression (Lewinsohn, Hoberman, Teri, & Hautzinger, 1985). While it was not at all age specific, it lent itself well to application to the elderly because of its emphasis on the interrelationship of events, thoughts, feelings, and behaviors. At the same time, Beck's basic theoretical approach was being refined and expanded. While he too recognizes these same reciprocal relationships, he places more emphasis on the role of cognitive appraisal and reprocessing (Beck, 1993), including the unearthing of biases in how information about oneself and one's world is evaluated and the development of alternative points of view. Most recently, Beck and colleagues have focused on the theoretical and clinical importance of linking specific dysfunctional beliefs to their underlying schemata, so that long-standing personality patterns may be altered as well (Beck, Freeman, & Associates, 1990). Given the fact that the elderly typically experience a disproportionate number of unchangeable negative events (such as loss of spouse and friends; older children being too preoccupied to spend much time with them; decline in income, health, and functional abilities; and changes in self-esteem resulting from major role losses for many), the emphasis on developing a more adaptive view of oneself and one's situation seems particularly appropriate. Of course, this often requires behavioral changes as well, but these always need to be processed cognitively so that their meaning and value can be ascertained and modifications made as needed.

The type of c/b therapy that we do, then, places primacy on the modification of dysfunctional beliefs, along with development of behavior patterns that are maximally reinforcing. A number of specific content and process issues that are unique to this therapy with the elderly are discussed by Thompson et al. (1991). A manual is also available that describes this approach in great detail, based on a 16- to 20-session model of individual treatment (Gallagher-Thompson & Thompson, 1992a). A lengthy case report is also available (Gallagher-Thompson & Thompson, 1992b). Briefly, several factors seem critical for maximizing the likelihood that a c/b approach will be effective with the elderly. First, the older client needs to be socialized into therapy, meaning that the roles and expectations of both client and therapist need to be articulated, as well as incorrect expectancies elicited, so that a working contract can be established. Second, the therapist needs to recognize sensory problems (particularly vision and hearing loss) and cognitive changes (however minor) that make it difficult for older adults to communicate in the therapy session as well as younger persons and that tend to affect homework assignments as well. Third, the pace of therapy tends to be slower, as more time is often needed to learn and practice the specific techniques. In most other respects, c/b therapy proceeds in a similar manner to the therapy with adults in general in terms of such factors as the high activity level of the therapist, the types of techniques used (e.g., recording dysfunctional thoughts, doing role plays, and figuring out ways to increase pleasant events in the client's life), and the incorporation of various concepts and behaviors for relapse prevention.

Efficacy of c/b with Elders

A summary of the efficacy of this particular approach, along with data on the effectiveness of other c/b interventions with clinically depressed elders, can be found in Teri, Curtis, Gallagher-Thompson, and Thompson (1994). In brief, our own work has centered on individual therapy with outpatient major depressives over age 60. The first study we conducted used a small sample ($N = 30$); in it, we compared cognitive therapy with behavioral therapy and a relationship-oriented therapy and found that there was significant pre–post change in all three conditions. However, those who received cognitive or behavioral therapy maintained their gains more at 1-year follow-up (Gallagher & Thompson, 1982, 1983; Thompson & Gallagher, 1984). In the second study ($N = 109$), cognitive and behavioral therapies were again compared, but brief psychodynamic therapy (following Horowitz's model; Morowitz et al., 1984) was used as the third condition. In the first part of this study, the active treatments were compared to a delayed-treatment control condition. It was found that little change occurred in the latter condition over the 6-week waiting period, whereas those in the active treatment conditions had already begun to improve on various symptom measures by that point. In the second part of the study, the three types of therapy were compared; the results were similar to those reported in the earlier research in that patients changed to a similar extent in all three conditions, based on pre–post assessments. This pattern held true for both 1- and 2-year follow-up data as well (Gallagher-Thompson, Hanley-Peterson, & Thompson, 1990; Thompson, Gallagher, & Breckenridge, 1987). In the third study, c/b therapy was used (representing a blend of the best features of each modality, as described above) in comparison with the use of the antidepressant medication despiramine, which was selected because of its relatively few anticholinergic side effects in the elderly (thus promoting compliance with its use). The two modalities were used alone or in combination in this three-group design ($N = 102$). Results were complex but, simply put, the combined condition showed some advantage over the cognitive therapy alone, which in turn was superior to the drug-alone condition (Thompson & Gallagher-Thompson, 1993; Thompson, Gallagher-Thompson, Hanser, Gantz, & Steffen, 1991). The final study (which focused on treating depression in a particular subset of older adults, namely, functioning as chronic caregivers to an impaired relative; $N = 66$) compared brief psychodynamic therapy (following Mann's model; Mann, 1973 with c/b therapy in an effort to determine which was more efficacious in the earlier versus later stages of the caregiving process, when demands on the caregiver were different. This hypothesis of therapy specificity was supported in that clients who had been caregivers for a period of 44 months or less responded better to the dynamic therapy, while caregivers for longer periods of time improved more if they received the c/b intervention (Gallagher-Thompson & Steffen, in press). These gains were also maintained at 1-year follow-up, suggesting that this individual difference variable may be usefully integrated into a model to assist the clinician in treatment selection for future clients (Beutler & Clarkin, 1990).

Returning now to the Teri et al. paper (1994), which contains outcome data from a total of about 20 studies (including both controlled clinical trials and case reports, as well as individual, group, and psychoeducational modes), we conclude that a significant body of research clearly supports the utility of c/b therapy for the treatment of late-life depression (and related affective distress). This body of literature was presented at the recent NIH consensus conference on this topic, where, unfortunately, the major recommendation was for treatment with antidepressant medication—not with any of the so-called psychosocial therapies, for which the available data were found lacking (NIH, 1992). This position may not remain tenable for very long, however, as new data emerge. For example, a recent meta-analysis of the efficacy of psychosocial treatments for geriatric depression, based on a total of 17 carefully controlled empirical studies (including studies done in individual, psychoeducational, group, or self-administered formats), found that treatments were reliably more effective than no-treatment conditions on both clinician-rated and self-report outcome measures (Scogin & McElreath, 1994). It was also noted that the obtained mean effect size of .78 compares quite favorably with the .85 effect size reported by Smith, Glass, and Miller (1980) in their pioneering meta-analysis of a much larger number of psychotherapy studies that were not focused on aging samples. This effect size

means that at posttreatment, patients who received a psychosocial therapeutic intervention (such as cognitive therapy, behavioral therapy, reminiscence therapy, bibliotherapy, or supportive treatment) averaged a bit over three-quarters of a standard deviation better on outcome measures than their counterparts who received no treatment or who were in a placebo control condition. Additionally, it was found that the effect size for studies employing cognitive therapy was .85, which (along with life review therapy, which will be discussed below) was impressively strong compared to the effect size of the other treatments that were studied.

Other Forms of c/b Therapy

Before returning to a discussion of the overall outcome literature at present, we will briefly report on a variant of cognitive therapy, developed in Australia, that is receiving increasing attention: *personal construct* therapy (Viney, 1986). Based on the theoretical work of George Kelly (1955), it posits that the elderly use their construct systems to make sense of what is happening to them; since multiple physical and psychological losses are common, older adults particularly need to have flexible construct systems in order to adapt. Those whose constructs are rigidly held, or frequently disconfirmed by their experience or by the views of others, tend to become depressed and develop other disruptive negative emotions. Therapy consists of a median of 10 individual sessions (which can be held in the home as well as in a practitioner's office) and focuses on redefining these constructs or beliefs by testing their viability and evaluating the extent to which they are confirmed or disconfirmed. In particular, constructs about independence and dependence are addressed, since achieving a balance in this domain is seen as critical to maintaining well-being in later life (Viney, Benjamin, & Preston, 1988). Viney et al. conducted a controlled empirical study ($N = 30$) to evaluate the efficacy of this approach, compared to no treatment for a 12-week period, and found that there was a significant reduction in depression and anxiety from pre- to posttreatment, with improvement in perceived competence and positive affect as well. However, the presenting problems or diagnoses of the patients before treatment were not clear, nor were standardized outcome measures used, thus limiting the comparability of this report to others in the field.

Next, we will consider the literature on the use of c/b therapies in a group format. Although the basic theoretical and technical aspects of c/b work would appear to lend themselves to utilization in a group therapy mode (see, e.g., Ellis, 1992; Rose, 1989; and Wessler & Hankin-Wessler, 1989), much less controlled research has been conducted on this type of intervention compared to individual therapy. This is undoubtedly due in part to the methodological difficulties of conducting such research, as described in Upper and Ross (1985), such as the need for diagnostic homogeneity and comparable distress levels at the outset, potential difficulties with overly dominant or submissive group members, and the technical skill required of the leaders. Few reports could be found, in either the clinical or empirical literatures, about group c/b therapy with older adults; the work of Beutler and colleagues is an exception and will now be described.

The clinical aspects of selecting group members, doing pretherapy preparation, organizing time in sessions, dealing with homework problems, and dealing with alliance and termination issues are well presented by Yost, Beutler, Corbishley, and Allender (1986). Results of a controlled clinical trial in which this method was used with 56 elderly major depressives were reported in Beutler et al. (1987). Briefly, they evaluated four conditions: cognitive therapy was used in combination with either placebo or alprazolam compared to either placebo or alprazolam alone. They found that those who received cognitive therapy reported significantly more change on a self-report measure of depression and on sleep efficiency, relative to nongroup-therapy subjects, in both pre–post comparisons and at 3-month follow-up. Also, those assigned to group therapy were less likely than their counterparts to terminate therapy prematurely. From these effects, the authors concluded that cognitive group therapy can be considered effective in ameliorating subjective depressive symptoms.

Finally, we will discuss the various psychoeducational approaches that have been developed within a c/b conceptual framework and implemented in a group format. Although some refer to them as group therapy, they are just as frequently described as classes or workshops designed to teach specific cognitive and behavioral skills that are targeted for specific problems, such as depressed mood or social skills deficits. Lewinsohn and colleagues pioneered this work with development of the "Coping with Depression" course for adults experiencing a unipolar depressive episode. It is available in manualized form (see Lewinsohn, Antonuccio, Steinmetz-Breckenridge, & Teri, 1984) and has been studied empirically by these authors in several different investigations (though none has focused on the elderly; see Clarke & Lewinsohn, 1989, for a review and summary of their generally positive research findings). This class format has been so well received by consumers that modifications have been developed for special populations such as high school adolescents and Native Americans. In our center, we have focused on older adults, developing a "Coping with Depression" class for mildly to moderately depressed elders (Thompson & Gallagher, 1983; Thompson, Gallagher, Nies, & Epstein, 1983). We have since renamed it the "Increasing Life Satisfaction" class in order to highlight that we are focusing on the development of positive affect, as well as the reduction of negative affect, and we have prepared a manual for this class (Gallagher, Lovett, & Thompson, 1988). We have also conducted several studies comparing its effectiveness to a waiting-list condition and have generally found improvement in self-reported depressive symptoms over the 12-week class period see Breckenridge, Thompson, Breckenridge, and Gallagher (1985) for more detailed results.

Most recently, we have have been using this approach in several research programs focusing on the treatment of psychologically distressed family caregivers (see Lovett & Gallagher, 1988, for preliminary results of one outcome study in which this class was found to be more effective than a 12-week waiting-list control condition for both reduction of depression and improvement in life satisfaction in a sample of older male and female caregivers). Final results of the research, involving about 150 persons, can be found in Gallagher-Thompson, Lovett, Rose, and Futterman (under review); in general, a similar pattern was obtained, along with an increase in the use of adaptive (rather than avoidant) coping skills with pre- to postintervention. A serendipitous finding of that research program was the observation that it was not feelings of depression, but rather feelings of anger (and angry behavior), that was most prevalent in the participants. Thus, a different class was developed to address this issue, called the "Anger Management" class. We have just completed a controlled outcome study in which the "Increasing Life Satisfaction" and "Anger Management" classes were compared to each other, and to a waiting-list control condition, for their efficacy in reducing psychological distress in a sample of 169 wives or daughters caring for a relative with Alzheimer's disease or a related form of cognitive impairment. Preliminary analysis of the results indicate that participants in both class conditions showed a marked reduction in angry, depressive, and anxious feelings from pre- to postintervention (compared to the waiting-list group), along with an increase in positive affect and a reduction of the perceived burdens of caregiving. A leader's manual has also been developed for the "Anger Management" class (Gallagher-Thompson, Rose, et al., 1992).

The final work we have done in this domain of psychoeducational interventions consists of modifying the "Anger Management" class to make it culturally sensitive and relevant to Spanish-speaking caregivers of Hispanic descent. Because of the increase in minority caregivers (particularly in the state of Calfornia) and the difficulties most experience when trying to obtain services, we decided to target this group for outreach, followed by offering them the opportunity to participate in a Spanish-language version of this class. Again, leaders' and participants' manuals have been developed and translated into Spanish Gallagher-

Thompson, Arguello, Johnson, Moorehead, & Polich, 1992). To date, about 50 Hispanic caregivers of dementia victims have completed this program. Preliminary analyses of pre–post changes (using translated measures of depression, burden, and anger) indicate that some measurable changes did occur, but the most meaningful outcomes seemed to involve behaviors that were not captured by the standard measures, such as asking for additional help from family members of refusing to feel guilty when not responding immediately to the demands of their demented relative. This information was provided in semistructured interviews conducted after the conclusion of the class and seems to support its usefulness in improving the emotional climate of the caregiving situation (Gallagher-Thompson, 1993). Clearly, more research is needed on the issue of whether this type of intervention is more or less effective when compared to a traditional support group type of service for minority caregivers in distress.

Psychodynamic (p/d) Theories and Therapies

Within the general framework of p/d or psychoanalytic theory, it is not possible to describe a single treatment strategy for working with elderly patients. Any number of variants can be found, each focusing on slightly different features in the treatment process, depending on their own particular biases. In a comprehensive review of p/d therapy with the elderly, Newton and her colleagues have identified writers in three major theoretical camps who have given serious attention to the problems of the elderly (Newton, Brauer, Gutmann, & Grunes, 1986). The developmentally oriented theorists (e.g., Gutmann, 1980) focus on the psychological challenges that typically arise in the late adult years and the problems encountered in working through them. These include problems with intimacy and autonomy as the structures of the family and the social network change, a shift from active to passive mastery as role responsibilities diminish, and the like. The self-psychologists, in particular Kohut (1972) and Lazarus (1980), have emphasized the impact of the aging process on the self. The onslaught of negative experiences accompanying the aging process, they feel, can weaken the psychological processes responsible for the maintenance of self-esteem. These include such factors as depletion of economic resources, loss of physical attractiveness and support network, and diminished sexual functioning. Finally, the traditional analysts are particularly interested in the effects of aging on intrapsychic processes such as internal drives, libido equilibrium, and so on (e.g. Berezin, 1963; Levin, 1965).

Although each camp may have slightly different therapeutic methods, all agree on the importance of internal psychological processes in coping with late-life problems. Furthermore, the successful outcome of these challenges is largely dependent on the manner in which early developmental issues were resolved. The experience of negative late-life events may well precipitate the reemergence of unresolved conflicts of earlier years that heretofore were successfully handled by reasonably intact internal resources.

Most p/d therapists agree that treatment objectives may be different for older patients than for younger ones. Many themes, such as grief for losses; fear of physical illness, disability, and death; and guilt and despair over past failures occur with greater regularity and often require different emphasis. Many p/d therapists (e.g., Pfeiffer & Busse, 1973) argue that supportive techniques are of prime importance in helping patients meet treatment objectives; this strategy greatly facilitates the reestablishment of previous defenses and improvement in self-esteem. More recently, however, other therapists (e.g., Myers, 1984) have argued that insight-oriented psychotherapy can be extremely effective with many psychologically healthier elderly patients. The criteria for selecting older patients for insight therapy are similar to those used with younger individuals, including diagnosis, general personality structure, cognitive flexibility, psychological-mindedness, and the ability to form a good therapeutic alliance.

When one reflects on the early negative view that Freud (1959a, 1959b) had regarding the use of psychoanalytic therapy with the elderly, it is noteworthy that so many p/d-oriented theorists have focused on the application of this model for the treatment of elderly patients. Most agree that, with some modifications, p/d therapy can be extremely effective in treating late-life mental health problems. Modifications suggested by most workers focus primarily on the relationship between the therapist and the patient and, to a lesser extent, on the actual process of the therapy. The therapist is encouraged to take a more active stance than is typically seen in therapy with younger individuals. Less formality and increased attention to concrete age-related problems facilitate the building of a strong alliance. Once this alliance is established, the therapist has an exceptionally powerful tool to help the patient shore up defenses and reinstate more positive self-perceptions. Because older individuals are frequently alone or lonely, this relationship can be doubly powerful by providing a replacement for many losses. For this reason, however, termination can be a greater problem. Many therapists argue that continued contact with the patient on a limited basis over an extended period near the end of therapy is preferable to a more traditional final termination. Transference issues may also be more varied than in younger patients. Rather than being centered on parental issues, transference may reflect issues related to the patient's spouse and children or other significant persons encountered in adult experiences. Similarly, countertransference may be influenced by the therapist's own unresolved issues with parents, by his or her own fears of aging, and by cultural stereotypes of what it means to grow older in our society.

With regard to the process of therapy, the therapist may need to be more flexible in setting the duration and frequency of sessions, as well as in the kinds of interactions with family members and other interested professionals who might be involved with the patient. Typically, the p/d therapies used with the elderly have been time-limited (in the 10- to 20-session range, comparable to that of c/b). Also, serious crises occur on a more regular basis, and the therapist may need to assume a very supportive role momentarily to assist the patient in coping with the immediate crisis before other therapeutic aims can again be considered.

Compared to the literature described above on the c/b approaches, few empirical studies have evaluated the effectiveness of p/d therapy with the elderly, although there are a number of case reports to suggest its efficacy (see, e.g., Lazarus, 1980; Myers, 1991; Rechtschaffen, 1959). Two carefully designed studies ($N = 5$ and $N = 8$, respectively) that have been published were conducted by Lazarus and colleagues (Lazarus et al., 1984, 1987). Outpatients over age 60 who were experiencing psychiatric distress (primarily diagnoses of adjustment disorder or dysthymic disorder) and who had a problem with a definable focus were seen for 10 to 15 sessions of individual treatment and were evaluated before and after the intervention by independent observers. Although no control or comparison conditions were reported in either study, Lazarus et al. (1984 and 1987) indicated that significant pre–post change occurred in the majority of those treated across several domains of outcome, including reduction in symptomatic distress, changes in the affects and defenses associated with each patient's focal issue, and an improved sense of self-esteem. The authors noted that one of the most striking findings was "the way patients used psychotherapy to restore their self-esteem and sense of mastery, and to validate their essential normalcy" (1987, p. 290). An unexpected finding in the second study was a differential response by gender: The female patients showed greater improvement earlier in the process than their male counterparts. However, because of the extremely small sample sizes and lack of control groups, these results are best viewed as tentative and in need of replication.

Control Mastery Theory

Silberschatz and Curtis (1991) offer another variant of the p/d approach, which is based on Weiss' (1991) theoretical point of view. This theory emphasizes the importance of patho-genic beliefs or false ideas in the emergence of psychopathology. These beliefs are formed as a result of experiences (usually traumatic) that occurred during the early developmental years, and although not necessarily, they are usually unconscious. They serve to alert the individual to the dangerous consequences of pursuing relevant life goals; thus, attempts to fulfill important aims are typically frustrated and/or prevented. Presumably, a person in distress who seeks therapy has somehow developed a modicum of strategy, containing both unconscious and conscious components, to work on changing specific pathogenic beliefs. In the course of therapy, change occurs as the patient's pathogenic beliefs are disconfirmed, thus permitting the patient to become more invested in the pursuit of desired ideas, wishes, affects, or behaviors that were heretofore unavailable.

No manual has been developed for implementing this therapy. Its proponents believe that this methodology does not lend itself to a systematic manual form, primarily because it is highly case specific and can in fact permit the introduction of any number of therapeutic strategies, depending on the nature of the problems to be addressed (Curtis, personal communication, June 18, 1993). This approach relies heavily on the *plan formulation method* to guide the course of therapy; this method is described in detail in Curtis, Silberschatz, Sampson, Weiss, and Rosenberg (1988). The method begins by formulating specific conscious goals unique to the patient, followed by an elaboration of factors or processes that serve to obstruct these goals. Most often, obstructions to goals emanate from pathogenic beliefs, which need to be tested empirically in order to disconfirm them. The primary factors in this process are the relationship with the therapist and the patient's ability to develop insight into the dysfunctional nature of these beliefs.

This approach has not been subjected to a traditional outcome evaluation in which it would be directly compared with other therapeutic methods. However, its effectiveness has been determined in several empirical studies in a manner that permits gross comparisons with other techniques. In these research investigations, patients were seen individually once a week for approximately 16 weeks (Curtis & Silberschatz, 1986; Silberschatz & Curtis, 1986). Evaluation includes the usual assessment of symptom intensity, plus other methods with greater relevance for the theoretical underpinning of this technique. These include a measure of target complaints, the Goal Attainment Scale, and a Plan Attainment Scale developed specifically for this research. In general, these researchers report that elderly patients with neurotic psychopathology show considerable benefit from this approach. For the most part, their work has been limited to elderly patients with an Axis I diagnosis who have minimal evidence of significant Axis II pathology. In summarizing their work over the past decade, the authors conclude that although elderly patients may present initially in therapy as more fixed, rigid, and defensive than younger patients, the severity of these characteristics is, for the most part, not sufficient to preclude the realization of substantial gains (Silberschatz & Curtis, 1991).

In terms of actual clinical procedures, control mastery therapists are permitted considerable latitude in making interventions. Depending on the specific components of the plan formulation, the therapist may at certain times become highly directive and at other times much more reflective. In order for this approach to be successful, however, the therapist must accurately appraise the patient's general plan for disconfirming pathogenic beliefs and come up with appropriate interventions that assist the patient in evaluating the validity of these beliefs. While this may involve any number of intervention strategies at times, usually the pathogenic beliefs are tested in the relationship with the therapist. Thus, a patient who experienced a devastating relationship with punitive parents in earlier years may subsequently develop a belief of being unworthy and susceptible to harm when relating to peers or authority figures. Through trial actions with the therapist, the patient may begin to test this belief by ignoring certain stylistic interaction patterns, assuming strong control of the therapy situation, and so on. Empirical studies (Silb-

erschatz & Curtis, 1986) provide support for the argument that if pathogenic beliefs are disconfirmed in the course of therapy, then the patient is likely to become more active and involved in the therapy process. If they are confirmed, then the patient may remain rigid and distant without becoming actively engaged.

Similarities between this approach and previously discussed cognitive and c/b forms of therapy are evident in both theory and methodology. Pathogenic beliefs are described—much like the beliefs emanating from Beck's schemas, discussed elsewhere in this chapter, or the irrational beliefs advanced by Ellis and his group. They develop as a result of earlier traumatic experiences, and typically have some instrumental value in assisting the individual to organize and cope with highly destructive and seemingly chaotic life events that might otherwise be catastrophically overwheming. They can be identified through guided exploration, and their validity tested through hypothesis formulation and subsequent experimental actions on the part of the patient. Indeed, a major focus of both therapies is to encourage evaluation of the beliefs that may at this point in life be counterproductive, and any ethically justified therapeutic strategies that might lead to this end are considered.

However, there is a difference in emphasis in that the control mastery position views the patient–therapist relationship as the primary agent in this process. In all likelihood, this is uppermost in the minds of these therapists as they target areas for productive work. Thus, it is not unreasonable to assume that the pathogenic beliefs most amenable to exploration in the therapeutic relationship take precedence in plan formulation. While appreciating the importance of the patient–therapist relationship, the cognitive (and c/b) therapist often emphasizes the importance of testing dysfunctional beliefs in other interpersonal settings. Thus, during the therapy hour, the therapist may work with the patient to develop strategies for evaluating negative beliefs or expectations with regard to other significant persons in the patient's life (rather than using the therapy relationship as a central vehicle for change).

Another distinction can be found in the emphasis on the unconscious. Control mastery theory holds that pathogenic beliefs are usually unconscious, and that the rudimentary plans that patients have for disconfirming these beliefs contain both unconscious and conscious elements. Patients may actually be engaging unthinkingly in certain behaviors, which otherwise have merit (such as being late for meetings or being characteristically oppositional), simply to test the validity of certain beliefs that are not readily identifiable. Thus, intentionality of purpose is attributed to processes beyond awareness, and this is viewed as a major tenet in any explanatory model used to develop a plan for therapy. Gaining insight into this process via tests in the therapeutic relationship then becomes pivotal for change. While older adults may require more time to achieve this, they are now regarded as good candidates for this form of therapy, particularly when no significant personality disorder is present.

Life Review Work: Erikson's Theoretical Perspective

This therapy is based on the seminal writings of Erik Erikson, who was the first p/d-oriented theoretician (and practicing clinician) to describe the developmental tasks of later life and to relate them to the psychotherapy endeavor (Erikson, 1959, 1982). In brief, Erikson regarded personality development as determined by the extent to which the individual successfully negotiates each of the eight developmental stages that he posited, concluding with the conflict between ego integrity and despair that marks the final stage. His view was that transcendence beyond despair could occur only when older adults were able to build and vicariously enjoy a future (for their families and/or society at large) that they personally would not live to see. Thus, those who have attained ego integrity are persons who have accepted their lives with no major regrets, are able to live with what they have become, and are able to find meaning in their lives at the final stages when those situations or relationships that previously gave meaning (such as work or marriage) are

no longer available or exist in a diluted (or very different) form.

From this perspective, an intervention strategy called the *life review* process was first described by Butler (1963). He viewed it as "a naturally occurring, universal mental process characterized by the progressive return to consciousness of past experiences, and, particularly, the resurgence of unresolved conflicts" (p. 66). As they undertake such a review, older persons ask such existential questions as these: Who am I? How did I live my life? When these questions can be answered in a generally positive manner, a sense of satisfaction results, along with an awareness of ego integrity (as noted above). Further, the life review is a systematic way to help older adults take stock of themselves and come to terms with their choices in life. According to Butler, "a major goal of the life review is to deal with the resurgence of unresolved conflicts which can now be surveyed and reintegrated" (1975, p. 412). Thus clients are encouraged to deal with "unfinished business," which, for older adults with significant depression, anxiety, or other negative affects, often means working through a process of self-forgiveness, along with forgiving others for real or perceived past transgressions. Techniques used include imagery, requesting recollections (in either structured or unstructured ways), writing down memories in a systematic way (e.g., by decade or major life events), and asking the client to tell his or her personal story to the therapist. Edinberg (1985) notes that in reviewing their lives, most people reactivate some memories that trigger guilt, anger, despair, or regret; each therapist must decide whether, at that moment in time, to comfort the person, encourage further expression of feelings, or move away from the subject. For these reasons, the life review process is highly individualized and cannot readily be done in a manualized form.

In the 30 years since Butler first proposed this approach, there has been tremendous interest in its use, particularly among applied gerontologists, who have viewed it as a powerful counseling tool (Waters, 1990). A large number of publications have resulted, some of which elaborate on the basic theory and its associated techniques, while others report findings from clinical and empirical studies. An excellent summary can be found in Disch (1988); see also Crose (1990), Sweeney (1990), and Boggs and Leptak (1991) for presentations of several newer modifications that have been made to the basic life review format, including the use of gestalt techniques, prompted early recollections, and drama to facilitate the process.

In general, the life review methodology has not been widely used in the primary mental health intervention with seriously distressed elders; more typically, it is used with the well elderly who are trying to gain perspective on their lives. Also, this is one intervention that has been more readily used in a group (rather than an individual) format. Waters (1990) discusses several stimuli that she has used to trigger the group process (such as music and memorabilia) and points out that life review groups can be fruitfully conducted with institutionalized elderly, as well as with the more able. A further development has been the publication of guidelines for conducting "autobiography groups" with older adults (see Birren & Deutchman, 1991, for a full description of this intervention, which has been manualized to allow for ready replication). These groups have been found to be popular in such settings as universities, senior centers, and elder residential settings and retirement communities.

Birren and Deutchman (1991) also have provided a brief review of the published literature on the efficacy of the life review in its many forms. From the more than 20 studies then available, they concluded that the life review is an effective method for increasing self-esteem and personal power, along with encouraging renewed interest in past activities or hobbies and supporting the development of friendships with other group members. However, very few controlled studies have been done; instead, anecdotal data have been reported in the majority of instances. An exception to this is the work of Haight (1988, 1992), in which a standard research design was used to evaluate the efficacy of life review (done individually, not in a group format) compared to a series of supportive conversations with a "friendly visitor" and to a no-treatment control condition. A total of 52 frail, homebound elderly were enrolled in the study, and 35 actually completed it through the 1-year follow-up. No mention was made of whether they had specific mental health problems in addition to their physical frailities. Haight found that those who completed the life review intervention (consisting of six 1-hour discussions with a trained counselor that took place in the older person's home) showed an increase in self-reported life satisfaction after the intervention. This continued as an upward trend at the 1-year follow-up (Haight, 1992). However, self-reported depression decreased in all three conditions from pre- to posttest. From these mixed results, Haight concluded that life review needs to be studied more carefully, with an effort made to systematize the intervention and to compare its value when done individually versus when done in a small-group format. Clearly, much more controlled research is needed before this type of intervention can be more strongly endorsed for elders with diagnosable mental health problems.

ETHNIC AND CULTURAL ISSUES IN PSYCHOTHERAPY

Within the past 10 years, the field of ethnogerontology has developed in order to understand more fully how ethnic and cultural issues affect the aging process in general and health practices in particular (Yeo, 1991). Although significant strides have been made in accumulation of knowledge, much of the focus has been on physical health problems, with little attention paid to the assessment and treatment of mental health problems (such as late-life depression) in elders of varying ethnic groups. For example, several recent studies have investigated the correlates of the high prevalence of diabetes in Hispanic elders and the high prevalence of hypertension in African-American elders. On the other hand, in a recent comprehensive review chapter on minority aging, Jackson, Antonucci, and Gibson

(1990) devoted only about one page to a discussion of psychopathology. Yet it is extremely important for psychologists and other mental health professionals to be attuned to cultural differences in the individuals they treat. In a cogent paper on the need for both knowledge and sensitivity, Landrine and Klonoff (1992) argue that health beliefs affect health practices, and health beliefs vary widely across cultures and ethnic backgrounds. For example, they cite a study by Murdock (1980) in which beliefs about the causes of various illnesses were investigated in 189 cultures throughout the world. It was found that only four cultures adhered to theories of natural causation (such as viruses, bacteria, accidents, and stress); the remainder endorsed theories of supernatural causation (such as mystical retribution involving punishment by the gods or other forces for violating certain rules of the community, and magical causation including sorcery and witchcraft). Certain cultures construe depression as resulting from "bad blood," while others view it as comparable to guilt that should be experienced to atone for one's transgressions. Clearly, how strongly such beliefs are held varies according to a number of factors, such as the extent of acculturation (or fitting in with the dominant culture), along with one's prior behavioral history and the types of beliefs and practices still used in the family at present. This is clearly a complex subject to which we cannot do justice in the space available; however, the interested reader is referred to a growing literature on the role of culture in the mental health of older persons of varied ethnic backgrounds (see, e.g., Gaw, 1993, for a psychiatric viewpoint, as well as Sue & Sue, 1990, for a psychological perspective).

Regardless of one's theoretical background, a key point is the need for caution in extrapolating the psychiatric epidemiology of one racial or ethnic group to other groups. What this essentially means is that little is known (at present) about the prevalence of most psychiatric disorders among the ethnic elderly; even less is known about efficacious treatment methods.

From a series of review papers written by the staff of the Stanford Geriatric Education Center, several findings about mental health, ethnicity, and aging have emerged. First, there is considerable doubt about the validity and reliability of most self-report measures with elders of color that are now used routinely with Caucasian elders. For minority elders whose first language may not be English and who may have trouble reading and writing in English, these measures may either under- or overestimate the true likelihood of psychopathology. However, there are some well-designed, small-scale studies that used appropriate measures and were conducted with cultural sensitivity; in such cases, prevalence rates of common disorders such as depression and chronic dysthymia tend to be higher for elder minorities than for Caucasians (see, e.g., Kemp, Staples, & Lopez-Aqueres, 1987, for data on depression in older Hispanics).

Second, because of changing values within many of the ethnic minority subcultures (e.g, less endorsement of filial piety by Asian-Americans and less *familismo* among Hispanic-Americans), there is more stress on those who have survived to old age. No longer can one assume that *la familia* comes first; because of more employment outside the home, fewer family members tend to be home to take care of frail or disturbed older relatives (Morioka-Douglas & Yeo, 1990). Third, ethnic elders are much less likely than Caucasians to seek or participate in psychotherapy of any kind (Yeo & Hikoyeda, 1993). This is similar to trends found with younger and middle-aged persons of color (Sue & Sue, 1990), although there is a growing literature suggesting that c/b types of interventions may be most efficacious (see Sue & Sue, 1990, for a fuller discussion of the various psychotherapeutic approaches found to be helpful with adult minority mental health clients).

Taken together, these findings suggest that this field is sorely in need of further research. Although there are many difficulties to be overcome in conducting this type of research (such as language differences, differences in how constructs are interpreted, differences in styles of relating to perceived authority figures, to name just a few), the projected increase in the proportion of minority elders over the next 10 to 20 years makes it imperative that these issues be addressed in a more concerted and systematic manner.

SUMMARY AND CONCLUSIONS

This chapter has reviewed the major theories and therapies in use with older adults today and has tried to point out their strengths and limitations. On balance, the cognitive and behavioral approaches have been shown to elicit the most consistent positive responses from distressed elders. However, many unanswered questions remain. Among the most pressing, from our point of view, are the following:

1. What are the "active ingredients" that promote change, regardless of the brand of therapy? We do not yet know what these critical ingredients are, and whether or not certain ones are unique for older adults.

2. What is the role of medication, either alone or in combination with psychotherapeutic methods, for achieving results, most notably in the treatment of affective disorders?

3. How can the older adult's family be involved in the therapy in a way likely to result in a more positive outcome? The field of family therapy with the elderly is just beginning to be established; at present, there is little consensus about how best (and when) to integrate other family members and when it is best to work without their input. Much remains to be learned about these and related issues.

4. What is the interrelationship of physical and mental health? Since so many elders experience at least one chronic disease, take prescription medications regularly, and have at least some degree of functional impairment, it is likely that a more reciprocal relationship among these two types of health exists than has been studied to date.

5. How can we keep elders contributing to

society in meaningful ways? This seems to be a key factor in the maintenance of mental health at any age. As Thompson has said: "The consistent finding of a high association between life satisfaction measures and active involvement in various social institutions or functions cannot be overemphasized" (1973, p. 70).

6. Finally, how can we begin to develop appropriate assessment and treatment methods for elders of color? This needs to become a priority within the field of geriatric mental health; it should prove to be a stimulating and creative endeavor.

Acknowledgment

Preparation of this chapter was substantially supported by Grants RO1-MH43407 and RO1-MH37196 from the National Institutes of Mental Health.

REFERENCES

Alexopoulos, G. S. (1991). Anxiety and depression in the elderly. In C. Salzman & B. D. Lebowitz (Eds.), *Anxiety in the elderly* (pp. 63–77). New York: Springer.

American Association of Retired Persons. (1990). A *profile of older americans*. Washinton, DC: Author.

Ames, A., & Molinari, V. (In press). Prevalence of personality disorders in community-living elderly. *Journal of Geriatric Psychiatry and Neurology*.

Beck, A. T. (1993). Cognitive therapy: Past, present and future. *Journal of Consulting and Clinical Psychology, 61,* 194–198.

Beck, A. T., & Freeman, A., and Associates (1990). *Cognitive therapy of personality disorders.* New York: Guilford Press.

Beck, A. T., Rush, J., Shaw, B., & Emery, G. (1979). *Cognitive therapy of depression.* New York: Guilford Press.

Berezin, M. A. (1963). Some intrapsychic aspects of aging. In N. E. Zinberg & I. Kaufman (Eds.), *Normal psychology of the aging process.* New York: International Universities Press.

Beutler, L. E., & Clarkin, J. F. (1990). *Systematic treatment selection: Toward targeted therapeutic interventions.* New York: Brunner/Mazel.

Beutler, L. E., Scogin, F., Kirkish, P., Schretlen, D., Corbishley, A., Hamblin, D., Meredith, K., Potter, R., Bamford, C. R., & Levenson, A. I. (1987). Group cognitive therapy and alprazolam in the treatment of depression in older adults. *Journal of Consulting and Clinical Psychology, 55,* 550–556.

Birren, J. E., & Deutchman, D. E. (1991). *Guiding autobiography groups for older adults: Exploring the fabric of life.* Baltimore: Johns Hopkins University Press.

Blazer, D., George, L. K., & Hughes, D. (1991). The epidemiology of anxiety disorders: An age comparison. In C. Salzman & B. D. Lebowitz (Eds.), *Anxiety in the elderly* (pp. 17–30). New York: Springer.

Bliwise, N., McCall, M. E., & Swan, S. J. (1987). The epidemiology of mental illness in late life. In E. E. Lurie, J. H. Swan, & Associates (Eds.), *Serving the mentally ill elderly: Problems and perspectives* (pp. 1–38). Lexington, MA: Heath.

Bloom, B. L. (1992). *Planned short-term psychotherapy: A clinical handbook.* Boston: Allyn & Bacon.

Boggs, D. L., & Leptak, J. (1991). Life review among senior citizens as a product of drama. *Educational Gerontology, 17,* 239–246.

Breckenridge, J. S., Thompson, L. W., Breckenridge, J. N., & Gallagher, D. (1985). Behavioral group therapy with the elderly. In S. Upper & S. Ross (Eds.), *Handbook of behavioral group therapy* (pp. 275–299). New York: Plenum Press.

Brink, T. L. (Ed.). (1986). *Clinical gerontology: A guide to assessment and intervention.* New York: Haworth Press.

Butler, R. N. (1963). The life review: An interpretation of reminiscence in the aged. *Psychiatry, 26,* 65–76.

Butler, R. N. (1975). *Why survive? Being old in America.* New York: Harper & Row.

Butler, R. N., & Lewis, M. I. (1986). *Aging and mental health* (3rd ed.). Columbus, OH: Charles E. Merrill.

Clarke, G., & Lewinsohn, P. M. (1989). The coping with depression course: A group psychoeducational intervention for unipolar depression. *Behavior Change, 6,* 54–69.

Crose, R. (1990). Reviewing the past in the here and now: Using gestalt therapy techniques with life review. *Journal of Mental Health Counseling, 12,* 279–287.

Curtis, J. T., & Silberschatz, G. (1986). Clinical implications of research on brief dynamic psychotherapy: I. Formulating the patient's problems and goals. *Psychoanalytic Psychology, 3,* 13–25.

Curtis, J. T., Silberschatz, G., Sampson, H., Weiss, J., & Rosenberg, S. E. (1988). Developing reliable psychodynamic case formulations: An illustration of the planned diagnosis method. *Psychotherapy, 25,* 256–265.

Disch, R. (Ed.). (1988). Twenty-five years of the life review: Theoretical and practical considerations. Special issue of *Journal of Gerontological Social Work, 12,* 1–148.

Dobson, K. S. (Ed.). (1988). *Handbook of cognitive-behavioral therapies.* New York: Guilford Press.

Dobson, K. S. (1989). A meta-analysis of the efficacy of cognitive therapy for depression. *Journal of Consulting and Clinical Psychology, 57,* 414–419.

Edinberg, M. A. (1985). *Mental health practice with the elderly.* Englewood Cliffs, NJ: Prentice-Hall.

Ellis, A. (1992). Group rational-emotive and cognitive-behavior therapy. *International Journal of Group Psychotherapy, 42,* 63–80.

Erikson, E. H. (1959). *Identity and the life cycle.* New York: Norton.

Erikson, E. H. (1982). *The life cycle completed.* New York: Norton

Farberow, N., Gallagher-Thompson, D., Gilewski, M., & Thompson, L. W. (1992). Changes in grief and mental health of bereaved spouses of older suicides. *Journal of Gerontology: Psychological Sciences, 47,* 357–366.

Finkel, S. (1991). Group psychotherapy in later life. In W. A. Myers (Ed.), *New techniques in the psychotherapy of older patients* (pp. 223–244). Washington, DC: American Psychiatric Press.

Fisher, J. E., & Carstensen, L. L. (1990). Behavior management of the dementias. *Clinical Psychology Review, 10,* 611–629.

Freud, S. (1959a). On psychotherapy. In S. J. London (Ed.), *The standard edition of the complete psychological works of Sigmund Freud* (Vol. 7, pp. 257–268). London: Hogarth Press. (Originally published 1905)

Freud, S. (1959b). Sexuality in the aetiology of the neuroses. In S. J. London (Ed.), *The standard edition of the complete psychological works of Sigmund Freud* (Vol. 3, pp. 261–285). (Originally published in 1898.)

Fry, P. S. (1986). *Depression, stress, and adaptations in the elderly.* Rockville, MD: Aspen.

Gallagher, D., & Thompson, L. W. (1982). Treatment of major depressive disorder in older adult outpatients with brief psychotherapies. *Psycho-*

therapy: Theory, Research and Practice, 19, 482–490.

Gallagher, D., & Thompson, L. W. (1983). Effectiveness of psychotherapy for both endogenous and nonendogenous depression in older adult outpatients. *Journal of Gerontology, 38,* 707–712.

Gallagher, D., Rose, J., Rivera, P., Lovett, S., & Thompson, L. W. (1989) Prevalence of depression in family caregivers. *The Gerontolgoist, 29,* 449–456.

Gallagher, D., Lovett, S., & Thompson, L. W. (1988). *"Increasing Life Satisfaction" class for caregivers: class leaders' manual.* Palo Alto, CA: Department of Veterans Affairs Medical Center.

Gallagher-Thompson, D. (1993). Final report to the State of California on grant: 91–12964: *Mexican-American Alzheimer's victims and their families: Development of a psychoeducational treatment program.* Unpublished report, available from the author.

Gallagher-Thompson, D., Arugello, D., Johnson, C., Moorehead, R. S., & Polich, T. M. (1992). *Como controlar la frustracion: Una clase para cuidantes.* Palo Alto, CA: Department of Veterans Affairs Medical Center.

Gallagher-Thompson, D., Hanley-Peterson, P., & Thompson, L. W. (1990). Maintenance of gains versus relapse following brief psychotherapy for depression. *Journal of Consulting and Clinical Psychology, 58,* 371–374.

Gallagher-Thompson, D., Lovett, S., Rose, J., & Futterman, A. (under editorial review). The impact of psychoeducational interventions on distressed family caregivers.

Gallagher-Thompson, D., Lovett, S., & Thompson, L. W. (1990). *Increasing life satisfaction class for caregivers: Class leader's manual.* Unpublished manual. Stanford, CA: Older Adult and Family Center, Stanford University School of Medicine and Palo Alto Veterans Affairs Medical Center:

Gallagher-Thompson, D., Rose, J., Florsheim, M., Jacome, P., DelMaestro, S., Peters, L., Gantz, F., Arguello, D., Johnson, C., Moorehead, R. S., Polich, T. M., Chesney, M., & Thompson, L. W. (1992). *Controlling your frustration: A class for caregivers.* Palo Alto, CA: Department of Veterans Affairs Medical Center.

Gallagher-Thompson, D., & Steffen, A. (in press). Comparative effects of cognitive/behavioral and brief psychodynamic psychotherapies for depressed family caregivers. *Journal of Consulting and Clinical Psychology.*

Gallagher-Thompson, D., & Thompson, L. W. (1992a). *Cognitive-behavioral therapy manual for the treatment of late-life depression.* Palo Alto, CA: Department of Veterans Affairs Medical Center.

Gallagher-Thompson, D., & Thompson, L. W. (1992b). The older adult. In A. Freeman & F. Dattilio (Eds.), *Comprehensive casebook of cognitive therapy* (pp. 193–200). New York: Plenum Press.

Gaw, A. C. (Ed.). (1993). *Culture, ethnicity, and mental illness.* Washington, DC: American Psychiatric Press.

Gilewski, M. J., Farberow, N. L., Gallagher, D. E., & Thompson, L. (1991). The interaction of depression and bereavement on mental health and the elderly. *Psychology and Aging, 6,* 67–75.

Gutmann, D. L. (1980). Psychoanalysis and aging. In S. I. Greenspan (Ed.), *The course of life: Psychoanalytic contributions toward understanding personality development. Vol III: Adulthood and the aging process* (pp. 489–517). (DHHS Pub. No. ADM-81-1000). Washington, DC: U.S. Government Printing Office.

Haight, B. K. (1988). The therapeutic role of a structured life review process in homebound elderly subjects. *Journal of Gerontology: Psychological Sciences Section, 43,* 40–44.

Haight, B. K. (1992). Long-term effects of a structured life review process. *Journal of Gerontology: Psychological Sciences Section, 47,* 312–315.

Hersen, M., & Van Hasselt, V. B. (1992). Behavioral assessment and treatment of anxiety in the elderly. *Clinical Psychology Review, 12,* 619–640.

Horowitz, M., & Kaltreider, N. (1979). Brief therapy of the stress response syndrome. *Psychiatric Clinics of North America, 2,* 365–377.

Horowitz, M., Marmar, C., Krupnick, J., Wilner, N., Kaltreider, N., & Wallerstein, R. (1984). *Personality styles and brief psychotherapy.* New York: Basic Books.

Hussian, R. (1981) *Geriatric psychology: A behavioral perspective.* New York: Van Nostrand Reinhold.

Jackson, J. S., Antonucci, C., & Gibson, R. C. (1990). Cultural, racial, and ethnic minority influences on aging. In J. Birren & K. W. Schaie (Eds.), *Handbook of the psychology of aging* (3rd ed.), pp. 103–123). New York: Academic Press.

Kelly. G. (1955). *The psychology of personal constructs.* New York: Norton.

Kemp, B. J., Staples, F., & Lopez-Aqueres, W. (1987). Epidemiology of depression and dysphoria in an elderly Hispanic population: Prevalence and correlates. *Journal of the American Geriatric Society, 35*, 920–926.

Knight, B. (1986). *Psychotherapy with older adults.* Newbury Park, CA: Sage.

Koenig, H. G., & Blazer, D. G. (1992). Epidemiology of geriatric affective disorders. *Clinics in Geriatric Medicine, 8*, 235–251.

Kohut, H. (1972). Thoughts on narcissism and narcissistic rage. *Psychoanalytic Study of the Child, 27*, 360–400.

Kroessler, D. (1990). Personality disorders in the elderly. *Hospital and Community Psychiatry, 41*, 1325–1329.

Landrine, H., & Klonoff, E. A. (1992). Culture and health-related schemas: A review and proposal for interdisciplinary integration. *Health Psychology, 11*, 267–276.

Lazarus, L. W. (1980). Self psychology and psychotherapy with the elderly: Theory and practice. *Journal of Geriatric Psychiatry, 13*, 69–88.

Lazarus, L. W., Groves, L., Gutmann, D., Ripeckyj, A., Frankel, R., Newton, N., Grunes, J., & Havasy-Galloway, S. (1987). Brief psychotherapy with the elderly: A study of process and outcome. In J. Sadavoy & M. Leszcz (Eds.), *Treating the elderly with psychotherapy* (pp. 265–293). Madison, CT: International Universities Press.

Lazarus, L. W., Groves, L., Newton, N., Gutmann, D., Ripeckyj, A., Frankel, R., Grunes, J., & Havasy-Galloway, S. (1984). Brief psychotherapy with the elderly: A review and preliminary study of process and outcome. In L. W. Lazarus (Ed.), *Clinical approaches to psychotherapy with the elderly* (pp. 15–35). Washington, DC: American Psychiatric Press.

Levin, S. (1965). Some comments on the distribution of narcissistic and object libido in the aged. *International Journal of Psychoanalysis, 46*, 200–208.

Lewinsohn, P. M., Antonuccio, D. O., Steinmetz-Breckenridge, J. L., & Teri, L. (1984). *The coping with depression course: A psychoeducational intervention for unipolar depression.* Eugene, OR: Castalia.

Lewinsohn, P. M., Biglan, T., & Zeiss, A. (1976). Behavioral treatment of depression. In P. Davidson (Ed.), *Behavioral management of anxiety, depression, and pain* (pp. 91–146). New York: Brunner/Mazel.

Lewinsohn, P. M., Hoberman, H., Teri, L., & Hautzinger, M. (1985). An integrative theory of depression. In S. Reiss & R. R. Bootzin (Eds.), *Theoretical issues in behavior therapy* (pp. 331–359). New York: Academic Press.

Lovett, S., & Gallagher, D. (1988). Psychoeducational interventions for family caregivers: Preliminary efficacy data. *Behavior Therapy, 19*, 321–330.

Mann, J. (1973). *Time-limited psychotherapy.* Cambridge, MA: Harvard University Press.

Morioka-Douglas, N., & Yeo, G. (1990). *Aging and health: Asian/Pacific Island American elders.* Stanford, CA: Stanford Geriatric Education Center Working Paper Series No. 3.

Murdock, G. P. (1980). *Theories of illness: A world survey.* Pittsburgh: University of Pittsburgh Press.

Myers, W. A. (1984). *Dynamic theory of the older patient.* New York: Jason Aronson.

Myers, W. A. (1991). Psychoanalytic psychotherapy and psychoanalysis with older patients. In W. Myers (Ed.), *New techniques in the psychotherapy of older patients* (pp. 265–279). Washington, DC: American Psychiatric Press.

National Institutes of Health Consensus Conference Statement: Diagnosis and treatment of depression in late life (1992). *Journal of the American Medical Association, 268*, 1018–1024.

Newton, N. A., Brauer, D., Gutmann, D. L., & Grunes, J. (1986). Psychodynamic therapy with the aged: A review. *Clinical Gerontologist, 5*, 205–229.

Pfeiffer, E., & Busse, E. (1973). Mental disorders in later life—affective disorders: Paranoid, neurotic, and situational reactions. In E. Busse & E. Pfeiffer (Eds.), *Mental illness in later life* (pp. 107–144). Washington, DC: American Psychiatric Press.

Pinkston, E., & Linsk, N. (1984). *Care of the elderly: A family approach.* New York: Pergamon Press.

Rechtschaffen, A. (1959). Psychotherapy with geriatric patients: A review of the literature. *Journal of Gerontology, 14*, 73–84.

Regier, D., Boyd, J., Burke, J., Rae, D., Myers, J., Kramer, M., Robins, L., George, L., Karno, M., & Locke, B. (1988). One-month prevalence of mental disorders in the United States: Based on five epidemiologic catchment area sites. *Archives of General Psychiatry, 45*, 977–986.

Rose, S. D. (1989). Coping skill training in groups. *International Journal of Group Psychotherapy, 39*, 59–78.

Schaie, K. W. (1989). The hazards of cognitive aging. *The Gerontologist, 29,* 484–493.

Schaie, K. W. (1990). The optimization of cognitive functioning in old age: Predictions based on cohort-sequential and longitudinal data. In P. B. Baltes & M. M. Baltes (Eds.), *Successful aging: Perspectives from the behavioral sciences* (pp. 94–117). Cambridge: Cambridge University Press.

Schoenberg, B., Kokmen, E., & Okazaki, H. (1987). Alzheimer's disease and other dementing illnesses in a defined United States population: Incidence rates and clinical features. *Annals of Neurology, 22,* 724–729.

Scogin, F. & McElreath, L. (1994). Efficacy of psychosocial treatments for geriatric depression: A quantitative review. *Journal of Clinical and Consulting Psychology, 62,* 69–74.

Shulman, S. (1985). Psychodynamic group therapy with older women. *Social Casework: The Journal of Contemporary Social Work, 10,* 579–586.

Silberschatz, G., & Curtis, J. T. (1986). Clincial implications of research on brief dynamic psychotherapy. II: How the therapist helps or hinders therapeutic progress. *Psychoanalytic Psychology, 3,* 27–37.

Silberschatz, G., & Curtis, J. T. (1991). Time-limited psychodynamic therapy with older adults. In W. Myers (Ed.), *New techniques in the psychotherapy of older patients* (pp. 95–108). Washington, DC: American Psychiatric Press.

Smith, M. L., Glass, G. V., & Miller, T. I. (1980). Benefits of psychotherapy. Baltimore: Johns Hopkins University Press.

Smyer, M., Zarit, S., & Qualls, S. H. (1990). Psychological intervention with the aging individual. In J. Birren & K. W. Schaie (Eds.), *Handbook of the psychology of aging* (3rd. ed., pp. 375–403). New York: Academic Press.

Steuer, J. L., Mintz, J., Hammon, C. L., Hill, M. A., Jarvik, L. F., McCarley, T., Motoike, P., & Rosen, R. (1984). Cognitive/behavioral and psychodynamic group psychotherapy in treatment of geriatric depression. *Journal of Consulting and Clinical Psychology, 52,* 180–189.

Sue, D. W., & Sue, D. (1990). *Counseling the culturally different: Theory and practice* (2nd ed.). New York: Wiley.

Sweeney, T. J. (1990). Early recollections: A promising technique for use with older people. *Journal of Mental Health Counseling, 12,* 260–269.

Teri, L., Curtis, J., Gallagher-Thompson, D. & Thompson, L. W. (1994). (press). Cognitive/behavior therapy with depressed older adults. In

L. S. Schneider, C. F. Reynolds, B. Lebowitz, & A. Friedhoff (Eds.), *Diagnosis and treatment of depression in the elderly: Proceedings of the NIH Consensus Development Conference* Washington, DC: American Psychiatric Press. (pp. 279–291).

Thompson, L. W. (1973). Psychological changes in later life. In E. W. Busse & E. Pfeiffer, (Eds.), *Mental illness in late-life,* (pp. 53–74). Washington, DC: American Psychiatric Press.

Thompson, L., Davies, R., Gallagher, D., & Krantz, S. (1986). Cognitive therapy with older adults. *Clinical Gerontologist, 5,* 245–279.

Thompson, L. W., & Gallagher, D. (1983). A psychoeducational approach for treatment of depression in elders. *Psychotherapy in Private Practice, 1,* 25–28.

Thompson, L. W., & Gallagher, D. (1984). Efficacy of psychotherapy in the treatment of late-life depression, *Advances in Behavior Research and Therapy, 6,* 127–139.

Thompson, L., Gallagher, D., & Breckenridge, J. S. (1987). Comparative effectiveness of psychotherapies for depressed elders. *Journal of Consulting and Clinical Psychology, 55,* 385–390.

Thompson, L. W., Gallagher, D., & Czirr, R. (1988). Personality disorder and outcome in the treatment of late-life depression. *Journal of Geriatric Psychiatry, 21,* 133–146.

Thompson, L. W., Gallagher, D., Nies, G., & Epstein, D. (1983). Evaluation of the effectiveness of professionals and nonprofessionals as instructors of "coping with depression" classes for elders. *The Gerontologist, 23,* 390–396.

Thompson, L. W., & Gallagher-Thompson, D. (1993). *Comparison of desipramine and cognitive-behavioral therapy in the treatment of late-life depression: A progress report.* Paper presented at the 27th Annual American Association for Behavioral Therapy Convention, Atlanta.

Thompson, L. W., Gallagher-Thompson, D., Hanser, S., Gantz, F., & Steffen, A. (1991). *Comparison of desipramine and cognitive/behavioral therapy for the treatment of depression in the elderly.* Paper presented at the American Psychological Association Convention, San Francisco.

Thompson, L. W., Gantz, F., Florsheim, M., Delmaestro, S., Rodman, J., Gallagher-Thompson, D., & Bryan, H. (1991). Cognitive-behavioral therapy for affective disorder in the elderly. In W. Myers (Ed.), *New techniques in the psychotherapy of older patients* (pp. 1–20). Washington, DC: American Psychiatric Press.

Tweed, D. L., Blazer, D. G., & Ciarlo, J. A.

(1991). Psychiatric epidemiology in elderly populations. In R. B. Wallace & R. F. Woolson (Eds.), *The epidemiologic study of the elderly* (pp. 213–233). New York: Oxford University Press.

Upper, S., & Ross, S. (Eds.). (1985). *Handbook of behavioral group therapy*. New York: Plenum.

U.S. Bureau of the Census. (1988). *Statistical abstract of the United States* (108th ed.). Washington, DC: U.S. Government Printing Office.

Viney, L. L. (1986). Expression of positive emotion by people who are physically ill: Is it evidence of coping or defending? In L. A. Gottschalk, F. Lobas, & L. L. Viney (Eds.), *Content analysis of verbal behavior in clinical medicine* (pp. 215–224). Berlin: Springer-Verlag.

Viney, L. L., Benjamin, Y. N., & Preston, C. A. (1988). Promoting independence in the elderly: The role of psychological, social and physical constraints. *Clinical Gerontologist, 8*, 3–17.

Waters, E. B. (1990). The life review: Strategies for working with individuals and groups. *Journal of Mental Health Counseling, 12*, 270–278.

Weiss, J. (1991). Part I: Theory and clinical observations. In J. Weiss & H. Sampson (Eds.), *The psychoanalytic process: Theory, clinical observation and empirical research* (pp. 3–138). New York: Guilford Press.

Wessler, R. L., & Hankin-Wessler, S. W. (1989). Nonconscious algorithms in cognitive and affective processes. *Journal of Cognitive Psychotherapy, 3*, 243–254.

Yeo, G. (1991). Ethnogeriatric education: Need and content. *Journal of Cross-Cultural Gerontology, 6*, 229–241.

Yeo, G., & Hikkoyeda, N. (1993). *Differential assessment and treatment of mental health problems: African American, Latino, Filipino, and Chinese American elders*. Stanford, CA: Stanford Geriatric Education Center Working Paper Series No. 13.

Yost, E., Beutler, L., Corbishley, A. M., & Allender, J. (1986). *Group cognitive therapy: A treatment approach for depressed older adults*. New York: Pergamon Press.

20
Brief and Crisis Psychotherapy in Theory and Practice

Julia Shiang
Bruce Bongar

In the past decade, mental health care providers have reported that an increasing percentage of their time is spent providing care within a limited time frame. The therapeutic forms most commonly employed are brief therapy and crisis intervention—in settings that range from university health care clinics to inner-city emergency rooms. Furthermore, these forms of therapy are used with all age groups and across most economic groups—from the middle-aged male who experiences normal developmental identity problems after losing a job to the child who experiences school phobia after a traumatic car accident.

When clients enter psychological treatment, they generally do not anticipate that their therapy will be prolonged, but rather believe that their problems will require a few sessions at most (Garfield, 1978). Indeed, clients typically come for psychological treatment seeking specific and focal problem resolution, rather than general personality "overhauls," as was assumed in providing the forms of long-term therapy of the past (Koss & Shiang, 1993). The median duration of therapeutic contact, regardless of the orientation of the therapist, is six to eight sessions (Garfield, 1986). Another pattern of care that is increasingly seen, especially in health maintenance organizations (HMOs), is

intermittent care, in which clients engage in therapy for short periods of time, terminate as problems are resolved, and then reenter treatment again when problems recur (Cummings & Vandenbos, 1979; Siddall, Haffey, & Feinman, 1988). Recent financial pressures to limit the payments for psychotherapy to a predetermined number of sessions have resulted in a practice climate in which many insurance companies advocate therapy modalities that are, in fact, brief or crisis treatment approaches.

Thus, it is imperative to investigate and understand both the specific and general contributions that each of these forms of therapy make in the study of human change. In fact, most of the research on the variables that affect outcome have utilized a brief therapy form. Rigorous research on brief therapy modalities has made a significant contribution to the enhancement of general and scientific theory about the ways in which people change and adapt to contextual differences. Research has found that 75% of the clients who benefit from brief therapy do so in the first 6 months of contact (Lambert, Shapiro, & Bergin, 1986). While the empirical studies on crisis therapy are not as numerous or as highly controlled, they too offer an opportunity to understand the impact of specific interventions with specific client problems.

In this chapter, we have chosen to make the distinction between brief therapies and crisis intervention/support (crisis-oriented) therapies. Discussions of crisis-oriented therapies have sometimes been subsumed under the general heading of brief therapies; here we have an opportunity to highlight their similarities and differences. As will become apparent in the following discussion, both general forms share a corpus of assumptions, but crisis intervention/support therapies are more highly focused on resolving the individual's personal reactions to the immediate precipitating events of the crisis. Correspondingly, the technical aspects of the two forms also differ.

Many researchers now agree that the question "Is psychotherapy effective?" has been addressed adequately by existing research (e.g., Smith & Glass, 1977; Smith, Glass, & Miller, 1980). There is also considerable empirical evidence showing that brief therapy, practiced in various forms, is efficacious with specific patient populations. The individuals who benefit from brief therapy are those in the mental health system whose lives are problematic in some specific areas (e.g., work-related stress, interpersonal problems), while in other areas they are functioning adequately (Koss & Shiang, 1993). In this review of the efficacy of the various therapies, we have chosen to narrow our focus. We ask not whether each of these forms of therapy is generally efficacious, but rather what specific changes predictably take place given a specific course of intervention. When a patient is actively engaged, we want to know the kind of change and "the *extent* or *degree* of change" (Garfield, 1981, p. 299), as well as those qualities and behaviors of both the therapist and the client that are associated with measurable positive change on the part of the client.

CASE PRESENTATION

In order to highlight the similarities and differences among brief and crisis therapy, we will present a case vignette. This will provide a way to apply the descriptions and empirical findings to actual practice.

Susan, a Caucasian female, age 42, has just ended a significant relationship of 2 years' duration. She states that she is worried because she realizes that she often "sabotages" her intimate relationships. She can't seem to rid herself of the idea that she will never be able to have a satisfying relationship. The precipitating factors that bring her into treatment are the recent breakup with her boyfriend and the death of her father 2 months ago. She also reports that she occasionally has thoughts of suicide.

To illustrate the differences between brief and crisis therapies, we will necessarily emphasize certain aspects of Susan's presentation as if she were the prototypical patient seeking the specific form of psychotherapy being illustrated. Due to the limited scope of this review, we will not be able to detail how all forms of therapy would consider and produce change for Susan, but will limit our discussion to contrasting and comparing two time-limited approaches with crisis intervention and support (crisis-oriented) therapies as they are practiced. We will focus on two commonly used time-limited therapy forms employed in clinical settings (the interpersonal approach and the cognitive-behavioral therapy), which will be compared to general crisis-oriented therapies. We have chosen to focus on these types of therapies because they would address the specific aspects of Susan's problem presentation. The therapies can then be differentiated by detailing the specific assumptions underlying their forms, the specific technical aspects (treatment formulations, stance of the therapist) of the forms, and the required contributions of the patient for a successful outcome.

There is general agreement in brief and crisis therapies that the therapist must take responsibility for determining and maintaining the focus of therapy (Koss & Shiang, 1993). However, positions vary as to what should be the focus of therapy. We will use the case study of Susan to illustrate variations in the focus and subsequent interventions among dynamic interpersonal, cognitive-behavioral, and crisis intervention/support approaches. In order to emphasize the matching of specific forms of therapy to patients' needs, we will attempt to be explicit about our rationale for selecting a specific approach. In describing the specific forms of therapy, we will present research findings and attempt to make explicit their application to the therapeutic setting.

Susan is presented as the prototypical patient who is motivated to seek one-on-one psychotherapy for a specific focal problem. It is important to note that a basic tenet of brief therapy is that growth and change continue beyond termination of the face-to-face interaction with the therapist. Consolidation of gains is assumed to take place within the context of normal developmental concerns.

In the final section of the chapter, we will briefly discuss training issues that concern both beginning therapists and supervisors based on our review of the different forms of therapy. We will conclude with a general summary and some conclusions regarding the practice of brief and crisis-oriented therapies.

BRIEF THERAPY

Approaches and Assumptions

One-on-one brief psychotherapy approaches are based on a number of different theoretical orientations: (1) psychodynamic, (2) behavioral, cognitive, and cognitive-behavioral, (3) eclectic, and (4) other verbal approaches (gestalt, etc.). The goals of therapy, problem formulations, and treatment plans all vary, but the principles presented in Table 20.1 apply to all approaches.

Each brief therapy approach uses these techniques in a manner that is consistent with its view of human change and the helping process. Practitioners of each approach determine how rigorously they apply their standard of selection and exclusion criteria. Theoretically, this involves an assessment of the characteristics of the patient's personality and an initial presentation that includes the types of problems that can be best served by the practitioner's therapeutic

approach. Adherence to these criteria is thought to be necessary because the limited time frame requires a concentration on specific issues that are amenable to change. Considerations of inclusion as well as exclusion criteria are important as factors that contribute to the probability of successful patient outcomes. We will not attempt to summarize in detail all the studies or issues on each of these factors; they have been discussed extensively elsewhere.

Comparative Studies of Brief Therapy

What do the research findings tell us about making treatment decisions that will best promote change for the patient Susan? Which type of brief therapy will produce an effective outcome that addresses her problems? Two relatively recent studies can help us make this decision. They both make use of a method of statistical analysis, called *meta-analysis*, in order to compare relatively similar studies based on a corrected treatment effect size. The first meta-analysis technique examined several different brief therapy approaches (Svartberg & Stiles, 1991). The authors chose 19 clinically relevant studies that met specific criteria to compare (1) short-term psychodynamic psychotherapies (STPP), (2) alternative therapies (AP) such as cognitive-supportive therapies, cognitive-behavioral therapies, experiential therapies and, attendance at self-help groups, and (3) no-treatment (NT) controls. They concluded the following: (1) STPP were superior to NT at posttreatment but inferior to AP both at posttreatment and at 1-year follow-up and (2) STPP were found to be less successful for treating depression, especially major depression, but (3) STPP and AP were equally successful with mixed neurotic patients. In discussing their results, Svartberg and Stiles point to the need to differentiate among different STPP approaches. For example, the research designs using STPP approaches differed in their formulation of a focus, in the application of techniques, and in the use of experienced or inexperienced therapists.

Meta-analysis was employed by Crits-

TABLE 20.1. Principles and Techniques That Guide Brief Therapies

Core set of principles that guide brief therapy:

1. Therapeutic goals are based on the view that patients are capable of changing throughout their life span.
2. The time required to achieve these goals is limited.
3. The development of a working alliance between therapist and patient is required to achieve the goals in a stated period of time.

Technical aspects that support the above principles:

1. The careful selection and exclusion of patients.
2. Rapid and early assessment of the patient.
3. Therapist actions that serve to promote the above principles. Among these actions are the maintenance of focus, high therapist activity, therapist flexibility, promptness of intervention, and addressing termination.

Source: Koss and Shiang (1993).

Christoph (1992), who conducted a review comparing studies of only those brief therapies based on a psychodynamic orientation. Eleven studies met the criteria for inclusion: (1) use of specific short-term dynamic psychotherapy (12 sessions minimum) guided by a treatment manual or manual-like guide, (2) use of experienced psychotherapists trained in the modality being offered, (3) use of a patient group (not an analogue), (4) comparison with a control group, and (5) reported data that allowed the calculation of effect sizes based on Cohen's *d* statistic (1977). These criteria are now increasingly being used to define high-quality research. Results indicate that brief dynamic therapy demonstrated large effects when compared with waiting-list conditions but was found to be only slightly superior to nonpsychiatric treatments. The largest effect size was found for the alleviation of target symptoms; 62% of the psychodynamically treated patients were more improved than nonpsychiatric comparison groups. However, comparisons across approaches showed that all psychiatric treatments and medications were equally effective.

The efficacy of cognitive therapy (CT) for the treatment of unipolar depression has been studied. CT has been found to be as effective as antidepressive medications (ADM) in numerous studies (Blackburn, Bishop, Glen, Whalley, & Christie, 1981; Dobson, 1989; Hollon, 1990; Robinson, Berman, & Neimeyer, 1990; Simons, Murphy, Levine, & Wet-

zel, 1986). However, differential effects have also been shown (Blackburn, Eunson, & Bishop, 1986); assessments of patients over time show that at 6-month and 2-year follow-up, subjects who had been treated with CT showed significantly fewer relapses than those treated with ADM. The same findings were replicated in several other studies with pools of subject suffering from acute depression (Kovacs, Rush, Beck, & Hollon, 1981).

How are we to determine which treatment will be most effective for Susan's set of problems? One might conclude from the first meta-analytic study that Susan would benefit from the group of therapies designated as alternate therapies (AP: cognitive-supportive, cognitive-behavioral, etc.), and that these would be more successful than dynamic therapies (STPP) if Susan is depressed. However, if she is diagnosed as being generally neurotic, then either AP or STPP would be suggested. The second study suggests that any of the STPP approaches would be useful and that some of her symptoms may be alleviated. At the same time, it is necessary to realize that because meta-analytic studies are based on many studies, the patients range in diagnosis from normal neurotics to severely disturbed. Do we actually expect every therapy to be able to treat all patients equally effectively? This expectation appears to ignore the requirement for selection and exclusion, as well as the need for a focal goal of the therapy—basic tenets of the short-term therapies.

It is quite possible that a patient's constellation of problems will be treated with different techniques, depending on the approach employed. Most clinicians realize that the patients included in the meta-analytic studies described above would not necessarily present with the same problems; that is, they did not all enter therapy with the same profile of symptoms, even if they were all diagnosed with depression. While assigning a diagnosis is standard fare for most clinicians, the diagnostic models of DSM-IV-R and ICD-9 are, unfortunately, not designed to determine what therapy is most appropriate, since the diagnosis itself has no direct relationship to the choice of therapy (Butcher & Koss, 1978). Furthermore, each patient enters therapy with specific characteristics that contribute to the particular manner in which he or she engages with the therapist. One approach that is increasingly being considered in the literature is the matching of specific problem constellations with specific forms of therapy that are, at least in manifest form, designed to address the specific problem. In other words, perhaps some therapies are better suited to address certain kinds of problems. How is the clinician to make informed choices? Here we are searching for the "active" ingredients of the therapies that contribute to positive outcome for specific patients.

Beutler and Clarkin (1990) have proposed a model that recognizes that "effective treatment is a consequence of increasingly fine-grained decisions. No effective treatment can be developed from information that is available at one point in time nor from decisions made on the basis of a static set of patient characteristics" (p. 20). In their model, called systematic treatment selection, they suggest four classes of variables that should be considered in the treatment decision process: (1) patient predisposing variables, (2) treatment contexts, (3) relationship variables, and (4) strategies and techniques. These classes of variables have the following characteristics: (1) each is part of an overall system, and each is therefore temporally and sequentially related to the others; (2) the variables are "activating" characteristics that describe both weaknesses and strengths (e.g., the patient's expectations and coping style can help determine to what degree the patient will engage in the therapeutic process); (3) the outcome of the interaction between the patient's presentation and the prior helping agencies must be considered at every decision point for further interventions; and (4) individual characteristics, as well as the situational context of the patient and therapist, must be considered.

Interpersonal Problems and Short-term Dynamic Interpersonal Therapies

Susan's presentation: Let us suppose that Susan come into a mental health clinic for the first time. She hopes that one-on-one therapy will be helpful to her; one of her girl friends "felt better" after being in therapy. Susan is the oldest child of a middle-class suburban family. Both her brother and sister have been married but are now divorced. An additional stress is that since her father's death, Susan's mother lives alone, and Susan worries about her mother's ability to manage on her own. Susan has been continuing in her daily job as a secretary, is able to talk in some detail about the supportive relationships in her past, and can talk articulately about her problems. She states, "I am feeling lonely and down ever since I broke up with my boyfriend. I guess somehow I knew it wasn't going to work out, even though we've been together two years. I suppose I did things to make it difficult. . . . I keep on ruining my relationships with men. Now I find that I'm avoiding social events." Since college she has had a number of boyfriends but says that she doesn't feel completely "at ease" with men.

After an assessment based on the model proposed by Beutler and Clarkin (1990), Susan is recommended for a course of short-term psychodynamic therapy. She meets the selection criteria. These approaches, such as interpersonal psychotherapy (Klerman, Weissman, Rounsaville, & Chevron, 1984), time-limited dynamic psychotherapy (Strupp & Binder, 1984), the use of a core conflictual relationship theme to define the therapy (Luborsky, 1984), and Silberschatz, Curtis, Sampson, and Weiss's control mastery approach (Curtis & Silberschatz, 1986) would, as part of the initial assessment, evaluate the quality of Susan's prior relationships (see Barber & Crits-Christoph, 1991). If Susan is now motivated to work on her problems and believes that the approach will help, clinical practice suggests that she may be able to make desired changes.

A number of assumptions and active ingredients underlie the interpersonal approaches to therapeutic change. One assumption related to the change process is that the patient's presenting symptoms (Such as Susan's avoidance of social events) are based on conflicts that are dynamically parallel to problems in long-standing interpersonal relationships. This is variously described as Menninger's (1958) triangle of insight (transference, significant others, parents), cyclical maladaptive patterns (Strupp & Binder, 1984), or the dynamic schemas and scripts of role-relationship models (Horowitz, 1991). To help relieve the symptoms, a primary goal is to articulate the parallel between present conflicts and prior maladaptive patterns.

An active ingredient of the interpersonal approaches is the building of the therapeutic alliance (Koss & Shiang, 1993). This requires that the therapist monitor and interpret selected aspects of the transference relationship to the patient, often in the context of the ongoing relationship. Gaston (1990) differentiated four independent aspects of the therapeutic alliance: (1) the therapeutic alliance, or the patient's affective relationship to the therapist, (2) the working alliance, or the patient's capacity to purposefully work in therapy, (3) the therapist's empathic understanding and involvement, and (4) the patient–therapist agreement on the goals and task of treatment. Although different definitions of the therapeutic alliance have been used in the past, these four categories have been repeatedly identified in empirical studies (Gomes-Schwartz, 1978; Hartley & Strupp, 1983; Marmar, Weiss, & Gaston, 1989).

Each of the psychodynamic approaches emphasizes specific techniques to address the development of the quality of the therapeutic alliance between patient and therapist. For example, in the approach of Strupp and Binder (1984), the therapist would attempt to provide Susan with a "new experience" in the development of a relationship. The therapeutic alliance would be addressed in the sessions by focusing on her expectations of the therapist and herself, the actual interactions that take place, and the practice of new aspects of the relationship. In theory, this challenges her past assumptions and behavior patterns concerning relationships in a manner that helps her make step-by-step changes toward practicing a new, more adaptive type of relationship. The process includes the facilitation of reality-based observations of herself and others, formulations of the impact of expectations, and, most importantly, practice in the new relationship.

Another ingredient is the determination of a specific focus for the therapy; in fact, this has been called the sine qua non of the brief psychodynamic approaches (Levenson & Hales, 1993). The therapist's adherence to a dynamic plan (based on the patient's pathogenic belief system) is strongly related to progress in therapy. This formulation describes the nature and etiology of the patient's problem (Perry, Cooper, & Michaels, 1987; Silberschatz & Curtis, 1986; Strupp & Binder, 1984). It also serves to focus the therapy on specific issues.

Let us consider the use of Strupp and Binder's (1984) time-limited dynamic psychotherapy (TLDP) with Susan. The therapist would determine (possibly in conjunction with the patient) the areas that are targeted for change. In Susan's case, the primary goal is to break her cycle of creating relationships that are nonsatisfying. To do this, the therapist would, over time, focus on the nature of her relationship with both her boyfriend and her father, the ways these relationships were similar and dissimilar, her expectations and behaviors in these relationships, and her wish for a different kind of relationship. It is the task of the therapist to (1) determine what aspects of the transference and the therapeutic alliance might be repetitions of her maladaptive interpersonal patterns and (2) in what ways the therapist must avoid reinforcing the maladaptive pattern, as well as (3) provide a new experience for the patient to promote change (Strupp & Binder, 1984).

In practice, the Strupp and Binder TLDP model suggests the identification of four structural elements of the patient's interpersonal transaction pattern. For Susan, her elements might be as follows:

1. *Acts of Self:* I don't get along with men. I am unattractive, and I feel badly about myself. When I am with other people, they see through me and I defer to them, especially men.

2. *Expectations About Others' Reactions:* When I show something about my real feelings, people get turned off. Most of the time, I think people either don't like me or can't be bothered. Men especially cut me off.

3. *Acts of Others Toward Self:* When I try to say what I think, people ignore me. Men overlook me, and much of the time I feel that people try to take advantage of me.

4. *Acts of Self Toward Self (Introject):* When others pay attention to me, I feel confused and unsure. This also happens when I feel excited or interested. I'm often not sure how to act, so I don't do anything or show only a little emotion. When men pay attention to me, I lose track of my own wishes.

These categories of action are outlined in the patient's "prototypic, maladaptive, cyclical interpersonal transaction pattern. If therapists systematically compare the structure of their formulations to this standard, then the format may also aid in recognizing when a tentative focus is incomplete and it may organize the pursuit of missing information" (Strupp & Binder, 1984, p. 76). Thus, the dynamic formulation will guide the therapist to be watchful for how the quality of interactions in the present transference tend to repeat Susan's past relationships. For example, the therapist might act in some manner that is perceived by the patient

as "acting just like my father." Here the therapist might have unwittingly exhibited some qualities that may be similar to the behaviors of men in the patient's life; addressing these interactions within the safety of the therapeutic setting will help bring the conflict right into the sessions in a more active manner. Providing the goal and set of foci thereby necessarily limits the nature of the therapeutic relationship, as well as the types of interpretations that are made. It helps clarify the new types of experiences the therapist is trying to provide for the patient.

Another method, the core conflictual relationship theme (CCRT) method (Luborsky, 1976, 1984), has also been found to be a reliable means of extracting central relationship themes as a focus of therapy. Spontaneous narratives about relationships told by the patient during psychotherapy can be analyzed into three general components: (1) the patient's main wishes, needs, or intentions toward others, (2) the responses of others, and (3) the responses of the self. In addition, responses of the self or others are rated as either positive or negative. The CCRT is then determined by those themes with the highest frequency in each of the three components. It is seen to reflect a conflict between, on the one hand, a constellation of wishes, needs, and intentions, and on the other hand, the responses of the self and others. Crits-Christoph and Luborsky (1990) found that while wishes had considerable stability over time, there was a slight decrease in the number of wishes when the later sessions were compared to the earlier ones. Positive change in therapy was determined by the even larger decreases over the course of therapy in the patient's total number of negative responses of others and the self.

Because several of the issues that brought Susan into therapy concern interpersonal relationships, Susan's case can easily be conceptualized using Luborsky's model (Luborsky & Crits-Christoph, 1990). In practice, core relationship themes would be identified by the therapist during the initial therapy sessions. Susan's narrative would be analyzed and classified, with an ear for the recurrent themes about her own wishes, needs, and intentions; her expectations about responses from others; and her typical ways of responding to herself. The result of the analysis would be a ranked set of key interpersonal themes drawn from Susan's life narrative and her interaction with the therapist in their sessions together. However, for our purposes, as an illustration, we will develop Susan's CCRT from her presenting information. Thus, the main entries on her CCRT "score sheet" might look something like this:

Wishes, Needs, Intentions	Responses from Others	Responses of Self
1. To be helped.	1. Are more independent than I am.	1. Am dependent.
2. To be accepted.	2. Are rejecting.	2. Am disappointed.
3. To be understood.	3. Are stronger than I am.	3. Feel unloved.

A brief glance at Susan's most important themes quickly identifies areas of potential conflict between her deepest needs and her expected and experienced responses from others. Susan's wish for approval and understanding is at odds with her experience of other people as disapproving, critical, and autonomous. Further, she generally describes herself as submissive, unfulfilled, and alone; her assessments about her own actions and her actual experiences confirm her expectations.

How reliably can these dynamic formulation be made? Horowitz, Rosenberg, Ureno, Kalehzan, and O'Halloran (1989) described a new method of aggregating psychodynamic formulations made independently by a number of clinicians to provide a standardized and reliable guide for therapy. They found that interrater reliability was greatest for formulations with a high proportion of interpersonal content.

Let us turn to an examination of empirical research. What aspects of the patient–therapist relationship have been found to be beneficial? A number of studies that employ the case study method (using small samples and intensive analysis) suggest the importance of attending to the interactional sequences and the patient's reaction to interventions. These methods help us clarify and examine what actually occurs in the "laboratory" of one-on-one interactions between the therapist and patient. One of these

avenues of inquiry focuses on the events that occur in-session, as well as the particular sequencing of events. Stiles et al. (1991) have used an assimilation model to understand the systematic sequence of changes that can be used to describe a patient's experience (memory, feeling, idea, impulse, wish, attitude) during psychotherapy. Using case studies, they have examined the interactional patterns that involve change. The model suggests that parallel transformations take place in both the cognitive and affective spheres—each with its own trajectory. The problematic experience is thought to be gradually assimilated into a new schema during the process of patient–therapist interactions.

Another method identifies those events determined to be significant or critical. The Therapeutic Impacts Content Analysis System (Elliot, James, Reimschuessel, Cislo, & Sack, 1985) and its shorter version, Brief Structured Recall (Elliot & Shapiro, 1988), have been used to measure the immediate impact of therapist interventions on patients. Results indicated that patients typically identified significant events in therapy that occurred in the last half of the session and that these events were approximately 5 to 10 minutes in duration. Significant events were generally interchanges between the dyad but were attributed by the patient mainly to the therapist. Patients reported that the most helpful interventions were those related to specific tasks as opposed to interpersonal issues. The main limitation of the study, as with most of these studies, was the small sample size. However, it is clear that the use of a small number of cases allows for a depth of knowledge that is essential for determining which intervention sequences are perceived as helpful to the therapeutic work.

The work of McCullough, Winston, Farber, Porter, Pollack, Laikin, Vingiano, and Trujillo (1991) also examines the interaction between therapist and patient. Their study is a comparative project that focused on two forms of brief therapy, short-term dynamic psychotherapy and brief adaptation-oriented psychotherapy, in 16 patient–therapist cases. The interaction sequences were reviewed using a process coding system developed by one of the authors. Their results indicated that in both forms of brief therapy, the frequency of patients' affective and defensive responses after a therapist's intervention accounted for 66% of the outcome variance. An interpretation by the therapist followed within 3 minutes by an affective response by the patient was related to improvement at termination, whereas a therapist interpretation followed by a defensive response by the patient was linked to a negative outcome. While there are inherent problems with the use of self-reports as measures of outcome, and while these findings are also based on a small sample, sequential analysis holds promise for understanding the types of interactional processes that contribute to a successful outcome. The work of Winston, Pinsker, and McCullough (1986) suggests that the role of identification is important to the patient; in supportive dynamic psychotherapy, patients have been found to change largely through issues related to their identification with the therapist rather than through the uncovering of dynamic conflict in their interpersonal patterns.

Another method of analysis, the Structural Analysis of Social Behavior (SASB) (Benjamin, 1982), has been found to be effective in determining which therapist behaviors can be categorized as helpful or harmful and how these behaviors relate to successful or poor outcomes (Henry, Schacht, & Strupp, 1986). The SASB provides a fine-grained, highly specific analysis of interpersonal events and allows for the coding of verbal statements into a number of categories. Henry et al. compared four therapists, each of whom saw a good and a poor outcome case (N-8). The good therapeutic outcomes were differentiated from the poor outcomes on interpersonal process variables such as helping and protecting, affirming and understanding, as well as blaming and belittling. Negative complementarity between therapist and patient was greater in the cases with a poor outcome. In the poor outcome studies, 22% of the therapist responses and 17% of the patient responses were coded as complex communications compared to the successful outcome studies, where the respective figures were 0% and 2%.

On the basis of these findings and others, we would expect the therapist to focus on the timing of interpretations, the patient's response to these interpretations, and the affect, behaviors, and situational variables of interpersonal relationships in the context of the relationship-as-lived in the therapeutic room.

Unipolar Depression and Cognitive-oriented Therapies

Susan's presentation: Susan walks into the community clinic, stating, "I keep on thinking that I'll never have a good relationship. I'm depressed, have no energy, can't sleep, and have no appetite. I don't go out and meet people because I know anyone I meet won't be interested. I've been feeling this way for the last three weeks. I tried some medications, but I don't want to take them anymore." With this presentation, Susan may now meet the diagnostic criteria for unipolar depression, but she has been noncompliant in taking medications.

After applying Beutler and Clarkin's (1990) methods of assessment, we find that Susan appears to be a person whose symptom presentation and problem list would be best addressed by treatment in one of the cognitive-oriented therapies. Her patterns of thinking contribute to her problems, and at this point in time she is not exhibiting suicidal ideation. Later, she may be more amenable to trying antidepressants. Cognitive-oriented approaches, such as cognitive restructuring (Beck, Rush, Shaw, & Emery, 1984), self-instructional therapy (Meichenbaum, 1977), and rational-emotive therapy (Ellis & Grieger, 1977), will focus the therapy on the patient's maladaptive belief systems and nonadaptive behaviors.

Let us consider the mechanisms of change that underlie the cognitive-oriented therapies. What are the active ingredients of these therapies that promote change? Cognitive-oriented therapies consider irrational beliefs (such as "I need to be perfect in everything I do or else I will fail") as the key to change. The cognitive theory of depression suggests that a latent cognitive schema based on erroneous beliefs and maladaptive information creates conditions whereby the person is in a ready state to become depressed. Once the schema is activated, negative mood states are thought to influence and perpetuate negative automatic thoughts (Beck, 1976). Beck calls the negative cognitive bias that is facilitated by the negative mood state the *cognitive triad* (Beck, 1976). In this model, the depressed individual is characterized by negative thoughts about the self, the world, and the future. These thoughts are maintained by systematic cognitive distortions.

Cognitive-oriented therapies operationalize this theory by helping patients recognize and readjust their patterns of thinking with structured techniques that focus the patient's thinking on pleasant events and promote the observation and blocking of negative automatic thoughts (cognitive disputation). In Susan's case, the first phases of treatment would help her to monitor her automatic thoughts and interpretations of her experience, as well as to recognize the connection between her thoughts, feelings, and behavior. Together, Susan and her therapist would generate a list of her typical thoughts. For Susan, the list might look something like this:

1. *Thoughts About the Self*
   I am unattractive.
   I am unsuccessful.
   I cannot sustain a relationship with a man.
2. *Thoughts About the World*
   No one cares about anyone else.
   Life is joyless, something to be "lived through."
3. *Thoughts About the Future*
   I will never have a satisfying relationship.
   I will always ruin things just when they seem to be going okay.

Once these thoughts are identified, Susan's therapist would help her examine the evidence for and against each interpretation. Eventually, Susan would be able to manage this process on her own, and her attributions about experience would become more reality-based. Thus, rather than typically making arbitrary or dichotomous statements about herself, she would begin to take a more balanced view of herself and others.

Persons (1989) suggests understanding patients' problems using a two-level model. At the first level, the patient is understood to have underlying psychological problems. These basic problems are manifested at a second level, where mood, behavior, and cognitions interact. The interdependence of these three components is illustrated by the work of Zeiss, Lewinsohn, and Muñoz (1979). Using cognitive therapy, behavior therapy, and supportive therapy to treat depressed patients, they found that interventions in one system created change in another system. For example, change in a behavioral area was shown to contribute to changes in mood and cognitions.

Barber and DeRubeis (1989) studied cognitive therapy and suggest that the learning of compensatory skills is another active ingredient promoting change. The patient learns a set of skills used to curtail negative thinking both during the acute episode and during the remission phase after the episode. The researchers suggest that greater patient change results from the development of these skills rather than from the generally accepted techniques of promoting accommodation of the patient's belief system to a more functional system.

The literature also suggests that practitioners should consider Susan's reactions to stress and life events. Research has consistently shown a relationship between stressful life events and depression (Billings & Moos, 1982; Thoits, 1983). Variables that act as mediators in this process include as the person's individual appraisals, personality characteristics, social supports, and coping methods. An assessment of Susan's problems would include an evaluation of her situation, the particular ways in which she tries to change her responses to these events, and her general social network. These will help the clinician predict her specific responses to stressors (Billings, Cronkite, & Moos, 1983;

Lazarus & Folkman, 1984) and could be addressed directly in a form of brief, supportive cognitive-oriented therapy.

In recent years, several cognitively oriented approaches have placed greater emphasis on the quality of the interactions between therapist and patient. Affective as well as cognitive factors have become important in determining the therapeutic outcome. Greenberg and Safran (1987), basing their ideas on the work of Gassner, Sampson, Weiss, and Brumer (1982), suggest that it is critical to allow patients to explore the interaction between their affective-cognitive processes (e.g., when the patient wants something but feels bad about wanting it). This process serves to allow "warded-off" material to emerge. Margolin and Fernandez (1985) have considered the impact of affect on dysfunctional behaviors associated with marital discord. Persons and Burns (1985) suggest that both technical and interpersonal interventions contribute to successful outcomes.

Another important issue that has been researched is that of relapse. If Susan finishes her course of therapy and positive change occurs, how likely is she to relapse? In other words, can change be maintained? One empirical study suggests that intermittent therapy may be helpful in maintaining gains from a course of therapy. In this study, patients suffering from recurrent unipolar depression were treated with a modified form of interpersonal psychotherapy (IPT-M) over the course of 3 years or for approximately 36 sessions (Frank, 1991). Although this study used a protocol that involved medications and a time frame that is somewhat longer than that of the typical time-limited brief therapy, it represents a prototype of intermittent therapy that may prove to be important to the maintenance of everyday functioning for certain types of patients diagnosed with unipolar depression. Patients were first treated for acute depression with imipramine and IPT-M. Those who were in stable remission for 20 weeks were then randomly assigned to one of five maintenance treatment cells: IPT-M alone, IPT-M with active imipramine, IPT-M with placebo, medication clinic with imipramine, or medication clinic with placebo. Patients were seen for 3 years on a monthly basis. A primary focus of the therapy was to identify interpersonal, cognitive, and somatic issues that were related to the onset of a depressive episode. Patients who received IPT-M alone or IPT-M plus placebo were in remission for an average of 10 months longer than patients receiving medication clinic with placebo (61 weeks vs. 21 weeks). This study suggests that if Susan's depressive symptoms can be successfully treated first, she may benefit from an intermittent course of interpersonal therapy alone that takes place over an extended period of time.

CRISIS INTERVENTION/SUPPORT THERAPIES

Approaches and Assumptions

Lindemann's (1944) classic study of the Coconut Grove Nightclub disaster, in which nearly 500 people died from a fire, provided one of the first models for the development of therapies based on the principles of crisis theory. "Prevention interventions" with survivors and family members of the fire victims provided immediate support and treatment as a response to the traumatic event. On the basis of this work, Lindemann was able to delineate the phases of grief that people predictably experienced in order to return to their prior level of functioning. With Lindemann's work as a model and its elaboration by Caplan (1964), crisis intervention/support or crisis-oriented therapies have evolved into a form of therapy that is generally provided at a time when the patient has experienced an extreme stressor such as rape, the diagnosis of cancer, an earthquake, or the death of a significant other. In the last decade, crisis-oriented therapies have also been found to be effective both on a one-on-one basis and when provided in a group treatment format (Budman, Demby, Feldstein, & Gold, 1984; Imber & Evanczuk, 1990). Generic crisis interventions are well described by Caplan (1964) and Klein and Lindemann

TABLE 20.2. Principles and Techniques That Guide Crisis Intervention/Support Therapies

Core set of principles that guide crisis intervention/support therapies

1. Therapeutic goals are based on the view that patients are capable of changing throughout their life span.
2. The time required to achieve these goals is limited.
3. The nature of the crisis and its impact must be clearly defined.
4. The acute nature of a crisis requires immediate intervention in order to restore the individual/group to its prior level of adaptive functioning.
5. A broad set of interventions may be employed, including one-on-one meetings, the use of medications, interventions with social support and community agencies (police, schools, government, hospitals, etc.), interventions with family members, etc.

Technical aspects of crisis intervention/support therapies

1. The crisis team emphasizes rapid assessment of the crisis and the person's reaction to it.
2. Interventions are reality-based, and are focused on the present crisis and on problems that have ensued.
3. The therapy may often require taking a systemic point of view; contact with family and social network members may be required for effective intervention.
4. The therapist may often be required to engage with the patient in multiple roles—as an educator, an advisor, a facilitator, etc. The techniques employed in crisis-oriented therapies are therefore somewhat different from those employed in general brief therapies.

(1961). Other approaches to crisis intervention are crisis therapy (Butcher, Stelmachers, & Maudal, 1984), the precipitating stress approach (Harris, Kalis, & Freeman, 1963), early access brief treatment (Jacobson, 1965, 1979), crisis-oriented psychotherapy (Levy, 1966), and approaches to supportive crisis therapy including dynamically oriented supportive psychotherapy (Coleman, 1960; Coleman & Zwerling, 1959), and crisis support therapy (Sifneos, 1972). In the following section, the discussion will be based largely on findings from clinical practice. While general efficacy studies indicate that measured improvement has been found in 60–70% of the clients who enter crisis-oriented therapies (Butcher & Koss, 1978; Kolotkin & Johnson, 1983), it is important to note that relatively little rigorous empirical outcome research has been conducted in this area. This is due, in part, to the fact that the emergency nature of the work means that people are often in and out of therapy, with little opportunity for evaluation at the end of the treatment. Other problems in conducting research are those that relate to determining comparable control groups, specifying the exact nature of the treatments, and defining meaningful outbcome criteria. People who seek treatment for crisis situations are, by definition, in inherently

difficult positions; it would be unethical not to put their specific needs before a research protocol.

Both the researcher and the practitioner realize that there are many ways in which brief therapies and crisis-oriented therapies overlap in their approaches and purpose. It is therefore not surprising that a number of the general principles outlined in Table 20.1 for brief therapies are the same as those that guide crisis intervention/support therapies as outlined in Table 20.2.

However, the acute onset of a crisis creates a number of specific issues that must be used to guide the formulation of the problem and the stated goals.

An immediate goal of crisis-oriented treatment is that the anxiety tied to the specific crisis is to be ameliorated in as timely a fashion as possible. Thus, the focus of change is on the person's specific emotional reaction to the crisis event (Ewing, 1990). In general, a *crisis* is defined as a specific event, which is generally viewed as a stressor by the patient or others, and which occurs in an acute manner. It precipitates specific symptoms that impede normal everyday functioning (Imber & Evanczuk, 1990). Budman and Bennett (1983) suggest that the definition of crisis should also include the feeling of loss or actual loss that accompanies the acute event. Caplan (1964) maintains that the reactions to the crisis are to be seen as normal even if the person suffers severe decompensation. Clinical experience has shown that the psychological disequilibrium that ensues after a traumatic event can create a time when patients are willing and able to address issues concerning the crisis and their ability to cope, as well as fundamental personality changes (Levenson & Hales, 1993). It is the patient's perception of the situation that can create "a turning point in the person's life" (Bard & Ellison, 1974, p. 68).

Ewing (1990) suggests a general model for the practice of crisis intervention that can be applied in general to crisis-oriented therapies. This model delineates six essential stages that guide the process of intervention: (1) delineating the problem focus, (2) evaluation, (3) contracting, (4) intervening, (5) termination, and (6) follow-up. Often this process can take place within a few hours or a few meetings. Thus, there is a general consensus that crisis management principally entails a pragmatic belief in therapeutic activism, delaying the patient's destructive impulses (if any), restoring hope, environmental intervention, and consideration of hospitalization (Ewing, 1990).

Hobbs (1984) suggests that a distinction be made between crisis *intervention* and crisis *support* therapy. Butcher et al. (1984) also suggest distinguishing between approaches based on the availability of ego reserves and the person's reaction to the immediate crisis. The patient's level of ego strength, coping, and personal reactions to the extreme stressor are critical in determining which approach is appropriate for a particular person. Based on the theories of coping and adaptation, the authors suggest that a dispositional crisis is one in which the individual's ability to cope is not threatened by the crisis situation. Such problems may be nonpsychological in nature and intervention could be as simple as finding the client a bed for the night. For example, if Susan has experienced a discrete crisis but is coping reasonably well and has a level of ego strength that predicts a normal resolution over

a relatively brief period of time, then she is suffering from a dispositional crisis. In contrast, there are instances where the individual believes that he or she cannot cope with the crisis. Decompensation or an inability to function may result; crisis therapy is recommended. In such cases, the therapist will examine the precipitating events and explore more adaptive means of coping. It is important to note that these are theoretical distinctions and are not based on outcome differences in empirical studies.

Let us now discuss some of the more Salient technical aspects of these approaches. An essential aspect of both crisis intervention and crisis therapy is that the therapist must gain a swift and clear understanding of the events that precipitated the crisis and their personal relevance to the patient. Thus, one of the first tasks is to determine the focus of the intervention so that the immediate crisis can be handled in an adaptive manner. Ewing (1990) states, "The key to an appropriate problem focus is almost always found in the client's description of the event(s) or situation(s) which precipitated his or her call for help" (p. 284). He suggests that once the therapist has established some initial rapport, it is appropriate to ask such questions as "Why now?" or "What has led you to seek help at this particular time?" (p. 284). The answers to these questions will usually provide important clues in determining the problem focus.

It is also essential to review the client's recent life experiences (e.g., family, work, social relationships, and sexual functioning) as well as the stressors related to the problem. In any crisis situation, it is assumed that the therapist will continue to assess the patient's mood and affect in order to screen for possible suicidal or homicidal ideation.

A history of past psychological treatment is essential to determine if the client is suitable for crisis treatment. A chronic history of maladjustment suggests that brief crisis intervention or therapy may be unsuccessful without making specific modifications in the level of involvement of the patient. Further, an active assessment of the patient's strengths and coping mechanisms will provide the first clues in determining meaningful interventions. Sometimes an intervention can be facilitated more swiftly by gathering this data through the use of standardized questionnaires such as the Beck Depression Inventory (Beck, 1976).

Butcher et al. (1984) state that the therapist must take an active role by articulating (1) a preliminary formulation of the patient's problem, (2) the contribution of the forces at work that resulted in conflict, and (3) the goals and means of help that are available. In addition, the empathic expression of the therapist's understanding of the emotional meaning of the hazardous situation can, in itself, serve to reduce anxiety and foster hope (Hobbs, 1984). Following these steps gives the patient an opportunity to integrate the therapist's perceptions, as well as to correct the information and impressions that go into formulating an intervention. The importance of the therapist's flexibility is emphasized in the work of Prazoff, Joyce, and Azim (1986), who suggest that the crisis situation requires the therapist to provide information, use reframing techniques, and provide immediate behavioral and cognitive interventions.

Crisis Interventions

In this approach, the focus of crisis interventions is on the resolution of the immediate crisis and restoration of the previous level of functioning. Crisis intervention is appropriate for those individuals who are in danger of decompensating but who possess adequate levels of ego reserves and have a history of adaptive functioning. The optimal therapeutic goal is improved functioning within 5–6 weeks (Caplan, 1964). For the patient Susan, the recent loss of her boyfriend combined with the recent loss of her father might be experienced as a crisis. She may come into the community clinic exhibiting signs of disorientation, inability to sleep, and a tendency to "break down crying at the smallest thing." She has called her employer for the last 5 days to say that she's sick and doesn't know if she can face the people on her work team. The immediate intervention is to find a way for Susan to return to her usual level of functioning.

In recent years, the rapid expansion of crisis intervention services has contributed to confusion about the meaning of the term *crisis intervention* (Kolotkin & Johnson, 1983). A number of crisis intervention programs have been developed for people who are admitted to clinics with specific problems such as rape, substance abuse, physical abuse, and sexual dysfunction (Roberts, 1990). In work with adolescents, it has been found that an intervention made in conjunction with the whole family can produce a greater impact than with the adolescent alone, especially if there is a threat of suicide (Lansley & Kaplan, 1968; Lewis, Walker, & Mehr, 1990). Other agencies may also become involved; interventions with women and children who have been repeatedly battered may include police-based crisis teams. This obviously requires an increased sensitivity to the need for strict confidentiality in order to keep the abusing husband from gaining access to families at risk (Roberts, 1990). Each of these modifications of the general crisis intervention approach attempts to carefully define the specific issues consequent to the crisis, as well as to clarify the specific procedures that address particular reactions.

According to Hobbs (1984), the first step in crisis intervention is to determine the degree of decompensation already present. For example, patients who are floridly psychotic, suicidal, or homicidal may require emergency hospitalization. Jacobson, Strickler, and Morley (1968) describe four levels of crisis intervention, all of which are effective with certain types of clients. The first level is environmental manipulation, whereby the helper serves as a referral source. The second level, general support, involves active listening without threatening or challenging the patient's basic personality structure. In the third level, the generic approach, a particular crisis is believed to have a similar meaning to most affected individuals, regardless of their personality dynamics. Generic crisis intervention requires that the therapist have techniques that are particularly helpful in resolving specific crises. The fourth level is the individual approach, which stresses understanding the personality dynamics of patients and helping them to develop insight into why the present situation developed into a crisis.

Crisis Support

In crisis support, the focus is on eliminating the factors that caused the crisis while offering ongoing support, guidance, and, in many cases, medication. Crisis support has been defined as being appropriate for those individuals who are in imminent danger of decompensating. In general, they exhibit limited ego reserves and have a history of chronic maladjustment to life's problems. Crisis emergency agencies such as suicide hot lines and parent and teenage hot lines often work with patients with these types of problems.

Crisis-support therapists employ techniques from orientations as diverse as behavioral, cognitive, cognitive-behavioral, and psychodynamic to obtain a detailed account of the behaviors, cognitions, and interpersonal dynamics associated with the dysfunction. With this information in hand, the therapist can focus on the areas that will provide the greatest leverage for change (Kendall, Vitousek, & Kane, 1991). Once there is agreement on the problem focus, adherence is monitored by both the patient and the therapist through the use of homework assignments, role plays, setting tasks, and so on. One example of this approach is Lazarus' (1989) multimodal approach. Assessment of a patient's "BASIC ID" allows the therapist to incorporate information on *Behavior, Affect, Sensation, Imagery, Cognition, Interpersonal,* and *Drugs/biology* into both the problem formulation and intervention plan. These elements are viewed as being interdependent; a change in one component is likely to produce change in other components. For our patient, Susan, her BASIC ID would summarize information about her presenting problem, as well as her habitual or preferential ways of moving through life. Based on the information presented in the vignette, Susan's BASIC ID might look something like this:

- *Behavior*
  Isolative
  Self-effacing
  Creates difficulties in relationships with men
- *Affect*
  Depression
  Anxiety and worry
  Loneliness
- *Sensation*
  Tension
  Feeling of heaviness
  Frequent headaches
- *Imagery*
  Pictures self as unattractive
  Imagines that she will always be alone
- *Cognition*
  "Men think I'm not worth bothering with."
  "I will never have a satisfying relationship."
  "My unhappiness is my own fault."
  "Suicide might be a solution."
- *Interpersonal*
  Dependent and demanding
- *Drugs/Biology*
  Exercises regularly
  Undereats when stressed

Let us consider how crisis-support therapy might be helpful to Susan. What modifications must be made if Susan suddenly becomes more active and considers suicide? For example, in Susan's BASIC ID, she is now actively suicidal; she has become overwhelmed by the loss of her father and boyfriend, is unable to work satisfactorily, and does not believe she possesses the ability to deal with her losses. The patient who presents with acute suicidal ideation forces the therapist to shift quickly to adopt a preventive approach that is reality-based.

It is well known that depression generally increases the risk of suicide. A large-scale prospective study of patients found that of the 954 patients with major affective disorders, 25 committed suicide. Hopelessness, loss of pleasure or interest, and mood cycling during the index episode differentiated the suicide group (Fawcett et al., 1987). In terms of practice, the researchers noted that, although suicide was a relatively frequent event in depressed patients, it still had a statistically low base rate; therefore, using cross-sectional measures was probably statistically unpredictable on an individual basis.

More specifically in Susan' case, it is important to set aside predetermined goals to help Susan through this crisis. Continual assessment of her suicidal thoughts and behaviors becomes the highest priority. Obviously, this level of attention is necessary regardless of whether the patient is being treated with interpersonal or cognitive-oriented approaches. Buie and Maltsberger (1989) point out that persons who are vulnerable to suicide often have not developed their own internal resources for self-soothing. These vulnerable individuals must look to resources external to themselves for a sense of comfort, and without these external resources, they experience aloneness (defined as a vacant, cold feeling of isolative and hopeless discomfort). Here, Buie and Maltsberger have elaborated on Kohut's position (Kohut, 1971) that people need to feel valuable, suggesting that immature, narcissistic individuals often use idealized or mirrored external others (self-objects) to feel a sense of value, and that when these self-objects are lost, vulnerable patients "fall prey to dangerous affects of worthlessness or aloneness (sometimes to both at once). Their survival is then in danger" (Buie & Maltsberger, 1989, p. 35). Also, the prudent clinician will be constantly on the lookout for any losses by the patient of external resources for self-worth or soothing. This leads us to consider the impact of crisis intervention/support therapies and the change that is fostered through their approaches.

It is interesting to note that Freud, like many present-day clinicians who deal with depression and self-destructiveness regularly in practice, came to adopt a pragmatic treatment attitude while developing psychoanalysis. In 1926, Freud wrote about a young patient, "What weighs on me in his case is my belief that unless the outcome is very good, it will be very bad indeed. What I mean is that he would commit suicide without any hesitation. I shall

do everything in my power to avert that eventuality" (Litman, 1989, p. 328).

For example, in looking at the most common emergency and crisis situation in clinical practice, the issue of patient suicidality, one powerful element in the treatment of suicidal patients is conveying to these patients that their lives truly matter to the therapist. Maltsberger (1989), in commenting on a clinical interview conducted by Havens (1989) with a chronically suicidal patient, pointed out that it is clear from the interview that Havens, if necessary, would be prepared to continue listening to the patient's despair for hours and hours rather than giving up hope, waiting for some spontaneous movement. The central concern here is that the psychotherapist become a self-sustaining object in order to counteract the highly corrosive affects of worthlessness and despair. Maltsberger quoted Elvin Semrad, speaking of Freida Fromm-Reichman: "that little old lady kept coming back and coming back and coming back and coming back until the patient could not stand it any longer. Something had to give. He used to say if you will stay with a patient long enough without surrender one day the patient will say to himself, 'If this doctor can care so much and be so interested in me, maybe I've got it wrong, maybe I've got something worthwhile that I can't see but he can.' But one must wait. You cannot be in a hurry" (Maltsberger, 1989, p. 415).

Jacobs (1989) concluded that using the empathic method in therapy with depressed and suicidal patients challenges the psychologist to be where the patient is—a place where "under ordinary circumstances, we would not choose to go. . . . We must be able to see death in its darkest moments to make it possible to see the light" (p. 341). In Susan's case, she may need a course of therapy that will, in essence, provide immediate relief in order to get her ready for longer-term therapy.

TRAINING ISSUES FOR THERAPISTS

The use of training manuals and manuals as guides for conducting therapy has recently gained greater credibility. Some advanced training programs have begun to use manuals to help therapists develop both a solid theoretical framework and the methods to practice that orientation. In 1978 the American Association of Directors of Residency Training conducted a survey of psychiatric residency programs. It was found that 88% offered a training experience in brief therapy; for 78% of the programs, it was a requirement. Many of these programs teach a manualized approach. However, it is sobering to realize that a survey of the clinicians actually practicing brief therapy in two states found that only a third had actually received formal training in brief therapy (Levenson, Speed, & Budman, 1992).

A number of research projects are now making use of manuals (Beck, Rush, Shaw, & Emery, 1984; Klerman, Weissman, Rounsaville, & Chevron, 1984; Luborsky & Crits-Christoph, 1990; Strupp & Binder, 1984). While it is foolish to expect that all moment-to-moment decisions in a therapy session can be made based on the use of a manual, it is still reasonable to expect that the decision-making process can be guided by the use of a manual. Unfortunately, many clinicians have not had formal training in brief therapy, yet they spend approximately 40% of their time providing some form of brief therapy (Levenson et al., 1992). The systematic training of clinicians in a specific form of brief therapy is a requirement for any outcome research that attempts to draw conclusions about the effectiveness of therapy. In reviewing research studies, it is clear that many projects do not actually train therapists in a systematic way in brief therapy before testing hypotheses. Training, supervision, and the use of manuals provide guidelines for the practice of brief therapy. No matter what theoretical orientation is espoused, systematic training begins to address the issues of reliable measurement—a key component of quality psychotherapy research. According to Koss and Shiang (1993), it has generally been found that (1) systematic training on the part of the therapist enhances patient outcome, lowers rates of attrition, and decreases recidivism, (2) the attitudes and values of therapists are im-

portant markers that affect their approach to providing therapy, (3) programmatic training has been shown to change therapists' attitudes concerning the provision of brief therapy, and (4) continual supervision is required to maintain adherence to the technical aspects of brief therapy.

CONCLUSIONS

In this chapter, we have tried to illustrate how a number of brief therapy approaches would address varying aspects of Susan's problems and, depending on the approach, the specific aspects of the therapy that would be emphasized. We have suggested that Beutler and Clarkin's (1990) systematic treatment selection provides the clinician with a structured decision-making process for determining which therapy approach will be more likely to produce beneficial results for patients.

We have presented a brief sketch of how Susan's characteristics and problems would be treated using psychodynamic and cognitive-oriented approaches. Next, we have considered crisis intervention/support therapies. In our attempt to make clear the distinction between brief and crisis intervention/support therapies, as well as to illustrate these differences with the use of a case example, we have not been able to be as thorough as we would like in our presentation of the therapeutic process and outcome. Consideration of both the clinical issues and the requirements of research programs would necessarily involve a discussion of the many complex issues that contribute to both processes. However, we have tried to show that research results can inform clinical decisions. We consider this approach to be most successful when the needs of the patient are thoroughly assessed and then, depending on the context, a treatment approach is offered that directly addresses the needs of the patient. Often, as most clinicians know, this is more easily said than done. Furthermore, these decisions often take place by inference or clinical intuition, and while they are often right on the mark, we frequently do not know what constellation of factors created the right climate for engagement and change. Then when we attempt to replicate our success, we are left in the vulnerable position of being unclear about what it was that contributed to success.

In conclusion, we would like to offer a few further thoughts on several general considerations that underlie much of the discussion in the chapter:

1. Should we expect all therapists to be equally effective for all people, regardless of their presentation? The predominant research paradigm appears to be based on this expectation. Isn't this much like asking for a vial of magic that will cure all problems? We now know enough about human development, change processes, and mental illness to realize that not all approaches will be equally effective with all populations.

2. We assume that clarifying the issues that contribute to assessment, selection, and exclusion for treatment (or designation to treatment groups), method of treatment, determination of specific outcome measures, and so on are essential for both good therapy and good research. Experimental research and the analysis of case materials are two overlapping methods of inquiry which will help determine what active factors contribute to change. Should people receive differential treatment based on their ability to relate to others, their prior history with the therapeutic community, or their diagnosis? What is the interaction of these factors in predicting long-term successful treatment? Without high-quality research that helps us to understand how these questions, among many others, are addressed by different approaches, we are still groping (largely in the dark).

3. The goal of therapy is to provide quality treatment to address the specific issues that the patient brings to therapy. Along the way, the patient may experience less suffering and more adaptive functioning. At times, treatment may focus on the immediate issues at hand. At other times, it may focus on long-standing problems that originated in early relationships with others. The patient may engage in crisis intervention/support therapy today and next week may need interpersonal therapy. After therapy, the patient may be able to face the problems of today in a more adaptive manner and achieve his or her goals.

4. One of the most important issues therapists and researchers face is that of how to facilitate change in patients. While we have generally relied on our clinical judgment and experience, we suggest that clinicians can now look to (and participate in) research endeavors that help us clarify the issues, consider the actual components involved in the process of therapy, consider the range of hypotheses that explain the variables that contribute to change, and concretize the means to achieve desired outcomes for our patients.

Our patients will be more competently served if we know how change occurs, what we can do to foster change, and what we must encourage our patients to try to do in order to produce change. Therefore, as practitioners, if we can find ways to conduct our clinical work while keeping in mind the parameters that constitute a quality research program, we will, in the long run, find ways to balance the requirements of scientific replication while serving the needs of individual patients.

Acknowledgments

The authors would like to thank Michael Wolfe, K. F. Lee Smithson, and Tish Kuljian for their helpful comments and contributions.

REFERENCES

Barber, J. P., & Crits-Christoph, P. (1991). Comparison of the brief dynamic psychotherapies. In P. Crits-Christoph & J. P. Barber (Eds.), *Handbook of short-term dynamic psychotherapy* (pp. 323–355). New York: Basic Books.

Barber, J. P., & DeRubeis, R. J. (1989). On second thought: Where the action is in cognitive therapy for depression. *Cognitive Therapy and Research, 13,* 441–457.

Bard, M., & Ellison, K. (1974, May). Crisis intervention and investigation of forcible rape. *The Police Chief, 41,* pp. 68–73.

Beck, A. T. (1976). *Cognitive therapy and the emotional disorders.* Madison, CT: International Universities Press.

Beck, A. T., Rush, A. J., Shaw, B. F., & Emery, G. (1984). *Cognitive therapy of depression. A treatment manual.* New York: Guilford Press.

Benjamin, L. S. (1982). Use of structural analysis of social behavior (SASB) to guide intervention in psychotherapy. In J. C. Anchin & D. J. Kiesler (Eds.), *Handbook of interpersonal psychotherapy* (pp. 190–212). New York: Pergamon Press.

Beutler, L. E., & Clarkin, J. F. (1990). *Systematic treatment selection toward targeted therapeutic interventions.* New York: Brunner/Mazel.

Billings, A. G., Cronkite, R. C., & Moos, R. H. (1983). Social-environmental factors in unipolar depression: Comparisons of depressed patients and nondepressed controls. *Journal of Abnormal Psychology, 92,* 119–133.

Billings, A. G., & Moos, R. H. (1982). Psychosocial theory and research on depression: An integrative framework and review. *Clinical Psychology Review, 2,* 213–237.

Blackburn, I. M., Bishop, S., Glen, A. I. M., Whalley, L. J., & Christie, J. E. (1981). The efficacy of cognitive therapy in depression: A treatment trial using cognitive therapy and pharmacotherapy, each alone and in combination. *British Journal of Psychiatry, 139,* 181–189.

Blackburn, I. M., Eunson, K. M., & Bishop, S. (1986). A two-year naturalistic follow-up of 38 depressed patients treated with cognitive therapy, pharmacotherapy and a combination of both. *Journal of Affective Disorders, 10,* 67–75.

Budman, S. H., & Bennett, M. J. (1983). Short-term group psychotherapy. In H. I. Kaplan & B. J. Sadock (Eds.), *Comprehensive group psychotherapy* (2nd ed., pp. 138–144). Baltimore: Williams & Wilkins.

Budman, S. H., Demby, A., Feldstein, M., & Gold, M. (1984). The effects of time-limited group psychotherapy: A controlled study. *International Journal of Group Psychotherapy, 34,* 587–603.

Buie, D. H., & Maltsberger, J. T. (1989). The psychological vulnerability to suicide. In D. G. Jacobs & H. N. Brown (Eds.), *Suicide: Understanding and responding: Harvard Medical School perspectives on suicide* (pp. 33–45). Madison, CT: International Universities Press.

Butcher, J., & Koss, M. P. (1978). Research in brief and crisis-oriented therapy. In S. Garfield & A. Bergin (Eds.), *Handbook of psychotherapy and behavior change* (pp. 627–670). New York: Wiley.

Butcher, J. N., Stelmachers, Z., & Maudal, G. R. (1984). Crisis intervention. In E. B. Weiner (Ed.), *Clinical methods in Psychology* (2nd ed., pp. 572–633). New York: Wiley.

Caplan, G. (1964). *Principles of preventive psychiatry.* New York: Basic Books.

Cohen, J. (1977). *Statistical power analysis for the behavioral sciences.* New York: Academic Press.

Coleman, M. D. (1960). Methods of psychotherapy: Emergency psychotherapy. In J. H. Masserman & J. L. Moreno (Eds.), *Progress in psychotherapy.* New York: Grune & Stratton.

Coleman, M. D., & Zwerling, I. (1959). The psychiatric emergency clinic: A flexible way of meeting community mental health needs. *American Journal of Psychiatry, 115,* 980–984.

Crits-Christoph, P. (1992). The efficacy of brief dynamic psychotherapy: A meta-analysis. *American Journal of Psychiatry, 149,* 151–158.

Crits-Christoph, P., & Luborsky, L. (1990). The measurement of self-understanding. In *Understanding transference: The core conflictual relationship theme method* (pp. 189–196). New York: Basic Books.

Cummings, N. A., & Vandenbos, C. (1979). The general practice of psychology. *Professional Psychology: Research and Practice, 10,* 439–440.

Curtis, J. T., & Silberschatz, G. (1986). Clinical implications of research on brief psychodynamic psychotherapy I. Formulating the patient's problems and goals. *Psychoanalytic Psychology, 3,* 13–25.

Dobson, K. (1989). A meta-analysis of the efficacy of cognitive therapy for depression. *Journal of Consulting and Clinical Psychology, 57,* 414–419.

Elliott, R., James, E., Reimschuessel, C., Cislo, D., & Sack, N. (1985). Significant events and the analysis of immediate therapeutic impacts. *Psychotherapy, 22,* 620–630.

Elliott, R., & Shapiro, D. A. (1988). Brief structured recall: A more efficient method for studying significant therapy events. *British Journal of Medical Psychology, 61,* 141–153.

Ellis, A., & Grieger, R. (1977). *Handbook of rational-emotive therapy.* New York: Springer.

Ewing, C. P. (1990). Crisis intervention as brief psychotherapy. In R. A. Wells & V. J. Giannetti (Eds.), *Handbook of the brief psychotherapies* (pp. 277–294). New York: Plenum Press.

Fawcett, J., Scheftner, W. A., Clark, D. C., Hedeker, D., Gibbons, R. D., & Coryell, W. (1987). Clinical predictors of suicide in patients with major affective disorder. *American Journal of Psychiatry, 144*, 35–40.

Frank, E. (1991). Interpersonal psychotherapy as a maintenance treatment for patients with recurrent depression. *Psychotherapy, 28*, 259–266.

Fremouw, W. J., de Perczel, M., & Ellis, T. E. (1990). *Suicide risk: Assessment and response guidelines.* New York: Pergamon Press.

Freud, S. (1917). Mourning and melancholia. *Standard Edition*, Vol. 14 (pp. 237–258). London: Hogarth Press.

Garfield, S. L. (1978). Research on client variables in psychotherapy. In S. L. Garfield & A. E. Bergin (Eds.), *Handbook of psychotherapy and and behavior change* (rev. ed., pp. 191–232). New York: Wiley.

Garfield, S. L. (1986). Research on client variables in psychotherapy. In S. L. Garfield & A. E. Bergin (Eds.), *Handbook of psychotherapy and behavior change* (3rd ed., p. 213–256). New York: Wiley.

Garfield, S. (1981). Evaluating the psychotherapies *Behavior Therapy, 12*, 295–307.

Gassner, S., Sampson, H., Weiss, J., & Brumer, S. (1982). The emergence of warded-off contents. *Psychoanalysis and Contemporary Thought, 5*, 55–75.

Gaston, L. (1990). The concept of the alliance and its role in psychotherapy: Theoretical and empirical considerations. *Psychotherapy, 27*, 143–153.

Gomes-Schwartz, B. (1978). Effective ingredients in psychotherapy: Prediction of outcome from process variables. *Journal of Consulting and Clinical Psychology, 46*, 1023–1035.

Greenberg, L. S., & Safran. J. D. (1987). *Emotion in psychotherapy.* New York: Guilford Press.

Harris, M. R., Kalis, B. L., & Freeman, E. H. (1983). Precipitating stress: An approach to brief therapy. *American Journal of Psychotherapy, 17*, 465–471.

Hartley, D. E., & Strupp, H. H. (1983). The therapeutic alliance: Its relationship to outcome in brief psychotherapy. In J. Masling (Ed.), *Empirical studies of psychoanalytic theories* (Vol. 1, pp. 1–38). Hillsdale, NJ: Analytical Press.

Havens, L. L. (1974). The existential use of the self. *American Journal of Psychiatry, 131*, 1–10.

Havens, L. L. (1984). The need for tests of normal functioning in the psychiatric interview. *American Journal of Psychiatry, 141*, 1208–1211.

Havens, L., (1989). Clinical interview with a suicidal patient. In D. G. Jacobs & H. N. Brown (Eds.), *Suicide: Understanding and responding: Harvard Medical School perspectives on suicide* (pp. 399–409). Madison, CT: International Universities Press.

Havens, L. L., & Palmer, H. L. (1984). Forms, difficulties, and tests of empathy. *Hillside Journal of Clinical Psychiatry, 6*(2), 285–291.

Henry, W. P., Schacht, T. E., & Strupp, H. E. (1986). Structural analysis of social behavior: Application to a study of interpersonal process in differential psychotherapeutic outcome. *Journal of Consulting and Clinical Psychology, 54*, 27–31.

Hobbs, M. (1984). Crisis intervention in theory and practice: A selective review. *British Journal of Medical Psychology, 57*, 23–34.

Hollon, S. D. (1990). Cognitive therapy and pharmacotherapy for depression. *Psychiatric Annals, 20*, 249–258.

Horowitz, L. M., Rosenberg, S. E., Ureno, G., Kalehzan, B. M., & O'Halloran, P. (1989). Psychodynamic formulation, consensual response method, and interpersonal problems. *Journal of Consulting and Clinical Psychology, 57*, 599–606.

Horowitz, M. J. (1988). *Introduction to psychodynamics: A new synthesis.* New York: Basic Books.

Horowitz, M. J. (1991). Person schemas. In M. J. Horowitz (Ed.), *Person schemas and maladaptive patterns* (pp. 13–32). Chicago: University of Chicago Press.

Imber, S. D., & Evanczuk, K. J. (1990). Brief crisis therapy Groups. In R. A. Wells & V. J. Giannetti (Eds.), *Handbook of the brief psychotherapies* (pp. 565–582). New York: Plenum Press.

Jacobs, D. G. (1989). Psychotherapy with suicidal patients: The empathic method. In D. G. Jacobs & H. N. Brown (Eds.), *Suicide: Understanding and responding: Harvard Medical School perspectives on suicide* (pp. 329–342). Madison, CT: International Universities Press.

Jacobson, G. F. (1965). Crisis theory and treatment strategy: Some sociocultural and psychodynamic considerations. *Journal of Nervous and Mental Disease, 141*, 209–218.

Jacobson, G. F. (1979). Crisis-oriented therapy. *Psychiatric Clinics of North America, 2*, 39–54.

Jacobson, G. F., Strickler, M., & Morley, W. E. (1968). Generic and individual approaches to crisis intervention. *American Journal of Public Health, 58*, 339–343.

Kendall, P. C., Vitousek, K. B., & Kane, M. (1991). Thought and action in psychotherapy: Cognitive behavioral approaches. In M. Hersen, A. E. Kazdin, & A. S. Bellack (Eds.), *The clinical psychology handbook* (pp. 596–626). New York: Pergamon Press.

Klein, D., & Lindemann, E. (1961) Preventive intervention in individual and family crisis situations. In G. Caplan (Ed.), *Prevention of mental disorders in children. Initial exploration* (pp. 283–306). New York: Basic Books.

Klerman, G. L., Weissman, M. M., Rounsaville, B. J., & Chevron, E. S. (1984). *The interpersonal psychotherapy of depression.* New York: Basic Books.

Kohut, H. (1971). *The analysis of the self.* New York: International Universities Press.

Kolotkin, R. L., & Johnson, M. (1983). Crisis intervention and measurement of treatment outcome. In M. J. Lambert, E. R. Christensen, & S. S. DeJulio (Eds.), *The assessment of psychotherapy outcome.* New York: Wiley.

Koss, M., & Shiang, J. (1993). Research on brief psychotherapy. In A. Bergin & S. L. Garfield (Eds.), *Handbook of psychotherapy and behavior change* (pp. 664–700). New York: Wiley.

Kovacs, M., Rush, A. J., Beck, A. T., & Hollon, S. D. (1981). Depressed outpatients treated with cognitive therapy or pharmacotherapy. *Archives of General Psychiatry, 38*, 33–39.

Lambert, M. J., Shapiro, D. A., & Bergin, A. E. (1986). The effectiveness of psychotherapy. In S. L. Garfield & A. E. Bergin (Eds.), *Handbook of psychotherapy and behavior change* (pp. 157–212). New York: Wiley.

Lansley, P. G., & Kaplan, D. M. (1968). *The treatment of families in crisis.* New York: Grune & Stratton.

Lazarus, A. A. (1989). *The practice of multimodal therapy.* Baltimore: Johns Hopkins University Press.

Lazarus, A. A., & Folkman, S. (1984). *Stress, appraisal, and coping.* New York: Springer.

Levenson, H., & Hales, R. E. (1993). Brief psychodynamically-informed therapy for medically ill patients. In A. Stoudemire & B. S. Fogel (Eds.), *Medical psychiatric practice* (Vol II, pp. 3–36). Washington, DC: American Psychiatric Press.

Levenson, H., Speed, J. L., & Budman, S. H. (1992, June). *Therapists' training and skill in brief therapy: A survey of Massachusetts and California psychologists.* Paper presented at the meeting of the Society for Psychotherapy Research,

Levy, R. A. (1966). How to conduct 6 session crisis oriented psychotherapy. *Hospital and Community Psychiatry, 17*, 340–343.

Lewis, R., Walker, B. A., & Mehr, M. (1990). Counseling with adolescent suicidal clients and their families. In A. R. Roberts (Ed.), *Crisis intervention handbook: Assessment, treatment, and research* (pp. 44–62). Belmont, CA.: Wadsworth.

Lindemann, E. (1944). Symptomatology and management of acute grief. *American Journal of Psychiatry, 101*, 141–148.

Litman, R. E. (1989). Suicides: What do they have in mind. In D. G. Jacobs & H. N. Brown (Eds.), *Suicide: Understanding and responding: Harvard Medical School perspectives on suicide* (pp. 143–154). Madison, CT: International Universities Press.

Luborsky, L. (1976). Helping alliances in psychotherapy. In J. L. Claghorn (Ed.), *Successful psychotherapy* (pp. 92–116). New York: Brunner/Mazel.

Luborsky, L. (1984). *Principles of psychoanalytic psychotherapy: A manual for supportive-expressive treatment.* New York: Basic Books.

Luborsky, L., & Crits-Christoph, P. (1990). *Understanding transference: The core conflictual relationship theme method.* New York: Basic Books.

Maltsberger, J. T. (1989). Discussion of Leston Havens' interview. In D. G. Jacobs & H. N. Brown (Eds.), *Suicide: Understanding and responding: Harvard Medical School perspectives on suicide* (pp. 357–360). Madison, CT: International Universities Press.

Margolin, G., & Fernandez, V. (1985). Marital dysfunction. In M. Hersen & A. S. Bellack (Eds.), *Handbook of clinical behavior therapy with adults* (pp. 69–728). New York: Plenum.

Marmar, C. R., Weiss, D. S., & Gaston, L. (1989). Toward the validation of the California Therapeutic Alliance Rating System. *Psychological Assessment, 1*, 46–52.

McCullough, L., Winston, A., Farber, B. A., Porter, F., Pollack, J., Laikin, M., Vingiano, W., & Trujillo, M. (1991). The relationship of patient–therapist interaction to outcome in brief psychotherapy. *Psychotherapy, 28*, 525–533.

Meichenbaum, D. B. (1977). *Cognitive-behavior modification*. New York: Plenum Press.

Menninger, K. (1958). *Theory of psychoanalytic technique*. New York: Basic Books.

Perry, J. C., Cooper, A. M., & Michels, R. (1987). The psychodynamic formulation: Its purpose, structure, and clinical application. *American Journal of Psychiatry, 144*, 543–550.

Persons, J. B. (1989). *Cognitive therapy in practice: A case formulation approach*. New York: Wiley.

Persons, J. B., & Burns, D. D. (1985). Mechanisms of action of cognitive therapy: The relative contributions of technical and interpersonal interventions. *Cognitive Therapy and Research, 9*, 539–551.

Prazoff, M., Joyce, A., & Azim, H. (1986). Brief crisis group psychotherapy: One therapist's model. *Group, 10*, 34–40.

Roberts, A. R. (Ed.). (1990). *Crisis intervention handbook: Assessment, treatment, and research*. Belmont, CA: Wadsworth.

Robinson, L. A., Berman, J. S., & Neimeyer, R. A. (1990). Psychotherapy for the treatment of depression: A comprehensive review of controlled outcome research. *Psychological Bulletin, 108*, 30–49.

Semrad, E. V. (1984). Psychotherapy of the psychoses. *Samiska* (published by the Indian Psychoanalytic Society), 8, 1.

Siddall, L. B., Haffey, N. A., & Feinman, J. A. (1988). Intermittent brief psychotherapy in an HMO setting. *American Journal of Psychotherapy, 62*, 96–106.

Sifneos, P. E. (1972). *Short-term psychotherapy and emotional crisis*. Cambridge, MA: Harvard University Press.

Silberschatz, G., & Curtis, J. T. (1986). Clinical implications of research on brief dynamic psycho-therapy II. How the therapist helps or hinders the therapeutic process. *Psychoanalytic Psychology, 3*, 27–37.

Simons, A. D., Murphy, G. E., Levine, J. L., & Wetzel, R. D. (1986). Cognitive therapy and pharmacotherapy for depression. *Archives of General Psychiatry, 43*, 43–48.

Smith, M. L., & Glass, G. V. (1977). Meta-analysis of psychotherapy outcome studies. *American Psychologist, 32*, 752–760.

Smith, M. L., Glass, G. V., & Miller, T. I. (1980). *The benefits of psychotherapy*. Baltimore: Johns Hopkins University Press.

Stiles, W. B., Morrison, L. A., Harper, D. A., Shapiro, D. A., Haw, S., K., & Firth-Cozens, J. (1991). Longitudinal study of assimilation in exploratory psychotherapy. *Psychotherapy, 28*, 195–206.

Strupp, H. H., & Binder, J. L. (1984). *Psychotherapy in a new key: A guide to time-limited dynamic psychotherapy*. New York: Basic Books.

Svartberg, M., & Stiles, T. C. (1991). Comparative effects of short-term psychotherapy: A meta-analysis. *Journal of Consulting and Clinical Psychology, 59*, 704–714.

Thoits, P. A. (1983). Multiple identities and psychological well-being: A reformulation and test of the social isolation hypothesis. *American Sociological Reviews, 48*, 174–187.

Winston, A., Pinsker, H., & McCullough, L. (1986). A review of supportive psychotherapy. *Hospital and Community Psychiatry, 37*, 1105–1114.

Zeiss, A. M., Lewinsohn, P. M., & Muñoz, R. F. (1979). Nonspecific improvements effects in depression using interpersonal skills training, pleasant activity schedules, or cognitive training. *Journal of Consulting and Clinical Psychology, 47*, 427–439.

III
RESEARCH METHODS, PROFESSIONAL ISSUES, AND NEW DIRECTIONS

21
Methods of Psychotherapy Research

Alan E. Kazdin

The overarching goal of psychotherapy research is to understand alternative forms of treatment, the mechanisms and processes through which these treatments operate, and the impact of treatment and moderating influences on maladaptive and adaptive functioning. In the context of research, psychotherapy serves as a laboratory for studying human interaction and individual differences in relation to specific types of interventions, processes, and outcomes. The task of understanding treatment and the manifold conditions that may affect processes and outcomes is daunting when one considers what therapy is, how and to whom it is applied, and methods of evaluating its impact.

The scope of treatments, client conditions to which they can be applied, and methods of evaluating their impact is vast.[1] First, over 400 psychotherapy techniques are in use for adults and over 200 for children and adolescents (Karasu, 1985; Kazdin, 1988). The range of investigations the alternative treatments could generate to establish their effectiveness and to examine the relative impact of viable treatments for a given problem is enormous. Second, almost 300 different forms of psychological syndromes or symptom patterns are currently rec-

ognized in diagnostic systems to which psychotherapy can be applied (e.g., *Diagnostic and Statistical Manual of Mental Disorders* [DSM-IV-R]; American Psychiatric Association, 1994). This count omits the many problems of living (e.g., life crises, stress) that do not necessarily meet criteria for recognizable disorders but often serve as the focus of psychotherapy. Finally, the methods of assessing treatment outcome are vast and include measures obtained from different informants (e.g., clients, clinicians, significant others in everyday contact with the client), assessment formats (e.g., paper-and-pencil measures, direct observations of behavior), and domains of functioning (e.g., affect, cognition, behavior) (Lambert, Christensen, & DeJulio, 1983). The possible interactions of techniques, disorders, and assessments are virtually infinite. Selection of the methods requires conceptualization of the treatment focus, techniques, relevant domains of process and outcome, and assessment devices to represent these.

This chapter discusses the role of research in drawing inferences about psychotherapy. The roles of assessment, research design, and data evaluation practices in psychotherapy research are highlighted. Salient methodological issues and practices central to therapy research are also presented. The chapter identifies the rationale and underpinnings of methods to investigate psychotherapy, to sample methods to address methodological issues and concerns, and to aid the investigator in studying interventions.[2]

INTERFACE OF GOALS AND METHODS OF RESEARCH IN PSYCHOTHERAPY

Questions Addressed by Psychotherapy Research

The effort to understand psychotherapy has been represented in different ways that emphasize treatment and other influences (e.g., patients, therapists, in-session processes) that may contribute to change (e.g., Goldfried, Greenberg, & Marmar, 1990; Lambert, Shapiro, & Bergin, 1986). Thus, as researchers,

we are interested in the impact of diverse treatments, on varied clinical problems, with clients of varying characteristics, and other manifold conditions that may mediate the outcome. At the concrete level of individual investigations, understanding how treatment operates and the factors that contribute to change can be translated into several specific treatment evaluation strategies that guide individual studies (Kazdin, 1992a).

Table 21.1 presents major strategies and the empirical questions they are designed to address. Individual strategies can be employed in a given study to evaluate some facet of treatment. Diverse strategies across multiple studies elaborate the range of factors that may contribute to treatment and represent a progression of research. At the most rudimentary level is the treatment package strategy. This is a useful place to begin when effective treatment has not been established in an area. Treatment is developed and tested against a control group. At that point, further questions may be addressed.

There is no necessarily fixed order in the

TABLE 21.1. Alternative Treatment Evaluation Strategies to Develop and to Identify Effective Interventions

Treatment Strategy	Question Asked	Basic Requirements
Treatment package	Does the treatment produce therapeutic change?	Treatment vs. no treatment or waiting-list control
Dismantling strategy	What components constitute necessary, sufficient, and facilitative therapeutic change?	Two or more treatment groups that vary in the components provided
Constructive strategy	What components or other treatments can be added to enhance therapeutic change?	Two or more treatment groups that vary in the components provided
Parametric strategy	What changes can be made in the treatment to increase its effectiveness?	Two or more treatment groups that differ in one or more facets of the treatment
Comparative outcome strategy	Which treatment is more or most effective for a particular condition and population?	Two or more different treatments for a given problem
Client and therapist variation strategy	On what patient, family, or therapist characteristics does treatment depend for its effectiveness?	Treatment as applied to separately to different types of cases, therapists, and so on
Process strategy	What processes occur in treatment that affect within-session performance and that may contribute to the treatment outcome?	Treatment groups in which patient–therapist interactions are evaluated within the sessions

strategies. Investigators often compare two or more viable treatment techniques that seem plausible for the problem. As an illustration, Szapocznik et al. (1989) compared structured family therapy and psychodynamic therapy to treat Hispanic boys (6–12 years old) referred for a variety of problems (e.g., conduct disorder, anxiety disorder, adjustment disorders). In the family therapy condition, families were seen. Treatment emphasized modifying maladaptive interactional patterns among family members. Psychodynamic therapy consisted of individual therapy with the child. Treatment focused on play, expression of feelings, transference interpretations, and insight. Diverse outcome measures were included to reflect changes unique to the individual treatments. In general, the results indicated that both groups attained equivalent reductions in behavioral and emotional problems at posttreatment. Both groups were better at posttreatment than clients in a nonspecific treatment control condition in which recreational activities were provided. Family therapy was superior to psychodynamic therapy on a measure of family functioning at a 1-year follow-up. However, generally there were no differences in child dysfunction at posttreatment and follow-up between treatment conditions. The use of a control group in this study was very helpful. If the two treatment groups were equally effective without this control, one could not determine whether the differences were due to nonspecific treatment influences such as attending sessions. The control group suggests that such minimal experiences did not lead to the types of changes associated with treatment.

Studies that contrast two or more competing treatments draw considerable attention, often because of the different theoretical views that are represented. In general, once a treatment is identified as promising, whether in a treatment package or in a comparative study, there are many questions that remain, and these take on increased importance. Subsequent studies may examine a particular characteristic of the cases or those who administer treatment (client–therapist variation) in relation to outcome or critical emergent processes, interactions, and relationship factors (process strategy) within the session. The manner in which treatments operate can be revealed in the contact of a broad portfolio of research that represents increasingly sophisticated questions about treatment.

The different strategies emphasize the importance of treatment *techniques* or procedures and their variations. The focus on techniques is represented by varying some aspect of a given treatment (parametric strategy), by deleting a component of treatment (dismantling strategy), adding new ingredients (constructive strategy), or by contrasting two or more different treatments (comparative strategy). At the same time, the goals of therapy research entail understanding how treatment operates, the factors with which treatment interacts, and the mechanisms of change within the therapy process. Two strategies listed in Table 21.1 carry much of the burden of this goal. Psychotherapy is concerned with individual differences, that is, with how different people respond to different conditions, as well as a variety of potential moderator variables. The client–therapist variation strategy focuses on the broad range of characteristics (e.g., client history, personality, family characteristics, cognitive processes; therapist experience and personality) that influence treatment process and outcome. Understanding the many factors that contribute to the outcome and theoretically driven investigations to evaluate them are high priorities in contemporary psychotherapy research (Beutler, 1991; Smith & Sechrest, 1991). The purpose of identifying factors is to explore how client and treatment characteristics combine to produce changes and what mechanisms account for their manifestation (Smith & Sechrest, 1991).

The mechanisms of change are also approached by the process evaluation strategy. This strategy includes studies devoted to understanding the unfolding of treatment; the experience of therapy by clients and therapists; relationship issues; and how all of these relate to change. Processes of therapy can reflect the dynamic features at a microscopic level. Processes are central to describe the structure and function of events, as well as to predict changes that appear at the end of treatment (Beutler, 1990).

As an illustration, Rounsaville et al. (1986)

examined the relation of alternative therapy processes in predicting the outcome for the treatment of depression. Patients ($N = 35$) received interpersonal psychotherapy for depression. Therapists ($N = 11$) who provided treatment were evaluated by their supervisors after observing tapes of several therapy sessions. Processes rated by the supervisors included therapist (exploration, warmth and friendliness, negative attitude) and patient factors (participation, exploration, hostility, psychic distress). Treatment outcome was assessed with measures of psychiatric symptoms, social functioning, and patient-evaluated change.

The results indicated that only one patient factor (hostility) was related to outcome on a measure of change completed by the patients. In contrast, therapist factors were much more strongly related to outcome. Therapist exploration was significantly and positively related to reductions in clinician evaluations of depression and patient-rated improvements. Therapist warmth and friendliness correlated significantly with improved social functioning and parent-rated improvements. These results convey the importance of specific therapist relationship characteristics in regard to treatment outcome.

In this study, no control or comparison was used. The purpose was to correlate specific processes with specific outcomes within a particular technique. Here too, this level of questioning is based on prior studies demonstrating that the treatment is effective when compared to alternative control conditions. After such demonstrations, it becomes meaningful to ask about the factors that contribute to change.

The full set of research strategies obviously can be used to understand individual treatment techniques and how they operate. At the same time, the nature and scope of the research agenda across different treatments, disorders, and problems of living draw our attention to a broader focus. The overriding goal is to understand fundamental processes related to the development, change, and alteration of affect, cognition, and behavior. Many processes central to therapy, such as patient–therapist interaction, may have generality across alternative treatments and clinical problems. We expect and seek to identify in research those processes that might be similar across the manifold treatments and the circumstances to which they can be applied. Thus, research in psychotherapy is designed not only to evaluate the impact and moderating influences of specific treatments but also to reveal fundamental processes and mechanisms of change that may transcend individual techniques.

The Role of Research

Research methods are designed to permit inferences to be drawn about psychotherapy and its effects. Many practices used in research help to simplify the situation so that the impact of specific variables can be isolated. We conduct research to help identify what variables have an effect and to ensure that our interpretation of the effect is the explanation of the effect. Stated another way, the purpose of research is to reach well-founded (i.e., valid) conclusions about the effects of a given intervention and the conditions under which it operates (Kazdin, 1992a). There are several domains of influence that can interfere with the ability to draw valid inferences. The main influences have been codified as types of experimental validity. Four types of experimental validity have been identified: *internal*, *external*, *construct*, and *statistical conclusion validity* (Cook & Campbell, 1979). Table 21.2 lists each type of validity, the issue to which each is addressed, and the major threats to validity. The threats to validity refer to those factors of the study that affect interpretation of the findings. Methodology, research design, and statistical evaluation are deployed to address, rule out, or make implausible these alternative threats.

Threats to validity vary in their subtlety and ease of control in research in general. For example, *internal validity threats* refer to a variety of influences that might explain those differences the investigator attributes to the intervention. Historical events, maturational processes, repeated testing (where there is pre- and

TABLE 21.2. Types of Experimental Validity, Questions They Address, and Their Threats to Drawing Valid Inferences

Type of Validity	Questions Addressed	Threats to Validity
Internal validity	To what extent can the intervention, rather than extraneous influences, be considered to account for the results, changes, or group differences?	Changes due to influences other than the experimental conditions, such as events (history) or processes (maturation) within the individual, repeated testing, statistical regression, or differential loss of subjects.
External validity	To what extent can the results be generalized or extended to persons, settings, times, measures, and characteristics other than those in this particular experimental arrangement?	Possible limitations on the generality of the findings because of characteristics of the sample, therapists, conditions, context, or setting of the study.
Construct validity	Given that the intervention was responsible for change, what specific aspect of the intervention or arrangement was the causal agent—that is, what is the conceptual basis (construct) underlying the effect?	Alternative interpretations that could explain the effects of the intervention—that is, the conceptual basis of the findings, such as attention and contact with the subject, expectancies of subjects or experimenters, or cues of the experiment.
Statistical conclusion validity	To what extent is a relationship shown, demonstrated, or evident, and how well can the investigation detect effects if they exist?	Any factor related to the quantitative evaluation that could affect interpretation of the findings, such as low statistical power, variability in the procedures, unreliability of the measurement, or inappropriate statistical tests.

Note: For further discussion of individual threats to validity in research in general or clinical and psychotherapy research more specifically, see Cook and Campbell (1979) and Kazdin (1992a), respectively.

posttreatment assessment), regression toward the mean, and related factors lead to changes over time and possibly to group differences. These factors generally can be controlled experimentally by assigning subjects randomly to groups, assessing subjects in the same way, and including a group that does not have the intervention so that influences occurring over time and experiences can be separated from the intervention. These are rather basic requirements and are met in most studies. More subtle influences are raised by other types of validity. For example, *statistical conclusion validity* refers to those factors related to evaluation of the data. Many such issues, such as selection of measures, sample size, and selection of statistical tests, can also influence conclusions.

Each type of validity raises critical points; not all potential threats to validity can be addressed in a given study because attention to one often has direct implications for another. For example, efforts to control and hold constant variables in the study are very important to minimize variability within the design. Selection of homogeneous subjects (rather than of all who volunteer to receive treatment), delivering and monitoring treatment carefully, and using therapists who are trained in a similar way and whose treatment is rigorously monitored may provide an excellent test of the treatment. As rigor, control, and monitoring procedures increase, the generality of the results (external validity) may be raised as an issue. Can the results be obtained when certain constraints, controls, and rigor are relaxed? The answer may or may not be important, depending on the purpose and research questions underlying the original study. In any given study of therapy, the priority accorded a particular type of validity and the threat to validity may vary. For this reason, methodology requires appreciation of the underlying concepts rather than application of design prescriptions and practices.

Types of experimental validity also illustrate the critical interplay between methodological and substantive issues in psychotherapy research. Consider the notion of construct validity, as highlighted in Table 21.2 An investigator may propose that cognitive therapy is effective for depression and may complete a study comparing this treatment with a no-treatment control. At the end of the study, assume that the treatment group is significantly (statistically) different from the no-treatment group. The investigator may wish to discuss the impact of cognitive therapy and perhaps even how cognitive changes lead to changes in depression. With the usual procedures and controls (e.g., random assignment, group equivalence prior to treatment), the threats to internal validity are largely controlled.

Given the design, issues of construct validity (interpretation of the basis for the differences) emerge. The treatment group may have changed for a variety of reasons (e.g., relationship with the therapist, catharsis, behavioral assignments) that have little to do with cognitions. Other groups added to the design (e.g., that include these other components, so that their impact can be separately evaluated) and various assessment procedures (e.g., the study of cognitive changes over the course of treatment and their relation to the outcome) could clarify construct validity. In short, the substantive questions and conclusions about treatment very much depend on the control conditions and assessment procedures of the study.

CORE FEATURES OF METHODOLOGY: AN OVERVIEW

Methodology refers generally to the principles, practices, and procedures that govern research. Methodology can be conceived as encompassing three general components: assessment, design, and data evaluation. *Assessment* refers to the systematic collection of data that permits one to describe a client's progress. *Design* refers ways of arranging the presentation or delivery of the intervention to facilitate drawing valid inferences. *Evaluation* refers to the ways in which the assessment data are examined to draw conclusions. The components work together to draw inferences and to rule out various factors that can compete with the ability to draw conclusions.

Assessment

Critical to research is the systematic collection of information. Assessment begins with identifying the construct of interest and deciding on the operations (measures) to assess the construct. The measure(s) constitute an operational definition of the construct, that is, a way of assessing the construct. Operational definitions are designed to approximate the domain of interest. For example, in therapy research we may wish to assess an individual's anxiety, depression, capacity for meaningful relationships, or interpersonal social skills. A measure of any one of these is deigned to sample the content of the domain and not necessarily to reflect all that we mean by the general concept.

In psychotherapy research, assessment is used to serve many different purposes. First, measures may be used in screening and subject selection. Clients with certain characteristics (e.g., level of anxiety) or clinical disorders (e.g., major depressive disorders) may be central to the study. Measures are administered to identify the sample of interest for inclusion in and exclusion from the study. Second, assessment often is important to evaluate processes in therapy itself. During the course of therapy, the investigator may be interested in measuring the relationship of therapist and client (e.g., therapeutic alliance) or specific processes (e.g., cognitions about oneself) considered to mediate change. Third, assessment is relevant to measure whether treatment was executed correctly. Videotapes of the treatment sessions may be evaluate to ensure that what was provided in treatment was actually carried out as intended. Finally, assessment is used to evaluate the outcome of therapy. Whether the client changed, how much change has occurred, and across what domains are of interest.

There are multiple methods of evaluating treatment. Projective techniques, objective personality tests (e.g., questionnaires, rating scales), and measures of overt behavior (e.g., direct observations of functioning) are primary examples. As a general rule, multiple methods are usually included in treatment evaluation. The rationale for multiple measures is that different methods of assessment sample different facets of the construct. For example, questionnaires, rating scales, and various inventories are the most frequently used measures in treatment evaluation. In such measures, it is useful to evaluate the perspective of different informants, such as the clients themselves and significant others (e.g., spouses, parents) with whom they interact. Therapeutic change may be reflected in these different sources of information, but the effects may vary.

There is a general consensus that outcome assessment needs to be multifaceted, involving different perspectives (e.g., patients, significant others, mental health practitioners), characteristics of the individual (e.g., affect, cognitions, behavior), domains of functioning (e.g., work, social, marital adjustment), and methods of assessment (e.g., self-report, direct observation) (Kazdin & Wilson, 1978; Lambert et al., 1983; Strupp & Hadley, 1977). The diversity of measures relevant to evaluate the outcome leads to multifaceted assessment batteries in individual outcome studies. The inevitable result often is ambiguity in comparisons of treatments. Professionals and lay persons alike often wish to know whether treatment "worked," which treatment was "more successful," or how many persons "got better." Although one can sympathize with these questions, the answers depend on the specific outcome measure. Different conclusions are quite possible, if not likely, as a function of different outcome measures (e.g., Szapocznik et al., 1989; Webster-Stratton, Hollinsworth, & Kolpacoff, 1989).

The differences in measures are not inher-ently problematic. However, from the standpoint of the design of a study, it is useful to identify in advance the goals of treatment and the primacy of alternative outcome measures in relation to these goals. Specification of the goals and their relation to specific measures will not reduce the ambiguity that different outcome measures produce. Yet, these strategies will permit stronger conclusions about the extent to which well-specified goals are achieved by a given technique.

Experimental Design

Design refers to the way of arranging the experiment to draw valid inferences about the impact of the variables of interest. The ways in which the conditions are arranged in the investigation vary widely in psychotherapy research. Group designs, single-group studies, and single-case research designs illustrate the diversity of design strategies. In *group designs*, several subjects are recruited for the investigation and assigned to various groups or conditions (e.g., treatment vs. no treatment). Clients in each group usually receive one of the treatment or control conditions. The effects of different experimental and control conditions among groups are evaluated statistically by comparing groups on the dependent measures. Preliminary assignment of subjects to groups usually is determined randomly to produce groups equivalent on factors possibly related to the independent variable (intervention) or that might also account for group differences on the measures (dependent variables). If groups are equivalent on such factors *before* the experimental manipulation or treatment, any differences among groups *after* the manipulation are assumed to result from the effects of different experimental conditions.

Psychotherapy research also is conducted with designs that do not rely on several cases or group comparisons. This is illustrated most clearly by investigation of a given individual, a few individuals, or one group over time. For example, in *single-case research*, one or a few subjects are studied. The dependent measures of interest are assessed on multiple occasions before, during, and after treatment (Barlow & Hersen, 1984; Kazdin, 1982). The manner in which the independent variable is implemented is examined in relation to the data pattern for the subject or group of subjects over time. Single-case designs can be used to address diverse research questions. The designs play a special role in the field because in clinical work a central concern is the treatment of individual clients.

The vast majority of studies of psychotherapy consist of group designs in which alternative treatment and control conditions are compared. Several group designs are used in therapy research (Kazdin, 1992a; Rosenthal & Rosnow, 1991). As an illustration, the most commonly used group design in psychotherapy research is the *pretest-posttest control group design*. The design consists of a minimum of two groups. The essential feature of the design is that subjects are tested before and after the intervention. Thus, the effect of the intervention is reflected in the amount of change from pre- to posttreatment assessment. In the true experimental version of this design, subjects are assigned randomly to groups either prior to or after completion of the pretest.

The pretest-posttest control group design enjoys widespread use in psychotherapy research because of the many advantages that derive from the use of a pretest (Kazdin, 1992a). First, the data obtained from the pretest allow the investigator to match subjects on different variables and to assign matched sets of subjects randomly to groups. Matching permits the investigator to equalize groups on pretest performance. Second and related, the pretest data permit evaluation of the effect of different levels of pretest performance. Within each group, different levels of performance (e.g., moderate vs. severe anxiety) on the pretest can be used as a separate variable in the design. Thus, the investigator can examine whether the intervention varied in impact as a function of the initial standing on the pretested measure. Third, the use of a pretest affords statistical advantages for the data analysis. By using a pretest, within-group (error) variability is reduced and more powerful statistical tests of the intervention,

such as analyses of covariance or repeated measures analyses of variance, can be applied than if no pretest were used. Fourth, the pretest allows the researcher to make specific statements about change. For example, an investigator can assess how many clients improved, as determined by a certain amount of change from pre- to posttreatment for each individual. Thus, in clinical research where individual performance is very important, the pretest affords information beyond mere group differences at posttreatment. Finally, by using a pretest, the investigator can evaluate loss of subjects (attrition) in a more analytic fashion than would be the case without a pretest. If subjects are lost over the course of the study, a comparison can be made of pretest data between those who dropped out and those who completed treatment. The analysis can raise and test hypotheses about who drops out of treatment and for what reasons.

Generally, in psychotherapy and psychotherapy research, the use of a pretest battery is often advisable for both clinical and methodological purposes. Pretest data serve as a basis to understand client functioning, to identify the scope of domains that might warrant treatment, and to invoke inclusion and exclusion criteria for providing a particular treatment or for considering cases for an investigation.

The evaluation of alternative treatment and control conditions in group research usually consists of investigation of a single variable (e.g., the effect of the treatment approach or some variation of a parameter of treatment). Investigation of a single variable in a study has its limitations. The main limitation is that it often raises relatively simple questions about treatment. The simplicity of the question should not demean its importance. In relatively new areas of research, the simple questions are the bedrock of subsequent research. However, more complex and refined questions can be raised to unravel the interrelations of multiple variables that can operate simultaneously to produce particular outcomes. A more intricate question might be raised by including more than one variable and asking whether certain treatments are more effective with certain types of therapists or clients. The latter type of question is somewhat more specific, entails evaluation of the separate and combined effects of two or more variables, and can yield a deeper level of understanding of how treatment operates.

Factorial designs allows the simultaneous investigation of two or more variables (factors) in a single investigation. Within each variable, two or more conditions are administered. In the simplest factorial design, two variables (e.g., therapist experience and type of treatment) would each consist of two different levels (e.g., experienced vs. inexperienced therapists and treatment A vs. treatment B). In this 2×2 design, there are four groups that represent each possible combination of the levels of the two factors.

A major reason for completing a factorial experiment is that the combined effect of two or more variables may be of interest—that is, their interaction. Many different interaction patterns are possible in therapy research even in the simplest version of the factorial design (two variables each with two levels) (Smith & Sechrest, 1991). Generally, the interaction means that the effect of one of the variables (e.g., treatment A or B) depends on the level of one of the other variables (e.g., experience level of the therapist). Stated another way, treatment may have different effects as a function of other conditions. The importance of interactions has been repeatedly underscored in the context of psychotherapy research to assess the extent to which the impact of a given treatment may depend on a host of other factors, such as who administers treatment, what type of client problem exists, under what conditions of administration, for how long, and so on (e.g., Beutler, 1991; Kiesler, 1971; Smith & Sechrest, 1991). The strength of a factorial design is that it can assess the effects of separate variables in a single study. This feature includes one of economy because different variables can be studied with fewer subjects and observations in a factorial design than in a series of single-variable studies of the variables one at a time. In addition, the factorial design provides unique information about the combined effects of the independent variables.

Data Evaluation

Evaluation refers to identifying whether change has occurred, is reliable, and departs from the fluctuations one would expect without the intervention. Evaluation relies on the assessment data that are examined systematically. In research, an initial purpose of evaluation is to examine the reliability of the findings, that is, whether the findings are consistent and reflect a veridical difference or change. Psychotherapy research, like psychological research more generally, relies primarily on statistical evaluation to determine whether groups receiving different conditions are reliably different on the dependent measure(s). Statistical evaluation consists of applying tests to assess whether the difference obtained on the dependent measure is likely to have occurred by chance. Typically, a level of confidence, or alpha (such as .05 or .01), is selected as the criterion for determining whether the results are statistically significant. A statistically significant difference indicates that the probability level is equal to or below the level of confidence selected, for example, $p < .05$. If the probability obtained in the study is lower than .05, most researchers would concede that group differences probably were *not* the result of chance but reflected a genuine relation between the independent and dependent variables.

To state that a relation in a study is statistically significant does not mean that there is necessarily a genuine relation between the variables studied. Chance is the one rival hypothesis that can never be completely ruled out. There may be no relation between the variables in fact but a statistically significant difference in the study because of a special or biased sampling of subjects and other factors. Nevertheless, by tradition, researchers have agreed that when the probability yielded by a statistical test is as low as .05 or .01, that is a sufficiently conservative level of confidence to permit one to conclude that the differences between groups or conditions are veridical (Cowles & Davis, 1982).

Essentially, statistical evaluation provides a criterion to separate probably veridical from possibly chance effects. Subjectivity and bias enter into the process of statistical evaluation, for example, in terms of the tests that are applied and the criteria for statistical significance (e.g., Berger & Berry, 1988; Cowles & Davis, 1982). Yet the goal of statistics is to provide a relatively bias-free and consistent method of interpreting results. The prevalent use of statistics does not imply that agreement on their value is universal. Diverse facets of statistical evaluation have been challenged, including the arbitrary criterion that a particular confidence level such as $p < .05$ represents, the all-or-none decision reached based on that criterion, the absence of information regarding the practical value of the relation, whether or not statistical significance is attained, and the likelihood that the null hypothesis on which tests are based is never really true (Chow, 1988; Kupfersmid, 1988; Meehl, 1978). Statistical significance is a function of many different features of an investigation, only *one* of which is whether there is a relation between the independent and dependent variables. Several issues related to a statistical evaluation influence the conclusions that are drawn (Kazdin, 1992a, 1992b).

Statistical significance does not really assess the practical or applied importance of treatment for individual patients. In therapy, we wish to produce an effect that makes a difference to the person who has received treatment. Thus, another criterion is the clinical significance of the change. *Clinical significance* refers to the practical value or importance of the effect of an intervention, that is, whether it makes any real difference to the clients or to others. Evaluation of the clinical or applied importance of the change usually is used as a supplement to statistical methods of determining whether group differences or changes over time are reliable. Once reliable changes are evident, further efforts are made to quantify whether treatment has moved the patient appreciably closer to adequate functioning, that is, whether the change is important.

Several methods of evaluating the clinical significance of treatment effects have emerged. Three general strategies can be delineated:

comparison with other groups, subjective evaluation, and social impact (Kazdin, 1992a). For example, one of the more commonly used methods to evaluate clinical significance involves comparing clients who complete treatment with other persons similar to them (e.g., in age, sex, socioeconomic status) who are functioning well in their everyday lives. Prior to treatment, presumably the patient sample would depart considerably from their well-functioning peers in the area identified for treatment (e.g., anxiety, depression, social withdrawal, aggression, tics). One measure of clinical significance is the extent to which the patient sample at the end of psychotherapy is indistinguishable from or well within the range of a normative, well-functioning sample on the measures of interest. To invoke this criterion, a comparison is made between treated patients and peers who are functioning well or without significant problems in everyday life or a normative sample.

As a typical example, in a recent study we evaluated alternative interventions for aggressive and antisocial children aged 7–13 (Kazdin, Siegel, & Bass, 1992). The effectiveness of three treatment conditions (problem-solving skills training, parent management training, or their combination) was evaluated. To assess clinical significance, the level of deviant behavior among youth who completed treatment was compared to the level of same-age and same-sex youth from nonclinic samples. Change was considered to be clinically significant if youth who received treatment fell within the normative range of scores that characterize children who are not referred for treatment on measures of functioning at home and at school. At post-treatment across the three conditions, respectively, 33%, 39%, and 64% of the youth fell within the normal range in relation to their behavior at home. These comparisons indicate that a high proportion of youth continued to remain outside of the normal range after treatment.

Clinical significance is obviously important. A treatment that produces a statistically significant change may not produce a change that makes a difference to the client and to those with whom the client interacts. The methods of clinical significance are not as well developed as those of statistical evaluation. Consequently, a number of fundamental issues regarding assessment and interpretation remain to be addressed (Kazdin, 1992a). Nevertheless, significant progress has been made in developing alternative methods and in applying these in treatment outcome studies (Jacobson & Revenstorf, 1988).

SALIENT METHODOLOGICAL ISSUES

Assessment, design, and evaluation are core features of methodology. In the context of psychotherapy research, several methodological issues arise in relation to these features. The issues affect the conclusions that can be drawn from research, the contribution of research to the knowledge base, and the extent to which the research can be replicated.

Identification and Specification of Clinical Dysfunction

Among the goals of treatment research is the identification of the persons for whom and clinical problems for which various treatments are effective. This goal raises fundamental questions about how to group or delineate cases in meaningful ways. In an obvious way, of course, each individual is unique and recognition of this in therapy is important. At the same time, progress requires identifying meaningful patterns and systematic differences as a function of various dimensions or categories. Differences by sex, age (e.g., children, adolescents, adults), stage (e.g., in life or in moral development), and problem (e.g., anxiety vs. personality disorder) may permit identifying individuals who are generally more or less responsive to a particular treatment.

The domains that are relevant to characterize the cases may be broad, including various subject and demographic variables (e.g., age, sex, race, ethnicity, socioeconomic status). Mention of the need for basic descriptive infor-

mation would seem to be obvious. Surprisingly, perhaps, evaluation of the reporting practices of psychotherapy research indicates that the majority of studies do not report information regarding economic status, race, and education of the participants (Francis & Aronson, 1990). Sex, age, and type of dysfunction are often omitted from research reports. Basic descriptive information is critically important because the variables may contribute to the generality (external validity) of the findings and may be relevant to further efforts to replicate treatment effects.

The scope, type, severity, and breadth of symptoms are particularly central. These characteristics reflect facets of dysfunction presumably underlying the rationale for treatment. Performance on diagnostic interviews and multidimensional scales that are relatively standardized or commonly used (e.g., Symptom Checklist 90, Minnesota Multiphasic Personality Inventory) provide data that are likely to permit comparisons across studies. The absence of such information increases the difficulty of determining the persons for whom treatment in a given study was effective.

In general, there is no standardized or agreed-on method of describing clinical dysfunctions that is in widespread use in psychotherapy research. Psychiatric diagnosis as a means of classifying clinical dysfunction is one way to describe dysfunction. Yet, diagnostic categories themselves are tentative hypotheses about how to organize symptom patterns. The patterns currently recognized vary in the extent to which they can be reliably assessed and validly delineated; this is not a criticism of diagnosis but rather a statement of the empirical status of delineating dysfunction. Even so, diagnosis can be a useful way of describing patients to facilitate communication, and in some cases data analyses, but it is only one way of delineating dysfunction.

Diagnostic assessment and the use of standardized assessments within a given domain of clinical dysfunction can facilitate accretion of the knowledge base. Without agreed-on systems or assessments, it is important to advocate the general principle, to wit, the scope, type, severity, and breadth of clinical dysfunction should be carefully assessed in treatment research. As part of the explicit description, it is useful to specify exclusion and inclusion criteria for case selection (Garfield, 1983). Inclusion and exclusion criteria clarify the boundaries of the sample and the presence or absence of other (comorbid) conditions than the primary condition of interest that might influence the findings. Explicit and thorough specification of the problem permits replication of findings of other investigators and optimizes the possibility of analyzing and reevaluating client characteristics across several studies.

Subject Assignment and Group Formation

In psychotherapy research involving group designs, the manner of assignment of subjects to groups is pivotal. Ideally, subjects are assigned randomly to groups to increase the likelihood that groups will not differ without the experimetnal manipulation or interventions. Random assignment consists of allocating subjects to groups in such a way that the probability of each subject appearing in any of the groups is equal. Usually this is accomplished by determining the group to which each subject is assigned by a table of random numbers.

Random assignment is important as a means of distributing characteristics of the sample among groups. There are several subject characteristics (e.g., age, sex, motivation for participation), circumstances of participation (e.g., how referred, order of appearance or entry into the study), and other factors that might, if uncontrolled, interfere with interpretation of group differences. In some studies, evaluating the impact of these variables may be the central purpose. In other studies, they might be regarded as "nuisance" variables that, if uncontrolled, may obscure interpretation. Random assignment is an effort to distribute nuisance variables unsystematically across groups. An advantage of random assignment is that it does not require the investigator to be aware of all of the important variables that might be related to the outcome of the investigation. Over an infinite number of subjects who are assigned to groups in a random fashion, the many different nuisance variables can be assumed to be distributed evenly among groups.

In a given study, random assignment does not necessarily produce equivalent groups. With random assignment, the likelihood that groups are equivalent increases as a function of the size of the sample. This means that with small samples, equivalence of the groups may not be assumed. This is especially relevant to studies of psychotherapy, where sample sizes typically are relatively small (e.g., 10–20 subjects per group) (Kazdin & Bass, 1989; Shapiro & Shapiro, 1983). When the total sample is relatively small (e.g., 24 subjects total in a two-group study), the likelihood that groups are *not* equivalent across a number of nuisance variables can be high (Hsu, 1989). The net effect is that at the end of the study, the difference between groups due to the intervention may be obscured or misrepresented because of the nonequivalence of groups (Hsu, 1989; Strube, 1991).

In general, random assignment remains vitally important as a concept and procedure. Interestingly, there is a belief that the procedure guarantees group equivalence in situations when this is not likely, that is, when the sample size is relatively small (Hsu, 1989; Tversky & Kahneman, 1971). Use of larger than usual sample sizes (e.g., >40 subjects in each group) or more precise preassignment blocking (e.g., into levels of dysfunction or types of cases by classifying participants in some way) can increase the confidence in the equivalence of groups.

Treatment Administration

Representativeness of Treatment

An important issue in designing a treatment outcome study is ensuring that the treatment will be fairly and faithfully represented. An investigator may wish to study a particular type of family therapy, for example. Obviously, it is important to ensure that the family therapy actually used in the study is a reasonable rendition of treatment based on current theory and practice. The representativeness of treatment warrants consideration before the study begins to ensure that the test is not a unique or idiosyncratic application of the treatment that has little relation to the treatment as usually conceived, researched, or practiced. The need to address this issue *before* carrying out the treatment has become especially clear in comparative outcome studies (e.g., DiLoreto, 1971; Paul, 1966; Sloane, Staples, Cristol, Yorkston, & Whipple, 1975). The results of such studies are often discounted by critics after fact because the specific treatments, as tested, did not represent their usual application in practice (e.g., Boy, 1971; Ellis, 1971; Heimberg & Becker, 1984; Rachman & Wilson, 1980; Roback, 1971).

As a more recent example, Snyder and his colleagues (1991; Snyder & Wills, 1989) reported a study that compared behavioral marital therapy and insight-oriented therapy for the treatment of marital discord. The results indicated no differences at posttreatment and at 6-month follow-up on several standardized and commonly used measures of marital adjustment. At a 4-year follow-up, a significantly greater percentage of couples in the behavioral condition had been divorced. An issue that has emerged is the representativeness of treatment (behavioral, insight-oriented) and the implications for interpretation of the findings (Collins & Thompson, 1988; Jacobson, 1991). Specifically, Jacobson (1991) noted that the insight-oriented treatment resembled behavioral marital training used in contemporary research and practice more than the behavioral treatment used in the study. Thus, both treatments in the study could be considered variations of behavioral management training rather than tests of competing treatments. The more effective versions, Jacobson maintained, is consistent with existing results from other studies on the impact of behavioral treatment.

As a general statement, efforts to evaluate treatment can profit from assurances that the treatments are representative of the approach or versions that the study is designed to test.

Currently there are no standard ways to evaluate at the inception of a study whether the treatment faithfully represents the intervention(s) of interest. One alternative is to develop the treatment in manual form and to submit the manual to proponents and practitioners of the technique (Sechrest, West, Phillips, Redner, & Yeaton, 1979). The experts can examine whether specific procedures are faithfully represented and whether the strength and dose of treatment (e.g., duration, number of sessions) are reasonable. The information so gained might be useful in revising the manual to represent treatment better. Another alternative is to rely on existing manuals of treatment for the techniques of interest, as discussed next.

Treatment Manuals

Treatment manuals consist of written materials to guide the therapist in the procedures, techniques, themes, therapeutic maneuvers, and actions. Over the past 10–15 years in particular, a large number of treatment manuals have emerged; they encompass psychodynamic, psychoanalytic, behavioral, cognitive, family, interpersonal, experiential, and other therapies (Lambert & Ogles, 1988; Luborsky & DeRubeis, 1984).[3] The manuals represent an effort to operationalize to the extent possible the practices that constitute "doing therapy" according to a particular approach. Clinical researchers recognize that manuals do not mirror or reflect all that transpires within treatment or the sessions any more than a "map is the terrain."

There are obvious methodological advantages to the development and use of treatment manuals. First, the codification of treatment in manual form permits therapist training in light of prespecified procedures and monitoring of adherence to these procedures. Both of these are likely to minimize variability in treatment delivery and to increase the sensitivity of the test that compares different treatment conditions (see Crits-Christoph et al., 1991). Second, the prospect of replication research is enhanced when manuals are available. Manuals provide explicit statements about how treatment is implemented, often on a session-by-session basis, which is extraordinarily helpful to researchers who wish to replicate treatment. Third, interpretation of treatment outcomes is enhanced when manuals are available. An example was noted previously in which the outcome results of two treatments were reinterpreted based on scrutiny of the manuals (Jacobson, 1991). Reinterpretation can raise hypotheses about potentially critical but neglected features of treatment within the manuals that would not otherwise be retrieved without codification of the intervention.

Beyond methodological advantages, it is worthwhile to note other advances that the development of treatment manuals provide. Manuals permit extension of treatments to clinical practice. The use of manuals allows persons involved in clinical practice to explore the impact of treatments investigated in research. This feature can help narrow the hiatus between research and clinical practice. In addition, within a given research program, manualized treatments can be revised. The accumulation of experience and research findings can be codified in manual revisions so that gains of an investigative team are not lost.

Although treatment manuals represent a methodological advance, they have raised concerns as well. In clinical research, one concern is that manuals may lead to rigid application of treatment without responding to the needs of the individual client, that complex processes of therapy cannot be adequately captured in manualized form, and that technique variables are emphasized and specified at the expense of other variables (Crits-Christoph et al., 1991; Dobson & Shaw, 1988). Manuals represent an effort to operationalize treatment. As with any operationalization effort, the result is not necessarily complete or reflective of all dimensions of interest. Concerns over manualized treatment also pertain to the potential absence of flexibility once a manual is written and implemented. Perhaps as manuals evolve, efforts will be made to make explicit how novel situations and circumstances are to be handled. Many departures from the manuals can be specified to permit more flexible manuals.

Treatment Integrity

A requirement of outcome research is to ensure the integrity of treatment, that is, that the procedures are carried out as intended (Yeaton & Sechrest, 1981). A number of interrelated concepts are encompassed by treatment integrity, including adherence, differentiation, and competence. *Treatment adherence*, the concept most central to the definition of integrity, refers to whether the therapists carried out treatment as intended. *Differentiation* refers to whether two or more treatments differed from each other along critical dimensions that are central to their execution. For example, statements by the therapist should vary between cognitive therapy and psychodynamic treatment; a study comparing these two treatments might assess whether treatments differed in several such dimensions that on a priori grounds ought to distinguish them. Treatments may be differentiated from one another along critical dimensions (e.g., Luborsky et al., 1982) but this does not necessarily mean that each was adhered to or met some absolute criterion used to define adherence. *Competence* refers to delivery of treatment as intended but with special skill. The notion entails quality of delivery over and above the criteria for adherence (Hill, O'Grady, & Elkin, 1992). The special skills can refer to those components that are consistent with but not encompassed fully by the treatment manual (e.g., timing of the therapeutic strategies, ability to invoke critical processes).

The breakdown of treatment integrity is one of the greatest dangers in outcome research. Interpretation of the outcome assumes that the treatments were well tested and carried out as intended. A number of outcome studies have shown no differences between treatment conditions in cases where individual interventions were not administered as intended, where treated patients in one condition received interventions from another condition, or where patients in a control condition received interventions they were not supposed to receive (e.g., Feldman, Caplinger, & Wodarski, 1983; Liberman & Eckman, 1981). The exemplary feature of these studies is that they provided data to permit evaluation of treatment integrity.

In psychotherapy outcome studies comparing two or more treatments, it is often the case that there are not statistically significant differences between these treatments (Kazdin & Bass, 1989). There are many interpretations of this finding related to theories about critical and common factors that transcend alternative models of therapy (Stiles, Shapiro, & Elliott, 1986). A number of methodological interpretations are viable as well. One interpretation has been the weak statistical power of such comparisons. Two other interpretations pertain to treatment integrity. It is possible that there is an unintended diffusion of treatments, that is, overlap in conditions that were inadvertently intended to be delivered to the separate groups. Also, it is possible that variability in implementing treatment within a condition was sufficiently great as to obscure group differences. Large variation in how individual treatments are carried out across patients with a given condition and failure to implement critical portions of treatments may also lead to no differences, as between two or more treatment conditions. In general, it is difficult to identify the role of lapses in treatment integrity in accounting for results in many studies because the assessment of treatment integrity in psychotherapy research is the exception rather than the rule (Kazdin, Bass, Ayers, & Rodgers, 1990; Moncher & Prinz, 1991).

In designing and implementing a psychotherapy study, there are several steps that can be performed to address treatment integrity. To begin with, the specific criteria, procedures, tasks, and therapist and patient characteristics that define the treatment can be well specified. Second, therapists can be trained to carry out the techniques. Some level of proficiency can be specified to operationalize the concept of therapist experience. In some studies, experience of the therapist is defined by the amount of time that the therapist has been in practice. By itself, this information has no necessary relation to proficiency or competence in carrying a particular technique and in executing treatment with integrity in a particular study (Kazdin, Kratochwill, & VandenBos, 1986). The training experience, however defined, obviously has important implications for how

faithfully treatment is likely to be rendered. Third, and related, when treatment has begun, it is valuable to supervise the therapists over the course of the study. Listening to or viewing tapes of selected sessions, meeting regularly with therapists to provide feedback, and similar monitoring procedures may reduce therapist drift (departure) from the desired practices.

Whether treatment has been carried out as intended can only be evaluated definitively after the treatment has been completed. This evaluation requires measuring the implementation of treatment. Audiotapes or videotapes of selected treatment sessions from each condition can be examined. Codes for therapist and/or patient behaviors or other specific facets of the sessions can operationalize important features of treatment and help decide whether treatment was conducted as intended (e.g., DeRubeis, Hollon, Evans, & Bemis, 1982; Wills, Faitler, & Snyder, 1987). An alternative might be to utilize information obtained from clients to identify differences among varied treatment conditions. For example, clients can report on the therapist's behavior after individual treatment sessions, and this information can be used to reflect the extent to which intended variations across conditions were achieved (Iberg, 1991).

Therapist Issues

Therapists and the Design of the Study

Treatment usually is administered by a therapist, trainer, or counselor. In the general case, it is important to make implausible the possibility that treatment outcome differences or the absence of differences can be attributed to therapist characteristics, competence, or execution of treatment unless evaluation of these latter features are of interest in the design of the study.

Different methodological issues emerge, depending on the characteristics of the study. If one treatment is being tested (e.g., treatment vs. no treatment or a waiting-list control condition), the major issue is ensuring that more than one therapist provides treatment in the study. With only one therapist, any intervention effects might be due to the impact of that therapist (Maher, 1978). This amounts to a therapist effect or a Treatment × Therapist interaction that cannot be detected by the design. If two or more therapists are utilized, then the effect of the therapist can be evaluated as part of the results and separated from the effects of the treatment being evaluated.

In a study with two or more treatments, other issues emerge. Depending on many practical issues as well as the specific treatments that are studied, a decision needs to be made on whether therapists as a factor should be crossed with or nested within treatment. When therapists are *crossed with* treatment, each therapist administers each of the treatment conditions in the investigation. Therapists can then be evaluated as a factor in the data analysis. Such analyses permit evaluation of the impact of therapists alone (as a main effect) and in combination (interaction) with treatment.

If therapists are *nested within* treatments, separate sets of therapists are used to administer the separate treatments. Thus, therapists administer only one of the treatments rather than all of the different treatments. The impact of therapists as a group cannot be separated from treatment effects. Any treatment difference can be reinterpreted as a difference in the therapists who provided the respective treatments. The alternative hypothesis of therapist effects cannot be treated lightly because different sorts of therapists might be attracted to different treatments. It is important to try to rule out the alternative hypothesis that therapist variables accounted for the results. To that end, such characteristics as age, gender, and professional experience should be similar across the sets of therapists administering alternative conditions. It may be difficult to match on other characteristics that in a given case might differentiate groups of therapists because the number of such therapists in any single outcome study typically is small (e.g., two or three therapists for each treatment condition). The small contingent of therapists may also preclude meaningful statistical evaluation of therapist attributes in relation to the outcome.

Purely from the standpoint of experimental design, crossing therapists with treatment is preferable because, theoretically, the portion of patient change attributed to therapists (therapist variance) can be separated from the portion due to treatment technique (treatment variance) and other variables included in the design. Yet in outcome studies, overriding reasons may dictate the nesting of therapists within treatments. An obvious advantage of nesting therapists is that therapists using a given technique can be selected for their background, skill level, commitment to, and enthusiasm for a specific technique. The alternative of having all therapists use all technique raises other problems, such as the differential skill level and background for the different techniques for a given therapist and among therapists. Also, each therapy technique may require considerable training and experience. Consequently, it may be unreasonable to attempt to train novices to master each technique.

Therapist Characteristics

It seems obvious that there will be differences among persons who administer treatment and that some of these differences will influence therapeutic change. The characteristics of therapists have been studied extensively (Beutler, Crago, & Arizmendi, 1986). A variety of therapist characteristics can play an important role in treatment outcome, such as level of empathic understanding, amount of experience, and degree of openness and directiveness, to mention a few.

Of interest here are the methodological considerations raised by the study of therapist characteristics. First, many different characteristics can be studied, and these may raise different sorts of problems. Subject and demographic characteristics (e.g., age, experience, treatment orientation) may be of interest. Alternatively, characteristics that emerge over the course of treatment (e.g., expressions of warmth, self-disclosure) can be evaluated as well. Selection of characteristics for investigation ideally relies on theory about the treatment, the clinical problem, and the clients to whom treatment is applied. Second, the study of therapist characteristics requires a sufficient number of therapists to evaluate different levels or degrees of the characteristic of interest. For example, evaluation of the impact of therapist warmth (high vs. low) is not well studied by utilizing two therapists to administer treatment. Several therapists are required, and they may need to be carefully selected for their initial characteristics.

Many considerations that might be raised in studying patients are somewhat neglected when therapists become the subjects. For example, sampling and sample size to provide statistically sensitive tests are obviously important. Typically, procuring therapists is much more difficult than procuring patients as subjects. The difficulty of obtaining large numbers of cases for the study of therapist characteristics has implications for the types of designs and tests that can be provided and the generality of effects beyond the specific characteristics of the sample that might be conveniently available. Also, with a relatively small number of therapists as subjects, analyses of the data to partial out potential influences (e.g., sex, race, experience, orientation) are extremely difficult. One possibility is to evaluate the effects of therapists with more lenient levels of significance (e.g., alpha of $p \leq .20$ rather than $p \leq .05$) so that therapist effects would not be overlooked due to low power (Crits-Christoph & Mintz, 1991).

Follow-up Assessment

Assessment immediately after treatment is referred to as *posttreatment* assessment; any point beyond that, ranging from weeks to years, typically is referred to as *follow-up* assessment. Follow-up raises important issues for psychotherapy outcome research, such as whether gains are maintained and whether conclusions can be reached at all given patient attrition. The majority of studies do not include follow-up assessment of therapy effects. For example, in our evaluation of psychotherapy research with children and adolescents, the majority of studies (59%) did not include follow-up assessment. Among studies that included follow-up, assessment typically takes place 5–6 months after treatment ends (Kazdin et al., 1990; Weisz, Weiss, Alicke, & Klotz, 1987).

Follow-up studies are critically important because the effects immediately after treatment are not always the same as those evident over time. Thus, fundamental conclusions about the efficacy of a treatment or the relative effectiveness of alternative treatments may vary greatly, depending on when assessments are conducted. In several studies, conclusions about the effectiveness of a given treatment relative to a control condition or another treatment differed as posttreatment and follow-up (Kazdin, 1988; Wright, Moelis, & Pollack, 1976). Thus, the treatment that appeared more or most effective at posttreatment did not retain this status at follow-up.

If we are to understand fully the extent to which treatments are effective, further research is needed to evaluate the long-term impact of interventions for alternative therapists and clinical problems. Different time periods reflect different questions, each of which is important in its own right. For example, we wish to know if therapy can produce change, whether gains are maintained, and whether long-term adjustment (e.g., in adulthood) is affected. Knowledge about the short- and long-term impact of treatment may help guide both the types of interventions that are selected and when and how they are to be used.

Attrition

Clients in a psychotherapy investigation traverse several stages, and which typically include pretreatment assessment, the course of treatment, posttreatment assessment, and then perhaps a period of follow-up. Over the time course, the loss of subjects is virtually inevitable. Indeed, one can expect a "decay curve" in which the number of persons who drop out of the study increases as a function of time (Phillips, 1985). The loss of clients during the course of an investigation has diverse methodological implications.

First and most obvious, subjects who drop out of an investigation are likely to differ from those who remain in the study. Dropouts may differ on a range of variables (e.g., diagnosis, severity of dysfunction, family history, past treatment experiences) that could interact with (moderate) the intervention in the outcomes that are produced. For example, in our own work on the treatment of antisocial children, we have found that patients who drop out of treatment are more severely impaired and come from families with greater stress and socioeconomic disadvantage than patients who complete treatment (Kazdin, Mazurick, & Bass, 1993). Clearly, conclusions about the effects of treatment may be restricted to a highly select group because attrition is not a random process.

Second, it is possible that characteristics of persons who drop out of separate groups or conditions within a study are not the same. There may be systematic differences in the conditions leading to attrition in ways that affect different types of people. Perhaps those psychotherapy subjects who did not wish to chat about their past and never considered their therapists to be like a father (transference) tired of psychotherapy and left; those behavior modification subjects who wished to discuss their early relationships with their parents were disappointed with role-playing in the sessions, and with homework assignments to practice new behaviors in everyday life, and dropped out. The subjects remaining in each of the groups and included in statistical comparisons may differ from each other in subject, demographic, and personality characteristics; this cannot be easily tested given the small sample sizes and the absence of information on a vast range of possible differences in these characteristics. Usually the number of attrition cases is too small to allow comparison of groups in a statistically sensitive way.

Third, the number of subjects who drop out may vary significantly between or among groups. For example, in a classic study of cognitive therapy, this form of treatment was shown to be superior in reducing depression in adults when compared to the use of medication (imipramine) (Rush, Beck, Kovacs, & Hollon, 1977). Interestingly, medication led to a significantly larger number of persons leaving

treatment before posttreatment assessment. Differential attrition across group itself is an interesting outcome and may indicate something important about treatment conditions. Treatments that generate relatively high attrition rates may be relatively aversive, place special demands on the clients, have untoward side effects, or perhaps simply not work. In the case of this study, differential attrition between the two treatment groups clearly raises questions for all comparisons at posttreatment. Were the two treatments differentially effective on measures of depression or were group differences due to differential selection? The question is not easily answered.

Finally, it is possible that so many subjects drop out that valid conclusions about treatment cannot be made. Upward of 50% of subjects who begin treatment may drop out (e.g., Pekarik & Stephenson, 1988; Vaile-Val, Rosenthal, Curtiss, & Marhohn, 1984). A recent review encompassing studies of child, adolescent, and adult treatment yielded a mean dropout rate of 46.9% of individuals who begin treatment (Wierzbicki & Pekarik, 1993). Selection biases are readily plausible. In some studies, loss of subjects at follow-up may be so high (e.g., almost 90%) as to preclude evaluation of the impact of alternative conditions in the original design (Feldman, Caplinger, & Wodarski, 1983). Even without such large losses, subjects who drop out of treatment decrease the sample size and hence may decrease the power of the study to detect group differences.

Several procedures and interventions have been explored to reduce subject loss (Baekeland & Lundwall, 1975; Flick, 1988; Stark, 1992). Examples include special orientation (pretreatment) interviews, various mailings during the course of treatment, reminders and novel methods of scheduling appointments, and monetary incentives or penalties. Development of interventions to combat attrition is likely to derive from efforts to understand factors that place clients at risk for premature termination from treatment (e.g., Kazdin et al., 1993) and from models of the critical factors that will help engage cases in treatment (e.g., Szapocznik et al., 1988). From a methodological perspective, statistical approaches to attrition have been developed and provide useful strategies to complement active efforts to minimize attrition. Statistical approaches utilize existing data (e.g., the last available data point) from subjects who drop out and utilize other data in the study to estimate what the lost data might reflect. These methods allow researchers to identify the likely bias that attrition introduces into the data and the conclusions that would be warranted if the lost subjects had improved, remained the same, or became worse (Flick, 1988; Howard, Krause, & Orlinsky, 1986; Little & Rubin, 1987).

Power to Detect Group Differences

A critical research issue is the extent to which an investigation can detect differences between groups when differences exist within the population. This notion is referred to as *statistical power* and reflects the probability that the test will lead to rejection of the null hypothesis (Cohen, 1988).[3] Power is a function of the criterion for statistical significance (alpha), sample size *(N)*, and the difference that exists between groups (effect size). An investigation must be sufficiently powerful to detect meaningful differences. Reviews of research spanning more than three decades of clinical research (Rossi, 1990) and psychological research in general (Sedlmeier & Gigerenzer, 1989) have revealed that the vast majority of studies continue to be quite weak in their statistical power.[4]

In many studies, alternative forms of psychotherapy or variations on a given type of psychotherapy are compared. No differences may be found. It may be that the treatments truly are equally effective. However, analyses have suggested that in the majority of psychotherapy studies, the power to detect differences is too weak if differences exist between the treatments (Kazdin & Bass, 1989). The usual sample sizes (10–20 per group) generally are much too small to identify differences. Much larger samples (70 per each group in a study) are needed to detect differences.

The weak power of therapy research is not a minor methodological annoyance. Rather, the neglect of power has major implications for interpreting research. Psychotherapy research is an area where the absence of difference (i.e., support for the null hypothesis) is often taken to be quite significant from conceptual and clinical perspectives (Frank & Frank, 1991; Luborsky, Singer, & Luborsky, 1975; Stiles et al., 1986). It may well be the case that treatments are similar in the outcome they produce and that "no difference" is the actual state of affairs. Yet, a plausible alternative is that the power of studies comparing alternative treatments is relatively weak.

PLANNING, IMPLEMENTING, AND EVALUATING AN OUTCOME STUDY

Questions to Guide Research

Alternative designs, methodological practices, and methods of data evaluation raise many options and decision points for the investigator. Many of the points can be translated into a set of questions the investigator might wish to consider in the design and execution of a study of psychotherapy. Table 21.3 presents salient questions that would be useful to address in planning, implementing, and reporting a study. Answers to the questions directly affect the quality of the study, its contribution, and its integration in the body of scientific evidence. The questions are discussed briefly below.

Sample Characteristics

Questions in Table 21.3 raise multiple issues regarding the sample and the clarification of its characteristics. In general, investigations could be improved by specifying the criteria of clinical dysfunction that served as the basis for selection of the sample. Frequently, investigators allude to the fact that patients were referred for treatment. This is of little use in terms of understanding the problems the patients present. Progress can be enhanced by specifying the inclusion and exclusion criteria for patient se-

TABLE 21.3. Selected Questions to Raise in Planning a Study of Psychotherapy

Sample Characteristics

1. Who are the subjects, and how many of them are there in this study?
2. Why was this sample selected in light of the research goals?
3. How was this sample obtained, recruited, and selected?
4. What are the subject and demographic characteristics of the sample (e.g., sex, age, ethnicity, race, socioeconomic status)?
5. What if any inclusion and exclusion criteria were invoked, that is, selection rules to obtain participants?
6. How many of those subjects eligible or recruited actually were selected and participated in the study?
7. With regard to clinical dysfunction or subject and demographic characteristics, is this a relatively homogeneous or heterogeneous sample?

Design

1. How were subjects assigned to groups or conditions?
2. How many groups were included in the design?
3. How are the groups similar and different in the way they are treated in the study?
4. Why are these groups critical to address the questions of interest?

Procedures

1. Where was the study conducted (setting)?
2. What measures, materials, equipment, or apparatus were used in the study?
3. What is the chronological sequence of events to which subjects were exposed?
4. What intervals elapsed between different aspects of the study (assessment, treatment, follow-up)?
5. What variation in administration of conditions emerged over the course of the study in ways that may introduce variation within and between conditions?
6. What procedural checks were completed to avert potential sources of bias in implementation of the manipulation and assessment of dependent measures?
7. What checks were made to ensure that the conditions were carried out as intended?
8. What other information does the reader need to know to understand how subjects were treated and what conditions were provided?

Therapists

1. Who are the therapists, and why are these individuals selected?
2. Can the influence of the therapist be evaluated in the design as a factor (as in a factorial design) or can therapist effects be evaluated within a condition?
3. Are the therapists adequately trained? By what criteria?
4. Can the quantity and quality of their training and implementation of treatment be measured?

Treatment

1. What characteristics of the clinical problem or cases make this particular treatment a reasonable approach?
2. Does the version of treatment represent the treatment as it is usually carried out?
3. Does the investigation provide a strong test of treatment? On what basis has one decided that this is a strong test?
4. Has treatment been specified in manual form or have explicit guidelines been provided?
5. Has the treatment been carried out as intended? (Integrity is examined during the study but evaluated after the study is completed.)
6. Can the degree of adherence of therapists to the treatment manual be codified?
7. What defines a completed case (e.g., completion of so many sessions)?

Assessment

1. If specific processes in the clients or their interpersonal environment are hypothesized to change with treatment, are these to be assessed?

2. If therapy is having the intended effect on these processes, how would performance be evident on the measure? How would groups differ on this measure?
3. Are there additional processes in therapy that are essential to or facilitative of this treatment, and are these being assessed?
4. Does the outcome assessment battery include a diverse range of measures to reflect different perspectives, methods, and domains of functioning?
5. What data can be brought to bear regarding pertinent types of reliability and validity for these measures?
6. Are treatment effects evident in measures of daily functioning (e.g., work, social activities)?
7. Are outcomes being assessed at different points in time after treatment?

Data Evaluation

1. What are the primary measures and data on which the predictions depend?
2. What statistical analyses are to be used, and how specifically do these address the original hypotheses and purposes?
3. Have the assumptions of the data analyses been met?
4. What is the likely effect size that will be found based on other treatment studies or meta-analyses?
5. Given the likely effect size, how large a sample is needed to provide a strong (powerful) test of treatment (e.g., power $\geq$ .80)?
6. Are these subdivisions of the sample that will be made to reduce the power of tests of interest to the investigator?
7. What is the likely rate of attrition over the course of treatment and of posttreatment and follow-up assessments?
8. With the anticipated loss of subjects, is the test likely to be sufficiently powerful to demonstrate differences between groups if all subjects complete the treatment?
9. If multiple tests are used, what means are provided to control error rates?
10. Prior to the experimental conditions, were groups similar on variables that might otherwise explain the results (e.g., diagnosis, age)?
11. Are data missing due to incomplete measures (not filled out completely by the subjects) or due to loss of subjects? If so, how are these handled in the data analyses?
12. Will the clinical significance of client improvement be evaluated, and if so, by what method(s)?

---

lection. Use of a specific diagnostic system such as DSM-IV or scores on a dimensional scale to describe or select patients would be helpful as well. Investigators invariably rely on diverse criteria. In any given study, the criteria ought to be specified, operationalized, and replicable.

Specification of the sample involves more than a clarification of the clinical dysfunction and criteria for selection. Subject and demographic variables, including, of course, age, sex, socioeconomic status, intelligence, and achievement, are prime candidates. These characteristics are often related to clinical dysfunction and adaptive functioning and may influence treatment efficacy. Race, ethnicity, and geographical locale (e.g., country, urban vs. rural area within a country) may be important to specify as well in order to describe the sample and to permit others to evaluate the potential role in generality of the results. The full range of subject and demographic variables that might be relevant in a given study or to future generations of meta-analysts who include the study in a larger data base cannot be elaborated a priori. As a general rule, it is useful to err on the side of careful description so that it is clear to others who was treated. Although the point seems obvious, very basic descriptors are routinely omitted from studies of psychotherapy, as reviewed earlier.

Design

There are many different ways in which the conditions of the investigation can be arranged. In the usual study of psychotherapy, conditions and variables of interest are evaluated in a group design. In such designs, methods for obtaining subjects, allocating subjects to conditions, and selecting conditions, treatments, or groups in relation to the hypotheses of interest need to be made explicit. As a broader guide, how threats to experimental validity (internal, external, construct, and statistical conclusion validity) are addressed in the design warrants consideration. The issues specific to the area of research may demand special attention in the study, such as why a particular group was or was not included if there is evidence that such a group is relevant for interpretation of the findings.

Although group designs dominate research, the consideration of alternative design options is critical. From the standpoint of the investigator, the question might be addressed by focusing on fewer subjects and more measures rather than on more subjects and fewer measures. The range of designs that have helped elaborate the characteristics of therapy provide multiple options for the researcher to consider.

Procedures

The procedures encompass what is to be done in relation to the subjects, therapists, treatment deliver, and related factors. Careful description of the procedures and means to ensure that the procedures are executed as intended are critically important. Studies conducted within clinical settings and with patient samples as a matter of course are subject to all sorts of procedural departures that can add variability to the study. Patients coming late (and attending only one-half of a session), incomplete questionnaires at pretreatment that are not detected until data entry, therapists omitting a procedure that is central, and a variety of other departures from the intended procedures are critical to monitor. Checks on procedures can mean a lot because they reflect on the quality of the study and the variability introduced into the design.

Therapists

It is valuable to specify characteristics of the therapists in a way similar to those that are identified for the patients. The relevant dimensions may vary but presumably include experience and level of training, age, sex, race, and ethnicity, to mention a few. In the usual study, therapists are described by referring to their experience, orientation, and professional degree. This is fine, but further information on skills in using the technique(s) in the study would be very helpful. The likelihood of replicating the findings of the study may be influenced greatly by knowing the characteristics of the therapists and the details of their training.

The reason(s) why a particular set of therapists are to be used may also be important. It is possible that the therapists were selected because of convenience or their availability to work on a project or because of a special therapeutic orientation. Selection for convenience (e.g., graduate student therapists) is not inherently undesirable. However, persons available to serve as therapists might have special skills, orientations, or status that could influence the generality of the results. Consequently, it is important to specify the characteristics that might be unique to those who were selected to serve as therapists.

An evaluation of the influence of therapists on the outcome is worthwhile to plan in the design if at all feasible. If each therapist administers each of the conditions, then the effects can be examined in a factorial design, as discussed previously. It is often the case that different therapists administer the different treatment conditions. In this case, for a given treatment, the investigator could evaluate the effects of therapists (A vs. B vs. C for Treatment 1). An evaluation of therapists is important to present even when a factorial design does not isolate the effects independently (i.e., statistically) of treatments.

Treatment

Several questions about the specific version of treatment are important to raise, including whether the version represents the treatment the investigator wishes to study, whether the version is a strong test, and whether the treatment could be followed and replicated by others. The use of treatment manuals facilitates training of therapists, replication of treatment by others, and evaluation of treatment integrity. Within the investigation, methods to ensure treatment integrity and evaluation of the extent to which treatments were faithfully rendered are critically important.

Assessment

It is very helpful to specify and then to assess processes within treatment that are assumed to mediate therapeutic change. Assessment of such processes as attributions and beliefs or self-esteem, if these are central to the technique of interest, can provide extremely valuable information. Apart from evaluation of the treatment outcome, the investigator can correlate changes in processes with changes in outcome. In effect, the study can become a test of the model of therapeutic change as well as treatment outcome.

Assessment of processes or mechanisms of change in treatment is important for methodological reasons, even among researchers who consider themselves primarily or exclusively interested in the treatment outcome. The reason has to do with construct validity, mentioned earlier, to wit, the extent to which the constructs of interest to the investigator can be considered to be the basis of outcome results. Group differences (e.g., treatment vs. controls) do not automatically provide insights into the reason for these differences. Data on intervening processes or constructs to which change is attributed can bolster the strength of the conclusions.

Central assessment questions pertain to the outcome assessment battery and the administration of this battery over time (e.g., Lambert et al., 1983). There is incomplete agreement on measures but general consensus that multiple domains of functioning need to be selected that directly reflect the basis for clinical referral. Usually this refers to reduction of symptoms in specific areas of functioning. In addition, it is important to examine prosocial or adaptive functioning. The ultimate adjustment of the case may derive not only from the reduction of symptoms but also from increases in positive adjustment in everyday life.

The timing of assessment is important too. Administration of the assessment battery prior to treatment usually is desirable on clinical and methodological grounds. Pretreatment data identifying the initial level and scope of dysfunction. Such data, also increase the power of the statistical analyses to evaluate treatment differences. Posttreatment assessment obviously is provided to evaluate the change after treatment. Follow-up assessment permits examination of the extent to which treatment effects are stable and/or change in relation to other treatment and control conditions within the study. Studies of diverse techniques cited earlier have shown that the conclusions drawn about the effects of a treatment or the relative effectiveness of alternative treatments may vary greatly over time. Different assessment occasions (e.g., posttreatment, 1-year and 2-year follow-up assessments) are difficult to obtain but very important to seek. The field of psychotherapy has only sparse data on the long-term (e.g., ≥5-year) impact of any treatment for any well-defined clinical dysfunction.

Data Evaluation

The manner in which data are to be evaluated is important to consider well in advance of data collection. No doubt completion of data collection will lead to novel analyses that may not have been considered at the outset of the study. The primary analyses and how they relate to the hypotheses warrant identification at the outset and at the design stage. Table 21-3 raises questions designed to draw attention to those data-analytic questions (e.g., anticipated effect size, power) that may influence the design itself. In addition to the statistical questions, the clinical significance of change warrants consideration.

General Comments

The questions highlighted previously alert the investigator to major considerations in the design of psychotherapy research. The questions and considerations they reflect are not intended to be complete, nor could they be in principle and practice, given the scope of psychotherapy research and the diversity of designs and variables. Underlying the questions are more general considerations that are useful guides as well.

First, it is important to be as explicit as possible about all facets of the study related to assessment, procedures, and data analyses. Usually, explicitness of one's procedures is advocated as a basis to permit subsequent replication of research. Yet, there is a more immediate basis for specification of procedures in concrete terms. Making details of the study explicit helps the investigator identify potential and actual departures from the integrity of procedures. The quality of study execution is critically important; explicitness in procedures facilitates checking to detect and prevent such departures. Replication of a study is a more distant goal; the initial task is to execute a high-quality investigation whose results are clear.

Second, the rationale for methodological decisions is useful to elaborate at the design stage. Why were these treatment conditions selected? Why these constructs and, for these constructs, Why these particular measures? Why this data-analytic method as opposed to other available options? And so on. These questions are less concrete but no less important. They become obviously important in the preparation of written reports of the study once the study is completed (Kazdin, 1992a). At the design stage, it is useful to self-challenge on each of the decision points to ensure that the rationale for the proposed design is well based. Occasionally, the rationale for using a particular procedure, method, design, or data-analytic procedure is based on the fact that the practice has appeared in the literature previously, perhaps even in one of the allegedly better journals. There is some merit in this point insofar as the use of common procedures and measures permits one to compare and combine separate studies in the knowledge base. At the same time, tradition can also transmit and perpetuate weak measures, methods, and data-analytic strategies.

SUMMARY AND CONCLUSIONS

The goals of psychotherapy research are to understand alternative forms of treatment, the mechanisms and processes through which these treatments operate, and the impact of treatment and moderating influences on client functioning. Methodology, research design, and statistical analyses are deployed in the service of these goals. The many practices that are used to study psychotherapy are not mere accoutrements of the research enterprise. The quality of the yield from individual studies and the conclusions reached about critical substantive questions rely heavily on research methodology.

Designing experimental research often is presented as a straightforward enterprise. At the most rudimentary level, the design includes an experimental and a control group. The experimental group receives some form of the experimental condition or intervention; the control group does not receive the intervention. Differences between the groups are considered to reflect the effect of the experimental manipulation. Although the basic comparison is well intentioned in principle, it greatly oversimplifies the bulk of contemporary research and the type of control procedures used in most psychotherapy studies. Methodology of psychotherapy research is a fascinating topic because of the many different ways in which studies can be completed, the advantages and disadvantages associated with the available design options, and the contribution of different designs to the results.

Methodology is directed at planning an investigation in such a way as to rule out competing explanations of the results. The better an investigation is designed, the fewer the alternative plausible explanations that can be advanced to account for the findings. Psychotherapy trials are very difficult to mount and usually costly in both time and money. A given investigator is not likely to conduct many research projects involving clinical treatments and samples given the complexity of individual projects and current life expectancies. Sound methodology is all the more critical. The cost of such studies warrants ensuring that the knowledge yield of individual projects is maximized.

This chapter has highlighted the diversity of methods and methodological issues of psychotherapy research. Assessment, design, and date evaluation are often assumed to be core features of and restricted to research. Many specific practices of research (e.g., randomly assigning subjects to groups in an investigation) are not relevant to clinical work in practice. However, methodology is not only a set of practices to guide research, but also a way of thinking about phenomena and systematizing the information we obtain to draw inferences. The thought processes reflect concerns about ways of operationalizing critical constructs, stating hypotheses about interventions and processes leading to change, and testing assumptions about interventions and their impact. The thought processes also entail bearing in mind the various threats to drawing inferences (i.e., those influences that may interfere with having the desired impact or with drawing conclusions about the agent of change).

The thought processes and many of the specific practices underlying research are quite relevant to clinical practice (Kazdin, 1993). Invariably, in our practice of psychotherapy with individual clients, we draw inferences, actively or passively make decisions on what we perceive, and so on. Methodology focuses on systematic and replicable ways of accomplishing these goals. Tenets of science (e.g., testing hypotheses, operationalizing critical concepts, fostering replication) can be used to advance the goals of psychotherapy in clinical practice as well as those of the larger research agenda. In this sense, methodology is not restricted to psychotherapy research. The thought processes as well as specific research practices (e.g., continuous assessment) can be used for decision making to benefit the client directly. This chapter focuses on several issues and practices that are central to therapy research but that also are relevant to evaluation and delivery of treatment in practice.

Acknowledgment

Completion of this chapter was facilitated by a Research Scientist Award (MH00353) and a grant (MH35408) from the National Institute of Mental Health.

NOTES

1. *Client* and *patient* will be used interchangeably in this chapter.

2. This chapter highlights several issues and practices of research design. A more extensive discussion of the topics is provided elsewhere (Kazdin, 1992a, 1992b).

3. Power (1-beta) is the probability of rejecting the null hypothesis when it is false. Stated differently, power is the likelihood of finding differences between the treatments when in fact the treatments are trutly different in their outcomes. Calculation of the power of a study is based on sample size (N), alpha (significance level), and effect size or the differences between the groups. For a given difference between groups and for a given alpha level (e.g., $p<.05$) an investigator can identify how large a sample is needed. The difference between groups (effect size) can be estimated as well based on prior studies and reviews of research (Kazdin, 1992a).

4. A number of publishers have devised book series designed to publish treatment manuals or books that approximate treatment manuals. Consequently, manuals for many treatments are available for clinical use.

REFERENCES

American Psychiatric Association. (1994). *Diagnostic and statistical manual of mental disorders* (4th ed.). Washington, DC: Author.

Baekeland, F., & Lundwall, L. (1975). Dropping out of treatment: A critical review. *Psychological Bulletin, 82,* 738–783.

Barlow, D. H., & Hersen, M. (1984). *Single-case experimental designs. Strategies for studying behavior change* (2nd ed.). New York: Pergamon Press.

Berger, J. O., & Berry, D. A. (1988). Statistical analysis and the illusion of objectivity. *American Scientists, 76,* 159–165.

Beutler, L. E. (1990). Special series: Advances in psychotherapy process research. *Journal of Consulting and Clinical Psychology, 58,* 263–264.

Beutler, L. E. (1991). Have all won and must all have prizes? Revising Luborsky et al.'s verdict. *Journal of Consulting and Clinical Psychology, 59,* 226–232.

Beutler, L. E., Cargo, M., & Arizmendi, T. G. (1986). Therapist variables in psychotherapy process and outcome. In S. L. Garfield & A. E. Bergin (Eds.), *Handbook of psychotherapy and behavior change* (3rd ed., pp. 257–310). New York: Wiley.

Boy, A. V. (1971). A critique by Angelo V. Boy. In A. O. DiLoreto (Ed.), *Comparative psychother-*

apy: *An experimental analysis* (pp. 233–245). Chicago: Aldine-Atherton.

Chow, S. L. (1988). Significance test or effective size? *Psychological Bulletin, 103*, 105–110.

Cohen, J. L. (1988). *Statistical power analysis in the behavioral sciences* (2nd ed.). Hillsdale, NJ: Erlbaum.

Collins, F. L., JR., & Thompson, J. K. (1988). On the use of symbolic labels in psychotherapy outcome research: Comment on Wills, Faitler, and Synder. *Journal of Consulting and Clinical Psychology, 56*, 932–933.

Cook, T. D., & Campbell, D. T. (Eds.). (1979). *Quasi-experimentation: Design and analysis issues for field settings.* Chicago: Rand McNally.

Cowles, M., & Davis, C. (1982). On the origins of the .05 level of statistical significance. *American Psychologist, 37*, 553–558.

Crits-Christoph, P., Baranackie, K., Kurcias, J. S., Beck, A. T., Carroll, K. Perry, K., Luborsky, L., McLellan, A. T., Woody, G. E., Thompson, L., Gallagher, D., & Zitrin, C. (1991). Meta-analysis of therapist effects in psychotherapy outcome studies. *Psychotherapy Research, 1*, 81–91.

Crits-Christoph, P., & Mintz, J. (1991). Implications of therapist effects for the design and analysis of comparative studies of psychotherapies. *Journal of Consulting and Clinical Psychology, 59*, 20–26.

DeRubeis, R. J., Hollon, S. E., Evans, M. D., & Bemis, K. M. (1982). Can psychotherapies for depression be discriminated? A systematic investigation of cognitive therapy and interpersonal therapy. *Journal of Consulting and Clinical Psychology, 50*, 744–756.

DiLoreto, A. O. (1971). *Comparative psychotherapy: An experimental analysis.* Chicago: Aldine-Atherton.

Dobson, K., & Shaw, B. F. (1988). The use of treatment manuals in cognitive therapy: Experience and issues. *Journal of Consulting and Clinical Psychology, 56*, 673–680.

Ellis, A. (1971). A critique by Albert Ellis. In A. O. DiLoreto (Ed.), *Comparative psychotherapy: An experimental analysis* (pp. 213–221). Chicago: Aldine-Atherton.

Feldman, R. A., Caplinger, T. E., & Wodarski, J. S. (1983). *The St. Louis conundrum: The effective treatment of antisocial youths.* Englewood Cliffs, NJ: Prentice-Hall.

Flick, S. N. (1988). Managing attrition in clincial research. *Clinical Psychology Review, 8*, 499–515.

Francis, J. R., & Aronson, H. (1990). Communicative efficacy of psychotherapy research. *Journal of Consulting and Clinical Psychology, 58*, 368–370.

Frank, J. D., & Frank, J. B. (1991). *Persuasion and healing* (3rd ed.). Baltimore: Johns Hopkins University Press.

Garfield, S. L. (1983). Editorial: Suggested recommendations for publication in the area of depression. *Journal of Consulting and Clinical Psychology, 51*, 807–808.

Goldfried, M. R. Greenberg, L. S., & Marmar, C. (1990). Individual psychotherapy: Process and outcome. *Annual Review of Psychology, 41*, 659–688.

Heimberg, R. G., & Becker, R. E. (1984). Comparative outcome research. In M. Hersen, L. Michelson, & A. S. Bellack (Eds.), *Issues in psychotherapy research* (pp. 251–283). New York: Plenum Press.

Hill, C. E., O'Grady, K. E., & Elkin, I. (1992). Applying the Collaborative Study Psychotherapy Rating Scale to rate therapist adherence in cognitive-behavior therapy, interpersonal therapy, and clinical management. *Journal of Consulting and Clinical Psychology, 60*, 73–79.

Howard, K. I., Krause, M. S., & Orlinsky, D. E. (1986). The attrition dilemma: Toward a new strategy for psychotherapy research. *Journal of Consulting and Clinical Psychology, 54*, 106–110.

Hsu, L. M. (1989). Random sampling, randomization, and equivalence of contrasted groups in psychotherapy outcome research. *Journal of Consulting and Clinical Psychology, 57*, 131–137.

Iberg, J. R. (1991). Applying statistical control theory to bring together clinical supervision and psychotherapy research. *Journal of Consulting and Clinical Psychology, 59*, 575–586.

Jacobson, N. S. (1991). Behavioral versus insight-oriented marital therapy: Labels can be misleading. *Journal of Consulting and Clinical Psychology, 59*, 142–145.

Jacobson, N. S., & Revenstorf, D. (1988). Statistics for assessing the clinical significance of psychotherapy techniques: Issues, problems, and new developments. *Behavioral Assessment, 10*, 133–145.

Karasu, T. B. (1985, March 1). Personal communication.

Karasu, T. B. (Ed.). (1990). *Treatment of psychiatric disorders: A task force report of the American*

Psychiatric Association (Vols. 1–4). Washington, DC: American Psychiatric Association.

Kazdin, A. E. (1982). *Single-case research designs: Methods for clinical and applied settings.* New York: Oxford University Press.

Kazdin, A. E. (1988). *Child psychotherapy: Developing and identifying effective treatments.* Elmsford, NY: Pergamon Press.

Kazdin, A. E. (1992a). *Research design in clinical psychology,* (2nd ed.). Needham Heights, MA: Allyn & Bacon.

Kazdin, A. E. (Ed.) (1992b). *Methodological issues and strategies in clinical research.* Washington, DC: American Psychological Association.

Kazdin, A. E. (1993). Evaluation in clinical practice: Clinically sensitive and systematic methods of treatment deliver. *Behavior Therapy, 24,* 11–45.

Kazdin, A. E., & Bass, D. (1989). Power to detect differences between alternative treatments in comparative psychotherapy outcome research. *Journal of Consulting and Clinical Psychology, 57,* 138–147.

Kazdin, A. E., Bass, D., Ayers, W. A., & Rodgers, A. (1990). Empirical and clinical focus of child and adolescent psychotherapy research. *Journal of Consulting and Clinical Psychology, 58,* 729–740.

Kazdin, A. E., Kratochwill, T. M. & VandenBos, G. R. (1986). Beyond clinical trials: Generalizing from research to practice. *Professional Psychology: Research and Practice, 17,* 391–398.

Kazdin, A. E., Mazurick, J. L, & Bass, D.(1993). Risk for attrition in treatment of antisocial children and families. *Journal of Clinical Child Psychology, 22,* 2–16.

Kazdin, A. E., Siegel, T., & Bass, D. (1992). Cognitive problem-solving skills training and parent management training in the treatment of antisocial behavior in children. *Journal of Consulting and Clinical Psychology, 60,* 733–747.

Kazdin, A. E., & Wilson, G. T. (1978). *Evaluation of behavior therapy: Issues, evidence, and research strategies.* Cambridge, MA: Ballinger.

Kiesler, D. J. (1971). Experimental designs in psychotherapy research. In A. E. Bergin & S. L. Garfield (Eds.), *Handbook of psychotherapy and behavior change: An empirical analysis* (pp. 36–74). New York: Wiley.

Kupfersmid, J. (1988). Improving what is published. A model in search of an editor. *American Psychologist, 43,* 635–642.

Lambert, M. J., Christensen, E. R., & DeJulio,

S. S. (Eds.). (1983). *The assessment of psychotherapy outcome.* New York: Wiley.

Lambert, M. J., & Ogles, B. M. (1988). Treatment manuals: Problems and promise. *Journal of Integrative and Eclectic Psychotherapy, 7,* 187–204.

Lambert, M. J., Shapiro, D. A., & Bergin, A. E. (1986). The effectiveness of psychotherapy. In S. L. Garfield & A. E. Bergin (Eds.), *Handbook of psychotherapy and behavior change* (3rd ed., pp. 157–211). New York: Wiley.

Liberman, R. L., & Eckman, T. (1981). Behavior therapy vs. insight-oriented therapy for repeated suicide attempters. *Archives of General Psychiatry, 38,* 1126–1130.

Little, R. J. A., & Rubin, D. B. (1987). *Statistical analysis with missing data.* New York: Wiley.

Luborsky, L., & DeRubeis, R. J. (1984). The use of psychotherapy treatment manuals: A small revolution in psychotherapy research style. *Clinical Psychology Review, 4,* 5–14.

Luborsky, L., Singer, B., & Luborsky, L. (1975). Comparative studies of psychotherapies: Is it true that "everyone has won and all must have prizes"? *Archives of General Psychiatry, 32,* 995–1008.

Luborsky, L., Woody, G. E., McLellan, A. T., O'Brien, C. P., & Rosenzweig, J. (1982). Can independent judges recognize different psychotherapies? An experience with manual-guided therapies. *Journal of Consulting and Clinical Psychology, 50,* 49–62.

Maher, B. A. (1978). Stimulus sampling in clinical research: Representative design reviewed. *Journal of Consulting and Clinical Psychology, 46,* 643–647.

Meehl, P. (1978). Theoretical risks and tabular asterisks: Sir Karl, Sir Ronald, and the slow progress of soft psychology. *Journal of Consulting and Clinical Psychology, 46,* 806–834.

Moncher, F. J., & Prinz, R. J. (1991). Treatment fidelity in outcome studies. *Clinical Psychology Review, 11,* 247–266.

Paul, G. L. (1966). *Insight versus desensitization in psychotherapy: An experiment in anxiety reduction.* Stanford, CA: Stanford University Press.

Pekarik, G., & Stephenson, L. A. (1988). Adult and child client differences in therapy dropout research. *Journal of Clinical Child Psychology, 17,* 316–321.

Phillips, E. L. (1985). *Psychotherapy revisited: New frontiers in research and practice.* Hillsdale, NJ: Erlbaum.

Rachman, S. J., & Wilson, G. T. (1980). *The*

effects of psychological therapy (2nd ed.). Oxford: Pergamon Press.

Roback, H. B. (1971). The comparative influence of insight and non-insight psychotherapies on therapeutic outcome: A review of experimental literature. *Psychotherapy: Theory, Research and Practice, 8*, 23–25.

Rosenthal, R., & Rosnow, R. L. (1991). *Essentials of behavioral research: Methods and data analysis* (2nd ed.). New York: McGraw—Hill.

Rossi, J. S. (1990). Statistical power of psychological research: What have we gained in 20 years? *Journal of Consulting and Clinical Psychology, 58*, 646–656.

Rounsaville, B. J., Chevron, E. S., Prusoff, B. A., Elkin, I. Imber, S., Sotsky, S., & Watkins, J. (1986). The relation between specific and general dimensions of the psychotherapy process in Interpersonal Psychotherapy of depression. *Journal of Consulting and Clinical Psychology, 55*, 379–384.

Rush, A. J., Beck, A. T., Kovacs, M., & Hollon, S. (1977). Comparative efficacy of cognitive therapy and pharmacotherapy in the treatment of depressed outpatients. *Cognitive Therapy and Research, 1*, 17–37.

Sechrest, L., West, S. G., Phillips, M. A., Redner, R., & Yeaton, W. (1979). Some neglected problems in evaluation research: Strength and integrity of treatments. In L. Sechrest, S. G. West, M. A. Phillips, R. Redner, & W. Yeaton (Eds.), *Evaluation studies: Review annual* (Vol. 4, pp. 15–35). Beverly Hills, CA: Sage.

Sedlmeier, P. & Gigerenzer, G. (1989). Do studies of statistical power have an effect on the power of studies? *Psychological Bulletin, 105*, 309–316.

Shapiro, D. A., & Shapiro, D. (1983). Comparative therapy outcome research: Methodological implications of meta-analysis. *Journal of Consulting and Clinical Psychology, 51*, 42–53.

Sloane, R. B., Staples, F. R., Cristol, A. H., Yorkston, N J., & Whipple, K. (1975). *Psychotherapy versus behavior therapy*. Cambridge, MA: Harvard University Press.

Smith, B., & Sechrest, L. (1991). Treatment of aptitude x treatment interactions. *Journal of Consulting and Clinical Psychology, 59*, 233–244.

Synder, D. K., & Wills, R. M. (1989). Behavioral versus insight-oriented marital therapy: Effects on individual and interspousal functioning. *Journal of Consulting and Clinical Psychology,. 57*, 39–46.

Snyder, D. K., Wills, R. M., & Grady-Fletcher, A. (1991). Long-term effectiveness of behavioral versus insight-oriented marital therapy: A 4-year follow-up study. *Journal of Consulting and Clinical Psychology, 59*, 138–141.

Stark, M. J. (1992). Dropping out of substance abuse treatment: A clinically oriented review. *Clinical Psychology Review, 12*, 93–116.

Stiles, W. B., Shapiro, D. A., & Elliott, R. (1986). Are all psychotherapies equivalent? *American Psychologist, 41*, 165–180.

Strube, M. J. (1991). Small sample failure of random assignment: A further examination. *Journal of Consulting and Clinical Psychology, 59*, 346–350.

Strupp, H. H., & Hadley, S. W. (1977). A tripartite model of mental health and therapeutic outcomes. *American Psychologist, 32*, 187–196.

Szapocznik, J., Perez-Vidal, A., Brickman, A., Foote, F. H., Santisteban, D., Hervis, O., & Kurtines, W. H. (1988). Engaging adolescent drug abusers and their families into treatment: A strategic structural systems approach. *Journal of Consulting and Clinical Psychology, 56*, 552–557.

Szapocznik, J., Rio, A., Murray, E., Cohen R. Scopetta, M., Rivas-Vazquez, A. Hervis, O., Posada, V., & Kurtines, W. (1989). Structural family versus psychodynamic child therapy for problematic Hispanic boys. *Journal of Consulting and Clinical Psychology, 57*, 571–578.

Tversky, A., & Kahneman, D. (1971). Belief in the law of small numbers. *Psychological Bulletin, 76*, 105–110.

Vaile-Val, G., Rosenthal, R. H., Curtiss, G., & Marohn, R. C. (1984). Dropout from adolescent psychotherapy: A preliminary study. *Journal of the American Academy of Child Psychiatry, 23*, 562–568.,

Webster-Stratton, C., Hollinsworth, T., & Kolpacoff, M. (1989). The long-term effectiveness and clinical significance of three cost-effective training programs for families with conduct-problem children. *Journal of Consulting and Clinical Psychology, 57*, 550–553.

Weisz, J. R., Weiss, B., Alicke, M. D., & Klotz, M. L. (1987). Effectiveness of psychotherapy with children and adolescents: Meta-analytic findings for clinicians. *Journal of Consulting and Clinical Psychology, 55*, 542–549.

Wierzbicki, M., & Pekarik, G. (1993). A meta-analysis of psychotherapy dropout. *Professional Psychology: Research and Practice, 24*, 190–195.

Wills, R. M., Faitler, S. L., & Snyder, D. K. (1987). Distinctiveness of behavioral versus insight-oriented marital therapy: An empirical analysis. *Journal of Consulting and Clinical Psychology, 55*, 685–690.

Wright, D. M., Moelis, I., & Pollack, L. J. (1976). The outcome of individual child psychotherapy: Increments at follow-up. *Journal of Child Psychology and Psychiatry, 17*, 275–285.

Yeaton, W. H., & Sechrest, L. (1981). Critical dimensions in the choice and maintenance of successful treatments: Strength, integrity, and effectiveness. *Journal of Consulting and Clinical Psychology, 49*, 156–167.

22
Issues in the Training of Psychotherapists

Richard P. Halgin
Robert A. Murphy

For most of the twentieth century, senior psychotherapists have struggled with the task of how best to impart the skills and techniques of therapeutic work to novices. As we approach the twenty-first century, the institutional structures (such as graduate programs, medical schools, and training clinics) are well established, and there is less concern than there was several decades ago about where psychotherapists would be trained and by whom (Abt, 1992). Although the training structures are in place, a great deal of uncertainty continues regarding the most effective strategies for training neophytes.

Complicating the task of training is the fact that so little is understood about how psychotherapy really works. For example, to what extent is successful psychotherapy attributable to the techniques introduced by the psychotherapist? To what extent is it the person of the psychotherapist and the quality of that individual's relationship with the patient that determine successful outcome? The research literature on psychotherapy outcome provides suggestions and trends about which factors seem to be central to psychotherapy success; however, comparatively little has been written about the ways in which the state of the art can

be most effectively communicated to beginners. In this chapter we will discuss what is known about pedagogy and propose approaches to training that are based on current understanding through a discussion of several related topics: (1) the relationship between science and clinical practice; (2) the nature of psychotherapy and how it works; (3) the development of psychotherapists; (4) pedagogical issues in the training of psychotherapists; (5) the evaluation of trainees; and (6) training psychotherapists for a changing society.

THE RELATIONSHIP BETWEEN SCIENCE AND CLINICAL PRACTICE

Psychotherapy is conducted by members of several professions other than psychology, including psychiatry, social work, counseling, and nursing. However, it seems fair to suggest that psychology (clinical psychology in particular), has played a central role in formulating a model of professional practice—that of the scientifically informed practitioner. In other words, the work of professional psychotherapists is informed by up-to-date theory and research. This is a notion that has prevailed for most of the twentieth century, and it is a principle on which sound training must rest. A brief review of the historical views regarding this blending of science and practice will set the stage for understanding the centrality of this approach to current psychotherapy training.

The history of professional psychology since the late 1800s has consisted of a mixture of science and practice interests. For example, Lightner Witmer, who coined the term *clinical psychology*, established a psychological clinic at the University of Pennsylvania in 1896 that was actually part of a psychology laboratory (Hilgard, 1987) and subsequently founded a journal, *The Psychological Clinic* (1907), providing a public forum for these previously disparate fields. Witmer had been trained in the experimental tradition but believed that by attempting to mitigate everyday human problems, psychologists could advance the scientific objectives of their discipline; furthermore, clinical methods could be refined by the application of experimental endeavors. In the 1920s abnormal and social psychology were regarded as overlapping fields (Allport & Prince, 1921–1922; Hill & Weary, 1983), providing many psychologists, particularly those who were social advocates, with an opportunity to bring these seemingly divergent pursuits together in synthesized professional endeavors.

A major impetus was provided for the advancement of this notion of building professional practice on a scientific foundation by the needs of the nation associated with World War II, particularly the mental health needs of returning veterans. When directors of the Veterans Administration (VA) were faced with large numbers of emotionally disturbed veterans, they turned to psychology for assistance and provided psychology with tremendous financial support for the training of practitioners. It is interesting to note that the VA set up training programs within hospitals and emphasized the importance of associating these programs with nearby universities (Hilgard, 1987). Implicit in this alliance was the notion that clinical endeavors within a psychiatric institution should be associated with scientific inquiry taking place on the university campus. In 1946

the National Mental Health Act was passed, from which grew the National Institutes of Mental Health (NIMH), an agency given the broad mission of promoting mental health and dealing with mental illness (Brand, 1965; Segal, 1975). NIMH would go on to become a major player in both clinical training and research, once again affirming the valued alliance between practice and science.

In the late 1940s the American Psychological Association recognized the importance of establishing curriculum requirements in the field of clinical psychology and called together a conference in Boulder, Colorado (Raimy, 1950). The 1949 Boulder Conference provided a definition of a clinical psychologist that would hold relatively constant for more than two decades; the clinical psychologist was to be a scientist-professional with training in both science and practice. In other words, graduate training that was limited to developing clinical expertise was regarded as insufficient; clinical psychologists were expected to be trained in and committed to scientific investigation of the phenomena associated with their work.

Although the ideal of this alliance between science and practice was admirable, the blending of the two has never been completely satisfactory. For example, clinical psychologists' ambivalent relationship to research was evidenced by their low publication rates (Clark, 1957; Levy, 1962; Pasewark, Fitzgerald, Thornton, & Sawyer, 1973; Secrest, 1975). Many questioned the wisdom of continued support for the scientist-professional model, and it is not surprising that an alternative training model emerged in the 1970s. At the Vail Conference in 1973 (Korman, 1976), a new training model emerged, that of the professional-scientist. Despite the reprioritizing of the relationship, science was not deleted as a core characteristic, but was still regarded as a defining feature of the role of the professional psychologist, who was trained as a practitioner and a knowledgeable consumer of psychological research. At present, there is certainly considerable variability in the extent to which practicing psychologists are engaged in research activities, but there is consensus in the field that the skilled clinician must be a consumer of the products of relevant scientific inquiry, ready and willing to apply newly acquired scientific knowledge within the clinical realm.

Although psychology has been the most visible player in promoting clinical practice that is informed by research and science, it is fair to conclude that professionals from the other mental health specialities, such as psychiatry, social work, and nursing, also value the importance of this approach. As we proceed in our discussion of the ways to teach psychotherapy, it is important to emphasize what should be considered a nonnegotiable component of solid training: Psychotherapy training models and approaches should be built on state-of-the-art research. First, educators should be acutely attentive to research on psychotherapy process and outcome. Second, attention needs to be given to research on psychotherapy training. In the sections to follow, we will briefly summarize the major points in each of these spheres.

THE NATURE OF PSYCHOTHERAPY AND HOW IT WORKS

For half a century psychotherapists, and their patients for that matter, have wondered about what makes psychotherapy work. One can conclude that the phenomenon would have become extinct by now if it involved nothing more than charlatanism. Four decades ago, Eysenck (1952) stirred up the profession by reviewing psychotherapy research and asserting that psychotherapy is not only ineffective but might even be detrimental for some patients.

Eysenck provoked a stampede of investigators who set out to disprove his claim. For example, Bergin (1971) drew a contradictory conclusion about the research and claimed that psychotherapy has a moderately positive effect. Using the premise that psychotherapy does work, the quest was initiated to understand which techniques in particular were effective. Luborsky and his colleagues (1975) raised some eyebrows in the profession when they concluded that, for the most part, specific techniques had little bearing on outcome. These

reviews, and the many others conducted around that time, were heavily criticized (Wierzbicki, 1993) and led to two groundbreaking meta-analyses of outcome studies (Smith & Glass, 1977; Smith, Glass, & Miller, 1980). In their 1977 article, Smith and Glass concluded that their meta-analysis demonstrated "the beneficial effects of counseling and psychotherapy" (p. 760) and "negligible differences in the effects produced by different therapy types" (p. 760). In their 1980 meta-analysis, Smith, Glass, and Miller reinforced their previous finding by reporting that "the results show unequivocally that psychotherapy is effective" (p. 124); however, they raised the possibility that therapeutic approach might make a difference by pointing out that "behavioral therapies were more effective than verbal therapies, which were in turn more effective than developmental therapies" (p. 124). The floodgates for subsequent meta-analysis had been opened, and in the years following the publications of Smith and his colleagues, numerous other inquiries would be conducted about whether psychotherapy works in general and which therapies work in particular (e.g., Andrews & Harvey, 1981; Bowers & Clum, 1988; Kazdin & Bass, 1989; Landman & Dawes, 1982; Matt, 11989; Prioleau, Murdock, & Brody, 1983; Searles, 1985; Shapiro & Shapiro, 1982; Whiston & Sexton, 1993). More than a decade of intensive evaluation of the issue of efficacy has provided psychotherapists with some reason to believe that their efforts are indeed worthwhile, but with little certainty about which efforts in particular are beneficial to their patients. If nothing else, the lesson that has been learned is that psychotherapists should be approaching their work from a scientific mindset. Similarly, trainees should be approaching the learning of psychotherapy with a healthy skepticism, attuned to the importance of developing, applying, and evaluating theories that are "rooted in science" (American Psychological Association, 1987, p. 4).

Basing our discussion on the assumption that psychotherapy works, we will now turn to a consideration of the characteristics that are essential for the trainee to appreciate. The definition of psychotherapy offered by Jerome

Frank (1982) is a succinct, yet powerful, statement about the nature of this intriguing phenomenon: "Psychotherapy is a planned, emotionally charged, confiding interaction between a trained, socially sanctioned healer and a sufferer" (p. 10). An appreciation of each phrase in this definition will help in understanding the complexity of the issues involved in training people to undertake this work.

A Planned Intervention

Psychotherapy stands in sharp contrast to casual helping relationships in which one person spontaneously provides advice, support, or feedback to someone else in an everyday relationship. Presumably, the psychotherapist bases the offering of help to another on some plan that rests on an assessment of the other person's needs and involves some predesigned techniques. All of these factors—assessment strategy, treatment plan, and techniques—are customarily rooted in one or more conceptual models. A glimpse at the history of psychology and psychotherapy during the twentieth century provides a view of very different theoretical models with correspondingly different intervention plans and techniques. Consider the differences in the assessments, treatment plans, and techniques formulated by proponents of psychoanalysis, client-centered therapy, behavior therapy, biofeedback, cognitive therapy, or pharmacotherapy.

The Relationship Between Theoretical Model and Choosing a Plan

The changing zeitgeist has affected the assessment, treatment plans, and techniques of psychotherapists throughout the century. It has been well documented that there are few theoretical purists adhering to narrow trends of a singular model of therapy. Although many therapists continue to draw on a particular theoretical orientation to guide their clinical endeavors, their practice rarely adheres to precise

tenets of their theory. Practicing psychotherapists have come to realize that no single orientation has all the answers (Lazarus, Beutler, & Norcross, 1992; Norcross & Newman, 1992; Whiston & Sexton, 1993), and instead have embraced eclecticism (Jensen, Bergin, & Greaves, 19990; Norcross, 1986; Norcross & Newman, 1992; Norcross, Prochaska, & Gallagher, 1989).

Although eclecticism prevails, there are some who have raised concerns about what is meant by this term (Dryden, 1984; Franks, 1984; Karasu, 1986; Lazarus, 1988). For many eclectic clinicians there is no plan, but rather a haphazard sampling from a smorgasbord (Lazarus et al., 1992) that lacks a systematic rationale or empirical verification (Eysenck, 1970). In place of careless and ill-conceived combinations of therapeutic techniques, Lazarus (1967) has proposed an approach, technical eclecticism, which involves a systematic process for selecting therapeutic procedures that is "built upon empirical demonstrations of the conditions, problems, and patients with whom different procedures are effective" (Lazarus et al., 1992, p. 12). Increasingly, it is being recognized that effective psychotherapy develops from explicit decision making and coherent treatment planning (e.g., Beutler, 1989; Beutler & Clarkin, 1990; Beutler & Consoli, 1992; Mahalik, 1990).

Defining Theoretical Approach

Experienced clinicians who are comfortable with their own approach to conducting psychotherapy can lose touch with how formidable a challenge this is for the beginning therapist. Early in training, most neophytes are exposed to statistics documenting the fact that most experienced therapists consider themselves eclectic. It is understandable, therefore, when the beginner also chooses such a label. For those who espouse eclecticism, the question arises: Can they really know *how* to be eclectic without having first been exposed to the traditional models of therapy from which experienced therapists have chosen their techniques? Rarely is the training curriculum of much utility to the aspiring eclecticist. Usually, models of therapy are taught in their historically pure forms (Andrews, Norcross, & Halgin, 1992), with the implication, for example, that behavior therapists limit their interventions to narrow behavior techniques and are unconcerned with feelings, personal history, family dynamics, and anything other than target behaviors. The vision that beginners have of a multitheoretical approach can be baffling, as they find themselves feeling puzzled by the mechanics of technique shifts and dismayed by a fear that their own attempts might prove to be awkward and disruptive (Wachtel, 1991). They are naive about the reality that "deep structure" integration takes a great deal of time and years of experience (Messer, 1992).

For some trainees, the choice of theoretical affiliation is simplified by espousing a single approach and taking comfort in the transient comfort of having a "home base." Such a choice can provide trainees with a conceptual framework that guides their professional development and offers a sense of confidence in the initially bewildering endeavor of psychotherapy (Frank & Frank, 1991; Teyber, 1992). By prematurely choosing an affiliation, they believe that they have eradicated ambiguity without yet realizing that the process is inherently and unavoidably ambiguous (Norcross, 1988). They may be seduced into a "camp" or "school" in which they become entrenched, perceiving any thought of deviating from the model as representing betrayal that engenders feelings akin to "separation anxiety" from a "mother" theory that has provided them with support and security (Norcross, 1988). In time, however, these individuals become disenchanted and frustrated by unsatisfying attempts to make all patients fit into the model.

In predicting the future, Lazarus et al. (1992) assert that "treatments of choice for selected clinical disorders will become standard practice" (p. 13) and that training programs will be faced with the challenge of ensuring exposure to and competence in multiple clinical procedures.

An Emotionally Charged, Confiding Interaction

There has been considerable discussion about what common factors (Karasu, 1986; Lambert, 1986; Patterson, 1989) are the core ingredients shared by different therapeutic approaches. In their review of 50 publications, Grencavage and Norcross (1990) concluded that "the single most frequent commonality was the development of a collaborative therapeutic relationship/alliance" (p. 377). Over and over in the literature, one reads about the therapeutic relationship as the sine qua non of successful intervention (Horvath & Symonds, 1991; Luborsky, Crits-Christoph, Mintz, & Auerbach, 1988; Marziali, Marmar, & Krupnick, 1981; Morgan, Luborsky, Crits-Christoph, Curtis, & Solomon, 1982; Orlinsky & Howard, 1986; Strupp, 1992; Teyber, 1992). It is described as "the foundation from which other activities are built" (Whiston & Sexton, 1993, p. 45).

The therapeutic relationship involves more than the ability to form a sensitive interpersonal relationship. It involves a focus on the well-being and growth of the patient (Guy, 1987). Perhaps more important than any other task for the beginner is the challenge of learning how to be involved with a patient in a manner that is appropriate and curative. There are countless pitfalls in learning this kind of intimacy, ranging from overinvolvement to phobic distancing from the patient. Somewhat surprising to some beginning therapists is the fact that they will relate in dramatically different ways to different patients. Lazarus et al. (1992) suggest that the relationship can be used prescriptively as the therapist learns to determine the "relationship of choice" (Norcross 1991) to be tapped with each patient.

The therapeutic relationship has been conceptualized in many ways, with the most prominent conceptualizations involving social influence (Strong, 1968) and working alliance (Bordin, 1979). In the social influence model, psychotherapy is seen as a "persuasion process in which the therapist's operational theory forms the content of *what* is persuaded, and the therapist's technology functions as the *means* of influence" (Beutler & Consoli, 1992, p. 266). Heppner and Claiborn (1989) reviewed 60 studies on the social influence model and concluded that the course and outcome of therapy can be influenced by myriad factors conveying power or influence, such as nonverbal behaviors, self-disclosure, and level of appropriate intimacy in the therapist's touch.

There is little question about the importance of the notion of a working alliance in the therapeutic relationship. It has been repeatedly documented that a primary contributor to positive therapy outcome is a relationship in which both patient and therapist feel emotionally bonded and are mutually affirming and respectful. As a result, therapy becomes a collaborative endeavor in which therapist and patient work together in their definition and pursuit of mutually defined treatment goals (Hartley & Strupp, 1983; Horvath & Symonds, 1991; Luborsky et al., 1988; Morgan et al., 1982; Orlinsky, & Howard, 1986; Whiston & Sexton, 1993).

Clinical supervisors and educators know that a major training challenge involves communicating to beginners the centrality of the relationship in the psychotherapy process. Later in this chapter we will discuss ways of undertaking this task.

THE DEVELOPMENT OF PSYCHOTHERAPISTS: BECOMING TRAINED, SOCIALLY SANCTIONED HEALERS

Continuing with our analysis of psychotherapy as proposed by Jerome Frank, we are brought to a discussion of the person of the psychotherapist. Who are these individuals who present themselves to society as healers? In order to capture the essence of the psychotherapist, it is helpful for us first to discuss what draws people to this profession.

Motivations for Becoming a Psychotherapist

People are drawn to this profession out of natural inquisitiveness (Guy, 1987), a desire for discovery (Marston, 1984), and a desire to understand the intricacies of human behavior; however, the primary motivation is presumably a desire to help people and to promote growth in others (Farber & Heifitz, 1981).

In addition to the laudatory motivations that attract aspiring clinicians, there are also some factors that are more complex and problematic. For example, some are drawn to this line of work out of a yearning for intimacy or power. Some have voyeuristic impulses that are gratified by learning about the private behaviors and fantasies of others. Some are narcissistically drawn to a position of control in which they are perceived as omniscient and influential (Bugental, 1964; Guy, 1987; Guy & Liaboe, 1986; Marston, 1984; Sussman, 1992). Some are hoping for a vicarious resolution of personal problems (Bugental, 1964; Ford, 1963; Goldberg, 1986; Guy, 1987; Sussman, 1992). Relevant to this latter notion is that of the "wounded healer" (Elliott & Guy, 1993; Goldberg, 1986; Guy, 1987; Scott & Hawk, 1986); in other words, some individuals with psychic "wounds" are drawn to the healing profession in the hope that they will be healed in the process of ministering to others.

In one avenue of research regarding the influences on choosing a psychotherapy career, researchers have investigated the role of family experiences and childhood trauma. Although some authors have questioned the prevalence of serious family problems in the lives of psychotherapists (Norcross & Guy, 1989), the bulk of research paints a dramatic picture. Many therapists come from families characterized by serious dysfunction and seek out a profession in which they hope to obtain the caring and closeness that they missed in childhood (Elliott & Guy, 1993; Ford, 1963; Guy, Tamura, & Poelstra, 1989; Liaboe & Guy, 1987; Raskin, 1978). In one interesting study Fussell and Bonney (1990) compared the childhood experiences of psychotherapists and physicists, and found that those in the therapist group had experienced more frequent parental death or absence due to prolonged illness, divorce, or separation. The psychotherapists viewed their families as less healthy and reported a greater likelihood than the physicists of having played a caretaker role within the family during youth. In other studies (Elliott & Guy, 1993; Racussin, Abramowitz, & Winter, 1981; Sussman, 1992), therapists reported having troubled families in which, as children, they had acted as nurturers or mediators.

Not only is family dysfunction influential in the choice of a career as a psychotherapist, but for many this factor appears to be connected to the specific therapeutic model with which clinicians affiliate and with their subsequent practice of psychotherapy. Rosin and Knudson (1986) evaluated the relationship between life experiences and the selection of either a psychodynamic or behavioral orientation, and found a positive correlation between a family history of psychological distress and the adoption of a psychodynamic orientation. Henry and his colleagues (1993) examined the effect of therapists' views of themselves on their learning of brief psychodynamic therapy; subsequent to training, therapists with controlling or hostile views of themselves adhered more stringently to the training protocols but also engaged in more interactions that were characterized as hostile to or critical to their clients.

For many psychotherapists, early life experiences and family roles form a general template for their work as psychotherapists. Presumably, individuals with troubled life experiences are choosing a career that is harmonious with their psychological needs (Goldberg, 1986) and are even selecting therapeutic approaches that may serve some curative role for their personal scars.

The Anxieties of the Neophyte Healer

As beginners embark on this new venture into the lives of other people, they encounter a host of anxieties that most have not anticipated. They fear that they will fail at their work, be vulnerable to authority figures such as supervisors, and have difficulty internalizing the healer role (Cohen, 1980; Gaoni & Neumann, 1974; Greenberg, 1980; Norcross, 1988). In addition to these concerns, they carry the burden of transitional stresses that can impair their profes-

sional functioning (Deutsch, 1985; Guy, Poelstra, & Stark, 1989). They are likely to become particularly distressed by "the undefined, complex, and ephemeral quality of psychotherapeutic endeavors" (Guy, 1987, p. 40).

A formidable challenge for beginners is the process of developing psychological-mindedness (Farber, 1985). They are thrust into a system in which their attention is directed to the understanding of human experiences, memories, and emotions—both in their patients and in themselves. This kind of scrutiny is typically very stressful for trainees and is likely to affect their relationships and their feelings about themselves (Farber, 1985; Guy, 1987). They are also especially at risk of exaggerated concerns and loss of clear boundaries between their own issues and the problems of those whom they are treating.

An additional stress for the novice is the commonly reported experience of feeling like a fraud or imposter (Guy, 1987). Based on a hidden but understandable doubt about personal competence as a therapist, the beginner may become paralyzed by a self-critique in which he or she imagines that peers and supervisors are observing one's seemingly gargantuan flaws.

Navigating the perilous waters of the initial training period causes many beginners to question the wisdom of their career choice. As they begin to learn to heal others, they become vulnerable to doubt about their own psychological stability and competence to help.

PEDAGOGICAL ISSUES IN THE TRAINING OF PSYCHOTHERAPISTS

Having discussed some essential contributors to successful psychotherapy, we now turn our attention to the cultivation of therapeutic technique and style in trainees. We work with the assumption that becoming an effective psychotherapist involves more than inherent qualities of personality. Although appropriate and sensitive interpersonal skill is a requisite, we believe that it is not a sufficient factor for determining the extent to which a therapist can help a patient. Even those who view psychotherapy as more of an art than a skill can acknowledge that most artists have benefited from being taught.

Excellent reviews of research on psychotherapy training have been published (e.g., Binder, 1993; Matarazzo & Garner, 1992). Rather than reiterate a review of the body of research on this topic, we will focus our discussion on critical issues that have emerged from the literature on psychotherapy training that inform proposals for innovative training models. Matarazzo and Garner (1992) note that for most of the twentieth century, two major lines of psychotherapy training have prevailed: (1) the didactic approach, which involves the conveying of knowledge and skills by a teacher to students, and (2) the supervisory approach, which involves a dyadic interaction focused on clinical cases. Didactic work can take place without the trainee actually being involved in clinical work, whereas supervision necessitates that the trainee have cases to present to the supervisor. In many instances both approaches are combined, sometimes formally and sometimes informally. For example, in some graduate school programs, the student may be taking formal courses in theory and technique with a concurrent psychotherapy practicum. In other cases, there is an attempt at careful intertwining of didactic and experiential work.

After reviewing a number of publications on psychotherapy training (e.g., Alberts & Edelstein, 1990; Bootzin & Ruggill, 1988; Buckley, Conte, Plutchik, Karasu, & Wild, 1982; Colenda, 1985; Ford, 1979; Garfield, 1977; Matarazzo & Patterson, 1986; Schiffman, 1987; Strupp, Butler, & Rosser, 1988; Wright, Horlick, Bouchard, Mathieu, & Zeichner, 1997). Binder (1993) points out that a core problem with the research on psychotherapy training is that there is minimal proof of its effectiveness. With tempered optimism, Binder acknowledges that a hopeful trend is emerging in training programs in which there is a combination of structured didactic and experiential components that teach specific procedures and skills, progressing from simple to more complex.

Structured Approaches to Teaching Psychotherapy Skills

As clinicians and researchers struggled for decades in their efforts to assess the effectiveness of psychotherapy, it became evident that psychotherapy was a difficult phenomenon to study because the process itself was so poorly defined. Several researchers made efforts to delineate specific techniques and styles of intervening, as well as ways to measure changes in therapeutic skills. For example, nearly three decades ago, Truax and Carkhuff (1967) attempted to operationalize some of the concepts of the client-centered model of intervention. Subsequently, Allen Ivey and his colleagues (Forsyth & Ivey, 1980; Ivey, 1980, 1983; Ivey & Authier, 1978) brought together client-centered and behavioral techniques in their development of *microtraining*, a program designed to teach interviewing skills such as attending behavior, reflection of feeling, summarization, and self-disclosure.

New attempts at introducing technical sophistication to psychotherapy training have arisen in well-respected programs for the study of psychotherapy process and outcome. In contrast to traditional texts that outlined a general system or theory of psychotherapy, treatment manuals were initially designed within research settings to provide specificity to the processes being studied. Strupp (1992) describes a treatment manual as being analogous to a cookbook or a flight plan, containing specific recommendations about appropriate techniques within a given theoretical model. Manuals also provide opportunities for assessing the extent to which a therapist adheres to the techniques. Manual-guided training emerged primarily within behavior therapy contexts (Bootzin & Ruggill, 1988) but has also been touted by proponents of other models including psychodynamic and interpersonal approaches (Luborsky, 1984; Rounsaville, O'Malley, Foley, & Weissman, 1988; Strupp & Binder, 1984), cognitive approaches (Beck, Rush, Shaw, & Emery, 1979), and humanistic models (Greenberg & Goldman, 1988).

Despite positive reports about the efficacy of

using manual-guided approaches to training that emphasize the acquisition of specific technical skills, there has been minimal implementation of such approaches outside of particular research contexts. Nevertheless, the early technique-focused models have been instrumental in setting the stage for the increased emphasis on the acquisition of specified skills commonly associated with pre- and post-training measurements. For example, several investigators assessed the role of practice on the acquisition of therapeutic proficiency (Errek & Randolph, 1982; Froehle, Robinson, & Kurpius, 1983; Hazler & Hipple, 1981; O'Toole, 1979; Robinson & Cabianca, 1985). In reviewing these studies, Alberts and Edelstein (1990) concluded that "training interventions containing some combination of instructions, modeling, feedback, and/or rehearsal lead to trainees' acquisition and demonstration of basic therapy responses" (p. 502). They also noted that investigators have reported that complex verbal skills can also be developed via technical training (e.g., Baker, Johnson, Kopala & Strout, 1985; Claiborn & Dixon, 1982; Kasdorf & Gustafson, 1979; Kurpius, Benjamin, & Moran, 1985).

The point raised by Bootzin and Ruggill (1988) in their review of behavior therapy training models seems apropos of other training models as well; they concluded that specific behavioral techniques can be taught but raised doubt about the generalizability of this learning to actual therapy settings. This same point was noted by Alberts and Edelstein (1990), who criticized training studies on methodological grounds, most notably pertaining to questions about the validity and utility of skills selected for training.

Binder (1993) pointed out that manual-guided training may be successful in bringing trainees to a criterion level of adherence to technical procedures but notes that at present there is insufficient evidence that such adherence improves the outcome of therapy. Binder also reported an interesting, somewhat ironic side effect of manual-guided training observed in the Vanderbilt II study in dynamic/interpersonal therapy (Henry, Schacht, Strupp, Binder, & Butler, 1993; Henry, Strupp, Butler, Schacht, & Binder, 1993); trainees acquired the prescribed techniques and improved their interviewing styles but simultaneously tended to act in ways that were more impatient with and critical of the patients.

As Strupp (1992) noted, accumulating research evidence leads us to recognize "that adherence to a set of techniques is no guarantee that a therapist practices skillfully" (p. 25). He went on to assert that "the practice of psychotherapy, like the practice of medicine, remains an art, only certain aspects of which are susceptible to specification and measurement" (p. 25).

Clinical Supervision

There is little question about the fact that the art and style of psychotherapy must be acquired through processes more intensive and personal than can be provided by manuals. Clinical supervision continues to be at the heart of psychotherapy training and is the most commonly used method (Binder, in press; Caligor, Bromberg, & Meltzer, 1984; Dewald, 1987). Despite the universality of this educational approach, relatively little research has been conducted on supervisory procedures and supervisory efficacy (Alberts & Edelstein, 1990; Binder 1993; Hess, 1987; Kennard, Stewart, & Gluck, 1987; Martin, Goodyear, & Newton, 1987; Matarazzo & Garner, 1992).

The bulk of the research and literature on supervision has been published during the past 15 years, prior to which time most supervisors relied on Dellis and Stone (1960), Eckstein and Wallerstein (1972), or Mueller and Kell (1972) for guidance. The supervision literature has grown dramatically in the past several years with the publication of innumerable articles, special journal sections, and a handful of respected books (e.g., Alonso, 1985; Stoltenberg & Delworth, 1988).

Clinical supervision is a dyadic relationship in which one person helps another to modify behaviors, affects, and cognitions in order to provide more effective services to patients (Hess, 1980). In characterizing the purpose of supervision, Stricker (1988) asserts that "(1) the patient's needs should be paramount in the therapeutic situation, (2) the therapist's interventions should be tailored to meeting these needs, and (3) the supervisor's role is to facilitate the occurrence of the first two conditions" (p. 180). The supervisor carries many responsibilities, ranging from the promotion of competency in the trainee to the inculcation of standards of professional and ethical practice (Vasquez, 1992).

The role of supervisor is multifaceted. As Guy (1987) notes, the supervisor serves as a teacher, journeyman, a facilitator, and an evaluator. The trainee seeks to learn the art of psychotherapy through this apprenticeship with a skilled clinician (Dewald, 1987; Goldfried & Padawer, 1982; Peterfreund, 1975). Significant pressures bear on supervision in that this relationship must incorporate and balance multiple foci, including the patient's need for competent treatment, the trainee's need for development, and the training program's evaluation of the student's progress (Norcross, 1988).

Characteristics of Good Supervision

Carifio and Hess (1987) reviewed the supervision literature and concluded that the ideal supervisor possesses "high levels of empathy, respect, genuineness, flexibility, concern, investment, and openness" (p. 244). They contended that good supervisors use appropriate teaching, goal-setting, and feedback techniques while being supportive, noncritical, and respectful. In good supervision, there is respect for honesty and psychic reality in the face of myriad pressures (Crick, 1991).

At the heart of effective supervision is a relationship. It has been established in the psychotherapy outcome literature that relationship factors are the most important determinants of positive outcome; similar importance can be attributed to relationship factors in supervision (Lambert & Arnold, 1987).

In defining a supervisory style that is more likely to succeed, Norcross (1988) proposed a collaborative approach in which the supervisor inquires about the supervisee's optimal way of learning and receiving feedback. The refinement of feedback to the learner is tremendously important in imparting skills (Matarazzo & Garner, 1992).

Characteristics of Bad Supervision

Despite the fact that the qualities of good supervision seem fairly evident, a disturbing amount of inadequate and counterproductive supervision takes places. Unfortunately, experience as a supervisor does not necessarily improve one's ability to supervise (Worthington, 1987). In their study of objectionable supervisory styles, Rosenblatt and Mayer (1975) found four styles to be particularly problematic: constrictive, amorphous, unsupportive, and therapeutic. In other words, supervision is likely to be viewed negatively when it is authoritarian (Allen, Szollos, & Williams, 1986), poorly defined, harshly judgmental, or inappropriately intrusive into the personal issues of the supervisee. Further, supervision can be contaminated when a supervisor constantly points out errors of commission and omission in order to demonstrate his or her superior knowledge (Marmor, 1953).

Supervision as a Developmental Process

In order to understand the nature of supervision, it is important to develop an appreciation of the fact that this phenomenon involves stages of change and growth. Developmental models of supervision have received a good deal of attention and empirical support (Hogan, 1964; Loganbill, Hardy, & Delworth, 1982; Stoltenberg, 1981; Stoltenberg & Delworth, 1988; Yogev, 1982). In Loganbill et al.'s (1982) conceptualization of supervision, there are three stages through which most supervisees pass: stagnation, confusion, and integration. During the stagnation stage, the beginner typically has a naive sense of security, deceptive stability, and simplistic black-and-white thinking. The confusion stage is characterized by instability, confusion, and conflict as the supervisee realizes that something is amiss and that the solution package is nowhere on the horizon. In the integration stage, the supervisee can reorganize and develop a new understanding, flexibility, and personal security.

As Norcross (1988) notes, the level of experience of the trainee usually calls for significantly different supervisory styles, with beginners more interested in the acquisition of specific skills, mid-level trainees more inclined to develop formulations, and advanced trainees most intrigued by the examination of personal dynamics affecting therapy. Stricker (1988) characterizes development as a process in which trainees "initially are most helped by a focus on technique, followed by more concentration on theory, and culminating with emphasis on transference and countertransference" (p. 177).

Methods of Supervision

Like psychotherapeutic techniques, supervisory techniques should be defined with several factors in mind. In part, the context dictates the methods that will be used. For example, a beginning therapist in a graduate program needs something different from supervision than is needed by a supervisee in postdoctoral training. The clinical needs of the patient influence the nature of the supervision as well. As Norcross (1988) points out, "the how of supervision (method) should parallel the what of supervision (content)" (p. 159). The therapist treating a patient who is in crisis will need an active and directive problem-solving approach, whereas a therapy that is focused on relational issues will benefit more from supervision concentrating on interpersonal issues in the supervisory relationship and the parallels with the therapeutic relationship.

Modeling

Although modeling has been shown to be particularly effective for teaching complex behaviors, this approach is used surprisingly little in teaching psychotherapy (Andrews, Norcross, &

Halgin, 1992). It is a common occurrence in training programs for senior clinicians to boast about therapeutic successes but provide little or no opportunity for trainees to observe them in their successful endeavors. Trainees are usually deprived of the opportunity to watch their teachers struggle with dilemmas that are such inherent parts of real-life intervention. As pointed out repeatedly, supervisory modeling has strong positive effects on the acquisition of clinical skills (Baum & Gray, 1992; Lambert & Arnold, 1987; Sifneos, 1984), and graduate students very much wish to observe the therapeutic work of their supervisors (Gandolfo & Brown, 1987). Unfortunately, all too often, supervisors feel vulnerable in exposing their work to a potentially critical audience, even in the form of a videotape (Goldberg, 1983; Heilveil, 1983).

Modeling of appropriate clinical style can take place at a level removed from the actual psychotherapeutic context. Within the teaching and supervisory context, the supervisor can model open-mindedness and synthetic thinking that encourage a sense of curiosity and incisive thinking (Norcross, 1988). Whatever form it takes, modeling can have long-lasting effects on the learner by demonstrating the complexity of real clinical problem-solving.

Process Notes

There has been considerable debate about the use of process notes in the context of supervision. Process notes have been criticized on the ground that they serve little use other than for the trainee to report therapy "heroics" (Norcross, 1988). Goldberg (1985) asserts that although process notes provide a great deal of information about how a supervisee thinks, they often lack objectivity.

Despite criticisms of the use of process notes, there is a place for this technique, usually as a supplement to other supervisory tools. Process notes can be instrumental in helping a supervisee step back and appraise themes within and across therapy sessions. They can serve as a context for the trainee's self-exploration regarding his or her involvement in the therapy from the viewpoint of analyzing reactions to the patient.

Observation and Taping

Many supervisors value the opportunity to observe directly the clinical work of their supervisees if the training setting has facilities such as one-way observation rooms. Alternatively, the therapy may be observed less directly by means of either videotape or audiotape. Some feel that in order to assess validly the acquisition of clinical skills, trainees must be regularly observed treating real patients (Binder, 1993; Norcross, 1988).

It is interesting to note that observation, even by means of taping, is not without its critics. Tennen (1988) asserts that observation and taping are major intrusions into the therapy that are likely to cause patients to feel like the objects of voyeuristic and exploitative motivations of the therapist; he believes that taping "severely compromises treatment" (p. 170).

Obviously, observation and taping must take place in a context in which the patient is informed about these processes and is given the opportunity to discuss his or her feelings about them. Although there may be some compromises, the overwhelming majority of clinicians and researchers who have published on these techniques characterize them as valuable (e.g., Baum & Gray, 1992; Benschoter, Eaton, & Smith, 1965; Chodoff, 1972; Gruenberg, Liston, & Wayne, 1969; Gutheil, Mikkelsen, Peteet, Shiling, & White, 1981; Hirsh & Freed, 1978). As Baum and Gray (1992) note, the use of a technique such as videotaping not only helps the supervisor to have a better sense of the patient, and therefore be more helpful, but also "fosters a greater sense of alliance between the therapist and the supervisor" (p. 220) in which their work can take on a collegial air.

Team Supervision

The supervisory dyad is the most common structure within which supervision takes place, but it is not the only model for providing supervision. In some contexts, group supervision is provided in lieu of one-to-one supervision. Although group supervision has the advantage of offering the learner opportunities to hear the viewpoints of several other clinicians, this model can be disadvantageous for trainees who feel vulnerable and insecure. Most trainees, especially beginners, benefit from a confidential exploration of personal challenges within the context of a one-to-one relationship. When group supervision is provided, it is best done as an adjunct to individual consultation.

The vertical team (Jarmon & Halgin, 1987) is a variant of group supervision that has been successfully incorporated into psychotherapy training as an adjunct to individual supervision. In this model, a group of five to seven trainees at varying levels of training meet weekly for case conferences that are led by a senior clinician, who also meets weekly in individual supervision with each of the trainees. Beginning clinicians observe the therapy conducted by the advanced trainees for a period of time, usually between 6 and 9 months. Following this observation period, trainees move into the second phase of participation on a vertical team and take on their own patients, usually two or three. In the third phase, customarily during the fourth or fifth year of training, advanced trainees assist the team leader in the supervision of junior-level students; their supervision is overseen by the team leader, and they also meet in a weekly seminar with other supervisors for a didactic/experiential discussion of their supervisory work.

The vertical team structure provides trainees with an important opportunity to share their work with peers, while at the same time taking advantage of the collected wisdom of those who have recently been in their place. Regardless of the stage of development or the level of experience, the opportunity to explore one's thinking with others is invaluable (Lewis, 1991). The vertical team model also affords advanced students a tremendous educational opportunity—to provide supervision at a relatively early point in their careers. It is well known that the responsibility for teaching others contributes to one's own learning. With adequate monitoring, supervisors-in-training are likely to become better therapists as a function of their training of others.

The Role of Personal Therapy

It seems to be a matter of common sense that personal experience with a phenomenon will inform one's understanding of the phenomenon. Thus, it would seem logical that a trainee's experience of having been a psychotherapy patient would enhance understanding of the psychotherapeutic process and provide an opportunity for enhanced empathy with one's patients (Ford, 1963; Storr, 1979; Wampler & Strupp, 1976). An additional presumed benefit of personal therapy is that it provides the trainee with an opportunity to observe the techniques of a senior clinician who can serve as a role model demonstrating the skills, confidence, and competence desired by the trainee (Guy, 1987). It is surprising to find that several who have considered this issue question whether there is demonstrable benefit for the therapist to have been in psychotherapy. Clark (1986) reviewed the empirical literature on the effects of personal therapy on the practice of therapy and found scant evidence for any beneficial impact. Clark did note, however, that researchers had not inquired sufficiently about the circumstances surrounding personal therapy. He suggested that personal therapy is possibly beneficial to the practice of those therapists actually in need of therapy due to psychological distress, but there is insufficient evidence to point to improved psychotherapeutic efficacy for those therapists already functioning at a higher level. In a similar vein, the variability of psychotherapy outcome must be considered. While psychotherapy itself is generally considered effective, not all therapies are effective. Any evaluation of therapists' own psychotherapy should take this variability into account.

Binder (1993) concurs that there is no empirical evidence that personal therapy enhances a therapist's performance and effectiveness. Nevertheless, there remains the general belief, perhaps on intuitive grounds, that the experience of personal therapy is helpful and desirable (Garfield & Kurtz, 1976; Goldberg, 1986; Guy, 1987; Guy & Liaboe, 1986). Norcross and Prochaska (1982) reported that the overwhelming majority of practicing therapists in their research sample who had undergone therapy saw it as a necessary contributor to their competence as psychotherapists.

Although there is no compelling empirical support for the correlation between personal therapy experience and proficiency as a psychotherapist, there remains a consensus that this experience must have some educational value. Beyond the educational benefit there is the therapeutic gain for the therapist. Perhaps the most salient rationale for recommending personal therapy to trainees is their need for personal growth and problem resolution. Repeatedly, investigators have reported that the majority of aspiring clinicians come to this profession with a comparatively greater number of personal problems and disturbed histories (Elliott & Guy, 1993; Guy et al., 1989; Murphy, 1993) than are found in peers entering other professions. It would seem judicious for trainees to work toward resolving some of their own problems before immersing themselves in clinical work, particularly those that might impair their objectivity and efficacy.

EVALUATION

A core variable in the training process is the evaluation of trainees. According to Robiner, Fuhrman, and Ristvedt (1993), supervisory evaluation has two purposes: (1) to provide feedback about skill levels and professional capabilities and (2) to provide objective assessment of competence and progress. To attain the first goal, supervisors "assist trainees in refining clinical skills and in recognizing personal issues that might be detrimental to effective practice" (p. 3). Work toward the second goal involves judging trainees' performance while "providing critical feedback about relative strengths and weaknesses" (p. 3).

The process of evaluation is an emotionally charged facet of the training relationship. Evaluators carry the burden of certifying that their students are competent to function in the profession. Patients approaching professionals for help expect that these individuals are competent to treat them (Pope & Vasquez, 1991; Vasquez, 1992). As Robiner et al., (1993) note, the construct of competence is nebulous for most educators, and it is therefore helpful to rely on operationalized criteria such as those articulated by the Joint Council on Professional Education in Psychology (Stignall et al., 1990) for use in the evaluation of psychology trainees. The criteria cover a broad range of variables, including the trainees's level of interpersonal functioning, professional judgment, assessment abilities, ethical adherence, and awareness of strengths and limitations.

Although the term *incompetent* may not be common in the evaluation of psychotherapy trainees, one does find reference to the concept of trainees being impaired. Lamb, Cochran, and Jackson (1991) assert that impairment is evident in a number of behaviors, such as a trainees's inability or unwillingness to acquire and integrate professional standards and skills into his or her repertoire or an inability to control personal stress that affects professional functioning.

Although the task of evaluation is a central part of the training of psychotherapists, Robiner and his colleagues (1993) note that supervisors are reluctant to give unfavorable ratings to substandard performance for several reasons, including apprehension about giving negative feedback and legal concerns. The personal issues of supervisors might also enter into this matter, as they feel responsibility for the inadequacy of the trainees, assuming that they themselves may have failed in the educational endeavor. They may wish to avoid a conflict with the trainees, and therefore opt for lenient ratings, which have become disturbingly pervasive (Robiner et al., 1993).

Finding an effective way to communicate critical observations about the work of a trainee involves both skill and art. Although centrally important in the process of facilitating growth, evaluations can also produce lasting damage, causing the trainees to become excessively defensive (Ward, Friedlander, Schoen, & Klein,

1985) or permanently insecure and self-critical. Clinical educators must strive to find an optimal balance of communicating criticism in a way that fosters growth rather than reinforces impairment. A multistep process can facilitate this task. First, as noted above, the successful supervisory relationship should be built on a foundation of trust. Second, the approach to corrective feedback should be formulated as a collaborative endeavor involving open, nondefensive discourse. At the point at which formal documentation is required, the supervisor should make a considerable effort to present the big picture, including both the strengths and deficits of the trainee and the course of change during the evaluation period.

TRAINING FOR A CHANGING MARKETPLACE

In addition to traditional issues of concern in psychotherapy training, there are emerging forces that must be considered. Most prominent is the pressure of the marketplace, particularly that associated with the tremendous growth in managed care. For the first time since the completion of their training, many psychotherapists are finding that they must answer to a case manager at an insurance company who wants to know specific details about the assessment, treatment plan, and goals of therapy before approving reimbursement.

Managed health care has been characterized as the most radical change ever in the delivery of mental health services (Zimet, 1991), with all of therapeutic practice being significantly influenced by the emphasis of managed care on short-term treatments for specific disorders, limited goals, and cost containment (Strupp, 1992). The managed care system emerged in response to what the insurance industry regarded as a financial catastrophe in the making as mental health care costs during the 1980s grew tremendously (Austad & Hoyt, 1992; Borenstein, 1990; Callan & Yeager, 1991; Hoyt & Austad, 1992; Zimet, 1989).

The tremendous impact of the managed health care movement has great bearing on how psychotherapy is taught. Whether it is because of changes in the marketplace or changes in the understanding of what constitutes effective psychotherapy, trends are becoming clearer about the future direction of the field. Norcross, Alford, and DeMichele (1992) asked 75 experts to predict changes in clinical interventions, modalities, and interventions and concluded that "psychotherapy will become more directive, psychoeducational, present-centered, problem-focused, and briefer in the next decade" (p. 155).

TRAINING FOR A CHANGING SOCIETY

As we approach the twenty-first century, the field will face new challenges as clinicians are called on to provide more services to previously underserved groups and to move away from the biases that have traditionally impeded clinical work. Increasing attention will be given to the therapeutic needs of an aging population and to the growing numbers of people who have been outside the focus of most clinicians, namely, the nonwhite and non-middle-class segments of society. Also, an improved understanding of gender issues will enlighten clinical work with both men and women. As the face of clinical work changes, so must the training of psychotherapists.

Clinicians will be increasingly called on to respond to the needs of aging individuals. In the last few decades, there has been a dramatic rise in the percentage of the U.S. population who are over 65—from 8 percent in 1950 to 12 percent in 1987 (U.S. Bureau of the Census, 1975; U.S. Department of Commerce, 1989). By the time current young adults are in their 60s, they will make up nearly one-quarter of the entire U.S. population. Despite the growing number of older adults in our population, psychotherapeutic services for them remain minimal. In fact, most psychotherapists avoid becoming involved in the provision of clinical services to older people, and psychologists in particular have lagged behind the other disciplines in recognizing aging as a specialty area

(Teri & Logsdon, 1992). In recent years there has been a detectable, but less than dramatic, increase in attention to these issues. For example, some texts have been published on the topic of providing psychotherapeutic services to older adults (e.g., Knight, 1986), and educators have been urged to include the topic of aging in curricula in the social and behavioral sciences (Parham, Poon, & Siegler, 1990). Nevertheless, formal training remains woefully lacking (Teri & Logsdon, 1992), and it is time for those who are training psychotherapists to attend to this educational deficit.

The minority population in the United States has grown dramatically during the latter part of the twentieth century as well, and their clinical needs are being increasingly recognized. Dramatic affirmative action efforts have brought greater numbers of people from minority groups into the mental health field (Comas-Diaz, 1992; Pion, Kohout, & Wicherski, 1989). Numerous publications on cross-cultural counseling and psychotherapy have appeared, but very little formal training in these areas has been included in the education of psychotherapists (Williams & Halgin, in press). Any psychotherapy training program that fails to attend to the special issues involved in treating members of minority groups is inadequately preparing aspiring therapists for work with countless patients who are not from white, middle-class America.

In a similar vein, training programs should be making a concerted effort to incorporate feminist perspectives in the educational sequence of psychotherapists. Feminist therapy is a philosophy of psychotherapy rather than a prescription of technique, a hybrid that grew from the interface between treatment of gender-role-related disorders and the application of a process of feminist analysis (Brodsky, 1980; Brown & Brodsky, 1992). Advances have been made in the establishment of a literature on feminist therapy that has contributed in major ways to the understanding of topics previously ignored, such as imbalances in power related to gender, sexual harassment and exploitation, domestic violence, and dual-career couple relationships. Unfortunately, the training of clinicians in how to understand and treat these phenomena has lagged behind. Although specialized centers have made an indelible mark (e.g., the Stone Center at Wellesley College and the Women's Therapy Centre Institute in New York), general psychotherapy training programs have given insufficient attention to these matters.

CONCLUDING COMMENTS

The field of psychotherapy has grown and changed in impressive ways during the past century. New markets have emerged, and innovative techniques have been developed. Standards of practice have been refined, and increased attention has been given to people previously regarded as being outside the mainstream. In a field with rapid changes, educators have struggled to keep up-to-date with what is happening in the real world.

Psychotherapy is a process that we still barely understand. We continue to debate what makes it work and why people pay money to a stranger in order to get help with life problems. With such distressing naiveté about the phenomenon, we are often at a loss in our struggle to determine the most effective way to educate those who will become our peers and our successors. In this chapter, we have tried to point out some of the complex issues involved in this challenging endeavor. We realize that many of our questions remain unanswered, but we have attempted to raise for discussion some of the matters that warrant critical attention in the very near future.

REFERENCES

Abt, L. E. (1992). Clinical psychology and the emergence of psychotherapy. *Professional Psychology: Research and Practice, 23,* 176–178.

Alberts, G., & Edelstein, B. (1990). Therapist training: A critical review of skill training studies. *Clinical Psychology Review, 10,* 497–511.

Allen, G. J., Szollos, S. J., & Williams, B. E. (1986). Doctoral students' comparative evaluations of best and worst psychotherapy supervision.

Professional Psychology: Research and Practice, 17, 91–99.

Allport, F. H., & Prince, M. (1921–1922). Editorial announcement. *Journal of Abnormal Psychology and Social Psychology, 16,* 1–15.

Alonso, A. (1985). *The quiet profession.* New York: Macmillan.

American Psychological Association. (1987). *General guidelines for providers of psychological services.* Washington, DC: Author.

Andrews, G., & Harvey, R. (1981). Does psychotherapy benefit neurotic patients? A reanalysis of the Smith, Glass, & Miller data. *Archives of General Psychiatry, 38,* 1203–1208.

Andrews, J. D. W., Norcross, J. C., & Halgin, R. P. (1992). Training in psychotherapy integration. In J. C. Norcross & M. R. Goldfried (Eds.), *Handbooks of psychotherapy integration* (pp. 563–592). New York: Basic Books.

Austad, C. S., & Hoyt, M. F. (1992). The managed care movement and the future of psychotherapy. *Psychotherapy, 29,* 109–118.

Baker, S., Johnson, E., Kopala, M., & Stout, N. (1985). Test interpretation competence: A comparison of microskills and mental practice training. *Counselor Education and Supervision, 25,* 31–43.

Baum, B. E., & Gray, J. J. (1992). Expert modeling, self-observation using videotape, and acquisition of basic therapy skills. *Professional Psychology: Research and Practice, 23,* 220–225.

Beck, A. T., Rush, A. J., Shaw, B. F., & Emery, G. (1979). *Cognitive therapy for depression.* New York: Guilford Press.

Benschoter, R. A., Eaton, M. T., & Smith, P. (1965). Use of videotape to provide individual instruction in techniques of psychotherapy. *Journal of Medical Education, 40,* 1159–1161.

Bergin, A. E. (1971). The evaluation of therapeutic outcomes. In A. E. Bergin & S. L. Garfield (Eds.), *Handbook of psychotherapy and behavior change* (pp. 217–270). New York: Wiley.

Beutler, L. E. (1989). Differential treatment selection: The role of diagnosis in psychotherapy. *Psychotherapy, 26,* 271–281.

Beutler, L. E., & Clarkin, J. F. (1990). *Systematic treatment selection: Toward targeted therapeutic interventions.* New York: Brunner/Mazel.

Beutler, L. E., & Consoli, A. J. (1992). Systematic eclectic psychotherapy. In J. C. Norcross & M. R. Goldfried (Eds.), *Handbook of psychotherapy integration* (pp. 264–299). New York: Basic Books.

Binder, J. L. (1993). Is it time to improve psychotherapy training? *Clinical Psychology Review, 13*, 301–318.

Bootzin, R. R., & Ruggill, J. S. (1988). Training issues in behavior therapy. *Journal of Consulting and Clinical Psychology, 56*, 703–709.

Bordin, E. S. (1979). The generalizability of the psychoanalytic concept of the working alliance. *Psychotherapy: Theory, Research, and Practice, 16*, 256–260.

Borenstein, D. B. (1990). Managed care: A mean of rationing psychiatric treatment. *Hospital and Community Psychiatry, 41*, 1095–1098.

Bowers, T. G., & Clum, G. A. (1988). Relative contributions of specific and nonspecific treatment effects: Meta-analysis of placebo-controlled behavior therapy research. *Psychological Bulletin, 103*, 315–323.

Brand, J. L. (1965). The National Mental Health Act of 1946: A retrospect. *Bulletin of the History of Medicine, 39*, 231–235.

Brodsky, A. M. (1980). A decade of feminist influence on psychotherapy. *Psychology of Women Quarterly, 4*, 331–344.

Brown, L. S., & Brodsky, A. M. (1992). The future of feminist therapy. *Psychotherapy, 29*, 51–57.

Buckley, P., Conte, H. R., Plutchik, R., Karasu, T. B., & Wild, K. V. (1982). Learning dynamic psychotherapy: A longitudinal study. *American Journal of Psychiatry, 139*, 1607–1610.

Bugental, J. F. T. (1964). The person who is the psychotherapist. *Journal of Consulting Psychology, 28*, 272–277.

Caligor, L., Bromberg, P. M., & Meltzer, J. D. (1984). *Clinical perspectives on the supervision of psychoanalysis and psychotherapy*. New York: Plenum Press.

Callan, M. F., & Yeager, D. C. (1991). *Containing the health care cost spiral*. New York: McGraw-Hill.

Carifio, M. S., & Hess, A. K. (1987). Who is the ideal supervisor? *Professional Psychology: Research and Practice, 18*, 244–250.

Chodoff, P. (1972). Supervision of psychotherapy with videotape: Pros and cons. *American Journal of Psychiatry, 128*, 819–823.

Claiborn, C., & Dixon, D. The acquisition of conceptual skills: An exploratory study. *Counselor Education and Supervision, 21*, 274–281.

Clark, K. E. (1957). *America's psychologists: A survey of a growing profession*. Washington, DC: American Psychological Association.

Clark, M. M. (1986). Personal therapy: A review of empirical research. *Professional Psychology: Research and Practice, 17*, 541–543.

Cohen, L. (1980). The new supervisee views supervision. In A. K. Hess (Ed.), *Psychotherapy supervision: Theory, research and practice*, (pp. 78–84). New York: Wiley.

Colenda, C. C. (1985). A survey of 10 psychiatry residence training programs on procedures for evaluating residents. *Journal of Medical Education, 60*, 886–888.

Comas-Diaz, L. (1992). The future of psychotherapy with ethnic minorities. *Psychotherapy, 29*, 88–94.

Crick, P. (1991). Good supervision: On the experience of being supervised. *Psychoanalytic Psychotherapy, 5*, 235–245.

Dellis, N. D., & Stone, H. K. (1960). *The training of psychotherapists*. Baton Rouge: Louisiana State University Press.

Deutsch, C. J. (1985). A survey of therapists' personal problems and treatment. *Professional Psychology: Research and Practice, 16*, 305–315.

Dewald, P. A. (1987). *Learning process in psychoanalytic supervision: Complexities and challenges*. New York: International Universities Press.

Dryden, W. (1984). *Individual therapy in Britain*. London: Harper & Row.

Eckstein, R., & Wallerstein, R. S. (1972). *The teaching and learning of psychotherapy*. New York: International Universities Press.

Elliott, D. M., & Guy, J. D. (1993). Mental health professionals versus non-mental-health professionals: Childhood trauma and adult functioning. *Professional Psychology: Research and Practice, 24*, 83–90.

Errek, H., & Randolph, D. (1982). Effects of discussion and role-play activities in the acquisition of consultant interview skills. *Journal of Counseling Psychology, 29*, 304–308.

Eysenck, H. J. (1952). The effects of psychotherapy: An evaluation. *Journal of Consulting Psychology, 16*, 319–324.

Eysenck, H. J. (1970). A mish-mash of theories. *International Journal of Psychiatry, 9*, 140–146.

Farber, B. A. (1985). The genesis, development, and implications of psychological-mindedness in psychotherapists. *Psychotherapy, 22*, 170–177.

Farber, B. A., & Heifitz, L. J. (1981). The satisfactions and stresses of psychotherapeutic work: A factor analytic study. *Professional Psychology, 12*, 621–630.

Ford, E. S. C. (1963). Being and becoming a psychotherapist: The search for identity. *American Journal of Psychotherapy, 17*, 472–482.

Ford, J. D. (1979). Research in training counselors

and clinicians. *Review of Educational Research,* 49, 87–130.

Forsyth, D. R., & Ivey, A. E. (1980). Microtraining: An approach to differential supervision. In A. K. Hess (Ed.), *Psychotherapy supervision: Theory, research and practice* (pp. 242–261). New York: Wiley.

Frank, J. D. (1982). Therapeutic components shared by all psychotherapies. In J. H. Harvey & M. M. Parks (Eds.), *The Master Lecture Series: Vol. 1. Psychotherapy research and behavior change* (pp. 5–37). Washington, DC: American Psychological Association.

Frank, J. D., & Frank, J. B. (1991). *Persuasion and healing* (3rd ed.). Baltimore: Johns Hopkins University Press.

Franks, C. M. (1984). On conceptual and technical integrity in psychoanalysis and behavior therapy: Two fundamentally incompatible systems. In H. Arkowitz & S. B. Messer (Eds.), *Psychoanalytic therapy and behavior therapy: Is integration possible?* (pp. 223–248). New York: Plenum Press.

Froehle, T. C., Robinson, S. E., & Kurpius, D. J. (1983). Enhancing the effects of modeling through role-play practice. *Counselor Education and Supervision, 22,* 197–206.

Fussell, F. W., & Bonney, W. C. (1990). A comparative study of childhood experiences of psychotherapists and physicists: Implications for clinical practice. *Psychotherapy, 27,* 505–512.

Gandolfo, R. L., & Brown, R. (1987). Psychology interns' ratings of actual and ideal supervision of psychotherapy. *Journal of Training and Practice in Professional Psychology, 1,* 15–28.

Gaoni, B., & Neumann, M. (1974). Supervision from the point of view of the supervisee. *American Journal of Psychotherapy, 23,* 108–114.

Garfield, S. L. (1977). Research on the training of professional psychologists. In A. S. Gurman & A. Razin (Eds.), *The therapist's contribution to effective psychotherapy: Empirical assessment* (pp. 63–83). New York: Pergamon Press.

Garfield, S. L., & Kurtz, R. (1976). Personal therapy for the psychotherapist: Some findings and issues. *Psychotherapy: Theory, Research, and Practice, 13,* 188–192.

Goldberg, C. (1986). *On being a psychotherapist.* New York: Gardner Press.

Goldberg, D. (1985). Process notes, audio, and video tape: Modes of presentation in psychotherapy training. *The Clinical Supervisor, 3,* 3–13.

Goldberg, D. A. (1983). Resistance to the use of video in individual psychotherapy training. *American Journal of Psychiatry, 140,* 1172–1176.

Goldfried, M. R., & Padawer, W. (1982). Current status and future directions in psychotherapy. In M. R. Goldfried (Ed.), *Converging themes in psychotherapy: Trends in psychodynamic, humanistic, and behavioral practice,* (pp. 3–49). New York: Springer.

Greenberg, L. (1980). Supervision from the perspective of the supervisee. In A. K. Hess (Ed.), *Psychotherapy supervision: Theory, research and practice,* New York: Wiley.

Greenberg, L. S., & Goldman, R. C. (1988). Training in experiential therapy. *Journal of Consulting and Clinical Psychology, 56,* 696–702.

Grencavage, L. M., & Norcross, J. C. (1990). Where are the commonalities among the therapeutic common factors? *Professional Psychology: Research and Practice, 21,* 372–378.

Gruenberg, P. B., Liston, E. H., Jr., & Wayne, G. J. (1969). Intensive supervision of psychotherapy with videotape recording. *Professional Psychology: Research and Practice, 16,* 605–610.

Gutheil, T. G., Mikkelsen, E. J., Peteet, J., Shiling, D., & White, H. (1981). Patient viewing of videotaped psychotherapy. Part II: Aspects of the supervisory process. *Psychiatric Quarterly, 53,* 227–234.

Guy, J. D. (1987). *The personal life of the psychotherapist.* New York: Wiley.

Guy, J. D., & Liaboe, G. P. (1986). The impact of conducting psychotherapy on psychotherapists' interpersonal functioning. *Professional Psychology: Research and Practice, 17,* 111–114.

Guy, J. D., Poelstra, P. L., & Stark, M. J. (1989). Personal distress and therapeutic effectiveness: National survey of psychologists practicing psychotherapy. *Professional Psychology: Research and Practice, 20,* 48–50.

Guy, J. D., Tamura, L. J., & Poelstra, P. L. (1989). All in the family: Multiple therapists per household. *Psychotherapy in Private Practice, 7,* 115–135.

Hartley, D. E., & Strupp, H. H. (1983). The therapeutic alliance: Its relationship to outcome in brief psychotherapy. In J. Masling (Ed.), *Empirical studies in analytic theories* (pp. 1–37). Hillsdale, NJ: Erlbaum.

Hazler, R. J., & Hipple, T. E. (1981). The effects of mental practice on counseling behavior. *Counselor Education and Supervision, 20,* 211–218.

Heilveil, I. (1983). *Video in mental health practice.* New York: Springer.

Henry, W. P., Schact, T. E., Strupp, H. H., Butler, S. F., & Binder, J. L. (1993). Effects of training in time-limited dynamic psychotherapy: Mediators or therapists' responses to training. *Journal of Consulting and Clinical Psychology, 61,* 441–447.

Henry, W. P., Strupp, H. H., Butler, S. F., Schact, T. E., & Binder, J. L. (1993). Effects of training in time-limited dynamic psychotherapy: Changes in therapist behavior. *Journal of Consulting and Clinical Psychology, 61,* 434–440.

Heppner, P. P., & Claiborn, C. D. (1989). Social influence research in counseling: A review and critique. *Journal of Counseling Psychology, 36,* 365–387.

Hess, A. K. (1980). Training models and the nature of psychotherapy supervision. In A. K. Hess (Ed.), *Psychotherapy supervision: Theory, research and practice* (pp. 15–25). New York: Wiley.

Hess, A. K. (1987). Psychotherapy supervision: Stages, Buber, and a theory of relationship. *Professional Psychology: Research and Practice, 18,* 251–259.

Hilgard, E. R. (1987). *Psychology in America: A historical survey.* New York: Harcourt Brace Jovanovich.

Hill, M. G., & Weary, G. (1983). Perspectives on the *Journal of Abnormal and Social Psychology:* How it began and how it was transformed. *Journal of Social and Clinical Psychology, 1,* 4–14.

Hirsh, H., & Freed, H. (1978). Pattern sensitization in psychotherapy supervision by means of videotape recording. In M. M. Berger (Ed.), *Videotape techniques in psychiatric training and treatment* (rev. ed., pp. 117–120). New York: Brunner/Mazel.

Hogan, R. A. (1964). Issues and approaches in supervision. *Psychotherapy: Theory, Research, and Practice, 1,* 139–141.

Horvath, A. O., & Symonds, B. D. (1991). Relation between working alliance and outcome in psychotherapy: A meta-analysis. *Journal of Counseling Psychology, 38,* 139–149.

Hoyt, M. F., & Austad, C. S. (1992). Psychotherapy in a staff model health maintenance organization: Providing and assuring quality care in the future. *Psychotherapy, 29,* 119–129.

Ivey, A. E. (1980). *Counseling and psychotherapy: Skills, theories and practice.* Englewood Cliffs, NJ: Prentice-Hall.

Ivey, A. E. (1983). *Intentional interviewing and counseling.* Monterey, CA: Brooks/Cole.

Ivey, A. E., & Authier, J. (1978). *Microcounseling: Innovations in interviewing, counseling, psychotherapy and psychoeducation* (2nd ed.). Springfield, IL: Charles C Thomas.

Jarmon, H., & Halgin, R. P. (1987). The role of psychology department clinic in training scientist-professionals. *Professional Psychology: Research and Practice, 18,* 509–514.

Jensen, J. P., Bergin, A. E., & Greaves, D. W. (1990). The meaning of eclecticism: New survey and analysis of components. *Professional Psychology: Research and Practice, 21,* 124–130.

Karasu, T. B. (1986). The specificity versus nonspecificity dilemma: Toward identifying therapeutic change agents. *American Journal of Psychiatry, 143,* 687–695.

Kasdorf, J., & Gustafson, K. (1979). Research related to microcounseling. In A. E. Ivey & J. Authier (Eds.), *Microcounseling: Innovations in interviewing, counselling, psychotherapy, and psychoeducation* (2nd ed.). Springfield, IL: Charles C Thomas.

Kazdin, A. E., & Bass, D. (1989). Power to detect differences between alternative treatments in comparative psychotherapy outcome research. *Journal of Consulting and Clinical Psychology, 57,* 138–147.

Kennard, B. D., Stewart, S. M., & Gluck, M. R. (1987). The supervisory relationship: Variables contributing to positive versus negative experiences. *Professional Psychology: Research and Practice, 18,* 172–175.

Knight, B. (1986). *Psychotherapy with older adults.* Beverly Hills, CA: Sage.

Korman, M. (1976). *Levels and patterns of professional training in psychology: Conference Proceedings, Vail, Colorado, July 25–30, 1973.* Washington, DC: American Psychological Association.

Kurpius, D., Benjamin, D., & Moran, D. (1985). Effects of teaching a cognitive strategy on counselor trainee internal dialogue and clinical hypothesis formulation. *Journal of Counseling Psychology, 32,* 263–271.

Lamb, D. H., Cochran, D. J., & Jackson, V. R. (1991). Training and organizational issues associated with identifying and responding to intern impairment. *Professional Psychology: Research and Practice, 22,* 291–296.

Lambert, M. J. (1986). Implications of psychotherapy outcome research for eclectic psychotherapy. In J. C. Norcross (Ed.), *Handbook of eclectic psychotherapy* (pp. 436–462). New York: Brunner/Mazel.

Lambert, M. J., & Arnold, R. C. (1987). Research and the supervisory process. *Professional Psychology: Research and Practice, 18,* 217–224.

Landman, J. T., & Dawes, R. M. (1982). Psychotherapy outcome: Smith and Glass conclusions stand up under scrutiny. *American Psychologist, 37*, 504–516.

Lazarus, A. A. (1967). In support of technical eclecticism. *Psychological Reports, 21*, 415–416.

Lazarus, A. A. (1988). Eclectism in behavior therapy. In P. M. G. Emmelkamp, W. T. A. M. Everaerd, F. Kraaimaat, & M. J. M. van Son (Eds.), *Advances in theory and practice in behavior therapy*. Amsterdam: Swets & Zeitlinger.

Lazarus, A. A., Beutler, L. E., & Norcross, J. C. (1992). The future of technical eclecticism. *Psychotherapy, 29*, 11–20.

Levy, L. H. (1962). The skew in clinical psychology. *American Psychologist, 17*, 244–249.

Lewis, J. (1991). *Swimming upstream: Teaching and learning psychotherapy in a biological era*. New York: Brunner/Mazel.

Liaboe, G. P., & Guy, J. D. (1987). Assessing the current stereotypes of the psychologists' family of origin. *Psychotherapy in Private Practice, 5*, 103–113.

Loganbill, C., Hardy, E., & Delworth, U. (1982). Supervision: A conceptual model. *The Counseling Psychologist, 10*, 3–42.

Luborsky, L. (1984). *Principles of psychoanalytic psychotherapy*. New York: Basic Books.

Luborsky, L., Crits-Cristoph, P., Mintz, J., & Auerbach, A. (1988). *Who will benefit from psychotherapy? Predicting therapeutic outcomes*. New York: Basic Books.

Luborsky, L., Singer, B., & Luborsky, L. (1975). Comparative studies of psychotherapy. *Archives of General Psychiatry, 32*, 995–1008.

Mahalik, J. R. (1990). Systematic eclectic models. *The Counseling Psychologist, 18*, 655–679.

Marmor, J. (1953). The feeling of superiority: An occupational hazard in the practice of psychotherapy. *American Journal of Psychiatry, 110*, 370–376.

Marston, A. R. (1984). What makes therapists run? A model for analysis of motivational styles. *Psychotherapy, 21*, 456–459.

Martin, J. S., Goodyear, R. K., & Newton, F. B. (1987). Clinical supervision: An intensive case study. *Professional Psychology: Research and Practice, 18*, 225–235.

Marziali, E., Marmer, C., & Krupnick, J. (1981). Therapeutic alliance scales: Development and relationship to psychotherapeutic outcome. *American Journal of Psychiatry, 138*, 361–364.

Matarazzo, R. G., & Garner, A. M. (1992). Research on training for psychotherapy. In D. K.

Freedheim (Ed.), *History of Psychotherapy: A century of change* (pp. 850–877). Washington, DC: American Psychological Association.

Matarazzo, R. G., & Patterson, D. R. (1986). Methods of teaching therapeutic skill. In S. L. Garfield & A. E. Bergin (Eds.), *Handbook of psychotherapy and behavior change* (3rd ed., pp. 821–843). New York: Wiley.

Matt, G. E. (1989). Decision rules for selecting effect sizes in meta-analysis: A review and reanalysis of psychotherapy outcome studies. *Psychological Bulletin, 105*, 106–115.

Messer, S. B. (1992). A critical examination of belief structures in integrative and eclectic psychotherapy. In J. C. Norcross & M. R. Goldfried (Eds.), *Handbook of psychotherapy integration* (pp. 130–165). New York: Basic Books.

Morgan, R., Luborsky, L., Crits-Cristoph, P., Curtis, H., & Solomon, J. (1982). Predicting the outcomes of psychotherapy by the Penn Helping Alliance Rating Method. *Archives of General Psychiatry, 39*, 397–402.

Mueller, W. J., & Kell, B. L. (1972). *Coping with conflict: Supervising counselors and psychotherapists*. New York: Appleton-Century-Crofts.

Murphy, R. A. (1993). *Influences on the career choice of psychotherapists*. Submitted for publication.

Norcross, J. C. (Ed.), (1986). *Handbook of eclectic psychotherapy*. New York: Brunner/Mazel.

Norcross, J. C. (1988). Supervision of integrative psychotherapy. In R. P. Halgin (Section Editor), *Issues in the supervision of integrative psychotherapy. Journal of Integrative and Eclectic Psychotherapy, 7*, 157–166.

Norcross, J. C. (1991). Prescriptive matching in psychotherapy: An introduction. *Psychotherapy, 28*, 439–443.

Norcross, J. C., Alford, B. A., & DeMichele, J. T. (1992). The future of psychotherapy: Delphi data and concluding observations. *Psychotherapy, 29*, 150–158.

Norcross, J. C., & Guy, J. D. (1989). Ten therapists: The process of becoming and being. In W. Dryden & L. Spurling (Eds.), *On becoming a psychotherapist* (pp. 215–239). London: Tavistock/Routledge.

Norcross, J. C., & Newman, C. F. (1992). Psychotherapy integration: Setting the context. In J. C. Norcross & M. R. Goldfried (Eds.), *Handbook of psychotherapy integration* (pp. 3–45). New York: Basic Books.

Norcross, J. C., & Prochaska, J. O. (1982). A

national survey of clinical psychologists: Affiliations and orientations. *The Clinical Psychologist*, 35, 1–2, 4–6.

Norcross, J. C., Prochaska, J. O., & Gallagher, K. M. (1989). Clinical psychologists in the 1980's: II. Theory, research, and practice. *The Clinical Psychologist*, 42, 45–53.

O'Toole, W. (1979). Effects of practice and some methodological considerations in training counseling interviewing skills. *Journal of Counseling Psychology*, 26, 412–426.

Orlinksy, D. E., & Howard, K. I. (1986). Process and outcome in psychotherapy. In S. L. Garfield & A. E. Bergin (Eds.), *Handbook of psychotherapy and behavior change* (pp. 311–381). New York: Wiley.

Parham, I., Poon, L., & Siegler, I. (Eds.). (1990). *Aging curriculum content for education in social-behavioral sciences.* New York: Springer.

Pasework, R., Fitzgerald, B., Thornton, L., & Sawyer, R. (1973). Icons in the attic: Research activities of clinical psychologists. *Professional Psychology*, 4, 244–249.

Patterson, C. H. (1989). Foundations for a systematic eclecticism in psychotherapy. *Psychotherapy*, 26, 427–435.

Peterfreund, E. (1975). How does the analyst listen? In D. P. Spence (Ed.), *Psychoanalysis and contemporary science. An annual of integrative and interdisciplinary studies* (Vol. IV, pp. 59–102). New York: International Universities Press.

Pion, G. M., Kohout, J., & Wicherski, M. (1989). *Characteristics of graduate departments of psychology.* Washington, DC: American Psychological Association.

Pope, K. S., & Vasquez, M. J. T. (1991). *Ethics in psychotherapy and counseling: A practical guide for psychologists.* San Francisco: Jossey-Bass.

Prioleau, L., Murdock, M., & Brody, N. (1983). An analysis of psychotherapy versus placebo studies. *The Behavioral and Brain Sciences*, 6, 275–310.

Racusin, G. R., Abramowitz, S. I., & Winter, W. D. (1981). Becoming a therapist: Family dynamics and career choice. *Professional Psychology*, 12, 271–279.

Raimy, V. (Ed.). (1950). *Training in clinical psychology* (by the staff of the Conference on Graduate Education in Clinical Psychology, Boulder, Colorado). New York: Prentice-Hall.

Raskin, N. J. (1978). Becoming—A therapist, a person, a partner, a parent. *Psychotherapy: Theory, Research, and Practice*, 15, 362–370.

Robiner, W., Fuhrman, M., & Ristvedt, S. (1993). Evaluation difficulties in supervising psychology interns. *The Clinical Psychologist*, 46, 3–13.

Robinson, S., & Cabianca, W. (1985). Effects of counselor's ordinal position when involved in role play practice in triads. *Counselor Education and Supervision*, 22, 365–371.

Rosenblatt, A., & Mayer, J. (1975). Objectionable supervisory styles: Students' views. *Social Work*, 18, 184–189.

Rosin, S. A., & Knudson, R. M. (1986). Perceived influence of life experiences on clinical psychologists' selection and development of theoretical orientation. *Psychotherapy*, 23, 357–362.

Rounsaville, B. J., O'Malley, S., Foley, S., & Weissman, M. (1988). Role of manual-guided training in the conduct and efficacy of interpersonal psychotherapy for depression. *Journal of Consulting and Clinical Psychology*, 56, 681–688.

Schiffman, S. (1987). Clinical psychology training and psychotherapy interview performance. *Psychotherapy*, 24, 71–84.

Scott, C., & Haw, J. (Eds.). (1986). *Heal thyself: The health of health care professionals.* New York: Brunner/Mazel.

Searles, J. S. (1985). A methodological and empirical critique of psychotherapy outcome meta-analysis. *Behaviour Research and Therapy*, 23, 453–463.

Sechrest, L. (1975). Research contributions of practicing clinical psychologists. *Professional Psychology*, 6, 413–419.

Segal, J. (Ed.). (1975). *Research in the service of mental health: Report of the Research Task Force of the National Institute of Mental Health* (DHEW Publication No. ADM 75-236). Washington, DC: U.S. Government Printing Office.

Shapiro, D. A., & Shapiro, D. (1982). Meta-analysis of comparative therapy outcome studies: A replication and refinement. *Psychological Bulletin*, 92, 581–604.

Sifneos, P. E. (1984). The current status of individual short-term dynamic psychotherapy and its future: An overview. *American Journal of Psychotherapy*, 38, 472–483.

Smith, M. L., & Glass, G. V. (1977). Meta-analysis of psychotherapy outcome studies. *American Psychologist*, 32, 752–760.

Smith, M. L., Glass, G. V., & Miller, T. I. (1980). *The benefits of psychotherapy.* Baltimore: Johns Hopkins University Press.

Stigall, T. T., Bourg, E. F., Bricklin, P. M., Kovacs, A. L., Larsen, K. G., Lorion, R. P., Nelson, P. D., Nurse, A. R., Pugh, R. W., & Wiens, A. N. (Eds.). (1990). *Report of the Joint Council on Professional Education in Psychology*. Baton Rouge, LA: Joint Council on Professional Education in Psychology.

Stoltenberg, C. D. (1981). Approaching supervision from a developmental perspective: The counselor complexity model. *Journal of Counseling Psychology, 28*, 59–65.

Stoltenberg, C. D., & Delworth, U. (1988). *Supervising counselors and therapists: A developmental approach*. San Francisco: Jossey-Bass.

Storr, A. (1979). *The art of psychotherapy*. New York: Methuen.

Stricker, G. (1988). Supervision of integrative psychotherapy: Discussion. In R. P. Halgin (Section Ed.), *Issues in the supervision of integrative psychotherapy. Journal of Integrative and Eclectic Psychotherapy, 7*, 176–180.

Strong, S. R. (1968). Counseling: An interpersonal influence process. *Journal of Counseling Psychology, 15*, 215–224.

Strupp, H. H. (1992). The future of psychodynamic psychotherapy. *Psychotherapy, 29*, 21–27.

Strupp, H. H., & Binder, J. L. (1984). *Psychotherapy in a new key: A guide to time-limited dynamic psychotherapy*. New York: Basic Books.

Strupp, H. H., Butler, S. F., & Rosser, C. L. (1988). Training in psychodynamic therapy. *Journal of Consulting and Clinical Psychology, 56*, 689–695.

Sussman, M. B. (1992). *A curious calling: Unconscious motivations for practicing psychotherapy*. Northvale, NJ: Jason Aronson.

Tennen, H. (1988). Supervision of integrative psychotherapy: A critique. In R. P. Halgin (Section Editor), *Issues in the supervision of integrative psychotherapy. Journal of Integrative and Eclectic Psychotherapy, 7*, 167–175.

Teri, L., & Logsdon, R. G. (1992). The future of psychotherapy with older adults. *Psychotherapy, 29*, 81–87.

Teyber, E. (1992). *Interpersonal process in psychotherapy: A guide for clinical training* (2nd ed.). Pacific Grove, CA: Brooks/Cole.

Truax, C. B., & Carkhuff, R. (1967). *Toward effective counseling and psychotherapy: Training and practice*. Chicago: Aldine.

U.S. Bureau of the Census. (1975). *Historical statistics of the United States: Colonial times in 1970 (Part I. Bicentennial ed.)*. Washington, DC: U.S. Government Printing Office.

U.S. Department of Commerce. (1989). *Statistical abstracts of the United States* (109th ed.). Washington, DC: U.S. Government Printing Office.

Vasquez, M. J. T. (1992). Psychologist as clinical supervisor: Promoting ethical practice. *Professional Psychology: Research and Practice, 23*, 197–202.

Wachtel, P. L. (1991). From eclecticism to synthesis: Toward a more seamless psychotherapeutic integration. *Journal of Psychotherapy Integration, 1*, 43–54.

Wampler, L. D., & Strupp, H. H. (1976). Personal therapy for students in clinical psychology: A matter of faith? *Professional Psychology, 7*, 195–201.

Ward, L. G., Friedlander, M. L., Schoen, L., & Klein, J. G. (1985). Strategic self-presentation in supervision. *Journal of Counseling Psychology, 32*, 111–118.

Whiston, S. C., & Sexton, T. L. (1993). An overview of psychotherapy outcome research: Implications for practice. *Professional Psychology: Research and Practice, 24*, 43–51.

Wierzbicki, M. (1993). *Issues in clinical psychology: Subjective versus objective approaches*. Boston: Allyn & Bacon.

Williams, S., & Halgin, R. P. (in press). Issues in psychotherapy supervision between the white supervisor and the black supervisee. *The Clinical Supervisor*.

Worthington, E. L. (1987). *Changes in supervision as counselors and supervisors gain experience: A review. Professional Psychology: Research and Practice, 18*, 189–208.

Wright, J., Horlick, S., Bouchard, C., Mathieu, M., & Zeichner, A. (1977). The development of instruments to assess behavior therapy training. *Journal of Behavior Therapy and Experimental Psychiatry, 8*, 281–286.

Yogev, S. (1982). An eclectic model of supervision: A developmental sequence for the beginning psychotherapy student. *Professional Psychology, 13*, 236–243.

Zimet, C. N. (1989). The mental health care revolution: Will psychology survive? *American Psychologist, 44*, 703–708.

Zimet, C. N. (1991). Managed care is here and is not going away. *The Psychotherapy Bulletin, 25*, 21–22.

23
Ethics in Psychotherapy

Gerald P. Koocher

FIRST, DO NO HARM

Ask psychotherapists about the ethics of their work and they wax philosophical, most likely as an intellectual defense against anxiety. Writing on the ethics of their craft, psychotherapists have variously described their craft as a science (Karasu, 1980), an art (Hale, 1976), the purchase of friendship (Schofield, 1976), a means of social control (Hurvitz, 1973), a source of honest and nonjudgmental feedback (Kaschak, 1978), and even as a means of exploring one's "ultimate values" (Kanoti, 1971). Questions about the worth of psychotherapy, its value as art or science, or the need to use trained experts to provide it have spanned decades of debate in the scientific literature (Eysenck, 1952; Garfield, 1981; Hogan, 1979; Marshall, 1980). Garfield (1981) noted, in reviewing 40 years of development, that the field has seen no significant breakthroughs, in spite of a large number of diverse therapies. The secretary for the proceedings of the Boulder Conference on the training of psychologists satirically noted: "We have left therapy as an undefined technique which is applied to unspecified problems with a nonpredictable outcome. For this technique we recommend rigorous training" (Lehner, 1952, p. 547). Still, many clients seek and apparently benefit from psychotherapy, while many professionals offer such services

and train others to do so as well. The cardinal underlying ethical principle is that of beneficence, as articulated in ancient times by Hippocrates in the dictum to "First, do no harm," and as paraphrased more recently: "Helping without hurting" (Pope & Vasquez, 1991).

PLACEBO EFFECT OR CURE?

The effectiveness of psychotherapy per se has long been a topic of spirited discussion. The matter of whether a placebo effect exists in psychotherapy is not at all in question. Although not well studied as an isolated phenomenon in recent years, there is good evidence that seemingly inert "agents" or "treatments" may be demonstrated to have psychotherapeutic effects (O'Leary & Borkovec, 1978; Piper & Wogan, 1970; Shapiro & Struening, 1973). From the client's viewpoint, it matters little whether improvement results from newly acquired empathic insights or a placebo effect. From the ethical standpoint, the central issue is client benefit. If the client improves as a result of the therapist's placebo value, so much the better. If, however, the client fails to improve, or if his or her condition worsens while under a therapist's care, the therapist is ethically obliged to take corrective action. In the case where the client's condition seems to be worsening, consultation with more experienced colleagues in an effort to find alternative treatment approaches becomes the first step. In the case where the client is not benefiting from therapy, the appropriate step is to terminate the relationship and offer to help the client locate alternative sources of assistance.

It is important to remember, however, that the course of psychotherapy is seldom a steady road of positive progress. Virtually any client may fail to show progress, regress, develop negative transference, or show only slow progress at some points in the course of psychotherapy. When encountering such problems, the first step one should take is to discuss the seeming impasse with the client. The second step might involve seeking consultation. A decision to terminate therapy or refer the client elsewhere should be made thoughtfully and with the sage advice of colleagues, rather than precipitously.

This chapter addresses five substantive areas of ethical problems in psychotherapy: the nature of the *treatment relationship*, the *special obligations of the therapist*, the *special difficulties of multiple-client treatment* (i.e., group, marital, and family therapy), *technique-related ethical problems* (e.g., sex therapy, hypnosis, behavioral approaches), and *unproven therapies*. A discussion of ethical issues related to the changing landscape of mental health care delivery is also included.

THE TREATMENT RELATIONSHIP

Therapeutic Contracting

If a client and psychologist are to form a therapeutic alliance, they must share some basic goals and understandings of their work together. In warning psychotherapists about how not to fail their clients, Strupp (1975) notes three major functions of the psychologist. First is the *healing function* or the alleviation of emotional suffering through understanding, support, and reassurance. Second is the *educational function*, which includes promoting growth, insight, and maturation. Finally, there is a *tech-*

nological function whereby various techniques may be applied to change or modify behavior. Strupp notes, "the [clients have] a right to know what [they are] buying, and the therapist, like the manufacturer of a product or seller of a service, has a responsibility to be explicit on this subject" (p. 39).

The notion of a client–therapist contract is not new, although attempts to define the parameters of such contracts are relatively recent (Everstine et al., 1980; Hale, 1976; Hare-Mustin, Marecek, Kaplan, & Liss-Levinson, 1979; Liss-Levinson, Hare-Mustin, Marecek, & Kaplan, 1980). This is not to say that therapists and clients must have formal or written documents outlining their relationship. Rather, it suggests that the therapist should assume responsibility to provide clients with the information they need to make decisions about therapy. This duty is underscored in the most recent revision of the American Psychological Association's (APA's) *Ethical Principles of Psychologists and Code of Conduct* (APA, 1992). The key principle is that the therapist should treat the client the way any consumer of services has a right to expect. This may include responding to clients' challenges about one's competence, attempting to resolve clients' complaints, and even using formal written contracts when indicated (Hare-Mustin et al., 1979), as well as initiating routine discussions of the structure of therapy, limits of confidentiality, and other aspects of informed consent.

The Client's Frame of Reference

Implicit in the contracting process is the assumption that the therapist will be able to take the client's unique frame of reference and personal psychosocial ecology into account when deciding whether and how to treat any given person. Therapists unfamiliar with the social, economic, and cultural pressures confronting women, minority group members, gay men and lesbians, and the poor may well fail to recognize the impact of these stresses in creating psychological problems. Conventional psychodiagnostic assessment training often emphasizes clients' own contributions to their problems, at times neglecting to consider the external forces that help to shape the clients' behavior. Counseling clients with culturally diverse backgrounds by psychologists who are not trained to work with such groups has been cited as unethical behavior (Keith-Spiegel & Koocher, 1985; Pedersen & Marsella, 1982).

Many subgroups of society including women, children, the elderly, and certain disadvantaged minorities are socialized in a manner that may accustom them to having their right to self-determination denied (Liss-Levinson et al., 1980). The therapist must be sensitive to these issues and to the general reluctance that an emotionally troubled client may have in asking important questions or raising certain needs. In such cases, the therapist must elicit the basic information needed to conclude a meaningful treatment contract.

Race and social class differences also demand the therapist's careful consideration. Many peoples of color have particular ongoing histories of trauma to which white middle-class psychotherapists may be insensitive. Examples include both day-to-day exposure to discrimination and official government policy such as the internment of Japanese citizens during World War II and Native Americans on reservations. In the latter case, official segregation led to land loss, poverty, cultural devastation, and alcoholism experienced by the many American Indian tribes.

On an individual level, white American society clearly responds to race and class issues in a manner that can be devastating for the person of color. For example, when a crime is committed in a predominantly white community and the alleged perpetrator is an African-American man, the vulnerability of such men in that community cannot be understated. A siege mentality can grip a community, with all African-American men being seen as suspects, regardless of whether or not they fit the description of the alleged perpetrator. The riots in Los Angeles following jury verdicts that cleared police officers who had been captured on videotape beating Rodney King, an African-American man, reflect the intensity of such community reactions.

Similarly, a poor homeless person from any ethnic group is at significantly greater risk in a legal proceeding or as a victim of crime than a well-to-do pillar of the community. This risk goes far beyond simple access to cash and, hence, top-quality legal representation. It also involves unspoken judgments about relative social worth and similar biases on the part of police, prosecutors, and juries (i.e., selected from residential or voter roles, which by definition exclude the peers of the unemployed homeless).

The point to be made here is that psychotherapists must educate and sensitize themselves to their clients' unique frames of reference. Therapists should strive for an awareness of their own biases and attempt to minimize them or avoid working with clients for whom such attitudes and beliefs can create a toxic rather than a therapeutic relationship.

Goal Setting

Another dilemma related to the client's frame of reference and goal setting for therapy is sometimes referred to as the *bait-and-switch* tactic. This term refers to the unethical strategy, sometimes used in retail sales, wherein a store may advertise a product at substantial savings to lure customers. Once they arrive, a salesperson will attempt to make the advertised product seem inferior and encourage the client to purchase a more expensive model. Williams (1985) draws an analogy between this practice and certain types of long-term psychotherapy. He describes the following comments from one of his clients describing a previous therapist:

> "My physician was concerned that there might be a psychological cause for my high blood pressure, so he sent me to see a psychotherapist. I was eager to go because I had become desperate for some kind of relief, and the medicine I took had too many bad side-effects. Psychotherapy was an approach I hadn't even considered. I walked into the therapist's office for my first ses-

sion. He greeted me and asked me to sit down, and we sat there looking at each other for a while. Finally, he asked me about my sex life, which I said was fine. We looked at each other some more, then he told me that the time was up. He expected to see me the following week, but I never went back. (p. 111)

In this case, the client had gone to see the therapist for help with hypertension. The next thing he knew, the topic of discussion was his sex life. In the client's view, the therapist had an agenda different from his own and expected the client to accept it without serious questions. If the client had explicitly chosen to discuss his sex life or any other issues on his own, or because the therapist indicated that some connection might exist between the topic and the presenting symptom, there would have been no unilateral switch and no ethical problem. If the client had decided to seek personal growth and exploration through treatment, there would also have been no problem. Instead, however, the story implies that the pursuit of these other issues was a unilateral and undiscussed decision of the therapist, intended, at least in part, to extend the duration of contact with the client. Perhaps this was therapeutically indicated and perhaps not, but in any case, it should have been discussed with the client. Williams notes that psychotherapy systems as diverse as psychoanalysis and gestalt therapy incorporate rationales for such bait-and-switch tactics (e.g., "the problem is really unconscious and the patient is unaware of the real meanings" or "anybody who goes to a therapist has something up his sleeve"), but a theoretical rationale does not make use of the technique ethical. It is clearly possible to retain one's theoretical integrity in any psychotherapy system, and still call on the client for active participation in setting goals and doing the work of treatment.

Conflicting Values in Psychotherapy

What of the situation where the goals and values of the client and therapist are at variance or the result of treatment may be more than the client bargained for? One of the most fundamental dilemmas related to therapy goals is whether to encourage a client to rebel against a repressive environment or attempt to adjust to it (Karasu, 1980). Issues related to abortion, sexual preference, religion, and family values are among the potential conflict areas. The therapist must be responsible for avoiding the imposition of his or her own values on the client.

In addition, the therapist must constantly ask, "Who is the client?" this is especially true when therapy is mandated, court ordered, or otherwise undertaken at the behest of a third party. For example, misguided judges will sometimes order therapy for children in contested divorce situations to convince the child to visit the noncustodial parent after the child has resisted doing so. Employers may order impaired workers to seek treatment. School officials may demand that a child perceived to have problems seek treatment as a condition of remaining in school. In each of these situations a third party is applying pressure for treatment, but the goals of that party may not be congruent with the goals of the actual client. In such cases, the therapist must carefully review the goals and treatment plan with the person to be treated. Therapy should generally not be undertaken if the client does not concur with the goals and methods to be used. In some situations (e.g., when a client is not competent to make such decisions independently), permission of a responsible guardian and basic assent of the client should be sought.

Consent to Treatment and the Right to Refuse

Consent issues in the context of psychotherapy demand special consideration because therapy unavoidably affects important belief systems and social relationships. This is well illustrated in the case study of Mary, a Christian Scientist with a socially reinforced obsessive disorder (Cohen & Smith, 1976). In a discussion of the ethics of informed consent in this case, it is clear that Mary experienced some sense of divided loyalty related to her religious practices as a result of psychotherapy. Coyne (1976) notes, "even the simplest intervention may have important repercussions for the client's belief system and social relationships" (p. 1015).

The information-giving and consent-getting processes of psychotherapists generally involve a discussion of goals, expectations, procedures, and potential side effects with clients (Everstine et al., 1980; Hare-Mustin et al., 1979; Noll, 1976, 1981). Clients might also reasonably expect to be warned about other foreseeable indirect effects of treatment. Obviously, no psychotherapist can anticipate every potential indirect effect of treatment, but a client who presents with marital complaints, for example, should be cautioned that therapy might lead to behavior or decisions that could end in the choice of divorce. Likewise, a client who presents with job-related complaints could be cautioned that he or she might choose to resign from work as a result of therapy. Such cautions are especially warranted when the therapist notes that the client has many issues that are being inadequately addressed and suspects that uncovering these issues (e.g., long-repressed anger) might lead to distressing feelings. Consider the married person who enters individual psychotherapy hoping to overcome individual and interpersonal problems and to enhance the marriage. What if the result is eventual harm to the marriage and a decision to dissolve it?

A client who does not like the specifications and the risk/benefit statement offered by the therapist can generally decide not to seek treatment or to seek alternative care, but some clients do not have such a choice. As noted above, these clients include potentially incompetent persons such as patients confined in mental hospitals and minors brought for treatment by their parents or guardians. It is important to recognize the rights and vulnerabilities of the hospitalized patient with respect to the ethics of psychotherapy.

In the case of *O'Connor v. Donaldson* (1975) the U.S. Supreme Court recognized for the first time a constitutional basis of a right to treatment for the nondangerous mentally ill patient. This ruling essentially said that the state could not confine such patients unless treatment was provided, but what if the patient does not want the treatment? A host of lawsuits asserting the right of mental patients to refuse treatment, especially those that involve physical interventions (e.g., drugs, psychosurgery, and electroconvulsive shock therapy), have highlighted special ethical problems (Appelbaum & Gutheil, 1980; White & White, 1981). In particular, the right of the patient to refuse medication has been described ironically as the "psychiatrist's double bind" (Ford, 1980) and dramatically as the "right to rot" (Appelbaum & Gutheil, 1980).

As nonphysicians, psychologists are not typically trained to use somatic therapies and have therefore rarely been the object of such suits, although as concerned professionals, they have been involved in the dialogue on the issues. One development predicted on the basis of these newly asserted rights to refuse medication and other somatic treatments is an increased demand for nonmedical treatment of psychological disorders, and hence a greater role for psychologists (White & White, 1981). There are instances where institutionalized clients have asserted the right to refuse psychological treatment, but these have generally been technique related (e.g., behavior modification) and are discussed later in this chapter.

Obtaining consent for treatment from a minor presents another set of issues. At the present time, only a few states permit minors to consent, independently of their parents, to psychotherapeutic treatment. In some states, such services could conceivably be provided as adjuncts to a minor's right to seek birth control, venereal disease, or drug abuse treatment without parental consent. But usually a parent's permission is needed in order to undertake psychotherapy with a minor client. When a child wishes to refuse treatment, there is, under many circumstances, no legal recourse even if the proposed treatment involves inpatient confinement (Melton, Koocher, & Saks, 1983). The courts have tended to assume that the mental health professional called on to hospitalize or treat the child at the parent's behest is an unbiased third party who can adequately assess what is best for the child. Some psychologists have argued that the best interests of parents are not necessarily those of children, and that mental health professionals are not always able to function in the idealized unbiased third-party role imagined by the court (Koocher, 1983; Melton et al., 1983; Weithorn, 1988).

Some decisions are too difficult to expect children to make independently. While it is clear that some children under age 18 may be competent to consent to treatment in the intellectual and emotional sense, it is also evident that many are not (Grisso, 1981, 1986).

OBLIGATIONS OF THE THERAPIST

At this point, it may seem that the many obligations of the psychotherapist to the client have been fully discussed; however, there are three special subareas of obligation that deserve highlighting. These include respect for the client, even the difficult or obnoxious client; the obligation to terminate a relationship when it is clear that the client is not benefiting from therapy; and the matter of malpractice. These are common factors related to ethical complaints. That is to say, few clients complain to ethics committees about a psychologist's failure to obtain treatment consent or adequately consider their cultural value system. Many complaints grow out of cases related to particularly difficult clients, failure to terminate a nonbeneficial relationship, and malpractice.

Exceptionally Difficult Clients

The definition of this type of client is a relative one, since the client who may prove difficult for one therapist could be easy for another. There are some types of clients, however, who would be considered difficult by virtually any therapist. These include the client who makes frequent suicidal threats; who is intimidating or dangerous; who fails to show up for appointments and/or fails to pay bills; who is actively decompensating and acting-out; who is overdependent, telephoning with urgent concerns at all hours of the day and night; or who harasses the therapist's family.

In working with difficult clients, it is essential that psychologists remain cognizant of their professional and personal limitations. This means knowing enough not to take on clients one is not adequately prepared to treat, or knowing enough to help clients in need of different services find them early in the relationship, rather than waiting until problems develop. Some categories of clients seem especially likely to evoke troubling feels on the part of the therapist. The client who is verbally abusive or sarcastic, or who does not speak very much during the session, can certainly generate a number of unpleasant feelings on the therapist's part. Substance abusers, individuals with borderline personality styles, and mentally retarded clients will occasionally be referred elsewhere by some therapists. There is nothing unethical about refusing to treat a client who stirs up troubling feelings or anger in the therapist. In fact, it is probably more appropriate to refer such clients elsewhere than to try to treat them while struggling with strong countertransference issues. However, it is important to minimize the risk and discomfort to all clients. One should therefore learn to identify those sorts of clients one cannot or should not work with, and refer them appropriately and quickly without causing them personal discomfort or stress. Still another type of difficult client is the one whose behavior or problems tend to interact with the personal psychological issues of the therapist to cause special countertransference situations.

The point here is that psychologists must strive for sufficient self-awareness to recognize their anger toward clients and make every effort to avoid acting-out or otherwise harming the client unnecessarily. There are many appropriate ways to handle anger toward a client, ranging from direct overt expression (e.g., "I am annoyed that you kicked that hole in my office wall, and I am going to charge you the cost of repairing it") to silent self-exploration (e.g., the client who stirs up countertransference feelings because of similarities to some significant other in the therapist's life). The client is always to be considered vulnerable to harm relative to the therapist, and the psychologist is obligated not to use the power inherent in the therapist's role to the client's detriment. If such problems occur more than rarely in a psychologist's career, it is likely that the therapist is practicing beyond his or her competence or has a personal problem that should be addressed.

Failure to Terminate a Client Who Is Not Benefiting from Therapy

Ethical problems related to the duration of treatment fall into this category—for example, the client who, by virtue of fostered dependency or other means, is encouraged to remain in treatment past the point of actual benefit. Such judgments are complicated by varying theoretical attitudes and orientations. Some therapists would argue: "If you think you need therapy, then you probably do." Others might argue: "If you are sure you don't need it, then you definitely do."

We recognize such biases in many of our colleagues and could choose two colleagues on opposite ends of the continuum for a test. A person might be selected at random and sent to each for a consultation. One would probably find the person basically well adjusted, while the other would probably find the same person in need of treatment. We might presume that one or the other is unethical, either for suggesting treatment where none is needed or for dismissing prematurely a person who is in need of help, but neither is necessarily the case. If the psychologist presents the client with the reasons why treatment is or is not needed and proposes a specific goal-directed plan, the client is in a position to make an informed choice. The therapist who sees emotional health may do so in the absence of symptoms, while the therapist who recommends treatment may sense some unconscious issues or potential for improved functioning. These views can and ought to be shared with the client.

From time to time, legitimate doubts will arise as to a client's therapeutic needs. When

this occurs, the client and therapist should discuss the issues, and the client should probably be referred for consultation to another practitioner. This procedure is also often useful when a client and therapist disagree on other major treatment issues or when a client's condition seems to be deteriorating despite the therapist's best efforts.

MULTIPLE-CLIENT THERAPIES

In marital, family, and group therapies the psychologist has more than one client. It is most unlikely that the best interests of one client in the treatment group will fully overlap with those of another. In certain groups, especially in marital and family work, it is more often the case that the needs or wishes of one member are quite different from those of another. Group therapies also require different techniques and training than individual therapies. They raise a host of other ethical issues, including matters of confidentiality, social coercion, and similar problems.

Marital and Family Therapy

Ethical guidelines dealing with a therapist's responsibility to clients, confidentiality, informed consent, and clients' rights are certainly ambiguous at times when considering the interaction of one psychologist with a single client. When a couple or multiple family members are involved in treatment, matters become even more complicated. Treatment will often involve a therapeutic obligation to several individuals whose needs are conflicting (Hare-Mustin, 1980; Hines & Hare-Mustin, 1978). Margolin (1982) cites several illustrations of such conflicts. She describes the mother who seeks treatment for her child so that the child will be better behaved, which may ease pressure on the mother while not helping her child. Margolin also cites the case of the wife whose goal is to surmount fears of terminating her marriage, while her husband's goal is to maintain the status quo (p. 789). A therapist in such situations must strive to ensure that improvement in the status of one family member does not occur at the expense of another. When such an outcome may be unavoidable (e.g., in the case of the couple whose treatment may result in the decision of one or both partners to seek a divorce), the psychologist should advise the couple of that potential outcome early in the course of treatment. In this situation, the therapist's personal values and therapeutic system are of critical importance (Hare-Mustin 1980; Hines & Hare-Mustin, 1978; Keith-Spiegel & Koocher, 1985, L'Abate, 1982; Margolin, 1982).

The APA Task Force on Sex Bias and Sex-Role Stereotyping (1975) found that family therapists are particularly vulnerable to certain biases. These include the assumption that remaining in a marriage represents the better adjustment for a woman and a tendency to defer to the husband's needs over those of the wife. The same report noted the tendency to demonstrate less interest in or sensitivity to a woman's career as opposed to a man's, and to perpetuate the belief that child rearing and children's problems are primarily in the woman's domain. The report also stated that therapists tended to hold a double standard in response to the extramarital affairs of a wife versus those of a husband.

Several authors have noted that the prevailing "therapeutic ideology" holds that all persons can and should benefit from therapy (Hines & Hare-Mustin, 1978; Silber, 1976). Some family therapists also insist that *all* members of the family must participate in treatment (Hare-Mustin, 1980; Hines & Hare-Mustin, 1978; Margolin, 1982). What does this do to a person's right to decline treatment? Must the reluctant adolescent or adult be pressured into attending sessions at the behest of the psychotherapist? We know that some children as young as 14 are as competent as adults to make decisions about treatment (Grisso, 1981, 1986), yet it is unclear how often such family members are offered a truly voluntary choice.

Obviously, coercion of any reluctant family member to participate in treatment would be unethical. This does not preclude a therapist's

urging that the resistant family member attend at least one trial session or attempting to address the underlying reasons for the refusal. The therapist who strongly believes that the *whole* family *must* be seen should not use coercion to drag in the reluctant member. Nor should such a therapist permit that reluctant member to deny treatment to the family members who wish to have it. In such cases, the therapist should provide the names of other professionals in the community who might be willing to treat the group desiring it. When the client in question is a minor, the therapist has a special duty to consider that client's needs as distinct from those of the parents (Koocher & Keith-Spiegel, 1990).

Still another issue that complicates marital and family therapy is the matter of confidentiality. Should a therapist tolerate secret keeping or participate in it? Should parents be able to sign away a child's right to confidentiality? The concept and conditions of confidentiality are somewhat different in the family context than in individual therapy. Couples often have difficulty in establishing boundaries and privacy with respect to their own lives and those of their children (Hines & Hare-Mustin, 1978; Margolin, 1982). Adult clients can and should be able to assert some privacy with respect to their marriage and to avoid burdening their children with information that is frightening, provocative, or simply beyond their ability to comprehend adequately. On the other hand, many attempts to maintain secrets are manipulative and do not serve the general goals of treatment.

The most reasonable way of handling this matter ethically is to formulate a policy based on therapeutic goals and define it for all concerned at the outset of treatment. Some therapists may state at the beginning of therapy that they will keep no secrets. Others may be willing to accept information shared in confidence in order to help the person offering it determine whether or not it is appropriate for discussion in the whole group. Still another option would be to discuss the resistance to sharing the information with the member in question, with the goal of helping that person to share the information with the family, if indicated. Secret keeping presents the therapist with the added burden of recalling which secret came from whom, not to mention the need to recall what was secret and what was not. The therapist who does not consider these matters in advance and does not discuss them early with family clients is certain to confront serious ethical dilemmas within a very short period of time.

Group Therapy

Psychotherapists may treat unrelated clients in groups for a variety of reasons, ranging from simple economy to specificity of the program. For example, a group may consist of recently hospitalized mental patients, divorced males, bereaved parents, or handicapped children. In such groups, the identified clients gather together to address similar emotional or social problems in a common supportive context. Other groups, however, may focus on enhancing personal growth or self-awareness as opposed to addressing personal psychodynamics or psychopathology. Rogers (1970) offered a sample listing of group types, including T-groups, encounter groups, sensitivity groups, task-oriented groups, sensory awareness or body awareness groups, organizational development groups, team building groups, and gestalt groups.

Group treatment has considerable potential for both good and harm. The influence and support of peers in the treatment process may facilitate gains that would be slow or unlikely in individual treatment. The group may also become a special therapeutic ecology within which special insights and awareness may develop. At the same time, however, there are significant hazards to group members when the group leader is not properly trained or is unable to monitor the experience adequately for all members. The group therapist has much less control over the content and direction of the therapeutic session than does the individual therapist. As a result, there is greater potential for individuals in the group to have unfavorable

or adverse experiences. Problems might include stresses resulting from confrontation, criticism, threats to confidentiality, or even the development of dependency on the group.

Discussion here will focus on two sets of related issues, first regarding groups intended as therapy experiences and, second, groups intended as *growth experiences*. The latter term is used in reference to short-terms group experiences, where individual development or growth rather than psychopathology is the focus. As used here, the term *group therapy* will generally refer to treatment for people seeking help in response to specific emotional or psychological symptoms, usually over a period of months or years rather than days or weeks, as in the growth experience programs.

The APA Guidelines for Psychologists Conducting Growth Groups (1973) make several important points, which can be generally categorized mandates for the psychologist leader to provide informed consent, ensure that participation is fully voluntary, conduct proper screening of participants, and carefully differentiate roles based on whether the group is intended to be therapeutic or educational. These guidelines make it evident that the responsibility for these obligations rests on the psychologist leading the group.

Lieberman, Yalom, and Miles (1973) list many participant vulnerability factors that therapists must consider in constructing and conducting groups. These factors include vulnerability to aggression, fragile self-esteem, excessive dependency needs, intense fear of rejection, withdrawal, transference to the group leader, internal conflicts aroused by group discussions, unreal expectations, and guardedness. In many ways, the group therapist's ethical burden is far greater than that of the individual therapist, since the psychologist conducting group therapy must consider the psychological ecology of the therapy or program as it affects a variety of different participants.

Confidentiality and privileged communication in group psychotherapy is also an important issue. The group context raises a variable not present in individual therapy since there are, by definition, more than two people in a position to disclose a confidence learned in the session (i.e., the therapist and at least one other client). In most jurisdictions there is no statutory privilege extending to material disclosed in group sessions to client members of the group (Slovenko, 1977). The therapist should therefore advise clients in two ways early in the group treatment process. First, the clients must be cautioned about the lack of legal protections (i.e., privilege) regarding information disclosed. Second, the therapist should encourage recognition of the importance to all group members of a mutually respectful duty of confidentiality regarding what each member says in the course of treatment.

Slovenko (1977) notes that therapists tend to be far more concerned about issues of confidentiality than are members of the group. One wonders whether clients in group treatment should reasonably be aware that gossip about sensitive material revealed in sessions may be communicated to others outside the group by their peers. As a result, clients might reasonably be expected to censor material about which they are particularly sensitive. Even so, the pressure toward self-disclosure in group therapy or even experiential growth programs may be intense, and therapists should have these issues in mind as the group sessions proceed.

SPECIAL TECHNIQUES AND ISSUES

Under the general heading of psychotherapy, there are a number of special techniques and issues that have attracted a sufficient number of ethics inquiries over time to warrant specific discussion. These include the issue of triage and intake procedures, as well as techniques associated with sex therapy, hypnosis, behavior modification, the use of psychological devices, and so-called coercive treatment techniques. The reasons such issues and techniques attract special ethical concerns is in part a function of the sensational nature of the context or style in which they are applied and in part a function of the special social concerns associated with the treatment issue (e.g., sexual practices and sex therapy or civil rights and coercive treatment programs).

Triage and Intake

Triage, a concept frequently applied in medical emergency situations, refers to a priority assignment to certain patients waiting to be seen. For example, a patient who has stopped breathing or who is hemorrhaging will be seen immediately, even if other, less severely injured patients must wait for an extended period in pain and discomfort. Likewise, a clinic with a long psychotherapy waiting list might move a suicidal client to the head of the list for treatment because of the urgent nature of the problem. At times, however, clients are not informed of such priorities, even if they are reasonable, with the result that clients may suffer needlessly rather than seeking alternative treatment. In some instances, the system of priorities or intake procedures may be ethically questionable.

These matters are well discussed by Levenson and Pope (1981), who also present with a sarcastic twist the ultimate abomination in triage policy:

> All slim, attractive, female patients will be moved automatically to the head of the waiting list . . . and will be assigned to male therapists on the basis of their seniority, clout, and ability to feign detachment and to deny countertransference in case conferences . . . those with Spanish surnames or accents of any kind will be referred elsewhere. (p. 482)

Sensitive and responsive intake and triage policies are important ethical issues and, as Levenson and Pope demonstrate, such policies actually lead to better interventions and improved utilization of services.

Sex Therapy

The very use of the word *sex* tends to capture immediately the attention of an adult audience, and when the term *sex therapy* is used, most mental health professionals think only of the most common presenting symptoms (i.e., impotence, premature ejaculation, anorgasmia, dyspareunia, vaginismus, and withdrawal from sexual activity). There are, however, a variety of other problems that might become the focus of sex therapy. These include hysterical conversion reactions with a sexual focus, the paraphilias (e.g., exhibitionism, pedophilia, voyeurism), gender dysphoria syndromes (e.g., transsexualism), physical developmental disorders (e.g., hypospadias), disease-related disorders (e.g., impotence associated with diabetes), and problems resulting from medical side effects, surgery, or traumatic injury to the sex organs (Meyer, 1976). Some clients may also present with varying degrees of concern about sexual functioning and homosexuality.

The American Association of Sex Educators, Counselors and Therapists (AASECT, 1980) has developed a code of ethics and training guidelines for individuals practicing in this specialized field. As their code of ethics and the complexity of the social, psychological, anatomical, and physiological factors that may be involved in sexual problems suggest, special skills and ethical sensitivities are required in this field of practice. Often, the style and substance of clinically appropriate sex therapy will differ dramatically from other therapeutic activities. For example, Lowery and Lowery (1975) claim that the most ethical sex therapy is that "which cures the symptom and improves the marital relationship in the briefest time and at the least cost" (p. 229). They also specify that neither insight-oriented treatment nor sex with the client satisfies these criteria. Clearly, special credentials are in order for any practitioner who desires to treat sexual dysfunction (AASECT, 1980; Meyer, 1976).

Emotional reactions linked to the nature of the problems treated are not limited to the general public. A fascinating debate began in the professional literature with the publication of a study describing highly specific behaviorally oriented masturbation procedures for inorgasmic women (Zeiss, Rosen, & Zeis, 1977).

This was followed by a critique entitled "Psychotherapy or Massage Parlor Technology?" (Bailey, 1978), which invoked ethical, moral, and philosophical (as well as social psychological) reasoning. This was followed by a comment describing Bailey's critique as "antiscientific" (Wagner, 1978) and, later, by a reasoned critique noting that value-free therapy does not exist and enjoining the therapist to involve the client fully in goal setting while conducting the least intrusive treatment (Wilson, 1978).

Perhaps the most dramatic focus of concern in the practice of sex therapy involves the use of sexual surrogates, that is, sexual partners used by some mental health professionals to assist certain clients by engaging in a variety of social and sexual activities for a fee. The use of surrogates is far more than a prescription for prostitution (Jacobs, Thompson, & Truxaw, 1975). Although they were initially used by Masters and Johnson with some single clients, the use of sex surrogates today is a more rare and atypical technique, with greater attention being paid to a host of other issues and techniques (Masters & Johnson, 1976). Still, some therapists may wish to use surrogates from time to time, although this may lead to substantial ethical and legal complications.

In some states, a mental health professional who refers a client to a sex surrogate may be liable for criminal prosecution under so-called procurement or pimping statutes. Some state laws could lead to prosecution under prostitution statues or antifornication laws, or even to rape charges, should some aspect of the relationship go wrong or come to the attention of a zealous district attorney. A variety of potential civil liabilities or tort actions are also possible if one marital partner objects to the other's use of a surrogate or if the client contracts a sexually transmitted disease from the surrogate. In such cases, the referring practitioner may have a vicarious liability and will most likely find his or her liability insurer unwilling to cover the resulting claim.

Sexual behavior is an emotionally charged, value-laden aspect of human life, and therapists working actively to alter such behavior must be appropriately cautious and sensitive to both community and professional standards. In such areas of practice, haphazard ethical practices and indiscretions are much more likely to lead to major problems for the client and practitioner than in almost any other realm.

Behavior Modification Techniques

As in the case of sex therapy, the application of behavioral techniques such as operant conditioning, classical conditioning, aversive therapies, and other types of physical interventions (e.g., physiological monitoring, biofeedback, stress management) requires specialized training of an interdisciplinary nature. This may involve training in anatomy and physiology, as well as analysis of behavior and application of learning theory. In addition, a keen awareness of one's limitations is needed, as in knowing when a medical consultation is indicated or when a certain instrumental procedure may edge toward the violation of a client's rights.

The application of behavioral techniques usually involves the assumption of a substantial degree of control over the client's environment. Generally, this takes place with the active involvement and consent of the client. In some instances, however, the client may be technically or literally incompetent to consent, as in the case of mentally retarded or severely psychotic clients. When the client is incompetent to consent fully and powerful environmental controls are enforced, special substituted judgment procedures using independent advocates may be needed (Koocher & Keith-Spiegel, 1990).

From time to time, there have been outcries in the mass media and public literature about the application of behavioral techniques in schools, prisons, and other settings. Many have called for, produced, or rebutted the need for specialized guidelines to be used in applying behavioral techniques (Davidson & Stuart, 1975; Geller, Johnson, Hamlin, & Kennedy, 1977; Stoltz, 1977; Thaw, Turkat, & Forehand, 1978). In actual practice, behavioral

therapies are no more or less in need of regulation than other forms of treatment that are also subject to abuse. Stolz (1977) reminds us that behavioral clinicians, like other therapists, should be governed by the ethics code of their profession, and that the ethics of all intervention programs should be evaluated in terms of a number of critical issues, such as circumstances and client intent.

The context and nature of decision making and treatment goal setting are critical (Stolz, 1978). These issues are well illustrated in a series of comments to a manuscript on alternatives to pain medication (Cook, 1975; Goodstein, 1975; Karoly, 1975). The original report focused on a 65-year-old man admitted to a psychiatric ward with symptoms of chronic abdominal pain and a self-induced drug habit to control the pain (Levendusky & Pankratz, 1975). He was successfully withdrawn from the drug using a treatment procedure that involved some deception and lacked fully informed consent. The ethical dilemma here is the matter of client involvement in making choices rather than the technique itself.

During a conversation hour at an APA meeting several years ago, B. F. Skinner spoke bemusedly about a controversy that seemed to focus on labels as opposed to practice. He noted that a school board had promulgated a threat to fire any personnel who used behavior modification. He then wondered aloud what would happen the next payday when "reinforcements" were handed out in the form of paychecks. This illustrated once again that it is not the technique itself that presents the ethical problem but the manner in which it is applied.

Unfortunately, not all psychologists who attempt to employ behavioral techniques are well trained in the underlying learning theory. Confusion regarding the distinction between the concepts of *punishment* and *negative reinforcement* is one example of a common problem. In other instances, aversive treatment protocols have occasionally been introduced without first trying less restrictive techniques. It is especially important that psychologists show careful concern for ethical problems inherent in the use of aversive stimuli with relatively powerless clients. This would include, for example, institutionalized, incarcerated, or incompetent individuals, as well as children or other persons not fully able to assert their rights.

Psychological Devices

The report of the APA Task Force on Psychologists' Use of Physical Interventions (1981) lists more than a score of instruments and devices used by psychologists for clinical assessment and psychotherapy. These include a variety of electrodes and monitors used in biofeedback training, as well as an assortment of color vision testers, dynamometers, audiometers, restraints, and even vibrators. Some of these devices are regulated by U.S. Food and Drug Administration, and most require specialized training for proper use. Detailed suggestions for the use of such devices have been published by R. L. and R. K. Schwitzgebel (1970, 1978) and Fuller (1978). Psychotherapists have also been involved in discussing problems associated with the use of lie detectors (Lykken, 1974; Szucko & Kleinmuntz, 1981), suicide prevention by means of computer-mediated therapy (Barnett, 1982), and therapy by telephone (Grumet, 1979). More recently, psychologists have become associated with 900 telephone numbers by which clients can phone in and be billed by the minute via their local phone company. Guidelines for these and other on-line therapies are now being debated, but few standards specific to these media exist.

The use of technology in the future of psychotherapy is likely to increase, along with related ethical complaints. For example, recent federal court decisions make it clear that local telephone companies will soon be in the cable television business. By the start of the twenty-first century, real-time psychotherapy by electronic audio and visual channels will almost certainly be routine. The basic ethical caveat is that psychologists should recognize the boundaries of their competence and the limitations or problems associated with new technologies (e.g., the potential for having confidential therapy sessions monitored by others while using electronic cable or cellular transmissions).

With respect to new electronics aids (e.g., biofeedback devices or computer-administered tests), it is important to avoid using unsafe or unproven devices, not to mention those that might prove dangerous to clients through electric shock or other hazards. Psychologists must also be mindful that they are not physicians and should never attempt to treat problems with possible organic causes without a collaborative relationship with a qualified physician. In addition, federal law may govern the licensing and use of some instruments. Psychologists are obligated to keep themselves abreast of these statutes and of the resulting obligations.

Coercive Therapies

As noted earlier in this chapter, psychotherapy has sometimes been considered a means of social control (Hurvitz, 1973) and has occasionally been compared in some ways with brainwashing (Dolliver, 1971; Gaylin, 1974). The use of *coercive persuasion*, *deprogramming*, and hypnotic suggestion techniques (Fromm, 1980; Kline, 1976) has been discussed from the viewpoint of client manipulation. That is to say, to what extent do certain psychological techniques permit the psychotherapist to manipulate or control the client by force or threat? Earlier in this chapter, we discussed the client's right to refuse treatment, and we cite these issues only as examples of techniques that from time to time have been the object of complaints.

In general, it is unethical for a psychotherapist to coerce a client into treatment or to impose certain goals or outcomes against the client's wishes. The subtler aspects of coercion are the most difficult to be sensitive to: group pressure, guilt induction, introduction of cognitive dissonance, attempts at total environmental control, and the establishment of a trusting relationship with a goal of effecting change in another person (Dolliver, 1971). It is critical that the psychotherapist attempt to remain aware of potentially coercive influences and avoid them without full participation, discussion, and choice by the client. The constant critical reexamination of the strategies and goals of treatment involving both client and therapist is the best means to this end.

UNTESTED OR FRINGE THERAPIES

From time to time, ethics complaints will develop in response to a new or unusual form of psychotherapy or allegedly therapeutic technique. Often these so-called treatments are of questionable merit or are frankly dangerous. There must be room for appropriate innovation and the development of new treatment strategies in any scientific field, but rigorous standards must be applied to avoid misleading or harming potential clients. No program of psychotherapy or psychotherapeutic technique should be undertaken without a firm theoretical foundation and scientific basis for anticipating client benefits. Such programs should be labeled as experimental, with appropriate informed consent when that is the case, and should be discontinued at the first indication that any harm is accruing to the clients.

Examples of some of the more questionable schools of psychotherapeutic thought include so-called past lives therapy, rage weekends, and harassment therapy. Some consider Scientology a type of fringe or unproven therapy as well. The work of Wilhelm Reich, which seems to have occasionally involved physical stimulation of clients to the point of orgasm (Reich, 1948), the body invasion technique of rolfing (Leland, 1976), and the dramatic stresses of implosive therapy (Stampfl, 1975) are all examples of therapeutic ideas at the outer limit of acceptability. The difficulty, of course, is that we have hardly reached the state of psychological science where precise evaluation of the therapeutic outcome for all interventions is possible. Still, some clear ethical problems do arise.

NEW PRESSURES

Managed care, the scope of practice limitations, hospital privilege access, and prescription privileges are a few of the issues that have begun to confront psychologists practicing psychotherapy in the past several years. Increasingly, the practice of psychotherapy is no longer governed solely by the client and therapist. The duration of treatment, determination of covered services, and eligibility for hospital admission increasingly require the practitioner to share detailed case formulations, data, and progress reports with insurance company or health maintenance organization reviewers. As psychologists acquire hospital admission privileges, they will need to deal with the precipitous discharges ordered by insurance companies. As nonphysician therapists acquire prescription privileges, they will have to deal with increased hazards. Some clients will suffer drug interactions and allergic reactions. Availability will also increase the hazard of practitioner substance abuse.

The three C's—caution, competence, and consent—will be the therapist's best allies in maintaining ethical practice during the coming evolutionary period. Caution will dictate careful preparation and assessment as a precursor to therapeutic intervention. Competence will require that psychotherapists acquire appropriate education and training before implementing new techniques. Maintaining competence will also demand continued professional development and learning throughout one's career. Consent will dictate thoughtful consideration of each client's need and involvement of all clients in setting the goals and parameters of therapy.

SUMMARY GUIDELINES

1. Psychotherapists should strive to reach explicit understandings with their clients regarding the terms of the treatment contract, whether written or informal. This includes some mutual discussion about the goals of treatment and the means to achieve these goals.
2. Psychotherapists are obliged to consider carefully the unique needs and perspec-

tive of each client in formulating therapeutic plans.

3. A psychotherapist's personal beliefs, values, and attributes may limit his or her ability to treat certain types of clients. Therapists should strive for awareness of such characteristics and limit their practices appropriately.

4. In certain circumstances, clients have specific legal rights either to receive or to refuse treatment. Psychologists should be aware of these rights and respect the underlying principles, even where no specific laws are in force.

5. Therapists should strive to recognize their own feelings with respect to each client, as well as the degree to which these feelings may interfere with therapy. In cases where the client does not seem to be benefiting or where the client's behavior is particularly problematic, the therapist should promptly consider alternative courses of action.

6. When the psychologist is treating more than one client at a time, as in group or family therapy, the rights of all clients must be respected and balanced. Therapists should also be sensitive to their own values with respect to the family or group and attempt to facilitate the growth of all concerned within their own value systems.

7. The psychologist conducting group treatment or educational programs should carefully define and articulate the goals, methods, and purposes of each group for each participant in such a manner as to permit each potential client a fully informed choice about participation.

8. In the application of special therapeutic techniques, including (but not limited to) sex therapy, behavior modification, hypnosis, and the use of psychological devices, psychologists must be certain that their training is adequate to use the technique in question.

9. When some symptoms or technique raise special emotional or public policy questions, the psychotherapist should be sensitive to the issues and discuss these, along with their implications, with the client. Psychologists are also obliged to keep abreast of evolving standards and regulations governing the use of specialized techniques and devices.

10. Coercion is not an appropriate part of a psychotherapeutic program. To the extent that subtle coercive pressures enter into a therapeutic relationship, the psychologist should attempt to ensure that these are not used to the detriment of the client.

11. Only well-validated approaches to treatment should be presented to clients as such. Experimental procedures must be described as such, and extreme caution should be used in the development of new modalities of treatment in order to minimize client risk.

REFERENCES

American Association of Sex Educators, Counselors, and Therapists. (1980). *AASECT code of ethics*, Washington, DC: Author.

American Psychological Association. (1973). Guidelines for psychologists conducting growth groups. *American Psychologist*, 28, 933.

American Psychological Association. (1981). *Task force report on psychologists' use of physical interventions*. Washington, DC: Author.

American Psychological Association. (1992). Ethical principles of psychologists and code of conduct. *American Psychologist*, 47, 1597–1611.

American Psychological Association Task Force. (1975). Report of the Task Force on Sex Bias and Sex-Role Stereotyping in Psychotherapeutic Practice. *American Psychologist*, 30, 1169–1175.

Appelbaum, P. S., & N. Gutheil, T. G. (1980). Drug refusal: A study of psychiatric inpatients. *American Journal of Psychiatry*, 137, 340–345.

Bailey, K. G. (1978). Psychotherapy or massage parlor technology? Comments on the Zeiss, Rosen, and Zeiss treatment procedure. *Journal of Consulting and Clinical Psychology*, 46, 1502–1506.

Barnett, D. C. (1982). A suicide prevention incident

involving use of the computer. *Professional Psychology, 13*, 565–570.

Cohen, R. J., & Smith, F. J. (1976). Socially reinforced obsessing: etiology of a disorder in a Christian Scientist. *Journal of Consulting and Clinical Psychology, 44*, 142–144.

Cook, S. W. (1975). Comments on ethical considerations in "self-control" techniques as an alternative to pain medication. *Journal of Abnormal Psychology, 84*, 169–171.

Coyne, J. C. (1976). The place of informed consent in ethical dilemmas. *Journal of Consulting and Clinical Psychology, 44*, 1015–1017.

Davidson, G. C., & Stuart, R. B. (1975). Behavior therapy and civil liberties. *American Psychologist, 30*, 755–763.

Dolliver, R. H. (1971). Concerning the potential parallels between psychotherapy and brainwashing. *Psychotherapy: Theory, Research, and Practice, 8*, 170–173.

Everstine, L., Everstine, D. S., Heymann, G. M., True, R. H., Frey, D. H., Johnson, H. G., & Seiden, R. H. (1980). Privacy and confidentiality in psychotherapy. *American Psychologist, 35*, 828–840.

Eysenck, H. J. (1952). The effects of psychotherapy: An evaluation. *Journal of Consulting Psychology, 16*, 319–324.

Ford, M. D. (1980). The psychiatrist's double bind: The right to refuse medication. *American Journal of Psychiatry, 137*, 332–339.

Fromm, E. (1980). Values in hypnotherapy. *Psychotherapy: Theory, Research, and Practice, 17*, 425–430.

Fuller, G. D. (1978). Current status of biofeedback in clinical practice. *American Psychologist, 33*, 30–48.

Garfield, S. L. (1981). Psychotherapy: A 40-year appraisal. *American Psychologist, 36*, 174–183.

Gaylin, W. (1974). On the borders of persuasion: A psychoanalytic look at coercion. *Psychiatry, 37*, 1–9.

Geller, E. S., Johnson, D. F., Hamlin, P. H., & Kennedy, T. D. (1977). Behavior modification in a prison: Issues, problems, and compromises. *Criminal Justice and Behavior, 4*, 11–43.

Goodstein, L. D. (1975). Self-control and therapist-control: The medical model in behavioral clothing. *Journal of Abnormal Psychology, 84*, 178–180.

Grisso, T. J. (1981). *Juvenile's waiver of rights: Legal and psychological competence.* New York: Plenum Press.

Grisso, T. J. (1986). *Evaluating competencies: Forensic assessments and instruments.* New York: Plenum Press.

Grumet, G. W. (1979). Telephone therapy: A review and case report. *American Journal of Orthopsychiatry, 51*, 574–585.

Hale, W. D. (1976). Responsibility and psychotherapy. *Psychotherapy: Theory, Research, and Practice, 13*, 298–302.

Hare-Mustin, R. T. (1978). A feminist approach to family therapy. *Family Process, 17*, 181–194.

Hare-Mustin, R. T. (1980). Family therapy may be dangerous for your health. *Professional Psychology, 11*, 935–938.

Hare-Mustin, R. T., Marecek, J., Kaplan, A. G., & Liss-Levenson, N. (1979). Rights of clients, responsibilities of therapists. *American Psychologist, 34*, 3–16.

Hines, P. M., & Hare-Mustin, R. T. (1978). Ethical concerns in family therapy. *Professional Psychology, 9*, 165–171.

Hogan, D. B. (1979). *The regulation of psychotherapists.* Cambridge, MA: Ballinger.

Hurvitz, N. (1967). Marital problems following psychotherapy with one spouse. *Journal of Consulting Psychology, 31*, 38–47.

Hurvitz, N. (1973). Psychotherapy as a means of social control. *Journal of Consulting and Clinical Psychology, 40*, 232–239.

Jacobs, M., Thompson, L. A., & Truxaw, P. (1975). The use of sexual surrogates in counseling. *The Counseling Psychologist, 5*, 73–76.

Kanoti, G. A. (1971). Ethical implications in psychotherapy. *Journal of Religion and Health, 10*, 180–191.

Karasu, T. B. (1980) The ethics of psychotherapy. *American Journal of Psychiatry, 137*, 1502–1512.

Karoly, P. (1975). Ethical considerations in the application of self-control techniques. *Journal of Abnormal Psychology, 84*, 175–177.

Kaschak, E. (1978). Therapist and client: Two views of the process and outcome of psychotherapy. *Professional Psychology, 9*, 271–278.

Keith-Spiegel, P. C., & Koocher, G. P. (1985). *Ethics in psychology: Professional standards and cases.* New York: Random House (currently published by McGraw-Hill).

Kline, M. V. (1976). Dangerous aspects of the practice of hypnosis and the need for legislative regulation. *The Clinical Psychologist, 29*, 2–5.

Koocher, G. P. (1983). Consent to psychotherapy. In G. B. Melton, G. P. Koocher, & M. Saks

(Eds.), *Children's competence to consent*. New York: Plenum Press.

Koocher, G. P., & Keith-Spiegel, P. C. (1990). *Children, ethics, and the law: Professional issues and cases*. Lincoln: University of Nebraska Press.

L'Abate, L. (1982). *Values, ethics, legalities and the family therapist*. Rockville, MD: Aspen Systems Corporation.

Lehner, G. F. J. (1952). Defining psychotherapy. *American Psychologist*, 7, 547.

Leland, J. (1976). "Invasion" of the body? *Psychotherapy: Theory, Research, and Practice*, 13, 214–218.

Levendusky, P. & Pankratz, L. (1975). Self-control techniques as an alternative to pain medication. *Journal of Abnormal Psychology*, 84, 165–168.

Levenson, H., & Pope, K. S. (1981). First encounters: Effects of intake procedures on patients, staff, and the organization. *Hospital and Community Psychiatry*, 32, 482–485.

Lieberman, M. A., Yalom, I. D., & Miles, M. B. (1973). *Encounter groups: First facts*. New York: Basic Books.

Liss-Levinson, N., Hare-Mustin, R. T., Marecek, J., & Kaplan, A. G. (1980, March). The therapist's role in assuring client rights. *Advocacy Now*, pp. 16–20.

Lowery, T. S., & Lowery, T. P. (1976). Ethical considerations in sex therapy. *Journal of Marriage and Family Counseling*, 1, 229–236.

Lykken, D. T. (1974). Psychology and the lie detector industry. *American Psychologist*, 29, 725–739.

Margolin, G. (1982). Ethical and legal considerations in marital and family therapy. *American Psychologist*, 37, 788–801.

Marshall, E. (1980). Psychotherapy faces test of worth. *Science*, 207, 35–36.

Masters, W. H., & Johnson, V. E. (1976). Principles of the new sex therapy. *American Journal of Psychiatry*, 133, 548–554.

Melton, G. B., Koocher, G. P., & Saks, M. (1983). *Children's competence to consent*. New York: Plenum Press.

Meyer, J. K. (1976). Training and accreditation for the treatment of sexual disorders. *American Journal of Psychiatry*, 133, 389–394.

Noll, J. O. (1976). The psychotherapist and informed consent. *American Journal of Psychiatry*, 133, 1451–1453.

Noll, J. O. (1981). Material risks and informed consent to psychotherapy. *American Psychologist*, 36, 916–918.

O'Connor v. Donaldson, 422 U.S. 575 (1975).

O'Leary, K. D., & Borkovec, T. D. (1978). Conceptual, methodological, and ethical problems of placebo groups in psychotherapy research. *American Psychologist*, 33, 821–830.

Parker, R. S. (1976). Ethical and professional considerations concerning high risk groups. *The Journal of Clinical Issues in Psychology*, 7, 4–19.

Pedersen, P. B., & Marsella, A. J. (1982). The ethical crisis for cross-cultural counseling and therapy. *Professional Psychology*, 13, 492–500.

Piper, W. E., & Wogan, M. (1970). Placebo effect in psychotherapy: An extension of earlier findings. *Journal of Consulting and Clinical Psychology*, 34, 447.

Pope, K. S., & Vasquez, M. J. T. (1991). *Ethics in psychotherapy and counseling: A practical guide for psychologists*. San Francisco: Jossey-Bass.

Reich, W. (1948). *The discovery of the orgasm: Volume One. The Function of the Orgasm*. New York: Orgone Institute Press.

Rogers, C. (1970). *Carl Rogers on encounter groups*. New York: Harper & Row.

Schofield, W. (1976). *Psychotherapy: The purchase of friendship*, Englewood Cliffs, NJ: Prentice-Hall.

Schwitzgebel, R. L. (1970). Behavior instrumentation and social technology. *American Psychologist*, 25, 491–499.

Schwitzgebel, R. K. (1978). Suggestions for the uses of psychological devices in accord with legal and ethical standards. *Professional Psychology*, 9, 478–488.

Shapiro, A. K., & Struening, E. L. (1973). The use of placebos: A study of ethics and physicians' attitudes. *Psychiatry in Medicine*, 4, 17–29.

Silber, D. E. (1976). Therapeutic ideology and the professional psychologist. *The Clinical Psychologist*, 24, 3–5.

Slovenko, R. (1977). Group psychotherapy: privileged communication and confidentiality. *Journal of Psychiatry and the Law*, 5, 405–466.

Stampfl, T. G. (1975, February). Implosive therapy: staring down your nightmares. *Psychology Today*, pp. 66–73.

Stolz, S. B. (1977). Why no guidelines for behavior modification? *Journal of Applied Behavior Analysis*, 10, 541–547.

Stolz, S. B. (1978). Ethics of social and educational interventions: Historical context and behavioral analysis. In A. C. Catania & T. A. Brigham (Eds.), *Handbook of applied behavior analysis*. New York: Irvington.

Strupp, H. H. (1975). On failing one's patient. *Psychotherapy: Theory, Research, and Practice.* 12, 39–41.

Szucko, J. J., & Kleinmuntz, B. (1981). Statistical versus clinical lie detection. *American Psychologist*, 36, 488–496.

Thaw, J., Turkat, I. D., & Forehand, R. (1978). Critical issues in behavior therapy. *Behavior Modification*, 4, 445–464.

Wagner, N. N. (1978). Is masturbation still wrong? Comments on Bailey's comments. *Journal of Consulting and Clinical Psychology*, 46, 1507–1509.

Weithorn, L. A. (1988). Mental hospitalization of troublesome youth: An analysis of skyrocketing admission rates. *Stanford Law Review*, 40, 1–46.

White, M. D., & White, C. A. (1981). Involuntarily committed patients' constitutional right to refuse treatment: a challenge to psychology. *American Psychologist*, 36, 953–962.

Williams, M. H. (1985). The bait-and-switch tactic in psychotherapy. *Psychotherapy: Theory, Research, and Practice*, 22, 110–113.

Wilson, G. T. (1978). Ethical and professional issues in sex therapy: Comments on Bailey's "Psychotherapy of massage parlor technology?" *Journal of Consulting and Clinical Psychology*, 46, 1510–1514.

Zeiss, A. M., Rosen, G. M., & Zeiss, R. A. (1977). Orgasm during intercourse: A treatment strategy for women. *Journal of Consulting and Clinical Psychology*, 45, 891–895.

24

The Modern Psychotherapist and the Future of Psychotherapy

Michael J. Mahoney

Any characterization of the modern psychotherapist and the future of psychotherapy must suffer from the necessary limitations involved in all generalizations. Psychotherapists are very diverse and difficult creatures to describe, and the practice of psychotherapy is clearly undergoing substantial transformations as we approach the end of the twentieth century. That diversity and those transformations did not emerge out of nothing, of course, and their sociocultural and historical contexts deserve at least brief mention.

HISTORICAL AND CONCEPTUAL CONTEXTS

Understanding the modern psychotherapist and anticipating the future of psychotherapy—to the limited extent that these are possible—both require an appreciation of how the present is situated and moving in relation to the past and the future. Unfortunately, all current discussions of this *problem of historicity* are necessarily complicated by the fact that the terminology of some of the most important works on this topic creates substantial conceptual and semantic hurdles. By most accounts of history and the arts, we are already living in or after an era

termed *postmodern* (Gergen, 1991; Madison, 1988; Tarnas, 1991). There are different renditions of meaning, of course, but *postmodernism* is not a school of thought or a neat collection of characteristics. It is, however, a popular term for some of the themes of activity and exploration that have emerged in the second half of the twentieth-century. Tarnas (1991) offered the following synopsis:

> the postmodern mind may be viewed as an open-ended, indeterminate set of attitudes that has been shaped by a great diversity of intellectual and cultural currents; these range from pragmatism, existentialism, Marxism, and psychoanalysis to feminism, hermeneutics, deconstruction, and postempiricist philosophy of science, to cite only a few of the more prominent. . . . The human subject is an embodied agent, acting and judging in a context that can never be wholly objectified, with orientations and motives that can never be fully grasped or controlled. The knowing subject is never disengaged from the body or from the world, which form the background and condition of every cognitive act. . . . Again, many sources contributed to this development—Nietzsche's analysis of the problematic relation of language to reality; C. S. Peirce's semiotics, positing that all human thought takes place in signs; Ferdinand de Saussure's linguistics, positing the arbitrary rela-

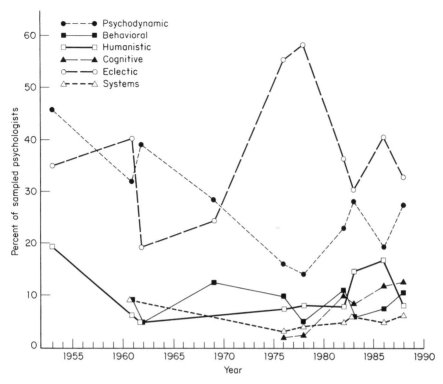

FIGURE 24.1. The relative popularity of different theoretical orientations among U.S. clinical psychologists between 1953 and 1988.

tionship between word and object, sign and signified; Wittgenstein's analysis of the linguistic structuring of human experience; Heidegger's existentialist-linguistic critique of metaphysics; Edward Sapir and B. L. Whorf's linguistic hypothesis that language shapes the perception of reality as much as reality shapes language; Michel Foucault's genealogical investigations in the social construction of knowledge; and Jacques Derrida's deconstructionism, challenging the attempt to establish a secure meaning in any text. (pp. 395–398).

Those interested in the history of ideas and the evolution of human knowing can now find many readable works that summarize and synthesize the major contributions in these areas (Boorstin, 1983; Mahoney, 1991; Manicas, 1987; Onians, 1951; Robinson, 1981; Tarnas, 1991; Wiener, 1974). What is most relevant to our understanding of the modern psychotherapist is that, for the most part, she or he has been trained to think, speak, and feel in technically

professional ways that often reflect only one of several possible alternatives. Even though estimates of the number of different kinds of psychotherapy are starting to approach 500, the vast majority of these can be comfortably situated in half a dozen superordinate categories. These *metatheoretical clusters* (families of related theories) include (1) psychoanalytic or—more broadly—psychodynamic, (2) behavioral, (3) humanistic (including experiential and existential), (4) cognitive, (5) eclectic or integrative, and (6) complex systems.

Figure 24.1 shows the combined results of 15 surveys of U.S. clinical psychologists between 1953 and 1988. The meaning of the data presented there is less obvious (to me, at least) than is the apparent variability of preferred theoretical orientations. It is clear, however, that psychotherapists and psychotherapy have been and are changing. In a broad and brief sweep, those changes include the following:

• A discernible decline in the long-standing domination of psychodynamic theory in psychotherapy.

• Substantial fluctuations in the popularity of eclectic or integrative perspectives (the Society for the Exploration of Psychotherapy Integration, begun informally in 1980, is one of the fastest-growing international groups in psychotherapy).

• The race for third place in this conceptual popularity contest has evidenced frequent shifts and substantial clustering and cross-fertilization (e.g., behavioral and cognitive psychotherapists are increasingly comfortable with the synthetic term *cognitive-behavioral*, and all four groups have shown signs of hybridization with one another).

Besides these changes in the popularity of different families of psychotherapies, there have been recent efforts to reexamine the meaning(s) of psychotherapy and hence the nature and role of the psychotherapist. Moreover, research on the effects of psychotherapy, and on the processes involved in producing those effects, has recently begun to converge on some important points of consensus. Let us address each of these developments before we conjecture about future possibilities for the therapist and his or her practice.

DEFINING PSYCHOTHERAPY AND THE PSYCHOTHERAPIST

Any attempt to characterize the modern psychotherapist must necessarily address the issue of defining psychotherapy and the psychotherapist. Most scholarly texts on the topic reserve these terms for developments associated with the beginning of the twentieth century. If what we mean by psychotherapy is the practice of a professional service specifically termed *psychotherapy*, this convention may be generally accurate. If we define psychotherapy as any form of interpersonal counseling related to personal problems and life's complexities, however, it should be clear that such practices have been used for several millennia under the rubrics of medicine, philosophy, and religion (Durant & Durant, 1935–1975; Frank, 1973).

In 1985 the Milton H. Erickson Foundation in Phoenix, Arizona, brought together a group of master clinicians and theorists for the first Evolution of Psychotherapy Conference (Zeig, 1987). The presenters were an impressive group: Aaron T. Beck, Bruno Bettelheim, Murray Bowen, Albert Ellis, Mary Goulding, Jay Haley, R. D. Laing, Arnold A. Lazarus, Cloe Madanes, Judd Marmor, James Masterson, Rollo May, Salvador Minuchin, Zerka Moreno, Erving Polster, Miriam Polster, Carl Rogers, Ernest Rossi, Virginia Satir, Thomas Szasz, Paul Watzlawick, Carl Whitaker, Lewis Wolberg, Joseph Wolpe, and Jeffrey Zeig. Each of these experts was asked to present his or her definition of psychotherapy and to discuss its goals and underlying assumptions. After several days of stimulating lectures and exchanges, it was clear that these respected authorities held widely ranging views on the nature of psychotherapy. This diversity was further explored in a later volume in which 81 psychotherapy experts were asked to respond to the same questions (Zeig & Munion, 1990). Once again, diversity of opinion was the rule rather than the exception. Consider, for example, the following range of selected definitions of psychotherapy from that volume:

Psychotherapy is a process in which a person who wishes to change symptoms or problems in living, or who seeks personal growth, enters into a contract, implicitly or explicitly, to interact verbally or nonverbally in a prescribed way with a person or persons who present themselves as helping agents. (Judd Marmor, p. 20)

Psychotherapy is the application of scientifically evaluated procedures that enable people to change their maladaptive behaviors, emotions, and cognitions themselves. (Paul M. G. Emmelkamp, p. 125)

Effective psychotherapy . . . consists of helping clients to clearly see and strongly dispute their conscious and unconscious imperatives, using a number of cognitive, emotive, and behavioral methods, and to thereby make themselves less disturbed and less disturbable. (Albert Ellis, pp. 146–147)

The question "What is psychotherapy?" presupposes that psychotherapy exists. I contend that it does not. Like mental illness, psychotherapy is a metaphor and, as an extended metaphor, a myth. . . . The term *psychotherapy* denotes various principles and practices of (secular) ethics. Every method or school of psychotherapy is thus a system of applied ethics couched in the idiom of treatment; each reflects the personality, values, and aspirations of its founder and practitioners. (Thomas S. Szasz, pp. 171–172)

Psychotherapy is the process of two people struggling with the issues of being alive in this world at this time. Both confront these issues, but the interest and needs of one, the client, have priority at all points. Psychotherapy attempts to disclose to the client the ways in which he keeps himself from the potential fullness of living and to ensure that he makes choices that are as aware as possible of these patterns. (James F. T. Bugental, p. 189)

Psychotherapy is a planned interpersonal process in which the less disturbed person, the therapist, attempts to help the more disturbed person, the patient, overcome his or her problems. (Sol L. Garfield, p. 239).

Psychotherapy is professional foster parenting with the deliberate function of facilitating the patient's effort to be more himself or herself. (Carl A. Whitaker, p. 256)

Psychotherapy endeavors to change people's assumptions about the nature of reality—assumptions they consider to be true, objective, platonic aspects of the "real" world. (Paul Watzlawick, p. 266)

Among other noteworthy aspects of the above definitions is their tendency to drift into issues of effectiveness (e.g., Ellis), intentions (e.g., Bugental, Garfield, Marmor, Watzlawick, Whitaker), and values (e.g., Emmelkamp, Szasz). My own attempt to render a definition

drew on the earlier works of Bowlby (1988), Frank (1961), and Guidano (1987, 1991):

Psychotherapy is a culturally relative special *relationship* between a professional helper and individual or group clients. Working from a *theoretical rationale* that includes basic assumptions about human nature and the processes of psychological *development*, the psychotherapist works with the client to create a safe, stable, and caring alliance in and from which the client can explore—often via ritualized techniques—past, present, and possible ways of experiencing self, world, and their dynamic relationships. (Michael J. Mahoney in Zeig & Munion, 1990, pp. 164–165.

There are points of consensus across these definitions, however, and they include the so-called three R's of psychotherapy: a relationship, rationale(s) for change, and rituals aimed at facilitating that change. This still leaves considerable room for diversity, of course.

The largest group of psychotherapy practitioners are neither psychiatrists nor psychologists (whether clinical or counseling), although bachelor-degreed "psychological assistants" probably clock more hours of actual client contact than practitioners in most other categories combined. Technically speaking, the most common current providers of psychotherapy are social workers and a heterogeneous group of master's-degreed counselors who are given license (though not always a written license) to practice under a variety of titles (marriage and family counselors, pastoral counselors, professional counselors, and so on). In most nations (including such leaders as Canada and the United States), the terms *psychotherapy* or *psychotherapist* and *counseling* or *counselor* are not legally defined. *Psychologist* or *psychological* and *psychiatrist* or *psychiatric* are the first terms whose use has come to be legally constrained in a few countries. This regulation of psychotherapeutic terminology is, of course, only a beginning, but it appears to have considerable momentum. Developments on several continents suggest that the use of these or other terms—as personal identifiers and labels for professional services—will soon be globally regulated by both national and international law.

THE MODERN PSYCHOTHERAPIST

And so, how should one characterize the modern psychotherapist? The easiest—and least informative—method might be to resort to a strictly data-based characterization. The extant data, which are inadequate in a number of ways, suggest that *the typical modern psychotherapist is a relatively young woman with a licentiate or a master's degree in social work or psychology.* The foregoing statement reflects a global average, of course, and not simply the statistics applicable to North American psychotherapists. Measures of central tendency in statistics are notoriously misrepresentative of the range and diversity of individual data points, however (Hermans, 1988; Lamiell, 1987). Beyond their obfuscation of individual differences, such statistics are also extremely sensitive to issues of sampling and methods of measurement. There are significant differences, for example, across continents, countries, and cultures. Characterizations that apply to one geographic region may be grossly inaccurate when applied to others. The majority of psychotherapists are not North American, yet statistics descriptive of U.S. and Canadian psychotherapists are often presented as if they were globally representative or ideal. This *hegemony* (dominant leadership) of North America in psychotherapy research and practice deserves serious reflection in our considerations of the modern psychotherapist and the future of psychotherapy (Fisher, 1989; Hall, 1990; Moghaddam, 1987; Rosenzweig, 1992; Simek-Downing, 1989; Tarnas, 1991; Urbina, 1989).

PSYCHOTHERAPY PROCESS AND OUTCOME

There was a time—and it was not that long ago—when psychotherapy process was considered a specialization separate from psychotherapy outcome. In other words, researchers interested in the processes of psychological change marched to a different drummer than researchers interested in the effects (outcome) of psychotherapy. Even a cursory glance at successive editions of the unofficial (but hardly disputable) authoritative text on psychotherapy research attests to the continuing convergence of these formerly estranged specializations (see *the Handbook of Psychotherapy and Behavior Change,* Bergin & Garfield, 1971; Garfield & Bergin, 1978, 1986, 1994). What goes on in a client's life—within and between therapeutic sessions—cannot be meaningfully separated from measurements intended to reflect the effects of that therapy on his or her quality of life and social functioning. With the exception of a few dogmatic skeptics, the burning question about psychotherapy is no longer whether it works but, rather, how, when, and with whom its effects are most salient and—equally important—how, when, and with whom it fails or does harm (Greenberg & Pinsof, 1986; Mahoney, 1991; Rice & Greenberg, 1984).

The three most popular research questions about psychotherapy in the third quarter of the twentieth century were (1) does psychotherapy work?, (2) how does psychotherapy work (when it does)?, and (3) are some psychotherapies better than others? (Mahoney, 1994b). The answers to these questions have been both puzzling and provocative. In brief relief, they seem to be that (1) yes, psychotherapy does work (although there are a minority of cases in which its effects appear to have been neutral or negative); (2) when it does work, psychotherapy appears to facilitate novel experiences (of self, life, others, world, work, and so on); and (3) the quest for "better" or "the best" psychotherapy has led to a realization that many ostensibly different approaches to therapy share important common ingredients that probably contribute to their reputation for success. What, exactly, are those ingredients?

This last question is one that is central to the psychotherapy integration movement discussed in previous chapters of this volume. There are at least two perspectives from which to approach it—namely, from the methods and findings of psychotherapy researchers and from

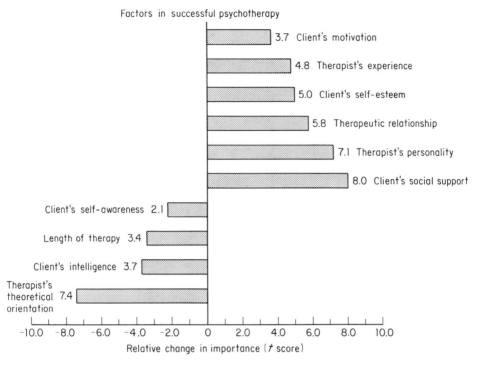

FIGURE 24.2. U.S. psychotherapists' view of the importance of different factors in successful psychotherapy, as rated currently and (retrospectively) at the beginning of their careers.

the reported experiences of psychotherapists and clients themselves. Looking first at the former, it is noteworthy that the best predictors of psychotherapy outcome are client variables, therapist variables, and therapeutic techniques, in that order (Bergin & Lambert, 1978). Techniques are, in fact, a "distant third" in that comparison, despite the fact that they have been a popular focus of professional training and research publications. In statistical analyses of the relative contributions of different factors in psychotherapy, the person (though not necessarily the personality) of the therapist appears to be at least eight times more influential than his or her theoretical orientation and/or use of specific therapeutic techniques in predicting the outcome of individual psychotherapy (Lambert, 1989).

Parallel conclusions were suggested by a retrospective study of psychotherapy researchers and practitioners (Mahoney & Craine, 1991). When asked to report the importance they now assigned to different factors in successful psy-

chotherapy in comparison with the importance they had presumed when they first began practicing, experienced practitioners showed the changes reflected in Figure 24.2. Over the course of their years of experience with clients, they had come to place more importance on their clients' motivation, self-esteem, and social support system and on their own experience, personality, and ability to facilitate a therapeutic relationship. Less important than they had originally expected were the length of therapy, their theoretical orientation, and their clients' intelligence.

Moreover, psychotherapists have consistently reported an acceleration in their own psychological development (whether they wanted it or not: Guy, 1987; Mahoney, 1991). A crystalline description of this process was offered by James F. T. Bugental (1978):

> I am not the person who began to practice counseling or psychotherapy more than 30 years ago. . . . And the changes in me are not solely those worked by time, education, and the life

circumstances shared by most of my generation. A powerful force affecting me has been my participation in so many lives.

   . . . My life as a psychotherapist has been . . . the source of anguish, pain, and anxiety—sometimes in the work itself, but more frequently within myself and with those important in my life. . . . Similarly that work and those relationships have directly and indirectly brought to me and those in my life joy, excitement, and a sense of participation in truly vital experiences (pp. 149–150).

The burdens and blessings of participating in so many lives in process are apparent in the above self-disclosure, and they are important to bear in mind as one continues the lifelong process of stretching to meet the developmental demands of psychotherapy clients.

If we look briefly at clients' reports of their experiences of therapy, yet another facet of this issue is revealed. The most common concerns presented by clients in psychotherapy cluster into four overlapping categories: intimacy and human relationships, the sense of personal agency and empowerment (control, capacity), openness to experience, and self-relationships (particularly guilt, self-esteem, and self-forgiveness) (Elliott & James, 1989). The most common dimensions of change reported by psychotherapy clients include developments in self-understanding (or *insight*), a greater range and comfort in emotional expression, and an increased sense of personal responsibility. Improvements in self-esteem, social skills, and hopefulness are also commonly reported after successful psychotherapy (irrespective of the original presenting concern or diagnosis).

ON PREDICTING THE FUTURE OF PSYCHOTHERAPY

As noted in the opening remarks of this chapter, the modern psychotherapist and the practice of psychotherapy are not only diverse, multicultural, and complex, but also in the midst of transformations the magnitude of which is difficult to discern. This should not be surprising, perhaps, given that we live in the most complex, rapidly changing period in human his-

tory. Indeed, it would be more surprising if contemporary psychotherapy were not reflecting and keeping pace with the rate and range of changes taking place in the lives and worlds outside the consulting room. Given this situation, however, any attempt to predict the future of psychotherapy (and the related fields of psychology and psychiatry) must necessarily be viewed as tentative conjectures rather than confident projections. This constraint has not prevented a number of writers from offering a range of observations and predictions on the past and future of these areas (Boneau, 1992; Norcross, Alford, & DeMichele, 1992; Norcross & Freedheim, 1992; Oltmanns & Krasner, 1993; Sechrest, 1992; Woodworth, 1937).

To place some of these observations and conjectures in historical perspective, a few recent and ongoing events deserve brief mention. At the time of this writing (August 1993), expressions of concern about the future of psychotherapy have focused on a number of portentious events in the field. These events include the following:

- In 1988 the 96-year-old American Psychological Association suffered a significant splintering over the power wielded in that organization by psychotherapy practitioners and other psychologists (mostly researchers and teachers). The American Psychological Society was formed that same year and has already become a significant voice for the priorities of scientific and pedagogical psychology. The result of this development has been an unfortunate widening of the gap between scientists and service providers in psychology.
- Throughout the 1970s and 1980s, psychotherapists petitioned to have their services covered by third-party payers (insurance companies and government programs). With the success of their petitions and reforms in the health care industry, however, what resulted was *managed health care*—a tightly controlled and regulated system in which clients were given access to limited forms of psychotherapy only if their diagno-

sis so warranted and, even then, only for a limited number of sessions and with substantial demands on psychotherapists for paperwork and justifications. Although some practitioners have viewed these results as disastrous, others have seen them as reasonable and challenging requests for the optimal use of resources (Austad & Berman, 1991).

• The issue of prescription privileges for nonmedical psychotherapists has generated considerable heat (and occasional flashes of light) over the last decade. A pilot project conducted by U.S. Army psychologists showed that nonmedical therapists could be trained to responsibly prescribe and monitor psychotropic medication with a wide range of clients. Although prescription privileges may broaden the repertoire of the nonmedical therapist, they have also raised controversial issues about professional identities and the presumed boundaries between mind and body that have long distinguished psychiatry and psychology.

Needless to say, one's interpretation of the foregoing events and their portent for psychotherapy must influence the images that appear in any crystal ball gazing.

John C. Norcross and his colleagues opted for an empirical alternative to the crystal ball (Norcross et al., 1992). They surveyed 75 psychotherapy experts regarding their predictions for the future of psychotherapy. The results were interesting. In the realm of technology, the experts predicted that the following techniques would be most likely to be used more frequently in psychotherapies of the future: self-change techniques, problem-solving techniques, audiovisual feedback, homework assignments, communication skills training, cognitive restructuring, live (in vivo) exposure, assertion/social skills training, self-control procedures, imagery and fantasy techniques, behavioral contracting, computerized therapies, didactic (teaching/advising) techniques, supportive techniques, and bibliotherapy. Aversive conditioning was rated as the technique most likely to decrease in frequency.

On the issue of psychotherapy providers, Norcross et al.'s sample of experts predicted that self-help groups, masters-degreed social workers, and psychiatric nurses were likely to be asked to increase their services, followed by doctoral-level clinical psychologists, masters-degreed counselors, and peer counselors. The relative amount of psychotherapy offered by psychiatrists was predicted to decrease slightly. Short-term therapies were predicted to increase in frequency, and long-term therapies were expected to decrease. In terms of theoretical orientations, the surveyed experts predicted that cognitive, integrative, and complex (family) systems approaches were most likely to exhibit substantial increases in popularity, while psychoanalysis and transactional analysis were most likely to decline. Other predictions of note were that the accreditation of training programs will become an increasingly important issue and that an increasing number of psychotherapists are likely to tend toward specialization (rather than general services) in their practice. There was little doubt that psychotherapy will continue to be needed and valued.

But perhaps the most interesting prediction offered by these experts was in response to the final question of the survey, namely, "What is the likelihood that a group of experienced psychotherapists can accurately predict the future of psychotherapy" (p. 157)? On a 7-point scale where 1 meant "very unlikely," 4 meant "uncertain," and 7 meant "very likely," the experts averaged a conservative response of 3.09 (with a 1.37 standard deviation). Overall, they tended to think it unlikely that their predictions would be accurate.

Another collection of predictions about the future of psychotherapy was published in 1992 by the Group for the Advancement of Psychiatry. The basis for their predictions was not described, but their pessimistic flavor is not difficult to discern. Consider, for example, their concluding remarks:

> In sum, the future psychotherapist, in this picture, is likely to be a woman with a degree other than medical, doing brief, most often group, psychotherapy within a managed care setting. A larger segment of society will have the

opportunity to obtain some brief psychiatric and possibly psychotherapeutic help, while long-term psychotherapy will be restricted to the very few who are wealthy enough to afford it outside of the managed health-care system. (p. 48)

Elsewhere in their report, they seem to bemoan the fact that, in the future, "the patient and therapist [will] have one eye on the cash register and the other on the clock" (p. 45). They also noted that the rising percentages of female practitioners in psychiatry and psychology portend unfortunate probabilities: "The historic consequences of the feminization of any vocation or profession have been a reduction in status and reduction in earning power in that area" (p. 5).

POSSIBLE CHALLENGES

The foregoing predictions and the contexts in which they were presented make it clear that psychotherapists in the future will face a host of challenges that may be difficult to anticipate, let alone deal with. Before concluding this chapter, let me speculate on a few more such challenges that are likely to face the intrepid practitioner of the twenty-first century.

The Balance of Centripetal and Centrifugal Trends

As a number of observers have amply noted, contemporary psychology is characterized by what appear to be opponent processes (Altman, 1987; Bower, 1993; Goldfried, 1982; Hermans, 1988; Koch, 1993; Miller, 1992; Prochaska, 1984; Tarnas, 1991; Weimer, 1982a, 1982b). While some of these processes reflect considerable and accelerating differentiation, specialization, and what some have termed *fragmentation*, others suggest that there are strong tendencies toward convergence, integration, and unification. The psychotherapist of the twenty-first century is likely to confront a number of ostensive dichotomies that may pull her or him in opposite conceptual and practical directions. Old and familiar boundaries between mind and body, self and society, and cognition and emotion—to name but a few—are in the throes of renegotiation, evidencing a dialectical development that might well have intimidated the likes of Hegel, Marx, and even Piaget.

The Embodiment of Psychotherapy

Another challenge facing twenty-first-century psychotherapy is the growing realization that mind (or head) and body are part of an integrally interdependent whole system. Contributions from cognitive science, health psychology, and psychotherapy process have made it increasingly clear that the "talking cure"—so named by its first famous client (Anna O.)—can no longer expect to remain an informational exchange between "talking heads" (Bruner, 1990; Fischer, 1987; Ford, 1987; Frick, 1982; Johnson, 1987; Lakoff & Johnson, 1980; Mahoney, in press; Merleau-Ponty, 1962, 1963; Montagu, 1978; Morgan, 1985). The psychotherapist—medically trained and otherwise—is being increasingly relied on to assess overall lifestyles in light of current research on happiness, health, and well-being (Argyle, 1987; Beiser, 1974; Warr, 1978). As noted in the earlier discussion of prescription privileges for psychologists, long-standing boundaries between the physical and mental dimensions of health are now being reexamined. While the psychotherapist of the future is unlikely to assume the responsibilities of a physical trainer or massage therapist, she or he is likely to be expected to incorporate embodiment issues into standard practices of assessment and service.

Confronting Complexity and Constraints on Human Plasticity

Another challenge that will face the psychotherapist of the twenty-first century is the realization that human lives are complex, unique, and ultimately constrained by circumstances well beyond the control of either client or therapist. At levels ranging from the basic biological to the sociocultural, the individual human being exhibits degrees of complexity and self-organization that were entirely unanticipated only half a century ago (Bienenstock, 1985; Bienenstock, Soulie, & Weisbuch, 1986; Cook, 1980; Dell, 1982a, 1982b; Dell & Goolishian, 1981; Gleick, 1987; Guidano, 1987, 1991; Hager, 1992; Hayek, 1964; Jantsch, 1980, 1981; Kauffman, 1993; Lewin, 1992; Maturana & Uarela, 1987; Morrison, 1991; Pattee, 1973, 1977, 1978; Prigogine, 1980; Prigogine & Stengers, 1984; Waldrop, 1992; Weimer, 1987; Zeleny, 1980, 1981). Moreover—although the resilience and *plasticity* (capacity for change) of individuals is undeniably impressive (Lerner, 1984; Mahoney, 1991)—it is equally clear that significant and enduring psychological change is much more difficult to effect than was once believed. A national survey of U.S. clinical psychologists revealed that the difficulties of psychological change were consistently acknowledged by cognitive therapists, eclectic-integrative therapists, existential-humanistic therapists, and psychoanalysts (Mahoney, Norcross, Prochaska, & Missar, 1989). Although the behavior therapists in the sample were significantly less inclined to rate psychological change as difficult, this difference disappeared in the subsample of behavior therapists who had themselves been in personal therapy.

Issues of Values, Ethics, and Spirituality

A challenge that is already beginning to confront turn-of-the-century psychotherapists has to do with the inevitable relationship between professional life counseling and issues of ethics, values, and spirituality. What is new about this challenge is not its contents so much as its recognition. For more than a century now, therapists have counseled clients about the right/wrong (best/worst, good/bad, wise/unwise) things to do in their individual life circumstances, but only recently has such counseling been openly acknowledged as overlapping with ethical, religious, and spiritual issues (Fulford,

1989; Kelly & Strupp, 1992; Payne, Bergin, & Loftus, 1992; Sperry, 1988; Vaughan, 1991; Walsh & Vaughan, 1980). The issues involved are perennial: life and death, the meaning(s) and value(s) of faith, family, fidelity, forgiveness, love, pain, patience, sacrifice, suffering, and self (Bugental, 1978; Friedman, 1967; Zweig, 1968). More than ever before, the psychotherapist of the twenty-first century is likely to be asked to address these issues and to help clients explore their past, present, and possibly developing feelings about them. There is little in modern textbooks to guide them, and the training of future psychotherapists is likely to be enhanced when such issues are included in the professional preparation of twenty-first-century psychotherapists (Bickman & Ellis, 1990).

The Person of the Therapist and Therapist Self-Care

There are, of course, myriad other challenges that face the future psychotherapist—for example, the "new views" of unconscious feeling and knowing (Bowers, 1987; Bowers & Meichenbaum, 1984; Ellenberger, 1970; Polanyi, 1958, 1966; Shevrin & Dickman, 1980), the implications of narrative and hermeneutic views of knowing for psychotherapy practice (Bruner, 1990; Madison, 1988; Messer, Sass, & Woolfolk, 1988; Neimeyer & Mahoney, 1995; Palmer, 1969), and the growing recognition that self-development is always embedded in family and social systems (Guidano, 1987, 1991; Mahoney, 1994a, 1994b; Sroufe, 1979; Stolorow & Atwood, 1992; Whitaker, 1989). Even more challenging than these, in my opinion, are the issues raised by the recent realization that the person of the psychotherapist—not necessarily her or his personality or character structure—may be the single most important variable (second only to client factors) in predicting the success of psychotherapy (Lambert, 1989). The message here is clear—namely, that what a therapist shares most extensively with clients are not theoretical rationales and technical rituals of change so much as himself or herself as another human being (albeit a professionally trained expert) struggling to cope with a complex, ambiguous, and rapidly changing world (Mahoney, 1991, 1994a, 1994b).

Ironically, the person of the therapist and his or her experience of psychotherapy is one of the most sparsely researched phenomena in the entire field. We know substantially more about the client's experience of therapy than we do about that of the therapist (Orlinsky & Howard, 1975). What does it feel like to be asked to counsel a life in process? What emotions are evoked when a client vividly describes his or her experiences of child abuse, rape, war, injustice, disaster, or tragedy? How does it feel to hear such stories all day long, day after day, week after week, year after year? What is it like when the therapist identifies with the client—that is, sees him or herself in the experience patterns described by the client? How does the therapist cope with his or her own continuing efforts at adaptation, development, and understanding?

To date, only two things are clear: (1) the practice of psychotherapy is a uniquely demanding and extremely stressful undertaking, and (2) therapist self-care—that is, self-awareness, self-acceptance, and active self-protection/propagation—are relatively low priorities in most professional training programs (Guy, 1987; Mahoney, 1991). The little research that does exist suggests that female psychotherapists are likely to come from home environments where there was conflict, trauma, or abuse, but that the developing therapists in these families were able to cope successfully with and/or "harvest" these difficulties in a healthy manner (Elliott & Guy, 1993; comparable data for males were not available at this time). Also evident is the fact that career psychotherapists exhibit increased vulnerability to anxiety disorders, burnout, depression, relationship problems, substance abuse, and suicide (particularly among female therapists). On the positive side, career therapists report accelerated psychological development, substantial improvement in self-esteem, and an increased appreciation for the importance of interpersonal relationships in their life quality.

All of this means, perhaps, that embarking on a career as a professional psychotherapist may entail more risks and benefits than the choices associated with being a(n) architect, artist, banker, businessperson, dentist, executive, manager, musician, researcher, scientist, or anything else. When your life is dedicated to the counseling of other lives, you cannot help but be involved. And when you are involved—even vicariously—in the complexities and vicissitudes of so many other lives, your own life cannot help but be influenced. You encounter situations, circumstances, and complexities that you never anticipated. You are forced to make judgment calls that have no firm footing in research, theory, or the teachings of your mentors. Fundamentally, psychotherapy is an existential exchange: A person seeking counsel (the client) asks for reassurance, advice, and predictions about choices and life situations. The professional counselor (therapist)—drawing on theory, research, training, and life experiences (both within and outside therapy)—attempts to offer cogent counsel on the same, with generous allowances for her or his limitations in experience, knowledge, and wisdom. Is there a more responsible or stressful role in contemporary society?

CONCLUDING REMARKS

My goal in this chapter has been to offer a brief overview of the complexities and issues facing both modern and future psychotherapists. In so doing, I have necessarily expressed my own limited and contextualized understanding of these matters. Needless to say, I believe that the therapist of today faces formidable responsibilities and challenges in a changing world, and that the psychotherapist of tomorrow is likely to be stretched even further by the ever-expanding demands of this developing profession.

REFERENCES

Albee, G. W. (1970). The uncertain future of clinical psychology. *American Psychologist*, 25, 1071–1080.

Allman, L. S., de La Rocha, O., Elkins, D. N., & Weathers, R. S. (1992). Psychotherapists' attitudes toward clients reporting mystical experiences. *Psychotherapy*, 29, 564–569.

Altman, I. (1987). Centripetal and centrifugal trends in psychology. *American Psychologist*, 42, 1058–1069.

Argyle, M. (1987). *The psychology of happiness.* London: Methuen.

Austad, C. S., & Berman, W. H. (Eds.). (1991). *Psychotherapy in managed health care: The optimal use of time and resources.* Washington, DC: American Psychological Association.

Beiser, M. (1974). Components and correlates of mental well-being. *Journal of Health and Social Behavior*, 15, 320–327.

Bergin, A. E., & Garfield, S. L. (Eds.). (1971). *Handbook of psychotherapy and behavior change.* New York: Wiley.

Bergin, A. E., & Lambert, M. J. (1978). The evaluation of therapeutic outcomes. In S. L. Garfield & A. E. Bergin (Eds.), *Handbook of psychotherapy and behavior change* (2nd ed., pp. 139–189). New York: Wiley.

Bickman, L., & Ellis, H. (1990). *Preparing psychologists for the 21st century: Proceedings of the National Conference on Graduate Education in Psychology.* Hillsdale, NJ: Erlbaum.

Bienenstock, E. (1985). Dynamics of the central nervous system. In J. P. Aubin, D. Saari, & K. Sigmund (Eds.), *Dynamics of macrosystems* (pp. 3–20). New York: Springer-Verlag.

Bienenstock, E., Soulie, F. F., & Weisbuch, G. (Eds.). (1986). *Disordered systems and biological organization.* New York: Springer-Verlag.

Boneau, C. A. (1992). Observations on psychology's past and future. *American Psychologist*, 47, 1586–1596.

Boorstin, D. J. (1983). *The discoverers: A history of man's search to know his world and himself.* New York: Random House.

Bowlby, J. (1988). *A secure base.* New York: Basic Books.

Bower, G. H. (1993). The fragmentation of psychology? *American Psychologist*, 48, 905–907.

Bowers, K. S. (1987). Revisioning the unconscious. *Canadian Psychology*, 28, 93–104.

Bowers, K. S., & Meichenbaum, D. (Eds.). (1984). *The unconscious reconsidered.* New York: Wiley.

Bruner, J. (1990). *Acts of meaning.* Cambridge, MA: Harvard University Press.

Bugental, J. F. T. (1978). *Psychotherapy and process: The fundamentals of an existential-humanistic approach.* Reading, MA: Addison-Wesley.

Cook, N. D. (1980). *Stability and flexibility: An analysis of natural systems.* New York: Pergamon Press.

Dell, P. F. (1982a). Beyond homeostasis: Toward a concept of coherence. *Family Process*, 21, 21–41.

Dell, P. F. (1982b). In search of truth: On the way to clinical epistemology. *Family Process*, 21, 407–414.

Dell, P. F., & Goolishian, H. A. (1981). Order through fluctuation: An evolutionary epistemology for human systems. *Australian Journal of Family Therapy*, 2, 175–184.

Durant, W., & Durant, A. (1935–1975). *The story of civilization.* 11 vols. New York: Simon & Schuster.

Ellenberger, H. F. (1970). *The discovery of the unconscious.* New York: Basic Books.

Elliott, D. M., & Guy, J. D. (1993). Mental health professionals versus non-mental-health professionals: Childhood trauma and adult functioning. *Professional Psychology: Research and Practice*, 24, 83–90.

Elliott, R., & James, E. (1989). Varieties of client experience in psychotherapy: An analysis of the literature. *Clinical Psychology Review*, 9, 443–467.

Fischer, R. (1987). On fact and fiction—The structures of stories that the brain tells to itself about itself. *Journal of Social and Biological Structures*, 10, 343–351.

Fisher, D. (1989). Boundary work: A model of the relation between power and knowledge. *Knowledge: Creation, Diffusion, Utilization*, 10, 156–176.

Ford, D. H. (1987). *Humans as self-constructing living systems: A developmental perspective on behavior and personality.* Hillsdale, NJ: Erlbaum.

Frank, J. D. (1973). *Persuasion and healing* (2nd ed.). Baltimore: Johns Hopkins University Press.

Frick, R. B. (1982). The ego and the vestibulocerebellar system: Some theoretical perspectives. *Psychoanalytic Quarterly*, 51, 93–121.

Friedman, M. (1967). *To deny our nothingness: Contemporary images of man.* Chicago: University of Chicago Press.

Fulford, K. W. M. (1989). *Moral theory and medical practice.* Cambridge: Cambridge University Press.

Garfield, S. L., & Bergin, A. E. (Eds.). (1986). *Handbook of psychotherapy and behavior change.* (3rd ed.). New York: Wiley.

Garfield, S. L., & Bergin, A. E. (Eds.). (1994).

Handbook of psychotherapy and behavior change. (4th ed.). New York: Wiley.

Gergen, K. J. (1991). *The saturated self: Dilemmas of identity in contemporary life.* New York: Basic Books.

Gleick, J. (1987). *Chaos: Making a new science.* New York: Viking Press.

Goldfried, M. R. (1982). *Converging themes in psychotherapy.* New York: Springer.

Greenberg, L. S., & Pinsof, W. M. (1986). *The psychotherapeutic process.* New York: Guilford Press.

Group for the Advancement of Psychiatry. (1992). *Psychotherapy in the future.* Washington, DC: American Psychiatric Press.

Guidano, V. F. (1987). *Complexity of the self: A developmental approach to psychopathology and therapy.* New York: Guilford Press.

Guidano, V. F. (1991). *The self in process: Toward a post-rationalist cognitive therapy.* New York: Guilford Press.

Guy, J. D. (1987). *The personal life of the psychotherapist.* New York: Wiley.

Hager, D. (1992). Chaos and growth. *Psychotherapy, 29,* 378–384.

Hall, J. P. (1990). Lessons from the First European Congress of Psychology. *American Psychologist, 45,* 978–980.

Hayek, F. A. (1964). The theory of complex phenomena. In M. Bunge (Ed.). *The critical approach to science and philosophy: Essays in honor of K. R. Popper* (pp. 332–349). New York: Free Press.

Hermans, H. J. M. (1988). On the integration of nomothetic and idiographic research methods in the study of personal meaning. *Journal of Personality, 56,* 785–812.

Jantsch, E. (1980). *The self-organizing universe: Scientific and human implications of the emerging paradigm of evolution.* New York: Pergamon Press.

Jantsch, E. (Ed.). (1981). *The evolutionary vision: Toward a unifying paradigm of physical, biological, and sociocultural evolution.* Boulder, CO: Westview Press.

Johnson, M. (1987). *The body in the mind: The bodily basis of meaning, imagination, and reason.* Chicago: University of Chicago Press.

Kauffman, S. A. (1993). *The origins of order: Self-organization and selection in evolution.* Oxford: Oxford University Press.

Kelly, T. A., & Strupp, H. H. (1992). Patient and therapist values in psychotherapy: Perceived changes, assimilation, similarity, and outcome. *Journal of Consulting and Clinical Psychology, 60,* 34–40.

Koch, S. (1993). "Psychology" or "the psychological studies?" *American Psychologist, 48,* 902–904.

Lakoff, G., & Johnson, M. (1980). *Metaphors we live by.* Chicago: University of Chicago Press.

Lambert, M. J. (1989). The individual therapist's contribution to psychotherapy process and outcome. *Clinical Psychology Review, 9,* 469–485.

Lamiell, J. T. (1987). *The psychology of personality: An epistemological inquiry.* New York: Columbia University Press.

Lerner, R. M. (1984). *On the nature of human plasticity.* Cambridge: Cambridge University Press.

Lewin, R. (1992). *Complexity: Life at the edge of chaos.* New York: Macmillan.

Madison, G. B. (1988). *The hermeneutics of postmodernity.* Bloomington: Indiana University Press.

Mahoney, M. J. (1991). *Human change processes: The scientific foundations of psychotherapy.* New York: Basic Books.

Mahoney, M. J. (Ed.) (1994a). *Cognitive and constructive psychotherapies.* New York: Springer.

Mahoney, M. J. (1994b). *Constructive psychotherapy.* New York: Guilford Press.

Mahoney, M. J. (in press). *The bodily self in psychotherapy.* New York: Guilford Press.

Mahoney, M. J., & Craine, M. H. (1991). The changing beliefs of psychotherapy experts. *Journal of Psychotherapy Integration, 1,* 207–221.

Mahoney, M. J., Norcross, J. C., Prochaska, J. O., & Missar, C. D. (1989). Psychological development and optimal psychotherapy: Converging perspectives among clinical psychologists. *Journal of Integrative and Eclectic Psychotherapy.*

Manicas, P. T. (1987). *A history and philosophy of the social sciences.* New York: Basil Blackwell.

Maturana, H. R., & Varela, F. J. (1987). *The tree of knowledge: The biological roots of human understanding.* Boston: Shambhala.

Merleau-Ponty, M. (1962). *Phenomenology of perception* (C. Smith, Trans.). London: Routledge & Kegan Paul.

Merleau-Ponty, M. (1963). *The structure of behavior* (A. L. Fisher, Trans.). Boston: Beacon Press.

Messer, S. B., Sass, L. A., & Woolfolk, R. L. (Eds.). (1988). *Hermeneutics and psychological theory: Interpretive perspectives on personality, psychotherapy, and psychopathology.* New Brunswick, NJ: Rutgers University Press.

Miller, R. B. (Ed.). (1992). *The restoration of dia-*

logue: Readings in the philosophy of clinical psychology. Washington, DC: American Psychological Association.

Moghaddam, F. M. (1987). Psychology in three worlds. American Psychologist, 42, 912–920.

Montagu, A. (1978). Touching: The human significance of the skin (2nd ed.). New York: Harper & Row.

Morgan, W. P. (1985). Affective beneficience of vigorous physical activity. Medicine and Science in Sports and Exercise, 17, 94–100.

Morrison, F. (1991). The art of modeling dynamic systems: Forecasting for chaos, randomness, and determinism. New York: Wiley Interscience.

Neimeyer, R. A., & Mahoney, M. J. (Eds.). (1995). Constructivism in psychotherapy. Washington, DC: American Psychological Association.

Norcross, J. C., Alford, B. A., & DeMichele, J. T. (1992). The future of psychotherapy: Delphi data and concluding observations. Psychotherapy, 29, 150–158.

Norcross, J. C., & Freedheim, D. K. (1992). Into the future: Retrospect and prospect in psychotherapy. In D. K. Freedheim (Ed.), History of psychotherapy: A century of change (pp. 881–900). Washington, DC: American Psychological Association.

Onians, R. B. (1951). The origins of European thought about the body, the mind, the soul, the world, time, and fate. Cambridge: Cambridge University Press.

Oltmanns, T. F., & Krasner, L. (1993). A voice for science in clinical psychology: The history of Section III of Division 12. The Clinical Psychologist, 46, 25–32.

Orlinsky, D. E., & Howard, K. I. (1975). Varieties of psychotherapeutic experience. New York: Teachers College Press.

Palmer, R. E. (1969). Hermeneutics: Interpretation theory in Schleiermacker, Silthey, Heidegger, and Gadamer. Evanston, IL: Northwestern University Press.

Pattee, H. H. (1973). Hierarchy theory: The challenge of complex systems. New York: George Braziller.

Pattee, H. H. (1977). Dynamic and linguistic modes of complex systems. International Journal of General Systems, 3, 259–266.

Pattee, H. H. (1978). The complementarity principle in biological and social structures. Journal of Biological and Social Structures, 1, 191–200.

Payne, I. R., Bergin, A. E., & Loftus, P. E. (1992). A review of attempts to integrate spiritual and standard psychotherapy techniques. Journal of Psychotherapy Integration, 2, 171–192.

Polanyi, M. (1958). Personal knowledge: Towards a post-critical philosophy. Chicago: University of Chicago Press.

Polanyi, M. (1966). The tacit dimension. New York: Doubleday.

Prigogine, I. (1980). From being to becoming: Time and complexity in the physical sciences. San Francisco: Freeman.

Prigogine, I., & Stengers, I. (1984). Order out of chaos: Man's new dialogue with nature. New York: Bantam Books.

Prochaska, J. O. (1984). Systems of psychotherapy: A transtheoretical analysis. Homewood, IL: Dorsey Press.

Rice, L. N., & Greenberg, L. S. (1984). Patterns of change. New York: Guilford Press.

Robinson, D. N (1981). An intellectual history of psychology. New York: Macmillan.

Rosenzweig, M. R. (1992). Psychological science around the world. American Psychologist, 47, 718–722.

Salthe, S. N. (1985). Evolving hierarchical systems. New York: Columbia University Press.

Sechrest, L. (1992). The past future of clinical psychology: A reflection on Woodworth (1937). Journal of Consulting and Clinical Psychology, 60, 18–23.

Shevrin, H., & Dickman, S. (1980). The psychological unconscious: A necessary assumption for all psychological theory? American Psychologist, 35, 421–434.

Simek-Downing, L. (Ed.). (1989). International psychotherapy: Theories, research, and cross-cultural implications. New York: Praeger.

Sperry, R. W. (1988). Psychology's mentalist paradigm and the religion/science tension. American psychologist, 43, 607–613.

Sperry, R. W. (1993). The impact and promise of the cognitive revolution. American Psychologist, 48, 878–885.

Sroufe, L. A. (1979). The coherence of individual development: Early care, attachment, and subsequent developmental issues. American Psychologist, 34, 834–841.

Stolorow, R. D., & Atwood, G. E. (1992). Contexts of being: The intersubjective foundations of psychological life. Hillsdale, NJ: Analytic Press.

Tarnas, R. (1991). The passion of the western mind. New York: Ballantine Books.

Urbina, J. (Ed.). (1989). El psicólogo: Formacion,

ejercicio profesional, y prospectiva. Mexico City: Universidad Nacional Autonoma de Mexico.

Vaughan, F. (1991). Spiritual issues in psychotherapy. *The Journal of Transpersonal Psychology,* 23, 105–119.

Waldrop, M. M. (1992). *Complexity: the emerging science at the edge of order and chaos.* New York: Simon & Schuster.

Walsh, R. N., & Vaughan, F. (1980). *Beyond ego: Transpersonal dimensions in psychology.* Los Angeles: Tarcher.

Warr, P. (1978). A study of psychological well-being. *British Journal of Psychology,* 69, 111–121.

Weimer, W. B. (1982a). Ambiguity and the future of psychology: *Meditations Leibniziennes.* In W. B. Weimer & D. S. Palermo (Eds.), *Cognition and the symbolic processes* (Vol. 2, pp. 331–360). Hillsdale, NJ: Erlbaum.

Weimer, W. B. (1982b). Hayek's approach to the problems of complex phenomena: An introduction to the theoretical psychology of *The Sensory Order.* In W. B. Weimer & D. S. Palermo (Eds.), *Cognition and the symbolic processes* (Vol. 2, pp. 267–311). Hillsdale, NJ: Erlbaum.

Weimer, W. B. (1987). Spontaneously ordered complex phenomena and the unity of the moral sciences. In G. Radnitzky (Ed.), *Centripetal forces in the universe* (pp. 257–296). New York: Paragon House.

Whitaker, C. (1989). *Midnight musings of a family therapist.* New York: Norton.

Wiener, P. P. (Ed.). (1974). *Dictionary of the history of ideas: Studies of selected pivotal ideas.* New York: Scribner.

Woodworth, R. S. (1937). The future of clinical psychology. *Journal of Consulting Psychology,* 1, 4–5.

Zeig, J. K. (Ed.). (1992). *The evolution of psychotherapy.* New York: Brunner/Mazel.

Zeig, J. K., & Munion, W. M. (Eds.). (1990). *What is psychotherapy? Contemporary perspectives.* San Francisco: Jossey-Bass.

Zeleny, M. (1980). *Autopoiesis, dissipative structures, and spontaneous social orders.* Washington, DC: American Association for the Advancement of Science.

Zeleny, M. (1981). *Autopoiesis: A theory of living organization.* New York: Elsevier North-Holland.

Zweig, P. (1968). *The heresy of self-love: A study of subversive individualism.* Princeton, NJ: Princeton University Press.

Index